Complete
Book of
New Zealand
Birds

First edition
Published by Reader's Digest Services Pty Limited (Inc. in NSW)
26–32 Waterloo Street, Surry Hills, NSW 2010
© 1985 Reader's Digest Services Pty Limited
© 1985 Reader's Digest Association Far East Limited
Philippines copyright 1985 Reader's Digest Association Far East Limited

National Library of Australia cataloguing-in-publication data
Reader's Digest complete book of New Zealand birds.
 Bibliography.
 Includes index.
 ISBN 0 949819 62 X.
 1. Birds—New Zealand. I. Reader's Digest Services.
 II. Title: Complete book of New Zealand birds.
598.29931

Half-title page: The kea *Nestor notabilis*.

READER'S
DIGEST

Complete
Book *of*
New Zealand
Birds

READER'S DIGEST   SYDNEY

The Reader's Digest Complete Book of New Zealand Birds
was edited and designed by Reader's Digest Services Pty Ltd, Sydney

CONSULTANT EDITOR

C. J. R. Robertson
Scientist, New Zealand Wildlife Service,
Wellington

CONTRIBUTORS

I.A.E.A. **I. A. E. Atkinson, MSc, PhD**
Scientist, Botany Division, New Zealand
Department of Scientific and Industrial
Research, Taita

A.B. **A. J. Baker, BSc, MSc (Hons), PhD**
Curator, Ornithology Department, Royal
Ontario Museum; and Assistant Professor
of Zoology, University of Toronto, Canada

D.J.B-G. **D. J. Baker-Gabb, PhD**
Biologist, Royal Australasian
Ornithologists Union, Australia

M.L.B. **M. L. Barlow, RGON**
Previously Council Member,
Ornithological Society of New Zealand

J.A.B. **J. A. Bartle, MSc**
Curator of Birds, National Museum of New
Zealand, Wellington

A.J.B. **A. J. Beauchamp, BSc (Hons)**
Doctorate Student, Victoria University,
Wellington

H.A.B. **H. A. Best, MSc (Hons)**
Scientist, New Zealand Wildlife Service,
Wellington

A.B.(2) **A. Blackburn, Lt. Col. (RL)**
Retired. Past President, Ornithological
Society of New Zealand

D.H.B. **D. H. Brathwaite**
Retired. Previously Regional
Representative, Ornithological Society of
New Zealand

N.B. **N. Brothers**
Technical Officer, Tasmanian Parks and
Wildlife Service, Australia

P.C.B. **P. C. Bull, MSc, DSc**
Retired. Previously Scientist, Ecology
Division, New Zealand Department of
Scientific and Industrial Research

T.A.C. **T. A. Caithness, BSc**
Scientist, New Zealand Wildlife Service,
Wellington

C.N.C. **C. N. Challies, BSc, PhD**
Scientist, New Zealand Forest Service,
Christchurch

J.L.C. **J. L. Craig, BSc, PhD**
Senior Lecturer in Zoology, Auckland
University, Auckland

D.E.C. **D. E. Crockett**
Council Member, Ornithological Society of
New Zealand, Whangarei

J.B.C. **J. B. Cunningham, MSc**
Doctorate Student, Canterbury University,
Christchurch

J.M.C. **J. M. Cunningham**
Previously Secretary/Treasurer,
Ornithological Society of New Zealand

M.D.D. **M. D. Dennison, BSc (Hons)**
Doctorate Student, University of Toronto,
Canada

M.E.D. **M. E. Douglas, BSc**
Technician, Zoology Department,
Auckland University, Auckland

P.D. **P. Dunn, MSc**
Tree Farmer, Dunedin

J.A.D.F. **J. A. D. Flack, PhD**
Previously Scientist, New Zealand Wildlife
Service

C.A.F. **Sir C. A. Fleming, KBE, BA, MSc, DSc,
FRS, FRSNZ, FMANZ**
Retired. Previously Chief Palaeontologist,
New Zealand Geological Survey; and Past
President, Royal Society of New Zealand

R.A.F. **R. A. Fordham, MSc, PhD**
Reader in Zoology, Massey University,
Palmerston North

N.C.F. **N. C. Fox, PhD**
Wildlife Department, Dyfed College,
Wales

P.J.F. **P. J. Fullagar, BSc, PhD**
Senior Research Scientist, Division of
Wildlife Research, CSIRO, Australia

A.S.G. **A. S. Garrick, BSc (Hons)**
Scientist, New Zealand Department of
Lands and Survey, Wellington

P.D.G. **P. D. Gaze, NZCS**
Technical Officer, Ecology Division, New
Zealand Department of Scientific and
Industrial Research, Nelson

B.J.G. **B. J. Gill, BSc (Hons), PhD**
Curator of Birds and Mammals, Auckland
Institute and Museum, Auckland

R.S.G. **Rev. R. S. Gray, MSc, BD**
Minister, Whakatane

L.G. **L. Gurr, MSc**
Retired. Previously Reader in Zoology,
Massey University

P.C.H. **P. C. Harper, BSc (Hons), PhD**
Lecturer, Department of Extension Studies,
Canterbury University, Christchurch

M.H. **M. Harrison, BSc**
Scientist, New Zealand Wildlife Service,
Wellington

G.H. **G. Harrow**
Previously Regional Representative,
Ornithological Society of New Zealand

J.R.H. **J. R. Hay, MSc**
Scientist, Royal Forest and Bird Protection
Society, Auckland

B.D.H. **B. D. Heather, MA**
Editor, *Notornis*, Journal of the
Ornithological Society of New Zealand

M.J.I. **M. J. Imber, MAgr Sc**
Scientist, New Zealand Wildlife Service,
Wellington

CH.I. **CH. Imboden, BSc, BCS (Hons), MA, PhD**
Director, International Council for Bird
Preservation, United Kingdom

J.R.J. **J. R. Jackson, MSc (Hons)**
Industrial Chemist. Previously Regional
Representative, Ornithological Society of
New Zealand

P.F.J. **P. F. Jenkins, BSc, PhD**
Senior Lecturer in Zoology, Auckland
University, Auckland

G.J. **G. Jones, MSc**
Science Teacher, Auckland

F.C.K. **F. C. Kinsky**
Retired. Previously Curator of Birds,
National Museum of New Zealand

C.L. **C. Lalas, MSc**
Doctorate Student, Otago University,
Dunedin

A.MacC. **A. MacCulloch, BSc**
Science Teacher, Kings College, Auckland

H.R.McK. **H. R. McKenzie, JP**
Deceased. Previously President,
Ornithological Society of New Zealand

D.G.M. **D. G. Medway, LLB, FLS**
Barrister and Solicitor, New Plymouth.
Researcher in Historical Ornithology,
especially of Cook's Voyages.

D.V.M. **D. V. Merton**
Principal Wildlife Officer, Protected
Fauna, New Zealand Wildlife Service,
Wellington

P.R.M. **P. R. Milliner, PhD**
Postdoctoral Fellow, Smithsonian Institute,
USA

J.A.M. **J. A. Mills, BSc, MSc (Hons), PhD**
Scientist, New Zealand Wildlife Service,
Wellington

R.B.M. **R. B. Morris**
Producer, TVNZ Natural History Unit,
Dunedin

P.M.M. **P. M. Morse, BSc**
Previously Technician, New Zealand
Wildlife Service

K.T.M. **K. T. Moynihan, BSc (Hons)**
Technician, New Zealand Wildlife Service,
Wellington

J.B.N. **J. B. Nelson, D Phil**
Lecturer in Zoology, University of
Aberdeen, Scotland

D.G.N. **D. G. Newman, MSc**
Scientist, New Zealand Wildlife Service,
Wellington

C.F.J.O'D. **C. F. J. O'Donnell, BSc (Hons)**
Scientist, New Zealand Wildlife Service,
Christchurch

R.J.P. **R. J. Pierce, MSc, PhD**
Contract Scientist, Royal Forest and Bird
Protection Society, Dunedin

M.H.P. **M. H. Powlesland, MSc**
Programmer, New Zealand Post Office,
Wellington

R.G.P. **R. G. Powlesland, MSc, PhD**
Scientist, New Zealand Wildlife Service,
Wellington

B.E.R. **B. E. Reid, BSc**
Scientist, New Zealand Wildlife Service,
Wellington

L.E.R. **L. E. Richdale, OBE, MA, DSc, FRSNZ,
FLS**
Deceased. Author of *Sexual Behaviour in
Penguins* and *A Population Study of
Penguins*

C.J.R.R. **C. J. R. Robertson**
Consultant Editor

H.A.R. **H. A. Robertson, BSc, D Phil**
Scientist, Ecology Division, New Zealand
Department of Scientific and Industrial
Research, Lower Hutt

P.M.S. **P. M. Sagar, MSc**
Scientist, New Zealand Ministry of
Agriculture and Fisheries, Christchurch

P.W.S. **P. W. Shaw, BSc**
Technical Officer, Entomology Division,
New Zealand Department of Scientific and
Industrial Research, Appleby

R.B.S. **R. B. Sibson, MA, Dip Ed**
Retired. Previously President,
Ornithological Society of New Zealand;
and Editor, *Notornis*

J.S. **J. Squire**
Ornithological Consultant, Queensland

A.S. **A. Stewart, MSc**
Doctorate Student, Auckland University,
Auckland

M.J.T. **M. J. Taylor, MA, D Phil, FNZIC, FRSC**
Associate Professor of Chemistry, Auckland
University, Auckland

R.H.T. **R. H. Taylor**
Scientist, Ecology Division, New Zealand
Department of Scientific and Industrial
Research, Nelson

G.F.v.T. **G. F. van Tets, MA, PhD**
Principal Research Scientist, Division of
Wildlife Research, CSIRO, Australia

G.A.T. **G. A. Tunnicliffe, MSc**
Curator of Vertebrate Zoology, Canterbury
Museum, Christchurch

E.G.T. **E. G. Turbott, MSc, FMANZ**
Retired. Previously Director, Auckland
Institute and Museum

W.J.M.V. **W. J. M. Vestjens**
Deceased. Previously Technical Officer,
Division of Wildlife Research, CSIRO,
Australia

J.W. **J. Warham, MSc, PhD**
Reader in Zoology, Canterbury University,
Christchurch

K.E.W. **K. E. Westerskov, MSc, PhD**
Associate Professor of Zoology, Otago
University, Dunedin

G.R.W. **G. R. Williams, MSc, PhD**
Deceased. Previously Director New
Zealand Wildlife Service, Professor of
Entomology, Lincoln College

M.J.W. **M. J. Williams, BSc (Hons), PhD**
Scientist, New Zealand Wildlife Service,
Wellington

E.C.Y. **E. C. Young, MSc, DIC, PhD**
Professor of Zoology, Auckland University,
Auckland

Foreword

by Sir Charles Fleming, KBE, BA, MSc, DSc, FRS, FRSNZ, FMANZ

Representing the combined efforts of a team of noted authors and photographers, and the editors and designers of Reader's Digest, Complete Book of New Zealand Birds *is a timely and comprehensive work encompassing every species of bird found in the New Zealand region. For a significant part of this century* New Zealand Birds *by W.R.B. Oliver, published in 1930 and now out of print, was the 'bible' of New Zealand ornithologists. To Walter Reginald Brook Oliver (1883–1957), this volume is dedicated in gratitude and respect.*

UNTIL 1930, THE ONLY comprehensive treatise on New Zealand birds was *A History of the Birds of New Zealand* by Walter Lawry Buller, which was first issued in 1873, with an enlarged second edition in 1888 and a Supplement in 1905. This expensive work, published in small editions, was authoritative in its day though never convenient to handle or readily available. Now, however, its main value is its first-hand account of species, habitats and distributions, some of which have unfortunately been lost or restricted.

For more than two decades after Buller's death in 1906, no recognised scientific authority on ornithology in New Zealand was produced. Then, in 1930, Oliver's *New Zealand Birds* appeared (Fine Arts [N.Z.] Limited, Wellington, 541 pages), a compact volume at a reasonable price. Here was the first handbook on our avifauna to incorporate concise scientific information on behaviour, numbers and distributions, changes in status during a century of environmental change, and modern approaches in taxonomy and ecology. The small edition soon became a collector's item.

W.R.B. Oliver was much more than a leading ornithologist. Born in Tasmania, he came to New Zealand as a boy. While working in the Customs Department he pursued his interests in natural history. In 1908 he took part in an expedition to the Kermadec Islands and after his return began to publish papers on their geology, fauna and flora. After serving overseas during the First World War, he left the Customs Department in 1920 to join the Dominion Museum staff, soon producing a second edition of T.F. Cheeseman's *Flora* and enrolling for a part-time science degree at Victoria University College. He became Senior Scholar in Zoology and gained his Master of Science with first class honours. Oliver continued to publish research in botany (for which he earned his Doctor of Science), palaeontology, and also on molluscs, birds and whales. When he was appointed Director of the Dominion Museum in 1928, he gave his enthusiastic support to the plans for a new museum which was opened in 1936. After his retirement in 1947, Dr Oliver first devoted himself to a revision of the moas and then to an enlarged and revised second edition of his *New Zealand Birds* which appeared in 1955, twenty-five years after the first edition. At the same time, he continued to publish papers on botany and fossil plants.

The second edition of *New Zealand Birds*, which was reissued as a facsimile reprint in 1974, reflects its author's individualism and unorthodox views on certain aspects of taxonomy; yet such are its virtues, in its comprehensive coverage of the subject and its wealth of illustration, that it became the text upon which hundreds of young ornithologists, including most of the contributors to the present work, have cut their teeth. Indeed, this volume was originally planned as a third edition of *New Zealand Birds*, but it soon became obvious that our knowledge of the taxonomy, ecology, behaviour and biogeography of New Zealand birds had progressed so much during the last quarter century that a completely new work was required.

The task of writing this book, like the production of the current checklist and field guide, has called for the collaboration of a team of authors, each of whom has contributed his own specialised knowledge to the text. All the contributors have depended to a considerable degree upon the pioneering work of Dr W.R.B. Oliver in past decades; we owe him much and acknowledge our debt by dedicating this book to his memory.

Wellington, 1984

Contents

Part 1 UNDERSTANDING BIRDS

NAMING AND IDENTIFYING BIRDS.. 12
FLIGHT: The versatility of feathers 12
           Defying the force of gravity 14
           Flying and landing.. 16
BIRTH AND SURVIVAL 19
LIVING TOGETHER: Safety in numbers 20
           Competition and courtship.. 22
HABITATS: Where New Zealand birds live.. 24
THE ORIGIN AND EVOLUTION OF NEW ZEALAND'S BIRDS 32

Part 2 BIRDS OF NEW ZEALAND

KIWIS Apterygiformes
KIWIS Apterygidae 36

PENGUINS Sphenisciformes
PENGUINS Spheniscidae.. 40

GREBES AND DABCHICKS Podicipediformes
GREBES AND DABCHICKS Podicipedidae.. 54

TUBE-NOSED SEABIRDS Procellariiformes
ALBATROSSES Diomedeidae 58
FULMARS, PETRELS AND ALLIES Procellariidae 67
STORM PETRELS Hydrobatidae 102
DIVING PETRELS Pelecanoididae.. 106

PELICANS, GANNETS AND ALLIES Pelecaniformes
TROPIC BIRDS Phaethontidae 108
PELICANS Pelecanidae 109
GANNETS AND BOOBIES Sulidae.. 110
SHAGS AND CORMORANTS Phalacrocoracidae 114
DARTERS Anhingidae 127
FRIGATE BIRDS Fregatidae 128

HERONS AND ALLIES Ciconiiformes
HERONS AND BITTERNS Ardeidae.. 129
IBISES AND SPOONBILLS Threskiornithidae.. 136

DUCK-LIKE BIRDS Anseriformes
SWANS, GEESE AND DUCKS Anatidae 138

BIRDS OF PREY Falconiformes
EAGLES, HAWKS AND ALLIES Accipitridae 152
FALCONS Falconidae.. 154

PHEASANTS, PARTRIDGES AND QUAILS Galliformes
PHEASANTS AND ALLIES Phasianidae.. 156

CRANES, RAILS AND ALLIES Gruiformes
CRANES Gruidae 164
RAILS Rallidae.. 165

WADERS AND GULLS Charadriiformes

OYSTERCATCHERS Haematopodidae 174
LAPWINGS, PLOVERS AND DOTTERELS Charadriidae 177
TURNSTONES, CURLEWS AND ALLIES Scolopacidae 190
STILTS AND AVOCETS Recurvirostridae 212
PHALAROPES Phalaropodidae 215
PRATINCOLES Glareolidae 216
SKUAS Stercorariidae 217
GULLS Laridae 221
TERNS AND NODDIES Sternidae 224

PIGEONS AND DOVES Columbiformes

PIGEONS AND DOVES Columbidae 237

COCKATOOS AND PARROTS Psittaciformes

COCKATOOS Cacatuidae 241
NEW ZEALAND PARROTS Nestoridae 244
ROSELLAS AND PARAKEETS Platycercidae 246

CUCKOOS Cuculiformes

CUCKOOS Cuculidae 252

OWLS Strigiformes

OWLS Strigidae 256

SWIFTS Apodiformes

SWIFTS Apodidae 259

KINGFISHERS AND ROLLERS Coraciiformes

KINGFISHERS Alcedinidae 260
ROLLERS Coraciidae 263

PERCHING BIRDS Passeriformes

NEW ZEALAND WRENS Xenicidae 264
LARKS Alaudidae 267
SWALLOWS AND MARTINS Hirundinidae 268
PIPITS AND WAGTAILS Motacillidae 270
CUCKOO-SHRIKES Campephagidae 271
ACCENTORS Prunellidae 273
WARBLERS, THRUSHES AND ALLIES Muscicapidae 274
SILVEREYES Zosteropidae 288
HONEYEATERS Meliphagidae 289
BUNTINGS AND ALLIES Emberizidae 293
FINCHES Fringillidae 295
SPARROWS AND WEAVERS Ploceidae 299
STARLINGS AND MYNAS Sturnidae 300
NEW ZEALAND WATTLEBIRDS Callaeidae 302
WOOD-SWALLOWS Artamidae 304
BELL MAGPIES Cracticidae 305
CROWS Corvidae 306

EXTINCT BIRDS 308
CLASSIFICATION BY ORDER AND FAMILY 309

INDEX OF SCIENTIFIC NAMES 314
INDEX OF COMMON NAMES 316
ACKNOWLEDGMENTS 319

The New Zealand kingfisher *Halcyon sancta vagans*.

Introduction

As many as 305 species of birds are known to breed in or visit the New Zealand region, and some of these—such as the tui and the rare kakapo—are found nowhere else in the world. Well-known introduced species, among them the starling, house sparrow and yellowhammer, comprise almost one-fifth the total number of species. However there are relatively few land and forest birds, as most birds of the New Zealand region are seabirds, waders or freshwater dwellers.

The migrant waders in particular—especially the rarer species and the vagrants that visit New Zealand and its outlying islands—attract a great deal of interest. 'Wader spotting', for some ornithologists and amateurs, has become an increasingly popular pastime—despite the difficulties of identification and the nature of the open, often remote, regions they favour.

Complete Book of New Zealand Birds is addressed not only to the ornithologist or the serious student, but to all New Zealanders who wish to improve their understanding of birds and enjoy the challenges and pleasures of bird observation and identification.

The book is divided into two sections. Part 1, Understanding Birds, explains some of the mysteries of bird behaviour—how they fly, navigate vast distances, deal with predators and competitors, maintain a constant food supply, find a mate and raise their young. The different kinds of New Zealand habitat, and how birds have been affected by the presence of humans, are also described. Part 1 concludes with a history of New Zealand birds—from their origins over two million years ago to their prospects for survival in today's increasingly threatened habitats.

Part 2, Birds of New Zealand, forms the core of the book. There are descriptions of every species of bird found in the New Zealand region and, with few exceptions, all descriptions are accompanied by a photograph of the bird. These remarkable photographs, many of them taken by the best of New Zealand's photographers and gathered from sources around the world, not only assist in identification in the field but provide enjoyable and informative browsing at home. Field notes support the general essays and sum up the features by which a bird can usually be recognised—such as its shape, distinctive markings, colour or flight pattern. The birds are arranged according to their classification, beginning with the most primitive species—the endemic kiwi—and ending with the introduced rook.

The book ends with descriptions of extinct species and explains the system of classification into order and family. An index of both common and scientific names provides quick and easy access to all species of birds described.

The Editors

Part 1 UNDERSTANDING BIRDS

Naming and identifying birds

PART 2, THE BIRDS OF NEW ZEALAND, presents descriptions of the appearance, distribution, habits and behaviour of every species of bird that visits the New Zealand region. The sequence of descriptions is according to classification, beginning with the more primitive species and ending with the most advanced species—the passerines, or perching birds. There are photographs of all but seven birds. The text describes the bird in two ways. The field notes, in italic type, are written in note form and provide a quick reference. A general essay then describes the bird's habitat, breeding behaviour, food and distinguishing feeding habits, distribution and abundance, and relations with humans.

Naming the bird

Every bird described is identified by two names—first, its common name, such as 'brown kiwi', and second by its scientific name. In the case of the brown kiwi this is *Apteryx australis*.

The scientific name is, by convention, always printed in italics, except where it occurs in an italic context. Every animal and plant is given a scientific name when it is classified as a separate species. A species is generally considered to be a group whose members can interbreed in the wild and produce fertile offspring. Closely related species are grouped into a genus, and the scientific name of a species also shows to which genus it belongs. Thus the Antarctic petrel is *Thalassoica antarctica*. The generic name always begins with a capital letter.

Most scientific names are derived from Greek or Latin, or a combination of both, as in the case of the Antarctic petrel. *Thalassoica* comes from the Greek word *thalassa*, meaning the sea, and *antarctica* (the Latin form of the Greek word *antarktikos*). Quite often the name of a person or country is latinised—the scientific name of Buller's mollymawk is *Diomedea bulleri*; the New Zealand falcon, *Falco novaeseelandiae*.

In some cases a triple name is used. The third name indicates the subspecies, or race; this is a level of classification awarded to birds of the same species that look different. For example, there are three subspecies of brown kiwi—the North Island brown kiwi *Apteryx australis mantelli*, South Island brown kiwi *Apteryx australis australis* and Stewart Island brown kiwi *Apteryx australis lawryi*.

The name of the person who originally described the species or subspecies, plus the date of the description, follows the scientific name. Brackets are used if the genus is no longer the same as that originally described.

Ornithologists are constantly reclassifying birds in the light of new studies. Some birds regarded as a separate species may become subspecies when they have been found to interbreed with other species. Conversely, some birds thought to be subspecies have been found to display sufficient differences to be reclassified as a separate species.

Classification by order and family

Animals are grouped into many other hierarchies besides species and genus. The Antarctic petrel, for instance, is grouped with fulmars, petrels, prions and shearwaters in the family Procellariidae. This family is, in turn, grouped with four other families in the order Procellariiformes, tube-nosed seabirds. This and 26 other orders of birds are grouped in the

Naming the parts 1

class Aves, which comprises all birds.

In this book the order and family to which each species belongs are shown at the bottom of each page; a more detailed classification by order and family of the birds found in the New Zealand region is given on pages 309 to 312. The classification generally followed is that of *The Annotated Checklist of the Birds of New Zealand* (and its Supplement) produced by the Ornithological Society of New Zealand. There are some minor differences in the sequence of species within a genus. In most cases the common names by which these birds are identified also follow the checklist.

For most people, an interest in birds begins with identification—with the pleasure to be had from being able to put the right name to a bird, whether it is studied at leisure in a city park or glimpsed fleetingly on a drive through the country. Success in identifying birds depends on knowing how to look at them. This is not simply a matter of being alert, but is a technique that can easily be learnt.

The most important clues to a bird's identity—the points to which special attention should be paid—are these: size; shape, including the shape and length of the bill; general colouring of the plumage, and particularly noticeable markings; behaviour (for instance how a bird feeds, or approaches its mate); call and song; and where the bird was seen.

Birds are adapted to fit into a particular habitat. The design of a bird's legs for example reflects the sort of habitat in which it lives: the heron for instance has long legs for wading through water. The shape of the bird's bill is also another distinctive feature which will help in the identification of a bird, and offers a clue as to the type of food it eats. The bill of the shoveler is flattened, so that it may sieve in mud, whereas the snipe has a long straight bill for probing the earth.

Since some birds visit New Zealand at only

certain times of the year, the season in which a bird is seen may be a clue to its identity. Flight pattern is another clue. Is it direct, undulating or meandering? Powerful or fluttering? Does the bird fly in rapid bursts or is its flight sustained? Its flight may be undulating—a fairly regular pattern of flapping and gliding. The method of flight is another significant factor. A bird may use its wings almost all the time in flapping flight or it may glide on outstretched wings; it may hover in one place or it may soar. Further points to watch for are the size and shape of the wings, the speed at which the wings move, and the depth of the wing-beats.

The field notes

This section consists of entries under the following headings: Status, Other Names, Size, Description, Moult, Voice, Distribution and Recognition.

STATUS: The status of the bird, which indicates at a glance the standing of the species in the New Zealand region, is the first entry in the Field Notes section. Seven kinds are described.

Endemic: These species, for example the kakapo or paradise shelduck, are found breeding naturally *only* in the New Zealand region.

Native: Although these species are found breeding in the New Zealand region naturally, they also breed in other localities outside the region. They include such species as the black-fronted dotterel, grey teal and welcome swallow.

Circumpolar: These species, among them several penguin races, are found breeding in the New Zealand region naturally, but also breed in most suitable locations in higher latitudes round the southern hemisphere.

Migrant: Species such as the far-eastern

curlew and the knot are classified as migrants. Although they do not breed in the New Zealand region, parts of the population visit the area on a regular, seasonal or periodic basis.

Straggler: These species, among them the little egret and the Mongolian dotterel, stray sporadically to the New Zealand region from breeding or migrating populations which occur elsewhere.

Vagrant: Species classified as vagrants are those found irregularly in the New Zealand region, either far from their natural range, or as a result of exceptional climatic events. The fork-tailed swift for instance breeds across eastern Asia, migrates to Australia, and some birds then drift to New Zealand.

Introduced: These species, mainly passerines, have been introduced to New Zealand solely by man. Notable examples are the starling and house sparrow.

OTHER NAMES: Many birds have a Maori name or an alternative English name—for instance, the morepork, known to the Maori as ruru, is also referred to as the New Zealand owl. The English names given are the alternative names by which the bird may be known in the New Zealand region. Each of these names is given an index entry.

SIZE: The length of each bird is given. Length is measured from the tip of the bill to the tip of the tail, and is rounded off to the nearest 10 mm. The main use of this measurement in identifying birds seen in the field is as a basis for visual comparisons between species.

DESCRIPTION: The bird's colour is described in detail, usually by working down the back

THE SHAPES OF EGGS

Birds' eggs vary greatly in shape. Some basic shapes are shown here, but all kinds of intergradations between them are to be seen. Birds of the same species lay eggs of the same shape.

round or spherical

pyriform or conical

elliptical or oblong-oval

long-oval or elliptical-ovate

and then down the front to the belly and undertail region, ending with the colour of the iris of the eye, the bill, and the legs. Different authorities sometimes use varying names for the same colour, especially subtle greys and browns; the accompanying photographs will provide guidance.

Some birds have two or more different plumages during the year. Certain feathers may be replaced by brighter ones for the beginning of the breeding season, and where this occurs, all plumages are usually described. Some birds change to an eclipse plumage, after the breeding season, which is

of much shorter duration than the true non-breeding season, or winter, plumage.

Young birds are called chicks or nestlings until they are able to fly. Chicks that are likely to be seen, such as ducklings, are described. The next stage is when a young bird wears its first plumage of true feathers. It is called a juvenile or fledgling. Next, the young bird is called an immature. This stage may last for several years in some species, and the birds may pass through several distinguishable plumage phases. Where there is a definite immature plumage this is briefly described.

MOULT: This describes both the timing and the various stages of the moult, and often the locality at which it occurs. Sometimes however, when a bird has been only rarely studied, little or no information can be provided.

VOICE: The sounds a bird makes may provide an important guide to its identification. Songs and calls are described. Sometimes calls can be phonetically transcribed—as *zit-zit-zit*, for instance—but others are so complex that they can only be described as 'harsh chattering sounds'.

DISTRIBUTION: Each species is distributed over a certain area, usually determined by the availability of suitable habitat and food. Within the range some birds are sedentary—they stay in one area throughout the year. The distribution notes are most extensive, however, for those birds which migrate between two places or wander nomadically.

RECOGNITION: This shaded panel picks out the essential features that allow quick recognition of the bird in the field.

Naming the parts 2

crown
forehead
lores
cere
cheek
bill
scapulars
wing coverts

ear coverts
nape
mantle
back
rump
upper tail coverts
tail

Flight: the versatility of feathers

TAIL FEATHERS usually number 10 to 12, although the pheasant may have as many as 24. They are mainly concerned with steering and maintaining balanced flight.

THE ALULA is attached to the bird's thumb and consists of three or four short vaned feathers. In normal flight it lies flat against the bird's wing but, at slow speeds, it is extended to prevent stalling.

TERTIARIES are the few flight feathers attached to the upper arm or humerus.

COVERTS are small contour feathers that overlie the quill bases of the larger feathers. They make the flight surfaces aerodynamically smooth.

SECONDARIES are flight feathers carried on the forearm. They sustain the bird in the air, providing 'lift'.

PRIMARIES are the largest of the flight feathers and the furthest away from the body. They propel the bird through the air.

Barb

Rachis

Barbule

Barbicels

Vane

Shaft

A FEATHER UNDER THE MICROSCOPE Shown microscopically, each barb of a vaned feather is revealed as a miniature feather. Every barb carries several hundred barbules, equipped with minute hooks—the barbicels. Each hooked barbule is able to interlock with its unhooked neighbour on the next barb.

I**T IS NOT THE POWER OF FLIGHT** that sets birds in a class of their own; for bats and insects can fly, and some birds cannot. What distinguishes them from all other animals, present or past, is that they have feathers.

The main functions of feathers—flight, heat conservation, waterproofing, camouflage and display—are all crucial to the existence of birds. How feathers evolved from reptiles so many millions of years ago remains a mystery. Yet they were fully developed in the earliest fossil, *Archaeopteryx*, 150 million years ago.

Feathers, whatever their origins, are of two main kinds: outer flight and contour feathers, which give the bird its shape and provide insulation, and inner down feathers, which provide an extra insulating coat. Filoplume feathers (the 'hairs' on a plucked fowl) are grown around the base of contour and down feathers; they seem to be degenerate feathers with no certain known function. Powder-down feathers, which are found in herons, bitterns and hawks, are the only feathers which grow continuously and are never moulted. Instead, their tips continually disintegrate into a fine, water-resistant powder, used in preening to waterproof and preserve the other feathers.

The structure of a flight feather

The typical flight contour feather is made up of a central shaft, hollow at its base for conveying nourishment, and becoming solid for strength further up, in a part called the rachis, where the two webs of the vane are supported. These webs reveal a fascinating interlocking system whereby hundreds of parallel barbs in turn carry barbules equipped with tiny hooks (or barbicels). Each hooked barbule interlocks with its unhooked neighbour on the next barb. To interlock separated barbs, a bird simply draws the feather through its beak a few times to restore the entire web. A ruffled feather can be restored to shape even by running it between a human finger and thumb.

Often, the vaned feather grows a secondary after-feather from a tiny opening at the point where the base and rachis meet. This after-feather is usually small and downy, and was probably developed as an extra layer of insulation against heat loss.

Down feathers are fluffy because their barbules have no hooks. Their main function is heat preservation—the same purpose as the semi-plume feathers which lie under the covering contour feathers. When a bird fluffs itself out in cold weather, it is giving itself a thicker blanket of warm air between its inner and outer covering of feathers. Conversely, in warm weather the bird often disarranges its outer feathers to speed up the process of heat loss.

Birds need effective insulation, especially against cold, because they live at what for a human would be fever heat: they must maintain a body temperature of approximately 41°C (106°F).

Body size is the main factor affecting the number of feathers on a bird. A large bird, such as a swan, can carry more than 25 000, while most small songbirds have 1500 to 3000.

Feather growth

Apart from powder-down feathers, which never stop growing, all fully formed feathers are dead structures, receiving nothing from the body but physical support. But at first each feather grows from a tiny papilla, or 'goose pimple', and is built up largely of the horny, lightweight substance keratin. During its growth period, the feather receives nourishment through its open-ended base.

Despite the 'fully clothed' appearance of most birds, feathers do not grow all over the body—except in rare cases such as the penguins —but in clearly defined feather tracts. Areas in between are naked; among birds with dense plumage, such as ducks, this area is reduced in size and often covered with down.

Apart from these featherless regions, many birds have developed brood spots—patches on the breast and belly from which feathers moult when the bird is incubating an egg. Feathers are such efficient insulators that they would keep much of the bird's body heat from the egg. When the feathers from them have moulted, the naked skin of the brood spots becomes warmer than normal, as swollen vessels carry more blood to them.

The moulting process

Feathers are continually subject to wear and are replaced at regular intervals. Old feathers are pushed out by the growth of new ones in the same follicles, giving the bird a regular series of plumages throughout its life.

In almost all birds, the feathers are replaced in sequence, a few at a time, and usually in pairs from either side of the body. There is a great deal of variation, but often the large wing and tail feathers begin to moult first, and this is followed by a progressive shedding of body feathers.

The loss of vital feathers renders some birds, for a time, particularly vulnerable and can seriously affect their capacity for survival. Birds cope with this vulnerability in a number of ways. For example, to ensure that penguins, most of which inhabit cold regions, have a uniformly warm coat, old feathers are not lost until the new have grown completely. When the new plumage has grown the bird combs off the old feathers with its feet and beak to complete the process of renewal.

Just as the penguin is in danger if old feathers are removed before renewal is complete, birds which depend greatly on their flying ability are in danger as they shed their flight feathers. During these flightless periods some birds seek the sanctuary of such places as marshes and lakes where food is readily available. Some species migrate to moult in traditionally safe areas.

It is difficult to establish firm rules as to why and when birds moult. Research suggests that a combination of factors may trigger the process: the length of daylight, action of the pituitary and thyroid glands, and changes in the reproductive organs.

Usually birds do not moult while breeding, during migration, or in times of food shortage. These are critical periods when extra energy is required to replace heat which is lost more rapidly as feathers are displaced. Yet some seabirds—which cannot risk moulting at sea on the wing—moult during their breeding season. For some species the period im-

Care of the plumage

An efficient system of feather maintenance is essential, not only for effective flight but for survival. Damaged or worn feathers hamper flight and dirty feathers may harbour parasites.

Preening is the most common cleansing activity. By nibbling individual feathers from the base outwards, birds repair small separations and restore a smooth flight surface. To cleanse the head area, a bird scratches with its feet. Bathing in water is another cleansing activity, one thought to have an additional function—it dampens the plumage so that oil from the preen gland may be spread more easily to water-proof and insulate. Two remarkable cleansing methods, insufficiently understood, are dusting, whereby small birds such as sparrows make scrapes in the ground and then work the dust into their feathers, and 'anting' (seemingly confined to songbirds), whereby a bird gathers ants and rubs them on its flight feathers.

BATHING
Fluffing up its body feathers, a Caspian tern beats its wings vigorously in water.

SCRATCHING
With wings closed, a kea reaches a leg forward to scratch its head feathers directly.

PREENING
A takahe nibbles its feathers between the tips of its bill, an activity all birds share.

mediately after the breeding season is the optimum time for moulting. Breeding areas are selected on the basis of a plentiful food supply and so a complete plumage can be achieved, in ideal conditions, in preparation for the long migration flights.

In its lifetime a bird may progress through a number of plumages, from natal down, through to juvenile, immature, partial 'pre-nuptial' and full adult display plumages. Some birds, especially migrants, have an interrupted moult which is completed in the winter quarters.

Birds as a class are the most vividly coloured of all backboned animals, though bright coloration is far from universal. The general rule is that the warmer and dryer the climate, the brighter the bird. New Zealand birds, in line with this rule, tend to be more drably coloured than those which live in Australia.

Two of the main functions of plumage colour seem to be contradictory, for one is self-advertisement and the other is self-concealment. In many species a balance is struck between these two needs; the male is brightly coloured, especially in the breeding season, and the female is camouflaged by drab coloration. This sex-based difference is particularly marked among ducks, in which the brown or grey females of some species tend to resemble one another more closely than they resemble their own males.

Brilliant plumage does more than simply attract the opposite sex; it serves also as a kind of flag or battle standard to warn off rivals when the bird is defending territory.

A third function of colour is to reduce wear and tear on feathers. Black feathers, for instance, contain wear-resistant pigments; the white wings of many seabirds are tipped with black, because the wing-tip feathers are those most likely to be scuffed and worn.

How birds obtain their colours

The different hues in the feathers of a bird are built up in two ways: by pigments and by the surface structure of the feathers themselves. Pigments known as melanins, produced in the body of the bird, give rise to colours ranging from blacks and browns to light tans. Those known as carotenoids, taken in with food and usually deposited directly on the feathers with little or no chemical change, produce bright yellows, oranges and reds.

Blue is not a pigment in feathers; it is caused by the structure of the barbs, which reflect blue light and filter through the rest of the spectrum to be absorbed by the dark melanin layer beneath. Green—except in a few cases— is produced in the same way, though the reflective part of the barb may be pigmented with melanin for olive-greens, or with carotenoids for brighter greens. White is produced by barbs which reflect almost all light.

semi-plume

filoplume

down

*vaned feather
with after-feather*

FOUR KINDS OF FEATHERS

The two basic types of feathers, from which the others seem to be derived, are vaned outer feathers and down feathers. Down feathers are fluffy because their barbs have no hooks. The vaned feather, with its long shaft of interlocked barbs, may have a small downy after-feather at its base. The filoplume is a hair-like feather with a vestige of barbs. (They have been developed as display plumes in some species.)

Flight: defying the force of gravity

SOARING AT CLIFFS Black-backed gulls and other seabirds are able to gain height by riding the updrafts that are caused when a wind hits cliffs or some other obstacle. Even with the wind offshore they can still gain height effortlessly by riding the eddies which curl upwards as the wind spills over the cliff edge.

THOUGH HUMANS HAVE BUILT flying machines and gradually unlocked many of the secrets of flight, a bird on the wing nevertheless remains a source of wonder and envy. To make flight possible, the body of a bird—the most efficient of flying machines—has evolved several noteworthy features. The most important are lightness and strength. Lightness is essential—and so the bones of the skeleton are extremely thin and, in many cases, hollow and criss-crossed with struts. In those parts of the skeleton where strength is paramount—such as the skull, chest region, pelvis and wing—the bones may fuse together.

A powerful musculature has evolved to facilitate powered flight. The most important muscles are those attached to the 'breast' which transmit their power through long tendons and provide the powerful downstroke. Muscles also extend and fold the wing while a series of tendons holds the feathers in their correct position.

The shape of a bird is another adaptation for flight. Whatever variations there may be to the shape, the body of a bird is always streamlined. As air passes over the body, friction must be reduced to a minimum, so feathers provide a smooth outer surface.

The most effortless form of flight is gliding. To do so a bird may simply launch itself from its perch, open its wings, and 'parachute' downwards. By losing height it travels forwards. This is the simplest form of flight as well as the most easily understood.

Aerodynamics in action

The aerodynamic design of a bird's body enables it to resist impediments to flight. For a start, the wing is designed to obtain lift. As air passes over the wing, the air travels faster over the upper rounded surface than it does over the lower surface. This is because it has further to go. The faster air travels across the surface, the lower the pressure it exerts on that surface. The pressure is therefore lower on the upper surface and lift is produced, counteracting the force of gravity.

If the air does not continue to flow at an adequate speed over the upper surface, lift is lost and it can be said that the bird stalls. To maintain a continuous flow of air and control turbulence, the bird projects its alula to smooth and control the air flow. (The alula is a tuft of feathers which can form a slot on the wing's leading edge.)

The passage of the air over the wing, though

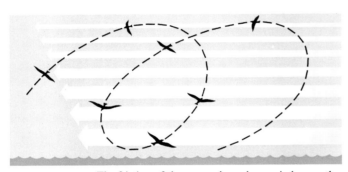

DYNAMIC SOARING The friction of the waves slows down winds near the surface of the sea. A gradient of velocities is set up, with the wind at its maximum speed 15 to 30 m above the waves. Birds such as shearwaters instinctively exploit this variation in wind speeds. They gain momentum on a high fast windstream, then wheel down to a lower level, using their momentum to rise again, this time against the wind.

STAYING IN THE AIR Air travels faster over the rounded upper surface of the wings as it has further to go. This creates pressure beneath the wings, which are hollowed, and a partial vacuum above them, resulting in the upward force known as 'lift'.

GAINING HEIGHT To climb higher, a bird tilts up the leading edge of its wings. The greater the angle between the wings and the airstream, the greater the turbulence. Too steep an angle, and the turbulence would break up the flow of air over the wings.

PREVENTING STALLING To prevent stalling the bird spreads the alula (normally folded against the wing) forward, to form a slot on the leading edge of the wing. Air rushes through, keeping the airstream over the whole wing fast and turbulence-free.

Moving on land and water:

LAND BIRDS

Though hopping is a most efficient way of moving from branch to branch, it is energy-consuming. Species such as starlings, which spend a good deal of time on the ground, have therefore evolved a way of moving on land which is more economical—walking. A bird walks on its toes, not on the entire area of its foot, because what looks like a knee joint is in actual fact closer to being a heel. Most birds have four toes, three pointing forwards and one, which is known as the hallux, pointing to the rear. In running birds such as the kiwi or weka this is little more than a stub, creating a minimum area of contact with the ground. The same result is achieved by sprinters running on the balls of their feet in a 100 m race. There are many variations to the legs and feet; these are in accordance with the bird's habitat and sometimes its food.

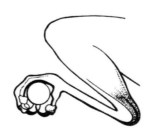

THE GRIP OF A PERCHING BIRD When a tui or a bellbird for instance settles on a small branch, so that it may stay attached, a mechanism comes into operation which locks the toes firmly around the branch. Flexor tendons passing down the back of its leg are automatically pulled taut over its ankle bone so that the toes curl in. The toes stay clamped around the perch as long as the bird is in the squatting position. They unlock only when the bird stands upright, releasing tension on its tendons.

WALKING
The hind claw of the pipit is elongated, to brace the bird and prevent it from falling backwards.

RUNNING
The kiwi frequently runs. Its shortened hind toe reduces the area of foot touching the ground.

HUNTING
The morepork's powerful talons are used for perching, and for seizing and killing its prey.

CLIMBING
Strong claws and two backward-pointing toes enable the parakeet to climb by gripping bark.

PERCHING
The backward-pointing toe of the greenfinch curls round to meet the other toes, clamping it to its perch.

BECOMING AIRBORNE: TAKING OFF FROM RIVERS, LAKES AND STRETCHES OF SEA

The object of any bird when it is about to take off is to get air moving over its wings at a speed that is fast enough to produce lift. Ducks, for instance, and many other waterbirds work up speed by pattering along the surface of a lake, river or stretch of sea, at the same time flapping their wings energetically until they gain sufficient momentum to fly into the oncoming airstream, or—alternatively—are thrown upwards by a collision with a wave.

it helps to create lift, also produces drag (a tendency to blow the wing backwards). The streamlined shape of the wing reduces drag—the leading edge, reinforced by bones, is blunt, rounded and stiff; and feathers ensure that the trailing edge tapers neatly to a point. The flatter the wing surface the less drag there is.

Taking off

Because a bird cannot become airborne unless it is moving against an airstream, it must either take off into the wind or make an airstream of its own. Most birds gain the initial impetus by jumping into the air, flapping their wings backwards and forwards rather than up and down, to create an airstream; or they take a short run, and push off strongly from the ground. Take-off is a special problem for some of the best flyers; specialisation in one direction often leads to under-development in another. The swift, airborne for much of its life, has poorly developed legs. To take off, it falls forward from a high ledge.

Once aloft, a bird may proceed forward either by flapping flight (which consumes a great deal of energy) or, if conditions are conducive, by gliding (which in its more complex forms involves soaring).

Those birds whose wings are equipped for soaring are able to take advantage of rising air. This way they need barely move their wings at all. Another method, common to seabirds, involves the use of the up-currents of air that are caused when wind strikes a cliff. In a method sometimes referred to as dynamic soaring, seabirds are able to take advantage of the friction caused by wind passing over the surface of the waves.

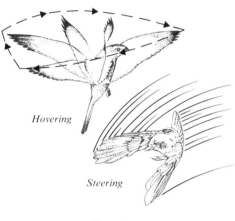

Hovering

Steering

Steering

Once in flight, a bird is able to adjust its course by bringing into play a number of factors. By tilting its body against the direction of motion the bird will be moved to one side—and so produce a turn. Its tail, and sometimes its feet, can also contribute to the steering process. Alternatively, by folding one wing, even slightly, the bird can reduce the drag on that side and begin to bank. The faster a bird is flying, the more precise and effective these operations will be.

Different species are able to capitalise on certain anatomical characteristics to steer successfully. For instance, a long tail enables the pheasant to twist easily through woodland habitat whereas the quail, though short-tailed, is able to bring into play its broad wings, for these provide an excellent control surface. In fast flight swallows keep their forked tail closed, but spread it to improve control in slower flight.

Hovering

Hovering is a most strenuous form of flight. To remain fixed over one spot—either to spy for food or, in the case of the hummingbird, to feed from a flower—requires lift without propulsion. This is achieved by energetically flapping the wings backwards and forwards. Falcons adapt a less demanding form of hovering. To maintain a fixed position in relation to the ground, they fly into the wind at the same speed as it is blowing them back.

special adaptations of legs and feet

WATERSIDE BIRDS

Most waders have long toes that are spread wide apart. This increases the area of foot that comes in contact with the ground so that the bird will not sink too readily in the soft mud of lake sides, riverbeds, swamps and marshes. Although they do not have webbed feet, some can swim on occasions. The conditions underfoot along stretches of water are extremely varied and the range of adaptations of the feet of wading birds reflects this. The shore in one area may be firm and dry, in another soft and marshy. Feeding habits of waterside birds are also varied. Gulls scavenge along the tide line; sandpipers wade in the shallows probing vigorously for molluscs, worms and small crustaceans. Long legs are an obvious advantage for birds which wade in the shallows to hunt prey.

SWIMMING BIRDS

Webbed feet and paddle-shaped toes help drive the swimming bird through the water. The feet must be able to move as much water as possible on the power stroke, and as little as possible on the recovery stroke. The amount of water that can be pushed back by the spread foot is a rough gauge of the importance of swimming in the life of each species. The rear positioning of the legs is marked in many swimming birds such as grebes and diving ducks. Just as a ship's propeller is located at the back of a ship, so the legs of these birds are at the ends of their bodies, providing power unimpeded by obstacles. This results in a rather ungainly inefficient movement on land, however, as the legs are positioned too far from the bird's centre of gravity.

WADING
Stilts have long, widely spaced toes adapted for walking on soft mud without sinking into it.

HALF-WEBBED TOES
The phalarope is a wader which feeds in the water. It has evolved semi-webbed feet for swimming.

THREE-WEBBED TOES
Webs between three toes increase the area of the mallard's foot, which is folded on the forward stroke.

FOUR-WEBBED TOES
Webs between all four toes powerfully propel shags and cormorants.

PADDLE-SHAPED TOES
The southern crested grebe spreads the paddle-shaped lobes on its feet to maximise the power stroke. They are folded back on the return stroke.

Flight: flying and landing

The bird begins its down-stroke

Air resistance bends wings into a propeller shape

Feathers fan open on the up-stroke

Wings sweep forward at end of the down-stroke

Each primary becomes a small propeller

Primaries snap back, ready for a new down-stroke

POWERED FLIGHT: WHAT HAPPENS WHEN A BIRD FLAPS ITS WINGS

FLAPPING FLIGHT IS MUCH more complex and requires more energy than gliding flight. Although all its subtleties are not yet understood, the basic facts have been established.

When they use their wings many birds use the inner parts of their wings as gliding wings to maintain lift, for they are held relatively steady. The large primary feathers, controlled by the hand, propel the bird.

The down-stroke, obtained when the great pectoral muscles drive the wing, is the power stroke. It is made with the feathers closed flat against one another, creating an unbroken airtight surface, so that the maximum amount of air resistance is encountered. The wing moves downwards and forwards and, as it does so, the primaries are bent back at their ends, shaping the wing into a propeller which pulls the bird forward.

During the up-stroke, which is mainly a recovery stroke, the primary feathers twist open (with an action similar to that of venetian blinds). This allows the air to pass easily through the gaps between them. On this stroke, the bird rotates its wing at the shoulder, increasing its angle of attack to maintain lift. The primary feathers are again bent back on this stroke and each individual feather becomes a small separate propeller. These feathers are regularly replaced by moulting.

During the up-stroke, the driving force of the primaries, although less powerful than on the down-stroke, is especially important for large, heavy birds. They cannot afford a 'wasted' stroke, especially on take-off or when climbing, and so their feathers do not open to the same extent as smaller birds.

In the complete cycle of a flapping stroke the wing-tips, which move faster and further than the rest of the wings, go through a figure-of-eight pattern, with a wide loop at the top. They complete the up-stroke with a rapid snap, which helps drive the bird forward.

An interesting flight variation is formation flying whereby birds such as geese, ducks and gulls fly in 'V' formations on long journeys. The eddies of air caused by a bird in flight represent much wasted energy. To conserve some of this energy, each bird gets extra lift from the slipstream of the bird flying in front.

Approaching and landing

Landing places great demands upon a bird's body. Wings play a major part in this process and the bird's undercarriage—feet, legs and tail, braced to withstand the transfer of weight—brings a complex range of factors into play.

A simple form of landing is, in many ways, an extension of gliding. To land gently, the bird must judge the landing position, glide down onto it just to the point of stalling and then gently alight on the landing place. If the bird finds it is approaching too quickly, it may dip down on the approach and then reduce momentum by gliding upwards. A more demanding method requires that, as the bird nears its landing position, it brakes by spreading its wings and tail and moving its body into a near-vertical position. It further reduces momentum by flapping its wings against the direction of flight. To prevent stalling, the alula are brought into play. The legs absorb the final shock.

A New Zealand falcon alights on a branch, wings and tail spread, and feet outstretched to absorb the shock of landing.

SHAPE
A bird's speed and manoeuvrability will be determined by such factors as whether the wing is long and pointed or short and broad; the camber or degree of curving; and the total area of wing surface in relation to weight.

SWIFT *High-speed flight demands swept-back wings, long and narrow to minimise turbulence. Such wings lack slots, which are a disadvantage in high-speed flight.*

ALBATROSS *Gliding is produced most effectively with long narrow wings. With such wings, flapping flight demands great muscular energy.*

PHEASANT *For rapid take-off, short broad wings, strongly arched for minimum lift, allow the pheasant to rise explosively.*

Birth and survival

SUCCESSFUL BREEDING demands a temporary change in a bird's behaviour pattern. Most species have a restricted breeding period—at roughly the same time, once a year; or, in some species, only once every two years. When conditions are most suitable for raising young efficiently, the male expresses its readiness for mating, often in elaborate courtship displays; a pair is formed and a nest-site chosen (though not necessarily in that order); and, singly or together, the partners construct a nest that is safe from predators. Once the female lays the eggs they are incubated until they hatch. The young must then be fed, sheltered and protected from enemies.

Most birds breed in territory they often fight to obtain. Not only is it a refuge for courting and mating; it must provide a suitable nest-site and, for some species, regular supplies of food. Frequently, birds form monogamous pairs—at least for part of the breeding season. In some species these pairs last for life; but in promiscuous species no such bond is formed. Mating is a relatively simple affair. Except for ducks and some flightless species, most birds have no external reproductive organs during mating. Mating involves a bringing together of the respective cloaca openings as the male bird (which has an evertible cloaca) mounts the female who moves her tail to one side.

Mammals, whose evolution is further developed than that of birds, reproduce their young inside their bodies. Birds develop their young outside their bodies—a distinct advantage for a creature so intricately designed for flight.

The eggs laid for incubation at one sitting are referred to as a clutch. The size of the clutch varies but it seems that a major factor is how many young the parent bird is able to care for successfully. Most seabirds lay only one egg, whereas some other species will lay more eggs during a season when food is abundant.

The egg nurtures the developing embryo. The germ cell from which it will grow lies on the upper surface of the yolk, which supplies fats and proteins. So that the germ cell remains uppermost, the yolk is encased in the tough vitelline membrane, which extends on both sides and attaches to the shell membranes as a twisted strand, the chalaza. Suspended in this fashion, the yolk is able to compensate for any chance movement. Albumen, which cushions the yolk against shock, is 90 per cent water and provides a further store of protein. The remarkably strong egg shell encloses the two sturdy membranes which surround the contents of the egg.

The embryo must be kept warm until the egg hatches. During this incubation period the male or female—sometimes both, in shifts—warms the eggs with its feet or with specially developed brood patches on its breast or abdomen. The king penguin keeps its single egg warm by supporting it on its feet and enveloping it in a fold of skin.

When the egg is hatched the young chick breaks through the shell with its egg-tooth (this disappears shortly after hatching). There are two types of young—precocial, which can run around within a few hours of hatching, and altricial, which are totally dependent.

Parental duties continue to be demanding once the chicks have hatched. The parents must clean the nest, protect the chicks from predators, keep them warm and, in the case of nestlings, provide a continual supply of food. Though chicks instinctively feed themselves, these skills are sharpened by practice. The parent bird continues to feed nestlings and very young chicks, partly in response to their begging. A common method of attracting attention is gaping, whereby the young open wide their bills displaying the bright pink interior (or gape). Gaping is often accompanied by squeaky, high-pitched calls.

The black shag often builds its nest of twigs, plants and debris in the branches of trees. The parent bird feeds its nestlings pre-digested fish.

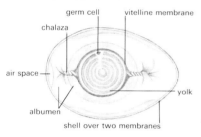
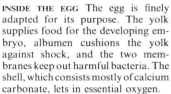

INSIDE THE EGG The egg is finely adapted for its purpose. The yolk supplies food for the developing embryo, albumen cushions the yolk against shock, and the two membranes keep out harmful bacteria. The shell, which consists mostly of calcium carbonate, lets in essential oxygen.

THREE-DAY-OLD BLACKBIRD NESTLING Unlike precocial young, which are born at a more advanced stage of development, altricial young are born blind, naked and totally dependent on their parents for food. While they are in the nest, these helpless young are also referred to as nestlings.

Nests: shelters for the young

A nest is a shelter in the battle for survival—a cradle in which eggs and the helpless young can be relatively safe from predators. Accordingly, birds often conceal their nests in unlikely or inaccessible places such as tall trees or remote islands, or cover them with camouflaging material. A nest can be the most rudimentary scrape in the ground or a remarkably intricate covered or hanging structure. Materials used in nest-building—which may be the sole responsibility of one sex or a joint effort—are mainly vegetable, and include sticks, seaweed, grass, leaves and bark. Animal materials such as feathers, wool, hair, cobwebs and droppings may be also used, and some birds surface or reinforce their nests with mud or line them with pebbles.

BLACKBIRD'S CUP NEST
A strong nest of grass, roots, moss and twigs, lined with mud.

GREBE'S FLOATING NEST
The southern crested grebe's floating platform of reeds and rushes.

STARLING'S HOLE NEST
The floor of a ready-made cavity, with nest material.

SWALLOW'S BRACKET NEST
A nail supports a nest of small straws, grass stems and mud.

SHEARWATER'S BURROW
A tunnel, one or two metres long, is excavated in well-drained soil.

Living together: safety in numbers

THE SOCIAL BEHAVIOUR of birds has great bearing on the success of many of their essential activities: feeding and sleeping, breeding and nesting, migration, safety from predators—and even learning. Instinct guides the passage of a bird through these major tasks, but many of these skills may be improved or perfected by learning.

Through trial and error, and continued practice, incorrect responses may be modified and corrected. This capacity for learning is limited however, for the bird possesses no unnecessary or extraneous skills. Its intelligent behaviour is confined to those skills essential to surviving in its natural habitat.

The safety of flocks

To perform instinctive activities, many birds gather together in groups—or flocks. Their lives are not so much 'sociable' as 'social'. A flock may be composed of birds of a single species or of mixed species, or consist solely of family groups, established pairs, or birds of one sex. Within small flocks especially, there is often a 'peck order' in which each bird gives way in turn to a more dominant bird.

Flocks are most frequently observed gathering at roosting areas or sources of abundant food. There is safety in numbers and flocking heightens awareness of the approach of predators. A solitary bird is less likely to notice the approach of a predator.

'Following reactions', which involve the immediate copying of one individual by another, are thought to assist in maintaining the cohesion of the flock, as do the recognisable markings (such as wing flashes) of many species. On the ground, flocks often synchronise such activities as feeding and drinking, preening, sleeping and hopping about. It is not entirely certain whether this is a result of following reactions or a direct reaction to a stimulus, such as an alarm call.

Living in colonies

Although most birds are solitary nesters, approximately 13 per cent of the world's birds live in colonies. In New Zealand, quite spectacular colonies of millions of pairs of sooty shearwaters have been recorded at The Snares. More than any other species, seabirds are the most colonial and each year, at breeding time, are likely to return in their thousands to favoured, secure sites on cliffs, beaches and islands. Land birds and waterfowl often breed in relatively small colonies of tens rather than thousands of birds.

The young of most colonial birds are particularly vulnerable and may not be immediately able to leave the nest. Living in large groups gives them greater protection. On the approach of predators, alarm-calls immediately alert other birds and a joint attack may repel the intruder. As egg-laying is usually a well synchronised activity in colonies, the young also have a greater chance of survival than they would if eggs or nestlings were available to predators over a more prolonged period.

Choice of a resting and sleeping site—or roost—is as important as the selection of a nest-site. It is a matter of survival. The roost may be in a sheltered position where wind, rain and extreme cold are unable to penetrate. It must also be one that is relatively safe from predators. Birds must maintain a constant body temperature and so conserving body heat is vital. Some small birds roost in clusters to obtain warmth from each other.

In a typical sleeping position a bird may hunch up and insert its bill under its feathers; some birds even sit down on their legs, covering them with their fluffed-up feathers to conserve warmth. The most unusual sleeping behaviour is that exhibited by the swift and some petrels, which seem to be able to sleep on the wing. Swifts are also among those species that are able to conserve body heat in extreme conditions by going into a state of torpidity, which allows the body's metabolic processes to slow down dramatically.

The struggle for food

The life of a bird is an almost constant demand for food. As birds fly they expend immense amounts of energy; this can be replaced only by consuming large amounts of food. Birds have no teeth and, in the case of insect-eating or flesh-eating birds, food is often ingested whole and broken down by the gizzard. Seed-eating birds have a more complicated digestive system that allows for storage of undigested food in the crop (an extension of the lower throat). The muscular walls of the gizzard—with the assistance of grit, which all seed-eating birds must consume regularly—grind down the food.

To replace supplies of energy and to maintain body heat, some birds spend up to 95 per cent of daylight hours searching for food. Birds respond to seasonal changes and will feast in times of plenty. Incubating birds may fast for several days at a time. The incubating emperor penguin, for example, must live for some weeks on reserves of fat.

The bill is a feeding tool. Its great variety of shape and form attests to the enormous range of foods upon which birds are able to feed. Of the seed-eating birds, only a few species eat seeds all year round. At certain times of the year, such as breeding times, they may eat insects. Similarly, few insect-eating birds rely upon insects as a regular source of food. In order to accommodate other types of food, the bills of these birds are not highly specialised and are sometimes referred to as all-purpose bills.

Many species of New Zealand birds feed predominantly on fish. Fish-eating birds are equipped with special adaptations, such as a sharp hook or serrated bill, to fix the slippery prey more securely in their bills.

Drinking is as important as feeding and methods vary: some birds scoop up water in their beaks; penguins eat snow; and seabirds remove the salt from seawater by transporting most of the salt, through the blood supply, to the nose. Their large nasal glands then excrete droplets of highly concentrated salt.

Below: A flock of white-fronted terns. This species is commonly seen foraging in flocks over shoaling fish, sometimes a few kilometres out to sea.

Right: A small colony of Auckland Island shags have established their nesting places along the rocky ledges of an island's precipitous cliff face.

The many shapes of bills: tools

PRISING

The oystercatcher strikes into the shell of its prey, prising it open.

TEARING

The New Zealand falcon tears flesh apart with its strong, hooked bill.

PROBING

The snipe uses its long, thin bill to probe soft earth for worms.

for every kind of feeding method

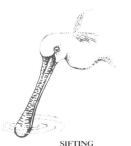

SIFTING

The spoonbill sifts animal organisms from shallows with its spatulate bill.

SPEARING

The dagger-like bill of the heron is ideally suited for spearing fish.

GRASPING

A spotted shag grasps slippery fish in its hooked bill.

Bird song

Bird song is often regarded as one of the most appealing aspects of bird behaviour, yet this apparently joyous outpouring has as its basis certain very practical functions.

A song is a complete set of notes formed rhythmically into a recognisable pattern of a characteristic length. Given the great variation of bird song amongst species and even within a species, this form of communication, like display, is a precise form of 'language', which is readily understood by other birds. Bird song is primarily concerned with defending territory and attracting a mate. Bird calls or call notes, which consist of up to five notes arranged in less 'musical' fashion, have a different function. Special 'contact notes' for example keep a flock together during migratory flight.

A very special language

Birds sing most extensively when there are increased daylight hours and, within the bird's body, increased hormonal activity. Often during this period birds are courting, establishing a pair-bond and nesting. In all these breeding activities bird song plays an important part. In most species it is only the male that sings, although some species of New Zealand birds—the tui, saddleback, bellbird and kokako—are notable for female song.

The male's song proclaims his sex and his species. The latter is significant as interbreeding of species is not usual. It is designed to attract a female and keep away other males. Essentially the male bird is defending its territory with a loud, repetitious and very distinctive vocal threat. Occasionally this becomes a vocal duel as two birds sing alternately with each other. This is known as countersinging.

Each bird may have a repertoire of as many as six to eight songs which announce its individuality. It may switch these songs throughout the day, although the reason for this is not known. Within the same species there are also local variations or 'dialects'.

A bird's ability to reproduce the basic sound pattern of its species is inherited. Usually a high standard of performance is reached only with practice and contact with its own species. There are exceptions, and some species reared in isolation from others of its species are able to reproduce perfectly a full repertoire of songs. An interesting variation is mimicry, in which one bird, such as the starling, mimics the songs and notes of other species.

Song duetting

In several New Zealand species that form pair-bonds lasting throughout the year, or even longer, song duetting between the male and female often occurs. One bird will begin its song and the other will join in. This phenomenon has been observed frequently in the saddleback. It has been suggested that this is a reassuring mechanism and it may also announce to other unpaired birds that this territory is occupied.

Antiphonal singing is a refinement of duetting, noted particularly in the fernbird, in which the call and subsequent response are so precisely co-ordinated that it is difficult to detect the separate contributions.

Though bird song appeals to humans, as birds are able to communicate over a roughly similar range of wavelengths, birds reproduce their sounds quite differently. A voice box, the syrinx, is located at the bottom of the trachea and sound is produced as air from the lungs is driven through its vibrating membranes. As birds have neither lips nor teeth they reproduce what are, to the human ear, vowel sounds rather than consonants.   P.F.J.

Living together: competition and courtship

With flippers raised, two rockhopper penguins direct their threat display at a royal penguin.

THE DRIVE TO ESTABLISH territory is a powerful and immensely important characteristic of bird behaviour. By establishing its own territory a bird gains vital access to food, roosting places, nest-sites and nesting materials, as well as a place where it can court its mate and safely rear its young.

The simplest definition of territory is 'any defended area'. A wide range of displays, often accompanied by song, assists birds in their defence of territory to which they have attached 'ownership'. There is usually little need to defend territory against birds of a different species, as they seldom take exactly the same food and are not rivals for mates—although they may be for nest-sites.

There is a general code of conduct to which most birds adhere: the owner of territory shows aggression only within its own defended area; and retreats when it is discovered trespassing in another bird's territory. Though there is inevitably competition for nest-sites, food and mates, it rarely develops into full-scale fighting. Natural selection ensures that birds whose aggressive drive leads them to the risk of being killed or maimed rarely live long enough to breed. Instead, when conflict looms, most birds advertise their ownership by an elaborate system of bluff—frightening calls and threatening physical displays—which usually stops short of violence.

Warding off the enemy

Apart from conflicts arising from competition for food and territory, many birds will boldly defend themselves if attacked. If spectacular displays and noisy song fail to frighten off a rival or predator, birds have a vast array of tactics to fall back on. Some species assume menacing postures—they increase their size by puffing out feathers or raising crests; or they may display striking plumage markings. The banded dotterel for example bends its legs and crouches forward to display to advantage its black chest patch; at the same time it ruffles its back feathers and spreads its tail. The shag erects its crest and the feathers on its neck and head; it then darts them forward suddenly, opening its bill wide to reveal a brightly coloured gape.

A bird's initial response to a rival or competitor is a mixture of appeasement and aggression. If unsure of whether to fight or flee the bird may adopt a sleeping position or suddenly begin to preen itself. Fights rarely fully involve more than two birds and are relatively bloodless. Perching birds flutter breast to breast, grappling with their bills; plovers use their feet as well. Grebes grapple in the water, bills interlocked, and try to repel the rival by forcing its head under water.

A contest—whether bluff or physical combat—ends when one bird concedes defeat. It may simply fly away or, if unable to do so, may enact a fresh set of stylised actions indicating submission. Alternatively, it may remain motionless, head withdrawn, and attempt to minimise or conceal its more threatening markings.

Developing the pair-bond

Territory is generally established by the male. Once a female has entered a territory, pair-formation, and later mating, can proceed with minimum interference from rivals. To attract and court a mate, some male birds have evolved special plumages and ornaments (crests, plumes and wattles) to emphasise the stereotyped displays distinctive of each species. For many species, song is also a special element in this form of communication.

In many species in which there is little variation between male and female plumages, birds may be aggressive towards one another in the early stages of courtship. Displays or ceremonies help establish a pair-bond. Another bird's response to the display of the male will indicate its sex; if the response continues to be aggressive rather than passive this indicates the other bird is also a male.

Among birds of similar plumage, courtship displays are often mutual. The southern crested grebe has an intricate courtship dance in which both sexes take part. Not all birds with similar plumages display together—in starlings, wrens and various pigeons, display is left to the male alone.

Once birds have become paired, the bond between them—so important for most species if they are to raise young successfully—is strengthened by special displays such as mutual preening, courtship feeding and showing

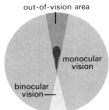
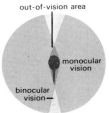

a nest-site. Mutual preening is characteristic of penguins, petrels, gannets, cormorants, shags and herons; all pigeons and doves; little owls; swifts and rooks. This preening is largely confined to the head and neck of the other bird, for these are areas of the plumage the bird cannot preen with its own bill. Birds sometimes assume a special preening invitation posture.

Courtship feeding is a widespread practice, particularly among species in which the female is responsible for incubation. In general, the female behaves like a begging chick and the male behaves as a parent would. Kingfishers and robins for example pass food from bill to bill; pigeons partially digest the food first, then pass the regurgitated food from bill to bill. The male kingfisher carries a fish to the female bird before mating. Courtship feeding, once regarded primarily as a bond-forming display, also has a practical dimension—it contributes to the nourishment of the female up to the period when she has finished brooding the young.

Mating displays, a prelude to mating, are not the sole preserve of the male bird. A female shag solicits by sitting in the nest with tail cocked while bending down and moving nest material. Mating then follows, during

The courtship 'dance' of the male kakapo.

which the male grips the female's neck in its bill and shakes gently.

In promiscuous species, in which no monogamous pair-bond is formed and males meet females only for mating, there is intense competition between males for females. This has resulted in the evolution of marked differences in size and appearance between the sexes. Usually larger and more brightly coloured, the males have evolved elaborate plumage features to accompany their highly ritualised displays. The females are dull in plumage, mainly because they need to be camouflaged when nesting.

The gannet demonstrates a wide range of seasonal displays. At the beginning of the nesting season there is often much competition among males for nesting sites. To proclaim his ownership of a site, the male performs a 'bowing display'. Dipping its bill from side to side, with wings held out, it gives a loud repeated threat call—'urrah-urrah'. Its 'advertising display' to prospective females, which fly over the territory repeatedly before landing, resembles a low-intensity form of bowing. When the female bird comes close, the male responds by flagging his head from side to side. If receptive, the female behaves submissively and faces away. Both birds may assume the 'pelican posture', in which the bill is tucked into the breast; this is thought to be a gesture of appeasement. After these preliminaries and mating, the male eventually surrenders the nest-site to the female. Gannets also perform special displays to indicate they are about to leave their mate on the nest. Similarly, throughout the breeding cycle, they perform a special 'greeting ceremony' whenever a bird joins its mate at the site. The returning bird flies into the site calling loudly, and its mate at the nest-site shakes its head rapidly, before vigorously greeting the returning bird and finishing with quieter mutual preening.

As part of their complex courtship display two New Zealand black-browed mollymawks fan their tails, and parry and riposte with their bills.

Habitats: where New Zealand birds live

WHERE A BIRD LIVES is intimately related to how it lives. A bird's survival in a particular habitat depends on a number of factors—food resources, nesting and roosting sites, and both the numbers and kinds of predators and food competitors present. Endemic birds that are already rare or which need large territories are those most vulnerable to change in their habitat. The species most likely to survive such changes are those that can adapt to a new habitat because they are not highly specialised.

New Zealand is a mountainous country—more than half the land rises above 300 m, and nearly a fifth above 900 m. Most of the country has a rainfall of between 1000 and 2000 mm per annum, but there are widely divergent extremes. The western side of some South Island mountains receives over 10 000 mm, and some eastern areas receive annually only 350 mm.

Forest appears to have covered much of New Zealand for the greater part of its geological history, and this was certainly the case when Polynesians settled a thousand years or more ago. Their influence gradually extended inland as more and more forest was cleared. When European settlement began in earnest in 1840, at least a quarter of the country was covered by scrub, fernland and tussockland induced by fire. As native forest shrank further, pasture increased to cover half the country and exotic pine forest expanded to occupy some three per cent of the land surface. The introduction of a variety of mammals (among them rats, stoats, weasels, ferrets, cats, dogs, deer, goats and pigs) and introduced birds from Europe caused further upheaval. The influence of introduced invertebrates (including European earthworms, slugs, snails, aphids, beetles and flies) is also significant.

The following description of 11 different kinds of habitat is one of convenience. Some birds do not recognise these boundaries; they may live in an area that includes parts of two or more habitats, or they may change their habitat according to the season.

NORTH ISLAND

Three Kings Islands

Parengarenga Harbour

Kaitaia

Bay of Islands

Kaikohe

Poor Knights Islands

Whangarei

Hen & Chicken Islands

Little Barrier Island Great Barrier Island

Kaipara Harbour

Hauraki Gulf

Cuvier Island

Mercury Islands

N

AUCKLAND

Manukau Harbour

Firth of Thames

Bay of Plenty

Mayor Island

White Island

Tauranga

Hamilton

East Cape

Whakatane

Taupo

Taumarunui

Gisborne

New Plymouth

Hawke Bay

Taihape

Napier

Hawera

Cape Kidnappers

Wanganui

Palmerston North

Kapiti Island

Masterton

WELLINGTON
Cook Strait

| 0 | 50 | 100 km |

Farmland (including cropland, orchards and swamps)

Upland forest and scrub

Lowland low-canopy forest and scrub

Lowland high-canopy forest

Subalpine and alpine vegetation

Exotic forest

Rivers and lakes are shown in white

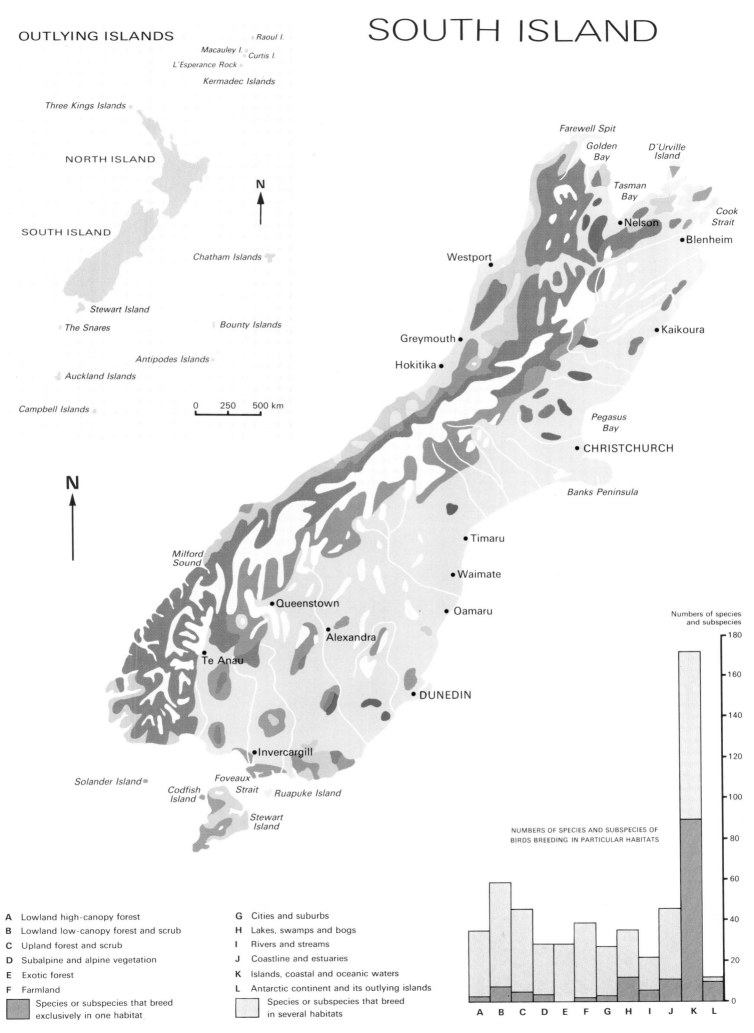

SOUTH ISLAND

OUTLYING ISLANDS

Raoul I.
Macauley I. Curtis I.
L'Esperance Rock
Kermadec Islands

Three Kings Islands

NORTH ISLAND

SOUTH ISLAND

Chatham Islands

Stewart Island

The Snares Bounty Islands

Antipodes Islands

Auckland Islands

Campbell Islands

0 250 500 km

N

N

Farewell Spit
Golden Bay
D'Urville Island
Tasman Bay
Cook Strait

Nelson
Blenheim

Westport

Kaikoura

Greymouth

Hokitika

Pegasus Bay

CHRISTCHURCH

Banks Peninsula

Milford Sound

Timaru

Waimate

Queenstown

Oamaru

Alexandra

Te Anau

DUNEDIN

Invercargill

Solander Island

Foveaux Strait

Codfish Island

Ruapuke Island

Stewart Island

Numbers of species and subspecies

NUMBERS OF SPECIES AND SUBSPECIES OF
BIRDS BREEDING IN PARTICULAR HABITATS

A Lowland high-canopy forest
B Lowland low-canopy forest and scrub
C Upland forest and scrub
D Subalpine and alpine vegetation
E Exotic forest
F Farmland

G Cities and suburbs
H Lakes, swamps and bogs
I Rivers and streams
J Coastline and estuaries
K Islands, coastal and oceanic waters
L Antarctic continent and its outlying islands

Species or subspecies that breed
exclusively in one habitat

Species or subspecies that breed
in several habitats

Habitats: forests and scrublands

EXOTIC FOREST Plantations of introduced softwoods, particularly radiata pine, supply most of New Zealand's timber, pulp and paper. They cover approximately 750 000 ha. Young plantations, less than seven years old, do not usually provide a suitable habitat for birds. Yet with increasing age and height, and sometimes an increasing undergrowth of native plants, greater numbers (mainly of insect-eating birds) become established as permanent residents.

In one study of a 30 year old pine forest, it was found that as many as 12 breeding species of birds inhabited a 20 ha stand. Chaffinch, whitehead, grey warbler, and blackbird were the most numerous with food sources including the ground, branches, cones, and foliage out to the tips of the needles.

Nectar and fruit-eating native birds—particularly the bellbird, tui and pigeon—also have been recorded in exotic forests. In the Nelson region it has been found that such birds cannot survive throughout the year in these forests unless patches of native forests are nearby. It is now known that bird numbers and diversity in pine forests will be favoured by the planting of relatively small blocks of trees, adjacent to stands of variable age; by protecting small areas of native forest, within or adjacent to the main plantation; and by reducing or eliminating burn-off.

The value, as bird habitats, of introduced hardwood plantations, particularly eucalypts, has yet to be investigated.

Exotic forest with a rich undergrowth of native plants commonly attracts great numbers of birds, mainly insect-eaters, as permanent residents.

UPLAND FOREST AND SCRUB Cooler temperatures, higher rainfalls and often greater cloud cover characterise the upland zone. In the northern half of the North Island, trees reach their upper limit at 1530 m. The timber line then decreases to 920 m in southern parts of the South Island. At any particular latitude, it is usually higher in the east than the west.

In northern parts of the North Island and some western parts of both islands, upland forests are dominated by non-coniferous trees, particularly kamahi (*Weinmannia racemosa*), tawheowheo (*Quintinia serrata*), tawari (*Ixerba brexioides*) and southern rata (*Metrosiderous umbellata*). Podocarps may or may not be present. Most upland forests, however, are dominated by southern beeches: *Nothofagus solandri* and *N. menziesii* (silver beech), both of which form timber lines.

Over the years, the undergrowth of these forests has been subject to change. Before European settlement, undergrowth was varied, with a high proportion of berry-producing shrubs. The introduction of deer, goats and opossums in the late nineteenth and early twentieth centuries resulted both in changes in the composition of the under-growth and, in places, to the canopy as well.

The range of bird species in upland forests is similar to that of lower altitude forests, but the proportions differ. It is apparent that some birds, including bellbirds, warblers and parakeets, tend to use upland forest mainly in spring and summer.

Most upland forest is dominated by species of southern beech interspersed with shrubs and ferns. It provides a suitable habitat for a variety of birds.

LOWLAND LOW-CANOPY FOREST AND SCRUB In the lowland areas, low-canopy forest is by far the more extensive woody habitat. It consists largely of trees left after the felling of podocarps for their prime-quality timber. Subsequent regrowth has restored forest cover, although such 'cut-over' forest is often very mixed. It is sometimes blanketed by tangled vines or thickets of cutty grasses (*Cortaderia* and *Gahnia* species) which grow along old logging tracks. This habitat can support almost all of the bird species found in high-canopy forest, although parrots and parakeets are rare.

On soils of low fertility many, mostly small, areas of hardwood forest still remain. They are dominated by one or two species of southern beech which may occur from sea level to the timber line. *Nothofagus truncata* extends into North Auckland but is absent from most upland forest. *N. solandri* has a much greater altitudinal range. These forests, though less varied in their composition, can support a considerable number of birds.

The area covered by lowland scrub exceeds that of forest. The most important species are small-leaved shrubs: manuka (*Leptospermum scoparium*), kanuka (*L. ericoides*), tauhinu (*Cassinia leptophylla*), and introduced gorse (*Ulex europaeus*). These species, which grow singly or mixed to heights varying from three to ten metres, have tiny windblown or small hard-coated seeds. Younger stands often form very dense, uniform thickets and do not support many birds. The more mature and varied scrub communities are used by a wide variety of native and introduced birds.

Some low-canopy forests seem devoid of birds, in marked contrast to others where numbers seem very high, particularly older secondary forest which developed after the burning of high forest during early settlement.

Forests of tall, long-lived podocarps are a favoured habitat of fruit-eating and nectar-eating birds.

LOWLAND HIGH-CANOPY FOREST New Zealand rainforest most closely resembles tropical rainforest, but does not support such a great variety of plant species. It is quite unlike either Australian eucalypt forest or the deciduous forests of the northern hemisphere.

Throughout the rainforest, the crowns of trees form two or three layers, at least one of which creates a dense continuous canopy. Here, there are about 36 significant species of evergreen trees. In any one place, however, the canopy is seldom composed of more than four species; usually one or two alone predominate.

The life span of these trees varies greatly. One group consists of very tall trees which live for 600 years or more. Among this group are the endemic conifers of the araucaria family (which includes kauris) and species belonging to the podocarp family (which includes totara, miro, rimu and kahikatea). Most native trees vary considerably in height and have a life span of between 100 and 300 years.

On the basis of canopy height, two types of lowland forest can be distinguished: high-canopy forest, which has at least a small proportion of trees (not less than five per cent) over 25 m tall, and low-canopy forest. In the past, high-canopy forest was the source of most of New Zealand's native timber; today, few large stands remain.

High-canopy forest includes small areas of closely growing, small-leaved podocarps formerly common on the central volcanic plateau of the North Island but also found on fertile alluvial flats. More predominant are large areas of non-coniferous trees with medium-sized leaves, where scattered podocarps often emerge above the remaining canopy.

Two further kinds of high-canopy forest are widespread on soils which are usually less fertile: the kauri forest of the northern North Island and small areas of southern beech forest which are dominated by red and silver beech (*Nothofagus fusca* and *N. menziesii*).

Because of its height and different canopy layers, high-canopy forest is able to provide birds with a variety of food sources. Its profusion of tree ferns, shrubs, lianas and epiphytes yields foliage, buds, berries, hard seeds and nectar; in addition, invertebrates may be hidden under bark, in litter or amongst foliage. Though the abundance and diversity of birds is high in tall forest, it is more pronounced in some areas than in others. For instance, insect-eating birds are more usual in beech forest.

Low-canopy forest in lowland areas often features a mixed undergrowth of ferns, thickets of grasses, tangled vines and, near the coast, nikau palms.

Habitats: the high altitudes, wetlands, cities and towns

SUBALPINE AND ALPINE VEGETATION At higher altitudes, the plant cover ranges from low forest—usually dominated by southern beeches—through various scrub and shrubland communities, to tussocklands. Above this again are open communities of small shrubs and herbs which reach their greatest variety in the mountains of the South Island.

In the wettest districts (with an average annual rainfall of 5000 mm), the subalpine 'moss forests' consist of short trees with twisted and much-branched trunks, often thickly covered with mosses and liverworts and dripping with water. Many such forests have been changed greatly by browsing deer.

That this is a much poorer habitat than the forest and scrub of lower altitudes is reflected by the relatively low numbers and diversity of birds. Above the timber line, introduced perching birds—particularly hedgesparrows and redpolls—are commonly found. Though few native birds have adapted to higher altitudes, the pipit is widespread and tits, bellbirds and brown creepers (the South Island only) inhabit subalpine scrub for a certain time each year. Keas, the rare kakapo, and great spotted and brown kiwis use this zone, although they range into forest at lower altitudes as well. In summer, the takahe feeds in Fiordland's alpine grasslands.

Near Boulder Lake, Nelson, subalpine forest edged by twisted trees is the habitat of the rock wren.

LAKES, SWAMPS AND BOGS In New Zealand there are over 750 lakes which exceed half a kilometre in length. As most have low nutrient levels they are unable to support dense populations of water plants or aquatic invertebrates. Bird numbers are therefore correspondingly low. Where lakes occur within farmed catchments, however, the added nutrients from manure and fertilisers result in abundant water plants and invertebrates—and greater numbers and variety of waterbirds.

Swamps—which contain open stretches of water for at least part of the year—are usually associated with high nutrient levels, and willows (*Salix* species), raupo (*Typha orientalis*), flax (*Phormium tenax*) and sedges (particularly *Carex* species) are widespread. Bogs, generally low in nutrient value, may be dominated by shrubs—particularly manuka (*Leptospermum scoparium*) and umbrella fern (*Gleichenia dicarpa*)—the restiad rush (*Empodisma minus*), and at higher altitudes, *Sphagnum* moss or hummock-forming sedges and herbs.

Although many lakes have been preserved for their scenic value, surrounding wetland habitats—including lake margins, swamps and bogs—have often been valued only for agricultural purposes. Consequently, these wetlands are one of the most threatened bird habitats in New Zealand. Thousands of hectares have been drained for farming, and flood control schemes have altered water levels. Their habitat value has been further threatened by fires, dumping of spoil from open-cast mining, and pollution from industrial wastes.

Wetland habitats pose some of the most challenging problems of protection and management. Areas of shallow water are necessary for the food supply of some freshwater birds such as dabchick, scaup and grey teal, and stability of water level is crucial both for the food supply of birds such as the black swan and for successful nesting of other birds such as the mallard, grey duck and crested grebe. The open margins of lakes provide areas for preening; clumps of sedges and rushes create cover for foraging and nesting; and the more complete covers of herbaceous plants or overhanging trees provide escape from predators. The diversity of bird species within a wetland is thus dependent on diversity of vegetation.

Swampland dominated by rushes, tall grasses such as toetoe and flax, herbs, and woody plants such as cabbage trees. Wetlands are usually high in nutrients.

RIVERS AND STREAMS In New Zealand, rivers and streams show every gradation—from deeply entrenched, swift-flowing torrents closely flanked by the walls of steep gorges to wide channels of more slowly moving water flowing across broad plains.

The density of the aquatic life which these rivers can support—both plant and animal—is closely related to their freedom from flooding, but high-intensity rainfalls with consequent floods can occur anywhere in the country at almost any time of the year. In stripping a riverbed, floodwaters remove algae and other water plants as well as greatly reducing the numbers of invertebrates. The effect is temporary, however, and the recovery time depends on the severity of the flood and the stability of the catchment.

In parts of the country still covered by native forest, river flats are colonised by woody plants such as kanuka, manuka and, where present in the surrounding forest, the various species of southern beech. However, most of the larger rivers pass through farmland or scrub, where the most common plants are broom, gorse, tree lupin and blackberry. Throughout the country, willows—initially introduced as a means of stabilising river banks—have become established along many kilometres of riverbed.

Although most streams support populations of several birds, particularly ducks, a greater variety of species occurs on broad riverbeds, notably on those crossing the eastern plains of the South Island. At least seven species, including the wrybill, South Island pied oystercatcher, black-fronted dotterel, black-fronted tern, and black stilt, breed only on drier stretches of riverbed. Apart from the insect life of the shingle banks, the mud at the water's edge provides sandflies, mayflies and certain species of water bugs. In shallow water, other foods for birds are the larvae of mayflies and caddis flies, many other invertebrates, and sometimes fish.

The braided riverbed of the Dart River, Otago, is the habitat of the South Island pied oystercatcher, banded dotterel, black-fronted tern and black-billed gull.

CITIES AND SUBURBS The completely built-up parts of cities and towns provide habitats for house sparrows, starlings and pigeons. Few other species have been able to adapt to this artificial environment so successfully.

These urban areas provide little vegetation beyond trees in the streets, weeds on waste ground and the lawns and borders of small gardens, so the most successful species in this man-made habitat are those which originally nested where vegetation was scarce.

House sparrows in particular have thrived since their introduction by the early colonists, despite the fact that bounties were placed on their heads early this century. In older suburbs, however, where garden trees have matured, from 15 to 20 species, both native and introduced, can be found as permanent residents or regular visitors.

Some enthusiasts actively seek to increase both the number and variety of birds by providing them with food, roosting cover and water for bathing; and these birds soon become comparatively indifferent to the presence of humans in a garden (although not to cats). Where sizeable patches of native bush are close by, the list of birds present can be lengthened to include the tui, pigeon and sometimes bellbirds. Many additional species reach the suburbs as occasional visitors.

A census of birds in the Dunedin Botanic Garden has indicated that high numbers can live in garden habitats—one hectare, for example, is able to support over 25 birds, the chief species being the song thrush, blackbird and silvereye.

At city rubbish dumps and abattoirs, black-backed gulls—feeding as scavengers—congregate in considerable numbers. Where airports have been built close to dumps, sewage outlets, gull colonies or the feeding areas of shorebirds, the risk of bird strike to aircraft is greatly increased. Scientists have tried many bird deterrent devices at airports, none of them wholly successful.

Habitats: farmland, coast, sea and islands

FARMLAND Pastures of grasses and clovers, carrying sheep and cattle, dominate farmland in New Zealand. As a result of the temperate moist climate, productivity is high, and in the north of the country grass growth continues throughout the winter. Mild winters may also explain why earthworm numbers are generally higher in New Zealand pasture soils than in Europe and America. Many other pasture invertebrates, not all introduced, are common and some such as the grass grub beetle (*Costelytra zealandica*), which is injurious to grass

Many introduced birds, and some endemic species, have adapted to the expansion of farmland.

roots, are sometimes eaten by birds. Hedgerows are few, as grazing areas are separated usually by post and wire fences. Shelterbelts are numerous but the variety of trees used is limited mainly to conifers.

Farmland has only become widespread since 1840. Its expansion has invariably affected traditional bird habitats, for example by restricting forest and scrub to ever-decreasing areas and by the draining of wetlands. Nearly two thirds of the birds that have adapted successfully have been introduced, and include European finches, the skylark, starling, white-backed magpie, Indian myna, pheasant and Californian quail. Some farmland birds, however, are self-introduced from Australia: the white-faced heron, spur-winged plover, and welcome swallow, which have only established and spread widely since 1940.

Among native species, the paradise shelduck, and probably the harrier, have increased their range and numbers as farmland has spread. Where trees are present other native birds may include the fantail, grey warbler, silvereye, shining cuckoo, morepork, kingfisher and weka.

Intensively cultivated cropland covers a relatively small area. Orchards are also small in total area, although they are increasing rapidly in number and are frequently subject to bird damage. Blackbirds, song thrushes, mynas and starlings are mainly responsible for the harm done to crops of cherries, plums, pears, strawberries and grapes.

ISLANDS, COASTAL AND OCEAN WATERS More than one third of New Zealand's breeding birds breed only on islands. The offshore islands—islands within 50 km of the mainland—were almost all greatly modified during Polynesian times, and many have been modified still further by Europeans. Yet these islands—especially the larger ones—are now important bird habitats.

The kinds of habitat are limited mainly to lowland and coastal forest, or scrub, much of it with a low canopy, but some taller forest occurs on the largest islands. Fewer species of introduced mammals, which on the mainland have proved to be both predators and food competitors, have reached these offshore islands. Some islands escaped them altogether. Furthermore, on many islands the vegetation has remained largely undisturbed since the Maori left them last century.

Several birds formerly common in parts of the mainland, notably the stitchbird, saddleback and New Zealand shore plover, have survived only on islands. The list would be longer had not ship rats invaded some islands. On Big South Cape Island, ship rats eliminated the only surviving populations of bush wren and Stewart Island snipe in the 1960s.

The great majority of burrowing and larger surface-nesting seabirds breed only on islands, whereas the breeding of many of the smaller petrels has become restricted to predator-free islands. Island size is much less critical for these birds as their food is taken at sea. Small islets can support colonies of burrowing petrels, or shags, terns, gulls, gannets, penguins and even albatrosses.

Almost a third of New Zealand bird species depend on the ocean for food—plankton, crustaceans, squid and fish. The availability of such food is controlled largely by the mixing of ocean currents. For example, a major ocean convergence extending down the southeastern coast of the North Island and then eastwards to the Chatham Islands forms a broad zone of nutrient enrichment; the enhanced marine life associated with this mixing of ocean currents is used by many species of oceanic birds. Many marine animals are bioluminescent (light-producing), thus allowing some petrels and albatrosses to catch them at night.

The outlying islands—Three Kings, Kermadec, Chatham, Snares, Auckland, Campbell, Antipodes and Bounty Island groups—are mostly nature reserves and lie at various distances greater than 50 km from the coast. In contrast to the offshore islands, they all support, to some degree, numbers of endemic plants and birds, especially the Chatham Islands. Most mainland habitats are represented on the outlying islands in some form, but they all show unique features resulting from the presence of endemic plants and the absence of characteristic mainland plants.

Burrow-nesting petrels and shearwaters are abundant on the outlying islands, and on some islands there are also dense colonies of penguins and the larger albatrosses and mollymawks, which are surface nesters. The feeding zones of some New Zealand seabirds extend as far as the Antarctic continent where four species of penguins breed, as well as a few species of petrels (including a storm petrel), skuas and a fulmar.

Some of the outlying islands have been, or are being, greatly modified by such introduced animals as sheep, pigs and goats, rats and cats. The expansion of fishing fleets and the increase in undersea oil and mineral prospecting mean that increased precautions are needed to prevent invasions of rats from ships, oil pollution or other gross modification from damaging what are quite irreplaceable habitats.

The coastal forest and scrub of the Chatham Islands supports high numbers of endemic birds.

Parengarenga Harbour sand dunes with a sparse cover of pingao, spinifex and toetoe. Terns, gulls, oystercatchers and dotterels are common coastal species.

COASTLINE AND ESTUARIES No other environment in New Zealand offers as much variety of bird habitat as the nearly ten thousand kilometres of cliffs, boulders, sandy beaches, and mud flats that make up the country's coastline. Soil slopes and remote bare areas, inaccessible ledges and caves provide nest-sites. Rock pools and platforms above low-tide level offer limpets and other shellfish, chitons and crabs as food supply, and beaches of boulders, gravel, sand, and shellbanks provide further feeding and nesting sites.

The mud flats of estuaries and lagoons are a rich source of shellfish, crabs and other invertebrates for wading birds. These habitats are mostly without higher plants, but where the coastline is building seawards there may be salt marshes or sand dunes. Salt marshes are usually covered by small semi-succulent herbs and, in northern North Island, mangroves. Young sand dunes usually support an open cover of grasses, particularly *Spinifex hirsutus*, pingao (*Desmochoenus spiralis*) and marram grass (*Ammophila arenaria*). Shrubby vegetation dominates older dunes.

The common birds of the coast are gulls, terns, oystercatchers, dotterels, herons and shags. The tidal mud flats of estuaries and lagoons are probably the richest of all habitats

The broad expanses of shell and mud flats at Firth of Thames are rich feeding sites for wading birds.

for bird life; their area has been estimated as about 100 000 ha. They are most numerous in the North Island, where the largest occur at Manukau and Kaipara Harbours. In the South Island, large estuaries and lagoons are restricted to Farewell Spit west of Golden Bay and the Fiordland coast.

In summer, estuaries and lagoons attract many species of Arctic-breeding waders. Their numbers exceed 150 000, with bar-tailed godwits and knots the most abundant. In winter, though most of the Arctic migrants have left, harbours are dominated by internal migrants: South Island pied oystercatcher and wrybill from South Island riverbed breeding grounds, stilts and banded dotterels. In northern estuaries two species of non-migratory wader, the New Zealand dotterel and variable oystercatcher, remain throughout the year with small numbers of migrant but temporarily non-breeding birds. It is not uncommon for a single estuary to contain five or more species of waders all feeding from the same area.

While natural forces, such as marine erosion, may create significant change in this environment over the years, man-made influences—such as pollutants and leisure vehicles—are today adversely affecting the quality of this rich habitat.   I.A.E.A.

The origin and evolution of New Zealand birds

BECAUSE OF NEW ZEALAND's long isolation from other land masses, her bird life has a special and very distinctive character. Many of the bird species occur nowhere else in the world; others are either highly unusual or especially primitive forms.

A total of 350 species of birds, either living or as fossil records, have so far been recorded from New Zealand and its outlying islands. Extinction has been the fate of many—in the period from roughly two million years ago to just before European settlement, some 45 are believed to have become extinct; and within the last 150 years a further seven species have, unwittingly, become extinct.

The evolution of New Zealand's bird life has been largely determined by events far back in geological history—the separation from the ancient southern supercontinent of Gondwanaland, and the advance and retreat of ice caps. Before the separation of continents there was some sharing of flora and fauna, and ancestors of the flightless species, the moas

and kiwis, were already present on the New Zealand segment. Significantly, snakes and mammals—both predators of birds—arrived in the Australian region after separation.

The land connections persisted until about two million years ago. As continents became progressively more isolated, the species of these major land masses became correspondingly more distinctive. The rest of the native fauna reached New Zealand by trans-oceanic dispersal, assisted by currents of sea and air.

During the interglacial periods, low-lying areas were inundated by the sea and the more prominent land masses became islands separated by large bodies of water. Birds and animals became isolated on these islands, and endemic species (species found nowhere else) developed. This has been particularly evident on the Chatham Islands.

The ice ages were characterised by climatic extremes, and many species adapted to warmer climates did not survive. Those species that did survive evolved in splendid isolation upon

a richly forested and predator-free land mass. Among them were many specialised and frequently flightless birds that were ill-adapted to survive the final episode in their evolutionary history—the arrival of man.

The most ancient colonisers, which are believed to have arrived over 136 million years ago, were the moas and kiwis. They were followed some 60 million years ago by three endemic families of birds—the New Zealand wrens, wattle birds and thrushes. Between two million and 10 500 years ago, 24 endemic genera established in the region, and a few species—such as the pukeko, pied stilt, banded rail and kingfisher—arrived within the last few hundred years.

The fossil record

The history of New Zealand birds can be compiled from three artificial but convenient divisions: the fossil, subfossil and recent periods. They correspond roughly to the pre-human, Polynesian and European periods respectively. The fossil record of the first two periods of the New Zealand region is limited. The four significant sources are caves, swamps, dunes and middens (refuse sites of the Polynesians). Though these sites have yielded a variety of species and indicated a wide distribution, they are still too recent to assist in clarifying the origins and evolutionary trends. Recorded from this fossil sample are a penguin, some moas and kiwis, an albatross, a 'bony tooth' and a goose. The more recent subfossil records are richer in variety and more numerous. They include pelicans; swans, geese and ducks; eagles and hawks; curlews and godwits; and nightjars. Most disappeared during the Polynesian occupation; the rest, after the arrival of the Europeans.

The third and most recent period in the history of birds in New Zealand is taken from the extinction of the last of the moas—assumed to have been about 1700. Today, the Checklist of the Birds of New Zealand lists a total of 305 species and races. (Nine of these are Antarctic birds of the Ross Dependency.) Of the remaining, 85 are stragglers and 20 either non-breeding migrants or regular visitors. This leaves a total of 191 species breeding in the New Zealand region. Apart from stragglers, the birds of Antarctica and oceanic and coastal species account for more than 42 per cent of New Zealand's bird life.

The Australian contribution is particularly important—25 families of Australian birds have representatives breeding in New Zealand. Since 1856, at least nine Australian

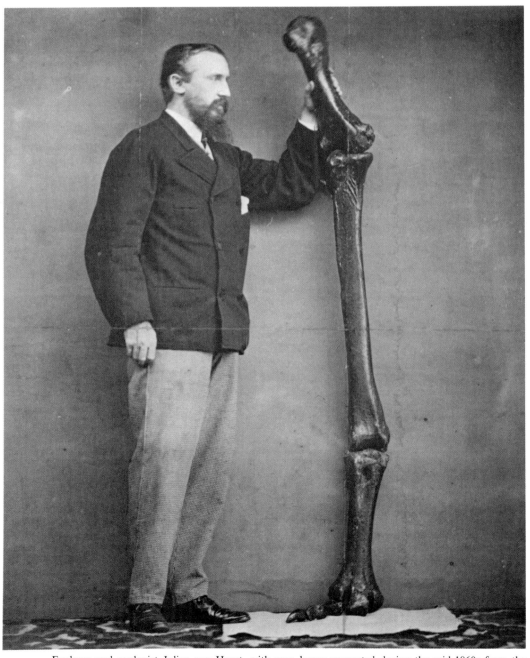

Explorer and geologist Julius von Haast, with moa bones excavated during the mid-1860s from the swampland of a sheep station in the North Canterbury region. The ancestors of these giant flightless birds —the tallest species may have stood more than three metres—were present at least 70 million years ago.

Dinornis maximus, the tallest of the moas.

Captain Cook's voyages to New Zealand

Captain Cook's three voyages to New Zealand between 1769 and 1777 yielded a fascinating and immensely valuable scientific record—an accumulation of writings, drawings and natural history exhibits which gave Europeans their first glimpse of a new world. Of particular interest to ornithologists were the very first descriptions of the bird life found in the New Zealand region.

On his first voyage Cook was accompanied by two distinguished botanists, Joseph Banks and Daniel Solander, and artist Sydney Parkinson, who drew many of the bird and animal specimens obtained during the voyage. However, the collection and preservation of botanical specimens took precedence, and few of the many birds collected were preserved. Most were eaten by the crew. The *Endeavour* voyaged in New Zealand waters for six months. Most of the birds recorded by Banks and described in fine detail by Solander were oceanic species; no detailed records were made of New Zealand land or shore birds.

Cook's second voyage departed England in July 1772. Johann Reinhold Forster was appointed official naturalist and his 17-year-old son George served as his assistant. A young Swedish botanist, Anders Sparrman, joined the voyage at Cape of Good Hope. The three formed a most efficient scientific team and, under the direction of Johann Forster, recorded approximately 150 bird species in detail and awarded them Latin names. Particularly significant

The Poa *(an early name for the tui) was painted by Robert Laurie from a specimen brought back to London by Captain Cook. As Plate IX of Peter Brown's* New Illustrations of Zoology, *published in 1776, it was the first published illustration of a New Zealand bird.*

contributions arose from their visits to Dusky and Charlotte Sounds. Sadly, Johann Forster's work remained unpublished in his lifetime and many species were subsequently described and named by other workers.

The second voyage proved to be of greater value to ornithologists than the first. Not only were Forster's descriptions numerous and detailed, but almost all were accompanied with an able drawing by his son. These drawings, now kept in the British Museum, are of great significance scientifically: 20 are type specimens for the species described. They include such New Zealand species as the paradise shelduck, grey duck, New Zealand wren, brown creeper and shining cuckoo.

Though no naturalist was appointed for Cook's third voyage, which arrived at Queen Charlotte Sound in February 1777, the *Resolution*'s surgeon, William Anderson, kept a journal in which he described new items of zoological interest. Though never published, his manuscripts in later years were of great use to ornithologists.

Altogether, about 60 bird species found in the New Zealand region were first described validly from specimens collected or paintings executed on Cook's three voyages to New Zealand. It is certain that Sir Joseph Banks was by far the chief recipient of the specimens collected. Of considerable importance scientifically, many were widely distributed by Sir Joseph and few are known to survive today. D.G.M.

---

species have established as breeders. They include a heron, spoonbill, duck, coot, swallow, silvereye and several species of plovers.

Some unusual characteristics

An intriguing feature of the species that have evolved in the New Zealand region is the relatively low number of land birds. These terrestrial species are mainly endemic; few have shown adaptive radiation—a process whereby a breeding population in a particular habitat or set of conditions evolves its own special features. Another unusual characteristic of New Zealand's birds is the high proportion of flightless species or those with weak flight. The absence of mammalian predators is generally regarded as the main reason for this. There is also a higher-than-usual incidence of melanism—the occurence of dark varieties—as displayed by the black stilt, black (Chatham Island) robin and the black phases of the oystercatchers. Another characteristic is the unusually large size of many species, not only of the moas (which included some of the world's largest birds) but of some species of waterfowl, parrots and owls.

Though all of New Zealand's bird species can be assigned to a major habitat type (for example 12 per cent of birds occupy lowland grassland and pasture), few terrestrial species have become so specialised that they exclusively occupy one particular plant commmuntity. For instance, there are none confined only to beech or kauri forest. Island species however tend to occupy broader niches than their counterparts on larger land masses. Competition for a particular habitat between introduced and native species does not yet appear to be significant. Most native terrestrial species inhabit heavy forest and scrub and are mainly insect-eaters. Introduced perching birds, accustomed to open country and deciduous woodlands, are mainly seed-eaters.

Migration, either within the country or to overseas destinations, is not as prominent a feature of birds in New Zealand as it is on the larger, less isolated land masses. Some species, such as the Pacific golden plover, eastern bar-tailed godwit, turnstone, knot and Arctic skua, breed in Arctic and subarctic regions

and winter in New Zealand. Other species (petrels, waders, skuas and terns) are regular visitors. Internal migration largely occurs in a north-south direction, with breeding in the south and a movement north in the summer. A few species, such as the banded dotterel and South Island pied oystercatcher, migrate inland to breed and then return to the coast. In bad weather, seasonal movement from high to low country is common.

In the main islands, a certain amount of breeding activity—pairing, mating, nesting, laying, incubating, hatching and fledging—takes place in every month of the year. The peak is from September to November, with activity less frequent from April to June. Some species begin consistently earlier than most others within the same range; other species begin consistently later. Some have a short well defined season; others an extended one. From year to year and from region to region, significant variations are caused by such

THE HOMING INSTINCT

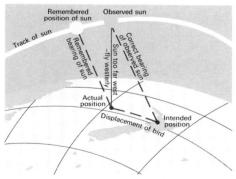

Many species migrate from the northern hemisphere to winter in New Zealand. One likely explanation of how they reach their destination is that birds use the same aids as man when steering a fixed course—the sun and the stars. In the diagram, a bird migrating to New Zealand from the north finds itself too far east of its destination. Remembering the position of the home sun at any given time, it realises that the sun has not moved far enough along its path for it to be in its 'correct' position—so it flies westward until the actual sun is at the same position along its path as the remembered sun. The bird is now on the correct line of longitude for home.

factors as weather, latitude, and food supply.

European settlement dramatically modified New Zealand's vegetation and, in consequence, the habitats of bird species—native forest was greatly reduced, exotic forests were established, and farmland expanded. The natural bird community was augmented by several species of introduced birds. They were brought to the country for many reasons—for sentiment or sport; because of the new country's poor numbers of land and freshwater species; and as a result of the misguided notions of biological control held by some agriculturalists. Many introduced species, such as nightingales and Hawaiian geese, failed to become established; others have proved to be ecological folly. Nevertheless, these acclimatised birds have today become a natural part of the bird community.

Many endemic species such as the saddleback, bush wren and kokako continue to show sensitivity to changes in the little remaining native environment. Others—brown kiwis, the fantail, bellbird, tui and weka—have shown surprising adaptability to altered circumstances. Opportunistic feeders such as harriers and black-backed gulls have become more widespread and abundant.

It has long been assumed that predatory animals—several species of rats, domestic dogs and cats, mustelids (ferrets, stoats and weasels), the hedgehog and the Australian opossum—have been responsible for the reduction and extinction of native species. Certainly there is direct evidence that when ships' rats infested some of the small islands on the southwestern coast, previously common species such as saddleback, bush wren and snipe virtually disappeared at once. Yet there are anomalies—larger flightless species such as wekas and kiwis seem able to survive successfully in the midst of populations of almost all the mammalian predators.

Though the destruction of habitats continues, there is a growing awareness and appreciation of the characteristic 'flavour' of the New Zealand environment. This factor, coupled with efforts to preserve endangered species, augurs well for the future of New Zealand's bird life. G.R.W. & P.R.M

A North Island brown kiwi foraging among litter on the forest floor.

THE KIWI

Apteryx species

The kiwi—a small, stocky, and flightless bird—is found nowhere else in the world. This largely nocturnal creature, whose main habitat is the forest floor, has been remarkable in its resistance to many of the factors which so adversely affected other endemic species of New Zealand birds.

The kiwi uses its long bill, with nostrils at the tip, to probe the earth for worms and insects.

The kiwi's legs, which are powerful and muscular, account for a third of its total weight.

The kiwi is the smallest of the flightless 'ratite' family, which also includes the ostrich, emu, rhea and cassowary. It is found only in New Zealand. When it was first described in 1813, a sceptical audience, believing itself to be the victim of a hoax, demanded to see a specimen of this strange, nocturnal, burrowing bird.

Certainly, the kiwi looks unlike other birds. Its wings, which end in a claw, are very small and it has no external tail. Its plumage—which is the same for both chicks and adults—is shaggy and hair-like, owing to weak barbs and a lack of aftershafts. About its face and at the base of its long and straight to slightly curved bill there are many long, sensitive bristles. Its body is cone-shaped, because of undeveloped flight muscles, and is topped with a strong neck and a small head. The kiwi's legs are powerful and muscular; they make up a third of its total weight.

Most birds are thought to have little or no sense of smell, but kiwis are an exception. The olfactory bulbs of the brain, which are part of the sense of smell, are very well developed, with a structure similar to that in mammals. They are the only birds with external nostrils at the tip of the bill. Kiwis are capable of locating foods by smell alone. There are several reports of kiwis in captivity sniffing their daily ration and refusing to eat it if it were not prepared by their usual keeper.

Hearing is also an important and well-developed sense. The ear openings are large and the kiwi can be seen cocking its head to direct its ear at distant or soft noises.

The kiwi skeleton differs from that of other birds, including other flightless birds. The kiwi's bones do not contain air sacs; they contain marrow. The eye sockets are not separated by a plate; they are divided by large nasal cavities—as in most mammals. Bones

that in other birds are developed to aid flight, are either reduced or absent. And in contrast with other flightless ratite cousins, which have only two or three toes, the kiwi has four.

They have small eyes, their vision is poor, and they avoid bright light. Though Stewart Island brown kiwis emerge from their burrows to forage at dusk or on overcast days, kiwis are essentially nocturnal. Thus, although they are found on all three main islands, as well as on Little Barrier Island and Kapiti Island, they are rarely seen.

In fact, kiwis are heard more often than seen. As they wander through the forest at night, they make a loud snuffling noise which is clearly audible many metres away. This is caused by the feeding kiwi forcing air out of its nostrils as it probes continuously with its bill. The characteristic call of the male, from which the bird's name is said to be derived, is a series of seven to 23 shrill, prolonged whistles, which ascend and descend slightly. The female calls a shorter, hoarser cry. These calls are heard at dusk, during the night and in the early morning. Each species has characteristic contact calls, but they are so similar that birds of one species are often attracted to, or respond to, the call of another species. When aggressive or alarmed, kiwis growl, hiss and loudly snap their bills.

The three kiwi species

The three species of kiwi include the brown kiwi *Apteryx australis,* the little spotted kiwi *Apteryx oweni,* and the great spotted kiwi *Apteryx haasti.* Though primarily birds of the indigenous rainforests, they are also found in scrub and native grasslands; and the brown kiwi also utilises exotic forests and pasture. The birds occur from sea level to alpine meadows. Nothing is known about the size of a kiwi's territory.

They are absent from many areas where, last century, they were known to exist. This is because of bush felling by European settlers and attacks by predators—both animal and human. Surveys carried out on the west coast of the South Island from Buller Gorge in the north to Haast in the south during 1977 showed that there were no kiwis in large tracts of forested country that, in the nineteenth century, were occupied by the little spotted kiwi. As this was the most familiar kiwi to early explorers, prospectors and settlers on the west coast, it was, presumably, the most common and widespread—particularly as it tends to be more secretive than the other two species. The disappearance of the little spotted kiwi from extensive areas of the west coast suggests that its small size may have made it more vulnerable to predators.

The Maoris killed some kiwis for food and to make kiwi feather cloaks, but this did not disrupt the overall distribution of the birds. Then, during the 1860s, prospectors and bushmen hunted the kiwi because of its gamey flavour. Collectors sent many specimens to overseas museums and zoos. However, the greatest number of kiwis were slaughtered between 1860 and 1890 to make feather trimmings and kiwi skin muffs for London fashion houses. One hunter working on the west coast killed more than 2200 kiwis before 1871. Most of these were little spotted kiwis.

With the decline of mining and prospecting at the end of the nineteenth century many dogs and cats were abandoned. Feral dogs and cats became widespread along the west coast of the South Island and the disappearance of ground birds, especially the little spotted kiwi, is perhaps mainly attributable to these predators. Wild pigs and stoats have also contributed to the decline of the kiwi.

Today, kiwis are fully protected by law. Nevertheless, large numbers are killed accidentally each year by traps set for the introduced Australian opossum. Others are destroyed in scrub or forest clearing schemes.

It is widely believed that kiwis live mainly on a diet of earthworms, but all three species are omnivorous. The stomach contents of 40 North Island brown kiwis included freshwater koura crayfish, earthworms, woodlice, millipedes, centipedes, slugs, snails, spiders, insects, seeds and berries. The stomach contents of another two kiwis consisted mainly of fibrous, grass-like plants.

Life on the forest floor

When they are feeding on earthworms kiwis probe their bills into the worms' tunnels and, by a back-and-forth levering action, enlarge them into a conical hole that is sometimes more than 12 cm deep and up to 10 cm wide at ground level. This is accompanied by frequent snuffling as the kiwis exhale forcefully, to clear soil from their nasal passages.

The kiwi appears to have no formal displays. It has little to display with—no tail, no visible wings and no obvious colour patches—although the long bill and flexible neck would allow many complex movements. Probably, there are no displays because of the kiwi's poor eyesight and nocturnal behaviour.

Kiwis breed throughout the year, although more eggs are laid from July to February. Like other flightless ratite birds, the male kiwi has a well-developed penis. In most female birds only the left ovary develops, but in kiwis both ovaries are functional; and if more than

one egg is laid in a breeding season, ovulation occurs alternately in each.

The age of sexual maturity is not known. The youngest pair to breed in captivity were a female reported to be two years old and a male said to be 14 months old. It is also not known at what age kiwis stop breeding. A captive female produced her last chick when she was over 15 years old. Males in captivity, just before they are ready to breed, sometimes leap and hop in great strides around their enclosure, then lie on their backs and kick their feet in the air. Or they roll, either 'head over heels' or sideways, down banks and slopes.

Males have been reported to fight vigorously when competing for females but the female, who will occasionally kick her smaller mate if she is not feeling receptive to his advances, is usually the more assertive. It is not known how long pairs stay together.

A young Maori woman wearing a traditional cloak which has been fashioned from kiwi feathers.

Once a partnership is formed, there is a lapse of about two months before the egg is laid. During this period the male, with some help from the female, prepares a nest. This is burrowed underground or sited in a hollow tree, under a log or in a rock crack. The floor and sides are usually lined with plants.

The birds mate about three weeks before the egg is laid and, at the peak of activity, three or more times a day. The male taps or strokes the female on her back near the base of the neck. She crouches low with her head stretched forward and resting on the ground. Once mounted, the male, lacking wings to stabilise himself, often maintains balance by grasping the hen's back feathers in his bill.

In the wild, clutches contain one or two or, very rarely, three eggs. In the brown kiwi, the interval between two consecutive eggs averages 33 days. Several days before laying, the female eats a great deal, but she fasts during the one or two days that just precede laying. In this period she walks with her legs wide apart, because of the large egg.

The eggs, especially in the little spotted kiwi, are proportionally larger, relative to the size of the female, than the eggs of any other

birds; and they contain the largest proportion of yolk. They have smooth, thin, white or greenish white shells.

For the first week or two of incubation, the egg is either left unattended for several days or the female incubates it. From then on, the male alone sits on the egg, which he warms with a large incubation patch. After 71 to 84 days the chick hatches. The male has ample fat reserves to survive irregular feeding during the nesting period. Some males fast for up to seven days at a time, while others leave the nest briefly on most nights to feed. On leaving the nest, the male frequently covers the eggs and burrow entrance with litter and, on returning, often brings in extra vegetation to maintain the nest lining. Sometimes, the male bathes when out feeding, perhaps to maintain the correct humidity in the nest.

There are unconfirmed reports that the female, with live food in its bill, sometimes enters the nest, probably to feed the incubating male, and also that she occasionally, for a brief period, incubates the eggs while the male is out feeding.

Caring for the young

The eggs are not usually turned in the nest, except accidentally by the sitting bird as it changes position in the confined burrow. When the clutch is greater than one, a viable egg may become buried and lost. Dead eggs and chicks are sometimes buried in the nest.

The embryo lacks an egg tooth and hatches by breaking the shell with its feet. At the time of hatching, the male blocks the entrance to the nest and, after the chick has emerged, eats some of the shell. The remainder is stamped down and buried in the nest. The newly hatched chick, which weighs between two thirds and three quarters of the fresh egg, is unable to stand. Its belly, swollen with yolk, rests on the ground and its legs splay sideways. The chick takes its first two or three ungainly steps when about 60 hours old, shuffling with its feet and legs on the ground. On the fourth day it stands, the next day it walks unsteadily on its toes and two days later it walks quickly and confidently.

During their first 72 to 84 hours the chicks probably do not feed, but then they receive some food which is carried in by the male. The chick, accompanied by the male, first leaves the nest to forage when it is six to eight days old and first eats with vigour when it is nine to 12 days old. At the end of its first 10 to 14 days the chick's weight will have decreased to 65 per cent of the hatching weight, but it can easily survive two weeks of partial fasting.

Unlike their parents, chicks up to the age of 30 to 35 days leave the burrow at any time of the day or night to feed. Only when they reach the age of about five weeks do they avoid bright light.

The adult weight is attained at about 12 months. In the wild, the average life span for kiwis is not known, but they are probably long-lived. At least two birds, a little spotted kiwi and a brown kiwi, have lived for 20 years or more in captivity.

The position of the external nostrils and the long olfactory passage may make kiwis vulnerable to certain respiratory, or even pulmonary, diseases. Several captive birds have died of pneumoconiosis, and probably this condition would develop also in wild birds, as dust and dirt are inhaled while feeding, particularly during dry periods.   B.E.R.

Brown Kiwi *Apteryx australis* SHAW & NODDER, 1813

The South Island brown kiwi is widespread in Fiordland and also present in the dry, low-lying podocarp and hardwood forest of the west coast.

ENDEMIC
North Island Brown Kiwi
A.a. mantelli BARTLETT, 1850.
South Island Brown Kiwi
A.a. australis SHAW & NODDER, 1813.
Stewart Island Brown Kiwi
A.a. lawryi ROTHSCHILD, 1893.

OTHER NAMES: *Rowi, tokoeka.*

SIZE: *500 mm.*

DESCRIPTION
ADULT: *Female larger. Plumage soft to the touch but 'harsher' in the North Island than in the 2, more southern, subspecies; varying in colour from pale grey-brown to dark rufous streaked with black. Sometimes, all-white plumage. Iris black. Bill usually light horn, but slate grey in Stewart Island brown kiwi.*
CHICK: *As adult.*

MOULT
Not known.

VOICE
Male calls 7 to 23 shrill, prolonged whistles, slightly ascending and descending. Female calls a shorter, lower, hoarser cry. A loud snuffling when feeding.

DISTRIBUTION
North Island brown kiwi:
Forested areas of the North Island as far south as the Manawatu Gorge. Little Barrier Island and, possibly, Kapiti Island.

South Island brown kiwi:
Fiordland south of the Hollyford River. Westland between the Okarito and Waiho Rivers; and between the Haast and Arawata Rivers.

Stewart Island brown kiwi:
Widespread throughout most of Stewart Island.

ORNITHOLOGISTS HAVE SEPARATED the brown kiwi into three subspecies: the North Island brown kiwi *Apteryx australis mantelli*; the South Island brown kiwi *A.a. australis*; and the Stewart Island brown kiwi *A.a. lawryi*.

The smallest of these is the North Island brown kiwi. Typically, it has a grey-black head and neck, a dark rufous back streaked with black, and paler grey-brown underparts. But birds have been sighted that range in colour from dark umber to pure white. Its feet are brown.

Once widespread in the North Island, it is now confined to the forested areas north of the Manawatu Gorge. Between 1910 and 1940 North Island brown kiwis were transferred to Little Barrier Island and Kapiti Island. The colonisation of Little Barrier Island has been so successful that the birds are common there, but on Kapiti Island the North Island brown kiwi is rarer.

The North Island brown kiwi inhabits all kinds of forest found on the island. It is most common in a mixture of podocarp and hardwood or hardwood and beech. But in some areas, such as North Auckland, it nests in manuka scrub, where it feeds on invertebrate ground animals from adjoining pasture lands. It is also successfully colonising some North Auckland exotic pine forests.

The South Island brown kiwi has grey-brown plumage, with a rufous tinge and black streaks. This kiwi is found mainly on the Fiordland and Westland coasts south of 43°S, but little is known about its habitat requirements. In Westland it appears to favour dry, undulating, low-lying podocarp and hardwood forests, but in Fiordland, it is found from sea level to tussock meadows above the timber line.

The Stewart Island brown kiwi is the largest of the three. It has grey-brown upper parts, streaked with black and rufous; and grey underparts streaked with brown. It has a slate grey bill that is darker along the ridge and blue-grey feet. B.E.R.

The largest of the brown kiwis, the Stewart Island brown kiwi is common throughout most of the island, where it favours forest and mountain scrub.

Little Spotted Kiwi *Apteryx owenii* GOULD, 1847

Quiet and placid by nature, the little spotted kiwi was the kiwi most familiar to early settlers and explorers.

ALTHOUGH MORE FURTIVE than the other two species, this was the best known kiwi to early European explorers, naturalists and settlers living on the west coast of the South Island. During the nineteenth century, the little spotted kiwi was found from the Marlborough Sounds to Fiordland, from sea level to over 700 m. It was also quite common on Mt Hector in the North Island.

Unfortunately, this small kiwi was particularly vulnerable to introduced predators, such as wild pigs, dogs, cats and stoats. Man also contributed directly to its decline: prospectors and bushmen fed on kiwi stew; collectors sent specimens to overseas zoos and museums; and thousands were slaughtered for their feathers.

Now it is absent from many forests where once it was numerous.

On Kapiti Island, several hundred birds, believed to be the descendants of five birds released in 1913, nest in open kohekohe or kanuka forest and feed also in adjacent pastureland.

Nothing definite is known about the type of habitat the little spotted kiwi prefers. It was reported by early observers as living in dry, open forest, as well as dense, wet forest and was seen in open country above the tree line.

The little spotted kiwi may consist of two subspecies. Small birds, similar to Gould's type specimen, were found in Marlborough and Nelson. Larger birds, including a white variety, occur on the western side of the Southern Alps. These are generally darker in colour, the brown bands proportionally wider on the upper surface.　　B.E.R.

Great Spotted Kiwi *Apteryx haastii* POTTS, 1872

The great spotted kiwi is confined to the western South Island and is most plentiful in mixed beech forest.

THE GREAT SPOTTED KIWI is most likely to be seen in the Tasman Mountains and the Paparoa Range. It is less common in Westland. Its varied habitat includes subalpine tussock; damp, mossy beech stands; dry, alluvial podocarp and hardwood forest; and scrub-covered coastal pasture. In a survey of the Paparoa Range in 1977 it was found from sea level to above 1000 m.　　B.E.R.

Emperor Penguin

Aptenodytes forsteri GRAY, 1844

THIS IMPRESSIVE BIRD, the largest of the penguin family, has been sighted only once on the New Zealand coast. Normally, the emperor penguin inhabits Antarctica, where it breeds under the harshest conditions to which any bird has adapted.

The long breeding cycle of the emperor penguin is timed so that the chicks will fledge in midsummer, when the winter icefields have broken and food is plentiful again. In April, breeding birds congregate on shelf ice that is sheltered by cliffs. To reach these colonies, the penguins often walk more than 200 km and expend as much as 1.5 kg of body fat. But by the time the young are ready to leave, the ice has broken, and they are near their feeding grounds in the open sea.

Emperor penguins do not prepare a nest, and both sexes fast until the female lays a solitary, conical egg. During the continuous darkness of the Antarctic winter, this egg is incubated by the male which holds it on its feet in a large pouch. Throughout the incubation period the male fasts while the female feeds at sea.

After 62 to 66 days, the chick hatches. It remains on the feet of the male and is fed a secretion from the parent's oesophagus. Soon the female returns to take over brooding, bringing in her stomach a huge meal of fish, squid or crustaceans for the infant bird. At about 40 days, the chick joins a crèche of other chicks. This frees both parents to hunt for and feed the young bird at long intervals, until it fledges at 140 to 165 days. While gathering food, adults will sometimes dive to a depth of up to 265 m.

The emperor penguin's behaviour enables it to survive the polar winter. Unlike other penguins, it is rarely aggressive towards its fellows, and incubating males and chicks huddle together in large groups. This cuts down heat loss by minimising the exposed area of the penguin's body. Studies of huddling males show that they lose half as much weight as birds fasting alone.

But, inevitably, bad weather kills some chicks and parental clumsiness accounts for other losses. The southern giant petrel attacks chicks on the ice while, at sea, leopard seals and killer whales have been known to take the birds.

The emperor penguin has few displays. In one, a courtship display, the bird first drops its bill onto its chest and utters a low note. It follows this by looping its neck upwards until its head is vertical, then it swings its head from shoulder to shoulder. This display is demonstrated by both lone birds and pairs.

J.W.

CIRCUMPOLAR

OTHER NAMES: *None.*

SIZE: *1150 mm.*

DESCRIPTION

ADULT: *Sexes alike. Head, throat and nape black. Large patches of white and yellow or white and orange extend from side of neck to top of breast. Back blue-grey. Underparts white, sometimes with yellow tinge on breast. Black band from underflipper to side of throat separates back and breast plumage. Flipper blue-grey above; white below with fine grey line along front edge and small dark patch at tip. Iris brown. Bill rather short, pointed, downcurved and partly feathered at base; with top and tip black; and orange, pink or purple patches on lower mandible. Legs and feet black, with outer sides of legs feathered.*
IMMATURE: *Neck patches pale, often yellowish grey; throat white to grey; bill black, sometimes with orange tinge below. Adult plumage gained at about 18 months old.*
CHICK: *Initially, silver-grey down above, and grey below; head black with white eye-mask. Secondary down thicker, darker grey above; head black; cheeks and throat white.*

MOULT

Breeders moult between December and February after a period at sea. Chicks moult into first feathers in November and December.

VOICE

Crowing, trumpeting and short calls indicate alarm and anger. Loud, sonorous buglings by returned parents are means of contacting chick once it has entered crèche.

DISTRIBUTION

One straggler reached Oreti Beach, Invercargill, in 1967. Breeds on ice, in at least 25 places, around the edge of Antarctica, often in large groups. At least 6 colonies in the Ross Sea. No fixed nesting territory.

RECOGNITION

Large, bulky bird with upright stance. Black throat sharply marked off from white or yellow of upper breast. Head often seems small in relation to body and feet. Walks, does not hop. Bigger than king penguin; bill more downcurved, shorter and feathered at base.

The emperor penguin is highly social and shows little aggression towards its fellows. It huddles in groups to conserve body heat during extreme conditions.

King Penguin

Aptenodytes patagonicus

MILLER, 1778

NATIVE

OTHER NAMES: *None.*

SIZE: *950 mm.*

DESCRIPTION

ADULT: *Sexes alike, although male usually larger. Head and throat black. Comma-shaped orange patch on either side of upper neck. Back silvery blue-grey. Tail black. Upper breast orange, shading downwards to yellow; rest of underparts white. Thin black line separates neck patches from back, runs towards throat and continues as broad line down each side of breast. Flipper blue-grey above. Underflipper white with blue-black area at base, blue-black band along front edge, and blue-black patch at tip of variable size, but often large. Iris brown, square when contracted. Bill pointed, slightly downcurved, mainly slate, with rear two thirds of lower mandible salmon pink or orange. Legs, feet, webs and soles dark grey to black.* IMMATURE: *As adult, but neck patches and throat yellow; grey-tipped feathers on crown; bill black with plates of lower mandible streaked pink or mauve.* CHICK: *Black and naked at first, then clad in thick brown down. Bill and legs black.*

MOULT

At Îles Crozet, adults moult between late September and the end of December, unsuccessful breeders from the previous season first. Immatures moult between late December and mid-February; chicks between October and December.

VOICE

Loud bugling calls, either long or short, used in displays. Short contact notes at sea.

DISTRIBUTION

Rare stragglers at Auckland Harbour; Moeraki (Otago); on the Auckland and Antipodes Islands; and on Campbell Island. Breeds on Macquarie Island; Îles Crozet and Kerguélen; Prince Edward, Marion and Heard Islands; Isla de los Estados; South Georgia; and the South Sandwich and Falkland Islands.

RECOGNITION

Large, upright bird with orange flash on upper breast. Walks, does not hop.

During breeding and moulting, king penguins resort to colonies on fairly flat land sheltered from prevailing winds.

A LARGE, ERECT AND DIGNIFIED BIRD, with a sleek black head and bright-orange neck patches, the king penguin could only be confused with its much rarer relative the emperor penguin. However, the king penguin is smaller and is soon distinguished by the dramatic flash of orange at the top of its breast and the thin black line that separates the neck from the back.

The breeding colony nearest to New Zealand is on Macquarie Island where there were about 13 000 chicks in 1960. Until the end of the last century, there was another, larger group of king penguins on the island, but after many of the birds were slaughtered for their oil, this colony was abandoned. Very occasionally, king penguins straggle to New Zealand.

When they come ashore to moult or to breed, king penguins return to sheltered, rather flat land which is near to sandy or stony beaches that allow easy access to the sea. Fish, cephalopods such as squid, and crustaceans form the bulk of the bird's diet.

King penguins lay from late November to early March. They do not construct a nest, but incubate the single white egg, oval or conical in shape, on their feet under a deep abdominal brood patch. The parents share the incubation period of about 53 days, dividing it into three or four long stints. The eggs hatch from late January to April.

The parents also take turns to guard and feed the almost naked newborn chick, which they continue to hold on their feet. At five or six weeks old, the young penguin, heavily clad in down, joins a crèche of other chicks. The growth of the young is halted by the winter and not resumed until the spring, so that they depend on parental feeding for a total of 10 to 13 months. Because of this king penguins breed on a three-year cycle, during which they rear only two chicks.

Young birds are prey to both species of giant petrel, while smaller chicks and eggs may be lost to skuas, Dominican gulls and sheathbills.

The king penguin adapts to captivity and breeds successfully far from the subantarctic region. J.W.

Yellow-eyed Penguin *Megadyptes antipodes* (Hombron & Jacquinot, 1841)

ENDEMIC

OTHER NAME: *Takaraka.*

SIZE: *760 mm.*

DESCRIPTION
ADULT: *Sexes alike, male generally larger. Feathers of top and side of head and below bill pale yellow with central streak of black; those on forehead and crown longer. Band of clear sulphur yellow from gape, around head and through eyes. Upper surface slate blue, each feather with central streak of black. Upper flipper blue-black, edged with yellowish white, narrower in front.*

Tail blue-black. Throat and side of neck brown-yellow. Breast, belly and underflipper, white. Iris lemon yellow. Bill mainly pale red-brown with part of upper bill and most of lower bill blue-white. Feet pink. Claws and edges of webs brown. Soles black.
IMMATURE: *Similar to adult except chin white; no yellow on head; and yellow head band only extends from bill to above and behind eye. Adult head band not developed till 14 to 18 months.*
CHICK: *Covered with brown down, second down a little lighter. Iris yellow-grey. Bill pink-brown. Feet white. Soles black.*

MOULT
Most moult during February and March, for about 24 days. Juveniles, non-breeding adults and failed breeders moult first while parents still feeding young. Breeding birds moult about 22 days after young have departed. Successful females tend to moult at same time each season, but males moult when partner does.

VOICE
Semi-musical voice, unlike harsh calls of many other penguins.

DISTRIBUTION
Breeds on coasts of Canterbury,

Otago and Southland; on Stewart and Campbell Islands; and the Auckland Islands. Straggles north to Cook Strait and westward in Foveaux Strait to the mouth of the Waiau River.

The yellow-eyed penguin, a rare sedentary species, does not breed in closely packed colonies; pairs are usually within sight or sound of neighbours.

THOUGH PROBABLY THE WORLD'S RAREST PENGUIN, the yellow-eyed penguin may nevertheless be seen throughout the year near the sea-facing scrub and forested slopes where it nests. At nightfall in particular, birds can be seen scrabbling out of the sea—where they hunt yellow-eyed mullet, red cod and squid—onto rocky and sandy beaches. From these landing places they sometimes climb considerable distances over difficult ground, before reaching the tops of grassy cliffs.

Since the 1950s, some of the mainland breeding grounds of this timid penguin have been disrupted, either by dogs or by human encroachment into the scrubby vegetation that the yellow-eyed penguin prefers. For this reason, perhaps, it has extended its range northwards to Banks Peninsula.

The breeding season begins in the last week of August, when the birds begin to stay ashore in the daytime, and lasts until the end of April when most healthy birds have completed their moult. There are more male yellow-eyed penguins than females, so the males do not secure a mate each season, and usually start to breed between three and 10 years, while females start a year earlier. Breeding pairs do not always stay together, probably because of the preponderance of males.

The pair build a shallow nest lined with dry vegetation and sheltered under a log or flax bush, in the end of a fallen tree or against a bank or cliff. The nests are spaced apart, yet close enough to allow the birds to see or hear their neighbours. Yellow-eyed penguins communicate with a complex system of calls and displays that vary

from trumpeting with their bills held vertically to violent trilling cries.

From approximately 11 September to 11 October, the birds lay one or two oval, white eggs. First-year breeders usually lay only one egg. The time of laying is determined by the female, which lays about the same time each year.

Both parents incubate the eggs and, unlike most birds, they do not always completely cover them. At first the penguins straddle the eggs, so that the first egg, and sometimes the second, is partially exposed. This may partly account for the variable incubation period, which lasts from 40 to 51 days with an average of 43. The first egg laid hatches first and two thirds of the second eggs hatch on the same day. About 80 per cent of eggs hatch, but only 15 per cent of the chicks survive to breed.

At about 106 days old, the young birds fledge, but over half of these soon die. Of the rest, a few return to the place where they were born and the others settle elsewhere. For a while, juveniles and non-breeding adults wander from place to place, but after five years of age, yellow-eyed penguins rarely move from their breeding grounds.

Externally, there is little difference between the sexes. In general, male yellow-eyed penguins are larger than females, although the weights of both sexes fluctuate a great deal throughout the year. The birds are at their heaviest when the moult begins, but by the time it ends they have lost 45 per cent of their weight. Then, during the winter, the penguins again increase in size until, for about four weeks before the eggs are laid, the female is larger than the male. L.E.R.

Adélie Penguin *Pygoscelis adeliae* (Hombron & Jacquinot, 1841)

THE ADÉLIE PENGUIN is a rare visitor to New Zealand from Antarctica. It winters at sea, hunting mainly small shoaling shrimps, but also in some areas amphipods, fish and cephalopods. In October, it congregates in colonies on exposed flats and slopes, up to 200 m high, on headlands, spits and islands. To reach these breeding grounds, the birds may walk as far as 100 km over ice. But in summer, when the ice breaks, the fledgling penguins are close to the open sea.

Unfortunately, the snow-free promontories where the Adélie penguin breeds have also been chosen as sites for the establishment of scientific stations and bases. The Adélie penguin is by no means an endangered species, but human disturbance, pollution and rubbish have disrupted some colonies.

When pairs are forming at the colonies, or when an established pair meet again, the male penguin performs a dramatic display. It begins this by stretching its closed bill vertically while waving its head from side to side and beating its flippers in a jerky and regular pattern. This is accompanied by the soft call of *ku-ku-ku-ku-ku-ku* which climaxes in a reverberating *kug-gu-gu-gu-ga-aaa*, with the head and neck fully extended, the eyes rolled down and back, the crest at the back of the head erect and the bill slightly open. The display is often completed by a soft *gurr-gurr-gurr-gurr*, called as the head is rocked from side to side and the bill is pointed towards the 'armpit' of the beating wings. In another display, a pair wave their heads while facing each other with upward pointed bills, flippers at their sides and calling a raucous *gug-gug-gug-gaa*.

The males return first to the colonies and re-establish the nest—a simple platform of small stones and rock chips—on its previous site. The eggs, generally two, are laid from early to mid-November. The second egg is usually slightly smaller than the first and laid about three days later. Incubation lasts about 35 days, with the second egg hatching one day later than the first. The parents share the incubation of the eggs, taking turns in long shifts of up to 17 days, during which they fast and lose up to 30 per cent of their body weight.

The newborn chicks are guarded for 22 to 25 days by their parents, until they gather in crèches for mutual protection. At 50 to 55 days old, in late January to mid-February, the fledglings leave the colony.

Mortality in adults is low, but as many as 70 per cent of the eggs and young may die. Nests and eggs may be nearly submerged by melting ice; Antarctic skuas snatch poorly guarded eggs and chicks; and leopard seals prey on birds at sea.　　　　C.J.R.R. & F.C.K

CIRCUMPOLAR

OTHER NAMES: *None.*

SIZE: *710 mm.*

DESCRIPTION
ADULT: *Sexes alike. Upper parts, including head, cheeks and throat, blue-black, changing with wear to black during breeding season and brown before moult. Tail black. Underparts white. Flipper black above with narrow white margin at rear; white below and sometimes with narrow black margin at front and black spot at tip. Iris red-brown. Prominent white eyelids. Bill short, feathered for half its length, chestnut red with black tip. Feet pale pink; soles black; claws dark brown. Pure albinos and individuals with light-coffee to dark-chocolate upper parts occur.*
IMMATURE: *Similar to adult, but upper surface bluer with throat and cheeks white. Adult plumage attained at first full moult in second year.*
CHICK: *First down short and dense, silvery to dusky grey with darker head; bill black. Second down, at third week, long thick dusky brown; bill black. Feathers start to appear from fifth week.*

MOULT
Not known.

VOICE
During certain displays males call ku-ku-ku-ku-ku-ku, *softly at first, but climaxing in resounding* kug-gu-gu-gu-ga-aaa, *followed by soft* gurr-gurr-gurr-gurr. *Pairs also call raucous* gug-gug-gug-gaaa *that varies in intensity and loudness. Young whistle shrilly when begging for food.*

DISTRIBUTION
Occasionally straggles north of 60°S to Macquarie Island. Twice recorded in the South Island. Breeds in large colonies around the Antarctic continent and on adjacent islands. Estimated 566 000 to 723 000 pairs breed at 26 places in the Ross Dependency.

RECOGNITION
Medium-sized stocky penguin. Blue-black and white body and white eyelids give it button-eyed appearance. When ashore, walks with outstretched flippers and head bent forward. Very gregarious, both at breeding colonies and at sea.

Little is known about the life of the Adélie penguin, except at its summer breeding grounds.

Gentoo Penguin *Pygoscelis papua* (FORSTER, 1781)

CIRCUMPOLAR

OTHER NAMES: *Johnny, Johnny penguin.*

SIZE: *760 mm.*

DESCRIPTION
ADULT: *Sexes alike, though at South Georgia female smaller in bill, flipper and foot. Head, neck and throat slate black, with white band across head from eye to eye, narrower in middle. Scattered white feathers give speckled effect to nape, sides of neck and shoulders. Rest of upper surface blue-black; rear of flipper edged with white. Underparts white. Underflipper white with dark front* edge and dark patch at tip. Eyelid white. Iris brown. Bill rather pointed, yellow to orange-red, with ridge and tip black. Feet and webs yellow to bright orange. Soles black. IMMATURE: *As adult but bill smaller, dull yellow. White on head and speckling may be less extensive, often not reaching to eye. Chin and throat may be grey rather than black.* CHICK: *Scant primary down dark grey on head and throat, grey on back, silver grey below. Iris dark blue initially, brown later. In thick secondary down head, throat and back dark grey; underparts white; upper flipper grey, edged at front with white; bill dull yellow at sides, black on top and at tip;* feet flesh-coloured.

MOULT
Adults return in March for annual moult. Most yearlings moult in February.

VOICE
Braying and trumpeting. Hissing when threatened.

DISTRIBUTION
Three or four sightings in New Zealand at Banks Peninsula, Dunedin, Bluff, and Campbell Island. Breeds at Macquarie Island; South Georgia; the South Orkney, South Shetland and Falkland Islands; Heard, Marion and Prince *Edward Islands; and Îles Crozet and Kerguélen. Birds of southern breeding populations leave their islands in winter but at northerly islands gentoo penguins can be seen throughout the year.*

RECOGNITION

Large penguin easily identified by bold white head band running across back of head and expanding into large white triangles above and behind eyes. Timid when approached.

OVER THE PAST TWENTY YEARS, there have been several sightings of the gentoo penguin on Campbell Island and mainland New Zealand. It is easily recognised by its white head band and the white feathers of the neck and shoulders, which give the bird a freckled appearance. Presumably, these stragglers came from Macquarie Island, the nearest breeding ground.

On the whole, gentoo penguins are sedentary: they either remain on their home islands or feed nearby on fish, crustaceans and cephalopods. In the winter, the Macquarie Island birds spend a lot of time on the beaches, particularly at night. During the summer, they travel inland and nest among fern or tussock. Often the location of these colonies varies slightly from year to year.

The range of the gentoo penguin is the subantarctic zone and birds from the warmer northern colonies lay before those at the southern end of the range. At Macquarie Island, colonies begin to form in early August and many nests are built by the middle of the month. Laying starts about 3 September and continues throughout the month.

As part of the courtship ritual, both sexes point their bills to the sky and trumpet loud crowing calls. Their orange bills and bright-orange mouths are especially prominent during these displays.

The nest is a large, well-made cup of tussock and other readily available vegetation. Gentoo penguins are a social species, but the nests are spaced far enough apart to prevent too many confrontations between neighbours, and at Macquarie Island there are seldom more than about 50 to a colony.

They lay two eggs, occasionally three, three or four days apart. The first is usually a little larger than the second. There is some evidence that if the first clutch is lost the gentoo penguin can lay another.

The parents divide the incubation period of 35 or 36 days into stints of about 24 hours. The chicks remain in the nest and are guarded by either parent for four or five weeks, until they join a crèche. Often only one chick is alive by this time. In the crèche, the parents probably feed their own young. The crèches tend to shift from colony sites towards the sea where the chicks can be fed more easily. The young birds fledge from mid-December to mid-January.

Some chicks are lost to skuas and giant petrels. At sea, birds are taken by leopard seals, fur seals and sea lions. On Macquarie Island adult gentoo penguins sometimes drown in the deep mud of elephant seal wallows. One of the most well known penguins, it has long been bred in captivity in northern hemisphere zoos.   J.W.

The gentoo penguin nests in summer, with laying fairly well synchronised within the colony. Incubation is shared by both sexes.

One display of the chinstrap penguin consists of mutual head waving, as birds face each other with upward-pointing bills and flippers at their sides.

Chinstrap Penguin *Pygoscelis antarctica* (Forster,1781)

THE CHINSTRAP PENGUIN is not afraid of intruders. With hackles bristling, it advances boldly towards them. And if this does not deter the interloper, the chinstrap penguin will stamp its feet, growl, hiss and attack with its bill and flippers.

Yet this is also a gregarious bird that breeds in dense rookeries. The largest of these colonies are on flat coastal areas. Sometimes plateaus are shared with *Eudyptes* penguins. When Adélie penguins nest on the same ground, the chinstrap penguins occupy the steeper, more broken land at the edges of colonies.

Chinstrap penguins return to the colonies in late October and early November. The males arrive first. The female lays in late November and early December although, in some northern colonies, the birds lay up to a month earlier. The nest is a low platform of pebbles and stone chips. A clutch usually consists of two greenish white eggs with a chalky coating, which both parents incubate in short stints of about three days. The chicks hatch after 35 days, although at the southern colonies incubation can take more than 38 days. At first, the parents guard the chicks, then the young birds join a loose crèche. They finally fledge from early February to mid-March.

Antarctic skuas take some eggs and young penguins, but adverse weather conditions account for most deaths.

Chinstrap penguins feed close to land, chiefly on krill and other crustaceans, as well as some fish. C.J.R.R.

CIRCUMPOLAR

OTHER NAMES: *Ringed penguin, bearded penguin.*

SIZE: *680 mm.*

DESCRIPTION
ADULT: *Crown black. Upper parts blue-grey. Cheeks, throat and underparts white. Thin black line extends from ear to ear downwards across throat. Tail long and black. Bill slim and black. Iris pale brown. Feet fleshy white.*
JUVENILE: *Smaller than adult. 'Chinstrap' acquired in first year. Some dark spotting on chin and cheeks. Mottled iris in first year.*
CHICK: *Newly hatched down silvery white. Longer second down grey, lighter on head and cheeks and even paler on chin and throat. Underparts vary from nearly pure white to pale grey.*

MOULT
Not known.

VOICE
Similar to Adélie penguin, but ecstatic display call is a low-pitched ah-kauk-kauk with bill open. Low growl and hiss when approached closely.

DISTRIBUTION
Straggles north to Campbell Island and the Antipodes Islands. Breeds in dense colonies of up to millions of birds on South Georgia; the South Sandwich, South Orkney and South Shetland Islands; and the Antarctic Peninsula. Also, in small numbers, on Bouvetoya; Peter Island; Heard Island; and the Balleny Islands.

RECOGNITION

White cheeks,
black crown and narrow
black 'chinstrap'.

White-flippered penguins come ashore only to moult or to return to their breeding grounds for the onset of laying. They nest along rocky coastlines.

Blue Penguin *Eudyptula minor* (FORSTER,1781)

ENDEMIC
Northern Blue Penguin
E.m. iredalei MATHEWS, 1911.
Cook Strait Blue Penguin
E.m. variabilis KINSKY &
FALLA, 1976.
White-flippered Penguin
E.m. albosignata FINSCH, 1874.
Southern Blue Penguin
E.m. minor (FORSTER, 1781).
Chatham Island Blue Penguin
E.m. chathamensis KINSKY &
FALLA, 1976.

OTHER NAMES: *Little blue
penguin, little penguin, fairy
penguin, korara.*

SIZE: *400 mm.*

DESCRIPTION
ADULT: *Sexes alike. Smallest of all
penguins. Upper surface blue, with
variations from pale to dark,
according to subspecies. Upper side
of flipper blue with 1 to 3 white rows
on rear edge. In white-flippered blue
penguin, broad white front band on*
*flipper. Tail very short and abraded,
usually blue, sometimes white in
Cook Strait and white-flippered blue
penguins. Throat grey; rest of underparts white. Iris usually silver-grey,
but dark grey or brown in Chatham
Island blue penguin. Bill black.
Feet white, pink when excited. Back
of legs, webs, claws, and soles black.*
IMMATURE: *As adult, but blue
colouring above brighter.*
CHICK: *First down usually black
above and light grey below, but
northern blue penguin uniformly
light grey. Second down changes
from black to chocolate brown above
and white below.*

MOULT
Northern blue penguin: *Late
December to early March. Lasts
about 2 weeks.*

Cook Strait blue penguin:
Period of moult not known.

White-flippered blue penguin:
*Late December to March, with a
peak around mid-January to mid-*
February. Lasts 15–21 days.

Southern blue penguin: *Period
of moult not known.*

Chatham Island blue penguin:
Period of moult not known.

VOICE
*At night, a long outbreathed moan
followed immediately by a shorter
inbreathed wail of higher pitch. A
growl when disturbed in the day. At
sea, a penetrating duck-like* quack
*especially just before coming ashore
at dusk. Chicks cheep when alone in
the nest and give a loud chirruping
call when being fed.*

DISTRIBUTION
Northern blue penguin: *The
northern half of the North Island,
including offshore islands.*

Cook Strait blue penguin: *The
coasts and islands of the southern
part of the North Island from Cape
Kidnappers south to Palliser Bay,
through Cook Strait and north to
about Cape Egmont. Also the coasts*
*and islands of the northern part of
the South Island from Karamea on
the west coast to Motunau Island on
the east coast.*

White-flippered blue penguin:
*The shores of Banks Peninsula and
Motunau Island.*

Southern blue penguin: *The
coasts of Otago and Southland south
to Foveaux Strait, Stewart and
outlying islands, and up the west
coast to about Karamea.*

Chatham Island blue penguin:
*The Chatham Islands at Chatham,
Pitt, South East, Mangere and Star
Keys.*

RECOGNITION

Blue upper parts. Mainly
nocturnal on land. Very vocal
at night from April to
August. At sea, only head and
small part of back above
water when not swimming.

THE BLUE PENGUIN IS THE SMALLEST of all penguins. It spends most
of the year at sea, where it hunts mainly small fish fairly close to
the shore. But during the breeding and moulting seasons, and
occasionally at other times, it comes on land at night to nest or
roost in dark crevices, caves, burrows or thick vegetation.

In winter and early spring, as the laying season approaches, the
birds start returning to their breeding areas. Gradually, the numbers coming ashore during the night increase and more and more
birds stay ashore during the day, often in pairs.

While pairs are forming, the birds are particularly noisy. During the
day, the penguins remain hidden, and the only clue to their presence is
an occasional growl. But, at night, blue penguins exchange their characteristic wailing call, which begins with a long outbreathed moan,
followed immediately by a shorter inbreathed wail of a higher pitch.

Blue penguin eggs are pure white when fresh, but soon they
become brown and discoloured. Often the first clutch is lost or
abandoned, but some birds lay another, two or three weeks later.

Both parents incubate the eggs alternately. When the chicks have
hatched, one of the parents remains on the nest until the young are about
25 days old. The chicks are then left alone during the day, and both
parents return at night to feed them, until the young leave for sea alone.

As soon as the chicks leave, the parents also depart for sea to
begin a period of intensive feeding. They gain up to 30 per cent of
their normal weight, then come ashore and fast while they moult.
They spend this time hidden in crevices or under thick vegetation.
Some birds return to their nests to moult; others choose the nests
of other pairs. The old feathers start to shed in five to seven days;
those on the flippers, face and lower back first, followed by those
on the breast and the rest of the head and back.

New Zealand's five subspecies

Five subspecies of blue penguin are found around the New Zealand
coast, and another subspecies, the fairy penguin *Eudyptula minor
novaehollandiae*, occurs in Australia.

The northern blue penguin, which breeds on the northern half of the
North Island, is a light Tyrian blue. It has an extensive breeding season
that lasts from July to February. On the whole, it is monogamous and
established breeders return each year to the same area of coast. As

competition for the best burrows is fierce, the nesting site may vary from year to year. Often, these sites are 200 to 300 m inland.

Invariably, northern blue penguins lay two eggs, two or three days apart. The incubation period lasts from 32 to 44 days with one chick hatching about 35 hours before the other. The fledglings leave the nest when they are 48 to 55 days old.

Outside the breeding season, northern blue penguins occasionally come ashore at night. They return to the same spot within a few metres. Sometimes, they will 'keep company' with another bird, which may not be the established breeding partner.

However, banding studies have also shown that some northern blue penguins travel far from their breeding grounds: up to some 300 km from where they were banded. These stragglers include adults as well as young birds, though not older established breeders.

The Cook strait blue penguin is found at the southern end of the North Island and the northern part of the South Island. It is Tyrian blue and sometimes has a white tail. This penguin tends to nest alone, occasionally in small groups. The nest itself is lined with dry grass or seaweed and the eggs are laid from early August to mid-November, with a peak in the second half of August. They usually number one or two, rarely three, and are laid one or two days apart. Both parents incubate them for 33 to 47 days, in shifts of about 16 hours. The chicks fledge when they are 49 to 60 days old.

The white-flippered blue penguin

The white-flippered blue penguin breeds around Banks Peninsula and Motunau Island. It is a bright columbia blue and has a characteristic white band at the front of its flipper. The nocturnal brayings of this penguin, commonly associated with pair behaviour, are familiar to the residents of Banks Peninsula, owing to its habit of nesting under boatsheds and other shoreline buildings.

The white-flippered blue penguin nests in loose-knit groups where, usually, neighbours can hear one another. Most of these colonies are within 25 m of the sea, although some are further inland. The penguins within a colony usually lay at the same time in September and October. Generally, they produce two eggs, but occasionally one or three. The incubation period lasts about 38 days, with the parents changing over every few days. The adults guard the chicks for 10 to 25 days, then when they are to 50 to 55 days old, the fledglings leave for sea.

Young white-flippered blue penguins disperse southwards to the coasts of South Canterbury, Otago and Southland. In the winter, they appear to travel northwards, as first-year birds have been recovered at Ruatoria and Gisborne. Older birds are more sedentary, although two-year-old penguins from Motunau Island have been found near Wellington and in Otago. Most young white-flippered blue penguins return to their birthplaces. They begin breeding when they are three years old and retain the same mate for life. Each year they return to the original nest-site.

When they are set near breeding areas, fishing nets are a hazard for white-flippered blue penguins. Birds damaged by oil slicks have been washed onto Canterbury beaches.

Little is known about the other two subspecies of blue penguin that occur in New Zealand. The southern blue penguin, which is found along the coasts of the southern part of South Island and around Stewart Island, is indigo blue. The Chatham Island blue penguin is confined to the Chatham Islands. Also indigo blue, it is distinguished by its dark grey or brown eye.

The fairy penguin, which is found in southern Australia and Tasmania, is a light Tyrian blue. It has a white tail and two white rows on the rear edge of its flipper. F.C.K., C.J.R.R., C.N.C. & G.J.

Southern blue penguins breed on the coasts of Otago and Southland from Oamaru south to Foveaux Strait, on Stewart and outlying islands, and also up the west coast of the South Island to about Karamea. Blue penguins arriving ashore to moult are much fatter than during the breeding season.

Royal Penguin *Eudyptes chrysolophus* BRANDT,1837

NATIVE
Royal Penguin
E.c. schlegeli FINSCH, 1876.

VAGRANT
Macaroni Penguin
E.c. chrysolophus BRANDT, 1837.

OTHER NAMES: *None.*

SIZE: *760 mm.*

DESCRIPTION
ADULT: *Forehead and crown blue-black with orange-yellow frontal band spreading backwards to orange plumes above eye. Feathers in centre and sides of crest golden yellow tipped with black, longer plumes drooping untidily across cheeks. Cheek and around eye white to grey or very rarely black. Lores and around upper mandible yellow. Upper surface blue-black, with tail coverts often white. Throat tinged with grey. Rest of underparts generally white. Upper side of flipper blue-black, with narrow white rear edge. Underflipper white, with dark front edge and black patches at tip and rear. Bill red-brown; bow-shaped when viewed from above. Fleshy triangular patches at base of bill, often bright pink. Iris red-brown. Feet and legs flesh pink. Toes brown. Soles black. Female smaller than male with darker face. Sometimes albino, part albino, part melanistic and greyish yellow colour variations occur.*
IMMATURE: *As adult, but head plumes of two-year-olds shorter and yellow.*
YEARLING: *Smaller in body and bill than adult, with small yellow crest, dull brown bill and brown to red-brown iris.*

MOULT
Not known.

VOICE
Not known.

DISTRIBUTION
Royal penguin: *Sightings in New Zealand occur mostly in summer. Stragglers have been found at Napier, Wellington, Waikouaiti and near Dunedin. Odd birds and pairs occur commonly on Campbell Island among rockhopper penguins and may moult there. Breeds at Macquarie Island in great numbers.*

Macaroni penguin: *Rare straggler to The Snares and Campbell Island. Breeds at the South Shetland, South Orkney and South Sandwich Islands; South Georgia; Bouvetoya; Marion, Prince Edward and Heard Islands; and Îles Kerguélen.*

THE ROYAL PENGUIN NESTS on Macquarie Island, in vast colonies which stretch from the shore to about 150 m above sea level. Most birds return each summer, after wintering at sea, but stragglers have been sighted on Campbell Island and mainland New Zealand.

Usually royal penguins do not start breeding until they are at least six years old. They lay two eggs in a shallow hollow lined with stones and grass. The birds incubate the eggs for about 35 days, the female taking the first stint which lasts about 14 days. Only one of the chicks survives. The male guards the nestling, while the female feeds it krill. After three weeks, the young penguin joins a crèche and is then fed by both parents at two or three day intervals. The chick fledges in late January and early February.

Between about 1890 and 1918, many royal penguins were killed for their oil. Now their main predators are southern skuas and giant petrels, which carry off chicks and weaklings.

The macaroni penguin, a rare visitor to New Zealand, is a close relative of the royal penguin and has been sighted several times during the summer, once on Campbell Island and three times at The Snares. This subspecies is generally smaller than the royal penguin and differs from the great majority of royal penguins in having black or dark grey cheeks, chin and throat. The macaroni penguin often breeds in very large colonies. Its breeding cycle is similar to that of the royal penguin, although, at Heard Island, macaroni penguins lay about a month later than royal penguins.　　　　　　　J.W.

The royal penguin winters at sea and during the summer months comes ashore to breed in large colonies. It usually begins breeding at six years.

Rockhopper Penguin

Eudyptes chrysocome (FORSTER, 1781)

The most plentiful of all species of crested penguins, the rockhopper penguin breeds successfully in New Zealand seas at Campbell, Antipodes and the Auckland Islands. Birds were once slaughtered for their crest tassels.

CIRCUMPOLAR
Rockhopper Penguin
E.c. chrysocome (FORSTER, 1781).

VAGRANT
Moseley's Rockhopper Penguin
E.c. moseleyi MATHEWS & IREDALE, 1921.

OTHER NAMES: *Crested penguin, tufted penguin.*

SIZE: *630 mm.*

DESCRIPTION
ADULT: *Sexes alike, though female smaller, particularly in beak. Head, cheeks and throat black; rest of upper surface blue-black. On back of head black crest merging into side tassels of long, silky, drooping yellow feathers arising from narrow yellow stripe above eye which does not extend to base of bill. Undersurface white. Underflipper white with narrow black band along front edge and black patches at tip and rear. Plate on top of bill bowed when viewed from above. Iris flat, geranium red. Bill red-brown, edged with flesh-coloured strips forming patch at angle of mouth. Feet white to flesh pink; soles black.*
IMMATURE: *Two-year-olds and some three-year-olds have shorter and more erect tassels; otherwise like adult.*
YEARLING: *Smaller than adult. Crest not developed. Eyebrow stripe faint. Throat paler. Iris and bill dull brown. Feet flesh-coloured with blackish soles.*
CHICK: *In primary down head blackish; rest of upper parts dark grey-brown; underparts white; bill black. Secondary down dark brown on head, throat, back and upper flipper; underparts white; iris brown; bill dark grey with horn-coloured tip; feet flesh-coloured with dark grey claws.*

MOULT
At southern islands, breeders moult at nests in April after about a month's fattening up at sea. Moulting period lasts about a month. At Macquarie Island, non-breeders in adult plumage moult in February. Yearlings moult in January and February.

VOICE
Particularly noisy penguin with wide range of harsh and strident squawks that vary noticeably from bird to bird.

DISTRIBUTION
Most plentiful of all crested penguins.
Rockhopper penguin: *Breeds in subantarctic zone at Campbell Island; the Antipodes and Auckland Islands; as well as the Falkland Islands; Marion, Prince Edward, Heard and Macquarie Islands; Îles Crozet and Kerguélen; and near Cape Horn. During non-breeding season from May to September disperses northwards. Many that reach the coasts of New Zealand and Australia are yearlings or other immatures that land in the summer to moult. A few reach The Snares each summer. Infrequent stragglers to mainland New Zealand usually found on the east coast of the South Island, but also seen at Preservation Inlet and as far north as Gisborne.*

Moseley's rockhopper penguin: *Breeds at Tristan da Cunha, Gough Island, Île Saint-Paul and Île Amsterdam. Stragglers sighted at Chatham Islands and Wellington.*

RECOGNITION

Spiky black fringe on crown, very narrow stripe above eye and long drooping yellow tassels. Bright red eye.

WITH ITS LONG YELLOW TASSELS and untidy black crest, the rockhopper penguin has a rakish look quite unlike other crested penguins.

It is a gregarious bird, both on land and at sea, and breeds in enormous colonies: one Campbell Island site numbered two and a half million penguins. These huge groups are governed by a hierarchical social system. At the top, the large and aggressive males dominate the smaller, more passive females. Then, breeding birds of both sexes dominate those adults which are not breeding; the non-breeders dominate yearlings, and so on. This order is effectively maintained by a range of calls and displays.

The aggressiveness of the males becomes apparent if a colony is approached when the males are incubating the eggs. The birds utter harsh cries, bob their heads up and down, and jab their beaks towards the intruder. In contrast, if a colony is crossed during the female's stint, many birds crouch protectively over their eggs.

Rockhopper penguins breed above the landing beaches, among boulders, scree, or tussock-covered slopes. Often these colonies also extend into coastal caves. To attract a female to his nest-site, the male rockhopper points his bill to the sky, trumpets a loud call, and swings his head from side to side. Unlike other crested penguins, this display is not repeated by the female. Instead, when the male begins to shake his head, the female reaches up towards him with her bill ajar and utters staccato calls that are barely audible above the male's louder cries. Once a pair are established, they stay together for life and return to the same nest-site every year.

Their nest is a shallow hollow in the ground, edged with stones, soil or plants, and sometimes lined with grass or fern. Nests are often spaced so closely that sitting birds can almost touch their neighbours' extended bills.

The timing of the breeding season is related to the temperature of the seas around the islands. The higher the mean annual temperature, the earlier the birds breed. In the islands to the south of New Zealand, rockhopper penguins lay mainly in November. On the Antipodes Islands they lay seven days earlier than on Campbell Island.

The female lays two eggs, three to five days apart. These are white with a blue-green cast and are elliptical or oval in shape. The first is smaller than the second.

The incubation period of 33 or 34 days starts when the second egg is laid and is shared by both parents. At first, the incubating birds change over frequently, then the male leaves and the female sits on the nest for about 14 days. The male takes over for the next 10 days and the female incubates the eggs for the last two days.

When the birds change over, they perform a noisy display. As the relieving bird approaches, they point their beaks towards each other and trumpet loudly. Often these yells are taken up by neighbouring penguins. When the relieving partner steps into the nest, the birds sometimes perform the courtship display. Or they point their bills to the sky, bray loudly and wave their flippers up and down. Normally only one egg hatches; the other is usually lost during quarrels or taken by skuas. If both hatch, one chick inevitably dies within a few days.

Both parents are at the nest when the young hatch. Then the male cares for and guards the chick while the female hunts for crustaceans and cephalopods to feed the infant bird. At about 26 days the chick joins a crèche of other chicks, but the parents continue to feed only their own offspring close to or on the nest-site. When they return from the sea, the adults stand on their nests and perform demonstrative bowing and trumpeting displays. They repel any chicks but their own.

Small or weak chicks are often lost to southern skuas. Those that survive fledge at about 70 days. Once at sea, the young penguin may fall prey to giant petrels, fur seals, sea lions or leopard seals.

In the past, people took eggs from Tristan da Cunha and around Cape Horn and slaughtered rockhopper penguins to make the crests into 'tassel mats'. Now the population of these penguins could increase as the decline in baleen whales has increased their food supply.

In 1968 a Moseley's rockhopper penguin reached the Chatham Islands, built a nest and stayed for two summers. This subspecies can be distinguished by its brilliant red eye, spectacular tassels and heavily marked underflipper. J.W.

The Fiordland crested penguin constructs its simple, sparsely lined nest with sticks and leaves. The parents incubate the eggs for about 33 days.

Fiordland Crested Penguin *Eudyptes pachyrhynchus* GRAY, 1845

ENDEMIC

OTHER NAMES: *Tawaki, thick-billed penguin, New Zealand crested penguin, Fiordland penguin.*

SIZE: *710 mm.*

DESCRIPTION

ADULT: *Head black. Rest of upper surface, throat, cheeks and tail blue-black. White base of cheek feathers often forms white stripes. Broad yellow band from bill passes over eye and ends in drooping crest often containing black feathers. Undersurface white. Upper flipper blue-black with narrow white rear edge. Underflipper white with narrow grey front edge, black tip and large dark brown patch at base. Bill red-brown, often ridged at base. Iris flat, grey-brown to, most commonly, purple-red. Feet white or pink. Claws brown. Soles and outer edges of webs, black. Female smaller than male with smaller bill and narrower stripe above eye.*
IMMATURE: *As adult, but dark brown iris.*
YEARLING: *Slim. Crest shorter than adult. White chin. Throat and cheeks suffused with grey. Brown bill.*
FLEDGLING: *Smaller and bluer than adult. Narrow yellow crest tipped with black. Chin pale grey. Black-brown bill with horn-coloured tip. Iris dark brown.*
CHICK: *First down silky. Second down dense fur-like coat: dark brown above, creamy white below. Bill glossy, dark brown. Legs flesh pink in front, dark grey behind. Edges of webs and claws brown; rest of webs flesh. Soles black.*

MOULT
Adults moult for 20 to 30 days in February and early March at breeding areas, often at nest-sites, after 60 to 80 days at sea. Yearlings moult in January and early February, often far from their birthplaces.

VOICE
Hissing and barking cries when threatened. Loud and complex grating calls are part of courtship display. At sea short barks used as contact notes.

DISTRIBUTION
Common in South Westland and Fiordland from Bruce Bay to Green Islets. Also nests on Solander Islands, Stewart Island and its outlying islands. Breeding attempted at Palliser Bay and Abut Head, Westland. Stragglers found around North and South Islands as far north as Bay of Islands, and at Campbell Island and Auckland Islands. Yearlings common on Snares in summer, but they do not return to breed there. Immatures straggle to southern Australia, Tasmania and Falkland Islands. Absent from breeding areas from March to June, but whereabouts not known.

THESE SHY BIRDS BREED along wet and isolated shores. They nest beneath rocks or in hollows at the roots of trees, on headlands, inlets, and in caves. Or they land on boulder beaches and make their way up to the heavy undergrowth of kie-kie, supplejack and ferns of the Fiordland rainforest. There the dense vegetation protects the young from extremes of heat and cold.

They probably do not breed until they are five or six years old but, once they are established, pairs usually stay together for life. In late winter or early spring the birds form a shallow hollow in the ground, which they line sparsely with sticks and leaves. These simple nests are spaced apart in loose clusters. The nest-site may vary from year to year. Over about four days, in early August, the penguins lay two eggs. These are dull white with a blue or green cast when fresh, and elliptical to oval in shape.

Both parents incubate the eggs for about 33 days, starting after the larger second egg has been laid. The male sits on the eggs for about 13 days, then the female takes over for about a fortnight. Usually the male is on duty at hatching. Many eggs are lost, but most pairs manage to hatch at least one chick. A few of the chicks that survive are eaten by stoats, and some die from a chill caught in heavy rain. Occasionally whole groups of birds are washed away.

The male fasts while he guards the surviving nestling and the female feeds it on crustaceans and cephalopods, usually in the evening or after dark. They hunt fairly close to the breeding grounds as the young are fed almost daily. At three weeks the chick joins a crèche of other chicks. The female continues to feed the chick, with some help from the male and the young birds fledge at about 75 days old, towards the end of November.

Fiordland crested penguins have a complex communication system based on calls and gestures. These indicate aggression or submission or readiness to mate; or they serve as a means of contact between a parent and its chick or between a pair. For example, a bird will avoid conflict when it passes other birds' nests by sleeking its feathers and hurrying forward with its flippers thrust in front. Or a bird will protect its eggs or chick by crouching over them and hiding its bill. On the other hand, a bird will resist an aggressor by hissing, uttering loud staccato cries, and even by lunging at its rival with open bill and flailing flippers. In this display the red bill is emphasised: the yellow crests lead the eye to the beak which, with the pink mouth and white cheek stripes, contrasts sharply with the dark face.

During courtship, males in particular point their bills to the sky and swing their heads through wide arcs so that the crest becomes a yellow blur. The pair preen each other and make trumpeting calls together. These cries are also used as recognition signals between partners as well as between a parent and chick. Trumpeting by one parent often results in the chick emerging from a crèche to be fed.

The remoteness of their nesting grounds means that Fiordland crested penguins are, apparently, affected little by man's activities, but of all the crested penguins this is the most timid when approached by people. If the birds are removed from nests in wet weather, eggs or chicks are likely to die.   J.W.

Snares Crested Penguin *Eudyptes robustus* OLIVER, 1953

ALTHOUGH STRAGGLERS MAY BE sighted elsewhere in New Zealand, Snares crested penguins breed only on The Snares. In early September, they come ashore to breed on open flat ground surrounded by tussock, or under the shade of trees and bushes or, occasionally, on rocky ledges. They breed in groups, each pair returning to the same nest for several years, until the surrounding plants die and the colony moves on. At other times, nesting grounds are abandoned for no apparent reason.

The nest itself is a shallow cup in the ground, edged with a variety of materials: plants, sticks, bones, stones or mud. The male returns first, at the beginning of September. At the end of September or in early October the birds lay two pale blue, oval eggs, four days apart. The first egg is smaller than the second. When they nest on exposed ground, the birds lay up to a fortnight later.

Both parents incubate the eggs for a total of about 33 days. For the first 10 days, they change over frequently, but then the male goes to sea and the female guards the eggs for about 12 days before the male returns to complete the incubation.

Neither parent feeds during their stints on the nest.

The birds lose many eggs during incubation and, even when both chicks are born, one soon dies so that the parents rear only one. The male fasts and guards the surviving chick while the female feeds it, usually in the evening or after dark, on crustaceans and cephalopods. At 20 days the chick joins a crèche, but the female, with some help from the male, continues to feed only her own offspring, even when other chicks beg. The parents must hunt within two or three days swimming distance of the colony as the chick is fed almost daily. The young penguins fledge in the middle of January when about 75 days old. Once at sea, the fledglings may be eaten by northern giant petrels, New Zealand fur seals, or Hooker's sea lions.

Male birds dominate females, and the old control the young. They communicate with a number of displays and calls: loud calls to resist aggression; mutual preening to avoid conflict; bowing, calling and trumpeting signals between partners, or between parents and chicks; and a head shake which means that communication is over. J.W.

ENDEMIC

OTHER NAMES: *Snares penguin, Snares Island penguin.*

SIZE: *730 mm.*

DESCRIPTION
ADULT: *Head black. Rest of upper surface, throat, cheeks and tail, blue-black. Pale grey to white base of cheek feathers sometimes seen. Narrow yellow band from bill passes over eye and ends in backwardly directed loose crest that is sometimes upstanding. Undersurface white. Upper flipper blue-black with narrow white rear edge. Underflipper white with narrow black front edge, variably sized black tip and large black patch at base. Bill red-brown with ridges across base of culmen. Plate on top of bill bowed when viewed from above. Flesh-coloured skin around base of lower mandible becomes triangle of flesh at gape. Iris flat, button-like, dull purple-red. Feet white to bright pink. Claws brown. Soles and outer edges of webs black. Occasionally part melanistic birds, with black underflippers, occur. Female like male, but smaller, particularly in beak, and stripe above eye often narrower.*
IMMATURE: *As adult, but iris dull brown.*
YEARLING: *Smaller than adult. Crest short and pale. Silver grey on chin and throat until moult at 15 months, then black. Bill dull grey-brown to blackish brown. Iris dull grey-brown to pale chocolate brown.*
FLEDGLING: *Smaller than adult. Black-brown bill with horn-coloured tip. Chin usually pale grey. Iris dark brown.*
CHICK: *First down dark brown above, white below. Bill black. Iris dark brown. Second down brown above, buff below.*

MOULT
When chicks have fledged, parents return to sea to feed. After about 70 days, breeders come ashore to nest-sites to moult. This takes 20 to 30 days between late March and early May. Yearlings moult in January and February and lose about 50 per cent of initial weight.

VOICE
Noisy when breeding, especially male. During courtship loud, throbbing grating calls, often based on pulses or throbs. Hisses and staccato barks when threatened. Short barks used as contact notes at sea.

DISTRIBUTION
Breeds only at The Snares. In 1969, 30 000 to 50 000 birds in 133 colonies. Straggles to the South Island; the Antipodes and Chatham Islands; Stewart, Solander and Macquarie Islands; and occasionally to southern Australia. Absent from The Snares from May to September, but whereabouts unknown.

RECOGNITION
Slightly larger than Fiordland crested penguin, usually with more black on underflipper. Shorter and squatter and with shorter flippers and tail than erect-crested penguin.

The male Snares crested penguin guards the chick at the nest for about 20 days. The chick then joins a crèche.

Erect-crested Penguin *Eudyptes sclateri* BULLER, 1888

ENDEMIC

OTHER NAMES: *Tawaki, big-crested penguin.*

SIZE: *710 mm.*

DESCRIPTION
ADULT: *Sexes alike, though female smaller, especially in bill (apparent among birds standing in pairs). Head, cheeks and throat velvety black. Rest of upper surface blue-black. Pale yellow band starts near gape, broadens above eye and ends in backwardly and upwardly directed erect brush-like crest that sometimes lies close to head. Tail long, blue-black. Undersurface white. Upper flipper blue-black, rear edge white. Underflipper white with broad black front edge linking black patches at tip and base with brownish black area at rear angle of flipper. Bill dark brown, plates edged with blue-white strips of exposed flesh forming triangle at gape. Iris brown. Feet white to pink; claws brown; soles black.*

IMMATURE: *As adult, but crest shorter.*
YEARLING: *Smaller than adult. Crest short and not erect. After moult, crest still short but brighter yellow and usually erect. Chin white. Cheeks pale grey. Bill yellow, with fleshy strips at base less pronounced than in adult. Underflipper as in adult.*
FLEDGLING: *Smaller and bluer than adult. Crest short, yellow. Cheeks and throat white. Chin grey-white. Bill black, tipped pale horn.*
CHICK: *Secondary down chocolate brown above, buff below.*

MOULT
After young fledge, parents go to sea to feed for about a month, before returning to nest to moult. At the Antipodes Islands breeders moult for 25 to 30 days in March and early April. Younger non-breeders in adult plumage moult for 26 to 27 days in February and early March and lose about half their weight. Yearlings moult in January and February when pale throat and cheeks replaced with black feathers.

VOICE
Sonorous calls, with more low frequency components than other crested penguins, sung deliberately and slowly. Loud honking cries, often with a mournful cadence, when sparring.

DISTRIBUTION
Breeds abundantly in large colonies on the Bounty and Antipodes Islands, and in small numbers at Campbell and Auckland Islands. Has attempted to breed on Otago Peninsula. Common straggler to the eastern North and South Islands and Cook Strait, but less common south of Dunedin. Also straggles to Macquarie Island, The Snares and the Chatham Islands, occasionally to southeastern Australia, Tasmania and even the Falkland Islands. Absent from breeding places from May to early September but precise wintering distribution unknown.

RECOGNITION
Large, tall penguin, with long tail and flippers. Underflipper has distinctive black front edge and black patches. Velvety black head feathers. Brush-like crest. Brown bill and iris. Triangular profile to throat, which is often distended like a pouch.

THE DEEP, BOOMING BRAY of the erect-crested penguin easily distinguishes it from other penguins. In fact, this resonant, mournful voice is so distinctive that if a lone erect-crested penguin calls while standing in a mob of other penguins, it can be identified immediately.

This gregarious bird nests on boulder beaches or on stones and tussock just above the shoreline. Some of these colonies spread into

Erect-crested penguins breed abundantly in large noisy colonies on the Bounty and Antipodes Islands.

caves or beneath overhanging cliffs. On the Antipodes Islands and on Campbell Island the birds breed amongst vegetation, next to rockhopper penguins, but on the Bounty Islands, they nest on barren stacks and islets with Salvin's mollymawks.

Because of the rocky coast, it is often difficult for the penguins to come ashore. On the Bounty Islands, the birds land in batches, diving beneath the surface a few metres from the rocks, then shooting up on a wave and clinging to the rocks with their bills, flippers and feet. Those that fall back into the sea come ashore later with another batch. Once on land, the penguins file up the slippery rocks, carefully avoiding the dirty plumage of birds about to enter the sea.

The breeding season is in spring and summer, the birds keeping the same partner from year to year. They arrive at the Antipodes Islands in early September and prepare a shallow hollow in the ground, which they rim with stones and sometimes line with grass. Nests are often so close together that neighbouring penguins are just beyond pecking reach of one another.

Before they mate the pair trumpet and bow a great deal. Then the female lies on her belly, props herself with the ends of her outstretched flippers and allows the male to climb on her back. He probes gently with his bill at her cheeks and nape, treads his feet and flips his flippers against her flanks as he brings the cloacae into position. After the climax, both remain still for a few seconds, then the male slides off and stands still with his head downturned and his bill tucked into one shoulder. He gives a quick head shake and then both relax.

In mid-October, the female lays two greenish-white eggs, elliptical to oval in shape, the first smaller. If the eggs are lost, the birds do not lay another clutch. The parents incubate the eggs for about 35 days. The chicks hatch in mid-November and are fed by the female. She returns to the nest towards evening, makes trumpeting noises with her beak pointed to the sky, and the chick appears from a crèche. In late January and early February, when they are about 75 days old, the young penguins leave for the sea.

Some eggs and chicks are eaten by southern skuas. Northern giant petrels swimming off the colonies also kill some birds.

Erect-crested penguins spend much time preening each other, which probably helps to reduce their aggressive tendencies and cement the pair-bond. This behaviour is seen whenever birds are together at their nests, both while breeding and during the moult. When one bird returns to the nest, both produce deep-throated yells with bills directed upwards. Trumpeting with the bill pointed forward, however, seems to be a threatening gesture between neighbours.

Erect-crested penguins feed on crustaceans and cephalopods. When they are rearing chicks, the parents hunt fairly close to the islands, as the young are fed almost daily. But nothing is known about their feeding areas for the rest of the year.   J.W.

Magellanic Penguin

Spheniscus magellanicus

(Forster, 1781)

VAGRANT

OTHER NAME: *Jackass penguin.*

SIZE: *700 mm.*

DESCRIPTION

ADULT: *Upper surface dark slate grey, more bluish in fresh plumage. Chin, throat and sides of head blackish or brownish black. White band above the eye loops down between nape and cheek and under chin to outline the face. Tail black. Underparts white with sporadic black feathers. Narrow U-shaped black band crosses breast and extends down sides breaking up into dark mottlings towards thigh. Between this band and black face mask a broad black collar across neck. Under surface of flipper white with black spotting. Iris brown. Skin around eyelids black. Bill brownish black with yellowish markings. Feet brownish black mottled with pale grey.* IMMATURE: *Paler than adult with dirty grey cheek and only one indistinct chest-band.*

MOULT
Not known.

VOICE
Not known.

DISTRIBUTION
One vagrant sighted in New Zealand. Millions of Magellanic penguins breed on coasts and islands of South America from Archipielago Juan Fernandez in the west to Patagonia and the Falkland Islands in the east. May make long dispersal movements northwards out of the breeding season. Straggles to South Georgia.

RECOGNITION
Medium-sized penguin with no crest. Conspicuous black and white bands on neck, face and upper breast.

Magellanic penguins feed and rear their chicks for 10 to 11 weeks before the young birds fledge.

ALTHOUGH THE WORLD POPULATION of Magellanic penguins is numbered in millions, so far, only one has reached New Zealand. In 1972 a live immature penguin was found in Hawke Bay. The generally tame behaviour of this bird indicated the strong possibility that it had been held captive on a ship and released in New Zealand waters.

The breeding grounds of the Magellanic penguin are on the other side of the Pacific on the coasts and islands of southern South America. In mid-September, the birds arrive at their colonies. Generally, they nest in underground burrows, but also on slopes or in shallow scrapes under bushes. They lay in October, and incubate for 43 or 44 days. The usual clutch is two, rarely one or three. They feed mainly on squid and small fish.   C.J.R.R.

New Zealand Dabchick *Podiceps rufopectus* GRAY,1843

ENDEMIC

OTHER NAME: *Weweia.*

SIZE: *280 mm.*

DESCRIPTION

ADULT: *Sexes alike, but male often larger. Crown and nape black. Side of head and neck dark brown. White filaments on top of head and on cheeks give grey tinge. Rest of upper parts black-brown. Flight feathers grey-brown, secondaries and base of inner primaries white, forming broad flash in flight. Chin and throat dark brown. Foreneck and upper breast dark chestnut, with brown streaks on lower breast, and large black-brown blotches on flanks and rear. Belly and underwing silvery white. Underside of flight feathers grey-brown. Tail short, narrow, black. White patch on each side of tail when displayed. Iris yellow. Bill short, tapering, black. Legs black on outer surface; olive-grey to yellowish on inner surface. Feet olive-grey with yellow edges. For a short time after breeding upper parts, neck and upper breast dark brown with little or no chestnut; chin and sometimes cheeks dull white; underparts silvery white; flank patches pale; iris pale yellow.*
IMMATURE: *As non-breeding adult but underparts, forehead and cheeks dull white; chin and throat dull white, at first mottled with black and with broad pale stripes extending back onto cheeks; upper breast pale buff at first, later chestnut; iris brown, fading to whitish or pale yellow; bill horn-coloured at first, later only lower mandible. Immature and post-breeding adult plumages confusing and need proper study.*
JUVENILE: *As immature but forehead to nape black; grey-buff stripe above eye; black stripe through brown eye; chin, flanks and belly white; flanks mottled yellow; throat, foreneck and upper breast yellow-buff.*
CHICK: *Short dense down. Top of head broadly striped black and rufous. Side of head, chin, throat and neck broadly striped black and white. Upper and underparts broadly striped black and buff. Breast and belly white. Bill horn-coloured with two black cross-stripes.*

MOULT
After breeding moults into nondescript eclipse plumage.

VOICE
Silent, except for chattering calls in breeding season.

DISTRIBUTION
The North Island.

RECOGNITION
Small, dark waterbird. Dumpy and short-necked. Tail-end slopes down to water. When alarmed white patches exposed on each side of tail. Darker and redder than hoary-headed grebe. Larger than Australian little grebe which has yellow spot at base of bill.

ONCE THE NEW ZEALAND DABCHICK bred in the South Island; now the species breeds only in the North Island. It inhabits small bodies of fresh water, especially where it is less than two metres deep and there is some dense emergent vegetation. These waters are usually sand-dune lakes and lagoons, larger inland lakes with shallow, sheltered inlets, or artificial farm dams.

Altogether there are an estimated 1100 to 1400 New Zealand dabchicks. The main breeding population is in the Rotorua and Taupo lakes district of the Volcanic Plateau. About another 200 birds nest in North Auckland. A few also breed in South Auckland, the eastern North Island and the western North Island.

After breeding, from about February to September, many New Zealand dabchicks congregate on larger, more open lakes and oxidation ponds, especially in the southern part of the North Island.

Although it has disappeared from the South Island, the New Zealand dabchick population is stable in the North Island. In fact it has benefited from the increasing number of farm dams, many of which suit its breeding habits, and also from the construction of sewage oxidation ponds, on which many birds spend the winter.

A wholly aquatic species

The New Zealand dabchick feeds mainly under water, generally diving headfirst without a splash, sometimes with a slight jump and a splash. Using its broadly lobed feet, with its wings held close to its body, it swims much faster under water than on the surface. It usually remains below for 20 to 30 seconds. Molluscs and insects are probably its main foods, but it also eats leeches, small fish, freshwater crayfish (koura) and the leaves of water plants. It brings fish and koura to the surface first to dismember them, and also snatches midges and other insects from the surface.

When mildly disturbed, the New Zealand dabchick swims away slowly and quietly on the surface, or under water in stages of up to 20 m. If it is strongly alarmed, it crash-dives, breast first, sending up a jet of water which may deter an attacking harrier. Sometimes a disturbed winter flock flies close to the surface with rapid wing-beats.

The New Zealand dabchick bathes with much splashing, raising its body vertically and flapping its wings vigorously. When preening, it often rolls sideways on the water, exposing its silver underparts.

Although an aquatic bird, the New Zealand dabchick is capable of sustained flight. During the winter it moves from lake to lake, flying only at night. It avoids land, and when on a rock or platform for mating moves clumsily.

The breeding season varies. On Manawatu dune lakes, some pairs engage in territory and courtship displays as early as June, but at other nearby lakes, some do not begin displaying until September. In general, egg-laying extends from late August to January. Chicks are seen in most districts from October to March, occasionally in early September, and as late as early May. In the warm thermal waters of the Rotorua lakes district, however, some New Zealand dabchicks may be found breeding at any time of the year and many pairs rear two broods. If a clutch is lost, the birds usually nest again and this is sometimes repeated five or six times.

Establishing a pair-bond

Three courtship displays have been described. In the head-turning display, the erect head is flicked rapidly from side to side. This is done by one or both birds of a pair. In another, the patter ceremony, the two birds mill about together, with their heads low, necks kinked, their folded wings held high and white rear-ends displayed. Both birds jerk their heads and utter quiet, low-pitched calls. Suddenly one rushes through the water away from the other, with a short pattering splash that ends in a glide. In a less common display, the diving ceremony, the pair face each other in turn, lowering their heads and thrusting their bills forward; then one dives under the other, which turns to watch the diving bird rise.

In an aggressive display to other New Zealand dabchicks, it lowers its head, kinks its neck, humps its back and makes short pattering rushes at the opponent. If the opponent is some distance away, the dabchick makes one or more low flights across the surface. This is then followed by a dive, at which the opponent usually dives too. Birds disturbed or defending their territories fluff out their rear-end feathers to reveal a white eye-like pattern on each side of the tail. When a bird is agitated, it bobs its head up and down, from side to side, and sometimes from front to back.

The nest is an untidy pile of waterlogged plants, mainly raupo brought up from the bottom of the lake. Usually it floats, anchored to plants or to overhanging branches. It is sometimes sited on a ledge at the water's edge, under an overhanging bank, in a small, partly submerged cave or even occasionally in a boatshed. It is always well hidden by plants, such as raupo, niggerhead or overhanging ferns. The top of the nest is only slightly above the water surface, so it is easily swamped by a rise in water level, by wave action in a wind, or by the surge caused by power boats. The birds approach it under water. Both sexes gather nest material, but only the female builds the nest sometimes within three days. Some nests, which reach over a metre to the bottom, have presumably been much used and constantly added to.

Breeding activities

Mating occurs out of the water on the nest, on a stone or other low platform such as waterlogged plant material placed at the water's edge. One bird crouches flat, jerking its head from side to side or it stands with its body hunched and its white rear-end displayed. When they mate, the active bird stands erect on the passive bird. After mating, the active bird moves forward over the head of the other and treads water briefly in an erect posture. Reverse mating, when the pair changes position, is common.

New Zealand dabchicks usually lay two rough-surfaced, elliptical eggs. At first they are blue-white, but in a few days they become stained from the nest. The laying interval is not known.

Both parents incubate, probably for two or three weeks. The chicks leave the nest immediately after hatching and swim with or ride on the backs of the adults. Sometimes one parent gathers the food and passes it to the other to give to the chick. The fledging time is not known. A new nest is sometimes built when the first brood is two or three weeks old; a lost clutch may be replaced within five or six days.

After breeding the New Zealand dabchick exchanges its bright breeding plumage for a nondescript eclipse plumage. At this moult, presumably as in grebes elsewhere, the wing feathers fall out simultaneously; until new feathers grow, the bird is unable to fly, but this has not been confirmed. At the next moult, grebes overseas moult their body and tail feathers only. The young probably moult gradually into a plumage like that of the adult eclipse plumage, and then moult into the breeding plumage. However, all these plumage changes need confirmation in the New Zealand dabchick.

Because the breeding season is extended, there is no clear moult period. At warm thermal waters of Volcanic Plateau all plumages may be seen at any one time. In the southern North Island most birds are in eclipse plumage by late March in some years, by mid-April in others; but by late April or late May they are darkening once more into breeding plumage. By July all are in breeding plumage again. B.D.H.

The nest of the New Zealand dabchick is a concealed pile of waterlogged plants. Unlike most grebes, it does not cover the eggs when it leaves the nest.

The Australian little grebe is usually seen singly or in pairs.

Australian Little Grebe

Tachybaptus novaehollandiae (Stephens,1826)

NATIVE

OTHER NAMES: *Black-throated grebe, Australasian little grebe, Australian dabchick.*

SIZE: *250 mm.*

DESCRIPTION
ADULT: *Sexes alike, but male slightly bigger. Head and neck glossy black. Chestnut patch from eye to neck and side of head. Upper parts sooty brown. Wing dark grey with white patch. Spot of bare yellow skin at gape. Chin and throat black. Breast and flanks light rufous, mottled and streaked. Rest of underparts silver grey to white. Iris orange to yellow. Bill short, thick, black with white tip. Legs and feet dark greenish grey.*
JUVENILE: *As adult with pale stripes and spots on head.*
CHICK: *Grey-black down with longitudinal white stripes on head, neck and back. Chestnut patch on crown. Iris dark brown. Bill yellow.*

Feet black.

MOULT
Not known.

VOICE
Loud, prolonged trill or chatter, sometimes called as duet. Short alarm note whit whit.

DISTRIBUTION
Stragglers from Australia first sighted at Arrowtown, Dargaville, and Lake Okareka. Recorded breeding 3 localities in South Island, 1977–79. Breeds in Australia, New Guinea, Java, Timor, Sulawesi, the Solomon Islands and the Moluccas.

ALTHOUGH AUSTRALIAN LITTLE GREBES rarely fly, several have straggled to New Zealand from Australia over the past 15 years and commenced breeding. These quiet, secretive birds are usually seen on freshwater ponds, small lakes, dams, streams and swamps.

Little is known about this grebe. It dives frequently and, whether hunting for food or escaping an intruder, disappears with hardly a ripple. When diving for food, it stays under water for an average of 15 seconds, but sometimes for twice that time.

It feeds mainly on insects, but also eats plants, molluscs and small fish. Unlike grebes that mainly eat fish, the insect-eating Australian little grebe does not need to prevent sharp, indigestible items, such as fish bones, from puncturing its intestines. Consequently, it eats feathers rarely and simply coughs up indigestible insect remains.

Like other grebes, the Australian little grebe builds a large floating nest anchored to reeds, branches or saplings. It lays, between September and January, four to six blue-white eggs, which soon become brown from the wet and decaying nest. Both parents incubate the eggs for 21 to 25 days. Both sexes also rear the brood and small chicks are often carried on a parent's back. Normally, two broods are reared each season, sometimes three. K.E.W.

Hoary-headed Grebe

Podiceps poliocephalus JARDINE & SELBY,1827

NATIVE

OTHER NAMES: *Hoary-headed dabchick, Tom Pudding.*

SIZE: *280 mm.*

DESCRIPTION
ADULT: *Sexes similar, but males larger and longer-billed. In breeding plumage upper parts grey-brown. Head and neck black but with long white hair-like feathers overlying black. Pale bar on wing. Upper breast pale buff; rest of underparts silky white. Iris golden yellow in male, ivory in female, finely speckled with black. Bill short, sharp, black with light tip. Legs and feet olive green. Non-breeding plumage similar, but top of head dark grey or black; throat and sides of head grey-white; upper breast loses buff tint; and bill mostly pale.*
IMMATURE: *Crown marked with black, buff, and white. Black spots and lines on sides of head. Iris brown.*
CHICK: *Downy young not adequately described.*

MOULT
Not known.

VOICE
Generally silent. Thin squeak when tending young. Soft chuff-chuff-chuff-purrr-ow near nest.

DISTRIBUTION
Breeds mainly in southern Australia and Tasmania. First straggled to The Snares in 1975. Since then also recorded at Te Anau, Maroroa, the Ashburton Lakes, Wanaka, Aupouri Peninsula, Manawatu, and Horowhenua.

The head of the hoary-headed grebe appears hoary only during the breeding season. At other times its head is unplumed and paler grey and white.

THE HOARY-HEADED GREBE takes its name from the long white hair-like plumes that cover its head during the breeding season. For the rest of the year these feathers are absent; the top of the head is dark grey or black and the side of the head is a paler grey-white.

This grebe is found on large areas of open water — often salt water — in swamps, lakes, estuaries and lagoons. Usually hoary-headed grebes are seen singly, in pairs or in small groups, but during dry periods they congregate in large flocks.

Unlike most other grebes, which fly mainly by night, the hoary-headed grebe flies readily during the day. Like other small grebes it often sunbathes. Over water, its flight is swift and close to the surface.

As yet few hoary-headed grebes have bred in New Zealand. In Australia, the species breeds from November to January or after the rains. It nests in groups of up to 400 pairs, each nest about a metre apart. The nest is built from algae and other water plants, and is often attached to emergent plants. The size of the clutch varies from three to six. At first the eggs are pale blue with many chalky nodules, but soon they are stained brown from the nest. H.A.B.

The southern crested grebe breeds only in the South Island, and is most commonly found on the lakes clustered in the headwaters of the large Canterbury rivers.

Southern Crested Grebe *Podiceps cristatus australis* GOULD,1844

NATIVE

OTHER NAMES: *Crested grebe, puteketeke.*

SIZE: *500 mm.*

DESCRIPTION
ADULT: *Upper parts dark brown. Black double crest on crown. Round chestnut ruff tipped with black on each side of head. Wing dark grey-brown with white along forearm and big white patch on secondaries. Long thin neck and underside silky white. Iris red. Bill thin, pointed, dark red-brown. Legs olive green. Male larger; thicker neck, longer bill, larger ruff and brighter plumage. Female usually*

white above and in front of eye.
JUVENILE: *As adult but no crown tufts or ruffs. Black-brown stripes on cheek and side of head until about 3 months old.*
CHICK: *Covered with down. Head and neck white with black spots and longitudinal stripes. On top of head a naked wedge, usually pink but red when excited; smaller naked areas in front of eye and on cheek. Back dark buff with brown-black longitudinal stripes. Underside white. Iris orange and yellow. Bill short, blunt, white-tipped, black in middle and red at base. Feet green-yellow.*

MOULT
Main moulting period probably

January to March, after the breeding season. Unlike the Australian population, which has a dull winter plumage, New Zealand birds retain their bright coloured breeding plumage all year long.

VOICE
Harsh honking or barking. Soft crooning notes as part of courtship display. Different guttural calls with each display and to attract young to feed. Shrill call from young when begging for food.

DISTRIBUTION
Australia and New Zealand. Breeds in the South Island: on highland lakes in Canterbury; on Westland

lakes; and on lakes in Fiordland. Rare straggler to the North Island.

RECOGNITION
Duck-sized waterbird that sits low in water when swimming. Head at right angles to long, thin neck. Back dark. Underside white. Long bill. Two large black tufts on crown. Chestnut, black-edged ruff on each side of head. Dives frequently without splashing, unlike shags and diving ducks.

THE SOUTHERN CRESTED GREBE is not a common bird in New Zealand and its numbers are declining. In 1980 it was estimated that there were no more than 250 adults. Natural floods dislodge some nests, but most interference is by humans. Birds are shot illegally for their plumage; nests are disturbed by boaters, anglers and holidaymakers. Nest-sites are damaged by the clearing of reeds, bushes and trees along the shore; and water levels are affected by hydro-electric installations.

More than half of New Zealand's southern crested grebes live in the Canterbury high country on two lake systems: the Ashburton Lakes and Lakes Alexandrina and Macgregor. The rest of the population is scattered throughout Westland and Fiordland. Although the population is small, southern crested grebes are possibly safest in Fiordland, where they breed in the Fiordland National Park.

Most lakes have only a few birds—often just a pair. The birds move from lake to lake within the same region, but generally do not migrate long distances. In Canterbury, for example, most birds stay in the high country, despite harsh, freezing conditions. Birds from the Ashburton Lakes, however, are thought to fly about 100 km south to Lake Alexandrina in response to weather conditions.

The southern crested grebe often spends its entire life on the freshwater lake where it breeds. It prefers clear lakes with a plentiful supply of small fish, insects and waterweeds. Ideally, the water is stagnant or slow moving, and shallow enough to allow the grebe to fish at depths of two to five metres.

In Canterbury, southern crested grebes inhabit alpine and subalpine lakes and tarns, usually surrounded with tussock grassland, willows, reed beds and open shoreline. Often these waters freeze over in winter, leaving little suitable habitat for grebes. On the west coast, grebes live on low altitude lakes, bordered with beech and podocarp forest. They rarely visit coastal brackish lagoons, and do not breed on them.

Excellent divers and swimmers, southern crested grebes obtain most of their food by diving. Surface feeding occurs rarely. When feeding,

they dive frequently, often remaining under water for 20 or 30 seconds, and sometimes as long as 60 seconds. During dives, the grebe moves faster than when it is swimming, holding its wings close to its body and propelling itself with its legs.

Adult grebes spend most of their day feeding. Both adults and young grebes eat feathers, which help form ejectable pellets and prevent sharp fish bones from entering and damaging the intestines.

Both sexes build the nest, a large mound of decayed and sodden weeds, willow twigs, grasses and leaves. The nest is always well-hidden by vegetation and usually built on water, up to 25 m from the shore. Normally the nest is attached to submerged vegetation and occasionally it is anchored to the lake bottom or shore.

The southern crested grebe's courtship ceremonies are a complex mixture of postures and gestures. Males and females take part in the displays, often carrying out the same rituals simultaneously, while facing each other. The simplest courtship display is the head-and-ruff-shaking ceremony which can be seen in all months of the year, although most commonly from late winter to summer. In another display, the so-called penguin dance, the birds dive, then surface, vigorously paddling their feet. Mating takes place on special platforms, usually built of twigs, close to the nest; the hen shows her willingness by crouching with neck stretched forward.

The breeding season is long—from October to May. Most birds lay between one and seven eggs in December and January, though the average clutch numbers two or three. The eggs are long and oval, pointed at both ends and chalky white at first, but soon stained rust-brown by mud from the nest.

Both parents incubate the eggs, which hatch in 23 to 29 days, at one or two day intervals. The young can swim after two days and dive after about a week, but they are dependent on their parents until about 11 weeks. When they are young, southern crested grebes are often seen riding on their parents' backs.   C.F.J.O'D. & K.E.W.

Wandering Albatross *Diomedea exulans* LINNAEUS,1758

CIRCUMPOLAR
Wandering Albatross
D.e. exulans LINNAEUS, 1758.
Snowy Albatross
D.e. chionoptera SALVIN, 1895.

OTHER NAMES: *Wanderer, toroa.*

SIZE: *1000–1350 mm.*

DESCRIPTION
ADULT MALE: *Head, cheek and nape white, sometimes with brown on centre of crown and nape. Back white, lightly pencilled with black. Tail white, sometimes with black tip. Underparts white, occasionally with fine brown-black zigzag bars on breast, flanks and thighs. Upper wing black-brown, black-tipped, with varying amounts of white in centre. Underwing white except for black tip and trailing edge. Iris brown. Bill horn-coloured, usually tinged pink. Legs and webs flesh-blue. Snowy albatross paler and much larger.*
ADULT FEMALE: *Darker than male. Brown cap or some brown feathers on crown. Body generally white, blotched with brown. Tail white with black tip. Upper wing black-brown with some white towards base and*
black tip. Underwing, iris, bill, and legs as male.
JUVENILE: *Fledgling dark brown except for white forehead, face, chin and throat. Upper wing dark brown, tipped with black. Underwing as adult. Iris brown. Beak horn to flesh-coloured. Progressive lightening of feathers from juvenile plumage to that of breeding adult.*
CHICK: *First down sparse, white on head and neck, tinged with grey on body. Second down very thick.*

MOULT
Breeding birds moult every other year when they miss breeding.

VOICE
Bill clapping, burring sounds and whistles during courtship. Clop clop when threatened. Throaty cries at sea when squabbling over food. Soft pipings from newly hatched chicks. High-pitched whistles and gurgling sounds from older chicks

DISTRIBUTION
Wandering albatross: *In New Zealand, breeds at Antipodes Island in large numbers; at Adams and Disappointment Islands in the*
Auckland Islands in very large numbers. At Campbell Island a few pairs only. Ranges around the subantarctic. Fairly common in New Zealand seas. Shifts northwards in the winter: some birds from the Antipodes and Auckland Islands visit southeastern Australia; others move into low latitudes towards South America.

Snowy albatross: *Breeds on Macquarie Island and subantarctic islands of the Indian and Atlantic Oceans. Straggles to New Zealand.*

RECOGNITION
Huge size. Short tail. Heavy bill. White underwing except for black tip and trailing edge. Flies with feet protruding slightly beyond tail. Smaller and often darker on body and tail than royal albatross. White-bodied wandering albatrosses and snowy albatrosses usually distinguished from royal albatross by black-brown on leading edge of upper wing.

AT SEA, THIS HUGE BIRD is usually seen alone. Flying with regular upward swoops, the wandering albatross glides almost effortlessly into, and at an angle to, the wind. Its range is the southern oceans of the subantarctic and the warmer seas around Gough Island and Tristan da Cunha in the South Atlantic. It rarely crosses the equator or enters the Antarctic pack ice.

Wandering albatrosses hunt squid and fish, but they also eat whatever else is available, including other seabirds. These opportunistic feeders rarely feed in pairs or groups, unless they are attracted to a large supply of food, such as a whale or seal carcass, or refuse from a ship.

The breeding cycle of the wandering albatross lasts about 11 months. Most birds nest every other year, unless the egg is lost or the small chick dies, in which case they return to lay the following year. Partners stay together for life and nest at the same place every time, usually in an area near where they were born. Sometimes eight year old birds lay eggs, but most wandering albatrosses are older when they begin breeding.

Some courtship displays, such as bill clapping, fencing, bowing and mutual preening occur at sea, but most are performed at or near a potential nesting site. In one display, the pair face each other, lower their heads, and with vibrating bills utter groaning sounds. In another, the birds face each other and with raised heads clapper their beaks. They then reach forwards to nibble at each other's throat and head and fence with their beaks.

In a more complex display, both birds rise to their feet, the male first. They face each other with wings fully spread, but with the tips drawn forwards, so that each wing forms a shallow arc directed at the partner. They also spread and cock their tails. The two birds step sideways and circle around, keeping two or three metres apart and facing one another. At intervals, one stretches forward and, with head slightly raised, vibrates its bill to produce a strange rubbery burring. At the climax of this display, the head is thrown back so that the bill points vertically and a powerful braying whistle is given as the bird breathes out. An inbreathed sigh follows, then the bill is suddenly lowered and tucked tightly into the breast. Sometimes, mating follows.

Similar displays are used by groups of three or four younger birds. These groups, or gams, form when a male calls and attracts unattached females to land nearby. The young birds continue displaying until the chicks are alone in their nests and the parents are foraging at sea.

Wandering albatrosses nest on flat ground that is within walking distance of a ridge for an easy take-off. The nest itself is a hollow cone of peat and grass that the female rakes up with her bill with some help from the male. In New Zealand these nests are usually sited in dips to shelter them from the wind.

Between December and February, they lay one elliptical or oval white egg that often has light red-brown speckling. Both sexes incubate the egg and usually the male takes the first stint. Every two or three weeks the parents change over.

The chick hatches in March or April and is brooded by both parents in turn for four to five weeks. Brooding stints are shorter than incubation ones, lasting about three days. The chick is fed by the returning parent. When guarding ceases, the infrequent visits of the adults are not co-ordinated. The rearing period extends through the winter until the chick flies away between January and early March, at about 278 days old.

When nesting birds are threatened, they clap their beaks and jab forward to grab any part of the intruder within reach. The bill of a wandering albatross is powerful, very sharp and readily draws blood.

Chicks that are alarmed draw themselves to their full height and turn to face the disturbance. If bill clapping does not deter the attacker, they sluice forth a stream of stomach oil, which is sometimes followed by the stomach contents.

Wandering albatrosses from the Antipodes Islands and Campbell Island are much darker than those from the Auckland Islands; and in all regions, the females are darker than the males. All wandering albatrosses gradually lighten in colour as they age. It takes about 20 years for both sexes to progress from the dark brown juvenile colouring to the whitest plumage. J.W.

The wandering albatross breeds every second year, and returns each time to the same nesting place.

Royal Albatross

Diomedea epomophora

LESSON, 1825

ENDEMIC
Northern Royal Albatross
D.e. sanfordi (MURPHY, 1917).
Southern Royal Albatross
D.e. epomophora LESSON, 1825.

OTHER NAME: *Toroa.*

SIZE
Northern royal albatross:
1000–1200 mm.
Southern royal albatross:
1100–1350 mm.

DESCRIPTION
ADULT: *Sexes alike, though male larger than female. In northern royal albatross body white, except for a few black-tipped feathers on crown and tail in fresh plumage. Upper wing mainly black-brown with white area at base. Underwing white, with irregular black edge from bend in wing to black tip. Bill large, pale-horn flushed with pink when chick rearing, with black line on cutting edges. Iris dark brown. Eyelid black, sometimes spotted white in older birds. Feet and legs blue-white flushing to pink at joints during chick rearing. Southern royal albatross similar, but front edge of wing white and wing coverts dusted and edged with white. Dark zigzag barrings on scapulars and upper wing coverts. Substantial white elbow patches in males.*
IMMATURE: *As northern adult, with smudgy dark markings on crown, central back, rump, flanks and tail, more pronounced in females.*
CHICK: *First down long and white, shorter on head. Second down, starting in third week, slightly darker. Bill pale pink; tip yellow-horn. Iris dark. Eyelid white at first, later black. Feet blue-white.*

The shallow-rimmed nest of the southern royal albatross is a substantial structure of tussock grasses and peat.

MOULT
Not known.

VOICE
Harsh scream when courting. Monotonous yapping between pairs. Aggressive bill clapping and hoarse roaring at intruders.

DISTRIBUTION
Northern royal albatross: *About 2700 pairs breed at the Sisters and about 5000 pairs at Motuhara in the* Chatham Islands; *about 15 pairs breed at Taiaroa Head on the Otago Peninsula. During breeding season seen in New Zealand waters from Cook Strait to East Cape. Disperses throughout subantarctic seas.*
Southern royal albatross: *About 7500 pairs breed at Campbell Island and about 60 pairs at the Auckland Islands. During breeding season seen in southern New Zealand waters north to Cook Strait. Disperses throughout subantarctic seas.*

THIS MAGNIFICENT BIRD, the largest of the albatrosses, spends most of its life gliding above the southern oceans. Sometimes, it is seen flying around fishing boats, waiting for scraps, but mostly the royal albatross hunts fish, crustaceans, salps and cephalopods, such as octopus and squid.

The breeding season is long. From egg-laying to the departure of the chick takes an average of 319 days. Because of this, successful breeders nest every other year. Only birds that have lost their eggs or their young chicks return the following season to breed again.

On the flat-topped islands of the Chathams, northern royal albatross colonies cover about 25 ha, with up to 800 nests per hectare. The nest, which has a shallow rim, is built from low bushes, small stones and peat. On the sloping land of Taiaroa Head the few nests are more substantial structures of grasses and dirt. At Campbell Island and the Auckland Islands the southern royal albatross builds a sturdy nest of tussock and peat, usually sheltered by small scrub or the lie of the land. At these colonies there are up to 20 nests a hectare.

Royal albatrosses pair for life and start to return to the colonies in September. Generally the male returns first, but often a pair arrives within a few hours of each other. The male re-establishes the territory and starts to build the nest. But this site is not always accepted by the female which may build a new nest. Royal albatrosses do not lay in old nests although the new nest is often close to the previous one.

During this period before egg-laying, the male spends about 44 per cent of his time at the nest-site compared with 26 per cent by the female. This gives the birds little time for synchronising mating, so that some pairs may not breed successfully for many years.

The courtship ritual of the royal albatross includes a harsh scream while the wings are closed and the head is held vertically. The ritual culminates in a distinctive display with the wings open and the head up. These displays are performed by one bird at a time.

The females lay from the end of October to the middle of December. Northern royal albatrosses mainly lay around the middle of November; southern royal albatrosses mainly lay at the beginning of December. Interbreeding between the two subspecies has only been recorded at Taiaroa Head.

The single egg is white with a slightly pitted surface and some red spotting at the larger end. Sometimes two females lay in the same nest, especially in dense colonies. Eggs from young females are long and narrow, becoming more rounded as the bird ages. Both parents incubate the egg in shifts of four to 10 days. The chick starts to call in the egg from 70 days and hatches after about 79 days.

The parents guard the newborn chick for about 36 days and the young fledge between 219 and 265 days old. The parents feed the chick until it leaves the nest, but in the last two or three weeks these feeds become smaller.

Young birds, adolescents and non-breeding adults fly eastwards across the Pacific and winter in the South Atlantic off the coast of Argentina. From there they continue flying around the subantarctic zone, across the South Indian Ocean and southern Australian seas, to return to their breeding grounds in New Zealand. In the Pacific the birds travel as far north as 20°S, but mainly they stay within the belt from 30°S to 60°S. Some chicks start to return to the colony at four years old, but young birds do not establish pairs and start breeding until they are about nine years old.

Before they select a mate, adolescent birds enjoy a social period of extensive displaying, or gamming. When they form pairs they spend a year of 'keeping company'. During this period, the birds are quieter and do not perform the full courtship displays seen earlier.

Bereaved birds go through the same stages of courtship and keeping company before they breed again. Most bereaved breeders, birds keeping company, and failed breeders leave the colony by the end of the chick guard stage, and the last non-breeding birds leave about six weeks after the guard stage.

This albatross is a long-lived bird. The mortality rate of breeding birds is only one or two per cent. The oldest known bird was over 54 years when it was recovered in 1982, after having been banded as a breeding adult in 1937.

C.J.R.R.

Black-browed Mollymawk *Diomedea melanophrys* TEMMINCK,1828

AT SEA, UNLESS IT IS QUARRELLING over food, the black-browed mollymawk is a silent bird. At its breeding grounds, however, it is noisy and belligerent.

When it arrives at the nest, the black-browed mollymawk fans its tail, lifts its wings, points its bill towards the nest and utters an aggressive braying *mbaaaa*. If it is threatened by other birds, it brays and waves its head from side to side. When defending territory, it calls a harsh, rapid, cackling *aahaahaahaaha,* with its bill vibrating and the orange skin stripe on its cheeks exposed. At the same time, it stretches its head and leans forward towards the ground.

The courtship display involves both of these calls as well as a two-tone bray, which descends on the second syllable. In this display, both birds fan their tails. They reach towards each other with a scooping head movement and the male gives a groaning roar. The female responds by reaching to pluck at the male's breast. Then both birds turn their heads over their shoulders and grunt a rapid *ug-ug-ug-ug* with their elbows raised.

All of these displays are interspersed with walking and rapid fencing, where the two birds parry and riposte with their bills.

Black-browed mollymawks pair for life and usually breed in large colonies on cliffs or hills near the shore. From packed soil and grass they build a bowl-shaped column with straight sides. The colonies are often wet and muddy, but the raised nests protect the eggs and chicks. Each year, the same pair return to the same nest, renovating it at the start of each season. Most of these nests last for many years, accumulating moss and algae on the base of the column.

The female lays a single blunt-ended egg which is dull white, with a ring of fine brown-red spots at the wider end. If this is lost, no replacement is laid. Sometimes, two females lay in the same nest. Most chicks take three or four days to hatch. The parents guard the young bird in shared shifts for about 21 days.

This mollymawk is divided into two subspecies: the nominate subspecies, the black-browed mollymawk, and the New Zealand black-browed mollymawk.

Breeding birds of the nominate subspecies return to Macquarie Island in early September and to South Georgia from late September.

They nest one and a half metres apart. Before the eggs are laid, the males spend most of their time at the nest-site, but the females are ashore for only 8 to 10 per cent of their time, mostly during the two days just before they lay. The eggs are probably fertilised successfully about 14 days before laying. Both parents incubate the eggs in shifts that last from one to 25 days. After about 68 days, the chicks hatch. They fledge when they are 116 days old. Birds of this subspecies eat krill, squid, fish, offal and rubbish from ships.

New Zealand black-browed mollymawks breed only on the northern part of Campbell Island, where in 1975 the population was estimated at 75000 pairs. They return to Campbell Island at the beginning of August and lay between 24 September and 8 October. The chicks fledge in mid-April.

Some ornithologists believe there are enough differences between the two races for them to be classified as separate species. When stragglers of the nominate subspecies have been observed in colonies of New Zealand black-browed mollymawks on Campbell Island, they walk through the colony with a scooping head movement, a display that is not seen in the New Zealand race. Also, the two subspecies do not respond to each other's calls.   C.J.R.R.

CIRCUMPOLAR
Black-browed Mollymawk
D.m. melanophrys TEMMINCK, 1828.

ENDEMIC
New Zealand Black-browed Mollymawk
D.m. impavida MATHEWS, 1912.

OTHER NAME: *Toroa.*

SIZE: *750–900 mm.*

DESCRIPTION
ADULT: *Sexes alike. In the black-browed mollymawk head white with dark grey mark above, in front of and behind eye. Body white with* back slate grey. Upper wing brown-black. White underwing edged with black, particularly along front edge, forming broad wedge at elbow. Iris dark brown. Bill yellow with pink tip. Narrow line of black skin around base of bill. Bare orange skin at gape. Legs and feet blue-grey. New Zealand black-browed mollymawk smaller; dark grey in front of eye stretches almost to base of bill and, in fresh plumage, continues as band of pale grey almost to nape; more black on underwing; iris honey yellow.*
IMMATURE: *As adult except dark line round eye not prominent; incomplete grey breast-band; underwing dark with pale area in centre; iris brown; bill dark brown with black tip, lightening with age and reaching full adult colour at about 5 years.*
CHICK: *Grey down with almost bare white mask around bill and sides of face. Bare black skin at gape. Iris dark brown. Bill jet black. Feet and legs pale grey.*

MOULT
Not known.

VOICE
Mainly silent at sea except for braying mbaaaa when squabbling over food. In the colony, both sexes vocal and aggressive. Main call is harsh rapid cackling aahaahaahaaha with vibrating bill. Braying mbaaaa on arrival. In mutual display, males give 2-tone bray descending on second syllable and groaning roar; both sexes grunt with rapid ug-ug-ug-ug.

DISTRIBUTION
Black-browed mollymawk: *The most plentiful of all mollymawks. Breeds in large numbers at Islas Ildefonso; the Falkland Islands; and South Georgia. About 150 pairs breed at the Antipodes Islands. Small numbers also nest at the Bishop and Clerks Island, Îles Kerguélen, Heard Island and Macquarie Island. Common in the Atlantic and Indian Oceans.*

New Zealand black-browed mollymawk: *Breeds at the northern part of Campbell Island. Juveniles move north from Campbell Island to southeastern Australian seas, the Tasman Sea and the Pacific Ocean from New Caledonia to Îles Marquises*

RECOGNITION
Medium-sized mollymawk with white head and pink-tipped yellow bill. Broad black margins on underwing.

The black-browed mollymawk is rare round New Zealand. Eye colour and plumage differ from the local subspecies.

Grey-headed Mollymawk *Diomedea chrysostoma* FORSTER, 1785

UNLIKE THE VOCIFEROUS BLACK-BROWED MOLLYMAWK, with which it shares its breeding grounds, the grey-headed mollymawk is generally a quiet and undemonstrative bird.

When a bird arrives at the nest, it calls a braying *mbaaaa* on one syllable. It defends its territory with a rapid, cackling *aahaahaahaaha* and at the same time vibrates its bill and exposes the orange skin stripe on its cheek. When skuas approach the nest too closely, the grey-headed mollymawk clatters its bill to produce an aggressive *clop clop*.

These mollymawks nest in large colonies on sea cliffs and hills near the shore. The nest itself is a column of packed mud and grasses with a bowl-shaped depression at the top. If a pair is successful in rearing a chick, it does not breed for another two years. As a pair uses the same nest each time it breeds, there are always many empty nests from absent pairs, which become covered with moss and lichen.

Each year about 11 500 pairs nest on Campbell Island. They start to return at the beginning of September when black-browed molly-mawks are already well established on the island. Both sexes spend only about 60 per cent of the time before egg-laying at the nest-site.

The courtship display is relatively simple. The male stretches its neck and, with slightly open and moving bill, moves it towards the female. The male then twists its head over its shoulder and grunts at its back between raised elbows. These initial movements are made slowly and deliberately. As the display increases in intensity, the male expands its neck when it reaches forward and utters a rasping groan. The female remains silent.

The pair also fence with their bills. First, the male pushes at the female and flicks the tip of his bill at the tip of her bill. Then, the birds walk slowly on their toes, the male sticking his head out and bobbing it up and down. This is followed with the male fencing at the female's feet; she responds with a high fencing action. At the end, the male often presents the female with nest material.

The female lays one egg, which is elongate, blunt-ended and white, with a ring of fine brown-red spots at the wider end. At Campbell Island, they lay between 28 September and 9 October. Both sexes incubate the eggs for about 72 days and on Campbell Island they hatch from 7 to 20 December. Most eggs take three or four days to hatch, and the young chick is guarded by the parents for about three weeks. The chicks depart from Campbell Island in early to mid-May, but are later at Macquarie Island.

At South Georgia grey-headed mollymawks feed on krill, fish, squid and lamprey, with some carrion from the sea. There is little information on the feeding habits of the Campbell Island birds but their diet is probably different, as there is no major krill source in New Zealand waters.

C.J.R.R.

CIRCUMPOLAR

OTHER NAME: *Grey-headed albatross.*

SIZE: *800–900 mm.*

DESCRIPTION
ADULT: *Sexes alike. Head, nape, neck and throat blue-grey. Black patch through eye. Just behind and below eye arched white stripe. Body white, except dark grey back and tail. Upper wing black-brown forming continuous dark band across back. Underwing white, clearly edged with black; front margin wider than rear edge, especially at base where it forms distinctive curve and at bend of wing where it forms black 'finger' patch. Iris brown. Bill glossy black with brilliant yellow-orange band along top and bottom; tip of bill dark pink. Bare skin at base of lower mandible and cheek stripe orange. Legs and feet blue-grey; webs flesh-coloured.*
IMMATURE: *As adult but head, neck, throat and upper breast darker grey; underwing grey-brown with black edges and small central white patch; bill dull black with horn tinge at base of upper bill plate. At four years old, head and nape streaked grey and white; lower mandible faint yellow; nail black; and ridge on top of bill pale yellow with black wash.*
CHICKS: *Grey down with almost bare white mask around bill and sides of face. Bill dark.*

MOULT
Not known.

VOICE
Harsh, rapid, cackling aahaahaahaaha *with vibrating bill. Short braying* mbaaaa *on one syllable.*

DISTRIBUTION
A bird of the southern oceans, usually seen in higher latitudes. Breeds on Campbell Island; South Georgia; Islas Diego Ramirez; Marion and Prince Edward Islands; Îles Crozet; and Macquarie Island. Juveniles from Campbell Island visit eastern Australia.

RECOGNITION

Grey head. Black and yellow bill. Underwing white with broad black front edge. Generally does not follow ships, but may congregate round fishing vessels.

The nest of the grey-headed mollymawk is a bowl-shaped depression supported by a column of packed mud and grass.

Yellow-nosed Mollymawk *Diomedea chlororhynchos* GMELIN,1789

THIS SMALL MOLLYMAWK, which breeds on subantarctic islands in the Indian and Atlantic Oceans, is a regular visitor to New Zealand seas. It feeds on fish, cephalopods and crustaceans, often with flocks of Australasian gannets.

From August to September, about 42000 pairs return to their breeding grounds. Both sexes build a cylindrical cone of mud and grasses between 30 and 60 cm high. These nests are usually sited on cliff ledges, plateaus or boggy valley bottoms. Sometimes, they are sheltered by trees and lush vegetation such as ferns or tussock.

Yellow-nosed mollymawks lay one egg, which they incubate for about 78 days. After it hatches, the parents guard the chick for two or three weeks. The young mollymawk leaves at about 130 days old.

There are two subspecies of the yellow-nosed mollymawk. Before 1975, only *Diomedea chlororhynchos bassi* had been found in New Zealand, but since then *Diomedea chlororhynchos chlororhynchos* has also been sighted.

D.c. chlororhynchos is identified by the pronounced black mark in front and below the eye; the light pearl grey of the head and nape, except for the cap; and the rounded base of the yellow bill stripe. Generally a solitary breeder, it lays in early September.

In *D.c. bassi*, the black eye mark is almost absent; the grey head colouring is confined to the cheeks; and the bill stripe is pointed at the base. This subspecies breeds in colonies of up to several hundred pairs and lays in early October.   C.J.R.R.

The yellow-nosed mollymawk *Diomedea chlororhynchos bassi* is most commonly seen at sea round northern New Zealand. It breeds in large colonies.

STRAGGLER
Yellow-nosed Mollymawk
D.c. chlororhynchos GMELIN, 1789.
Yellow-nosed Mollymawk
D.c. bassi MATHEWS, 1912.

OTHER NAMES: *None.*

SIZE: *700–750 mm.*

DESCRIPTION
ADULT: *Sexes alike. Head white with varying amount of light grey; black mark in front and below eye; white line behind eye. Body white except for slate-brown back and tail. Underwing white, with narrow black edges, slightly wider on front edge; primaries black. Iris brown. Bill slender and glossy black with yellow stripe along top ridge; tip of nail pink. Gape and cheek stripe orange. Feet and legs blue or pinkish blue; webs flesh-coloured.*
JUVENILE: *As adult but head wholly white; back of neck pearl grey; black eye-patch not well developed; bill wholly black.*
CHICK: *Grey down, paler face. Chin and throat almost naked. Bill black.*

MOULT
Not known.

VOICE
In courtship and territorial display a rapidly repeated he-e-e-e-ek-eg-gee-geee and a harsh bray. Aggressive bill snapping or clopping by chicks to discourage intruders.

DISTRIBUTION
Visits New Zealand waters.
D.c. chlororhynchos: *Breeds on Tristan da Cunha and Gough Island.*
D.c. bassi: *Breeds on Prince Edward Island; Îles Saint-Paul and Amsterdam.*

Black-footed Albatross

Diomedea nigripes

AUDUBON,1839

VAGRANT

OTHER NAME: *Black gooney.*

SIZE: *700–750 mm.*

DESCRIPTION
ADULT: *Sexes alike, but male generally larger. Head and upper parts grey-black, often with brown tinge; breast and belly slightly paler. Circle of white feathers round base of bill. Small triangular white patch below eye. Sometimes rump sprinkled with white. Outermost primaries straw-coloured, visible when wing extended. Tail black. Underwing brownish, sometimes with paler stripe along its length. Undertail coverts and around vent often white. Iris brown. Bill glossy, chestnut brown, darker at tip. Feet, webs and nails black.*
IMMATURE: *As adult, but more dusky brown, including undertail coverts.*

VOICE
At sea, series of deep calls and squeals when squabbling over food. On land, bill clacks, quacks and high-pitched squeaks during mutual displays.

DISTRIBUTION
Ranges across North Pacific with only one sighting south of the equator. Breeds from Minami-Tori-Shima in the west, to the Hawaiian Leeward Chain in the east.

A bird of the North Pacific, the black-footed albatross has been sighted only once in the southern hemisphere.

THE BLACK-FOOTED ALBATROSS has been sighted only once in the southern hemisphere, in 1884 at Dusky Sound. It is primarily a bird of the North Pacific, and rarely ranges south of about 20°N.

The species is found in both pelagic and coastal waters. It breeds in the northern winter, from November to about mid-June, and nests in colonies on sandy beaches and atolls. It is a social species with a wide range of displays and calls.

The black-footed albatross follows ships, picking up food from the surface. It also eats fish and crustaceans.   J.W.

Buller's Mollymawk *Diomedea bulleri* ROTHSCHILD, 1893

BULLER'S MOLLYMAWK BREEDS in New Zealand, on small outlying islands. It spends the rest of the year at sea, where it may follow ships, scavenging for food. Its exact non-breeding distribution is unknown, but it has been sighted on both sides of the South Pacific, off the coasts of Chile and off eastern Australia.

Pairs stay together for life and usually return to the same nest-site. They nest alone or in small groups. The nest itself is usually a pillar of mud and vegetation. In this, the birds lay a single egg which is white and often speckled with red-brown spots at the blunt end.

Buller's mollymawks are long-lived birds. The adult mortality rate is as low as 11 per cent, and birds banded when they were already breeding were still alive 23 years later.

There are two subspecies of this mollymawk: the southern Buller's mollymawk and the northern Buller's mollymawk. Some ornithologists believe that these two subspecies are so different that they should be reclassified as separate species.

The southern Buller's mollymawk, which breeds at The Snares and Solander Island, builds a nest on steep tussock slopes or under *Olearia* forest, sometimes as far as one kilometre from the coast. The birds return in December and lay in January or February. The males arrive first, but they stay ashore for less than half of the period before egg-laying. The females are present for even less time, returning finally to the nest about two days before they lay. Both sexes incubate the egg, in long stints that last up to 12 days. From late August to mid-October the chicks fly from the colonies.

On The Sisters, the northern Buller's mollymawk nests on cliffs and ledges. At Motuhara, it breeds on the flattish island top, with a few birds nesting on the cliffs. Cliff-nesting birds often gather rock chips and mud to form a rim to the nest, but the rocks usually crush or break the egg. The first birds return about 9 September. They lay from the end of October through November, with most eggs being laid between 4 and 16 November. Both sexes incubate the eggs in stints of one to four days. The parents guard the chicks for 21 days and the young fledge in early to mid-June.

C.J.R.R.

ENDEMIC
Southern Buller's Mollymawk
D.b. bulleri ROTHSCHILD, 1893.
Northern Buller's Mollymawk
D.b. platei REICHENOW, 1898.

OTHER NAMES: *None.*

SIZE: *750–800 mm.*

DESCRIPTION
ADULT: *Sexes alike. In southern Buller's mollymawk cheeks, chin, nape and back light grey. Forehead white. Small dark grey line above eye. Narrow white patch at lower rear of eye. Underparts white. Tail and upper wing black-brown. Underwing white, edged broadly at front and narrowly at back with black. Iris brown. Bill dull black at sides; top ridge, nail and broad band along lower mandible yellow. Strip of orange skin on cheek and at base of lower mandible. Feet and legs flesh-blue. Northern Buller's mollymawk similar but forehead light silver grey; back, cheek, chin and nape darker silver grey; stripe above eye more pronounced and reaches base of bill.*
IMMATURE: *As adult, but bill horn-coloured with black tip and sides.*

CHICK: *Long, pale, smoky grey down; shorter on chin and face.*

MOULT
Not known.

VOICE
Bray and aggressive cackle.

DISTRIBUTION
Southern Buller's mollymawk:
About 5000 breed at The Snares and 2000 on Solander Island. Seen at sea south of the South Island; around the Auckland Islands; off the coasts of Chile and eastern Australia.

Northern Buller's mollymawk:
About 24 000 pairs breed at Motuhara and about 2000 pairs at The Sisters at the Chatham Islands. Seen at sea off the eastern coast of the North Island from Cook Strait to East Cape; and off the Chilean coast.

The southern Buller's mollymawk returns each year to the same nest-site to lay a single egg which is incubated by both sexes.

Salvin's mollymawk builds its nest on flat ground or rock ledges, on islands which have no vegetation. It breeds from September to April.

Shy Mollymawk *Diomedea cauta* GOULD,1841

ENDEMIC
White-capped Mollymawk
D.c. steadi (FALLA, 1933).
Salvin's Mollymawk
D.c. salvini (ROTHSCHILD, 1893).
Chatham Island Mollymawk
D.c. eremita (MURPHY, 1930).

OTHER NAMES: *None.*

SIZE: *900–1000 mm.*

DESCRIPTION
ADULT: *Sexes alike. Head, throat and neck vary from pale to dark grey, sometimes with white or grey cap, according to subspecies. Dark grey eyebrow stripe from behind eye almost to base of bill. Indistinct white eye crescent. Back usually dark grey, but medium grey in Salvin's mollymawk. Underparts white. Upper wing black. Tail grey. Underwing white with narrow black border and black patch at base of front edge of wing. Iris dark brown. Bill varies according to subspecies. Legs and feet fleshy blue-grey.*
IMMATURE: *Inadequately described. Head and neck grey. Throat pale grey. Underwing as adult. Bill generally dark with black tip, gradually changing to breeding adult form.*
CHICK: *Pale grey down. Iris brown. Legs flesh-coloured.*

MOULT
Not known.

VOICE
Bray and aggressive cackle.

DISTRIBUTION
White-capped mollymawk:
About 64 000 pairs breed on Disappointment, Auckland and Adams Islands in the Auckland Islands. Sea distribution not well known, although banded birds have been recovered in South Africa.

Salvin's mollymawk: *About 76 000 pairs breed on the Bounty Islands and a few hundred on the Western Chain islets at The Snares. Ranges from New Zealand to the South Pacific and South Atlantic coasts of South America.*

Chatham Island mollymawk:
About 4000 pairs breed on the Pyramid at the Chatham Islands. Ranges to the central South Pacific and Bass Strait. Rarely seen in New Zealand coastal waters.

RECOGNITION
Largest mollymawk. Pale underwing with narrow black border and black spot at base of front edge. Head pattern varies according to subspecies. White-capped and Salvin's mollymawks avidly follow fishing vessels for scraps.

LITTLE IS KNOWN ABOUT THE LIFE and habits of this bird, the largest of the mollymawks. Most of its breeding grounds—on the slopes and rocky ledges of small islands off the coasts of New Zealand—are rarely accessible to ornithologists.

Like other mollymawks, the shy mollymawk performs a wide range of courtship displays with braying and cackling calls. The pair build a bowl-shaped pillar of mud, which they reinforce with vegetation or feathers. In this, the female lays a single egg, which is white with a pitted surface and some fine red spotting at the blunt end. Both parents incubate the egg and, after it hatches, guard the newborn chick for about three weeks.

In New Zealand, there are three subspecies of the shy mollymawk: the white-capped mollymawk, Salvin's mollymawk, and the Chatham Island mollymawk.

The white-capped mollymawk takes its name from its white head. On its cheeks, there is sometimes a pale grey wash that may extend to its nape and throat. Its bill is an almost uniform, bluish horn colour with a pale yellow tip.

This mollymawk breeds in colonies on steep slopes or wide ledges among tussock and succulent vegetation such as *stilbocarpa, anisotome* and *pleurophyllum*. Laying starts about 20 November and hatching starts at the beginning of February, with the young fledging in mid-August. The white-capped mollymawk feeds on cephalopods, fish and salps as well as fish offal from boats.

Salvin's mollymawk has a medium grey head, throat and neck with a light grey crown. The primaries are entirely black. The sides of the bill are grey-green; the top ridge is pale horn, becoming slightly yellow at the base; the bottom edges of the lower mandible are striped horn; and the tip of the lower mandible is brown.

The breeding season of Salvin's mollymawk extends from September to April. It nests on rock ledges or relatively flat ground. As there is no vegetation on its breeding islands, it reinforces the nest with penguin feathers. These nests are spaced so that there is one nest about every two square metres; they vary in height from 15 mm to 40 cm and are about 37 cm wide. Salvin's mollymawk feeds on cephalopods, fish, salps and scraps from scavenging behind boats.

The Chatham Island mollymawk has a dark grey head, throat and neck which extends into a dark grey back. The crown is slightly paler than the rest of the head. Its bill is bright yellow with a dark brown tip to the lower mandible.

The Chatham Island mollymawk nests on rock ledges or flat ground where there is little vegetation. The females lay between 20 August and 15 September. There is little information on the incubation period, but one egg is known to have hatched after 66 days. In April the young leave. The Chatham Island mollymawk eats cephalopods, fish, salps and krill.   C.J.R.R.

Light-mantled Sooty Albatross *Phoebetria palpebrata* (FORSTER, 1785)

CIRCUMPOLAR

OTHER NAME: *Pee-oo.*

SIZE: *800–900 mm.*

DESCRIPTION
ADULT: *Sexes similar, but male slightly larger. Head mainly sooty brown; blackish between upper mandible and eye; and incomplete white eye-ring at rear of eye. Body grey-brown, with back ash grey, shading into darker head and rump. Wing mainly dark slate brown, but primaries grey-black with white shafts, except at tip. Tail grey-black with white shafts. Underparts ash grey. Iris brown. Bill shiny black with narrow blue or violet stripe on side of lower mandible. Legs and feet blue-grey.*
IMMATURE: *Similar to adult but quill shafts and bill stripe browner; white eye-ring duller.*
CHICK: *First down grey, lighter on side of head. Second down long and light grey on body; shorter and darker*

on head; white on face. Bill black. Feet grey-black with pale grey toes.

MOULT
Not known.

VOICE
Penetrating pee-arr.

DISTRIBUTION
Breeds on Campbell, Auckland, Antipodes, Macquarie and Heard Islands; Prince Edward Islands; Îles Crozet and Kerguélen; and South Georgia. Ranges throughout subantarctic and Antarctic waters as far south as heavy pack ice. Rarely found north of 40° S.

RECOGNITION

Sooty-brown albatross.
Dark head and wings contrast
sharply with pale back.
Pointed tail and long
slender wings.

THE LIGHT-MANTLED SOOTY ALBATROSS flies gracefully above the southern oceans, where it feeds on cephalopods, crustaceans and fish, as well as dead seabirds and waste from ships. Sometimes it is seen trailing the same ship for a long period. Primarily a bird of the open sea, it comes ashore to breed on remote subantarctic islands.

Between 5000 and 10 000 light-mantled sooty albatrosses breed in New Zealand. Usually they nest alone on the ledges of coastal cliffs and inland peaks where there is some vegetation. These sites provide both shelter from the wind and plants for building the nest. They sometimes breed in small groups. These colonies are either in areas

beyond the reach of sheep on Campbell Island or of pigs on Auckland Island. The nest is always next to steeply falling ground, which allows the bird to take off easily and soar away on the updraft.

The inaccessibility of these breeding sites has made this a difficult bird to study. They mate for life and, almost certainly, breed only every other year. If a pair successfully rear a chick, they will not nest the following breeding season.

At Campbell Island, the first birds return early in October and during that month re-establish their nesting territories and pair relationships. Breeding birds usually return to the same general area, although they build a new nest each time. Young birds normally spend at least one season in courtship and pair formation before breeding.

The displays of the light-mantled sooty albatross include pointing, thrusting and scooping with the bill, as well as mutual preening. Its call is a distinctive and penetrating *pee-arr*. It begins with a shrill outbreathed note with the head up and the bill open, and is followed immediately by a lower, quieter inbreathed note with the bill closed and pointing downwards.

The birds build a low cone-shaped nest of mud and grasses. The nest is begun by the male while he occupies and defends the site, but most of the work is completed by the female. Throughout incubation, both sexes repair the nest.

On Campbell Island, the birds lay in the last week of October and the first week of November. The single egg is white with red-brown spots at the broader end. Both parents incubate it. They sit for periods of 12 to 17 days for the first four shifts, then for increasingly shorter periods as hatching approaches.

The chicks hatch early in January after about 67 days, taking an average of three days to break out of the shell. The parents then guard the chick for about 19 days, until it flies from the nest in late May or early June.

The life expectancy of the light-mantled sooty albatross is long; one banded bird was recovered alive after 20 years.   C.J.R.R.

The light-mantled sooty albatross builds a low nest of mud and grasses on high peaks inland from the coast, or on ledges of coastal cliffs.

Antarctic Petrel

Thalassoica antarctica (GMELIN, 1789)

The Antarctic petrel, sighted rarely in New Zealand, breeds on cliff ledges.

STRAGGLER

OTHER NAMES: *None.*

SIZE: *430 mm.*

DESCRIPTION
ADULT: *Sexes alike. Head and upper parts chocolate brown. Broad white stripe along rear edge of upper wing. Rump white. Tail white with broad brown tip. Throat and sides of neck mottled light brown, shading into white underparts. Underwing white with broad brown front edge. Iris brown. Bill brown, pale olive at sides. Feet flesh-coloured.*
JUVENILE: *Slightly darker than adult. Bill amost black.*
CHICK: *Pale grey down on upper parts, foreneck and breast. Head and belly white. Bill dark grey. Feet grey.*

MOULT
Not known.

VOICE
Rapidly repeated cack cack cack. Chirring and cackling calls.

DISTRIBUTION
Circumpolar. Breeds on the Antarctic continent at at least 9 known widely scattered localities, up to 250 km inland. Ranges around the continent to 50°S in the zone of pack ice and icebergs. Straggles to northern and western New Zealand. First New Zealand record Northland (September 1973).

RECOGNITION

Conspicuous medium-sized petrel. Dark head and upper parts. White underparts. White rear edge to upper wing. Tail white with brown-black tip.

FLOCKS OF ANTARCTIC PETRELS feed in the Southern Ocean on surface organisms and flotsam. They hover with wings outspread and heads pointed into the wind, making flat plunges into the water. Krill forms the bulk of their prey, but they also catch pteropods, cephalopods, fish and medusae. And although they seldom follow ships, large assemblies of birds also gather around whaling fleets. By day they generally come ashore and often roost on icebergs.

Primarily a bird of the Antarctic, this medium-sized petrel is seldom seen in New Zealand. It was first sighted in September 1973 in Northland. In the following five years, four more birds were seen; then in July, August and September 1978 large numbers were washed ashore on western beaches.

It breeds amongst rocks or on cliff ledges. The birds arrive at these breeding grounds from early to mid-October and scrape a shallow bare depression for a nest. They sometimes collect small stones to surround the egg.

Courting birds sit face to face in the nest and preen each other's head and bill. In one display, a bird lowers its bill to its breast, then slowly raises and extends its neck until its bill lies horizontally on its back. The pair also wag their heads. These displays are accompanied by a variety of chirring, soft clucking and cackling calls. Sometimes displays at the nest are interrupted by short flights out to sea.

One egg is laid late November or early December. After an incubation period of more than 45 days, the egg hatches in mid-January. A quarter of the eggs may be killed by bad weather. Both parents tend the chick, which flies in late February.   C.J.R.R. & F.C.K.

Antarctic Fulmar

Fulmarus glacialoides (SMITH, 1840)

CIRCUMPOLAR

OTHER NAMES: *Silver-grey fulmar, southern fulmar.*

SIZE: *450–500 mm.*

DESCRIPTION
ADULT: *Sexes alike. Upper parts light blue-grey, but paler on head and neck, which may be almost white. Outer primaries mainly black. White inner webs of outer primaries and nearly all-white inner primaries form white rectangular patch on upper wing. Forehead, face, underparts and underwing white. Iris brown. Bill pink, with horn-coloured band, black tip and light blue nasal tubes. Legs flesh-coloured with irregular brown stains, especially on outer toes.*
CHICK: *First down mainly white with blue-grey wash on back. Second down light grey on upper parts and flanks shading to white on forehead and underparts. Bill mostly pink, as adult. Iris hazel. Feet flesh-coloured.*

MOULT
Not known.

VOICE
At breeding grounds, shrill and piercing, rapidly repeated kew-kew-kew, often compared to cackle of a rooster. Soft guttural droning or croaking at courtship.

DISTRIBUTION
Regular winter straggler to New Zealand as far north as the Auckland west coast and the Bay of Plenty. Breeds on the Antarctic continent and offshore at Bouvetoya; Peter I Island; the South Shetland, South Orkney, South Sandwich, and Balleny Islands. Non-breeding birds disperse into subtropics following cold currents along the western coasts of southern land masses.

RECOGNITION

Large, pale, gull-like petrel. Pale grey above and white below with rectangular white patch on upper wing.

The Antarctic fulmar appears to be a regular winter straggler to New Zealand.

DURING WINTER these pale gull-like petrels may migrate to the seas around New Zealand—more than 600 were recorded in 1975. Their summer feeding grounds are the icy waters of Antarctica. Generally breeding in colonies, the birds avoid heavy pack ice and congregate on the steep cliffs of the Antarctic continent and its outlying islands. The nest is simply a shallow hollow in the ground, lined with stone chips and usually sited in a crevice or on a ledge sheltered from the wind.

When pairs are forming, the two birds take turns to perform the courtship display, sitting either head to head or side by side. One bird, with bill half open and feathers raised, moves its head from side to side, and calls a rolling, chuckling cry. Or it stretches its neck, and with slightly open bill, utters a long outbreathed call. When defending its nest-site, the bird points its head forward and lunges with its bill open very wide. Occasionally it spits oil at intruders.

The breeding season extends from October to March. The birds mate about 17 days before laying a single egg between late November and mid-December. Both parents incubate the egg for 43 or 44 days until it hatches in mid to late January. Then the parents guard the chick for 15 to 18 days. About 51 days after hatching, in mid-March, the young bird flies.

Extreme weather kills 40 per cent of eggs and 25 per cent of chicks. Skuas eat some abandoned eggs and young chicks.

Antarctic fulmars feed mainly on krill, cephalopods, amphipods and fish. They also scavenge offal from ships and whaling stations and, sometimes, take small sick birds.   C.J.R.R. & F.C.K.

Southern Giant Petrel

Macronectes giganteus

(GMELIN, 1789)

NATIVE

OTHER NAMES: *Nelly, stinker, giant fulmar.*

SIZE: *850-950 mm.*

DESCRIPTION

ADULT: *Sexes alike, but male larger. Two colour types. In dark birds, body dark brown to grey. Crown, neck, face and throat often white. Plumage often mottled because of pale edges to contour feathers. Upper and underwing dark brown to grey, often with pale front edge. Iris off-white, grey or brown, or mixed grey and brown. Bill heavy, horn-coloured with pale shiny green nail. Prominent nostril tube extends three fifths along ridge of bill. Legs and feet grey. In white birds body white, usually with some black spots or patches. Iris white or grey, but usually brown. Bill as dark adult. Feet grey, rarely flesh-coloured or flesh and grey.*

IMMATURE: *Dark bird has chocolate brown plumage; brown iris; bill, feet and legs as adult. White bird like adult, but iris brown.*

FLEDGLING: *Either satin black or white. Iris brown. Bill as adult. Feet grey.*

CHICK: *Dark chicks have pale grey down, replaced at about 2 weeks by coarser, curly grey down. Iris brown. Bill and feet as adult. White chicks wholly white. Iris brown. Feet grey, rarely pale blue or flesh-coloured.*

MOULT

Body moult during incubation. At Signy Island, main moult of breeders is delayed until chicks have laid down food reserves, but by mid-March most breeders are in wing moult. Failed breeders shed flight feathers earlier.

VOICE

Guttural, growling and whinnying calls in threat and courtship displays. Also bill snapping when threatened. Piping from chicks.

The eggs and young of the southern giant petrel are vulnerable to bad weather and avian predators.

DISTRIBUTION

Breeds at South Georgia; Marion, Macquarie and Heard Islands; the South Shetland and South Orkney Islands; Îles Crozet; and on islands off the Antarctic mainland. Common visitor to coastal New Zealand. Much less common out at sea.

WHEN NESTING, THE SOUTHERN GIANT PETREL is even more timid than its close relative, the northern giant petrel. When a breeding group is disturbed, one or two of the more timid birds desert their nests and flee with flailing wings. This, in turn, upsets the other birds in the colony so that they too take to the air, leaving the skuas, sheathbills and wekas with a feast of eggs or chicks. When a brood is lost no chicks are reared that season as the petrels do not lay another clutch until the following year. If a traditional colony site is persistently disturbed, for example following establishment of a nearby field station, the birds abandon the site altogether.

The colony nearest to New Zealand is on Macquarie Island, but this petrel is a common visitor to the New Zealand coast. Many of these wanderers are fledglings that have travelled north and eastwards on westerly winds. Others are older birds that return to the same feeding area every year.

Southern giant petrels are seen most often in New Zealand in the summer when they flock around the outfalls of freezing works, and inshore fishing boats. Dead birds cast ashore are usually found between July and December. From May to June southern giant petrels are scarce in New Zealand waters.

Usually the southern giant petrel nests or roosts on exposed saddles, hillsides and raised beach terraces, often on the exposed western sides of islands. From such elevated sites the bird takes off easily into the prevailing wind. A few southern giant petrels nest in less exposed situations among tussock grass. At Macquarie Island the birds return to roost in winter, even in snow, but farther south at Signy Island the birds leave during May and June.

The breeding season lasts throughout the summer, but varies from island to island. At Macquarie Island most birds lay between 5 and 11 October and the chicks fly in late March and April. At the colder, more southerly islands, the breeding season is later—at Signy Island the birds do not lay until November and the chicks fledge in late April or May. When northern giant petrels breed at the same island, they lay at different times. At Macquarie Island, for example, the breeding season of the northern giant petrel is about six weeks later than that of the southern giant petrel.

Southern giant petrels mate for life and return to the same nest each year. The nests vary in design. Some are little more than depressions in the ground or moss, lined or rimmed with a few stones. Others are cups, made of grasses and other vegetation. The nests are grouped fairly closely, about three metres apart on open land. At Macquarie Island in 1962 there were 70 colonies with an average of 41 chicks in each colony. But at Signy Island there were 92 colonies with an average of 27 nests.

About 14 days before it lays, the female leaves to feed at sea. Both sexes incubate the single elliptical or oval white egg for about 60 days, the male taking the first spell. This first stint lasts about two days. Successive stints last about a week, but tend to become shorter towards the end of the incubation period.

At Macquarie Island most eggs hatch between 2 and 20 December and at Signy Island they hatch around 12 January. The newborn chick remains in the nest, and is usually guarded for 15 to 26 days by both parents in turn. In particularly severe weather the parents may guard the chick for longer.

During the guard stage the chick is fed about once a day by one of its parents. After that it usually gets a meal every three or four days. Male chicks are commonly heavier and larger-billed than females. For six to 14 days at the beginning of winter the chick loses weight until attempting its first flight when it is about 118 days old. Many eggs and chicks die—bad weather kills them or heavy snow makes them easy prey for skuas.

Most southern giant petrels have a dark brown or grey back, rump, tail and wings, and are paler on the head and breast. But some birds—up to about 12 per cent—are white, usually with a few black spots or patches. These birds are white from birth and retain the same colouring throughout their lives. The darker birds, on the other hand, are grey as chicks, black as fledglings, and chocolate brown as immatures. Some dark birds still have their chocolate brown imma-ture colouring when they start to breed. Studies have indicated that dark and pale birds mate at random.

This petrel feeds on land less often than the northern giant petrel. At sea it scavenges around any large food source such as a dead whale. Southern giant petrels also eat other seabirds, fish, krill, other crustaceans and cephalopods.

When the body temperature of the southern giant petrel is raised, blood flows quickly through its webs to cool the bird. Similarly, when its webs hit icy water, blood rushes through them to prevent a cold shock to the tissue and its sensory and motor nerves.   J.W.

Northern Giant Petrel *Macronectes halli* MATHEWS, 1912

THE FEEDING HABITS of the giant petrel have earned it the nickname 'vulture of the Southern Ocean'. It flocks around carrion such as seals, whales, penguins and rabbits. When a group of petrels squabble over a carcass, they sway their heads, extend their wings, ruffle their nape feathers and fan their tails. Sometimes, they glide behind ships, waiting for refuse to be thrown overboard. But despite their nickname, giant petrels do not always scavenge; they also feed on fish, krill and cephalopods.

The northern giant petrel ranges around the southern seas in subantarctic and temperate regions. In New Zealand it breeds on Campbell Island, Antipodes Island, the Chatham Islands, the Auckland Islands and Stewart Island. It wanders to both the North and South Islands, although it does not nest there, and is fairly common in coastal waters, especially around Cook Strait ferries and Banks Peninsula.

The northern giant petrel is very similar to the southern giant petrel and, in fact, it was not until 1966 that they were recognised as two separate species. Before then, all sightings of giant petrels in New Zealand were recorded as southern giant petrels. The northern giant petrel is identified by the red-brown or pink tip to its bill. Both species begin with black-brown plumage and progressively lighten with age, but northern giant petrels never become white-headed or even all-white, as some southern giant petrels do. Chicks of both species have brown eyes, but the colour lightens more rapidly in the northern giant petrel than in the southern bird. Thus, a dark-plumaged bird which has grey or white eyes is a northern giant petrel.

In New Zealand, the species often nests in the shelter of heavy tussock or against rocks. The nest is a shallow cup about 65 cm wide, built from grasses and other plant matter, and often sited on headlands, beach terraces and the edges of plateaus overlooking the sea. From these high grounds, the birds can launch themselves easily into the air.

Northern giant petrels nest in groups of various sizes. Breeding groups studied at Antipodes Island, for example, were small—each comprised about 20 nests, spaced about three metres apart. These birds have been known to form mixed breeding colonies with their close relative, the southern giant petrel.

Courting birds preen each other and wobble and sway while making soft braying calls. When a pair mates, the male strops his bill across the female's. This produces a loud clicking sound that can be heard some distance away. At the climax, the male stops moving his head and swings his tail sideways to bring the cloacae together.

The birds start laying in early spring. Sometimes they build nests as early as June but usually they lay from mid-August to early September. The single white egg is elliptical to oval in shape, and is incubated by both parents for about 59 days. The male takes the first and the last shifts so that usually he sits for five shifts, the female for four. Most nesting failures occur during the egg stage.

Between about 19 October and 5 November the egg hatches, and for two or three weeks the chick is covered by one or other parent. From then on it is left alone, except when the parents visit briefly to feed it. The chick finally walks or flies from its nest in February, at about 108 days old. Adult birds still visit the nest after the chicks have left, and may begin repairing it in February or March.

Chicks and, sometimes, adults that are threatened defend themselves by spitting stomach oil. But these petrels are timid birds. Even when they are hatching eggs or brooding newborn chicks, the adults flee if people approach them closely. Then, skuas or wekas find the abandoned egg or chick easy prey.   J.W.

NATIVE

OTHER NAMES: *Nelly, stinker, Hall's giant petrel, giant fulmar.*

SIZE: *800–900 mm.*

DESCRIPTION
ADULT: *Sexes alike, but male larger and heavier-billed than female. Feathers often have silky sheen. Head, upper parts and wings dark brown to dark grey, crown usually darker than back. Underparts grey to pale brown-grey, with breast usually paler than rest. Variable amount of white on cheek, forehead and throat. Feathers may appear scalloped due to light edges, creating freckled effect on forehead, crown, mantle, wing coverts and upper breast. Iris usually grey to off-white, often flecked with brown and appearing white at a distance; rarely black. Bill heavy, horn or brown-horn in colour; tip of bill tinged red-brown to dark pink. Prominent nostril tube extends along three fifths of bill. Legs and feet dark grey.*
IMMATURE: *Rate of change from sooty black of fledgling to paler adult plumage varies. Most immatures chocolate brown with little scalloping at edges, but paler on cheeks, base of bill and throat. Iris brown. Bill and foot as adult.*
FLEDGLING: *Male larger and heavier-billed than female. Glossy, sooty black feathers. Iris brown. Bill less red-brown than adult. Feet as adult.*
CHICK: *First down ash grey above, extending onto back of head like skull cap; white below. Second down uniform grey. Iris brown. Bill horn-coloured; tip brown-pink. Legs and feet dark grey.*

MOULT
No precise details available. Some loss of body feathers when nesting. Wing moult after chicks fly.

VOICE
Not fully described. Whinnying, guttural growling and bill snapping when threatened. Piping from chick.

DISTRIBUTION
Breeds at Macquarie Island; Marion Island; Îles Kerguélen and Crozet; and South Georgia. Also nests in small numbers at Motuhara and the Sisters in the Chatham Islands; Antipodes Island; at Rose, Ocean and Adams Islands in the Auckland Islands; at Campbell Island; and at Nelly Island in Port Pegasus, Stewart Island. Common at the Snares, but does not nest there. Often seen in New Zealand coastal waters, especially around Cook Strait ferries and Banks Peninsula. In winter, young birds disperse north and eastwards. Banded Campbell Island birds have been found in Argentina. In 1966, a banded straggler from Îles Crozet reached New Zealand.

RECOGNITION
Thickset bird with fan-shaped tail and huge bill. Red-brown to pink bill tip, noticeable even when flying, distinguishes it from southern giant petrel. Pale on face, throat and usually on foreneck and upper breast. Glides well.

The chick of the northern giant petrel, a rather timid bird, is guarded by either parent for up to two or three weeks.

Cape Pigeon *Daption capense* (LINNAEUS,1758)

ENDEMIC
Snares Cape Pigeon
D.c. australe MATHEWS, 1913.

MIGRANT
Cape Pigeon
D.c. capense (LINNAEUS, 1758.)

OTHER NAMES: *Cape petrel,*
pintado petrel.

SIZE: *400 mm.*

DESCRIPTION
ADULT: *Sexes alike. Head and mantle*
black, except for throat which is
speckled white. Shoulder, back and
upper tail coverts white with terminal
black spots giving speckled
appearance. Outer wing coverts
black; inner wing coverts white with
black spots. Primaries black, with
large amount of white on inner webs.
Secondaries white with black tips.
Tail white with black tip. Chin
black. Lower body white, with black-
tipped feathers on side of neck, chest,
flanks and thighs. Underwing coverts
white with distinct black border.
Undertail coverts white, with black
near tip. Iris dark brown. Bill black.
Legs and feet black with fleshy
patches on webs.
JUVENILE: *Like adult, except for*
narrower bill.
CHICK: *First down dark grey, except*
for bare areas under wing and around
base of bill and eye. Second down at
10 days, dark grey above and off-
white below.

MOULT
At the South Orkney Islands body
moult begins end of December, during
incubation. Successful breeders begin
wing moult in mid-February when
young near fledging. Failed breeders
may begin wing moult within a week
of egg or chick loss.

VOICE
Raucous chattering cac-cac, cac-cac
when feeding at sea.

DISTRIBUTION
Cape pigeon: *Ranges around the*
southern seas, as far north as the
Tropic of Capricorn in winter.
Breeds on the Antarctic mainland
and many Antarctic and subantarctic
islands, including Heard and Peter I
Islands; the Palmer Archipelago; the
South Shetland, South Orkney,
South Sandwich and Balleny
Islands; Bouvetoya; South Georgia;
Îles Crozet and Kerguélen. Regularly
wrecked on New Zealand beaches.

Snares Cape pigeon: *Large*
numbers breed on The Snares at Main
Island, the Daption Rocks and the
Western Chain. Also breeds on the
Antipodes, Bounty and Campbell
Islands. Regularly wrecked on
beaches of New Zealand mainland.
Seen in New Zealand coastal waters
and Tasman Sea during non-
breeding season from April or May to
November.

RECOGNITION

Medium-sized petrel with
distinctive black and white-
patterned upper parts and
mainly white underparts.

THIS NOISY SEABIRD FEEDS in flocks, pecking at the surface of the water and occasionally diving to reach deeper prey. It also follows ships, scavenging for scraps.

It comes ashore to breed in colonies on cliff faces. Some birds begin breeding when they are four years old, but most start in their fifth year. They nest on ledges, in crevices or under rock overhangs which protect them from the prevailing winds. The birds scrape a shallow bowl in granite fritter or peat and usually line it with granite chips, although some bowls are lined with dead vegetation and bird bones.

The Cape pigeon lays a single white elliptical egg which both parents incubate for about 45 days. The newborn chick is brooded continuously for up to 10 days and then guarded for up to 15 days. It steadily increases in weight until, about three weeks after hatching, it weighs the same as an adult. The parents continue to feed the chick until it fledges, from 47 to 57 days after hatching. During the breeding season Cape pigeons defend their nests by spitting stomach oil at intruders. However away from the nest-site they are gregarious.

This petrel is divided into two subspecies: the nominate subspecies, the Cape pigeon *Daption capense capense*, and the Snares Cape pigeon *D.c. australe*.

The two subspecies are easily confused, but the nominate subspecies is larger and has a paler back. Banding results show that birds of the nominate subspecies which breed on the South Orkney Islands visit New Zealand. The diet of this subspecies varies from place to place. Cape pigeons found off Peru hunt fish, crustaceans and squid. At Heard Island they eat siphonophores and krill, and at the South Orkney Islands feed mainly on krill.

At The Snares, Snares Cape pigeons begin laying in the second week of December and the eggs hatch between the third week of November and the first week of January. Eggs and chicks are not attacked by predators, but wind and rain account for some losses, especially where nests are exposed. About 67 per cent of eggs survive to become flying birds. Snares Cape pigeons feed on neritic crustaceans.

The Cape pigeon is also called pintado—Portuguese for 'painted'. Its scientific name *Daption* is an anagram of pintado.   P.M.S.

Once it has hatched, the Snares Cape pigeon reaches adult weight after three weeks of guarding by the parents.

The snow petrel is the only all-white plumaged petrel. It breeds on the Antarctic mainland and outlying islands, often nesting in sheltered crevices.

Snow Petrel *Pagodroma nivea* (FORSTER, 1777)

THIS HANDSOME BIRD, the only all-white plumaged petrel, is a rare straggler to New Zealand. The snow petrel is almost entirely restricted to the colder Antarctic seas, where flocks may perch on the ridges of icebergs. In the air it glides occasionally, but more often hovers over the water, flying erratically with short, rapid wing-beats.

It breeds in colonies on the Antarctic mainland and outlying islands. These nesting grounds are sited on cliffs and slopes, often facing into the prevailing wind, so that snow will not drift and bury the birds. In some areas the birds are present at the colonies all year, but at others only from mid-September to early November.

The nest is a simple pebble-lined scrape, usually placed in a deep rock crevice with overhanging protection, although sometimes it is fully exposed from above.

The snow petrel lays one white egg between late November and early December. Both sexes incubate for 41 to 49 days. After the egg hatches, the parents guard the chick for about eight days. The young bird fledges at 42 to 50 days, between late February and mid-May.

About 50 per cent of eggs are lost, and 10 to 15 per cent of chicks die. Antarctic skuas are the most serious predators, but severe weather conditions can cause adults to abandon eggs and chicks.

At sea the snow petrel feeds mainly on small fish, and also consumes some cephalopods, krill and other molluscs. Ashore birds may eat carrion, such as seals, whales and penguins, and they occasionally scavenge refuse.　　　　　　　　　　　　　　　　　C.J.R.R. & F.C.K.

NATIVE
Lesser Snow Petrel
P.n. nivea (FORSTER, 1777).
Greater Snow Petrel
P.n. major BONAPARTE, 1856.

OTHER NAMES: *None.*

SIZE: *300–350 mm.*

DESCRIPTION
ADULT: *Sexes alike. All white, except for small patch of black feathers in front of eye of lesser snow petrel. Greater snow petrel larger, and in poor light underwing may appear pale grey in flight. Iris dark. Small black bill. Blue-grey feet.*
JUVENILE: *Same as adult, but with faint grey zigzag barring on back and grey wash on tips of primaries.*

MOULT
Not known.

VOICE
Mechanical chirring note when mating. Guttural teck-teck-teck, similar to that of tern, when defending nest. Calls used to recognise individuals and sexes. Male and female calls differ in sound frequency.

DISTRIBUTION
Lesser snow petrel: *Breeds on the Antarctic continent up to 350 km inland. In the Ross Dependency at Franklin, Possession and Ross Islands; and Edisto Inlet near Cape Hallet. Also at Scott Island; the South Orkney and South Sandwich Islands; South Georgia; and Bouvetoya. Rarely ranges north of 60°S. Straggles to New Zealand.*

Greater snow petrel: *Breeds at Adélie Coast and the Balleny Islands.*

RECOGNITION

Only all-white petrel. Flies erratically with short rapid wing-beats and glides infrequently. Rarely seen swimming.

Grey-faced Petrel

Pterodroma macroptera gouldi (HUTTON, 1869)

ENDEMIC

OTHER NAMES: *Oi, muttonbird.*

SIZE: *410 mm.*

DESCRIPTION
ADULT: *Sexes alike. Plumage mainly sooty black, becoming browner with wear. Filoplumes sometimes visible on head and neck, particularly in male. Feathers of breast and belly have white bases. Lores, chin and throat grey. Underwing dark grey. Iris dark brown. Bill black, tinged horn with age. Feet black.*
FLEDGLING: *As adult, but blacker.*
CHICK: *First down sooty. Main down grey.*

MOULT
Wing and tail feathers replaced at sea between January and April. Body feathers replaced gradually after breeding and may not all be replaced until incubation period of next breeding season. Failed breeders begin body moult as early as September, while still visiting breeding grounds.

VOICE
Commonest calls are ooo-i, in flight and on ground, and wik-wik-wik in flight. Deep bo-r-r-r from single birds in flight and on ground. Kek or kik and squeak and shrieks from pairs and groups in flight. Si-si-si and loud screeches to repel invaders from burrows.

DISTRIBUTION
Breeds around and on the North Island from the Three Kings Islands in the north, along the west coast on islets and headlands as far south as Pukearuhe, and along the northeast coast on numerous headlands and well over 100 islands and islets as far south as Gisborne. Main colonies are on the Mokohinau, Mercury and Aldermen Islands; White and Motuhora Islands; and the Hen and Chickens group. Resident throughout the year in the South Pacific Ocean and Tasman Sea from 30°S to at least 47°S, and from the east coast of Australia to at least 145°W.

The grey-faced petrel is the most common breeding petrel in northern parts and islands round the North Island.

RECOGNITION
Grey face. Rises easily from the sea and soars with high arcs. Rarely follows ships. Solitary, except when resting on sea in small groups.

AROUND THE NORTHERN PART of the North Island, the grey-faced petrel is the most common breeding petrel. A nocturnal bird, it flies to and from its feeding grounds only between sunset and sunrise. Usually it feeds in the open ocean, mainly east of the North Island and further than 100 km from the coast. During the breeding season this feeding range extends to at least 600 km from the colony. On the long flight back to the colony, food for the chick is partially digested.

The prey of the grey-faced petrel is mainly nekton and zooplankton that migrate to the surface each night. Much of the bird's prey are bioluminescent species—marine creatures which, like the firefly, give off light. This suggests that it may rely on the light organs of some of its prey to detect them at night.

At sea the grey-faced petrel is usually seen alone. Sometimes small groups rest on the surface. Ashore it breeds in loose colonies, and pairs or groups of up to 12 birds can be seen flying and chasing one another above the burrows. These aerial displays are accompanied by a range of loud and soft calls.

It nests in burrows between one and three metres long, usually under forest or scrub. All nesting sites are less than 400 m above sea level. When the natural vegetation is cleared by fire the birds continue to nest at the colony. On larger islands, such as Little Barrier Island, they breed only at the top of sea cliffs but they nest all over smaller islands.

The grey-faced petrel does not migrate. It breeds in the winter, the first birds returning to the colony in late February. The male spends more time than the female at the colony. He cleans out the burrow and prepares the nest, a simple depression, usually lined with leaves or twigs, but sometimes bare. In April and early May the birds mate, then feed at sea for about two months. From late May to late June only non-breeders visit the colony. Some of these birds settle in burrows prepared by breeding pairs. When they return the ensuing conflict is often fatal to the egg.

Growth of the egg, a prolonged process in most petrels of this genus, is even longer in the grey-faced petrel. This slow development has been attributed to the bird's habit of breeding during winter, when there is less food available.

The female lays between 21 June and 29 July, with the peak of laying around 4 July. A single white egg is produced each season—it is not replaced if damaged or lost. Most eggs are incubated for about 55 days and some that survive periods of desertion are incubated for up to 60 days. The female incubates until relieved by the male or until her weight becomes critically low, forcing desertion. The male usually arrives to incubate three or four days after laying but may arrive from a week or more before to two or three weeks afterwards. The three main incubation spells, of which two are undertaken by the male, average 17 days in length. To compensate for their weight loss during these fasts, birds arriving to incubate are about 100 to 200 g above average weight. Incubating birds spend most of the time in deep sleep; they normally leave the nest only to excrete outside, and only at night.

The chick takes about five days to hatch out of the egg. It is looked after by one of its parents, usually the female, for three days at most. From then on it is rarely attended except when being fed. For about the first two weeks it is fed on half the nights but this soon changes to approximately two large feeds a week, one from each parent.

The young depart at about 120 days. Occasionally they fly with down still on their necks, bellies or backs, but they are usually fully fledged and weigh approximately the same as adults. Most leave towards the end of December. The older chicks leave their burrows to exercise their wings, excrete and explore the neighbourhood for several nights before they leave.

On Motuhora Island, breeding success varies from less than one per cent to nearly 40 per cent. This stable population is controlled primarily by the food available during the breeding season. Also, Norway rats eat deserted eggs and kill up to 20 per cent of young chicks; and not all breeding birds are successful in securing nest-sites. The long breeding season makes heavy demands on the parents, so that if a chick is reared, the birds may not breed successfully in the following season. Most colonies seem to be stable or increasing, but on Little Barrier Island birds have been almost annihilated by feral cats.

This is the muttonbird of the North Island Maori. Between 3000 and 8000 fledglings were once harvested annually at the larger colonies. They were plucked, cleaned, cured and stored until eaten. Now many colonies are legally protected in reserves and wildlife refuges, and fewer birds are killed. Only the Mokohinau and Aldermen Islands are now birded at all regularly. Licences are issued to those who have a hereditary right to take the birds.

Over 10000 grey-faced petrels have been banded, mostly on Motuhora Island. Only one has been recovered from overseas—from the central east coast of Australia. Banding shows that amongst breeding birds the annual mortality rate is less than six per cent. This indicates a life expectancy of at least 16 years. Birds banded as fledglings and later recaptured show that they are seven years or older when they first breed.   M.J.I.

White-headed Petrel *Pterodroma lessonii* (GARNOT,1826)

BY DAY THIS NOCTURNAL BIRD is rarely seen near its breeding places; but at night the white-headed petrel performs noisy aerial displays. In groups of two to five, the birds dash along in high speed chases, calling out to each other a staccato *wi-wi-wi* or *wik-wik-wik*, a more protracted *tew-i, tew-i* or a drawling *oooo-er*.

They breed in the summer, keeping the same partner and returning to the same nest every year. In early September the birds arrive at the colonies to prepare the nest. They do not lay until late November to mid-December, the egg hatches in February, and chicks and adults leave in late May or June. Thus this species is absent from its breeding grounds for only about 11 weeks.

The white-headed petrel nests in burrows that, in some cases, are sited to protect the young from westerly and southerly winds. The surrounding vegetation varies. At Îles Crozet, the few known nests are in ground covered with vegetation, and at Antipodes Island the birds burrow beneath *Poa* tussocks. But at Îles Kerguélen and Macquarie Island the tunnels are on almost barren ground with only a sparse covering of *Acaena* and *Azorella*.

The elevation of the breeding tunnels also varies. At Antipodes Islands and Îles Kerguélen they are sited on both low and high ground, whereas at Macquarie Island the birds nest on higher ground.

It is often possible to detect birds nesting in a burrow as they moult white feathers near the entrance. The nest chamber, lined sparsely with dead plants, is at the end of a tunnel one or two metres long. There the temperature is much more constant than outside the burrow.

The birds lay one white, oval egg, which both parents incubate alternately for 59 or 60 days. After it hatches, the parents guard the downy chick for one to three days, then they leave it alone during the day. The underground chick gradually gathers grasses, leaves and feathers around itself and builds up a substantial cup. At night, both parents feed the chick, fairly frequently at first, less often later. The chick reaches the weight of an adult at 50 to 70 days, after which time its weight continues to rise until it falls during late fledging.

From about 70 days old chicks threaten intruders by hissing, darting their bills forward and ejecting small amounts of stomach oil. They also scream with fear when attacked or hauled from their burrows. One chick was observed to fly at about 102 days old.

White-headed petrels feed far from the nest, sometimes travelling to the South Atlantic. They eat mainly cephalopods. At Îles Crozet they also eat crustaceans and at Antipodes Island lantern fishes and mysids.

Skuas kill many of these shy and unaggressive birds. At Macquarie Island feral cats also eat about 11 000 white-headed petrels each year. As well as these heavy losses, Macquarie Island birds have to cope with interference from rabbits and attacks from introduced wekas which enter the burrows and take eggs and small chicks. At the Auckland Islands petrels are attacked by New Zealand falcons.   J.W.

NATIVE

OTHER NAMES: *None.*

SIZE: *430 mm.*

DESCRIPTION
ADULT: *Sexes alike. Head very pale grey, flecked with darker grey, appearing white at a distance. Cheek white with black patch in front of and below eye. Nape and mantle pale grey shading into darker grey on back and rump. Upper wing dark grey to brown-grey, with M-shaped brown-black band across fully spread wings visible at close quarters. Tail white, finely powdered with grey. Throat and underparts, including undertail coverts, white. Underwing grey. Iris brown. Bill stout, black. Legs mainly flesh-coloured, but brown-black on outer toes, joints and front half of webs.*
JUVENILE: *As adult but no worn and brown feathers such as usually occur in older birds.*
CHICK: *First down grey. Legs and webs pale flesh. Bill black-brown. Second down thicker; grey above, dull white below. Feet gradually darken along toes and front half of webs.*

MOULT
Breeders moult contour feathers while incubating. Moult of flight feathers delayed until well after chicks have flown in May, perhaps until August. In many birds at Macquarie Island, flight quills still not fully grown when birds return in late August. Birds cast ashore in New Zealand in August and September usually in wing moult.

VOICE
In the air, series of sharp calls wi-wi-wi or wik-wik-wik; more drawn-out tew-i, tew-i; and long, slurred oooo-er. Sitting birds utter stream of high-pitched si-si-si cries. Loud wailing scream when attacked. Chicks chirrup when being fed.

DISTRIBUTION
Ranges around the subantarctic. Breeds abundantly at the Antipodes Islands, the Auckland Islands and Macquarie Island; and in smaller numbers at Îles Crozet and Kerguélen. Not migratory, but seen plentifully about 320 km east of Wellington in winter and early spring, which probably reflects a seasonal northward movement from the southern islands. Birds cast ashore throughout year, especially from June to September; most washed onto North Island beaches but also records from Westland, Christchurch and the Chatham Islands.

RECOGNITION
Fairly big petrel. White head and underparts; dark back and underwing. Separated from white-headed Kermadec petrels by paler upper parts and black patch around eye. Distinguished from grey petrel by white head and undertail. At sea usually seen alone. Swift and impetuous flight, often sweeping high into the sky and gliding well.

The white-headed petrel nests in burrows and lines the nest chamber sparsely with plants. Young birds are particularly endangered by skuas and feral cats.

Lord Howe Island is the only known breeding locality of the providence petrel which breeds solely in winter. It has been sighted once in New Zealand.

Providence Petrel *Pterodroma solandri* (GOULD, 1844)

A BIRD OF THE COOL or subtropical waters of the Pacific Ocean, the providence petrel nests only on Lord Howe Island. In 1975, about 27 000 pairs were breeding on Mt Gower, with up to 5000 pairs per hectare. The total breeding population is probably more than 96 000 pairs. However its distribution at sea during the non-breeding season is still a mystery.

The birds return to their breeding colonies in late February or early March and stay there until at least November. The nest is located in a chamber at the end of a burrow about one metre long. It is often substantial and made from a pile of dry *Dracophyllum fitzgeraldii* leaves and shredded palm fronds. The female lays a single white, elliptical egg around mid-May. The parents incubate the egg for about eight weeks and the chick hatches by mid-July. Tail and flight feathers grow in October and it fledges from early November.

There is little information on the diet of the providence petrel, though adults at the breeding colonies have regurgitated cephalopods, crustaceans and small fish.   P.J.F.

VAGRANT

OTHER NAMES: *Solander's petrel, brown-headed petrel, big-hill muttonbird, bird-of-providence.*

SIZE: *400 mm.*

DESCRIPTION
ADULT: *Sexes alike. head brown-grey. Face has scaly appearance,* caused by pale feathers with dark edges at base of bill and on chin. Body generally dark grey, mottled slate grey across mantle and paler grey on breast and belly. Underwing has large and distinctive patch formed by creamy white bases to outer flight feathers and pale outer coverts with dark tips. Iris brown. Bill black. Legs and feet black, sometimes irregulary patterned with pale grey flesh, often on legs but especially on inner webs.
IMMATURE: *As adult.*
CHICK: *Down uniform dark grey. Shortly after hatching legs pale grey and feet almost white. Gape pink.*

MOULT
No details available, but birds are in fresh plumage when they return to Lord Howe Island in March.

VOICE
Rapidly uttered, screeching kir-rer-rer, kik-kik-kik-kik *in flight. Trilling* ker-rer, kuk-kuk-kuk, ker-rer *on ground at breeding colony.*

DISTRIBUTION
Breeds in winter at Lord Howe Island. Infrequently sighted at sea except in region of Lord Howe Island. Ranges across the northern Tasman Sea, occurring in moderate numbers off the eastern coast of Australia. Immature and non-breeding birds common in the western North Pacific during the breeding season. Sighted at Muriwai in January 1921.

RECOGNITION

Large brown-toned petrel. Stubby black bill. In favourable light, head and underwing dark, contrasting with paler, almost buff underbody. Underwing patches, mottled face, and grey mantle distinguish it from other dark petrels and shearwaters.

Juan Fernandez Petrel *Pterodroma externa externa* (SALVIN, 1875)

VAGRANT

OTHER NAME: *White-necked petrel.*

SIZE: *430 mm.*

DESCRIPTION
ADULT: *Forehead white, mottled with dark brown where it merges with dark grey-brown crown. Upper surface between crown and rump grey to grey-brown, nape sometimes paler. Primaries and central tail quills brown-black. Inner web of outermost primary mainly white; inner webs of other primaries white at base. Secondaries, greater wing coverts and outer tail quills dark grey. Black open-M pattern across upper surface in flight. Below and behind eye black. Undersurface from throat and cheek to undertail coverts white.* Underwing mainly white but narrow grey-black strip, mottled with white, along front. Iris dark brown. Bill black. Feet flesh-colour, with ends of webs and toes black.
FLEDGLING: *Like adult but greyer above.*
CHICK: *Slaty grey down.*

RECOGNITION

Large dark grey and white petrel. Distinguished from similar white-naped petrel by paler brown-grey crown; no whitish collar; narrower and paler dark stripe on underwing; generally more white on inner webs of primaries; and darker outer tail feathers.

MOULT
Takes place in wintering area during northern summer and autumn.

VOICE
Very vocal at breeding grounds; main flight call is drawn-out coo *followed by shorter* cuck, cuck.

DISTRIBUTION
Breeds in very large numbers on Isla Mas Afuera in Archipielago Juan Fernandez in the eastern South Pacific. Main wintering area south of Hawaiian Islands, where non-breeders present all year. Rare vagrants reach the western South Pacific.

THE JUAN FERNANDEZ PETREL is the most abundant breeding bird on Isla Mas Afuera. Feral cats kill some of them, but there have been conflicting reports of the severity of this predation. Little is known about the habits of this bird. Remains of cephalopods have been found in stomachs. It is very vocal at its breeding grounds, where it nests in burrows up to three metres long. These burrows contain downy chicks during February and March, suggesting that the petrels lay in November and December and that the young depart in May or June. After the breeding season the entire population migrates to the North Pacific, eastward almost to the coast of Mexico. Only one confirmed vagrant has reached New Zealand.   M.J...

White-naped Petrel *Pterodroma externa cervicalis* (SALVIN,1891)

NATIVE

OTHER NAMES: *Black-capped petrel, Sunday Island petrel.*

SIZE: *430 mm.*

DESCRIPTION

ADULT: *Crown of head to below eye brown-black. Forehead white, but mottled with black where it merges with crown. Hind neck and side of neck white mottled with dusky grey. Mantle grey, the feathers black with broad, ash grey edges. Wide brown-black M pattern across wings and back. Greater wing coverts grey above. Primaries mainly black, inner webs brownish and white at base.*

Secondaries slate, with paler fringe and mainly white inner web. Innermost secondaries brown-black. Upper tail coverts slate. Central tail feathers slate-black; side ones slate grey, but whiter at base of inner webs; and 2 outermost feathers mainly all white. Undersurface white including cheeks and undertail coverts. Underwing white, except for black strip, slightly mottled with white. Iris brown. Bill black. Feet flesh-coloured, with tip of webs and toes black.
FLEDGLING: *As adult but lighter above wing to pale feather margins.*
CHICK: *Dove grey down, with abdomen and central strip on throat and chest white.*

MOULT
Not known.

VOICE
Described only as a 'peculiar cry'.

DISTRIBUTION
Breeds in considerable numbers on Macauley Island in the Kermadecs. Only 2 storm-blown birds have reached the New Zealand mainland: one inland from the Bay of Plenty in April 1968 and a fledgling inland north of Gisborne in 1977. At sea, seen regularly north of the North Island from 33°S, though sightings more common west and north of the Kermadec Islands. Main wintering area apparently in

the central Pacific between the equator and the Hawaiian Islands. Straggles to Japan.

UNTIL RECENTLY, ORNITHOLOGISTS thought the white-naped petrel was extinct. Feral cats annihilated the population of less than 500 pairs which bred on Raoul Island and no other breeding place was known to exist. Then in 1969 birds were discovered nesting in considerable numbers on nearby Macauley Island, where it has few enemies. Kiore rats are present on the island, but they appear to be vegetarians.

The white-naped petrel shares these breeding grounds with wedge-tailed shearwaters, black-winged petrels and Kermadec petrels. It has a fixed breeding season in the summer and nests in burrows. During October, breeding birds arrive back at the colony and most of the courtship, burrow preparation and mating occurs in November. After this period, the birds leave the colony for about a month.

They return to lay one white egg between 26 December and 2 January and this hatches in late February. The fledging period is between 100 and 125 days. On Raoul Island the young were in down during March and April, and growing feathers in May. M.J.I.

Phoenix Petrel *Pterodroma alba* (GMELIN,1789)

VAGRANT

OTHER NAME: *Christmas Island petrel.*

SIZE: *350 mm.*

DESCRIPTION
ADULT: *Sexes alike. Body mainly brown-black, darker on upper parts. Throat and line round eye whitish. Lower breast and belly white. Underwing mostly black, but greater coverts white with dark tips forming narrow, diagonal white bar, and a few pale feathers near front edge of underwing. Undertail coverts white with grey-black bands. Bill black. Feet pink, with tips of webs and toes black.*

MOULT
Not known.

VOICE
Not known.

DISTRIBUTION
Breeds in the tropical Pacific at Christmas, Henderson, and Ducie Islands; Oeno Atoll; the Phoenix Islands; Îles Marquises and Tuamotu. Does not range far from this region. Four birds sighted on Raoul Island in 1913; and one seen over Curtis Island in the Kermadecs.

The phoenix petrel has no fixed breeding season. It nests in a small surface scrape under low vegetation.

THE PHOENIX PETREL RARELY strays far from the tropical Pacific. Yet in 1913, four of these birds were found on the forest floor at Raoul Island. Apart from a recent Curtis Island sighting, this is the most southerly record of this species, and the sighting of four birds together probably means that they were not vagrants. If, as seems likely, a small, tenuous colony of Phoenix petrels once bred on Raoul Island, it may have been destroyed by feral cats.

This tropical petrel has no fixed breeding season and there were eggs and young of all ages at Christmas Island in February. Unlike petrels to the south, it does not burrow, but nests on the surface, scraping a hollow beneath bushes or other low plants. It lays one white egg, but there is no information on how it incubates and rears the chick.

Phoenix petrels probably feed at night. Their main food is cephalopods, such as squids, but they also eat fish. M.J.I.

Mottled Petrel *Pterodroma inexpectata* (FORSTER,1844)

A summer nester, the mottled petrel frequents cool and cold oceanic waters. It nests in burrows or in holes among rocks.

ENDEMIC

OTHER NAMES: *Scaled petrel, Peale's petrel, rainbird, korure, titi.*

SIZE: *340 mm.*

DESCRIPTION
ADULT: *Sexes alike. Upper parts grey, darker on head and rump. Most of upper wing grey; with secondaries and their coverts narrowly edged with white. Black-brown M-shaped band across wing when opened. Tail grey. Forehead looks scaly as feathers grey with broad white edges. Cheeks white, mottled black, with black patch below eye. Lores, chin and throat white. Upper breast and flanks white; dotted and mottled with grey which merges into grey breast and belly. Belly often looks patchy as white patches show through grey feathers. Underwing white, with grey edges, dark tip and broad black band running diagonally from bend of wing towards body. Iris dark brown. Bill robust, black. Legs and webs flesh pink with front of webs and toes black.*
JUVENILE: *As adult, but in fledgling no brown and faded feathers, and edges of contour feathers and coverts edged finely with white.*
CHICK: *First down medium grey, sometimes brownish, slightly lighter underneath. Occasionally, throat and belly white. Iris blue. Bill black. Legs grey to white with flesh-coloured webs. Second down darker grey. Iris brown. Feet and webs variegated flesh and black.*

MOULT
Breeding birds moult flight and tail feathers in the North Pacific after migrating.

VOICE
Far-carrying ti-ti-ti, *often followed or preceded by deep, resonant note. Abrupt* wik, *or longer* gor-wik. *Harsh rasping cries when fighting over burrows.*

DISTRIBUTION
Breeds on and around the southern South Island: on an islet between Cascade and Awarua Points; at the Shag Islands in Dusky Sound; around Preservation Inlet; and on an islet in Lake Hauroko. Around Stewart Island nests on Codfish Island; Big South Cape Island; and possibly on the Solander Islands and islets in Port Pegasus. At The Snares breeds on Main Island; Broughton Island; and on several off-lying stacks. Rarely seen at sea near New Zealand. Occasionally seen by day near its breeding islands. Beach-wrecked specimens found in many parts of New Zealand, particularly in the North Island in the summer months. Straggles to southeastern Australia, Tasmania and the South Pacific. Seen on the pack ice off Antarctica during the summer. Spends the southern winter along the subarctic front in the North Pacific Ocean. Some birds, presumably immatures, remain in the North Pacific during the northern winter.

AT ONE TIME THE MOTTLED PETREL may have bred on the mountains of the North and South Islands and on Banks Peninsula; but if so, the firing and clearing of forests and attacks from introduced mammals have ensured that it has all but disappeared from these areas. It is possible that some still breed there, perhaps in the Hauhungaroa Range east of Taumaranui. Today, the mottled petrel is common only around Stewart Island, its outlying islands and at The Snares.

At sea this petrel often flies alone, ignoring ships. It flies fast above cool waters, careening and soaring high into the sky.

On land it breeds in colonies, nesting in burrows about one metre long or in holes among rocks. The nest is in a chamber lined with grasses and other plants. Sometimes the colonies are as low as 10 m above sea level, but more often they are higher. At The Snares the burrows are driven beneath tussock grass on steep slopes and cliffs around the edges of the islands. But at Codfish Island, the burrows are often sheltered under a forest and fern canopy.

At The Snares, the birds mate for life and return to the same nest every year. They breed in the summer, returning in late October and laying in December. The eggs hatch from late January to mid-February and the chicks fly between May and early June.

Birds arrive at the colonies after sunset, slightly earlier in rain or mist and slightly later under clear skies. At night they perform aerial displays, in groups of two or three, dashing and twisting at high speed. These displays continue for five or six hours in summer, until the birds leave before dawn.

A variety of calls accompanies these flights. The most commonly heard cry is a far-carrying *ti-ti-ti*, which the birds call from both the air and the ground. This complex cry is a strident, hysterical giggle based on eight to 15 staccato syllables that begin with a quiet introduction and have a low-pitched ending. Each syllable is a simple cry with strong harmonies, during which the frequency rises and falls. Another call is a deep, resonant note heard only at short range and often followed or preceded by the *ti-ti-ti* sequence. This deep note is sometimes followed by an abrupt *wik*, the complete call sounding like *gor-wik*.

Before they mate, the birds may caress and preen each other with their bills. After mating, the female leaves to feed at sea and form her egg.

Both parents incubate the single, dull white elliptical egg in fairly equal stints of about 13 days, for a total of about 50 days. The male takes the first long stint. As with other burrowing petrels, eggs uncovered for several days may still hatch, although the incubation period is accordingly longer.

About four days after the egg first cracks the chick hatches. Either parent is present. They brood the chick for a few hours to about two days, then the parents leave the burrow during the day. Usually they feed the chick during the first two hours after dark. Often the parents take turns to feed the young petrel but some chicks are fed on two or three successive nights by the same parent. When intruders enter the burrow, the chick lunges forward, sometimes spitting stomach oil. The nestling period of this species is not yet determined, but it appears to be from 90 to 105 days.

Mottled petrels eat squid and small fish. Off Kamchatka they have been seen fluttering above the water like storm petrels, feeding on dead pollock floating on the sea.

To the Maoris, this petrel is known as the korure and was one of the petrels harvested as muttonbirds. A few are still taken on islands where both this petrel and the sooty shearwater breed. On land the mottled petrel's natural enemy is the southern skua and skua-killed birds are common at most breeding places. Wekas have inflicted serious losses on the large population on Codfish Island. No one has actually reported seeing a weka killing a mottled petrel but the numerous corpses found under heavy scrub and fern suggest that a predator other than the resident skuas is responsible. This appears to have been confirmed recently when most of the wekas were removed from Codfish island and the number of corpses fell.

The survival of the mottled petrel depends on the isolation of its nesting islands. It is safest of all at sanctuaries like The Snares where muttonbirding is prohibited and where there are no introduced mammalian predators, but it probably nests at many unrecorded places along the Fiordland coasts and on islands and islets of both the west and east sides of Stewart Island. At The Snares, the survival of adult birds is quite high. Over three seasons an average of 73 per cent of banded birds survived to the following year and some live birds must have been overlooked each year.　　　　J.W.

RECOGNITION

Medium-sized petrel. Grey upper surface, dark belly, light undertail and dark diagonal slash across white underwing. Tail shorter and more rounded when fanned than that of soft-plumaged and Kerguelen petrels.

Soft-plumaged Petrel *Pterodroma mollis mollis* (GOULD, 1844)

NATIVE

OTHER NAMES: *None.*

SIZE: *340 mm.*

DESCRIPTION
ADULT: *Sexes alike. Slate above, head slightly darker. Forehead looks scaly as feathers edged with white. Black patch in front of eye extends into eye socket. Back and tail ash grey, except outer tail feathers white, freckled with grey. Upper wing grey, except primaries sooty black and broad black stripe across upper wing coverts. Cheeks white, lightly barred with grey. Underparts white except* for more or less well-defined grey chest-band and dusting of grey on flanks. Underwing grey with dark front edge and small white, central patch. Undertail coverts white. Undertail plumes grey. Iris brown. Bill fairly stout, black. Legs flesh pink. Toes and front of webs black-brown.*
JUVENILE: *As adult.*
CHICK: *Down grey, paler below. Bill black. Feet similar to adult.*

MOULT
Birds collected at Antipodes Island in mid to late February had nearly all re-grown wings but most were completing regrowth of tail quills.

VOICE
In the air, low musical moan, lasting 1 or 2 seconds and often repeated several times. Typically ends in sudden whik.

DISTRIBUTION
Breeds at the Antipodes Islands; Tristan da Cunha; Gough Island; Îles Kerguélen and Crozet; Marion Island; and on subtropical islands in the North Atlantic. Fairly rare in New Zealand seas. Only 4 records from mainland New Zealand: juvenile male found alive in the Hutt Valley in May 1971; dead female on a Bay of Plenty beach in November 1971; and dead birds at Raukaka Beach, Auckland, in December 1974 and Petone Beach in June 1978. Fairly common visitor to Australian seas and dead birds found on Western Australian beaches presumably originate from Marion Island and Îles Crozet.*

UNTIL RECENTLY IT WAS THOUGHT that soft-plumaged petrels did not breed in the Pacific Ocean. Then, in February and March 1969, they were seen and heard flying over the Antipodes Islands. No nests were found, but as this is not a migratory species and the nearest breeding island, at Îles Crozet, is over 8000 km away, it is unlikely that these birds were visitors. Since then there have been four sightings on mainland New Zealand. One of these, a dead female found on a Bay of Plenty beach in November with a large yolk in her oviduct, was probably an Antipodes Island bird on its pre-laying exodus. In November 1978 more birds and burrows were examined at the Antipodes Islands but no eggs were found.

Possibly these birds arrived not long ago from a more distant colony. But more likely, an established colony of soft-plumaged petrels was overlooked. In recent years, it has become popular to search beaches for dead seabirds, so that sightings of rare birds are now more common. Also, previous visits by biologists to the Antipodes Islands usually lasted only a few hours or at most a few days, whereas the 1969 group was ashore for six weeks.

In the North Atlantic the soft-plumaged petrel breeds on subtropical islands, but in the southern hemisphere it inhabits subantarctic and sometimes Antarctic seas. At sea it is a solitary bird, and feeds on fish, cephalopods and ships' refuse.

At night above its breeding grounds it flies at high speed in groups of two or three, evidently in pursuit flights. On Marion Island it nests on vegetated hillsides overlooking the sea, and at Îles Crozet on the flanks of well-drained valleys.

One North Atlantic colony breeds in the winter, but in the southern hemisphere this is a summer breeder. It returns to land in August or September and lays eggs in November or December. The eggs hatch in late January or early February and the young fly in May. At the Antipodes Islands egg-laying probably peaks in mid-December.

This petrel lays one white egg. Little is known about the chick except that it is naked at the end of its first day and growth is slower than in chicks of the Kerguelen petrel.

The soft-plumaged petrel's main enemy on land is the southern skua, noted for its attacks on seabirds. J.W.

An elusive bird in New Zealand seas, the soft-plumaged petrel is a fairly common visitor to Australian waters. It breeds mainly during summer.

New Caledonian Petrel

Pterodroma leucoptera caledonica NAUROIS, 1978

A New Caledonian petrel at the entrance to its nesting burrow.

ONLY A FEW YEARS AGO this petrel was discovered nesting along the central mountain chain of New Caledonia. The breeding places located so far are on the steep, densely forested sides of remote valleys at heights of 400 to 550 m. The nesting burrows are half to one metre long, in the soil or among and under loose rock. Wild pigs dig open the burrows and eat the birds.

The New Caledonian petrel lays around the end of December. As yet there is no information on egg dimensions, incubation or chick-rearing. Probably incubation takes place in January and February, the chick is reared from late February through April, and it fledges in May. The New Caledonian petrel eats mainly small squid, but also small fish and probably crustaceans, such as prawns.

It is closely related to Gould's petrel *Pterodroma leucoptera leucoptera*, which breeds on Cabbage Tree Island, at the entrance to Port Stephens on the east coast of Australia. Over the past 40 years 18 New Caledonian petrels have been beach-wrecked on the west coast of New Zealand. Many of these corpses have been sighted in the autumn between March and June. But until ornithologists were aware of the New Caledonian subspecies, all sightings in New Zealand were attributed to Gould's petrel. M.J.I.

VAGRANT

OTHER NAMES: *None.*

SIZE: *300 mm.*

DESCRIPTION
ADULT: *Sexes alike. Forehead freckled, feathers black with white borders. Crown, hind neck and rump soot-coloured. Below and before eye black. Back and upper tail coverts ash grey, with pale tips to feathers in fresh plumage. Tail grey, central feathers with sooty tips, outer pair of feathers with white inner webs,* *sometimes with light freckling of pale grey near tip. Primaries brown-black with white wedge at base of inner webs. Secondaries grey, with inner webs white except at tips. Lesser and secondary coverts brown-black. Greater coverts grey edged with white. Lores and undersurface white. Underwing white with black stripe along front edge from primaries to wrist and fading out diagonally inwards. Iris dark brown. Bill black. Feet pale blue, with outer toe and front two thirds of middle and inner toes and front half of webs brown-black; irregular dark spots on* *tarsus; claws black.*
CHICK: *Not described.*

MOULT
In the wintering area.

VOICE
No information available, but Australian subspecies calls kek-kek-kek.

DISTRIBUTION
Breeds only on the main island of New Caledonia. During breeding season ranges south as far as the South Westland coast. Often seen along shipping routes in the southern *Tasman Sea. Cast ashore on the North Island at Waipu, Muriwai Beach, Waikato Heads, Otaki Beach and Titahi Bay. After breeding migrates to the eastern tropical Pacific.*

RECOGNITION

Very dark upper parts with pale back. Similar to Gould's petrel, but slightly larger, with paler back, white inner webs to outer tail feathers.

Chatham Island Taiko

Pterodroma magentae (GIGLIOLI & SALVADORI, 1868)

IN THE AIR THE FAST-FLYING Chatham Island taiko is easily distinguished from other seabirds. Its white breast, belly and undertail coverts contrast sharply with the black-brown of its upper parts. Also, the primary feathers of its dark underwing have a silvery sheen that in direct light, such as a low sun, sometimes appears as white markings.

However, this extremely rare bird is hardly ever seen. During expeditions to the Chatham Islands between 1972 and 1983 only 23 birds were positively identified by banding and measurements. A further 20 were sighted, but these may have included some of those already handled.

Most of the information about the sea distribution of this bird comes from the original research of Giglioli and Salvadori who, in 1867, observed the Chatham Island taiko in an area between 800 km and 3300 km east of the Chathams. Only one other observation, carried out in 1970, seems well substantiated. According to these reports, the Chatham Island taiko feeds along the rich waters of the subtropical convergence and then disperses after breeding to the east of the Chatham Islands.

There is no recent evidence of breeding, but earlier accounts describe how the Chatham Island taiko bred in the Tuku Gully region in the southwest of the main Chatham Island. The birds nested in peaty soil near sea cliffs and on ridges. Fledglings were taken in March and April, which suggests that it breeds in the spring, a theory supported by a bird examined on 1 December 1978 which had a distinct brood patch.

The native Polynesian people, the Morioris, ate large numbers of the Chatham Island taiko, but the annual slaughter of what was then a plentiful species probably had little effect on the overall numbers. Europeans brought domestic cattle, sheep and pigs to the Chatham Islands and these were later joined by dogs, cats and rats. The introduction of these animals and the pastoral development of the taiko's breeding grounds caused a steady decline in its population. The introduction of the eastern weka in 1905 and that of the opossum around 1928 posed further serious threats to the bird's existence. Both the weka and the opossum use burrows as retreats. D.E.C.

The Chatham Island taiko, one of the rarest seabirds in the world.

ENDEMIC

OTHER NAMES: *Magenta petrel, tchaik of the Moriori.*

SIZE: *380 mm.*

DESCRIPTION
ADULT: *Sexes alike. White scalloped feathers on forehead merge into dark crown. Line of white-tipped feathers above eye. Intense sooty black in front of eye. Upper parts brown-black with wing coverts, tail and sides of body paler. Below bill, white feathers merge into dark band across foreneck. Breast and belly white. Underwing black-brown with highly reflective sheen on primaries. Undertail coverts white flecked with grey. Iris brown. Bill lead grey to black. Feet rich flesh colour; outer half of toes and webs black.*
JUVENILE: *Not known.*

MOULT
Five birds examined between *1 December and 1 January were in fresh plumage, though one bird still had outer primaries growing on 1 January.*

VOICE
Not recorded.

DISTRIBUTION
Rare bird that breeds only at the Chatham Islands. Feeds along the subtropical convergence. After breeding disperses east of the Chatham Islands.

RECOGNITION

Dark underwing with highly reflective silvery sheen on primary feathers. In flight, white breast, belly and undertail coverts very obvious. Black webs and pink legs silhouette against white undertail coverts.

Early this century Kermadec petrels were harvested in their thousands as muttonbirds. Introduced feral cats and Norway rats further reduced their numbers.

Kermadec Petrel *Pterodroma neglecta neglecta* (SCHLEGEL, 1863)

NATIVE

OTHER NAMES: *None.*

SIZE: *380 mm.*

DESCRIPTION
ADULT: *Sexes alike. Plumage varies from pale to dark. In intermediate colouring: front of crown mottled brown and white. Feathers of top of head, side and back of neck brown with white edges. Rest of upper surface dark brown; except long scapulars, primary feathers, and tail black; and shafts of primaries white or ivory. Forehead, lores, side of face, line over eye and undersurface white. Underwing mainly dark grey-brown with white patch at base of primaries; smaller white area inside this patch; and some pale feathers near elbow. Undertail coverts white freckled with brown. Iris dark brown. Bill black. Feet pale flesh-coloured, with ends of webs and toes black.*
FLEDGLING: *Darker and more uniformly coloured than adult.*
CHICK: *Long down varies from light to dark grey.*

MOULT
Main moult before breeding.

VOICE
Long drawn-out ow *followed by* coo *repeated several times, especially when flying in evening.*

DISTRIBUTION
Breeds at the Kermadec Islands on Herald Islets, and on Macauley, Haszard, Curtis, and Cheeseman Islands; Lord Howe, Rapa, Ducie and Henderson Islands; Iles Tuamotu; Oeno Atoll. Ranges in South Pacific between 20°S and 35°S. Non-breeders range into North Pacific and have been recorded from the Philippines, Hawaiian Islands and Mexico. Two specimens found on Muriwai beach, west Auckland. One bird has visited Cuvier Island, off Coromandel Peninsula each summer since 1973. It made a nest, but failed to find a mate.

RECOGNITION

Medium to large petrel. Conspicuous divided white patch on outer underwing. Relatively short, square tail. Pale primary shafts distinguish it from providence petrel.

AT THE BEGINNING OF THIS CENTURY, more than 200 000 Kermadec petrels bred on Raoul Island. Many of their young were harvested as muttonbirds and in the first three weeks of April 1908, over 2000 were slaughtered. After killing, plucking and cleaning the birds, the hunters opened them out and rubbed in dry salt. Then they put the petrels in brine for a day and smoked them for another day before storing the birds in casks, covered in their own oil. In this way the meat kept for up to three years. Undoubtedly, muttonbirding reduced the species'

numbers, but introduced feral cats and Norway rats were even more destructive and eventually they wiped out the Kermadec petrel from Raoul Island.

At Raoul Island the petrels were observed arriving at the breeding places in late August. They nested on the ground in a shallow hollow. First the bird went under a log or bush, fluffed out its feathers, and stood up. It then leaned forwards on its breast and scratched the earth backwards with both feet at once. Within half an hour it had scraped a dip about 20 cm across and 6 cm deep. It lined this with sticks and leaves. After the nest was completed, mating soon followed and the petrel left the island.

Two or three weeks after mating, between the end of October and the beginning of December, the females returned to Raoul Island to lay one white egg. The birds incubated this for about 51 days and by the end of January most eggs had hatched. The chick was fed by the parents for over three months, during which time it became very fat. Most of the young flew in April and May but a few late ones were seen during the first week of June. All adults had left by the end of May.

On the smaller Kermadec Islands, 6000 to 10 000 pairs breed. At the Meyer Islands, the birds used to breed mainly during the winter. They laid from late February to early April and the young departed between late August and October when about 120 days old. Now they also breed in the summer on the Meyer Islands.

At the Kermadec Islands, Kermadec petrels eat mainly cephalopods and crustaceans; elsewhere, cephalopods, particularly squids.

The plumage of this petrel varies from pale to dark with many shades in between. In the lightest birds, the head, neck and undersurface are pure white, except for brown freckles on the forehead and crown. The rest of the upper surface is pale ash brown with darker primary feathers. The darkest specimens, however, are sooty black above with paler edges to the forehead feathers, and grey-brown below. The distinctive underwing pattern does not vary with the rest of the plumage. Often several characteristics go together. Thus, dark birds usually have dark feet, light birds pale feet, and birds of intermediate plumage bluish feet. But this is not invariable as the different colour variations are inherited separately.   M.J.I.

A migratory bird, Cook's petrel breeds on offshore islands and often nests in burrows which wind among tree roots. It is a particularly agile climber.

Cook's Petrel *Pterodroma cookii* (GRAY, 1843)

ENDEMIC

OTHER NAME: *Titi.*

SIZE: *300 mm.*

DESCRIPTION

ADULT: *Sexes alike. Forehead white with grey freckling above bill. Narrow white line above eye. Black patch in front of and below eye, blending with grey behind eye. Feathers of crown, nape, mantle, lower back, side of neck, side of breast and upper tail coverts grey, with white edges when fresh. White edges remain on front of crown and sides of neck and breast. Roughly triangular black-brown area on rump. Upper wing mainly black, browning with wear. Secondaries and greater coverts grey-black, their exposed parts narrowly edged with white, outlining dark wide M across wings. Inner webs of primaries white at base, forming white wedge into black tip. Central tail feathers grey with black-brown tips. Outer webs of side tail feathers grey or speckled with grey, and inner webs pale grey, speckled or white, outermost pair always palest. Underparts white. Boundary between grey upper parts and white underparts mottled. Underwing white, except front edge from tip to bend of wing narrowly mottled black and grey, this strip petering out diagonally across underwing. Iris dark brown. Bill relatively long and slender, black. Legs, most of inner third of foot and inner two toes blue. Webs mainly pale yellow, rest of toes and ends of webs black.*
FLEDGLING: *Similar to adult, except pale-edged contour feathers of upper surface make it appear paler. Exposed upper surface of primaries black.*
CHICK: *First down slate, with white stripe of short, thick down on throat and belly. Long second down pale grey above.*

MOULT
Mostly in the wintering area. Non-breeders and failed breeders begin body moult before leaving breeding places.

VOICE
At night, vocal in flight above breeding places and over landmarks on flight paths. Calls nasal-sounding kek-kek-kek or nga-nga-nga, usually 3 times in succession and sometimes, at its colonies, in a long sequence. Borr and subdued oo-i heard only above the breeding grounds. Generally silent on ground.

DISTRIBUTION
Possibly 100 000 breed on Little Barrier Island; less than 20 pairs on Great Barrier Island; and about 100 pairs on Codfish Island. At night, on flights between colonies and feeding grounds, passes over North Auckland peninsula, especially near Kaipara Harbour; Cuvier Island; Motuhora Island; possibly across the land separating Bay of Plenty from northern Hawke Bay; possibly across the Tararua Range; and across Stewart Island. Winters in the eastern central Pacific mainly between 13°S and 23°N. Straggles to the Aleutian Islands.

RECOGNITION

White below and dark above, with head and neck paler. M pattern across wings and back sometimes visible. Distinguished from black-winged petrel by lack of black band on underwing, and from Stejneger's petrel by pale crown. Hard to separate from Pycroft's petrel but sightings south of Cook Strait probably Cook's petrel.

TO ENSURE AN EASY TAKE-OFF this forest-nesting petrel scales trees. It prefers to climb sloping trees, especially those projecting above the forest canopy, but it can also haul itself up vertical trunks that are clad in kidney fern. It breeds in permanent burrows, often on a ridge or on steeply sloping land where there is a choice of take-off sites.

This is a typically noisy gadfly petrel at night above its nesting places, but it also calls as it flies over landmarks on its flight paths. During the summer, from November to January, it is heard regularly over Cuvier Island and Great Barrier Island and, less often, over Motuhora Island and over the North Auckland peninsula. This flight call is a nasal-sounding *kek-kek-kek* or *nga-nga-nga* that sometimes sounds like the quack of a duck. An entirely different sound, heard on nights when the birds are very active and noisy, is caused by the birds performing high-speed dives. Their wing or tail quill feathers vibrate to produce a bleating goat-like sound.

The breeding season

The breeding season extends from late August to early April in the north and about three or four weeks later on Codfish Island. The birds prepare the burrows and mate between September and mid-October. The burrows are usually one to three metres long, sometimes up to five metres. They wind among tree roots, usually in rather heavy soil. In places the soil is shallow and the birds build the nest of leaves and twigs against impervious bedrock. In heavy rain such nests are flooded and the eggs die. After they have mated the birds leave the burrow to feed at sea for four or five weeks.

On Little Barrier Island, they lay one white, oval egg between 24 October and about 5 December, with a peak from 7 to 12 November. On Codfish Island, they lay around 12 December.

The total incubation period is about 49 days. For the first few days the female incubates the egg. After this, the pair alternate for three main incubation spells, each lasting about a fortnight. Finally the female completes the incubation. Sometimes it is difficult for the birds to incubate continuously, especially during the male's last main spell, as he has to recover condition quickly during the female's main stint. If the birds desert the egg, kiore often eat it. In fact, as incubation progresses, these rats learn that a meal can be found in the burrows with little effort, and towards the end of the incubation period a day, at most, is the survival time of a deserted egg.

Most chicks hatch at the end of December and the females guard them for from 12 hours to three days, after which they are rarely accompanied by a parent during the day. After the short guard period the adults feed the young petrels about every second night and after two weeks this is reduced to about once every three nights. By this time a chick can consume in one meal all that a parent can bring to it. The chicks grow very fat and usually attain weights between 300 and 440 g. Before the young fledge, at about 88 days old, the parents desert them for 10 days or so and their weight falls to around 206 g.

The fledglings spend only a few nights exercising their wings and exploring take-off sites. During this period, the young birds sometimes find themselves unwittingly up large, often epiphyte-covered trees. But they persevere and after a few crashes, they eventually take flight and leave the forest, probably not to set foot again on land for the next five years. They depart between 15 March and 15 April, with a very high proportion leaving between 20 and 31 March. In some years, perhaps because of misty weather, a few drift into Auckland and are found grounded in its suburbs.

Cook's petrels feed at night from near the water's surface, catching cephalopods (especially squid), their main food, and fish and crustaceans. They range to the east of both main islands and in the Tasman Sea north of about 40°S. In the north, an important feeding ground is over 150 km offshore between East Cape and Cape Palliser. The Codfish Island birds feed east of Otago.

After the breeding season they migrate to the eastern central Pacific, between 13°S and 23°N, where large numbers of Cook's petrels are seen in June and July. The birds are away from New Zealand between May and August, but probably they do not all migrate together. Most non-breeders leave the breeding grounds in February, successful breeders in March, and chicks follow in late March or early April. A few birds may remain at the colonies.

On Little Barrier Island, the population is almost stable despite the attacks of feral cats which have killed many fledglings, non-breeders and breeders. Now kiore kill young chicks and severely maul older chicks, although they seem unable to kill them. On Great Barrier Island, bush rats kiore and feral cats threaten the small colony. On Codfish Island, the Stewart Island weka was introduced in about 1900 and by 1966 had almost annihilated its population of Cook's petrels. These predatory birds kill the petrels on the ground at night, with a swift stab of the beak to the petrel's skull.

Many years ago, adult and young Cook's petrels were taken for food by Maoris. The young birds were caught at the colonies and the adults were lured towards a fire. On overland flight paths the hunters made a clearing on a hilltop. In the evening darkness, as the titi flew inland, the muttonbirders lit a fire. Many birds were attracted to the flames and were captured when they landed or were struck with poles as they flew overhead. The birds were then prepared for eating or preserved in their own fat.   M.J.I.

The Chatham Island petrel, a relatively primitive bird, is among the rarest of New Zealand's petrels.

Chatham Island Petrel

Pterodroma axillaris

(SALVIN, 1893)

ENDEMIC

OTHER NAME: *Ranguru.*

SIZE: *300 mm.*

DESCRIPTION
ADULT: *Sexes alike. Feathers of upper surface mainly slate with darker edges. Shoulder and upper wing coverts black. Primary feathers of upper wing black, with white wedge extending out from base of inner web. Outer tail feathers mottled ash brown and white. Forehead and lores white freckled with black. Black around eye. Rest of face and underparts white. Broad black front edge on inner half of underwing. Rest of underwing white. Iris brown. Bill black. Legs, first joint of mid and inner toes, and inner part of webs flesh-coloured; rest of feet black.*
IMMATURE: *Not described but probably paler above due to pale feather edges.*
CHICK: *Not described.*

MOULT
Not known.

VOICE
Main flight call is tee repeated 3 times, similar to cry of black-winged petrel.

DISTRIBUTION
Breeds only on Rangatira Island in the Chatham Islands. From June to early November its whereabouts not known but probably moves northwards or eastwards into the Pacific Ocean.

RECOGNITION

Very rarely seen at sea. Distinguished from similar black-winged petrel by extensive black on inner half of underwing.

FEWER THAN 20 SPECIMENS of this rare petrel have been banded. It breeds only on Rangatira Island in the Chatham Islands and has never been sighted beyond this region.

The Moriois, the Polynesian inhabitants of the Chatham Islands, killed and ate these petrels, but subfossil bones show that few birds were taken, compared to the numbers of taikos, broad-billed prions and diving petrels that were slaughtered. In the 1930s sheep grazed on the breeding grounds of the Chatham Island petrel and the closely cropped vegetation made it easy for southern skuas to kill them. In 1955 the sheep were removed and since then, the vegetation has grown rank, so that now it is more difficult for skuas to attack these petrels.

The Chatham Island petrel is no longer threatened directly, but it competes on its breeding grounds with prions and diving petrels which have been forced off the two main islands of the Chathams by predators. At sea, it competes with black-winged petrels, whose numbers are increasing. One of the first *Pterodroma* species to exist, the Chatham Island petrel is scarce apparently because of its primitiveness. Compared to other *Pterodroma* petrels, it has fewer calls, simpler intestines and a shorter breeding season.

Very little is known about the breeding habits of this petrel, as fewer than 20 nesting burrows have been identified. These are on the lower northern and eastern parts of Rangatira Island, below 100 m and scattered amongst burrows of countless broad-billed prions, white-faced storm petrels and common diving petrels. Probably, Chatham Island petrels share their burrows with broad-billed prions and, as the prions and diving petrels return to the breeding grounds first, this may be another reason for the scarcity of the Chatham Island petrel.

The tunnels are dug in deep crumbly loam under the bush and anyone walking over them must take great care not to plunge into the nests. Outside the low forest, the birds burrow under bracken, rank grass and *Muehlenbeckia* vines. The burrows vary greatly in structure and the only constant shape is that of the tunnel entrance, which is about 10 cm wide by 7 cm deep and just admits an adult hand. The petrels gather dead leaves and strip low-growing plants to make the nest. They mate in early December.

The female lays one white, ovoid egg. Only four have been found. These were laid during the last 10 days of December or the first 10 days of January. The young most likely fledge in May. Most observations of birds at the colony have been made from December to early March.

The food of the Chatham Island petrel is probably similar to that of other small gadfly petrels. Remains of small squid and bioluminescent fish have been found in dead birds' stomachs.   M.J.I.

Stejneger's Petrel *Pterodroma longirostris* (STEJNEGER, 1893)

OBSERVATIONS BY ORNITHOLOGISTS strongly suggest that Stejneger's petrel breeds on Isla Alejandro Selkirk in the Archipielago Juan Fernandez off the eastern coast of Chile. Neither eggs nor chicks have been found, but nesting burrows tunnelled below dense fern groves on the island's high plateau Cerro de Los Inocentes have been attributed to this species of petrel.

The birds are abundant around the archipelago from October to April and this has led to one suggestion that they breed there in the southern summer. To support this are the recordings of moulting birds in the northwest Pacific between June and November.

Sightings of *Pterodroma longirostris* have also been made in the northeast Pacific and around New Zealand, but it is thought that these indicate the wide dispersal of non-breeders, rather than any pattern of migration by breeding adults. J.A.B.

VAGRANT

OTHER NAMES: *None.*

SIZE: *260 mm.*

DESCRIPTION
ADULT: *Sexes similar. Forehead white, with slight mottling along centre line and on crown to level of eye. Black patch around, below and behind eye. Crown and nape grey-black contrasting with medium grey back and rump. Grey extends onto side of breast, forming conspicuous* patch. *Upper wing and tail brown-black. Underparts white, except for dark narrow band along front edge of underwing, near bend of wing. Inner webs of underwing primaries light grey fading to white at base and centre. Iris brown. Bill black. Legs and feet pale blue, with dark grey on outer toes, joints, and claws.* IMMATURE: *Probably same as adult.* CHICK: *Not known.*

MOULT
Between June and January. Probably breeders moult between June and August; younger birds later.

VOICE
Not known.

DISTRIBUTION
Breeds on Isla Alejandro Selkirk at Archipielago Juan Fernandez. Feeds around the Archipielago Juan Fernandez during the breeding season before migrating to the subtropical northwest Pacific from June until October or November. Non-breeders sighted in northeast Pacific in November and in New Zealand between November and January.

Pycroft's Petrel *Pterodroma pycrofti* FALLA, 1933

Pycroft's petrel nests in burrows in sparse colonies, and avoids the dense colonies of other species.

ON THE GROUND, Pycroft's petrel is a quiet bird. The only sounds from its breeding places are an occasional screech or squawk in times of stress, a growl from a lone bird, a soft crooning from a pair in their burrow or cackles from a group of unemployed birds. In the air however it calls noisily—either a chirping high-pitched *zip-zip* or a strident low-pitched *te-te*.

Small groups of birds nest together in burrows that are spaced apart and usually away from the dense colonies of other species. They breed below 200 m, on well-drained sites in both soft, crumbly soil and in stiffer, clay soils. The tunnels vary in size from 0.3 to 1.5 m long and usually contain an enlarged section where the birds gather together twigs and leaves to form a nest.

The breeding season most likely begins in October when the birds prepare the burrows, and mate. They lay one white egg between 23 November and 6 December, with a peak of laying about 28 November. It is not known how long the incubation period lasts. The parents take turns to sit on the egg, the male taking the first main stint of 14 days. The parents desert the egg if they have not put on enough extra weight to allow them to fast as they incubate. Most chicks hatch by the end of January. It is not known when they depart, but breeding success is often low.

The only terrestrial predators of this petrel are kiore and tuatara. On Hen Island kiore eat deserted eggs. At Aorangi in the Poor Knights Islands, tuatara may evict adult petrels from their burrows but it is not known if any deaths result.

Little is known of the feeding habits of Pycroft's petrels, and only the remains of small cephalopods have been found in the birds' stomachs. J.A.B.

ENDEMIC

OTHER NAMES: *None.*

SIZE: *280 mm.*

DESCRIPTION
ADULT: *Sexes alike, though head of male larger. Upper parts medium grey, extending down side of breast, slightly darker on head and neck, and shading to brown-black on upper wing, rump, and main tail feathers. Conspicuous dark patch below eye. Underparts white. Narrow band of dark grey on front edge of underwing, widest at bend of wing, before fading away diagonally towards axillaries. Iris dark brown. Bill black. Legs and feet pale violet-blue, with outer toes, joints, and claws dark grey.* IMMATURE: *Probably same as adult.* CHICK: *Not known.*

MOULT
Not known.

VOICE
Noisy in flight, with repetitive calls. High-pitched cicada-like zip-zip *and* tzi-tzi. *Harsh, loud and low-pitched* te-te.

DISTRIBUTION
Endangered species; world population less then 500 pairs. Breeds off the east coast of northern New Zealand at Stephenson Island; Aorangi, Poor Knights Islands; Hen and Chickens; Mercury Islands. Sea range not known. Storm-killed specimens have been cast ashore in northern New Zealand, between Cape Maria van Diemen and Tauranga. Probably migrates to the North Pacific, but no records from outside New Zealand waters.

Black-winged Petrel
Pterodroma nigripennis (Rothschild, 1893)

A swift, summer-breeding bird, the black-winged petrel nests in burrows, rocky crevices or on steep rocky terrain overlooking the sea.

NATIVE

OTHER NAMES: *None.*

SIZE: *300 mm.*

DESCRIPTION
ADULT: *Sexes alike. Forehead freckled dark grey and white. Lores mainly white. White line, freckled grey, over and behind eye; black patch mottled at edges, through and below eye. Feathers of upper surface mostly ash grey with pale margins; darker on crown. Long scapulars, patch on rump, median upper tail coverts, most of upper wing coverts and primaries black. Greater wing coverts and secondaries slate grey with pale edges. Inner webs of primaries white at base. Tail slate grey, black at tip, outer feathers white mottled grey. Underparts white. Sides of neck and upper breast grey, sometimes tending to form collar or extending as bars towards throat and along flanks. Underwing white with very prominent black band on front edge from tip to between bend of wing and elbow, then petering out diagonally across wing. Iris dark brown. Bill black. Feet flesh-coloured; ends of webs and toes and all of outer toe black.*
FLEDGLING: *As adult, except for paler edges to most contour feathers on upper surface.*
CHICK: *Pale grey down, except for white band from chin to white belly.*

MOULT
Not known.

VOICE
Noisy at night and sometimes by day over colonies. Loud tee-tee-tee, *sometimes followed immediately by a call similar to the meow of a cat. Sometimes both calls uttered separately, either in the air or on the ground.*

DISTRIBUTION
Probably breeds on all the Kermadec Islands, on the Three Kings Islands, on Portland Island and on Îlots de Bass. Frequents, and probably breeds at Norfolk, Philip and Lord Howe Islands; the Chatham and the Poor Knights Islands; islets off New Caledonia; and Tonga. May start breeding on headlands in the far north of New Zealand. At sea during breeding season ranges mainly west, north and east of the North Island, from west of Taranaki to the Chatham Islands. Regularly seen northwards from North Cape and east of East Cape as far south as Wairarapa. Frequently recorded in the Tasman Sea. After breeding season migrates to the northern central Pacific, where considerable numbers present from May to October between 5°N and 25°N.

RECOGNITION

Small size. White underparts with conspicuous black band on underwing. Uniform grey plumage from crown to mantle. Similar to collared petrel which usually has more distinct collar.

WITH RAPID WING-BEATS and steeply banking arcs, the flight of the black-winged petrel is fast and swooping. During the breeding season birds at sea, as well as those visiting the breeding colonies, chase one another, soar high and call a loud *tee-tee-tee*. Birds at the colonies also utter a complicated cry like the meow of a cat.

About a million black-winged petrels nest on Macauley Island. Smaller numbers breed on the other islands in the Kermadec group, on the Three Kings Islands and on the Îlots de Bass. In recent decades the black-winged petrel has also extended its range to Norfolk Island, Philip Island, Lord Howe Island, the Chatham Islands, the Poor Knights Islands, Portland Island in Hawke Bay, islets off New Caledonia and probably to Tonga. At all of these new discoveries numbers have increased, but it is difficult to prove that the birds actually breed there. So far, much of the increase may be from immigrants. However, on at least some of these islands, there could be small, established colonies that were previously overlooked.

This petrel breeds in the summer. At the Kermadec Islands the birds first arrive in mid-October and at the Chatham Islands a month later. Usually they nest in a burrow approximately half to one metre long, but sometimes they use a rocky crevice. On the Chatham Islands, some black-winged petrels have wandered into the burrows of broad-billed prions. Groups of black-winged petrels looking for new breeding places favour the top of steep, rocky terrain overlooking the sea, where burrowing can be difficult.

At the Kermadec Islands, the black-winged petrel lays from late December to mid-January. Fledglings are thought to leave in May, but little is known about incubation and chick-rearing. Food is mainly squids and prawns, but again there is little precise information.

Feral cats kill black-winged petrels on Raoul Island, on the headlands of northern New Zealand and on Pitt Island in the Chatham Islands. Each year southern skuas are killing more and more birds on Rangatira in the Chathams. (Birds have been visiting the summit of Rangatira for over ten summers.) But the large colonies in the Kermadecs are free of predators and it is from these that the emigrant birds probably originate.   M.J.I.

Kerguelen Petrel *Lugensa brevirostris* (LESSON,1831)

KERGUELEN PETRELS BREED on subantarctic islands in the Indian and South Atlantic Oceans. At sea they range from near the subtropical convergence to the Antarctic pack ice, feeding on cephalopods and crustaceans. Some solitary, wind-drifted birds have reached the western shores of New Zealand in late winter or early spring.

Their breeding season is short, perhaps because they rely on crustaceans which are plentiful during the summer. In late August and early September breeding birds return to their islands. They court and mate in September, but build most of the nest while they incubate.

They breed in waterlogged burrows that vary in length from one to three metres. Tunnels are often found around the coast or at the bottom of valleys, except on Gough Island where they are above 300 m. Birds raise the nest with plants to place the egg in a drier position.

After they have mated the birds leave their islands for about three weeks. In early October they return to lay. The single white egg is incubated by both parents in four main shifts. Few birds desert their eggs, and after about 49 days, in late November, the egg hatches. The parents guard the chick for only one or two days and after a surprisingly short period, about 60 days, the young bird leaves. Most chicks depart in late January and only a few remain into February.

At all of their breeding places, southern skuas attack Kerguelen petrels and on Est Island they kill many fledglings as the young birds are leaving. On Possession Island, black rats will eat chicks as soon as the parents stop guarding them. In fact, on this island, rats could eventually exterminate the remaining small colonies. At Îles Kerguélen and Marion Island feral cats kill some birds.

In anatomy and biology Kerguelen petrels differ from petrels within the genus *Pterodroma*. Unlike gadfly-petrels, the skull surrounding the eye-sockets is expanded and flared outwards to accommodate the relatively large eyes. In most *Pterodroma* species, such as the soft-plumaged petrel, the upper intestine is helically twisted. But in Kerguelen petrels, the upper intestine, from the gizzard to about halfway to the cloaca, is a simple tube, as in most petrels, fulmars and shearwaters, and a few gadfly-petrels.   M.J.I.

The Kerguelen petrel occurs in New Zealand mainly as a wind-drifted vagrant.

VAGRANT

OTHER NAMES: *None.*

SIZE: *360 mm.*

DESCRIPTION
ADULT: *Sexes alike. Plumage exceptionally thick and soft. Feathers of upper surface dark grey with pale edges, darker around eyes. Upper wing grey-black, with grey edges to wing coverts; inner webs of primaries paler. Tail grey-black. Face and throat mottled grey. Undersurface dark grey to brown-grey. Undersurface of primaries and edges of axillaries pale grey. Edges of underwing coverts white, at least when fresh. Bases of all feathers pale grey. Iris brown. Bill black, very narrow in proportion to its depth. Feet brown-grey to purple-grey; claws black.*
FLEDGLING: *As adult but greyer, with pale feather edges more prominent.*
CHICK: *Uniform grey down.*

MOULT
Noticed in late January, so occurs soon after breeding season. Quill moult completed by June; body moult continues into September. Most beach-wrecked birds in fresh plumage.

VOICE
Very quiet when flying over nesting places. About an hour after dusk birds come in from the sea uttering a call like chee-chee-chay, *but after a brief period of infrequent calls they are silent again.* See-see-see *when disturbed in their burrows during the day.*

DISTRIBUTION
Breeds on Tristan da Cunha; Gough Island; the Prince Edward Islands; Îles Crozet and Kerguélen. Ranges from near the subtropical convergence to as far south as the pack ice. Uncommon in the South Pacific but occasionally seen near 60°S eastwards from 145°W. Occurs in New Zealand seas only when wind-drifted, especially non-breeders in August and September.

RECOGNITION

Medium-sized petrel. Large head. Distinctive pale grey undersurface of primaries contrasts with darker underparts. Smaller and greyer than grey-faced petrel. Usually solitary.

Blue Petrel *Halobaena caerulea* (GMELIN,1789)

ITS BLUE-GREY UPPER PARTS, white underparts and white-tipped tail distinguish the blue petrel from other petrels. In general appearance it looks like a large prion, but its swift flight is higher arcing and less erratic than that of the prions. Normally the blue petrel flies alone and occasionally follows ships.

It is a regular visitor to New Zealand in the winter and spring. As this is not a migratory species it is not known whether these stragglers are breeding birds that have dispersed north and eastwards after the breeding season or wandering juveniles. Possibly they are blown into the Tasman Sea by southwesterly gales.

The blue petrel breeds in dense colonies, nesting in burrows dug into hillsides. Grass often grows prolifically over these burrows, and much of the adjacent ground is bare. The burrows themselves are one to three metres long, tortuous and often interconnecting or with two entrances. The birds build a nest of grass and lay one white, ovoid egg.

The breeding season is from spring to summer. At Marion and Prince Edward Islands and at the Îles Crozet, courtship and burrow preparation take place in August and September, egg-laying in October and hatching in late November or early December. The incubation period is about 46 days and the fledging period about 60 days, with young leaving in late January or early February. At the Îles Kerguélen the breeding season occurs about a month later than at the more northerly colonies.

At South Georgia the birds feed on small fish and krill. This is supplemented by other crustaceans including deep-sea prawns, amphipods and copepods. Lantern-fish and antarctic cod may make up 55 per cent of the diet. They also eat some squids. Often they range far from the colony when seeking food.

Southern skuas kill blue petrels at all the breeding places, and on Macquarie and Marion Islands feral cats attack them.   M.J.I.

STRAGGLER

OTHER NAMES: *None.*

SIZE: *300 mm.*

DESCRIPTION
ADULT: *Sexes alike. Lower forehead white; upper forehead mottled brown and white. Crown, nape and patch round eye slate-black. Line above eye white. Upper parts, side of neck and side of upper breast blue-grey. Long scapulars dark grey with white edges. Outer webs of outer primaries black-brown; inner webs white. Outer webs of inner primaries blue-grey; inner webs white. Tail blue-grey with white outer feathers and conspicuous white tip. Throat, centre of breast and rest of undersurface white. Iris brown. Bill blue with top and nasal tubes black. Feet blue. Webs flesh-coloured. Claws black-brown.*
FLEDGLING: *Probably generally paler.*
CHICK: *Uniformly slate-coloured.*

MOULT
Not known.

VOICE
At night, kuk-kuk-kuk-coo-oo *from inside burrows or on the ground. Usually silent when flying over breeding grounds at night.*

DISTRIBUTION
Breeds at South Georgia; Marion and Prince Edward Islands; Îles Crozet and Kerguélen; and Macquarie Island. Ranges around Antarctica from the pack ice to the subtropical convergence, though it is rare in the South Pacific. Regular visitor to New Zealand seas from June to November.

RECOGNITION

Blue-grey; white below. Conspicuous white-tipped tail. Black cap. Dark sides of neck and upper breast.

Thin-billed Prion *Pachyptila belcheri* (MATHEWS, 1912)

AT SEA THE THIN-BILLED PRION is a less gregarious bird than other prions. It often flies alone or in the company of only a few others. Immature birds are common, if irregular, visitors to New Zealand shores from late May to late September. Adult thin-billed prions are sighted rarely in New Zealand, but they are often found among birds cast upon Western Australian beaches.

Most of these wanderers are from colonies at the Îles Kerguélen and Îles Crozet in the Indian Ocean. A few birds breed on stacks off Macquarie Island. The thin-billed prion also nests in large numbers on off-lying islands of the Falkland Islands. Although birds from these nesting sites forage far into the western South Pacific, they are not known to reach New Zealand.

This prion feeds at night, catching amphipods, squid and small fish from the sea's surface. It is a voracious feeder and as many as 100 amphipods, which may comprise a quarter of the bird's net weight, have been taken from one bird's stomach. The thin-billed prion rarely approaches ships, unless they are stationary. P.C.H.

MIGRANT

OTHER NAME: *Slender-billed prion.*

SIZE: *250 mm.*

DESCRIPTION
ADULT: *Sexes alike. Upper parts pale blue. Conspicuous white lores and white stripe above eye. Black open-M marking across upper wings and small black tail tip. Underparts white. Iris sepia brown. Bill of medium length, very narrow, blue. Legs and feet lavender blue. Webs cream or grey.*
IMMATURE: *Similar to adult but wing pattern dark grey; and bill and feet duller.*
YOUNG: *First down grey-brown. Second down longer, smoky grey.*

MOULT
Body moult begins near end of breeding season. Full moult normally completed by May or June.

VOICE
On land, raucous grating or cooing.

DISTRIBUTION
Breeds at Îles Kerguélen, Îles Crozet and on off-lying islands of Macquarie Island and the Falkland Islands.

> **RECOGNITION**
> Small, pale prion. Narrow bill. Small black tail tip.

Broad-billed Prion *Pachyptila vittata vittata* (FORSTER, 1777)

A broad-billed prion at its nest under a building at the Chatham Islands. Its bill is specially adapted for feeding.

NATIVE

OTHER NAMES: *Whalebird, scooper, blue-billy, parara.*

SIZE: *280 mm.*

DESCRIPTION
ADULT: *Sexes alike. Body blue-grey with conspicuous black open-M pattern across upper wings. Tip of tail black. Underparts white. Bill broad and deep, iron grey, with lower mandible mauve and each side of upper mandible fringed with buff to cream-coloured comb-like lamellae. Iris sepia brown. Legs pale blue. Webs cream-coloured.*
IMMATURE: *As adult, but plumage slightly paler. Inner primaries often edged with white.*
CHICK: *First down dark grey. Second down longer, smoky grey.*

MOULT
After the breeding season from early February, to April. Non-breeding birds often moult some distance from breeding grounds during July and August while other birds are breeding.

VOICE
On land, a raucous grating or cooing rerky-rik-ik repeated continuously. Silent at sea.

DISTRIBUTION
Found abundantly in New Zealand offshore waters, particularly near the subtropical convergence. Breeds in millions at the Chatham Islands and on islets in Foveaux Strait.

> **RECOGNITION**
> Large beak, at its widest part as broad as the bird's head.

IN THE SHAPE AND FUNCTION of its remarkable beak, the broad-billed prion is unique among petrels. Its bill, as wide as its head, is fringed with small comb-like growths called lamellae. When the bird is feeding, these lamellae act as filters. The prion scurries rapidly over the sea, immersing its beak and swinging its head from side to side. By this method it draws water into its mouth, then quickly forces it out again by moving its large, fleshy tongue upwards. Small crustaceans are strained through the lamellae and swallowed.

This is a common seabird in New Zealand seas and breeds in millions at the Chatham Islands and on islets in Foveaux Strait where food is plentiful. It nests in burrows which it digs with its enormous beak, kicking the earth away with its webbed feet.

After mating, the birds return to sea for several weeks while the female forms the single white egg. She lays this between late August and mid-September. Both parents incubate the egg alternately for about 48 days. For a few days they continually guard the newly hatched chick, then they leave it alone in the nest during the day, returning only after nightfall to feed it. When it is about 53 days old, in mid-December, the fledgling leaves. Normally, by the first week in January the breeding season is over but in years of poor food supplies some chicks stay until the third week of January. Sometimes, there is so little food that very few chicks survive to leave the islands.

After the breeding season, broad-billed prion moult their faded and worn plumage gradually. This ensures that they can fly well throughout the moult. Immediately after the moult, birds begin returning to the breeding places. Throughout the non-breeding season, birds visit the colonies in varying numbers, so that on most nights of the year, some are found ashore. P.C.H.

Antarctic Prion

Pachyptila desolata desolata (GMELIN, 1789)

CIRCUMPOLAR

OTHER NAME: *Dove prion.*

SIZE: *270 mm.*

DESCRIPTION
ADULT: *Sexes alike. Upper parts blue-grey with conspicuous black open-M marking over upper wings and black tip to central tail feathers. Lores white, barred or flecked with dark grey. Eye-patch of dark feathers before and under eye. Small white eyebrow. Undersurface white. Iris sepia brown. Bill blue, moderately broad. Lamellae small, sometimes visible at gape when bill closed. Feet blue. Webs cream-coloured.*
IMMATURE: *Paler than adult.*
CHICK: *First down smoky blue-grey. Second down longer and paler.*

MOULT
Begins in last weeks of breeding season, and normally completed by May or June. Precise timing varies amongst age groups.

VOICE
Throaty cooing in burrows and when flying over land at night. Silent at sea.

DISTRIBUTION
Breeds at the Auckland, South Orkney and South Sandwich Islands; Îles Kerguélen; Macquarie, Scott and Heard Islands; and South Georgia. Widespread and often abundant in all cooler waters of the Southern Ocean, except the central Pacific.

RECOGNITION

Medium-sized prion with rather prominent bill. Dark crown and dark eye-patch accent small white eyebrow stripe. Conspicuous collar of dark blue-grey extends over thickset neck. Distinct, open-M wing marking. Tail appears long in relation to head.

At sea, Antarctic prions are gregarious birds, forming huge flocks to feed in plankton-rich areas.

BETWEEN MAY AND SEPTEMBER, winter storms regularly cast young Antarctic prions ashore on the New Zealand mainland. This seabird ranges throughout the cooler waters of the Southern Ocean, except for the central Pacific where there are no islands and food is scarce. But where food is plentiful, such as in the Scotia Sea, it feeds in huge flocks. In the New Zealand region it nests at the Auckland Islands and on Macquarie and Scott Islands. It is not known whether any of these birds fly right around the pole, but young birds explore areas much larger than they will use as adults. Immature Antarctic prions have been seen as far north as Java and as far south as the ice encircling Antarctica.

Although some of the nesting islands of this prion are separated by thousands of kilometres, the breeding schedule remains the same. The birds return to their colonies at night in late October, and from early November they clean out and reoccupy the burrows. Experienced breeders arrive first to defend their nest-sites from other Antarctic prions.

Birds usually nest under *Azorella* cushions, or under tall tussock grass *Poa flabellata*. Where there is soil, they dig tortuous burrows, occasionally over a metre in length. Sometimes the birds nest in rock crevices instead of burrows, particularly in high latitudes where the ground is hard.

The single white egg represents about 22 per cent of the female's total body weight. Birds lay from mid to late December and both sexes incubate the egg in shifts of about three days. Between late January and late February, after about 45 days, the egg hatches. The young spend 43 to 54 days in the nest, fed at night by both parents. A week or so before fledging it usually weighs more than its parents—up to 200 g compared to the adult weight of 118 to 182 g.

At South Georgia the chick is fed chiefly on crustaceans, including *Euphausia superba*, amphipods and copepods. Chicks also eat fish and cephalopods.

Few eggs or chicks die. Some are buried in heavy snow, others starve when there are local food shortages. The main predator is the rapacious southern skua, which catches and eats Antarctic prions in large numbers. They catch their victims at daybreak as they leave their burrows; skuas rarely catch a prion on the wing. At Macquarie Island, the introduced Stewart Island weka and feral cats prey on nesting prions.

After the breeding season, Antarctic prions leave their nesting places for the winter. P.C.H.

Salvin's Prion *Pachyptila salvini salvini* (MATHEWS, 1912)

RECOGNITION

Similar to Antarctic prion, but with longer and wider bill and more conspicuous lamellae fringing upper mandible. Immatures easily confused with adult Antarctic prions.

MIGRANT

OTHER NAMES: *Medium-billed prion, lesser broad-billed prion, Marion Island prion, Crozet Islands prion.*

SIZE: *280 mm.*

DESCRIPTION
ADULT: *Sexes alike. Upper parts blue-grey. Conspicuous black open-M marking over upper wings. Black tip to central tail feathers. Lores white, barred or flecked with dark*

MILLIONS OF SALVIN'S PRIONS breed in the Indian Ocean on Marion and Prince Edward Islands and at Îles Crozet. In the winter adults and young migrate westwards to South Africa and eastwards to Western Australia. Some birds regularly reach New Zealand waters. These are mainly emaciated immature birds that have lost over 40 per cent of their weight since leaving the islands of their birth. The young prions travel further than the adults so that they familiarise themselves with a vast area in which to find food and new breeding locations.

Little is known about the diet, except that it includes krill, amphipods and small squid. P.C.H.

grey. Eye-patch of dark feathers before and under eye. Small white eyebrow. Undersurface white. Iris sepia brown. Bill blue, fairly long and broad. Feet blue. Webs cream-coloured.
IMMATURE: *As adult, but paler.*
YOUNG: *First down dark grey. Second down longer, smoky grey.*

MOULT
Commences during the last weeks of the breeding season, and is normally completed by May or June. Precise timing varies amongst age groups.

VOICE
On land, raucous grating or cooing.

Salvin's prion straggles regularly to New Zealand waters.

Silent at sea.

DISTRIBUTION
Breeds in millions on Marion and Prince Edward Islands and at Îles Crozet. In winter, immatures and some older birds migrate to South Africa to the west and to New Zealand to the east.

One of New Zealand's most abundant petrels, fairy prions occur in offshore subtropical waters. They select rock crevices, caves and burrows for their nest-sites.

Fairy Prion *Pachyptila turtur* (Kuhl,1820)

CIRCUMPOLAR

OTHER NAMES: *Titi-wainui, narrow-billed prion.*

SIZE: *230 mm.*

DESCRIPTION
ADULT: *Sexes alike. Upper parts blue-grey with conspicuous black open-M marking across wings and broad black tip to most of tail feathers. Facial pattern indistinct. Underparts white. Iris sepia brown. Bill short, blue. Legs blue. Webs light grey.*
IMMATURE: *As adult, but with slightly paler plumage.*
CHICK: *First down grey-brown, 15 to 20 mm long. Second down 20 to 30 mm, smoky grey.*

MOULT
After the breeding season, adults disperse into the Tasman Sea for 2 months to moult. Younger birds

moult in December.

VOICE
On land, raucous grating or cooing from the burrows. Less calling on the wing. Silent at sea.

DISTRIBUTION
In New Zealand breeds on the Poor Knights, Trio, Stephens, Brothers, Motunau and Open Bay Islands; The Snares; Chatham and Antipodes Islands; and islets off Stewart Island, Akaroa and Otago. Seen in offshore subtropical waters from North Cape to Foveaux Strait. Other populations throughout subantarctic zone.

RECOGNITION

Common small blue-grey petrel. White underparts. Short, blue bill.

FAIRY PRIONS PATROL THE SEAS in large, loose flocks. They alight on the water only to feed, retrieving their prey in their short beaks. They are voracious feeders, and fill their distensible glandular stomachs with up to 30 per cent of their body weight in food. Their diet is a variety of zooplankton, including amphipods, krill, pteropods and small fish.

Flocks of fairy prions sometimes number a thousand birds, but their blue and white upper parts camouflage them well. If the sun is low, however, it flashes on their white undersurfaces as they dip over a swell, before the birds vanish beyond the crest of a wave.

Fairy prions are one of New Zealand's most abundant petrels, and are seen in offshore waters from North Cape to Foveaux Strait and on their breeding grounds on numerous stacks and islands from the Poor Knights Islands to the Antipodes Islands. They occur in largest numbers east of Northland and in Cook and Foveaux Straits.

Dead birds are often washed onto high tide lines after storms.

Rough seas, poor food supplies in winter and spring, and the loss of fat reserves when battling against westerly winds all contribute to these deaths. This is one of the smallest prions. In good condition it weighs 110 g, but those cast ashore by storms are usually starved and very thin, weighing between 65 and 97 g. Of these storm-killed birds, there are as many males as females, which indicates that winter flocks are composed equally of both sexes.

Fairy prions nest in vast, noisy colonies. At the largest, on Stephens Island in Cook Strait, there are about a million birds. They nest in rock crevices, caves or burrows up to 80 cm long. They line the nest chamber with materials that are easy to carry into the burrows, such as stiff leaves and twigs. Birds in warmer climates begin breeding up to a month earlier than their southern relatives.

From mid-October to late November, depending on the latitude, the birds lay a single white egg. Both parents incubate it for 44 to 50 days in shifts of one to five days, with an average of three days. Incubating birds lose about eight grams in body weight a day. When the nestling hatches, the parents guard it continuously for up to five days, then they desert it by day. Both parents visit their offspring nightly, feeding it soon after their arrival.

At the more southerly islands, moonlight affects the return of the birds. This is probably an old racial instinct to avoid aerial predators, such as the highly successful southern skua which captures and eats large numbers of prions throughout the summer breeding season. Tuataras also devour prions, although more often they snap at fledglings in burrows causing them either fatal injury or forcing them to leave their burrows prematurely. Nevertheless, mortality is usually low on the breeding grounds. About three quarters of hatchlings fledge. The number of fledglings that survive to adulthood, however, is only about six per cent. Summer storms in late January and early February kill many young prions before they can build up their fat reserves and feeding expertise.

Fairy prions can live to be a good age. Two birds banded as adults in 1963 were still raising young in 1982. As prions do not breed successfully until they are four or five years old, these birds were estimated to be at least 23 years old. P.C.H.

Fulmar Prion *Pachyptila crassirostris* (MATHEWS,1912)

Fulmar prions do not range far from their subantarctic breeding grounds. At sea they are characterised by their conspicuous looping flight.

THE FULMAR PRION FEEDS alone or in small groups, taking crustaceans, pteropods, squid and small fish from the sea's surface. It is easily confused with the more common fairy prion. At sea it has a distinctive looping flight and in the hand it can be identified by its larger beak. If the width of the hook of the upper mandible is over 4.5 mm the bird is probably a fulmar prion.

This is the rarest of the three prions that breed in New Zealand. Its populations are small and the birds do not fly far from their subantarctic breeding grounds. Fewer than a dozen fulmar prions have been seen on the main islands of New Zealand.

The fulmar prion nests on lava outcrops or on steep cliffs overlooking the sea, either in the shelter of small rock crevices or in tunnels under the surface. At the Pyramid, in the Chatham Islands, it burrows into the mud nest-mounds of the Chatham Island molly-mawk. Because its nests are often inaccessible, very little is known about the fulmar prion's breeding behaviour. The nest usually consists of a pile of stone chips about two metres away from the crevice opening. The birds lay a single white egg in mid-November and the chick hatches about 46 days later. The fledgling leaves between mid-February and mid-March.   P.C.H.

NATIVE

OTHER NAMES: *Cliff prion, thick-billed prion.*

SIZE: *240 mm.*

DESCRIPTION
ADULT: *Sexes alike. Upper parts blue-grey with conspicuous black open-M marking across wings and* broad black tip to most tail feathers. Facial pattern indistinct. Underparts white. Iris sepia brown. Bill robust, blue. Legs blue. Webs light grey.
IMMATURE: *As adult, but with slightly paler plumage.*
CHICK: *First down grey-brown. Second down longer, smoky grey.*

MOULT
Adults moult after breeding season; non-breeders in December.

VOICE
Gurgling or wheezy squeaking while at nest. Silent at sea.

DISTRIBUTION
Breeds at the Western Chain of The Snares and at the Chatham, Bounty, Auckland and Heard Islands. Straggles to mainland.

RECOGNITION

Separated from the fairy prion by more robust beak. Distinguished at sea by characteristic looping flight.

Grey Petrel *Procellaria cinerea* GMELIN,1789

WHEN IT DIVES FOR FOOD, the grey petrel plunges into the sea from heights of up to eight metres. Its prey is mainly squid, with some fish. It also scavenges among ship's refuse and gathers around whale carcasses and other carrion. One of the few New Zealand petrels that flies over its nesting islands in daylight, the grey petrel can be seen—especially in the late afternoon—interspersing its glides with a strange, rapid wing action, rather like that of a duck.

In New Zealand, it breeds on Antipodes, Bollons, Campbell and possibly Jacquemart Islands. At one time there was a large population of grey petrels on Macquarie Island, but most, if not all of these birds have been killed by introduced cats. Few grey petrels have been banded in New Zealand, but one ringed in 1969 at Antipodes Island was recovered near Wellington in 1977.

This is one of the least studied of Southern Ocean petrels. It breeds in the winter. At Antipodes Island and at Tristan da Cunha the first birds return in mid-February. They lay in April, May and June, and the chicks fly between mid-September and mid-December. At Îles Crozet, the breeding cycle is a little earlier. No displays have been described, but newly arrived birds sit on the top of tussocks and rocks and advertise their presence by calling for long periods.

The grey petrel breeds in colonies and nests in burrows, which it digs in flat or sloping peaty soil that is covered with vegetation. On Campbell Island it breeds on Mount Eboule at 308 m, but on Antipodes Island it nests on the plains and slopes down to 20 m above sea level, and on Bollons Island it breeds in the main ridge. At Antipodes Island, burrows are intermingled with those of the white-chinned petrel.

The burrows are fairly dry and between one and three metres long. In the chamber at the end of the tunnel, the birds build a nest, in which they lay a single white egg. It is not known how long the incubation period is. A young bird that was observed at Îles Crozet flew between 10 and 20 September at about 111 days old. Fleas have been known to infest burrows in which chicks were reared.

At Antipodes, Bollons and Gough Islands skuas kill a few birds, particularly fledglings. Norway rats appear to kill all chicks on Campbell Island.

J.W. & M.J.I.

CIRCUMPOLAR

OTHER NAMES: *Pediunker, brown petrel, great grey shearwater.*

SIZE: *480 mm.*

DESCRIPTION

ADULT: *Sexes alike, but female slightly smaller. Upper parts medium grey. Crown, wings, tail and rump darker, with pale edges to wing coverts. Tail short, wedge-shaped. With wear upper surface becomes brown-grey. Face and sides of neck pale grey. Underparts, including throat white, except underwing, axillaries and long undertail coverts ashy brown. Iris brown. Side of bill grey-green; ridge on top and groove on lower bill black; nail horn-coloured. Feet grey-flesh. Webs yellow-flesh with front edges black.*
IMMATURE: *As adult. In fledgling, feathers of upper surface have pale edges and there are no old brown feathers.*
CHICK: *Down lead grey. Feet flesh-coloured. Webs yellow.*

MOULT

Breeders may shed contour feathers when nesting. Birds arriving back at Antipodes Island between mid-February and March were completing regrowth of flight quills.

VOICE

Short moan followed by explosive, sustained bray, given from ground or prominence especially after sunset.

DISTRIBUTION

Breeds on Antipodes, Bollons, Campbell, Prince Edward, Marion and Gough Islands; Tristan da Cunha; Îles Crozet and Kerguélen; possibly on Jacquemart Island; and formerly on Macquarie Island. Ranges around the subantarctic seas, sometimes extending northwards along cool currents. Not usually seen south of 55°S, but straggles to the Antarctic pack ice. Few sightings at sea around mainland New Zealand, but sometimes beach-wrecked birds found on the coast, especially between September and January.

RECOGNITION

Large, rather stout-bodied grey and white petrel. Uniform grey upper parts. White belly. Dark underwings.

A winter breeder, the grey petrel is one of the least studied subantarctic petrels. Some birds have been seen as far south as the Antarctic pack ice.

Though mainland colonies of the black petrel no longer exist, the breeding population is found on Great Barrier Island and Little Barrier Island.

Black Petrel *Procellaria parkinsoni* GRAY,1862

ENDEMIC

OTHER NAMES: *Taiko, Parkinson's petrel.*

SIZE: *460 mm.*

DESCRIPTION
ADULT: *Sexes alike. Sooty black, becoming browner with wear. Successful breeders often tinged with russet, particularly on belly. Iris dark brown. Bill yellow-horn, dark at very tip; black on lower part of nasal tubes, in front of nostrils, on upper part of lower mandible and skin between horny plates. Feet black.*
FLEDGLING: *Uniformly black. Bill ivory to blue-white, gradually changing to pale yellow-horn during first 5 years.*
NESTLING: *Slate grey down; second down paler and longer.*

MOULT
Birds in heavy wing moult seen in wintering area in April, presumably non-breeders. Breeders moult later, also in wintering area.

VOICE
On the ground, far-carrying, repeated, staccato clack *from unmated birds, mainly males. Heard on Great Barrier Island from November to the beginning of April. Sometimes subdued version when pair meet. Startling honk from chick disturbed on nest. Silent in flight.*

DISTRIBUTION
Breeds on Little Barrier and Great Barrier Islands. At sea, found off North Island, particularly in the outer Bay of Plenty and north and east of East Cape from October to early July. Also present in small numbers in the Tasman Sea, south to about 42°S, and in Tasman Bay. Winters in the eastern tropical Pacific from March to November.

RECOGNITION

Separated from flesh-footed shearwater by darker body, black feet and stronger flight. Similar white-chinned petrel is larger with paler bill. Similar Westland black petrel is larger with darker bill tip.

WHEN HUNTING FOR FOOD the black petrel ranges far from its breeding places. Often it flies over 500 km, seeking its prey of deep-sea squid. It catches these cephalopods at night, when they migrate into surface waters. Most of its prey have organs which give off light, but it is not known if this helps identification. As well as squid, the black petrel eats some fish and scavenges from ships. It does not dive to catch food. Instead, it probably flies above the water and makes shallow plunges.

This was the largest type of muttonbird available to North Island Maoris, and so it was highly valued. Maoris carefully conserved the colonies. The birds were caught in May. A flexible stick, split at the end, was pushed into the burrow until the bird was located. The stick was then twisted in the bird's down and the bird was gently pulled out. It was killed by biting its head; and the stomach, with its oily contents, was cut out with the bill and thrown away. The birds were then plucked, singed, and roasted until the fat was extracted. Afterwards they were placed in a vessel made of totara bark and covered with the fat. Preserved in this way, the meat kept for a long time. Black petrels may still be killed occasionally for food on Great Barrier Island.

Some 800 pairs breed on Great Barrier Island with little interference

from rats and feral cats. There was once a very large colony on Little Barrier Island, but now only about 100 pairs breed there; the birds were almost annihilated by cats. Black petrels also once bred on the lower coastal mountain ranges of the North Island and the northwestern South Island, but these colonies were wiped out by cats, stoats and dogs, and by opossums taking over the birds' burrows.

The breeding season extends from October to early July. The first birds return in the first week of October, but others are as late as the end of November. They nest in burrows, one to three metres long, dug into soil or peat at the top of ridges and often winding among tree roots. On Great Barrier Island the nest is often simply placed in a cavity under overhanging tree roots or in a hollow log. Because so many young birds are killed by cats, such exposed sites are no longer used on Little Barrier Island. The nest chamber is usually spacious and often lined with *Dracophyllum* leaves. The male does nearly all the early work, cleaning out the burrow and bringing the nest material. His mate makes few visits. After mating the birds leave for sea for about 22 days.

They return to lay one white egg, usually between 5 and 10 December. Soon after laying, the male takes over incubation. There are three main incubation shifts, each lasting about 17 days, the female finishing with a short final spell. The birds very rarely desert the egg and most chicks hatch in the first week of February after 57 days.

The parents guard the chick for longer than most burrow-nesting petrels: for most of the first 10 days, one of the parents looks after the chick by day. The feeding routine then settles down to a parental visit every three or four days, each parent visiting once a week. They bring such huge meals that the chick grows erratically to reach over one kilogram. Before it leaves, its weight declines to slightly above adult weight. After about 105 to 110 days, the young petrel departs.

The fledgling is not shown where to take off by its parents. The adults fly from trees projecting above the forest, or other open high points to which they may walk 100 m or more. The chick has to find its own way out of the forest. While its many abortive attempts help develop flying ability, the resulting crashes away from the safety of the nest place the bird in great peril from cats. Most chicks spend part of 7 to 14 nights outside their burrows before they leave successfully.

The chicks leave between April and July, with a peak around 20 to 25 May. They have been found soon after at Auckland, Tokoroa, Lake Taupo, Masterton and Palliser Bay, which suggests that initially they head southeastwards. Very few fledglings are beach-wrecked. Young birds do not revisit the breeding places until they are five years old.

About 300 birds have been banded, in almost equal numbers, from the two colonies. There have been no distant recoveries. One bird banded as an adult was recovered dead after 12 years and two months, and so was at least 17 years old. One banded as a chick was recaptured incubating six years later just 15 m from where it was born. M.J.I.

Westland Black Petrel *Procellaria westlandica* FALLA,1946

ENDEMIC

OTHER NAMES: *None.*

SIZE: *510 mm.*

DESCRIPTION
ADULT: *Sexes similar, female tends to be smaller. Plumage uniformly sooty black. Iris dark brown. Large bill bicoloured, strongly developed dark grey tip contrasting with mainly cream-coloured nostrils, sides and underneath. Legs, feet and claws black.*
FLEDGLING: *As adult, but pale parts of bill white rather than cream.*

MOULT
Wing and tail moult completed by April. Body feathers replaced in March, April, May, September.

VOICE
From the ground or burrow, a wide variety of harsh calls and cackles mostly coo-roo-rah. *Does not normally call in flight.*

DISTRIBUTION
Breeds only on west coast of the South Island, south of Punakaiki River. During breeding season, from March to November, ranges over continental shelf waters between Cape Egmont and Foveaux Strait to the west, and between East Cape and Banks Peninsula to the east. From December to March, whereabouts unknown.

RECOGNITION

Largest of all burrow-nesting seabirds. When resting on the water, floats high, like a gull, giving it a distinctly 'fat' appearance. Large contrasting cream and dark grey bill separates it from white-chinned petrel.

OVER THE LAST 20 YEARS, the Westland black petrel has doubled its population to well over 9000 birds. An abundance of food and a lack of predators—both animal and human—probably account for this large increase.

In 1966, big trawlers started to fish regularly off the west coast of the South Island. Such large-scale fishing expanded until, in 1977, around 120000 tonnes of fish were caught within 200 km of the Westland black petrel's breeding grounds south of the Punakaiki River. The result is that fish waste now forms the bulk of its diet during the breeding season, and is frequently fed to chicks. However, it has not entirely replaced other sources of food: these birds still eat pelagic squid, and are often seen feeding at night on planktonic crustaceans.

Although there are wild cats and dogs, as well as wekas, stoats, weasels and black rats in the vicinity of the breeding colony, they do not prey on adult Westland black petrels. Occasionally, cats eat chicks, but the adult birds are so strong and ferocious that they repel animal attackers.

For most of the year, its sea range is the continental shelf just north of the subtropical convergence. The only records away from New Zealand are from eastern Australia and Chile. From December to March, its habitat is unknown. During this time it moults its flight feathers.

The Westland black petrel breeds on low coastal hills of soft siltstone. Nests are mostly located below 200 m, on the steep sides of valleys, usually underneath tall forest with a dense understorey of lianas.

The breeding season, longer than that of many other petrels, is from February to December. In mid-February the first few birds return to clean out and extend the burrows, and by mid-March most males have returned. In April the males visit the colony at least twice a week and stay for periods of up to four nights. They occupy their burrows on as many nights as possible to re-establish ownership of their burrows. There is much fighting between males with burrows and those without.

The females visit the colony much less frequently than the males and rarely stay for more than 24 hours. During the three weeks before they lay they rarely come ashore at all. The males continue to visit the colony, although less often and for shorter periods than in early April. This allows them to gain weight for the first incubation shift.

Egg-laying dates are remarkably constant from year to year. Females begin to lay from 12 May, with a peak around 23 May, and by the end of May most birds have laid. Both parents incubate the white egg, with the male taking the first shift, if he is on land. Many males remain ashore from early May, so that they will be there when the females return to lay.

The egg hatches between 15 and 27 July, with a peak between 20 and 26 July, after an average of 64 days incubation. After it hatches, the parents guard the chick continuously for about two weeks, although this guard stage sometimes varies from a few days to six weeks.

The young fledge over an extended period, from 5 November to 26 December. In recent years most birds have left between 18 and 22 November. Chicks that leave in December are probably the progeny of inexperienced parents. Most chicks leave at about 125 days old, but some chicks are much older than this. This long period of chick development may be partly the result of irregular feeding. Both parents feed the chick—sometimes on the same night—but on average each parent returns to the colony only once every three nights.

Westland black petrels do not always breed every year. One or two successful years may be followed by a break of one or two years, during which the birds visit the colony without breeding. In other cases, they lay an egg but later desert it. The weight of adults in years when they do not breed seems normal. Throughout the breeding season the population on the breeding grounds is made up of breeding birds and their chicks, failed breeders, burrow-holding pre-breeders, pre-breeders without burrows, and non-breeding adults which have previously bred. There are always far more non-breeding than breeding adults. 　　　　J.A.B

Today, the Westland black petrel has no human predators, though many birds were once caught for food: by Maoris, between 1600 and 1820, and later by miners.

White-chinned Petrel *Procellaria aequinoctialis* LINNAEUS,1758

CIRCUMPOLAR

OTHER NAMES: *Shoemaker, Cape hen.*

SIZE: *540 mm.*

DESCRIPTION
ADULT: *Sexes alike. Sooty black, browning with wear. Chin usually white, sometimes few white feathers, occasionally none. Bill pale horn colour; black in front of nostrils and on groove of lower mandible; dark at very tip and on lower edge of nasal tubes. Feet black.*
FLEDGLING: *Black. Chin as adult. Bill ivory to bluish horn, with dark parts as adult.*
CHICK: *Down long, grey-black at first, then slate grey. Feet grey, gradually darkening.*

MOULT
Little known, except that it takes place during winter between breeding seasons.

VOICE
Chattering trill from non-breeders and unmated birds on ground. Rarely calls in flight.

DISTRIBUTION
Breeds at the Auckland Islands on Auckland, Adams and Disappointment Islands; at the Campbell Islands on Campbell, Dent and possibly Jacquemart Islands; and at Antipodes Island. Also at South Georgia; the Falkland Islands; Marion and Prince Edward Islands; Îles Crozet and Kerguélen; and Inaccessible Island. Sea range extends from the Antarctic convergence at about 55°S to about 30°S, particularly in winter, and to about 10°S off Chile and Peru. Around New Zealand, much more abundant to the south and east than in the Tasman Sea; reaches latitude of Cook Strait in summer, and the far north in winter.

RECOGNITION
Large black petrel with pale bill. Lazy and powerful flight. Often follows ships. Paler bill tip distinguishes it from very similar Westland black petrel.

AN ALTERNATIVE NAME FOR the white-chinned petrel is the shoemaker. This refers to its chattering call which may sound like a cobbler stitching a shoe. The bird produces this high-pitched trill by vibrating its throat with the beak wide open and pointing slightly upwards. On summer nights at the nesting islands non-breeding birds fill the air with their chorus, calling from the ground, either outside their burrows or from tussock tops.

The white-chinned petrel ranges throughout the southern oceans in the subantarctic zone, feeding mainly on squid, but also on some fish and crustaceans, such as medium-sized rat-tail fish, large amphipods and shoaling crabs. These animals are caught at night when they come near the surface. Presumably the white-chinned petrel flies above the surface, plunging into the water when it sights its prey. But, as with other feeding petrels, its foraging habits are a mystery. It also makes shallow dives to scavenge refuse thrown off ships.

During the breeding season white-chinned petrels begin arriving at the nesting places in the afternoon. Most fly silently above until it is dark; some land and hurry to their burrows to avoid southern skuas. Calling begins after dusk when more birds arrive and most land.

The tunnels vary in shape and are between one and two metres long. The birds dig into peaty hummocks or hillsides which offer better drainage in the frequently waterlogged terrain. Even so, water often lies at the entrance or flows through part of the burrow. To protect the nest, built in a spacious chamber, the birds mound up earth—the wetter the site, the more they raise the nest. The number of nests to a site depends on the terrain: on the plains they are spaced out, but on well-drained hillsides they may be closer together.

At Marion Island and Îles Crozet, the birds breed from mid-September to early May and at South Georgia, Îles Kerguélen and Antipodes Island, about two weeks later.

At Îles Crozet they court and mate for a month from mid-September to mid-October, when about a third of the nests are occupied each day. The birds visit the colony for between one and six days, the females spending more time at sea than the males. After they have mated, the birds feed at sea for two or three weeks.

They return to the nest to lay a single white egg. At Antipodes Island, over half the female birds lay between 26 November and 3 December, but at Îles Crozet most birds lay earlier, between 8 November and 22 November.

Both parents share the incubation. About four days after laying the male takes over. The main incubation spells range from four to 13 days with an average of 12.5 days for males and 8.5 days for females. Each bird has three or four spells. At Îles Crozet as many as 75 per cent of eggs are deserted and do not hatch.

If the parents have stayed on the nest, the egg hatches after about 58 days. The parents guard the nestling for only two to four days. At Possession island, in some years, rats have killed nearly half the young on the parents' departure. When they are about 59 days old, the chicks reach a maximum weight of 1200 to 1740 g. They leave at about 94 days old, slightly below adult weight, between 920 and 1230 g.

At some colonies, such as on Antipodes Island, southern skuas attack white-chinned petrels when smaller prey, such as prions, small *Pterodroma* petrels and little shearwaters are scarce. Because of their size, the adult birds are a match for skuas, unless the skuas attack in pairs, which they have learnt to do on Antipodes Island.   M.J.I.

A white-chinned petrel crouches in its nesting burrow in moist soil, its large white egg left exposed. The birds breed in summer.

North Atlantic Shearwater

Calonectris diomedea borealis CORY,1881

VAGRANT

OTHER NAMES: *Cory's shearwater, Mediterranean shearwater.*

SIZE: *480 mm.*

DESCRIPTION
ADULT: *Head and hind neck grey-brown, faintly mottled. Rest of upper parts mainly dark brown, with pale edges to most feathers. Quill feathers of wing and tail, primary coverts and scapulars black. Long upper tail coverts with white tips. Underparts* mainly white except underwing irregularly edged with dark brown, particularly on primaries, and faint grey-brown barring on axillaries, flanks and sides of undertail coverts. Tail slightly wedge-shaped. Iris brown. Bill dull yellow, brownish just behind tip. Feet pale flesh; outer toe, sides of joints and webs dusky.

MOULT
Takes place outside breeding season, between September and February.

VOICE
Flight call kaa-ough, uttered 3 or 4 times. Very noisy at breeding grounds at dusk and dawn. Silent at sea.

DISTRIBUTION
Breeds on islands in the North Atlantic, then migrates to South Atlantic. Recently sighted well out from Africa in southwest Indian Ocean. Straggles to New Zealand.

RECOGNITION
Very large shearwater. Browner upper parts, white underwing and yellowish bill separate it from grey petrel.

The North Atlantic shearwater is a rare vagrant to Australasian seas.

AFTER NESTING ON ISLANDS in the North Atlantic Ocean, this shearwater journeys south to spend the northern winter in the South Atlantic and Indian Oceans. The few birds that were carried well beyond their normal range to New Zealand in 1934 and 1979 were presumably caught up in the prevailing westerlies south of 35°S.

Generally North Atlantic shearwaters are gregarious birds at sea. Their flight is powerful, with slow wing-beats and long glides. In strong winds, they 'shear water' with the tips of their wings and soar upwards. They dive rarely, but plunge just beneath the surface to catch squid and fish. Sometimes they follow ships, scavenging among refuse.

At sea this bird is silent, but on its breeding islands it is a typically noisy shearwater. It nests mainly at low altitudes, often not far above sea level. It places its poorly made nest in rocky niches, under rocks, in caves, occasionally in burrows or sometimes on the ground under thick vegetation. From April the birds arrive back at their colonies. They mainly lay during a brief period in late May and early June, and the eggs hatch in July. When they are about three months old, at around the end of October, the young shearwaters leave the colony. From late November to March the breeding grounds are deserted.

Traditionally local people have harvested thousands of well-grown young birds, and now eggs and adults are also taken.　　　　M.J.I.

Buller's Shearwater

Puffinus bulleri SALVIN,1888

BULLER'S SHEARWATERS RARELY dive for their food. They alight on the water with wings half open and lunge this way and that to catch and gulp down their swift-moving prey of fish and crustaceans. They fly close to the surface, using their broad wings and long tails to wheel slowly and glide.

This seabird is seen rarely from the New Zealand mainland but it breeds in enormous numbers on the Poor Knights Islands. In late August and early September large flocks return from the North Pacific. In October, the birds pair and prepare the nesting burrows. Usually they reclaim the same burrows they have used in previous years. These are normally dug in soil and are one to one and a half metres long, but sometimes they are located in rocky crevices. The birds vigorously defend their burrows from intruders and invariably the long term occupants win any territorial dispute.

About 26 October the birds mate. The females leave for a month, although the yolk part of the egg takes only 18 days to form. The birds return to lay during the last days of November. Both parents incubate the egg in shifts of four or five days. In late January the chick hatches.

The parents feed the young bird on regurgitated fish, krill *Nyctiphanes australis* and, occasionally, small cephalopods. When they are about 90 days old, between mid-April and the first week in May, the fledglings leave the islands.

The Buller's shearwater usually vigorously reclaims the nesting burrow it has used the year before.

Until the early nineteenth century Maoris lived on the Poor Knights Islands and hunted the young shearwaters. Since the early 1920s the islands have been a Flora and Fauna Reserve. Pigs, feral since the Maoris were killed by another tribe, preyed heavily on the birds and disrupted their breeding burrows. In 1936 the pigs were exterminated and since then this shearwater has increased considerably. Now the only predators are tuataras which share the shearwater burrows.　　　P.C.H. & M.J.I.

RECOGNITION
Large, slender body, with broad wings. Grey upper parts with conspicuous dark open-M marking across wings and back. Dark cap. Long, wedge-shaped, dark-tipped tail. White underparts. Flies with slow wing-beats, even in light winds.

ENDEMIC

OTHER NAMES: *Grey-backed shearwater, New Zealand shearwater.*

SIZE: *460 mm.*

DESCRIPTION
ADULT: *Sexes alike. Crown and upper hind neck sooty brown. Lores, ear coverts, lower hind neck, sides of neck, scapulars, secondaries, greater wing coverts, upper tail coverts, rump and flanks mouse grey or darker, with* paler edges to most feathers. Primaries and their coverts black. Middle and lesser wing coverts black-brown. Tail quills black except 2 side ones mouse grey. Underparts and underwing white. Iris dark brown. Nasal plates, top and tip of bill black; side of bill blue-grey; bottom of bill blue. Outer leg and 2 outer toes black; inner parts flesh-blue. Webs cream to mauve-grey.
IMMATURE: *Pale edges to mantle and wing feathers. Tips of undertail coverts often flecked with grey.*

YOUNG: *First down long, grey; paler below. Second down smoky blue-grey.*

MOULT
Adult birds moult after breeding. Non-breeders moult in summer.

VOICE
Braying and howling in the air and on the ground at the breeding colonies. Silent at sea.

DISTRIBUTION
Over 2 million nest on the Poor Knights Islands, the only known breeding place. Solitary birds found in burrows on 2 islands off eastern Australia, and prospecting for burrows at the Three Kings Islands. During winter migrates to subtropical North Pacific, although exact movements not known. Non-breeders seen in summer on coasts of the North and South Islands as far south as Banks Peninsula; to the Chatham Islands in the east; and Farewell Spit and Greymouth in the west. Other non-breeders summer off Peru and Chile.

The wedge-tailed shearwater breeds on all islands of the Kermadec Group. Its call has been likened to the growls and snarls of brawling cats.

Wedge-tailed Shearwater *Puffinus pacificus* (GMELIN, 1789)

NATIVE

OTHER NAME: *Black burrower.*

SIZE: *460 mm.*

DESCRIPTION
ADULT: *Upper parts mainly sooty brown; feathers of back and wings with paler edges; primaries and tail quills black. Undersurface usually dusky brown; paler on chin, throat and foreneck. Some birds have white underparts from throat to belly; and white underwing with broad dark edges and dark axillaries. Iris brown. Bill dark lead colour, with* black tip. Legs, webs and toes white-flesh colour.*
NESTLING: *Dark ash grey, with throat and breast paler.*

MOULT
In the wintering area.

VOICE
Deep growl followed by shorter, high-pitched snarl, rendered as ka-koo-er or kuk-oo-kuk.

DISTRIBUTION
Breeds on all the Kermadec Islands, on islands off eastern and western Australia, and on innumerable islands and islets throughout the Indian and Pacific Oceans, in the tropics and subtropics. Occasionally, single birds beach-cast on the North Island west coast. Dark birds found at Otaki in June 1962, at Waiuku in November 1966, and on the Auckland west coast in April 1978 probably came from the Kermadec Islands, Norfolk or Lord Howe Islands or from eastern Australia. Pale birds found on the Wellington west coast in January 1962 were probably from the North Pacific. Wedge-tailed shearwaters from the Kermadec Islands spend June to October in the southeastern North Pacific.*

THE CACOPHONY OF CALLS that arises from a colony of wedge-tailed shearwaters resembles the yowls and snarls of an alley of cats. Birds on the ground produce this discordant sound; once in the air, they are usually silent.

In October, after wintering in the North Pacific, wedge-tailed shearwaters return to their breeding grounds on the Kermadec Islands. A few birds are seen over nearby seas in August, but they are probably on their way to Lord Howe Island or eastern Australia, where wedge-tailed shearwaters breed up to two months earlier.

These shearwaters nest in burrows in deep, crumbly, often sandy soil. The tunnels vary in length from half a metre to two and a half metres. The birds clean out the burrows and remake their nests from October to about 25 November, then they leave the colonies to feed at sea for about three weeks. At the Kermadec Islands they begin laying about 12 December, reaching a peak on 17 or 18 December, and by the end of the month the birds have finished laying.

Both sexes alternately incubate the single, white, ovoid egg for 50 to 55 days. Usually the chick hatches during the first half of February. The young leave after about 90 days, mainly during May, with the last fledglings departing in the first week of June. The adults desert their offspring before they can fly, leaving the chicks to live on their fat reserves while they complete fledging.

Cyclones occasionally wreak havoc in the breeding colonies, flooding burrows, blocking them with rubble, or even obliterating them. In such conditions, up to half the eggs and chicks may be destroyed. In the years that follow such damage, more birds than usual forego the burrows and lay on the surface.

Little is known about the wedge-tailed shearwater's feeding habits. It eats cephalopods, fish and crustaceans which it takes from near the surface. It feeds in flocks, both at night and during the day, with other tropical seabirds, but especially with sooty terns.

Cats and rats have killed many birds on Raoul Island. At other colonies, where there are no introduced predators, these shearwaters have no evident enemies. M.J.I.

Flesh-footed Shearwater

Puffinus carneipes GOULD, 1844

AROUND DUSK AND DAWN flesh-footed shearwaters hunt small squid, crustaceans and little fish. During the day they catch small fish driven to the surface by larger, predatory ones, and trail boats (especially fishing vessels) to feed on scraps and waste thrown overboard. Usually they take their food from near the sea's surface, but they also dive and steal bait from fishing lines.

Essentially birds of warm waters, they range around the North Island during the breeding season, from September to May, and even wander as far south as the subtropical convergence.

After the breeding season they migrate northwards and winter in the North Pacific near east Korea and Japan, and off the west coast of North America. Some non-breeders remain off California well into the northern summer, though they probably return in the same year to the southwest Pacific. As they have also been seen in the western North Pacific in August, a month before they return to New Zealand, most probably do not follow a circular migratory route in the North Pacific.

In the last few days of September they return to their breeding places. They nest in burrows that are usually about one metre long, although sometimes they are twice that length. Usually these burrows are close together as on Coppermine and Karewa Islands, but on some islands, such as Hen Island, they are interspersed among burrows of other species. Sometimes grey-faced petrels share the same burrows or compete for the use of them.

The tuatara lizard also lives on some of its breeding islands, for example Hen and Chickens, and Kerewa Islands. Shearwaters and tuataras often share the same burrows. Tuataras apparently use the shearwater burrows for shelter from enemies and extremes of temperature, and for finding food.

Between mid-November and mid-December, the birds lay a single white long-oval egg. Usually this hatches during January. The parents guard the chick for up to three days then they leave it alone during the day. Initially the adults feed the chick about every second night but these visits become less frequent as the chick grows and becomes able to take as much food as its parents can bring. The young fly in late April and early May, at about 92 days old.

Flesh-footed shearwaters have few predators. Until recently, Maoris hunted well-grown young birds for food. Now virtually all the nesting places of this shearwater are wildlife reserves and muttonbirding only occurs illicitly, if at all. Kiore rats live at most colonies but are little more than scavengers. Adult flesh-footed shearwaters frequently become hooked up in fishing lines, particularly long-lines, when stealing baits, and sometimes they are netted during tuna-trawling operations in the Bay of Plenty.　　　M.J.I.

The flesh-footed shearwater at sea is an active surface feeder and scavenger.

NATIVE

OTHER NAMES: *Pale-footed shearwater, toanui.*

SIZE: *450 mm.*

DESCRIPTION
ADULT: *Sexes alike. Body brown-black, slightly paler on face and underparts; darkest on head. Quill feathers of wing and rounded tail sooty black. Bill pale cream, with top and tip brown. Feet flesh-coloured, with webs pale brown at tips.*
JUVENILE: *As adult.*
NESTLING: *Sooty grey, paler below. Bill blue-grey, darker at tip. Feet flesh-grey.*

MOULT
Presumably at winter quarters.

VOICE
On the ground and sometimes in the air, repeated short gug, followed by hoarse crooning ku-koo-ah, stressed in middle. This is repeated 3 to 6 times, becoming increasingly strident until the koo becomes a scream and finally a rapidly dying splutter. Quiet cackles from courting birds. Less calling on moonlit nights.

DISTRIBUTION
Breeds on the Hen and Chickens; the Mercury and Aldermen Islands; Karewa Island in the western Bay of Plenty; the main Sugar Loaf Island off New Plymouth; and in small numbers on Trio and Titi Islands in Cook Strait. Elsewhere breeds in large numbers on Lord Howe Island; on many islands off the southwestern coast of Australia; and on Île St-Paul. During the breeding season ranges around the North Island, wandering as far south as Foveaux Strait and the Chatham Islands. New Zealand and Lord Howe Island birds winter in the North Pacific.

RECOGNITION
Buoyant, slow-flapping flight and all-dark underwing distinguish it from sooty shearwater. Dark face, pale bill and less soaring flight separate it from grey-faced petrel. Similar flesh-footed shearwater has browner plumage, pale feet, less powerful flight and more rapid wing-beats.

Though wide-ranging, the Christmas Island shearwater is not a common bird.

Christmas Island Shearwater *Puffinus nativitatis* STREETS, 1877

RECOGNITION
Sooty brown shearwater. Dark bill and legs. Short, rounded tail. Differs from sooty shearwater in smaller size and entirely dark underwing; and from wedge-tailed and short-tailed shearwaters in smaller size and less pointed wings. Light and graceful flight and, unlike short-tailed shearwater, seldom banks steeply. Wing-beats stiffer and faster than in wedge-tailed shearwater.

VAGRANT

OTHER NAMES: *Christmas shearwater, black shearwater.*

SIZE: *350 mm.*

DESCRIPTION
ADULT: *Uniformly dark. Upper parts sooty brown; underparts slightly lighter. Throat sometimes grey. Tail short, rounded. Iris brown. Bill black. Legs dark brown.*
NESTLING: *Sooty black down.*

MOULT
Breeding birds begin to moult primary feathers during last week or two of feeding chicks. Rest of moult takes place after leaving colony.

VOICE
Described as 'humphing and barking'.

DISTRIBUTION
Breeds on the Hawaiian, Line and Phoenix Islands; Îles Tuamotu and Australes; and Ducie and Henderson Islands. One specimen found ashore near Dargaville.

THIS SHEARWATER BREEDS on islands over a large area of the tropical and subtropical central Pacific Ocean. But nowhere is it a common seabird and its world population is small. Many of its traditional breeding sites were disrupted during the Second World War when essential breeding cover was removed as vegetation was cleared for airports and military installations. The introduced vermin which accompanied the military occupation are still preventing the populations from recovering.

Usually the Christmas Island shearwater feeds close to its breeding islands, mostly on small fish up to 8 cm in length and squids. On rare occasions, small crustaceans are taken. It does not appear to migrate and the only sighting in New Zealand is of a single bird that was found ashore near Dargaville in February 1976. Probably this was carried south by a tropical storm.　　　D.E.C.

Although they may be seen alone at sea, on land sooty shearwaters are a highly social species, particularly at nesting places after dark.

Sooty Shearwater *Puffinus griseus* (GMELIN, 1789)

THE SOOTY SHEARWATER FLIES fast with stiff wings, swooping high above the sea. Sometimes, when it banks to descend, its white underwings flash in the sun. Near the surface it often intersperses this soaring flight with a few quick wing-beats, although it also glides, without any apparent effort, just a few centimetres above a heaving sea. In calm weather it beats its wings more often and flies close to the surface. If the sea is still and the weather sunny, a raft of these brown seabirds resting on the surface looks from a distance like a slick of oil.

At sea the sooty shearwater is seen either alone or, particularly when it has found a shoal of fish or crustaceans, in a flock. The birds assemble over a shoal and attack the fish together, often with white-fronted terns joining in the melee. They dive under water and chase their prey by swimming with powerful strokes from their flexed wings. In New Zealand seas sooty shearwaters feed mainly on squid, small shoaling fish, amphipods, krill and *Munida*. In the North Pacific they eat squid, anchovies and sand eels.

At sea this shearwater is at home in cold to temperate waters. On land it breeds on exposed headlands and islands where it can burrow into the soil beneath grasses, herbs or trees.

The sooty shearwater once bred on many headlands of mainland New Zealand and still nests around Banks and Otago Peninsulas. But these remaining mainland colonies seem doomed as mammalian predators such as cats and stoats take their toll. The sooty shearwater breeds successfully in small numbers on many islands off the coast, such as at Hen and Chickens; White, Motuhora, Kapiti, Mana, Stephens, Open Bay, Taieri and Green Islands; and at the Three Kings, Gavalli, Mokohinau, Aldermen and Trio Islands. However, the largest numbers of what is probably New Zealand's most abundant breeding bird are on islands around Stewart Island. Where the soil is strong enough this highly social bird breeds within a metre of other birds and a single island may contain millions of sooty shearwaters.

Most birds remain with the same partner and return to the same nest each year, but there is also a good deal of change and at least 16 per cent of birds change partners between breeding seasons. A few birds return to the breeding colony at three years old, but usually not until they are four years old. Some probably start breeding at six years old.

Birds are active after dark at their nesting sites, although at the Snares they come ashore in broad daylight. Young pre-breeders are particularly busy. One bird preens the head of another or, while one bird preens itself, it allows another to preen it too. This may lead to mating.

The breeding season

At The Snares the first birds appear overhead about 11 September. They alight about 10 days later and start to refurbish their nesting burrows. A few birds nest on the surface in caves or under boulders, but most nest in a chamber at the end of a burrow up to one and a half metres long. They line this sparsely with leaves, twigs or sticks. Some birds leave during the first three weeks of November but return to lay a single white oval or elliptical egg about 22 November. Further north at Taieri Island they lay about a week later. Both sexes incubate the egg in shifts that vary from three to more than 12 days. The relieved bird usually leaves just before daylight on the night its partner appears.

After 53 days, the egg hatches. The parents brood the chick for the first day and night, then gradually desert it during the day. They feed the chick on the day of hatching, but then irregularly. Some meals are so large that the chick's weight doubles overnight. But during the last three weeks of the feeding period the parents bring smaller meals. Well-fed chicks are heavier than their parents when the adults leave to begin their migration northwards. When their parents have left, the chicks lose weight and come out from their nests after dark to exercise their wings. Most young leave the breeding grounds in the last week of April or the first week of May.

After the breeding season, the sooty shearwater migrates to spend the southern winter in the North Pacific. In late March the non-breeding or 'unemployed' birds probably form the van of the migration. In the first half of April successful parents form the main body of the northward exodus and often can be seen from headlands along the Southland and Otago coasts. The last of these successful adults are joined by fledglings from about 20 April to mid-May.

Some authorities believe the birds fly in a clockwise direction around

the periphery of the Pacific Ocean. If this is the case, the birds fly up the western side of the Pacific, past Japan where they are common offshore in May and June. They then drift gradually eastwards across the North Pacific where they feed and moult. This brings them to the waters off British Columbia, from where they travel southwards. Huge flocks are seen off California in August and September before their return to the southwest Pacific. When the birds cross the tropics they fly fast and do not feed.

But not all sooty shearwaters fly around the edges of the Pacific Ocean. Some birds have been seen flying northwest in the central Pacific near Hawaii in March, April and May, and southwards from September to November. Like other migrating sooty shearwaters, they flew singly and appeared neither to rest nor feed.

Some pre-breeders remain in northern waters during the southern summer, possibly a few also stay behind in the southwest Pacific during the southern winter. Sooty shearwaters are also present in coastal waters off South Africa throughout the year, especially in the winter, but it is not yet known whether any of these are New Zealand birds. A few sooty shearwaters are seen flying westwards in summer along the ice-edge between about 60°S and 70°S in the Australian Antarctic sector. The origin of these birds is also not known.

Although this is a powerful and aggressive shearwater, it sometimes falls victim to attacks by southern skuas and northern giant petrels. Sometimes the chicks are emaciated and small boned compared with normal fledglings because of food shortages. In May 1961 a 'wreck' of such young birds occurred along the South Canterbury coast.

Muttonbirding

Of all the various petrels serving as 'muttonbirds' in New Zealand this is the most important. The Maoris around Stewart Island still harvest squabs for sale and for their own consumption. They extract the birds' fat and sell it for soap-making, lubricating oil and other purposes. The feathers are also sold to Europeans.

Muttonbirding begins on 1 April. Formerly the birders travelled by sea, but now many hire a helicopter. For the first four weeks or so the young birds are captured in their burrows. If the birder is unable to reach the chick by thrusting in an arm, a hole is dug above the place where the nesting chamber is reckoned to be, the bird taken out, and the hole carefully plugged with the sod that was removed. Towards the end of the season, during the first three weeks of May, the birds are taken at night. The lighted torches of totara bark once used have been replaced with electric torches. The birds are usually killed by a blow on the head with a stick, care being taken not to injure the body.

The down and feathers are removed and the birds hung up overnight. Next day the wings, legs and head are cut off and the birds split open, cleaned and dry salt rubbed in. In this condition they are packed in casks until they are transferred to large tins. Preserved like this, the birds keep for a year or more. A second method of preserving the birds is to cook them in their own fat.

Preserved birds are boiled until they have softened and the salt has been removed. Then they can be roasted.   J.W.

RECOGNITION
Larger and darker than short-tailed shearwater, with longer bill and, usually, white lining to underwing. Separated from larger flesh-footed shearwater by dark bill, pale wing lining and dark feet; from wedge-tailed shearwater by short, fan-shaped tail, pale wing lining and dark feet.

NATIVE

OTHER NAMES: *Titi, New Zealand muttonbird.*

SIZE: *430 mm.*

DESCRIPTION
ADULT: *Sexes alike. Upper parts black-brown with wing quills and tail blacker. Underparts grey-brown with pale grey bases to many feathers, particularly on chin, throat and belly. Underwing grey, mottled with black-brown along edges; coverts in centre white or grey-white with dark shafts. Undertail grey-brown. Iris dark brown. Bill rather slender, grey-black. Legs flattened at sides, black-brown on outside, purple-flesh colour on inside. Webs purple-flesh colour.*
IMMATURE: *As adult.*
NESTLING: *First down dark grey above, slightly paler below. Bill light blue-grey. Second down appears at about 8 days old, slightly darker than first down. Feathers first show at 31 to 35 days on scapulars and rapidly spread elsewhere.*

MOULT
At the northern wintering grounds. Adult birds have been found in various stages of wing and body moult between May and August. Others, found moulting as early as February, were probably pre-breeders.

VOICE
Asthmatical croonings when courting on the ground, sometimes described as ku-ah-ku-ah-ku-ah-krek, with emphasis on the outbreathed ku. *Sometimes this rises to hysterical screams in ardent males, before ending abruptly. Females often voice quieter, lower-pitched calls as duets with their partners. At sea flocks cackle over shoals of fish.*

DISTRIBUTION
In New Zealand region, headquarters the islands around Stewart Island. Breeds in small numbers on many islands around the coast: Three Kings Islands; Cavalli Island; Hen Island, Mokohinau and Aldermen Islands; White Island, Rurima Rocks, Motuhora Island; Kapiti and Mana Islands, Stephens Island, The Trios; Open Bay Island off Jackson Bay; Green and Teieri Islands near Dunedin. Further offshore breeds on the Chatham, Antipodes and Auckland Islands; The Snares; and on Campbell, Solander and Macquarie Islands. Also breeds on islands near Cape Horn; at the Falkland Islands; and on islands off Tasmania and New South Wales. Winters in the North Pacific.

A powerful and aggressive shearwater, the sooty shearwater is very sensitive to interference during incubation.

Short-tailed Shearwater *Puffinus tenuirostris* (TEMMINCK, 1835)

Perhaps Australia's most abundant bird, the short-tailed shearwater is a regular straggler to New Zealand shores.

MIGRANT

OTHER NAMES: *Tasmanian muttonbird, slender-billed shearwater.*

SIZE: *400 mm.*

DESCRIPTION
ADULT: *Sexes alike, but female slightly smaller with more slender neck. Mainly brown-black above, slightly paler on throat and underparts. Wing quills and short, rounded tail black. Underwing coverts grey. Iris brown. Bill rather short, lead grey. Legs grey-black to grey-brown and often flesh-coloured on inside. Webs grey.*
IMMATURE: *As adult.*

MOULT
Wing and tail feathers moulted in North Pacific at end of post-nuptial migration.

VOICE
Silent in flight. On the ground squealing, crooning and sobbing notes uttered in rhythmical sequence.

DISTRIBUTION
Breeds on islands off the southeastern Australian coast, in Bass Strait and around Tasmania. Winters in the North Pacific, around the Aleutian Islands and in the Arctic Ocean to 71°N. Straggles to mainland New Zealand, Raoul Island and Macquarie Island.

> **RECOGNITION**
>
> Smaller and paler than sooty shearwater with shorter, darker bill, and no white patch on underwing. Dark legs, short bill and short tail separate it from wedge-tailed shearwater; smaller size, dark beak and dark legs from flesh-footed shearwater.

THIS SHEARWATER, WHICH BREEDS in vast colonies on islands off Tasmania and the southeastern coast of Australia is a common visitor to New Zealand.

In late April and early May, short-tailed shearwaters fly swiftly north to winter in the North Pacific and Arctic Oceans. Sometimes, in May and June, young birds at the start of their migration are washed onto New Zealand beaches. In August the adult birds start to return south, with immatures and non-breeders following later, although some probably remain in northern seas. At the end of this long flight, many birds, especially immatures, die in the seas off southeastern Australia. Often the birds have been facing headwinds and presumably have found feeding difficult. In some years large numbers are also wrecked on New Zealand shores, especially on the west coast. This was the case in October and November 1968, when many dead birds were washed onto Southland beaches and around Waikanae after persistently strong westerlies.

Occasionally in midsummer, flocks of short-tailed shearwaters fly offshore from mainland New Zealand in the Hauraki Gulf and Bay of Plenty. At the same time of year some birds are also washed onto New Zealand beaches.

Breeding birds arrive back at their islands in the last week of September. They keep the same partner and nest-site each year. After mating the birds leave for sea. They return to lay one egg about 25 November. Both sexes incubate in long stints of 10 to 14 days for a total of 53 days. The parents feed the chick at night, frequently at first, less often later, and finally desert it for about 14 days. The chick leaves at about 94 days old between the third week of April and the first week of May, after its parents have begun their northward migration.

Short-tailed shearwaters feed on crustaceans, small pelagic fish and cephalopods. J.W.

Manx Shearwater *Puffinus puffinus puffinus* (BRUNNICH, 1764)

VAGRANT

OTHER NAME: *Common shearwater.*

SIZE: *350 mm.*

DESCRIPTION
ADULT: *Sexes alike. Upper parts, including wings and tail slate black. Chin, throat, breast and belly white. Black upper parts and white underparts merge into grey on side of neck and upper breast. Underwing white with dark tip and rather broad dark trailing edge. Leading edge of underwing grey owing to mottled slate grey feathers which sometimes extend as triangle towards centre of wing. Long axillaries blunt ended, white with black or grey tips. Under-tail coverts white with side ones dusted or banded with black on outer webs; central coverts black towards tip. Thighs black. Iris dark brown. Bill slate black, paler on lower mandible. Webs and inside of leg pink; outside of leg and outer toe pink and black; other toes and claws black.*
JUVENILE: *As adult.*

MOULT
Main wing moult occurs in winter quarters after breeding.

VOICE
Cu-cu, coo-er *over breeding places.*

DISTRIBUTION
Breeds on islands in the North Atlantic and migrates to the South Atlantic. One straggler reached the Wellington west coast in June 1972.

> **RECOGNITION**
>
> Upper parts blacker than fluttering shearwater. Slightly larger than Hutton's shearwater. Rather stiff-winged flight with much turning and gliding. In the hand identified by white underwing coverts with grey leading edge.

The Manx shearwater is normally confined to the Atlantic Ocean.

IN JUNE 1972, an immature male Manx shearwater was found dead on the Wellington west coast. The only other specimen to reach Australasia was one recovered in South Australia. Presumably, these birds were blown across the Pacific on westerly winds from their wintering grounds in the South Atlantic. They breed on islands in the North Atlantic, then in July they begin the long migration towards South America. The adults return northwards between late February and early April, but immature birds sometimes remain in the South Atlantic until they are four years old.

On the wing the Manx shearwater, a medium-sized shearwater, is easily confused with the fluttering shearwater and with Hutton's shearwater. In fact, the three species are so similar that some authorities believe them to be members of the same species.

The Manx shearwater eats small fish and cephalopods. J.W.

Hutton's shearwaters gather at the entrance of a snow-covered burrow in the Seaward Kaikoura Range. Dry snow tussock lines the nest chamber.

Hutton's Shearwater *Puffinus huttoni* MATHEWS, 1912

ENDEMIC

OTHER NAMES: *Titi, pakaha, muttonbird.*

SIZE: *360 mm.*

DESCRIPTION
ADULT: *Sexes alike, but female probably smaller. Upper parts dark brown, extending below eye and onto side of lower neck. Wing and tail quills black. Underparts white. Underwing coverts mottled white and light brown to grey with dark shafts. Long axillaries slightly pointed, brown, and occasionally white-tipped. Side undertail coverts flecked with brown. Iris brown. Bill long, slender, dark grey. Inside of leg light pink to dark pink and mauve; outside of leg dark grey. Feet pink.*
JUVENILE: *As adult.*
NESTLING: *First down mid-grey; second down light grey.*

MOULT
Breeders begin in mid-March; non-breeders and failed breeders in early February.

VOICE
On breeding grounds and during nightly flights to and from the land to the ocean, rapid cackling calls kouw-kouw-kouw-kouw-kee-kee-kee-kee-aaah. *Pairs chuckle to each other inside burrows. High-pitched piping from chick, to which parents respond with deep croon.*

DISTRIBUTION
Breeds abundantly in the Seaward Kaikoura Range and possibly on the Inland Kaikoura Range. Absent from breeding grounds from mid-April to end of August. At sea found abundantly throughout spring, summer and early autumn from Otago Peninsula to Cook Strait and the Wellington west coast. Winters in Australian seas. Some birds present on Kaikoura coastal waters April to August.

landmarks. If these are obscured, they become disorientated. From September to March, when southeasterly storms with thick fog and cloud envelop the Kaikoura Ranges, the shearwaters crash regularly.

After the breeding season, some Hutton's shearwaters migrate to Australian seas. It is possible that they circumnavigate Australia. Birds have been found along the coast from northern Queensland, down to Garie, near Sydney in New South Wales, west to Bunbury, Western Australia, and recently in the north of Western Australia. Non-breeders have reached the shores of Tasmania.

At sea, this bird is very quiet, apart from an occasional excited cackle when it is feeding. But at its breeding grounds and during its nightly flights to and from its feeding grounds, it is extremely noisy. From September to February, the breeding grounds sound like a large poultry farm when the hens are laying, with the birds in the air and about the burrows calling incessantly.

Like other petrels, Hutton's shearwaters probably begin breeding in their third or fourth year. The first birds arrive at their breeding burrows during the last week of August and the first week of September. By mid-September, vast numbers are ashore at night even though in some seasons the burrows are deeply covered by snow. Some burrows are occupied continuously from mid-September. The birds clean the burrows throughout September and early October.

The burrows vary in length from 0.6 m to 2.5 m. The nest chamber is a little bigger than the approach tunnel. The birds line the nest with dry snow tussock and white shearwater feathers. The same nests are used year after year.

The birds mate during the second and third weeks of October and lay mainly during the last week in October and the first two weeks in November. When heavy snow falls the birds delay laying for up to a fortnight. Young birds without a burrow lay on the surface.

The chick hatches between the end of December and mid-January, after about sixty days. The parents guard it continuously for the first few days, then leave it alone in the burrow during the day. From an average hatch weight of about 65 g the chick grows rapidly to as much as 600 g five weeks later—nearly double the weight of its parents. Most young birds fledge in mid-March, when they are about 80 days old. Sometimes fledging is delayed by snowfalls.

In the nineteenth century, Maoris on the Kaikoura coast regularly harvested Hutton's shearwaters in the nearby ranges. Stoats now account for many birds, but fortunately the lack of a reliable food in the winter, when the shearwaters are absent from the breeding grounds, keeps the stoats at a level compatible with the birds' survival. New Zealand falcons take some birds when they return to the ocean just before dawn on moonlit mornings.   G.H.

HUTTON'S SHEARWATER BREEDS only on the South Island. It nests in burrows among tall snow tussocks and clumps of low alpine scrub between 1200 m and 1800 m above sea level.

During the breeding season, from the end of August to mid-April, it feeds along the east coast of the South Island, usually no further than 70 km from the shore. Sometimes as many as 20 000 birds flock along the Kaikoura coastline, within a few metres of the shore. In summer the bird favours the sheltered bays of Banks Peninsula, although it also forages along the open coastline. It eats small fish, which it catches by diving with wings half outstretched. Late in the day, before its nocturnal flight back to the nesting grounds, the birds flock on the surface of the water about a kilometre offshore just north and south of Kaikoura Peninsula, east of the breeding sites.

They find their way back to their breeding grounds by local

Fluttering Shearwater *Puffinus gavia* (FORSTER,1844)

ENDEMIC

OTHER NAMES: *Pakaha, Forster's shearwater.*

SIZE: *330 mm.*

DESCRIPTION

ADULT: *Sexes alike. Upper parts black-brown, becoming browner with wear. Primaries, secondaries and tail almost black. Undersurface white. Underwing coverts white, except leading edge mottled grey-brown. Axillaries grey-brown, almost square-ended and white-tipped. Side of head to well below eye and side of neck grey-brown, with indistinct boundary between dark upper parts and white underparts. Iris brown. Bill mainly lead-coloured, black on top; lower mandible purplish with black tip. Feet dull flesh colour, brown on outside of tarsus and on outer toe. Claws black.*

FLEDGLING: *Often grey bloom to upper surface just after leaving burrow.*

MOULT

In February and March after breeding. Particularly vulnerable during wing moult in stormy conditions.

VOICE

Flight call is ka-hek *like the cackle of a fowl, repeated about 6 times with increasing tempo and ending in a slurred note. Higher pitched than the call of the sooty shearwater but lower pitched than that of the little shearwater. Similar calls from the ground at breeding colonies.*

DISTRIBUTION

Breeds only in New Zealand on the Three Kings, Poor Knights and Moko-hinau Islands; Hen and Chickens; Saddle Island, and possibly others off the west coast of Great Barrier Island; islets off the east coast north of Auckland; numerous islands and islets in the Bay of Plenty including Mercury and Aldermen Islands, and Rurima Rocks; East Island off East Cape; Cook Strait Islands including Stephens Island, the Chetwode and Trio Islands; and several islets within the Marlborough Sounds. At sea extends as far south as South Canterbury during autumn and winter and very rarely to near the Chatham Islands. Some, mainly young birds, migrate to eastern Australia in winter and stay into early summer. Stragglers reach New Caledonia and Vanuatu.

RECOGNITION

Rather small, dark brown and white shearwater. Larger and browner than the little shearwater. Distinguished in the hand from similar Hutton's shearwater by white underwing and undertail coverts; and square-ended and white-tipped axillaries.

THE FLUTTERING SHEARWATER FLIES with rapid, stiff wing-beats, interspersed with very short glides, usually close to the water's surface. It catches its food by diving, sometimes from the air, but more often from the surface. In fact, it spends more time settled on the sea, in groups or flocks, than most other shearwaters and petrels. Under water it pursues its prey to depths of over 10 m, propelling itself with feet and wings.

There is no detailed study of its diet, but observations show that it eats small coastal fish, particularly pilchards and sprats, as well as coastal krill. Each winter, flocks of fluttering shearwaters invade Wellington harbour and plunge into the murky depths in pursuit of small fish. Red-billed gulls, white-fronted terns, gannets, flesh-footed shearwaters and Buller's shearwaters often feed with fluttering shearwaters.

The fluttering shearwater inhabits inshore or continental shelf waters, rather than the open sea. It breeds only in New Zealand, on well-vegetated islands and islets from Cook Strait to the Three Kings Islands in the north. In August the first birds come ashore. They prepare nesting burrows which are up to two metres long or simply cavities under rocks. Between early September and mid-October, perhaps even later, they lay a single, white, oval egg. Both sexes share incubation, probably for about 53 days. The chick usually hatches during November, and remains in its burrow until late January or February, and occasionally until early March.

Maoris once hunted the young, but this is now illegal and has virtually stopped. On Little Barrier Island feral cats destroyed a colony of fluttering shearwaters. Cats and Norway rats annihilated a large colony on Motuhora Island; rats still infest the island and possibly prevent the shearwaters from recolonising it. During the breeding season, the birds sometimes call at night as they fly along the shores of Motuhora Island, but none have been observed on the ground since 1925. In the winter bad weather kills some birds, mainly young ones, and their corpses are cast onto beaches. M.J.I.

The fluttering shearwater breeds only in the New Zealand region and nests mainly in burrows in fairly dense colonies on well-vegetated islands.

Little Shearwater
Puffinus assimilis
GOULD, 1838

ENDEMIC
Kermadec Little Shearwater
P.a. kermadecensis MURPHY, 1927.
North Island Little Shearwater
P.a. haurakiensis FLEMING &
SERVENTY, 1943.

NATIVE
Subantarctic Little Shearwater
P.a. elegans GIGLIO & SALVADORI,
1869.

VAGRANT
Norfolk Island Little Shearwater
P.a. assimilis GOULD, 1838.

OTHER NAMES: *Allied shearwater,
whistler.*

SIZE: *300 mm.*

DESCRIPTION
ADULT: *Upper surface slate to slate-
black, with grey bloom in fresh
plumage. Underparts, including lores,
face, underwing and undertail coverts
white. Axillaries white, sometimes
with grey spots. Division between
black above and white below slightly
mottled or freckled grey. Iris dark
brown. Bill black along top, light blue
to lead-coloured on sides. Feet light
blue, with outer margin of outer toe
and claws black. Webs pale yellow to
flesh-coloured.*
NESTLING: *Dark grey above. Abdomen,
band from throat to abdomen white.*

MOULT
At sea, after the breeding season.

VOICE
*High-pitched cackling call wah-i-
wah-i-wah-i-wah-ooo, given from
the air, the ground and burrows.
Subantarctic little shearwater calls
series of high-pitched notes, almost
whistles, in closely repeated sets of
about 4 syllables.*

DISTRIBUTION
Kermadec little shearwater:
*Breeds on the Herald Islets off Raoul
Island; on Macauley, Haszard,
Curtis and Cheeseman Islands; and
possibly on Raoul Island. Young
birds beach-cast on the west coasts of
New Zealand.*

North Island little shearwater:
*Breeds on islands off the northeast
coast of the North Island at Hen and
Chickens; Stephenson Island; and the
Cavalli, Poor Knights, Mokohinau
and Mercury Islands. Ranges from
about North Cape to Bay of Plenty.
Rarely straggles south to Hawke Bay.*

Subantarctic little shearwater:
*Breeds in small numbers on Star
Keys and Little Mangere Island in
the Chatham Islands; and in huge
numbers on Bollons, Archway, Inner
Windward, and probably Outer
Windward and Leeward Islands in
the Antipodes. Ranges widely over
adjacent seas, to the South Island,
the vicinity of the Bounty Islands
and to Auckland Islands.*

Norfolk Island little shearwater:
*Breeds on islets off Norfolk and Lord
Howe Islands.*

Small numbers of the North Island little shearwater breed on islands off the northeastern coast of the North Island.

THIS SMALL, BLACK-AND-WHITE shearwater keeps close to the sea's surface, and in choppy seas stays inside the troughs of waves. It flies with rapid wing-beats interspersed with short glides, diving often to catch squid, crustaceans and small fish.

It nests in burrows that vary in length from a third of a metre to two metres. The birds dig these tunnels in well-drained soil or peat, or among rocks. At the northern end of its range, the little shearwater begins breeding in the winter, but further south, the subantarctic little shearwater does not start breeding until the spring. The northern birds return to their colonies between January and March. They clean the burrows in April and May, then throughout the courtship and incubation periods they gradually build a nest from small amounts of leaves, twigs and grasses.

There is no accurate information on incubation and fledging times for New Zealand little shearwaters, but the subspecies *Puffinus assimilis tunneyi*, which breeds in Western Australia, incubates its egg for 52 to 58 days and rears the chick in 70 to 75 days. At first the parents feed the chick frequently, even twice nightly. But after a few days, the adults stay away during the day, and seven to 10 days before the fledgling departs, the parents abandon it altogether.

The breeding birds are away from the colonies for only one to three months. During this period they moult. On the whole this is a sedentary species, with no long-distance migrations, although possibly the subantarctic little shearwater ranges widely across the subantarctic.

There are four subspecies of little shearwater found in New Zealand: the Kermadec little shearwater, the North Island little shearwater, the subantarctic little shearwater, and the Norfolk Island little shearwater.

The Kermadec little shearwater breeds on the Kermadec Islands and feeds in the surrounding seas. In November and December, immediately after the breeding season, young birds are frequently washed ashore on the coasts of the North Island. Possibly they summer just west of mainland New Zealand. This subspecies is identified by the pattern of dark spots on the axillary feathers. Birds lay from about 10 June to the end of July, with a peak at the end of June. The fledglings leave between mid-October and the first week in December. Feral cats kill a few birds at the breeding grounds.

The North Island little shearwater breeds in small numbers on islands off the northeastern coast of the North Island. Usually it flies alone or in pairs and is slightly larger than the Kermadec bird. It lays from early July to mid-August and the fledgling departs in November and December. As well as crustaceans and fish, it also eats small cephalopods such as the young octopod *Argonauta*. Kiore eat deserted eggs and young chicks.

The subantarctic little shearwater breeds on Gough Island and at Tristan da Cunha as well as on islands off New Zealand. Over 100 000 pairs nest on the Antipodes Islands and about 150 pairs breed on the Chatham Islands. It also visits the Auckland Islands, but does not breed there. Birds which may have come from the Antipodes Islands occur in the southeastern Pacific. This bird differs from the other New Zealand subspecies in that the feathers of its neck, back, upper wing coverts, secondaries, and upper tail coverts are edged with white. This is most apparent in newly fledged birds and least noticeable in adults in worn plumage. The crown is darker than the back and this darkness extends to just below and behind the eye. The lores are speckled. The long axillaries have grey tips.

The subantarctic little shearwater lays between the end of August and 10 October, with a peak about the middle of September. The young fledge in January and February. Their food includes krill and young *Nototodarus* squids. At all of its breeding places, southern skuas attack the subantarctic little shearwater and on Bollons and Archway Islands they are the predominant source of food for the skuas.

The Norfolk Island little shearwater occasionally wanders to the west coast of Auckland from its breeding places off Lord Howe and Norfolk Islands. It is smaller, with less grey on its axillaries.   M.J.I.

RECOGNITION
Small, black-and-white shearwater, much darker above
than fluttering, Hutton's and
Manx shearwaters.

Leach's Storm Petrel *Oceanodroma leucorhoa leucorhoa* (VIEILLOT, 1817)

OTHER NAMES: *Fork-tailed storm petrel, Leach's petrel, Leach's fork-tailed petrel.*

SIZE: *190 mm.*

DESCRIPTION
ADULT: *Mainly black-brown with grey bloom in fresh plumage. Darkest on crown, lesser upper wing coverts, primaries and their coverts, outer secondaries and tail. Browner below. Pale grey-brown diagonal bar on upper wing. White rump patch partly divided by central dark line. Throat and face slate. Underwing ash grey. Tail forked. Iris dark brown. Bill and feet black.*

MOULT
After breeding. Quill feathers replaced first, often while migrating.

VOICE
Two main calls given at colonies at night: chatter is rapid sequence of 8 or more staccato notes, last ones a slurred trill, given in flight or on ground; chirr is continuing sequence of rising notes which, after an ik, start again at the lower pitch, given from ground.

DISTRIBUTION
Breeds on islands in the North Pacific from northern Japan to Alaska, western Canada and western USA, and in the North Atlantic from the northeastern United States, eastern Canada, Iceland and the Faeroe Islands to northwestern Scotland and Norway. Migrates south to winter in the tropics of both oceans. Non-breeders present all year in the tropical Central Pacific. Rare visitor to New Zealand.

RECOGNITION

At very short range, all-black feet and forked tail separate it from Wilson's storm petrel. Flight faster and stronger than that of Wilson's storm petrel, and does not skip or patter on sea.

Leach's storm petrel attracts mates with aerial displays and frequent calls.

THIS SEABIRD OF THE northern hemisphere winters in the tropics of the Atlantic and Pacific Oceans. Often, it travels as far as 15°S and, very rarely, it straggles to New Zealand. A dead bird was cast ashore on the west Auckland coast in August 1922, two birds were blown by storms in April and August 1978, and two more birds reached the Chatham Islands in November 1980. The last two are the only Leach's storm petrels ever recorded coming voluntarily to land in the southern hemisphere. Both gave typical courtship calls to attract mates.

Leach's storm petrel breeds in colonies, mostly on small offshore islands that are unlikely to be invaded by predators such as rats. The bird nests in burrows, mainly in soil or among rocks, arriving at its breeding islands in late April or early June. It lays in June or July and the egg hatches between July and early September. The chick fledges between mid-September and late November at 63 to 70 days old.

The bird's diet consists largely of zooplankton and small fish. It is most likely a nocturnal feeder and, probably to assist digestion, consumes pellets of pumice and, nowadays, plastic.

Storms kill some birds, particularly when they are moulting their flight feathers. At night gulls kill many Leach's storm petrels around the breeding colonies. Introduced mammals, such as rats, cats, dogs and foxes also threaten the birds.   M.J.I.

Wilson's Storm Petrel *Oceanites oceanicus* (KUHL, 1820)

Wilson's storm petrels dabbling for their staple diet of krill.

OTHER NAME: *Wilson's petrel.*

SIZE: *190 mm.*

DESCRIPTION
ADULT: *Sexes alike. Brown-black with grey bloom in fresh plumage. Darker on crown; browner below. Pale diagonal wing-bar across upper wing coverts. Inner secondaries pale. White rump. Sometimes bases of belly feathers white. Iris dark brown. Bill and feet black. Webs orange-yellow with black edges.*
JUVENILE: *Similar to adult but white edges to belly feathers and white spot on ear coverts, which fade with wear.*
NESTLING: *Uniformly grey-black.*

MOULT
Adults moult during non-breeding season in wintering area. First-year birds moult in early summer.

VOICE
Normally silent at sea but sometimes twitters when feeding in a flock. Also twitters at breeding colonies, but main call, from nest or ground nearby, is monotonous grating chirp.

DISTRIBUTION
Breeds at many places on the coast of Antarctica and adjacent islands, particularly on the Antarctic Peninsula, the Ross Sea coasts and other places free of ice in summer. Also breeds on South Georgia; the South Shetland and South Orkney Islands; Heard Island; Îles Kerguélen; and around Tierra del Fuego. Winters in the extreme east and west central Pacific, the Indian Ocean and the North Atlantic to about 45°N. Migrates past New Zealand in small numbers.

RECOGNITION

At close range rather long, yellow-webbed feet extending beyond square tail distinguish it from Leach's storm petrel. In the Tasman Sea pale upper wing-bar separates it from dark white-bellied storm petrels.

AFTER THE BREEDING SEASON, the Wilson's storm petrel migrates northwards from its Antarctic and subantarctic nesting sites. Birds from the Ross Sea and colonies south of Australia apparently fly to the tropical Indian Ocean, to the seas immediately north and northwest of Australia, and to near the Marshall Islands. Most travel to the west of Australia, but some fly through the Tasman Sea and wind-drifted birds reach New Zealand. Altogether, about 40 Wilson's storm petrels have been sighted in New Zealand seas or found on beaches, mainly between March and May when the birds migrate north or in November and December when they return south.

This is the only Antarctic petrel that protects its young from predators by nesting only in holes and crevices. Usually it breeds in rocky areas, such as scree slopes, where it builds a nest of small pebbles with shells and bones from earlier nests. Sometimes nests become ice-bound. At low latitudes, where peat or soil are available, birds dig burrows and line the nests with fragments of plants.

The first birds return to the colonies between 5 and 11 November. In late November or December, they lay one egg which both parents incubate alternately for a total of about 42 days. In Antarctica most chicks leave the colonies in March at about 54 days, but at the more northerly colonies, where the breeding season is up to one month later, the fledglings depart in April. Skuas eat many Wilson's storm petrels and in high latitudes bad weather kills many chicks.

In the Antarctic, krill are the staple diet of the Wilson's storm petrel, although it also eats amphipods, small squid and small fish. Occasionally, it also scavenges at mammal carcasses, behind ships and at whaling operations for waste oil. It most likely takes the same prey in its winter quarters. When alarmed it releases a reddish oil which it stores in its stomach. Birds feed mainly in the open sea, but also close to the edge of continental shelves, particularly on migration.   M.J.I.

Grey-backed Storm Petrel *Garrodia nereis* (Gould, 1841)

THE GREY-BACKED STORM PETREL never strays far from its subantarctic breeding islands. It visits its nesting grounds virtually all year round, returning only at night.

The breeding season extends from August to March, a month later at the southern colonies. It nests on the surface in grass or sedge tussocks, at the base of flax, among ferns, under any other covering vegetation or in crevices. Sometimes nests have an entrance tunnel, but many do not. Usually burrows are spaced well apart and often they are hard to find. The nest itself is made from leaf fibres.

Often it shares its breeding grounds with other storm petrels. At the Chatham Islands it nests with white-faced storm petrels; on Gough Island it breeds among white-faced and white-bellied storm petrels; and at numerous places it nests with black-bellied storm petrels. But the grey-backed storm petrel does not compete with these birds for nest-sites. They are all burrowing or hole-nesting species and the grey-backed storm petrel nests in crevices only occasionally. However there is often competition among grey-backed storm petrels for nests, and so two or even three eggs may be laid in the same nest. When this happens often none survive.

The birds begin laying in late September, but some do not lay until late December. The white egg, speckled with red near the larger end, represents about 30 per cent of the bird's weight. Both parents incubate the egg for 39 to 45 days, in stints that average about five days. The incubation period varies as the birds may desert the egg for short periods during bad weather. Sometimes the birds abandon the egg more frequently and when this happens the egg dies. The chick leaves at any time between January and March, when it is about 50 days old. When it departs, it usually weighs the same as an adult bird.

Skuas, harriers and, in the Falkland Islands, short-eared owls eat grey-backed storm petrels, but none of these predators threaten the colonies. Because of their small size and exposed nests, however, grey-backed storm petrels are very vulnerable to introduced predators and in some cases these have driven the birds off the larger islands of their breeding archipelagos.

The grey-backed storm petrel's food is almost entirely crustacean zooplankton. Chicks are fed a small amount of regurgitated krill and amphipods, but mainly the well-grown young of the stalked barnacle *Lepas australis*. The free-swimming young of this barnacle live in the subantarctic and grow exceptionally large before settling and forming shells. It is probably the only barnacle that could provide enough food for a storm petrel. By feeding on this barnacle during the breeding season, the grey-backed storm petrel competes little for food with other storm petrels.   M.J.I.

CIRCUMPOLAR

OTHER NAMES: *None.*

SIZE: *180 mm.*

DESCRIPTION
ADULT: *Head, nape, neck, upper breast, much of upper wing and outer edge of underwing grey-black, becoming browner with wear, especially on forehead. Mantle, scapulars, median wing coverts, rump and upper tail coverts grey, paling towards rear. Feathers of mantle have white edges or tips, especially when fresh, and dark shafts. Usually narrow white tips to secondaries and some inner primaries. Tail square, feathers pale grey, with broad black tips, less prominent on side feathers. Rest of undersurface white, with some grey mottling on flanks and undertail coverts. Iris dark brown. Bill and feet black.*
CHICK: *Dark grey down.*

MOULT
Breeding birds moult February to May.

VOICE
Generally silent. Low, regularly repeated wheezy chirp, like that of an insect, uttered by unmated birds on nests or on ground.

DISTRIBUTION
Breeds at the Auckland, Antipodes, and Chatham Islands; and probably on islets off Campbell Island. Also breeds at the Falkland Islands; South Georgia; Gough and Prince Edward Islands; and Îles Crozet and Kerguélen. Inhabits subantarctic waters, extending near or into the Antarctic zone at South Georgia and Îles Kerguélen. Ranges north to the subtropical convergence and as far as 30°S near New Zealand. Often seen in the southern Tasman Sea.

RECOGNITION
Small, dark storm petrel with white belly. Darting flight in wave troughs. Usually seen alone at sea.

The grey-backed storm petrel will often share its breeding ground with other storm petrels. A surface nester, it does not compete for burrows as nest-sites.

White-faced Storm Petrel *Pelagodroma marina* (LATHAM, 1790)

ESSENTIALLY A BIRD of the open ocean, the New Zealand white-faced storm petrel is sometimes seen in coastal waters during the breeding season, from August to March. With both legs lowered and thrusting together, it flaps its wings occasionally and bounds from wave to wave as if on springs. Once the young have fledged, the birds migrate east, then northwards to the eastern tropical Pacific. When travelling out in the ocean, their flight is slightly erratic, but swift and purposeful. They fly close to the surface, their long legs retracted.

White-faced storm petrels feed mainly at night on crustaceans and small fish that migrate to the surface. Feeding is more difficult when the moon is bright, as fewer animals come to the surface.

They breed in colonies which vary in size from a few hundred pairs to over a million pairs on Rangatira Island in the Chatham Islands. In the north the birds return in mid-August, and in the south about two to four weeks later. They nest in burrows usually not more than half to one metre in length. They prefer well-drained sites and prepare a nest of leaves at the end of the burrow. In the north most lay in the last two weeks of October, at the Chatham Islands in the first two weeks of November, and in the south between early November and early December. The elliptical egg is white with red spots at the larger end.

Both sexes incubate in spells of one to nine days, most spells lasting four or five days. Often the parents desert the egg for up to four days, so that the incubation period varies between 45 and 59 days. If uninterrupted, incubation probably lasts about 40 to 43 days, as is the case with other storm petrels.

For about the first two and a half days after hatching, the parents guard the chick. It is then left alone for increasingly longer periods, and after about the tenth day, parents return only to feed the chick at night. In the week before the chick leaves, the parents feed it half as often and bring smaller meals. At 30 days the chick weighs between 62 and 67 g. This declines to about 50 g when it fledges at about 57 days.

When food is scarce, the chicks become torpid and use less energy to increase their chances of survival. In the southern colonies, skuas kill many birds. Whole colonies have been destroyed by rats in the northeast, by cats on Pitt Island and by wekas on islets off Stewart Island. Maria Island was recently invaded by rats, but they were poisoned before they eliminated the storm petrels. Lizard Island has been invaded by kiore from nearby islets.

In the Chatham Islands the legs of these birds are sometimes tied together with filaments. This is caused by a parasitic flatworm *Distomun filiferum* whose intermediate host is the krill *Nematoscelis megalops*. The flatworm's filaments become entangled round the birds' legs when they are feeding on shoals of krill. In some years, when infestations are severe, many birds have both legs tied together by numerous entangled flatworms, and many die after becoming entangled in ferns and creepers at the breeding grounds.

There are three subspecies of the white-faced storm petrel found in New Zealand. The most common is the New Zealand white-faced storm petrel, which breeds on many islands off the three main islands, as well as on the Chatham and Auckland Islands. The Australian white-faced storm petrel occurs on migration off the far north of New Zealand from April to June. It differs from the New Zealand race in having more white on the face and sides of the breast, and an almost square tail. The rare Kermadec storm petrel is found around the Kermadec Islands. This subspecies is similar to the Australian race, but differs from all other white-faced storm petrels in having a white rump. It is most likely that Kermadec storm petrels are merely young Australian white-faced storm petrels. M.J.I.

ENDEMIC
New Zealand White-faced Storm Petrel
P.m. maoriana MATHEWS, 1912.
Kermadec Storm Petrel
P.m. albinclunis MURPHY & IRVING, 1951.

VAGRANT
Australian White-faced Storm Petrel
P.m. dulciae MATHEWS, 1912.

OTHER NAMES: *Takahi-kare-moana, frigate petrel, J. C. bird, skipjack, dancing dolly.*

SIZE: *200 mm.*

DESCRIPTION
ADULT: *Sexes alike. Crown grey-black, browning with wear. Neck, sides of neck and mantle grey-brown. Feathers of back, scapulars and* upper wing coverts dark brown, with paler edges. Rump and upper tail coverts usually pale grey, but white in Kermadec storm petrel. Primaries and their coverts, secondaries and tail brown-black. Forehead, lores, wide stripe above and behind eye white. Band in front and below eye brown-black. Undersurface white, except sides of breast grey, and undertail coverts usually white with some grey markings. Iris dark brown. Bill and feet black. Webs pale yellow.
NESTLING: *Long, pale grey down.*

MOULT
In the wintering quarters: adults from May to August; younger birds later.

VOICE
Silent in flight. Main call, often duetted, has been rendered as scratchy tiu-tiu-tiu, tiu-tiu, tiu-tiu-tiu, tiu-tiu. *Twittering and cooing from birds in burrows. Mouse-like squeaks from birds on ground.*

DISTRIBUTION
New Zealand white-faced storm petrel: *Breeds on the Poor Knights, Cavalli, Mokohinau, Mercury, Aldermen, Auckland and Chatham Islands; numerous islands around Stewart Island; the Noises; Cow and Motuokino Islands off Coromandel; Sentinel Rock in Cook Strait; Motunau Island in Bay of Plenty; Motunau Island off Canterbury; and Motumahunga Island, New Plymouth. Winters in the eastern tropical Pacific off Peru, Ecuador and Galapagos Islands.*

Kermadec storm petrel: *Breeding grounds unknown, but found only close to the Kermadec Islands and once off eastern Australia. Possibly these are • yearling Australian white-faced storm petrels.*

Australian white-faced storm petrel: *Breeds on islands off western, southern and eastern Australia. Birds presumably from eastern colonies migrate past northern New Zealand in autumn to winter between the Kermadec Islands and Fiji. One beached on the west coast near Auckland in May 1983.*

> **RECOGNITION**
> Pale bird with white underparts and grey upper parts. No white rump, except in rare Kermadec storm petrel. When retracted, feet extend beyond slightly forked tail. Skips off water using feet.

The white-faced storm petrel is particularly vulnerable to such predators as skuas, rats, cats and wekas.

Black-bellied Storm Petrel *Fregetta tropica* (GOULD, 1844)

Black-bellied storm petrels breed in scattered nests, visiting them after dark.

CIRCUMPOLAR

OTHER NAMES: *None.*

SIZE: *200 mm.*

DESCRIPTION
ADULT: *Sexes alike, though female tends to be larger. Upper parts grey-black with black on head and wing and tail quills. Rump white. Throat and undertail black. Chin sometimes mottled white. Usually central line down belly black, but sometimes belly streaked with black, and sometimes almost entirely white. Rest of underparts white, except black leading wing edge. Iris dark brown. Bill and feet black.*
CHICK: *Long, dark grey down.*

MOULT
After migration to the tropics.

VOICE
Thin high-pitched whistle, lasting about 4 seconds at or inside nest-site. Softened version from pair on nest.

DISTRIBUTION
Breeds at the Auckland, Antipodes, South Shetland, South Orkney and South Sandwich Islands; Bouvetoya; Prince Edward and Heard Islands; South Georgia; and Îles Crozet and Kerguélen. Winters in the tropical and subtropical Pacific, Indian and Atlantic Oceans. Straggles to the Solomon and Samoa Islands, Îles Marquises and northern Peru.

RECOGNITION

Tail square to slightly rounded. Black line on belly separates it from white-bellied storm petrel but line often difficult to see and not always present. Sometimes follows ships. Skips off sea using feet.

ALTHOUGH THE BLACK-BELLIED STORM PETREL nests on many islands in the South Pacific, South Atlantic and Indian Oceans, it breeds in large numbers at only a few places, such as on Elephant Island in the South Shetlands and Prince Edward Island. In the New Zealand region it nests on the Auckland and Antipodes Islands where it shares its breeding places with grey-backed storm petrels. On these islands its nests are scattered widely so that, although at first the birds seem scarce, their numbers are thought to be large.

The breeding season extends from September to May. Some breeders return in early September, but most do not appear until after mid-September. The black-bellied storm petrel visits its breeding places only after dark. At the Antipodes and Auckland Islands it uses rather short burrows in well-drained sites such as peaty hummocks or in the banks of streams. But at the South Shetland and South Orkney Islands, where there is little soil and vegetation, it nests in rocky niches.

Like other petrels, the male spends more time than the female at the nest before laying. He continues to visit the nest even when the female goes to sea to feed for eight to 15 days.

Between mid-October and the end of January the female returns to lay one, elongated-oval egg that is white with minute black, grey and brown-red spots and faint red streaks around one end. The egg makes up over a quarter of the female's weight.

The parents share the incubation equally in shifts of about three days. Very few birds desert the egg. When they do, it is usually because of bad weather, such as heavy snow which can cover nest-sites at high latitudes. After 38 to 44 days the chick hatches and the parents guard it for a day. Unless snowdrifts block the entrance to the nest or storms delay their return, the parents feed the chick almost every night. By the time it is 23 days old the young bird weighs more than the adults. If food is not available the chick goes into a torpid state. Normally the young petrel fledges after 65 to 71 days, between February and April. Southern skuas kill a few birds at the breeding grounds.   M.J.I.

White-bellied Storm Petrel *Fregetta grallaria* (VIEILLOT, 1818)

NATIVE

OTHER NAMES: *None.*

SIZE: *190 mm.*

DESCRIPTION
ADULT: *Head, upper breast and most of upper surface sooty black, mantle feathers with white tips when fresh. Throat feathers have white bases. Usually rump, lower breast, belly, undertail coverts and central underwing coverts white, with some grey flecking on flanks and undertail, and edge of underwing black. Sometimes rump, lower breast, belly and undertail coverts black with white bases to feathers, or colouring between these two extremes. Iris dark brown. Bill and feet black.*
CHICK: *Long, grey down.*

MOULT
Not known.

VOICE
Monotonous shrill piping call from ground or nest.

DISTRIBUTION
Breeds at Macauley and Curtis Islands in the Kermadec group; Tristan da Cunha; Lord Howe; Gough and Rapa Islands; Archipielago Juan Fernandez; and probably at Islas San Felix and San Ambrosio. At sea seen north of New Zealand, east of Northland and off Farewell Spit. Storm-blown specimens found in Northland and near Wanganui. After breeding, apparently disperses northwards into the tropics.

RECOGNITION

Most birds have white belly and rump. Tail square; feet do not project in flight. Darker birds rarely seen, except near Lord Howe Island. Lack of bar on upper wing separates it from Wilson's storm petrel. Fast and sometimes erratic flight. Sometimes uses its feet to skip off the sea.

The elusive white-bellied storm petrel at the entrance to its burrow.

IN 1966 THE WHITE-BELLIED STORM PETREL was discovered breeding in New Zealand when a dead fledgling was found on Macauley Island. No live birds were sighted, but this is not surprising as at all of its breeding islands nests are scattered and often hard to find.

Because of its elusiveness and probably its rarity, little is known about the breeding habits of this storm petrel. On Lord Howe Island it nests in burrows about 35 to 40 cm long. Elsewhere it nests in rocky crevices and cavities. In January, and probably later, it lays one egg that is white with pink or red spots at the larger end. The young birds leave the breeding grounds between late April and July.

Virtually nothing is known of its food, but probably, like many other storm petrels, it eats krill and myctophids.

The classification of this species needs more study. The typical race breeds in the eastern South Pacific. Larger birds—almost the size of black-bellied storm petrels—breed on Rapa and Gough Islands and on Tristan da Cunha. At Lord Howe Island, half the birds are darker than other white-bellied storm petrels. A small colony may survive on an islet off Île Saint-Paul in the Indian Ocean.   M.J.I.

The New Zealand diving petrel generally breeds on small islands. Diving petrels are the most aquatic of all petrels and swim under water in search of food.

Common Diving Petrel *Pelecanoides urinatrix* (Gmelin,1789)

NATIVE
New Zealand Diving Petrel
P.u. urinatrix (Gmelin, 1789).
Subantarctic Diving Petrel
P.u. exsul Salvin, 1896.

OTHER NAMES: *Kuaka, Chatham Island diving petrel, Kerguelen diving petrel.*

SIZE: *200 mm.*

DESCRIPTION
ADULT: *Sexes alike. Upper surface glossy black. Upper wing brown-black; with white edges to secondaries and some short scapulars; and inner webs of primaries dusky brown. Sometimes tips of tail feathers white. Side of neck and sometimes breast grey with white tips. Undersurface mainly*
white; with underwing coverts mainly pale brown-grey and flanks and undertail coverts washed with grey. Iris brown. Sides of bill parallel at base, tapering towards tip, black, with lower edges of both mandibles purplish. Feet cobalt blue. Webs almost black.
JUVENILE: *As adult.*
NESTLING: *First down pale silver-grey above and white below with grey-brown area at vent. Second down similar, but darker grey above.*

MOULT
Soon after breeding, although subantarctic diving petrel begins to moult primaries before chicks have departed.

VOICE
Aptly described by the name kuaka.
Soft call often repeated beginning with coo, *sometimes slurred, and ending with short, higher pitched* aka. *Uttered while flying over nesting area, from ground or from burrow. Sometimes pair in nest chamber call duet.*

DISTRIBUTION
New Zealand diving petrel:
Ranges throughout coastal waters. Breeds on many islands around the North Island from the Three Kings Islands to Bay of Plenty and on islets off the Taranaki coast; on islands in Cook Strait; the Chatham and Solander Islands; islands around Stewart Island; The Snares; and on islets around the south and east of the South Island. Elsewhere breeds in small numbers on islands off southeastern Australia.

Subantarctic diving petrel:
Ranges in subantarctic seas, mainly coastally. Breeds on the Antipodes and Auckland Islands, and possibly on islets and stacks off Campbell and Macquarie Islands. Elsewhere breeds on Heard, Prince Edward and Gough Islands; Îles Kerguélen and Crozet; and South Georgia.

RECOGNITION

Cannot be distinguished from South Georgian diving petrel at sea. In the hand identified by darker underwing and inner webs of primaries, and longer bill with parallel-sided base that tapers towards tip.

THE MOST AQUATIC OF ALL PETRELS, diving petrels use their legs and wings to swim under water in search of food. They feed during the day, but probably most at dusk and dawn when their prey of crustacean zooplankton is nearer the surface. They fly much less than other petrels, as they feed close to land and do not migrate. The apparent effort of their whirring flight, with its incessant wing-beats, as they move directly and horizontally not far above the sea, gives the impression that they are ill-fitted to this form of locomotion. When their wings no longer propel them, they plummet to the sea or ground.

The common diving petrel is found throughout the year in New Zealand coastal waters and around the outlying southern islands. It nests in burrows in soil or peat in well-vegetated terrain, such as under tussocks, coastal forest or scrub. Sometimes part of the burrow is wet but the nest itself must be dry. Often the burrows are long and tortuous and dug relatively deep, reaching to 0.6 m below the surface. At other times they are located in very shallow soil at the storm tideline around the edge of an island.

This petrel visits its breeding places at any time of year, though it is less likely to do so immediately after the breeding season when it moults. Many birds return to the breeding grounds in April. Most are young birds and other pre-breeders seeking vacant burrows or preparing new burrows and looking for mates. Breeding birds do not begin courtship and nest-making until between June and August.

The breeding season varies from year to year, by as much as 14 days. It also varies with latitude, becoming later towards the south. At Green Island in northern New Zealand the birds lay between 7 August and 4 September. At the Chatham Islands most birds lay during September and early October. At Whero Island, they lay from 11 September to 9 November with a peak between 23 September and 13 October. And in the subantarctic they lay during October and early November. Thus laying extends over about three months.

The birds leave for sea before laying but it is not known for how long or whether both sexes go. There is little information on the early stages of breeding but one pair observed incubated their egg for 53.5 days. At Whero Island the parents change over almost every night, but at Green Island they often leave the egg unattended by day. However the embryo is very resistant to chilling, and one chick hatched nine days after being deserted at the pipping stage.

After hatching the chick's eyes are closed for about 12 hours and it opens them only occasionally until it is three days old. The parents take turns to guard it continuously for seven to 15 days. They feed the young bird almost every night. Often both parents bring food, and during the first week or two they feed the chick at any time. The chick grows fairly regularly to a maximum weight of 145 to 150 g at 37 to 48 days of age, which is about 20 per cent above adult weight. On departure the fledgling weighs about the same as an adult—between 124 and 131 g. On Green Island, young birds leave at about 50 days, but at South Georgia, they are usually about 54 days old. The first chicks leave about 22 November in the north and the last chicks leave about 28 February in the south. Many chicks fly off, but often they blunder their way down to the sea and eventually swim away.

The young return to their colonies at an early age, although often not to where they hatched. Some come back as non-breeders at one year old and 70 per cent may breed at two years old.

While southern skuas are the chief enemy of the common diving petrel at its more southerly breeding places, animals introduced to breeding islands, either accidentally or intentionally, are generally a more serious threat. Norway rats have wiped out common diving petrels on Mayor, Motuhora, Kapiti and Campbell Islands. Wekas have considerably reduced their numbers on islets off Stewart Island. Feral cats have annihilated the subantarctic subspecies on Marion Island and are probably mainly responsible for the bird's absence on Macquarie Island.

Two subspecies of the common diving petrel are found in New Zealand: the New Zealand diving petrel and the subantarctic diving petrel. The New Zealand diving petrel is identified by its parallel-sided bill that tapers abruptly towards the tip, its black tail, and the pale grey sides to its neck. It eats mainly krill.

The distinctive bill of the subantarctic diving petrel is parallel-sided at the base, but it soon narrows and then tapers gradually towards the tip. Its tail feathers are tipped with white; and a grey mottling usually extends across the lower foreneck and upper breast, sometimes in a broad band. It feeds on amphipods, young stomatopods, copepods and krill. M.J.I.

South Georgian Diving Petrel *Pelecanoides georgicus* Murphy & Harper, 1916

CIRCUMPOLAR

OTHER NAMES: *None.*

SIZE: *170 mm.*

DESCRIPTION
ADULT: *Sexes alike. Upper parts glossy black. Upper wing tinged brown, with diagonal white bar across scapulars, and inner webs of outermost 3 primaries mainly white. Forehead and lores tinged brown. Cheeks, sides of neck and sometimes foreneck grey. Underparts white, with flanks, axillaries and undertail variably marked or tinged with grey. Iris brown. Bill fairly short with tapering sides, black, lower mandible partly blue. Feet blue, usually with black stripe along back of tarsus. Webs dark grey.*
NESTLING: *Rather dense, dark grey to almost sooty grey down, darker on crown.*

MOULT
Probably at sea after breeding.

VOICE
Squeaks repeated in phrases of 5 to 10. At Codfish Island, single call of kuueek.

DISTRIBUTION
Breeds on Codfish Island off Stewart Island; on Heard, Marion and Prince Edward Islands; Îles Crozet and Kerguélen; and South Georgia. Ranges at sea near its breeding places.

RECOGNITION

Probably cannot be distinguished from other diving petrels at sea. In the hand identified by white inner webs of three outermost primaries; white underwing; rather short, tapering bill; boomerang-shaped nostrils; and usually black stripe down back of tarsus. Smaller than common diving petrel.

Before nesting begins, the South Georgian petrel must often clear the blocked entrance to its old burrow.

THE ONLY BREEDING COLONY of South Georgian diving petrels in New Zealand is a small group of 30 to 40 pairs on Codfish Island. This petrel once nested on the Auckland Islands, but the last sighting was in 1943. In the nineteenth century birds were also found on Macquarie Island, but none have been seen there this century.

The Codfish Island birds feed in the seas around their breeding places, catching krill, small fish and young cephalopods. At Heard Island they eat mainly copepods and at South Georgia the adults feed chicks primarily on *Euphausia superba*.

The birds visit their colonies only during the breeding season. They nest in burrows dug in barren, unstable terrain such as scree, scoria or sand where there is little competition for burrowing space with other petrels. Often the burrows collapse during the non-breeding season and the entrances become blocked. At the beginning of the nesting season the birds usually have to do some digging to open out their burrows. It is not known whether or not they have to dig new burrows frequently but probably, like other petrels, they have a precise knowledge of the location of their old burrow. Each burrow is usually deep, tortuous, and one to two metres long.

The breeding season varies according to the latitude. On Codfish Island at 46°S, burrow excavation begins before 22 September but further south on South Georgia at 54°S the birds start burrowing on 27 October. They lay at South Georgia from about 19 November to 31 December and at Codfish Island about a month earlier.

The birds do not desert the colony before they lay. Both sexes take turns to incubate the single, white, ovoid egg for a total of about 46 days. At South Georgia the eggs hatch throughout January. The parents feed the chick every night. At 35 days old the chick weighs about 41 per cent more than an adult, but by the time it departs at about 45 days old it weighs about the same as an adult. By the end of March the colonies are deserted.

Southern skuas kill small numbers of adults at most breeding places, and sometimes dig out and kill chicks in nests near the surface. Colonies on Macquarie Island may have been wiped out by rats, cats and wekas. Sea lions have destroyed colonies on the Auckland Islands. M.J.I.

White-tailed Tropic Bird *Phaethon lepturus dorotheae* MATHEWS,1913

VAGRANT

OTHER NAMES: *Bo'sun bird, yellow-billed tropic bird.*

SIZE: *380 mm.*

DESCRIPTION
ADULT: *Sexes alike. General colour glossy white. Strong black upcurved stripe from gape through eye to neck. Head feathers have black bases. Flank feathers, inner secondaries and scapulars black with narrow white edges. Central black bar in secondary wing coverts. All primaries have black shafts. Four outermost primaries have black outer web, white tip and broad black margin on inner web. Tail white with 2 long centre feathers. Iris dark brown. Bill yellow. Feet and webs grey and black.*
IMMATURE: *White with black bars extensively above and on flanks. Scapulars and inner secondaries black with broad white edges. Outer*

primaries black on outer webs. Eye-stripe as in adult. Iris dark brown. Bill pearl grey.

MOULT
Body moult at sea after breeding, but wing moult may begin during nesting. Tail streamers moulted alternately.

VOICE
Rattling t-t-t-t and tick calls in flight. Sometimes a harsh scream.

DISTRIBUTION
Breeds on islands in the tropical western and central Pacific. Straggles to New Zealand.

> **RECOGNITION**
>
> Medium-sized white bird with yellow bill and white tail streamers. Translucent wings.

White-tailed tropic birds nesting in the crevice of a rock.

THE WHITE-TAILED TROPIC BIRD, more agile in flight than the red-tailed tropic bird, breeds on islands in the tropical Pacific and very occasionally straggles south to New Zealand. No birds were recorded until January 1973, when a juvenile was found at Bay of Plenty. In 1979, three more juveniles were recovered: at Dargaville in February; at Taranaki, also in February; and at Muriwai in June. Two birds were also picked up at Ninety Mile Beach in March and May 1983. This species breeds throughout the year. It nests in a tree fork, hollow, or scrape in the ground that is bare of nesting material, and lays one egg. It eats squid, flying fish and other small fish.   D.G.N. & F.C.K.

Red-tailed Tropic Bird *Phaethon rubricauda roseotincta* MATHEWS,1926

The long streamer tail feathers of the red-tailed tropic bird were much sought after by Maoris for decoration and barter.

NATIVE

OTHER NAMES: *Bo'sun bird, amokura.*

SIZE: *460 mm.*

DESCRIPTION
ADULT: *Sexes alike. General plumage pink-white. Black upward curving stripe from base of gape through and behind eye. Shafts of outer primaries black. Inner secondaries and flank feathers black with wide white edges. Tail white with black shafts. Two centre tail feathers longer with red extensions. Iris brown. Bill red. Feet and webs grey and black.*
IMMATURE: *Upper surface, flanks and sometimes tail strongly barred with black. Eye-patch as in adult. No tail streamers. Bill blue-black. Feet as in adult.*

MOULT
Appears to be continuous except when breeding.

VOICE
Main call ratchet-like pirr-igh in flight. Harsh clinging rattle from sitting birds and those approaching nest. Guttural call from birds on nest calling to those flying overhead.

DISTRIBUTION
In New Zealand, breeds on Raoul, North Meyer, South Meyer, Nugent, Dayrell, South Chanter and Macauley Islands in the Kermadec group. Straggles to the North Island: in recent years birds found at Awanui, Muriwai Beach, in the Rangitoto Channel, off East Cape and on Lake Taupo.

THE MAORIS OF THE NORTH CAPE region prized the long tail streamers of the red-tailed tropic bird. After easterly gales it is said that they systematically searched the coast for these birds. Feathers they found were either used as decoration or sent to southern tribes in exchange for greenstone.

Usually red-tailed tropic birds feed alone, often hundreds of miles out to sea. They eat squid and fish in similar proportions and catch their prey by diving from heights of 15 m or more and staying under water for up to 25 seconds.

They breed either singly or in loose colonies where their nests are 20 to 30 m or more apart. Occasionally birds return to Raoul Island in the winter, but more often they arrive at the end of October and during November. Courting pairs

sometimes fly in vertical circles, their red tail streamers bent downwards and their webbed feet spread on either side of the tail. They fly one above the other near the potential nest-site.

They nest in hollows on the ledges of sea cliffs or forested cliffs near the shore. Between mid-December and mid-January they lay one oval egg. The colour of this egg varies but usually it is pink with red-brown spots and blotches. Both parents incubate the egg, changing over daily. The downy chick hatches between mid-January and mid-February and remains in the nest. At first the parents feed it on squid, then later they also bring it fish. The young bird fledges within three months, during April and May. Birds also breed on Norfolk and Lord Howe Islands.   D.G.N. & F.C.K.

> **RECOGNITION**
>
> Large pink-white bird with red bill. Often long dark red tail streamers, but sometimes broken. Translucent wings.

Australian Pelican *Pelecanus conspicillatus* TEMMINCK, 1824

PERHAPS IT IS SURPRISING THAT, apart from prehistoric remains, so few Australian pelicans have been recorded in New Zealand. In Australia this bird is found throughout the mainland and on offshore islands in sheltered and shallow bays, estuaries and inland waters, wherever there is both a large body of water and plenty of food. When it is not feeding, it rests on sandpits, rocks, and the limbs of large trees.

Usually these are social birds that form dense flocks for flying, feeding, resting and breeding. When flying long distances they spiral upwards on a thermal updraft and then glide down to the next updraft. Occasionally, they use a laborious flapping flight. When they take off from water, they kick both feet together.

Pelicans feed mainly on fish, but also on crustaceans, insects, small tortoises and other aquatic animals. To capture its prey, it reaches down into shallow water with its long neck, bill and huge throat pouch. Often several pelicans, either in a line or a circle, do this in synchrony.

The pelican also uses its bill as a prop when it stretches a wing or a leg sideways. At times its pouch serves as an evaporative cooling surface. It cares for this large pouch by stretching it inside out over the breast, or by flapping it back and forth with the bill either pointing down and slightly open or with the neck stretched upwards and the bill closed.

If there is enough food and shelter, pelicans breed at any time of the year. In one courtship display both sexes ripple their pouches like flags in a breeze, sometimes clapping their bills at the same time. In another, males swing their open bills from side to side with the head high. Males also throw objects in the air and catch them. They threaten other males by thrusting their bills forward, opening and snapping them shut at the same time. When only one male is left with a female, she leads him to a nest-site. They step slowly, holding their bodies upright with their necks arched backwards, their bills resting on the lower part of their necks and their wings slightly raised.

They nest on the ground on small islands or on partly submerged lignum bushes. The female builds the nest with sticks and debris gathered by the male. She lays two eggs which the pair incubate on their webbed feet for 32 to 35 days.

The parents guard the chicks for the first four weeks, then the young join a crèche. At first, the adults feed their offspring on a fluid that flows down the inside of the parent's bill. When they are two weeks old, the chicks stand inside the parent's pouch to feed on regurgitated food. Later they take food directly from the adult's throat. Some chicks, after they feed, go into convulsions, perhaps because of breathing difficulties. They fledge at three months. Before they are four months old, they start to forage for themselves.   G.F.v.T.

The Australian pelican is widespread throughout Australia but straggles rarely to New Zealand.

VAGRANT

OTHER NAME: *Spectacled pelican.*

SIZE: *1700 mm.*

DESCRIPTION
ADULT: *Sexes alike, but female smaller with much smaller bill. Most of head, neck and body white. Back of head and neck grey. Upper wing black except large white patch and long secondary coverts. Eye-ring yellow. Throat pink-yellow. Underwing coverts, sometimes with black line. Black rear-pointing V on rump. Tail black. Iris brown. Bill pale blue with pink ridge. Legs and feet dark slate blue. At start of breeding grey, black or white crest on nape; front two thirds of throat bright red and rear one third pink; with broad blue-black line on each side of throat and blue-black border along base of throat. During nesting throat turns orange-pink and blue-black line turns bright red.*
IMMATURE: *Plumage white and black with similar pattern to adult, but with short secondary coverts. Bill and throat pink. Legs and feet grey.*
JUVENILE: *Plumage white and brown with similar pattern to adult. Short secondary coverts. Head white, grey or brown. Throat and eye-ring pink. Bill pink with orange tip. Legs and feet brown-grey.*

MOULT
Gradual moult with no flightless period.

VOICE
Grunting sounds away from nesting areas. During breeding orrh-orrrh-orrrha, thu-thu-thuh, ah-ah-ahha, uh-uh-uh-uhhr *and soft* oh-oh-oh.

DISTRIBUTION
Breeds in Australia. A number of sightings in New Zealand: in 1890 on the Wanganui River; in August 1976 on the northern Wairoa River; in November 1977 in Southland; and December 1977 to June 1978 in south Canterbury.

RECOGNITION
Only pelican likely to be seen in New Zealand. Naked eye-ring separated by feathers from naked face. Very long bill with terminal hook. Short broad tail. Short legs with all four toes united in web.

A young pair of Australasian gannets greet each other with the mutual display. Various displays and calls regulate the social activities of breeding birds.

Australasian Gannet *Sula bassana serrator* GRAY,1843

NATIVE

OTHER NAMES: *Takapu,
Australian gannet, solan goose.*

SIZE: *910 mm.*

DESCRIPTION
ADULT: *Sexes alike. Body mostly
white. Crown and nape golden buff.
All primaries black. Three innermost
secondaries white, remainder usually
black. Lesser upper primary wing
coverts black, white or mixed.
Remainder of upper and underwing
coverts white. Central tail feathers
black; side feathers white. Iris silver-
grey with yellow tinge. Bill light
blue-grey horn with black cutting
edges. Eyelid blue. Lores naked.
Throat pouch grey-black. Feet and
webs slate grey with blue-green or
yellow stripe on front of leg and toes.
Claws light horn.*
IMMATURE: *Plumage varies with age.
After first full moult crown and
nape pale yellow to golden. Back at
first white with scattered black*

*feathers on lower back and rump;
later white. Two of 3 innermost
secondaries white. Four black coverts
on alula, changing to white. Greater
secondary upper wing coverts,
tertiaries and scapulars mostly black
at first, then mostly white.
Underwing coverts at first smoky
grey and mottled dark grey-brown,
then generally white. Tail changes
from black, or black and white, to
adult form over 3 or 4 years. Rest of
plumage as adult.*
JUVENILE: *Head, neck, upper breast
and thighs white, heavily streaked
with dark grey-brown. In males
variable amount of yellow in crown
and nape. Feathers of back and
upper wing dark grey-brown with
white tips, giving speckled
appearance. Lower breast, belly and
undertail coverts white. Primaries,
secondaries and tail feathers black.
Median and lesser underwing coverts
dark grey-brown mottled with white.
Greater underwing coverts white
with some grey smudging. Iris dark
brown. Bill, eyelid, naked facial*

skin, legs and feet slate-black.
NESTLING: *Naked black skin at
hatching. First down from fourth
day sparse, short, grey-white.
Second down at 2 or 3 weeks longer,
thicker and white; covers entire
body, except for face. Face and bill
black. First feathers appear in tail
at 6 weeks. Down shed completely at
12 weeks.*

MOULT
*Coincides with end of breeding
season; varies according to age and
colony. In Cape Kidnappers birds,
first full moult starts in males in
September, females in October of
first year; concluded by following
January. Subsequent full moult
occurs somewhat later each year.*

VOICE
Harsh urrah-urrah-urrah, *higher
pitched in males during landing,
greeting and solo displays. Soft
sibilant groan at departure from nest
and occasionally in flight. Harsh
aggressive quacking in colony.*

DISTRIBUTION
*In New Zealand, breeds at the
Three Kings, Poor Knights and
Mokohinau Islands; Mahuki, Bush,
Horuhoru, Oaia, Gannet, White,
Nugget and Little Solander Islands;
and North Auckland, Muriwai,
Hawke's Bay, Tolaga Bay and the
Marlborough Sounds localities.
Ranges around the continental shelf
and in harbours and river mouths.
Most plentiful north of Cook Strait,
but reaches the Auckland, Campbell
and Chatham Islands. Also breeds
on Norfolk Island and islands along
the coasts of Tasmania and southern
Australia.*

RECOGNITION

Large white bird with
contrasting black trailing edge
to wing and pointed tail with
black centre. Dives steeply
from up to 30 m for food. At
sea seen singly or in flocks.

WHEN GANNETS FEED THEY DIVE into the sea from heights of up to 30 m. Above deep water they suddenly drop vertically with their heads outstretched and their wings partly folded. Just before they hit the water the birds stretch their long wings fully backwards. Often they enter the water at 145 km/h. Inflatable air sacs beneath the skin on the breast and lower neck cushion the shock of impact, as does the absence of external nostrils. In shallow water they dive more obliquely.

Their prey is small fish, such as anchovies, pilchards, yellow-eyed mullet and garfish, as well as some small squid. Under water the birds swim beneath the fish and swallow all but the largest before returning to the surface within a few seconds. They repeat this action many times and the sight of a large flock of gannets fishing is often a good guide to fishermen.

Australasian gannets are on the increase in New Zealand. Their estimated numbers have probably more than doubled from 21 000 breeding pairs in 1947 to 43 000 in 1980. Usually they nest in dense colonies on flat or moderately sloping ground, although there is one cliff-nesting colony on the Poor Knights Islands. As with other gannets, most of the colonies are on offshore islands, except for major mainland colonies at Cape Kidnappers. The total breeding population for the Australasian gannet in both Australia and New Zealand was estimated at 53 000 pairs in 1980. A colony was recently begun in the north Tasman Sea at Norfolk Island.

The breeding colonies

Generally, these colonies are deserted outside the breeding season. The return of the birds depends on the latitude of the colony and the availability of food. The further south the colony, the later the breeding season. At Cape Kidnappers, breeding birds return in increasing numbers from the end of July, while birds may return to Horuhoru Island four or five weeks earlier. Male birds return first and occupy sites on or close to previous nests.

As a rule gannets mate for life, although the pair may separate during winter when they are away from the colony. They do not begin breeding until they are at least four years old and, by the time they are eight years old, most have started breeding. Young males attempting to breed for the first time arrive at the colonies later than experienced breeders. First they must establish a territory. Normally this is at the edge of the colony, as most of the central area is taken by previous occupants. They then attract a female and form a strong pair-bond before they breed. Consequently, young birds breed later in the season than established pairs.

During courtship gannets combine stylised movements with their striking plumage in a number of displays. They perform these on the nest-site, defending it against all challengers. To attract a female to its nest-site, a male bird stands with its head and bill raised and slowly flags its bill from side to side.

To intimidate an opponent without fighting, the Australasian gannet uses one of several signals that vary in intensity. In the least aggressive of these threats the bird remains sitting or standing quietly, then lunges slowly towards the other bird with its bill closed. In a similar, but slightly more forceful display, it opens its bill. If either of these displays proves inadequate, the bird might lunge forward quickly with its bill open, its neck fully extended and its wings flicked up behind its neck. Sometimes this action is repeated in quick succession. A more aggressive variation of this includes a sharp upward flick of the tail with the bird advancing off the nest-site towards the other bird. When one bird wants to appease another, it will often bow its head and point its bill downwards.

In one commonly performed territorial display that is accompanied by a loud guttural call, a bird raises itself and slightly spreads its half-folded wings. It then waggles its head from side to side and lowers it in a gentle bow towards its feet and under its wing. This smooth, swinging bow is made from one to eight times. Following the final bow the bird coils in its neck and points its bill down the front or side of its breast.

Displaying at the nest-site

When a mate arrives at the nest-site it faces the resident bird. Both birds raise their heads and call together, each touching the tip of the other's bill as they shake their heads. They intersperse this with slow bows towards the nest over the other bird's neck. Sometimes the birds, especially the female, hold their wings well out from their bodies. At the end of the display, they often preen each other on the head, throat and neck, with rapid movements of their bills.

When a departing bird leaves its mate on the nest it points its head upwards and, slightly raising its wings, rotates slowly, raising and lowering its feet at the same time. It then crouches and leans towards the outside of the colony. If it is close to the colony edge it flies a few wing strokes, then lands with a soft sighing groan. If it is well inside the colony it extends its neck horizontal to the ground and rushes towards the edge rapidly flailing its wings. Just before it takes off, the bird leans its neck forward and crouches with wings partly extended.

As soon as the pair-bond is formed or re-established by mating, the male takes off to gather nesting material, leaving the female to guard the site. The main nesting material is seaweed, but often the birds add grass and other plant material. Males hunting for nest material raid unattended and carelessly guarded nests, sometimes dragging whole nests back to their own site. The male, on returning to the site, presents the material to the waiting female. Both birds carefully shape the material into a rough bowl, adding more plants until they have built a substantial nest. They dig dirt and rake it towards the nest. This, along with their faeces, helps to cement the nesting material. Nests are usually built about one metre apart, just out of pecking range from neighbouring sites.

At Cape Kidnappers the birds lay from about 20 September to mid-December, with a peak in mid-October. Incubation starts immediately and is shared by both sexes, although the male spends slightly more time on the nest. The average incubation shift is about 27 hours. As gannets have no brood patches they incubate the egg between their feet. They place their highly vascularised webs over the egg and their body feathers form an effective insulation barrier that maintains the correct temperature. The single pale blue-green egg is elongate and elliptical, heavily covered with a white chalky layer and streaked with blood when laid; but it soon changes to a muddy brown with dirt from the nest.

Often, if the egg is lost during early incubation, the female lays another within two or three weeks. On rare occasions there are two eggs in the clutch. Sometimes twin chicks survive, but usually one dies, even if both hatch.

After about 43 days the chick pips the shell and the parent transfers it to the top of its feet to prevent crushing the young chick. The chick takes 24 to 36 hours to hatch.

At hatching, the chick weighs 60 to 65 g. Its eyes are closed for about three days. The parents brood and guard it for about four weeks, after which it may be left alone at the nest. They feed the young bird by regurgitation. In the early stages the chick begs with a high-pitched peeping. Later it also sways its head from side to side, while keeping the tip of its bill near that of the adult. When feeding, the chick inserts its head into the adult's open gape to receive the partly digested food. Very small chicks are fed an almost liquid paste, while well-developed chicks are fed almost whole fish. Sometimes the same parent feeds the chick several times in one day and when there is no more food it avoids the chick's begging by turning its bill away. Fishing trips rarely seem to be longer than 12 to 15 hours and mostly they feed after sunrise and before sunset. The probable feeding range of most breeding birds is within 160 km of the colony, but birds from Cape Kidnappers have been recovered as far north as East Cape and as far south as Paremata.

The rapid growth of the chick

The weight of the chick increases rapidly. At three weeks it weighs about 900 g, at four weeks 1500 g, and at six weeks 1900 g. When it reaches adult weight, at about six and a half weeks, it looks considerably larger because of its heavy layer of down. Its peak weight of about 3200 g is reached between 11 and 13 weeks and coincides with the final growth of its flight feathers. In the final two weeks before departure it exercises and builds up strength for the first flight. It fledges between 93 and 115 days after hatching. The last chicks depart from Cape Kidnappers during May and the colony is then deserted, except for the occasional roosting adult, until the start of the next breeding season.

Most juveniles spend the first year in Australian waters, especially on the east coast south from the Tropic of Capricorn, and also in Bass Strait, with some moving as far as Western Australia. Very few return to their natal colony at one year; about three to five per cent return at two years old and 25 to 30 per cent at three years old. By the time they are six years old most have returned to New Zealand. Few birds cross the Tasman Sea again; they disperse in New Zealand waters during the non-breeding season.

Only about 20 to 30 per cent of all flying chicks survive to return to their breeding colony. Banding shows that the oldest 80 per cent of the chicks have a higher chance of survival. In breeding birds there is an annual mortality of about five per cent.

The mean life expectancy of an Australasian gannet is between 16 and 20 years. The oldest known-age birds at Cape Kidnappers have reached 28 years. One bird that was banded as an adult had reached an age of over 33 years.

C.J.R.R.

The brown booby frequently dives from heights of 10 to 15 metres to pursue its prey, continuing the pursuit by swimming under water.

Brown Booby *Sula leucogaster plotus* (FORSTER, 1844)

VAGRANT

OTHER NAMES: *Brown gannet, common booby, Brewster's booby, white-bellied booby.*

SIZE: *720 mm.*

DESCRIPTION
ADULT: *Wings, back and tail dark brown. Head, neck and upper breast brown, ending in sharp line where white undersurface begins. Face, bill and feet usually lime green to yellow. Iris grey or brown.*
IMMATURE: *Upper surface less uniform brown than in adult. Tail paler at tip. Head, neck and undersurface grey-brown.*
CHICK: *Largely naked at hatching. Sparse white down after 1 week; thicker down at 3 or 4 weeks. Primaries visible at 4 weeks. Bare skin on face tinged with green. Feet*

pale green. Bill blue-grey.

MOULT
In adult begins before breeding and then suspended until after chick hatches.

VOICE
Harsh quacking or honking from female. Sibilant whistle, hiss or chuff from male.

DISTRIBUTION
Most common booby in the southwestern Pacific. Straggles to New Zealand.

RECOGNITION

Sharp demarcation between brown upper breast and white lower breast.

THE BROWN BOOBY IS SOMETIMES SEEN in New Zealand, fishing close inshore for squid and flying fish. It dives from heights of 10 to 15 m then pursues its prey under water, propelling itself with its feet and wings. It stays submerged for up to 40 seconds.

It prefers to breed on cliffs or steep and broken land, but also nests on flat, vegetated ground. The young wander for the first few years and at the earliest breed in their third year. They do not always return to the island of their birth and sometimes they breed on different islands in different years. Often mates remain together, however, and nest on the same site in successive seasons. The breeding cycle varies from place to place, with some birds breeding about the same time every year and others breeding less often and at different times of the year.

The male marks out his territory and defends it with flailing wings and jabbing beak. He attracts a female by pointing his bill towards the sky. As part of the courtship ritual, they both jab each other with their bills and parade around the territory, tucking their bills into their wings or pointing them sideways and upwards. Sometimes, they preen each other, but not as often as other gannets and boobies. The male also gathers nesting material and presents it to his mate.

The pair build a substantial nest in which the female lays one or two eggs. On average she lays the second egg five days after the first. Both parents share incubation, and about 65 per cent of eggs hatch. When two chicks hatch, one always dies. Both parents feed the young bird. After between 85 and 105 days the chick flies for the first time, although the parents continue to feed it for another one or two months.

The number of chicks that fledge varies enormously depending on the availability of food. But once they reach adulthood, mortality is probably less than six per cent. In some areas, people take eggs, young and adults for food or bait. J.B.N.

Masked Booby *Sula dactylatra personata* GOULD,1846

THE MASKED BOOBY WANDERS throughout the tropics, often foraging more than 1000 km from the nearest land. It hunts alone or in small groups. When it sights its prey of squid or flying fish it plunges into the sea from heights of up to 100 m, although generally it dives from less than 25 m. Sometimes, to increase its speed, the falling bird beats its primary feathers rapidly.

Most birds breed for the first time at three years old, rarely at two. Young birds sometimes nest on islands other than the one on which they were born. They generally breed every year, over a period of 33 to 40 weeks, although occasionally they miss a year.

Masked boobies prefer to nest on flat open ground or barren slopes, but they are adaptable birds and also breed among boulders, vegetation, on outcrops and, rarely, on ledges. The nest is a mere scrape with no additional material. Masked boobies have several displays. Sexual displays include pointing the bill skywards or walking with the bill turned up and away from the other bird. To defend its territory, a masked booby jabs with its beak or waves its head.

The female lays either one or two eggs which are chalky white over a blue surface. Both parents incubate the clutch in shifts of 12 to 25 hours. The first egg hatches after 44 days; the second after 43 days. The second egg is smaller than the first. Masked boobies never rear two chicks, but 22 per cent of the chicks that survive to fledging are from second eggs.

The parents feed the young bird for about 118 days before it flies and they continue to feed it a further 56 to 60 days before it leaves the colony. The number of chicks that live to leave the colony varies considerably. Amongst adult birds, the annual mortality rate is about six per cent, with a mean life expectancy of about 16 years.

In some areas, such as the Caribbean, masked boobies' eggs are gathered for food; and in some cases the bird itself is eaten. Introduced mammals, such as pigs and cats, attack the birds on some islands. Frigate birds snatch food from masked boobies.   J.B.N.

NATIVE

OTHER NAMES: *White booby, blue-faced booby, whistling booby.*

SIZE: *860 mm.*

DESCRIPTION
ADULT: *Sexes alike, but female slightly larger. Plumage dazzling white except for black flight and tail feathers. Facial skin black. Iris yellow. Bill varies from orange to yellow, but often pink, especially in female. Legs and feet dull orange to* lead grey with purple tinge.
IMMATURE: *Mainly brown above and white below. Brown slowly replaced by white. Bill grey-horn, turning yellow.*
CHICK: *Sparse white down when hatched. Thick down by 4 weeks old. Facial skin grey, becoming pale blue. Bare throat skin cream to pink. Bill and feet dark grey.*

MOULT
In adult, begins before breeding cycle is suspended, then resumed after chick hatches, and continues while chick being fed.

VOICE
During courtship male calls thin whistle whee-ee-oo *in descending pitch for 2 or 3 seconds. Female calls loud shout or honk that varies in pitch and loudness.*

DISTRIBUTION
Ranges to at least 32°S in the Tasman Sea. Nests at the Kermadec Islands on Meyer, Macauley, Dayrell, South Chanter, North Chanter, Curtis and Haszard Islands. *Also breeds in eastern Australia; on Norfolk and Lord Howe Islands; and widely in the Coral Sea. Related subspecies widely distributed throughout tropical seas of the world.*

The masked booby, distributed throughout the tropics, has a broad repertoire of ritualised displays used mainly for courtship and to defend territory.

The great cormorant inhabits sheltered inland and coastal waters and, as long as food is plentiful, will breed at any time of the year.

Great Cormorant *Phalacrocorax carbo* (LINNAEUS, 1758)

ENDEMIC
Great Cormorant
P.c. steadi (MATHEWS &
IREDALE, 1913).

OTHER NAMES: *Kawau-tua-
whenua, black cormorant, black shag.*

SIZE: *880 mm.*

DESCRIPTION
ADULT: *Sexes alike. Generally black
with blue-green sheen. Erectile black
crest behind middle of nape. Upper
wing coverts grey-brown with broad
black borders and bronze sheen. Base
of tail feathers grey. Plumage fades
to dark brown with sandy edges to
coverts. Throat and triangle above
gape yellow. White, grey and buff
throat patch starting behind eye. Iris
green. Bill grey with dark ridge.
Legs and feet black. At start of
breeding, throat black with yellow
spots; eye-ring black with light blue
nodules; triangle above gape orange-
red; and sometimes sparse white
plumes on side of upper neck and
dense white plumes on side of rump.*
IMMATURE: *Mottled dark and light
brown, variable amount of white on
foreneck, breast, belly. Iris green.*
JUVENILE: *As adult but plumage
silky; iris brown; no erectile crest.*
NESTLING: *Skin dark slate blue with
top of head, throat and bill pale
pink-yellow. Later covered with
sooty grey-brown down. Throat*

becomes yellow. Legs and feet black.

MOULT
Gradual, with no flightless period.

VOICE
*During pair formation call of male
loud and raucous; that of female soft
and husky, becoming louder during
incubation. Usually silent away from
breeding grounds.*

DISTRIBUTION
*In New Zealand, ranges around
inland and coastal waters of the
3 main islands and the Chatham
Islands. Vagrants from southeastern
Australia straggle to Lord Howe,
Norfolk and Macquarie Islands; The
Snares; Campbell Islands. Also
found on the shores of the North
Atlantic Ocean; mainly on inland
waters in Eurasia, Africa, Australia.
Rare vagrant to New Guinea,
Indonesia and Christmas Island.*

RECOGNITION
Mainly all-dark cormorant
with prominent yellow throat.
At start of breeding throat
turns black with yellow spots.
Stout bill with large hook.
Strong, long wings and long
tail. Flies with head held high
and neck S-shaped.

With its strong, hooked bill, it grabs small animals on the body and swallows them immediately. Medium-sized fish it seizes from behind the gills and brings to the surface. It tosses them in the air and swallows them head first. When it catches freshwater crayfish it shakes off the claws; it chews all crustaceans several times before ingesting them. In the Far East, people collar great cormorants to prevent them swallowing, and use the birds to fish for them.

This cormorant forages in sheltered inland waters, estuaries and coastal bays. Normally it hunts by day. Once it has finished feeding, it flies to a nearby perch to rest, digest its meal and dry its feathers before returning to its roosting or nesting area. If it is rearing chicks, it digests its own meal first and then catches food for its offspring.

Great cormorants congregate in dense flocks for feeding, resting, breeding and flying. When they fly they flap their wings several times and then glide. Before they take off from water, they dry their wings by shaking them backwards and forwards. When swimming rapidly under water and when taking off from water they kick both feet down and backwards together, but when swimming slowly above and below water they kick their feet alternately. Sometimes they beat the water's surface with their wings, then dip head, neck and shoulders under water. Mates, siblings, and parents and offspring preen each other.

They roost and nest in trees, bushes and tussocks on cliff ledges, rocks and sand spits. Although a few birds start breeding before the end of their second year, most do not breed until they are one or more years older. Provided there is sufficient food and shelter, they breed at any time of the year, building nests from sticks, twigs, plants and debris.

Attracting a mate

The male selects a nest-site which it defends against other males, and on which it advertises for a mate. The female chooses a male and approaches him cautiously. After he accepts her, she builds the nest, mainly with material he brings her. They mate on the nest, which they continue to build during the egg and chick stages. When the cormorants change over, the bird on the nest-site closes its wings and droops them down beside its body, while the bird outside the nest folds its wings well up, covering its back. A bird on the nest holds its crest down, but beside the nest its crest is up, unless it is alarmed.

To attract a mate, or to call a mate to the nest, the male, or rarely the female, waves its wings. It moves the tips up and outwards, exposing and covering its white rump patches. As the display increases in intensity the bird points its closed bill, neck and fanned tail vertically

To MANY ANGLERS, the great cormorant is a troublesome bird. Either it fishes in trout streams and ponds, or it gets caught in nets, traps and lines. But where other species are available, the great cormorant rarely feeds on commercial or game fish. In fact, its prey include a wide variety of small and medium-sized fish, including eels and trout; crustaceans, and other arthropods, including ants and spiders.

It sights its prey from as high as 80 m above the water's surface, spirals rapidly down and, a few metres above the water, brings its feet forward for landing. As soon as it touches the water, the bird dives.

upwards, while its body remains horizontal with its breast pressed down and its rump raised.

To acknowledge the arrival of its mate, the bird swings its head back through a vertical arc. As its head moves back it opens its mouth wide. Males call a loud *ah, arr, kroh,* or *eh-eh-eh,* whereas females call a soft *f-f-f . . ., sh-hi-hi . . ., fhi-fhi-fhi . . .* or *heh-eh-eh . . . .* Males, but not females, pull the head backwards until the nape touches the rump. Then the head rotates from side to side. At the same time, the male utters a rattling, gargling *rooo, r-r-r . . .* or *rooorr.* In this display, the body is horizontal and the tail raised. The bird is silent as it swings its head to the forward position.

Displays at the nest

Males and females on the nest also greet their mates by stretching neck, head and closed bill forward about 30° above the horizontal, with the body horizontal and the tail raised about 30° above the horizontal.

When approached by a cormorant other than its mate, the bird on the nest-site may respond by grabbing a nearby twig or a piece of nest material and shaking it vigorously. This is believed to show its readiness to defend the nest-site. Sometimes males call *ahr-roo-roo.*

A bird confronts an intruder with its bill open wide and its throat bulging. It moves its head back and forth and sideways with irregular neck movements. Males threaten with a raucous barking *tock-gock-gock . . . cock* and females with a soft, hoarse, puffing *fhi-fhi-hi-hi . . . .* In this threat display the body is held horizontally, the wings are partly spread sideways and downwards, and the tail is fanned and raised almost vertically.

When there is no cause for alarm cormorants and shags leave their nesting area slowly and deliberately. Before they take off, the neck is vertical and the closed bill tilted slightly. The front of the throat is straight and sometimes it pulsates to produce a purring *r-r-r . . . .*

When a bird arrives at the nest-site it kinks its throat. At the same time, males that are not holding nest material make a loud, raucous, barking and repetitive *kro-kro-kro . . ., gorr-gorr-gorr . . ., rahr-rahr-rahr . . ., arre-arre-arre . . ., roh-roh-roh . . .* or *reh-reh-reh . . . .* Females make a soft, hoarse, puffing, repetitive *ghi-ghi-ghi . . ., fee-hi-hi . . .,* or *for-for-for.*

When a female lands near an advertising male, she flattens her head and throat and raises her crest. Often the male makes a loud roaring *rooo* sound and the female utters a soft *fhi.* In another courtship display that is a symbolic flight, the birds hop.

The great cormorant lays four, elliptical eggs that are pale blue-green and covered with a thin chalky layer. They lay these two days apart and incubate them under their webbed feet for 27 to 31 days. During hot sunny weather, eggs and small chicks depend on their parents' shade for survival. The parents guard the nest in turns, changing over at least three times a day, until the chicks are able to ward off predators. The chicks stay in the nest for about four weeks and fledge at seven weeks. Both parents feed them until they lose contact a week or more after fledging.

When chicks beg for food they reach up with their necks stretched, bills closed and throats kinked. Older chicks spread their wings and flap them back and forth as they prod their bills at their parent's throat. They call a squeaky and repetitive *thue-tjue-tjue- . . . .* In response to very small chicks, the parent lowers its head with its mouth open and pointing backwards. It feeds the chick a regurgitated fluid from a trough formed by its lower bill and its throat pouch. Older chicks take partly digested food from the throat and gullet of their parents, and are fed less frequently than small chicks. When begging for water the chick directs its open bill silently upwards.   G.F.v.T. & W.J.M.V.

The little black cormorant is distinguished by its slender form and long tail.

Little Black Cormorant
Phalacrocorax sulcirostris (Brandt, 1837)

NATIVE

OTHER NAME: *Little black shag.*

SIZE: *610 mm.*

DESCRIPTION
ADULT: *Sexes alike. Generally black. Upper wing coverts grey with broad black borders and purple sheen. Plumage fades to dark brown with sandy edges to coverts. Throat blue with thin buff, grey or white line. Iris green. Bill blue-grey with dark ridge and base of lower bill blue. Legs and feet black. At start of breeding, short white plumes on side of head, over eye and scattered over head and upper neck; ring of blue-green nodules around eye; throat violet.*
JUVENILE: *Plumage dark silky brown. Iris brown. Assumes adult colouring late in first year.*
NESTLING: *Dark skin. Later black down with naked purple-grey crown.*

MOULT
Gradual, with no flightless period.

VOICE
At resting, roosting and nesting areas male makes ticking, whistling and croaking sounds and female probably silent. On the water, flocks and rafts audible at least a mile away splashing and making ticking and croaking calls.

DISTRIBUTION
On inland waters, more common in the North than the South Island. Inland and estuarine waters of Indonesia, New Guinea, Australia and southwestern Pacific islands. Straggles to Lord Howe and Norfolk Islands.

RECOGNITION

Small, slender cormorant with long tail. All-dark plumage. Thin, slender, hooked bill. Flies with neck S-shaped and head held high.

ALTHOUGH THE LITTLE BLACK CORMORANT often forages in large flocks, it is not a common New Zealand bird. At times, its numbers increase suddenly, but usually this is due to an influx of migrants from Australia. It feeds in small, sheltered, inland waters on a wide variety of little fish, including young mullet, carp and eel, as well as crustaceans and insects. It pursues most of its prey under water, grabbing it with its strongly hooked bill.

Usually it builds its nest of sticks, twigs, plants and debris high up in trees or bushes, rarely on the ground. As long as it has sufficient food and shelter, this cormorant breeds at any time of the year, but in New Zealand the peak periods of nesting and egg-laying are from October to November and April to May. It lays four elongate-oval eggs which are pale blue with a chalky outer layer. The parents incubate the eggs and protect small chicks on their webbed feet. They feed the chicks a regurgitated fluid from a trough formed by the lower bill and the throat pouch. Older chicks take partly digested food from the throat and gullet of their parents. In hot sunny weather the adult bird shades its young and pours water into their open bills.

Many of the displays of the little black cormorant are similar to those of the great cormorant. A male greets its mate by first moving its bill back and calling *hack,* then uttering *ak-he* as it rotates its closed bill above its rump. The male may also perform a bout of wing-waving. This may sometimes end with a gargling display similar to that of the great cormorant. When a female greets its mate it is silent. When an intruder appears the bird on the nest first raises its upper neck feathers and stretches its neck and closed bill towards the intruder. Later it darts its head back and forth with its bill slightly open and its wings partly spread. The male calls a harsh *ake-ake-ake . . .,* while the female probably threatens silently.

A bird about to take off from the nest-site stands with its neck and body in line about 45° to the horizontal, its closed bill sloping down and its tail almost horizontal. It flattens its head feathers and raises its neck feathers below the nape to form a broad ruff. Its throat pulsates as it calls *t-t-t . . . .* When a male returns to the nest, it whistles *ou-tu-tu.* Later in the breeding season this changes to a hoarse *hack-hack-hack* or a croaking *krah-krah-krah.*   W.J.M.V. & G.F.v.T.

Pied Cormorant *Phalacrocorax varius* (GMELIN, 1789)

COMPARED TO OTHER CORMORANTS and birds of the same species in Australia, the pied cormorant in New Zealand is remarkably tame. This fearlessness is probably because it was rarely persecuted before the arrival of the Europeans and has been fairly safe since.

There are fewer than 10 000 pied cormorants in New Zealand. Most inhabit sheltered and shallow marine inlets, bays and estuaries. Some live inland on large lakes and rivers. They eat a variety of fish, but mainly yellow-belly flounder and yellow-eyed mullet. When they dive from the water, birds often jump clear of the surface before plunging beneath it. Generally they take fish between 6 and 15 cm long, although sometimes they kill carp up to 22 cm long and short-finned eel up to 50 cm. Pied cormorants also eat crustaceans, such as snapping shrimp and spiny crayfish. An adult bird eats less than 500 g of fish a day, but an almost fully grown chick eats up to 800 g of food.

In New Zealand, pied cormorants roost and nest in trees and bushes, mainly pohutukawa and southern rata. They build a nest of sticks, twigs, plants and debris. A few birds breed before the end of their second year, but most begin breeding at least a year later. Providing there is enough food and shelter, they breed at any time of the year, and the peak seasons for egg-laying are from August to September and from March to April.

They lay three or four or, rarely, five eggs. These are elliptical, with one end slightly more pointed than the other, pale blue and heavily coated with a chalky layer. Each egg is laid two days apart. The incubation period varies from about 31 days for the first egg, 29 days for the second, 27 days for the third and 26.5 days for the fourth egg. The parents take turns to guard the nest, changing over at least three times a day, until the chicks are able to ward off predators. At about four weeks old, the chicks leave the nest. They fledge between 47 and 60 days old. Both parents continue to feed their young for up to 80 days after fledging.

The displays of the pied cormorant are similar to those of the great cormorant. To attract a mate, the male waves its wings silently at a rate that varies from once to twice per second. When a pair is forming at the nest-site, they raise their neck feathers to form broad ruffs. The male warns intruders with a harsh guttural *arhk, arrh-eh* or *eeh-h* and the female makes soft hissing sounds. Before leaving the nest-site, the bird bulges its throat forward, and if it is a male, calls a ticking *t-t-t* .... During this display the base of the neck pulsates and the bill opens and closes slightly in time with the ticking sound. As a male approaches the nest-site, it whistles a high-pitched *prit-prit-prit* ..., *rick-tick-tick* ..., or *prrr-prit-t-t-t-t* ... in time with its wing-beat. Chicks beg with a *wee-wee-wee* .... Males coming in to feed their chicks call them with a hoarse *urr-urr-urr* ....

A male pied cormorant acknowledges the arrival of its mate by swinging its head backwards and forwards. As it moves its head back, and for the first half of the forward movement, it holds its mouth wide open and bulges its throat. At the same time, the bird calls a slow loud screeching *aahr, whee-eer* or *whee-eh-eh-eh*. In the second part of the forward movement the male rotates its head from side to side with its bill closed and throat bulging. At the same time it calls a loud gargling, gobbling or barking *quog-wog-wog-wog, goh-goh-goh-goh, gug-gug-gug* or *cooee-cooee-cooee*. Both the screech and the gargle vary a great deal in the sound and number of syllables. Often at the end of this gargle the male keeps its stretched head and neck forward in a pointing display and slowly raises its breast. The females perform a similar, but silent display. Males and females also acknowledge the arrival of their mate by bulging the throat, holding the neck in the shape of an S and directing forward the wide open bill, which they move slowly back and forth. At the same time the tail is raised. The male calls *eeeh-eh-eh*.

G.F.v.T., P.R.M. & W.J.M.V.

The pied cormorant is the most tame of the cormorants and a strong swimmer.

ENDEMIC
Pied Cormorant
P.v. varius (GMELIN, 1789).

OTHER NAMES: *Karuhiruhi, pied shag, yellow-faced cormorant.*

SIZE: *810 mm.*

DESCRIPTION
ADULT: *Sexes alike, but female smaller, especially in bill. Plumage black above and white below, often with prominent black spur on side of head. Sheen on back green. Upper wing coverts dark grey with thin black borders and bronze sheen. Upper parts fade to dark brown with sandy edges to coverts. Base of tail feathers white or grey. Face yellow. Throat and triangle above gape salmon pink. Fleshy wattles in front of eyes which sometimes extend as thin spurs above eye-ring. Eye-ring and below eye green-blue. Iris green. Bill grey with dark ridge. Legs and feet black. At start of breeding, few short white nuptial plumes on crown and hind neck; throat and triangle above gape intense red-pink; face bright yellow and area around eye turquoise.*
IMMATURE: *Upper parts mottled dark and light brown. Underparts brown and white, sometimes all brown. Face yellow. Around and below eye grey. Throat pale pink. Iris green. Bill horn-coloured with dark ridge.*
JUVENILE: *Upper parts silky dark brown. Underparts streaked white and dark grey. Face and throat cream or pale yellow. Around and below eye grey. Iris dark brown. Bill pink-white or pale grey with dark ridge.*
NESTLING: *Naked when hatched, skin pink, then black. Facial area pale yellow. Bill pale cream. Later down dark brown above, white below.*

MOULT
Gradual, with no flightless period.

VOICE
During pair-formation loud and raucous calls from males and soft hissing from females. Usually silent away from resting, roosting and nesting areas.

DISTRIBUTION
Sheltered and shallow marine waters and large inland lakes and rivers of the 3 main islands. Also on islands off the east coast from North Cape to East Cape. Rare vagrant at The Snares. Common around mainland Australia on marine waters and rare on inland lakes and rivers. Rare vagrant to Tasmania.

RECOGNITION

Black and white plumage with naked yellow patch in front of eye. Long stout bill with large hook. Weak short wings and long tail. Flies with head and S-shaped neck held high.

Little Pied Cormorant
P.m. brevirostris GOULD, 1837.

OTHER NAMES: *Kawaupaka,*
white-throated shag, frilled shag,
little river shag, little cormorant,
little shag.

SIZE: *560 mm.*

DESCRIPTION
ADULT: *Sexes alike. Upper parts*
black. Upper wing coverts dark grey
with broad black borders. Face
yellow. Underparts all or partly
white, border starting above bill with
white area over eye. White plumage
varies from only on throat and sides
of head, to breast and belly mottled
black and white, to all white below.
Sometimes white plumage stained
yellow or orange. Naked part of
throat yellow. Iris dark brown. Bill
yellow with black ridge. Mouth-
lining light blue. Legs and feet black.
At start of breeding black crest on
forehead and erect white frills on
side of crown; face dark grey; throat
orange; bill orange with dark ridge.
JUVENILE: *Either all black or black*
above and white below with border
starting below eye. Bill black with
base of lower bill red. Assumes adult
colouring late in first year.
NESTLING: *Naked black skin, with*
throat pouch red. Later, down black
with bald crown pink. Around bill
pink, later white. Bill black.

MOULT
Gradual, with no flightless period.

VOICE
Cooing and croaking at nesting area.
Squeaking and sucking sounds from
chicks.

DISTRIBUTION
Inland and coastal waters of 3
main islands; Indonesia, New
Guinea, Australia and southwestern
Pacific Islands. Birds probably from
Australia straggle to Lord Howe
and Norfolk Islands and have bred
at Campbell Island.

RECOGNITION
Small, tubby cormorant with
short, stubby bill, long tail
and broad wings. Some birds
identified by white thighs.
Flies with neck S-shaped and
head held high.

The nest of the little pied cormorant is constructed with material gathered by the male. The female lays four eggs.

Little Pied Cormorant *Phalacrocorax melanoleucos* (VIEILLOT,1817)

ALONG ROCKY SEASHORES, in bays, estuaries and small inland water bodies, the little pied cormorant hunts crayfish, other crustaceans, fish and insects. It pursues most of this prey under water, swimming with its feet to the side of its body in the manner of grebes and ducks. It grabs fish and crustaceans by its short, strong bill and, in the case of crayfish, shakes them until their claws drop off. Fish too large to be swallowed it drops on shore.

This bird takes off much more steeply than other cormorants, at an angle of about 45°. It roosts and breeds in trees and bushes and occasionally in reeds or on rocks, and builds a nest of sticks, twigs, plants and debris. Near Auckland birds breed between August and March, with most females laying in September or early October.

Its four eggs are elliptical, pointed, and pale blue with a chalky outer layer. The male bird chooses the nest-site and the female builds the nest, with material gathered by the male. Once the eggs are laid, both parents bring extra nest material. The bird on the nest droops its wings, exposing its back, and the bird beside the nest folds its wings well up.

When a male is looking for a mate it stands upright and raises its closed wings. It then sits, stands up again and lowers its wings. This display is performed either once or twice at irregular intervals, or for some minutes at a rate of two or three times per minute. When it sits, the bird holds its head vertically, with bill closed and forehead crest raised. It ruffles its body feathers and raises its tail.

A male greets an actual or potential mate by standing upright with its forehead crest raised and bill closed. It then swings its head and open bill through a vertical arc forward and down, until the head is almost upside down or—if it is perched on a branch—below the feet. Sometimes, it repeats this after two or three seconds. During this display the male raises its tail slightly and calls a guttural cooing *oo-oo* or *oo-oo-oo* as it swings its head downwards.

When a male arrives with nest material it calls a repetitive *uck-uck-uck*. Before the birds change over they utter the same call with their mouths open and directed forward, their forehead crests raised and their heads swaying. Later in the breeding sequence and especially when a bird arrives to feed the chicks, it calls a repetitive soft *uk-uk-uk*. Before flying or hopping from one part of the colony to another it coos a harsh *oo-oo-oo*. When it lands it holds its head up and forward, with its throat bulged, and its mouth open and directed forward. When threatened by other birds the little pied cormorant extends its neck, gaping its open bill at the intruder.   W.J.M.V., G.F.v.T. & M.J.T.

King Shag *Leucocarbo carunculatus* (GMELIN, 1789)

WITH A TOTAL POPULATION of fewer than 500 birds, the king shag is one of the world's rarest shags. It lives only around Cook Strait and the Marlborough Sounds, where it roosts and nests on the barren rocks of small islands. It forages in sheltered inlets and bays, catching fish, such as blue cod, sole and sand eels. When it leaves the water, it dries its wings by beating them back and forth. Like other subantarctic shags it does not spread out its wings to dry.

Sometimes king shags swallow pebbles, but the reasons for this are unclear. Perhaps, the pebbles reduce buoyancy and act as ballast when the bird dives under water; or they may assist in pellet regurgitation or offset hunger pangs.

The breeding season of the king shag varies from year to year and from colony to colony, probably depending on the weather and the availability of food. It builds a nest of ice plant, grass and other plants on bare sloping rocks. Its two eggs are elliptical and pale blue with a chalky surface.

To attract a female, a male swings its head through a vertical arc, sometimes bumping its head on its rump. The body remains horizontal, with tail raised, wings drooped and head and neck feathers pressed down. Sometimes, when a pair greet each other, they lower and raise their heads in front of their bodies. Their bills are closed, their bodies horizontal and their tails lowered.　　　　G.F.v.T.

ENDEMIC

OTHER NAMES: *Carunculated shag, Marlborough Sounds shag, rough-faced shag, Cook Strait cormorant.*

SIZE: *760 mm.*

DESCRIPTION
ADULT: *Sexes alike. Upper parts black with blue sheen. Upper wing coverts dark purple-brown with green sheen and narrow indistinct black borders. White wing, shoulder and back patches. Base of tail feathers white. Underparts white, starting at side of throat. White line on underwing. Throat and face slate grey. Mouth-lining orange-red. Eye-ring blue. Iris hazel-grey. Bill grey-pink. Caruncles at base of bill yellow. Legs and feet grey-pink. At start of breeding long black crest on forehead and short black crest on nape; throat and face blue-grey; mouth-lining red; caruncles orange.*
IMMATURE: *Upper parts brown with green sheen. Underparts white. No caruncles. Upper bill brown. Lower bill white. Face, legs and feet flesh-coloured.*
NESTLING: *Black skin, later covered with sooty brown down. Upper bill and tip of lower bill brown-black. Rest of lower bill and throat blue-white or pink. Bare skin on head black. Iris green-grey. Legs and feet brown.*

MOULT
Gradual, with no flightless period.

VOICE
No information on calls at resting, roosting and nesting areas. Silent elsewhere.

DISTRIBUTION
Cook Strait and the Marlborough Sounds.

RECOGNITION
Only shag with pink feet in the Cook Strait and Marlborough Sounds area. Prominent caruncles at base of bill. Short broad wings. Flies with head held lower than body. Differs from pied cormorant in that black and white border starts at side of throat.

One of the rarest shags, the king shag nests only on the small, rocky islands of Cook Strait and Marlborough Sounds.

The Stewart Island shag has two colour forms and typically nests and roosts on the bare rocks of headlands and small islands.

Stewart Island Shag *Leucocarbo chalconotus* (GRAY,1845)

ON THE BARREN, SLOPING ROCKS of headlands and small islands the Stewart Island shag builds a tall nest, one to one and a half metres high, of grass, peat and debris, cemented with faeces. To line the nest bowl, it gathers dry grass. The breeding season varies from year to year and from colony to colony, probably depending on food supplies and the weather. It lays two or three eggs which are elliptical and pale blue with a rough chalky outer layer. When the chicks are a week old they beg for food with a squeaky *ah-whee-ah*.

The male that is looking for a mate holds its body upright with its bill closed and tail raised. It swings its head back to its rump. Occasionally, it opens its bill slightly and calls *borr*. To show recognition, both sexes open their bills wide and move their heads slowly back and forth in front of their bodies. At the same time, their bodies are horizontal with their breasts pressed down and their rumps raised. The male calls a soft *eh-eh-eh* and the female remains silent.

A bird that is about to leave the nest-site opens its bill slightly and points it downwards. It stands upright, with the top of its neck arched and its forehead crest raised. On arrival at the nest, a bird kinks its throat, and if it is a male, calls a repetitive *corr-corr-corr.* . . . It then arches its neck forward and downward with the head higher than the body and its closed bill horizontal. It keeps its crest and crown feathers down but raises its neck feathers and bulges its throat.

Stewart Island shags forage for bullheads in sheltered sea inlets and bays, and rest on the bare rocks of headlands.   G.F.v.T.

ENDEMIC

OTHER NAMES: *Bronze shag, Gray's shag.*

SIZE: *680 mm.*

DESCRIPTION
ADULT: *Sexes alike. Upper parts black with blue sheen. Upper wing coverts dark brown with green sheen and narrow black border. Sometimes white wing, shoulder and back patches. Base of tail feathers white. Underparts black or white or mixed, starting from side of throat. Face dark purple-brown. Caruncles yellow. Throat dark purple-brown or* shiny *light red. Mouth-lining orange. Eye-ring blue. Iris dark golden brown. Bill pale brown, pink or grey with dark ridge. Legs and feet pink. At start of breeding long black crest on forehead; short black crest on nape, long white nuptial tufts on sides of crown and some plumes elsewhere on head and neck; caruncles red; eye-ring iridescent purple-blue; and mouth-lining red.*
IMMATURE: *Upper parts dark. Sometimes white wing and back patches. Underparts dark brown or white, or mixed. Face dark brown. Eye-ring grey. Gape yellow. Iris pale brown. Bill light grey or sandy with dark ridge. Legs and feet* flesh-coloured.
NESTLING: *Naked black skin, later covered with grey down, sometimes mottled white below. Upper bill, face and naked crown grey. Lower bill and throat pale iridescent blue with black patches.*

MOULT
Gradual, with no flightless period.

VOICE
Males bark at roosting and nesting areas. Silent elsewhere.

DISTRIBUTION
Fewer than 5000 birds around Stewart Island and the southern end of the South Island.

Bounty Island Shag

Leucocarbo ranfurlyi

OGILVIE-GRANT, 1901

ENDEMIC

OTHER NAMES: *None.*

SIZE: *710 mm.*

DESCRIPTION

ADULT: *Sexes alike. Upper parts black with blue sheen. Upper wing coverts dark-brown with green sheen and narrow indistinct black borders. White wing patches. Sometimes white back patches. Throat orange-red. Face red, orange or purple. Eye-ring red. Base of bill orange or yellow. Underparts white, starting at side of throat. Sometimes 1 or 2 lines on underwing. Iris light brown. Bill brown or pink with dark ridge and light tip. Legs and feet pink with grey smudges around top of tarsus and on toes. Nails dark brown.*
IMMATURE: *Brown above and white below. Sometimes, brown spots or broad band on white foreneck. Iris brown.*
JUVENILE: *Throat grey. Face and eye-ring brown. Iris pale brown. Bill brown-flesh colour.*

MOULT
Gradual, with no flightless period.

VOICE
At resting, roosting and nesting areas, males make soft purring and ticking sounds audible only a metre or so away and females are silent except for soft, puffing sounds during mating. Silent elsewhere.

DISTRIBUTION
Fewer than 600 birds at the Bounty Islands in 1978.

RECOGNITION

Only shag at the Bounty Islands. Black and white plumage. No caruncles at base of bill. Yellow or orange at gape. Short broad wings.

To build its nest the Bounty Island shag gathers brown seaweed which it combines with feathers, stones and mud.

TO GATHER THE BROWN SEAWEED *Marginariella,* with which it builds its nest, the Bounty Island shag dives over 10 m into very rough seas. The surging waters are thought to loosen the seaweed, which on land soon dries out to a sticky consistency. The birds combine it with feathers, mud, stones and debris to construct a nest about 35 cm wide and up to 15 cm high. As the surface of the seaweed hardens it binds the nest.

The shags space these nests about a metre apart from centre to centre on skyline ridges or on the ledges and alcoves of cliffs. During the months of October and November the female lays two or three eggs. Both parents take turns to guard the nest.

When they are breeding, females leave the nesting area shortly after dawn to forage and return during the middle of the day. Males forage during the afternoon when their mate has returned. Before the birds leave they regurgitate a green or pink pellet of food remains and pebbles, with a soft *gock-gock-gock* ... sound. They also dive a few times for seaweed to strengthen the nest. They feed far out to sea, mainly on small fish and octopus. They also eat small hermit crabs. Regurgitated pellets were found to contain pebbles, small snails, bivalve shell fragments, sea urchin spines and bits of coral. When they dive for food from the water, they usually jump higher than a body length before plunging beneath the surface.

The Bounty Island shag forms pairs and builds a nest in the same way as the great cormorant. The male advertises the nest-site by swinging its head backwards and forwards. As its head reaches its rump, its body usually becomes vertical. At the same time, its bill opens, then snaps shut as its head returns to the forward position. During this display, the bird raises its tail almost vertically and droops its wings down beside its body. It calls a soft *hargh.* When a bird is on

or near the nest-site its forehead crest is raised. It forms a prominent line around its neck and throat by depressing its crown feathers and raising its neck feathers.

Birds greet each other with their bills wide open, directed forward and sometimes slightly up, moving back, forth and sideways in front of their bodies. During mating males call a soft *he-he-he* .... They threaten intruders by opening their bills wide, bulging their throats and moving their heads back, forth and sideways. Sometimes males call a soft *borr-borr-borr.*

Just before a Bounty Island shag leaves its nest-site it holds its head high with its bill closed or slightly open and sloping slightly downwards. This posture closely resembles that of the great cormorant. Usually the neck is almost vertical, but arched slightly, so that the head is rather forward. The breast and the belly pulsate. Males sometimes make a ticking *t-t-t* ..., but females are silent. Males also make this sound and pulsate their breast when they are about to rise from their nest to let their mate take over incubation.

As it arrives at the nest-site a bird kinks its throat, in a fashion similar to the pied cormorant and the emperor shag. Nearer the nest, males sometimes call a soft *herr-herr-herr* ..., *corr-corr-corr* ... or *horr-horr-horr* .... After landing the bird raises its head with its bill horizontal and its throat bulged. It holds its neck and body almost vertical and lowers its tail.

In short flights around the colony, the bird arches its neck and holds its closed bill downwards. Males sometimes start with a soft ticking *t-t-t* ... call and end with a soft *aw-orgh.* When they walk through the nesting colony the birds arch their necks and point their closed bills downwards.

G.F.v.T. & C.J.R.R.

Chatham Island Shag *Leucocarbo onslowi* FORBES,1893

THE CHATHAM ISLAND SHAG shares its breeding islands with both the Pitt Island shag and the great cormorant. All three birds fish in the surrounding seas, but they nest and roost apart. While the Chatham Island shag rests and breeds on the exposed rocks of headlands and small islands, the Pitt Island shag prefers the sides of cliffs, and the great cormorant inland swamps.

The Chatham Island shag builds its nest of ice plant, grass and other plants on level and sloping rocks not far above the high tide line and the spray zone. Between September and December it lays three eggs, oval to elliptical in shape, and pale blue with a chalky outer layer.

A male that is looking for a mate holds its body almost vertical and moves its head back towards its rump. Its bill may be either closed, slightly open or wide open. It repeats this movement up to 13 times in quick succession. Sometimes it brings its head down beside its body. It also raises its tail and droops its wings. Occasionally it makes a loud *orgh, rogh* or *borr* as it moves its head back. A male bird that is threatened calls *ergh*.

When a bird is about to leave the nest-site it opens its bill slightly and points it downwards, holding its body upright. Females remain silent but males call *t-t-t* .... On arrival at the nest-site, a male calls a repetitive *corr-corr-corr* .... Then the bird lowers its head to the level of its breast and holds its closed bill horizontal.

A bird on the nest greets its mate or potential mate by opening its bill wide, directing it forward and moving it back and forth in front of its body. During this display males make a loud barking *heh-heh-heh* ... and females call a soft puffing *ghff-ghff-ghff* ...

The Chatham Island shag feeds on small fish about 10 cm long, which it hunts in bays, inlets and along sheltered shores.   G.F.v.T.

ENDEMIC

OTHER NAMES: *None.*

SIZE: *630 mm.*

DESCRIPTION
ADULT: *Sexes alike. Upper parts black with blue sheen. Upper wing coverts dark grey-brown with green sheen and narrow indistinct black borders. Sometimes, white wing and back patches. Base of tail feathers white. Underparts white, border starting at side of throat. White line on underwing. Face, throat and mouth-lining orange. Caruncles yellow. Eye-ring blue. Iris brown. Bill grey-brown. Legs and feet pink. At start of breeding black crest on forehead; caruncles and base of lower bill orange-red; throat and mouth-lining bright red; face dark purple; and eye-ring purple-blue.*
IMMATURE: *Brown above and white below. Sometimes white wing patches and sandy brown back patches. Throat and face brown. Eye-ring pale blue. Iris green-brown. Bill pale blue-grey with dark ridge. Legs and feet pink.*
FLEDGLING: *Throat pale blue-white. Face brown-black. Iris grey-brown. Upper bill dark horn colour; lower bill blue-white at base and horn colour at tip. Legs and feet brown-black.*
NESTLING: *Naked when hatched. Later covered with smoky brown down with tufts of white filoplumes.*

MOULT
Gradual, with no flightless period.

VOICE
At resting, roosting and nesting areas males make barking and ticking sounds. Silent elsewhere.

DISTRIBUTION
Fewer than 5000 birds around the Chatham Islands. Main colonies, with about 530 nests, at Star Keys.

RECOGNITION
Only shag with pink feet around the Chatham Islands. Black and white plumage. Caruncles at base of bill. Short broad wings. Flies with head held lower than body.

The arrival or departure of the male Chatham Island shag at a nest-site is usually accompanied by calls and displays.

Campbell Island shags commonly rest on intertidal rocks and rocky headlands after foraging. Non-breeders roost separately from nesting and courting birds.

Campbell Island Shag *Leucocarbo campbelli* (Filhol, 1878)

ENDEMIC

OTHER NAMES: *None.*

SIZE: *630 mm.*

DESCRIPTION
ADULT: *Sexes alike. Upper parts and most of foreneck black with blue sheen. Upper wing coverts dark purple-grey with green sheen and narrow indistinct black borders. Sometimes white wing patches. Base of tail feathers white. Face dark purple. Line above and spot below gape yellow. Throat, mouth-lining and behind yellow gape spot red. Underparts white, starting at side of throat. Iris dark brown. Legs and feet pink with dark grey smudges. At start of breeding long black crest on forehead; long white nuptial plumes scattered on side of head; gape line and spot orange.*
IMMATURE: *Dark brown above and white below, patterned like adult. Throat and mouth-lining dull yellow-orange. Face dull purple. Legs and feet dull orange, pink and grey. Iris grey-brown. Bill light orange-brown merging into yellow or orange at base and gape.*
NESTLING: *Skin black. Throat and lower bill pink. Later covered with grey down.*

MOULT
Gradual, with no flightless period.

VOICE
At resting, roosting and nesting areas males bark rarely. Silent elsewhere.

DISTRIBUTION
Fewer than 10 000 birds at Campbell Island and adjacent stacks, rocks and islets.

> **RECOGNITION**
> Black and white plumage. No caruncles. Prominent yellow line above gape and yellow spot below. Red behind yellow spot. Short broad wings. Flies with head held lower than body.

CAMPBELL ISLAND SHAGS HUNT in large flocks. First they fan out in a line, dip their heads in the water and beat the surface with their wings. Then together they jump into the air before disappearing beneath the surface. Once submerged they swim long distances, probably catching small crustaceans and fish. The birds reappear scattered across the surface, but before they dive again they swim towards each other and regroup. Their feeding grounds are both far out to sea and in bays and inlets near the shore. Sometimes, other seabirds, such as Cape petrels, Antarctic terns and red-billed gulls feed with Campbell Island shags.

When they have finished foraging, the shags rest on intertidal rocks and barren headlands. Non-breeding birds roost separately from nesting and courting birds. When a shag lands at a crowded roost, it keeps its head down with its bill closed and pointing downwards. After a while it relaxes and raises its head.

They breed in large sea caves or on vertical cliffs in alcoves and on ledges beneath overhanging rocks. Their nests are built from tussock grass, other plants and debris. Little is known about the breeding cycle, but adults are in nuptial plumage in June, and fully grown chicks seen in November suggest that the birds lay from about August to December. Often skuas harass nesting Campbell Island shags and try to steal their eggs. Sometimes, however, Antarctic terns nesting in small caves near the shag colonies mob the skuas and prevent them from landing near the shags' nests.

At the nest-site, the shags usually display their forehead crests. They also depress their crown feathers and raise their neck feathers to outline their napes. The male chooses a nest-site and advertises for a mate. He gathers the nest material and the female builds the nest. The bird on the nest droops its wings to expose its back; the bird outside the nest folds its wings well up.

A male advertising for a mate holds its body horizontal, presses its breast down and its rump up. It swings its head backwards and forwards sometimes bouncing it on its rump. The position of its tail varies from being down below the horizontal to being up and forward. Its bill is either slightly open or wide open, its crest is down and, as in most of its displays, the bird is silent.

When a pair greet each other they open their bills wide and move them back and forth in front of their bodies as well as sideways and towards the rear, at a rate varying from once to twice per second. During this display, the head and neck plumage is sleek, the body horizontal, the wings droop beside the body and the tail is up. Alternatively, two birds may lower and raise their heads. They either stand side by side with their heads going up and down in front of them, or they face each other and alternate between moving their heads up and down several times on one side and several times on the other side. As the head goes down there is a flash of red as the throat bulges.

Both males and females respond to intruders by worrying the nest with their bills. Sometimes they confront the other bird with a wide open bill and bulging throat. At the same time the bird moves its head back and forth and sideways.

Before a bird leaves the nest-site it holds its head high with its closed or slightly open bill sloping slightly downwards. Usually its neck is almost vertical with a slight bend in the upper neck so that the head is somewhat forward. Occasionally the neck is horizontal and rarely is it arched higher than the head. The belly and the breast pulsate about two times a second, but no sound is made. A bird arriving at the nest kinks its throat and, if a male, occasionally calls *korr-korr-korr*. After it has landed it holds its head high and somewhat forward, with its closed bill horizontal and its upper neck bulged where there is a white patch of feathers.

G.F.v.T.

Auckland Island Shag *Leucocarbo colensoi* BULLER, 1888

THE AUCKLAND ISLAND SHAG BREEDS in alcoves, on ledges or along the tops of very steep cliffs. It makes its nest either on a tussock or on the ground under overhanging rocks, bushes or trees. Such cover helps protect the eggs and chicks from southern skuas. When overhead plants die and rot, the shags abandon the nest-site for one that is more secure. High tides, another danger, often wash away nests.

The birds gather mainly tussock straws and some twigs, bracken, seaweed, peat, mud and debris, and space their nests about 75 cm apart from centre to centre. Between November and February, at three-day intervals, they lay three oval, pale blue eggs with a smooth outer chalky layer. The first egg hatches after about 29 days, the second after 26 days. Usually, the parents rear only two chicks, which they guard until the young are strong enough to ward off other birds.

Auckland Island shags hunt a small crustacean *Munida subrugosa* either far out to sea or in bays and inlets. During nesting the female forages from shortly after dawn to the middle of the day. When she returns, the male leaves and comes back before dusk. Before a bird departs it gathers more nesting material and regurgitates a wrinkled pellet of food remains. When a bird is about to regurgitate, its neck swells up and, if it is a male, it calls an accelerating *gock-gock-gock* . . . . If a female, it calls a shoft *ff-ff-ff* . . . . Usually a red-billed gull gobbles up the pellet.

Auckland Island shags form pairs in the same way as great cormorants. When it advertises for a mate, the male swings its head back and forth with its bill closed or open, its tail raised and its wings drooping. As its head reaches back to its rump, its body becomes almost vertical and it calls a loud *ahr, arr, ohr, bar, borr, orr* or *orrgh*. It may also perform the display silently. It repeats this movement many times at a slow irregular rate.

Mated birds greet each other by moving their wide-open bills back and forth in front of their bodies. Their breasts pulsate. Males make a loud raucous barking *ah-ah-ah* . . ., *eh-eh-eh* . . . or *he-he-he* . . . and females are either silent or utter a soft, barely audible, *ff-ff-ff* . . ., *fee-fee-fee* . . ., *eh-eh-eh* . . . or *hegh-hegh-hegh* . . . .

A threatened male calls either a single *argh* or *ergh* or a repetitive *erh-erh-erh* . . ., *ehr-ehr-ehr* . . . or *err-err-err* . . . . Females either threaten silently or make soft *gf-gf-gf* . . . or *ff-ff-ff* . . . sounds. A bird that is alarmed raises its head, its neck becoming vertical and sleek.

A bird about to take off from the nest-site stands erect with its neck arched higher than its head. It directs its half to slightly open bill forwards and downwards as its breast pulsates. Sometimes males call a ticking *t-t-t* . . ., *eh-eh-eh* . . . or *hu-hu-hu* . . . . After take-off the feet sometimes touch above the tail. Birds arriving at the nest-site kink their throats. Males may call a repetitive *ergh-ergh-ergh*.   G.F.v.T.

ENDEMIC

OTHER NAMES: *None.*

SIZE: *630 mm.*

DESCRIPTION
ADULT: *Sexes alike. Upper parts black with blue sheen. Upper wing coverts dark purple-grey with green sheen and narrow indistinct black borders. Broad black band across foreneck prominent in some and poorly developed, spotty or absent in others. Sometimes white wing patches. Rarely white shoulder patches. White back patches on some males. Base of tail feathers white. Face dark purple. Eye-ring pink or shiny purple. Line above and below gape yellow. Mouth-lining orange-red. Throat red. Underparts white, starting at side of throat. Black plumage fades to brown in December and January when eggs are hatching. Iris dark purple or brown. Bill dark brown. Legs and top of feet pink with dark grey smudges, soles dark grey and nails black. At start of breeding long black crest on forehead; bill dark grey with orange tip to lower bill; eye-ring shiny violet-purple, gape lines orange and somewhat warty. During nesting crest becomes shorter.* IMMATURE: *Dark brown above, white below. Sometimes brown band or spots across foreneck; white or sandy brown wing and back patches.* NESTLING: *Naked grey or black skin, later covered with grey down. Throat and lower bill pink.*

MOULT
Gradual, with no flightless period.

VOICE
At resting, roosting and nesting areas males make barking and ticking sounds and females make soft, almost inaudible, puffing sounds. Silent elsewhere.

DISTRIBUTION
Fewer than 5000 birds, mainly at the northern and southern ends of the Auckland Islands.

RECOGNITION

Only shag at the Auckland Islands. Black and white plumage. No caruncles. Prominent yellow line above and below gape. Prominent eye-ring, paler than face. Short broad wings.

The Auckland Island shag constructs its bulky nest with tussock straws, twigs, bracken, seaweed, peat, mud and debris.

Emperor Shag *Leucocarbo atriceps* (KING, 1828)

FROM ITS ROOSTING SITES on barren rocks just above the spray zone, the emperor shag commutes in large flocks to its foraging grounds out at sea or in inlets, bays and tide pools. The birds leave before ten in the morning and return by four, flying with short, broad wings, somewhat like bats. When they dive from the water to catch crustaceans and fish, they usually leap clear of the surface first.

This shag ranges around the South Pole on the Antarctic Peninsula, at southern South America and on subantarctic islands. In the New Zealand region 600 pairs breed in 14 colonies on Macquarie Island and a further 100 pairs nest on nearby Bishop and Clerk Rocks. It is surprising that, given the wide range of this bird, it has not strayed a few hundred kilometres to the Auckland and Campbell Islands. It may well be a distinct species.

The emperor shag breeds for the first time at the end of its second or third year. In June, it displays its nuptial plumage of a black forehead crest, white plumes and orange caruncles. In the following month the birds start to build nests of tussock grass, moss, mud and debris, usually on sloping rocks so close to the high tide line that storms often wash the nests away. About 20 cm high and 50 cm wide, these nests are positioned one or two metres apart from centre to centre. The birds lay between late September and mid-January. If flooding destroys nests and eggs the birds replace them within a month.

The three ovoid-elliptical eggs are pale blue with a chalky outside layer. The parents incubate them for 33 days and in late November or early December the eggs start to hatch. From the middle of January the chicks wander up to five metres away from the nest, but the parents still feed them at the nest. By March most chicks have left the nest. During this stage, siblings often stay together when away from the nest. For a short period in May the rookery is completely deserted, the nests have disintegrated and the rocks are washed clean, but at all other times the colony is occupied by paired birds.

When pairs are forming, the male holds its body upright, swings its head back through a vertical arc until its crown and nape touch its rump and then swings it forward again. Sometimes the bird sits with its breast raised during this display; at other times it stands on either both or only one foot. As it swings its head, it opens its bill wide and sometimes calls *eeh-oh*, *oh-arr*, *heh-who* or *heh-hah* with the first syllable during the back stroke and the second during the forward movement. At the same time, it raises its tail, droops its wings down beside its body and presses down its head and neck feathers.

A bird greets its mate by directing its open bill forward and sometimes slightly upwards with its neck straight and vertical, its body horizontal and its tail varying from down to almost vertically upwards. It droops its wings down beside its body. Early in the breeding season, the male barks a loud, slow, repetitive *heh-heh-heh* ... and the female hisses. Later the male calls *oh-oh-oh* ....

Males threaten intruders by swinging their wide open bills sideways and back and forth. They bark a raucous *harrr* which changes to a growling *wirrr* sound as the bills lock during fighting. Females hiss.

Birds about to take off from the nest-site open their bills slightly and pulsate their breasts. The female is silent, but the male calls *t-t-t* .... Once airborne, males sometimes call a loud *owh*. Birds arriving at the nest-site kink their throats and close their bills. Males utter a repetitive *orgh-orgh-orgh* ..., *ooh-ooh-ooh* ... or *oo-ah-oo-ah-oo-ah* .... If the nest has chicks the male calls *oh-oh-oh* .... After landing, the bird lowers its head and upper neck straight out in front of its breast. Its throat remains kinked or bulged and its bill closed. It holds its tail down. Males call *whoo* and females hiss.

Before birds fly from one part of the colony to another, however short the distance, they arch their necks and direct their open bills downwards. Males call a ticking *t-t-t* ..., then when they land they utter a gargling or warbling *ah-grrrg* or *ah-worgh*.

When a bird walks through or near the nesting colony—especially a male gathering nesting material or a female in search of a mate—it arches its upper neck and holds its closed bill against the base of its neck. It forms a ridge of feathers along its nape by depressing its crown feathers and raising its upper neck feathers. It folds its wings tightly on top of its back and holds its tail down.   G.F.V.T., N.B. & W.J.M.V.

ENDEMIC
Emperor Shag
L.a. purpurascens (BRANDT, 1837).

OTHER NAMES: *Subantarctic king shag, blue-eyed shag, imperial cormorant, Macquarie Island shag.*

SIZE: *710 mm.*

DESCRIPTION
ADULT: *Sexes alike. Upper parts black with blue sheen. Upper wing coverts brown-black with green sheen and thin indistinct black borders. Sometimes white wing and shoulder patches. Base of tail feathers white. Face and above gape black with yellow spots. Throat orange-brown with yellow spots. Underparts white, starting at gape. White line on underwing. Iris dark brown. Eye-ring blue. Bill grey with horn-coloured patch near tip of lower bill. Caruncles yellow. Mouth-lining red with front along inside of bill black. Front of legs and base of feet pink. Back of legs and tips of feet purple-grey. At start of breeding black crest on forehead; caruncles orange; sometimes a few white plumes on head, neck and back. Later in breeding season, many females and some males have worn upper wing coverts.*
IMMATURE: *Upper parts brown with green sheen. Underparts white. Wing patch pale brown. No caruncles.*
NESTLING: *Shiny black skin with pink throat when hatched. Later, sooty brown down and pink or white face.*

MOULT
Gradual, with no flightless period.

VOICE
At resting, roosting and nesting areas male makes barking and ticking sounds and female hisses.

DISTRIBUTION
Macquarie Island and nearby Bishop and Clerk Rocks. Along shores and islands north and south of Antarctic convergence, including Antarctic Peninsula; tip of South America; the Falkland, South Shetland, South Orkney and South Sandwich Islands; Îles Crozet; South Georgia; Marion and Heard Islands.

RECOGNITION
Only black and white shag known to occur at Macquarie Island. Flies with head held below body axis.

A breeding pair of emperor shags at their nest. Parents incubate their three pale blue eggs for 33 days.

Spotted Shag *Stictocarbo punctatus* (SPARRMAN, 1786)

ENDEMIC
Spotted Shag
S.p. punctatus (SPARRMAN, 1786).
Blue Shag
S.p. steadi (OLIVER, 1930).

OTHER NAMES: *Parekareka, ocean shag, crested shag, flip-flap, blue shag.*

SIZE: *730 mm.*

DESCRIPTION

ADULT: *Sexes alike. Crown, hind neck, back, belly, thighs, tail and upper foreneck black. Pale grey base to tail feathers. Wings grey-brown with primaries browner. Black tips on upper wing coverts. Throat, face and eye-ring green. White stripe from above eye, down side of neck, to side of breast, with variable amounts of grey when breeding. White line obscured by dark feathers at end of breeding. Sometimes white line along base of throat. Lower foreneck and breast grey. Iris dark brown. Bill orange-brown with dark ridge and cream-coloured bar at base of lower bill. Legs and feet orange. At start of breeding, long black crests on forehead and nape; long white plumes on head, neck, back, rump and thighs; throat dark blue; eye-ring blue; around and below eye to gape blue-green. Blue shag has darker wings and narrower white stripe on side of neck.*
IMMATURE: *Grey-brown above and grey-white below. Dark tips on upper wing coverts. Upper foreneck and hind neck dark grey. Throat, face and eye-ring yellow. Stripe on side of neck pale grey. Slight grey crest on forehead. Iris dark brown. Bill yellow-pink.*

JUVENILE: *Upper parts dark grey with small white filoplumes. Upper wing coverts grey-brown with thin border and black tip. Underparts pale grey. Iris green. Eye-ring pale green. Bill, face, legs and feet brown-yellow.*
NESTLING: *Skin dark grey. Face, legs and feet flesh-coloured. Later, dark grey-brown down above, and white down with grey-brown spots below. Naked crown. Throat and mouth-lining orange-pink. Dark line through eye. Iris dark brown. Legs and feet grey.*

MOULT
Gradual, with no flightless period.

VOICE
At resting, roosting and nesting areas male makes loud grunts. Silent elsewhere.

DISTRIBUTION
Spotted shag: *Rocky shores and headlands of the North and South Islands.*

Blue shag: *Rocky shores and headlands of Stewart Island and the western coast of the South Island.*

RECOGNITION
Only shag around the three main islands with green face and black spots on tips of upper wing coverts. Very slender bird with long, slender wings and short stubby tail. Long slim bill with small terminal hook.

The spotted shag has the most striking breeding plumage of New Zealand's shags and cormorants. It frequents the rocky coast of the three main islands.

AT THE START OF THE BREEDING season the spotted shag is the most striking and elegant of the New Zealand shags. Black crests appear on its forehead and at the back of its head; long, white plumes are scattered over its head and upper parts; its dark brown eye is ringed with blue and this, in turn, is surrounded by a patch of bright green. The spotted shag displays this plumage in its courtship rituals, holding its prominent forehead and nape crests erect.

The male advertises for a mate by raising its partly folded wings and flapping them about four times per second. It points its closed bill upwards and brings its head down to its back. Sometimes it deflects its bill towards the female and brings its head and neck in a tight S-curve down beside its shoulders, but with the bill still pointing upwards.

A male greets a female by slowly swinging its stretched head and neck from the base of its tail to the ground in front. The neck acts as a pivot to the rapidly vibrating head. In another display the male holds its head upside down below the base of its arched neck and points its partly open bill back and downwards. Both sexes greet their mate by moving the head slowly up and down, with the closed bill pointing upwards. In a variation of this display, the bird also raises its body up and pulsates its breast. Or the bird opens its bill, points it upwards and moves its head backwards and forwards above its back.

When approached by a shag other than its mate, the bird on the nest-site worries the nest in a demonstrative but ineffectual manner with its bill. Sometimes it worries the tail of its mate instead. Males may confront intruders with a loud *hergh-hergh.*

Before a bird flies away from the nest-site it faces the nest, stretches its neck and raises its head up and slightly forward. It drops its closed bill and points it in the direction of its intended take-off. It slightly inflates its throat, but its lower neck remains thin so that its head and neck have a club-shaped appearance. Sometimes the throat pulsates slowly a couple of times. The bird then lowers its breast, spreads its wings and with a powerful kick launches itself from the cliff. Its brightly coloured feet move beside its tail. The bird does not relax its head and neck posture until it is some distance from the cliff.

A bird arriving at the nest-site kinks its throat and, if it is not carrying any nest material, opens its bill wide. With its bill directed down and forward the male calls a loud repetitive *ergh-ergh-ergh ....* Once it has landed the bird stretches its neck and raises its head up and slightly forward. During most displays on or near the nest-site the tail is raised about 45° above the horizontal.

The breeding season of spotted shags varies from year to year and from colony to colony, depending primarily on the availability of food, and local weather conditions. It builds its nest of ice plant, grass and twigs on the alcoves of steep cliffs, plucking grass when the ground has been softened by rain. The usual clutch size is three. The eggs are elliptical with blunt ends and pale blue with a chalky outside layer. These are usually laid three days apart and incubated for 28 to 31 days. The parents take turns to guard the nest, changing over at least three times a day, until the chicks are strong enough to fend off predatory birds. The parents feed the chicks approximately four times a day at the nest, even after the young birds have fledged and left the nest at about nine weeks old.

The spotted shag hunts far out to sea and in bays, inlets and estuaries, catching fish and planktonic crustaceans under water. When it dives directly from the water, it usually jumps into the air first. It also swallows pebbles, perhaps to reduce buoyancy under water, or to facilitate the regurgitation of indigestible food remains. It is possible that these pebbles serve to offset hunger pangs. After it has fed, it rests on cliffs, with its wings spread out to dry. When the spotted shag lands or takes off, it spreads its large, webbed feet on either side of its tail to almost treble its surface area.

G.F.v.T.

At the start of the breeding season the Pitt Island shag has dense concentrations of long white nuptial plumes on its hind neck.

Pitt Island Shag *Stictocarbo featherstoni* BULLER,1873

LIKE ITS CLOSE RELATIVE the spotted shag, the Pitt Island shag builds a nest of ice plant, grass and other plants in the alcoves of steep cliffs. It lays three oval-elliptical eggs that are pale blue with a chalky outside layer. The birds start laying in August and by December all the chicks have fledged and left their nests. They feed either far out to sea or close inshore in bays and inlets.

The displays of the Pitt Island shag are similar to those of the spotted shag. A male silently advertises for a mate by waving its wings up and outwards about four times per second, pointing its closed bill upwards. Pairs sometimes greet each other by swinging their heads backwards and forwards through a 90° arc. Or they bow their heads so that the partly open bill touches the ground either vertically or sloping

forwards. The male confronts intruders with a loud gargling *ooh-argh, eh-argh-argh* or repetitive *argh-argh-argh* sounds. Sometimes male birds leave the nest-site to chase away other Pitt Island shags, but not other species.

Before a bird flies away from the nest-site, it raises the feathers at the top of its neck and bulges its throat to display lines of iridescent blue-green warts on a black background edged with yellow. The throat and breast pulsate and the male calls a soft ticking *t-t-t* . . . . When it returns to the nest, the bird kinks its throat, flattens its head to one side and—if it has not brought any nesting material—holds its bill wide open. The male calls a loud repetitive *ergh-ergh-ergh* . . . or *ergh-oh-ergh-oh-erhg-oh* . . . .   G.F.v.T.

ENDEMIC

OTHER NAME: *Double-crested shag.*

SIZE: *630 mm.*

DESCRIPTION
ADULT: *Sexes alike. Upper parts blue-black, with upper neck black. Upper wing coverts glossy grey-green with black tips. Base of tail feathers pale grey. Underparts grey. Face warty and grass green. Throat, rear*
of belly and thighs black. Iris red-brown. Bill black with light brown tip and cream-coloured bar at base of lower bill. Mouth-lining brown-black. Legs and feet orange. At start of breeding long black crests on forehead and nape; with tufts of long white plumes on hind neck and scattered elsewhere on head and neck. When bulged, throat black with lines of blue-green warts.
IMMATURE: *Dark brown above, light brown below; plumage pattern as in adult. Throat, face, legs and feet*
yellow or orange. Iris grey-brown. Bill grey-brown with dark ridge.

MOULT
Gradual, with no flightless period.

VOICE
At resting, roosting and nesting areas male makes grunting, gargling and ticking sounds. Silent elsewhere.

DISTRIBUTION
Rocky shores and headlands of the Chatham Islands.

RECOGNITION

Only shag at the Chatham Islands with green face and black tips to upper wing coverts. Slender bird with long slender wings, short stubby tail and slender bill with small terminal hook. Flies with neck and head almost horizontal.

Darter

Anhinga melanogaster PENNANT,1769

VAGRANT

OTHER NAMES: _Snake-bird, needle-beaked shag._

SIZE: _900 mm._

DESCRIPTION
ADULT MALE: _Mostly black. White or pale brown stripe from below eye, along side of head and side of upper neck. Upper wing streaked and spotted white, silver grey or pale brown. Underparts of young males irregularly patched with white or dark brown. Throat and eye-ring yellow. Iris yellow. Bill yellow with brown ridge. Legs and feet pink and yellow._
ADULT FEMALE: _Grey above and white or pale buff below. Head and neck stripe white with black border._
IMMATURE: _Similar to female, but head and neck stripe, streaks and spots on upper wing less distinct. Upper wing coverts shorter._
JUVENILE: _Brown-black above. Pale brown below. Flight feathers of wing and tail black. White head and neck stripe incomplete and without dark_ border. _Streaks and spots on upper wing silver grey or pale brown. Iris pale yellow or pale brown._

MOULT
Flight feathers shed together. Tail moult gradual.

VOICE
Clicking sounds away from nesting area. During nesting, harsh kah, _explosive_ khaah, tjeeu, krrr _and_ kururah, _as well as hissing._

DISTRIBUTION
Tropical and warm temperate Africa, the Middle East, southern and southeastern Asia, New Guinea and Australia. One New Zealand record.

RECOGNITION
Heron-like head and neck, very long tail and large wings. Short legs with all four toes united in a web. Bill pointed, no terminal hook.

THE DARTER TAKES ITS NAME from its method of fishing. Stalking its prey under water, it darts its head rapidly forward to spear a fish on the pointed tip of its slightly open bill. On surfacing, it shakes the fish loose, grabs it with its serrated beak and swallows it head first. Fish make up most of the darter's food, but it also eats insects and small tortoises. It forages in sheltered water bodies and sometimes swims with only its head and long, curved neck above the surface, which has earned it the alternative name of snake-bird.

No live darters have been sighted in New Zealand. The only record is of a skin found nailed to a shed at Hokitika in 1874. But if several birds were to cross the Tasman Sea from Australia they would find plenty of suitable feeding and breeding grounds.

Darters roost and nest in trees and bushes over water or in reed beds. They breed at any time of the year, if there is enough food and shelter. They incubate their clutch of two to six eggs on their webbed feet. Normally, chicks fledge at about 40 days. Darters are fiercely territorial. The males lay claim to large feeding, nesting and roosting areas, which they defend from other male darters, although they tolerate waterbirds from different families.

When they fly, darters spiral up on thermal updrafts, then glide down to the next one. They take off from the water by kicking both feet together. Sometimes they climb bushes or trees to gain height before launching themselves into the air.   W.J.M.V. & G.F.v.T.

A darter spreads its wings to dry them in the sun. Though darters are closely related to cormorants they can be distinguished from them by their S-shaped neck.

Greater Frigate Bird *Fregata minor* (GMELIN, 1789)

A male greater frigate bird flies over a nesting island, displaying to the female by inflating its throat pouch.

VAGRANT

OTHER NAMES: *Frigate bird, man-o'-war bird, Pacific man-o'-war bird.*

SIZE: *1000 mm.*

DESCRIPTION
ADULT MALE: *Mostly black. Brown bar on upper wing. Green sheen on head and back. Throat pouch red. Eye-ring black. Iris dark brown. Bill blue-grey. Legs pink-buff.*
ADULT FEMALE: *Larger than male. Dark above; obvious brown bar on upper wing and back of neck. Throat and breast to sides of belly white or light grey. Eye-ring blue. Iris brown. Bill blue-grey. Legs red-brown.*
IMMATURE: *Head and neck white mottled with rust. Mantle and wing coverts brown-black. Belly and flanks white. Throat pouch light grey. Rest of body black. Eye-ring blue. Iris dark brown. Feet and legs yellow-white.*

MOULT
Adult moult may be delayed at least until towards end of fledging period.

VOICE
Silent except when coming in to land, displaying, fighting or chasing. Female approaching perch calls wiiiiiik-wiiick-wick-wickwick-wick; male calls long, drawn-out teeeeeuu-teeuu-teu-tutu.

DISTRIBUTION
Breeds on tropical islands of the Atlantic, Indian and Pacific Oceans. Straggles to New Zealand.

RECOGNITION

Male separated from lesser frigate bird by all-dark plumage; female by white throat.

IN CALM WEATHER ESPECIALLY, this piratical bird snatches both food and nesting material from other seabirds. Most of its victims are terns and boobies, or birds grounded by broken wings. In rough weather, however, the greater frigate bird does more of its own hunting. It catches flying fish in mid-air, picks other fish and squid from the water's surface, and grabs young turtles and crabs from the beach. It also steals eggs and small chicks from tern nests. It drinks on the wing, scooping water from freshwater pools on land.

The greater frigate bird breeds on tropical off-shore islands between January and October. As part of its courtship display, the male inflates its bright red throat pouch. When incubation begins this pouch becomes less and less prominent.

Occasionally the greater frigate bird visits the New Zealand region. Since 1861, there have been at least 12 sightings—at the Kermadec Islands, Whangarei, Clevedon, Lake Kimihia, Lake Tarawera, Tauranga, Castle Point, Masterton, Cape Farewell and Westport.   D.G.N. & F.C.K.

Lesser Frigate Bird *Fregata ariel ariel* (GRAY, 1845)

VAGRANT

OTHER NAME: *Man-o'-war hawk.*

SIZE: *800 mm.*

DESCRIPTION
ADULT MALE: *Entirely black except for white patch on each flank extending onto base of underwing. Blue sheen on back of head. Red throat pouch sometimes visible. Eye-ring black. Iris dark brown. Bill black with grey tip. Feet brown-black.*
ADULT FEMALE: *Larger than male. General plumage black with brown wing-bars. Throat black. Throat pouch purple. Breast and sides of belly white. Eye-ring red. Iris red-brown. Bill light grey with brown tip. Legs and feet pink or red.*
IMMATURE: *Head and neck white mottled with rust. Mantle and wing coverts brown-black. Throat pouch light grey. Belly and flanks white. Rest of body black. Eye-ring blue. Iris dark brown. Bill lead grey.*

Feet and legs yellow-white.

MOULT
Adult moult appears to be delayed until at least towards end of fledging period.

VOICE
Silent except when coming in to land, displaying, fighting or chasing. Male approaching perch calls series of short whistles; female calls harsh chuck-chuck-chuck; in both sexes, notes accelerate and drop in pitch as birds descend.

DISTRIBUTION
Breeds in the tropical Pacific Ocean. Straggles to New Zealand.

RECOGNITION

Long narrow wings with deeply forked tail. Long beak with hooked tip.

A female lesser frigate bird with chick. The species can neither walk nor swim.

FRIGATE BIRDS ARE THE MOST AERIAL of seabirds. They can neither walk nor swim and generally come ashore only to breed or to pick up food they have forced other birds to drop. The lesser frigate bird is as buccaneering as the greater frigate bird and harasses other seabirds, such as sooty terns and boobies, until they disgorge their food. It also takes young turtles and crabs from beaches, as well as squid from the sea's surface.

These birds nest in colonies on islands off Queensland, Fiji, New Caledonia and other locations in the tropical Pacific Ocean. Between May and December it rears one chick in a nest of sticks, grass and debris placed in a tree, bush or occasionally on the ground.

Winds and storms carry lesser frigate birds to New Zealand. Between 1907 and 1970 at least 13 birds were sighted, mainly from the North Island, although one bird reached Cook Strait and another, the Chatham Islands. Then in 1971 a storm swept several lesser frigate birds towards the Northland coast and the number of sightings was doubled. One bird over Kaipara Harbour harried gannets, gulls and terns. Specimens have been recovered from Ninety Mile Beach, Pahi, Auckland, Panmure, Little Barrier Island, Te Kuiti, Umutoi, Wellington, Scott Point and the Chatham Islands. Others have been sighted at Te Werahi, Houhora Harbour, Waiheke Island, Langholm, Bush Island (Coromandel) and Nelson.   D.G.N. & F.C.K.

The white-faced heron, first recorded breeding in 1941, is now New Zealand's most common heron. It is able to exploit most types of wetland habitat.

White-faced Heron *Ardea novaehollandiae novaehollandiae* LATHAM,1790

NATIVE

OTHER NAME: *Blue crane.*

SIZE: *660 mm.*

DESCRIPTION
ADULT: *Sexes alike. In non-breeding plumage generally blue-grey, with lower breast and abdomen lighter, and main flight feathers darker. Upper breast feathers bordered with chestnut. Forehead, face, and throat white. Iris yellow-green. Bill dark grey or black. Legs and feet olive-yellow. In breeding season legs and feet turn pinkish; blue-grey plumes develop on back; upper breast feathers lengthen; and chestnut colouring intensifies.*
IMMATURE: *Similar to adult, but lacks white on face; brown on breast, and plumes.*

MOULT
Probably February to April after breeding, with further partial moult about June, before back plumes grow.

VOICE
In flight, guttural grr-aw *repeated at short intervals. Similar call, with added* gow-gow-gow, *when alighting at nest. Alarm call higher-pitched* wrink.

DISTRIBUTION
Throughout New Zealand in wetland habitats; the Kermadec and Chatham Islands; Campbell and Macquarie Islands; Australia; New Guinea; Indonesia; and western Pacific Islands. Still expanding north and east from Australia.

RECOGNITION

Blue colour. Distinguished from reef heron by white face, pale legs and contrasting wing surfaces—dark above and light below.

WHITE-FACED HERONS were occasionally sighted in New Zealand in the nineteenth century. These may have been blown-away strays from Australia. Breeding however was not confirmed until 1941. In the early 1960s numbers of the species exploded and it is now the most common heron in New Zealand. The key to its success is its wide choice of diet and its ability to exploit most kinds of wetland habitat. The bird does as well on rocky shores, sandy beaches and mud flats as it does on city sewage treatment ponds. Big flocks winter on seasonally flooded lowland pastures, swamp margins and inland lake shores. They wander up rivers, often as far as bush-clad mountain regions, and they throng around the dams and creeks of hill-country farms.

Trout fishermen were alarmed by this invasion of their favourite streams. But studies of stomach contents showed that white-faced herons within range of trout-stocked rivers fed substantially on crustaceans, worms, spiders, molluscs, insects and vegetable matter.

Only half of the birds examined had eaten any fish, and many of those were bullies *Gobiomorphus*—predators of trout fry. The proportion of trout fingerlings eaten was extremely small. Researchers concluded that this heron's impact on trout fisheries was probably beneficial, as they removed weaker and smaller fry, or at worst neutral.

Foot-raking is a characteristic hunting method of the white-faced heron. It strides through the shallows, pausing every two or three metres to stretch out a leg and drag its foot rapidly back and forth, apparently to disturb small fish and invertebrates. It may stir the bottom by turning around two or three times as it rakes, before darting off. Often the wings are slightly spread, as if to shade the water surface and increase the bird's ability to see below.

Almost nothing is known of this bird's courtship displays. One of a pair was observed following the other slowly along a branch with its head lowered and its head feathers and back plumes raised. It attempted to break off sticks, which suggests a presentation ritual like that of the reef heron. In courting flights birds fly with necks outstretched, calling vociferously.

Nesting starts as early as June in the far north, but birds in colder regions do not breed until early summer. The peak of the breeding season is probably in October. Pairs nest alone or in scattered groups. They always choose tall trees—especially the crowns—near but not necessarily beside water. The nest is the heron's usual platform of sticks, but smaller than that of other species and so loose that the pale blue-green eggs may be seen from below. Three to five eggs are normally laid. Incubation, shared by the parents, takes about 25 days. Rivalry among the chicks seems to be intense and it is rare for more than two to be alive after their first 10 days. They stay in the nest for the whole six weeks of fledging—unlike other heron chicks—and remain with their parents until the next breeding season.

When nesting is over, the white-faced heron is more social than any of New Zealand's other herons, except for the cattle egret. Flocks of 20 or more feed together, and it is not uncommon to find 50 to 100 in a single night roost. No evidence has been gathered of population movements, and they are considered to be a fairly sedentary species; but observation of numbers suggests some northward shift in autumn as well as a movement from the hinterland to lower-lying coastal areas in winter.   M.J.W.

White-necked Heron

Ardea pacifica LATHAM,1801

When feeding, the white-necked heron stalks slowly in shallow water.

VAGRANT

OTHER NAME: *Pacific heron.*

SIZE: *760 mm.*

DESCRIPTION
ADULT: *Sexes alike. Body dark slate with green gloss above. Head, neck, upper breast mainly white; neck front black-tipped. Chestnut or purple patches on crown, upper breast, back of neck. Lower breast, abdomen and undertail dark slate, streaked with white. White patch at bend of black upper wing. Iris yellow-green. Facial skin usually blue. Bill, legs, and feet black. At breeding time, long, thin maroon nuptial plumes develop on back.*

MOULT
Not known.

VOICE
Guttural; typical heron's alarm croak.

DISTRIBUTION
Throughout Australia near freshwater shallows.

RECOGNITION

Dark, glossy body contrasting with white head and neck. White patch at bend of dark wing obvious in flight. Slow wing-beat.

ONLY THREE SIGHTINGS of the white-necked heron have been recorded in New Zealand—at Methven, mid-Canterbury, in 1952, near Whakatane in 1978 and at Houhora, Northland, in 1981. Its rarity is surprising, because it is fully nomadic in habit and in Australia it seems to be the only heron capable of suddenly moving into new areas in large numbers. It is essentially a solitary species with little apparent social organisation. It does not appear to defend any breeding area against other birds of its species or other herons. If a number of birds are in a group together they simply feed over the same area, almost ignoring each other.

The nest is typically a heap of sticks, poorly arranged, sometimes built up to 30 m above water. Dead trees standing in water are said to be a favoured nesting site. The white-necked heron has a variable breeding season that depends on rains and the availability of food. A slow and deliberate hunter, it eats a wide range of animals, including small reptiles, fish, crustaceans, frogs and aquatic insects.   M.J.W.

Little Egret *Egretta garzetta immaculata* GOULD,1846

THE FIRST LITTLE EGRET recorded in New Zealand stayed on the Hawke's Bay coast for more than a year in 1951–52. Three more were reported before 1957, and in that year at least 10 came in company with a substantial invasion of other Australian birds. Since then little egrets have been sighted almost every year, mostly between April and November, suggesting an annual winter migration. They are not known to breed in New Zealand.

This is essentially a bird of the water—a feature that helps to distinguish it from the cattle egret and intermediate egret. In New Zealand it is mostly an estuarine inhabitant, with occasional sightings on lakes near the coast. Only two sightings have been made on swampland or flooded pasture. It is a highly active feeder, seldom motionless. Often it stirs shallow estuarine or lake waters with a foot, or rakes material such as weed out of the way to reveal fish and other prey; then it may run rapidly in pursuit. The wings are sometimes partly opened. Food consists of fish, frogs, crustaceans, aquatic insects and large land insects.

Little egrets are often seen in the company of other egrets, particularly white herons, and occasionally cattle egrets. They roost communally at traditional sites in trees and nest in colonies, usually in association with other herons and egrets.   M.J.W.

STRAGGLER

OTHER NAMES: *None.*

SIZE: *560 mm.*

DESCRIPTION
ADULT: *Sexes alike. In non-breeding season plumage entirely white. Bill black. Iris and facial skin yellow. Legs black. Feet yellow. In breeding season 2 plumes on back of head, many others on back and breast; and facial skin may turn red.*
IMMATURE: *White feathers, sometimes tinged salmon-buff along outer scapulars, tail, undertail coverts.*

MOULT
Not known.

VOICE
Silent except at breeding colony.

DISTRIBUTION
Tropical and temperate Africa, Europe, Asia, western Pacific, Australia. Straggles to New Zealand estuaries and coastal lakes, mostly at Waikato, Northland and Nelson.

RECOGNITION

Small white heron. Black bill and legs. Flies with slow wing-beat and head tucked in against body.

The little egret, its nest an untidy platform of sticks and leaves.

White Heron

Egretta alba modesta

(GRAY, 1831)

NATIVE

OTHER NAMES: *Eastern great white egret, great white heron, white egret, large egret, kotuku.*

SIZE: *910 mm.*

DESCRIPTION

ADULT: *Sexes alike. In non-breeding plumage entirely white. Iris yellow. Bill yellow with brownish tip. Facial skin yellowish green. Legs and feet black. In breeding plumage back plumes extending up to 100 mm beyond tail; bill black, sometimes with slightly yellow base; facial skin green; and eye reddish.*
IMMATURE: *Like adult in non-breeding plumage. Small back plumes in second year; and probably mature in third year.*
CHICK: *Down yellowish white, longer and upright on crown. Bill dull yellow with black tip. Legs black.*

MOULT

Complete adult moult February to May. Back feather moult July and August. Juveniles moult body feathers February to May.

VOICE

Typical heron croak in flight or when disturbed. Variety of low, guttural noises and gratings at nest.

DISTRIBUTION

Breeds in Westland. Rest of year found throughout New Zealand around shallow freshwater or estuarine wetlands and lakes. Also in Australia, the South Pacific, tropical Asia and Japan. This and related subspecies found worldwide in tropical and temperate regions.

RECOGNITION

Pure white.
Biggest of white-coloured herons. Black legs.
Long yellow bill.

The white heron, which in Maori folklore was a symbol of anything rare and beautiful, is a bird of shallow wetlands.

IN MAORI ORATORY, the most exquisite compliment is to liken someone to the kotuku. It symbolises everything rare and beautiful. In recent years there has been a permanent population of 100 to 120 white herons in New Zealand (about half of them of breeding age). Populations in the past are not thought to have exceeded this number. Irruptions from Australia occasionally boost the population, but the newcomers do not seem to breed here; instead they find their way back, or disperse to the east or south, to Macquarie Island, the Chatham or Auckland Islands.

The country's only breeding site is in a predominantly kahikatea forest beside the Waitangiroto River, near Okarito in south Westland, where white herons nest in association with spoonbills and shags. It was declared a fauna and flora reserve in 1941 and is closely patrolled in the breeding season. Adult birds start arriving from all over the country in August, and take part in elaborate courtship rituals before they lay in late September or October. Males build small platforms from which they advertise themselves to the females. Displays by the male include a spectacular raising of the nuptial plumes, with the neck erect, the bill snapping and the wing feathers flicking. Once a female is attracted, the pair preen each other and intertwine their necks, wings and bills. Then the female builds the real nesting platform—a heavy construction of twigs and tree-fern fronds woven together and topped by smaller twigs. Such nests are made at heights of three to 13 m above the water, in kowhais, kamihis or the crowns of tree-ferns.

Three to five pale bluish green eggs are laid. Incubation, shared by the parents, takes about 25 days. The young start to clamber from the nest about three weeks after hatching, and fledge in a further three weeks. On average, one or two per nest are successfully hatched, and nearly all survive to fledging. The breeding season is over by around the end of December and all birds disperse in January. The young may associate with one or both parents for a short time after, but white herons, though they roost communally at night, are solitary feeders. Mortality must be high among the juveniles, for the total population remains almost static.

White herons are birds of shallow wetlands. They inhabit estuarine harbours, the shores of lakes and ponds, river banks and stream margins. They are never far from water, although they will forage in wet pasture. At night or when not feeding they roost in trees.

Hunting techniques may involve stalking in the shallows, occasionally jumping up and down or foot-stirring, or simply standing and waiting. Sighting prey, a bird characteristically kinks its neck with the head slightly drawn back. Then the whole neck swings down and the head darts forward. Small fish and eels, frogs and tadpoles, insect larvae and shrimps make up the main diet. But white herons sometimes spear mice and birds such as ducklings, chickens and silvereyes—and even small kingfishers. At Okarito, the birds get most of their food from the lagoon nearby. Their breeding season coincides with the upstream migration of whitebait *Galaxias attenuatus*. It probably provides the bulk of their nesting diet, and of the food they regurgitate to their chicks.

The Maoris used the nuptial plumes of the kotuku to adorn the heads of their chieftans. Captured birds were kept in cages and plucked at intervals. In the 1870s, after Europeans discovered the Okarito breeding site, the species was almost exterminated to satisfy a fad for feathers in women's hats. The number of nests was reduced from 25 in 1871 to six in 1877. Little further notice was taken of the white heron until 1940, when there were only four nests at Okarito. The subsequent recovery of breeding numbers has been a triumph of conservation policies and the kotuku is now the official symbol of the New Zealand Wildlife Service.

P.M.M. & M.J.W.

The young of the reef heron are carefully brooded by at least one adult during their early life, but after the first week they are left entirely unguarded.

Reef Heron *Egretta sacra sacra* (GMELIN, 1789)

NATIVE

OTHER NAMES: *Blue reef heron, eastern reef heron, blue crane, blue heron, matuku-moana.*

SIZE: *660 mm.*

DESCRIPTION
ADULT: *Sexes alike. In non-breeding plumage dark blue-grey all over, darker on upper surface. Lower breast and belly feathers tinged brown. White patch or streak on chin or throat, not obvious in field. Iris yellow. Bill yellow and brown. Facial skin and legs yellowish green. Some reef herons in tropics entirely white; with yellow bill and iris; and yellow-green facial skin and legs. In breeding plumage long plumes on back; shorter plumes on breast; long feathers on crown; bill and facial skin turn brighter yellow; and iris turns orange-red.*
IMMATURE: *Plumage browner. Iris brown or brownish yellow. Bill brown. Facial skin and legs grey.*
CHICK: *Down dark grey. Bill and legs flesh-coloured.*

MOULT
Adults probably start full post-breeding moult about February. Post-juvenile moult probably March-April.

VOICE
Guttural croaking, often with bill-snapping when breeding. Alarm call crr-aw. Soft mewing at nest.

DISTRIBUTION
Coasts of the 2 main islands, though more abundant in north; Stewart Island; and the Chatham Islands. Straggles to the Auckland Islands. Also occurs in coastal Australia; the southwestern Pacific; Southeast Asia; and Japan.

RECOGNITION

In New Zealand blue colour with no white on face. In flight, distinguished from white-faced heron by lack of contrast between upper and lower wing surfaces.

REEF HERONS IN NEW ZEALAND are at the southeastern limit of their mostly tropical range, and for that reason alone may never be common. An apparent decline in numbers over the past 30 to 40 years may indicate a subtle change in coastal climate; or it may be that man-made physical changes—reclamations, pollution and the removal of the old wooden wharves that used to provide roosts—along with the generally increased use and disturbance of coasts, have driven the birds away. They have a distinct preference for rocky shores, but also inhabit estuarine areas and hunt over mud flats. Though seldom seen on sandy beaches, they are not frightened to live near cities.

A solitary feeder, the reef heron seems to establish its own territory as it hunts in rock pools or on mud flats at the water's edge. It may stalk stealthily, suddenly darting its neck forward when small fish or crustaceans come within range, or it may run in pursuit of prey, darting its bill from side to side. Feeding is regulated by the tides, and it is common for this species to hunt both in daylight and in darkness. The reef heron is known as a hijacker of food, invading the nesting colonies of terns and stealing fish brought for the chicks.

Little is known of courtship, although it certainly involves aerial displays—swooping, banking and chasing—with one or both of the birds holding the neck outstretched for short distances. Sticks are carried on some of these flights. Courting pairs have also been seen on the ground, dancing around each other with necks arched and nuptial plumes raised.

Nesting starts in late September and is probably at its peak in October and November. Eggs found as late as February are almost certainly replacement clutches, laid after the loss of an earlier nest. Nests are typically located in dark and gloomy sites, such as crevices and caves on cliffs or rocky islets, under flax clumps or pohutukawa roots at the water's edge, or low in overhanging trees. Boat wreckage and the lower timbers of disused wharves have also been used. Reef herons are solitary nesters. The nest material consists almost entirely of sticks, with seaweed, grass or flax sometimes entwined. Flimsy at first, nests used for several seasons become bulky with the addition of new material each year.

Two or three—rarely four—pale greenish blue eggs are laid at two-day intervals. They are incubated by both parents for 25 to 28 days. Chicks scramble out of the nest about three weeks after hatching, returning only at feeding time. Early in their life, their parents delay feeding them for about half an hour after hunting, so that the regurgitated food is partly digested. This waiting period is progressively shortened, and by the time the young are fledged, in six weeks or less, they are eating wholly undigested small fish. The young remain with the parents for two or three weeks after fledging, but then the family breaks up completely.

The reef heron is the most solitary of all New Zealand herons, and will defend its feeding territory from others of its own kind. It seems tolerant of other species within its feeding range, however, and may join them at high-tide resting places and evening roosts. M.J.W.

Intermediate Egret *Egretta intermedia* (WAGLER,1829)

VAGRANT

OTHER NAME: *Plumed egret.*

SIZE: *620 mm.*

DESCRIPTION
ADULT: *Sexes alike. In non-breeding plumage entirely white but may appear cream. Bill yellow-orange, with black line of gape reaching to below eye—not beyond it as in little egret and white heron. Iris and facial skin yellow. Upper legs yellow-brown, lower legs and feet black. In breeding plumage long white plumes develop on breast and back, not on head. Bill orange with yellow tip. Facial skin green. Iris red. Upper legs reddish.* IMMATURE: *Feathers more yellowish. Upper legs dark.*

MOULT
Not known.

VOICE
Guttural noises at nest. Loud croaking alarm call.

DISTRIBUTION
Northern and eastern Australia, New Guinea, the Moluccas, eastern Asia and tropical Africa. Rare straggler to New Zealand.

RECOGNITION

Small white heron. Yellow bill. Different upper and lower leg colouring. Slow wing-beat.

THE FIRST INTERMEDIATE EGRET reported in New Zealand was a mounted specimen found in a collection seized by the Wildlife Service in Palmerston North. It was said to have been obtained at the Manawatu River mouth in the early 1970s. This specimen was in full breeding plumage, with breast plumes and long, lacy back plumes cascading past its tail. The only other record in New Zealand is of a single bird feeding among maize stubble in the lower Waikato in 1979.

Yet this is essentially a wetland bird that forages along the shorelines of swamps, lakes and irrigation dams; amongst mangroves; and at the edges of estuaries and coastal lagoons. It wades in shallow water, searching for a wide range of aquatic insects, fish, amphibia and crustaceans. Sometimes it feeds territorially in shallow water; at other times it hunts in flocks, especially on land.

It is a more social species than the little egret or the white heron. Shy and wary of other egrets, it often flocks up when alarmed and roosts colonially at night. This gregariousness disappears at the beginning of the breeding season, however, and it is extremely aggressive at pair formation and nest-building time. M.J.W.

The intermediate egret nests colonially in low trees overhanging water.

Nankeen Night Heron *Nycticorax caledonicus* (GMELIN,1789)

THERE HAVE BEEN AT LEAST 15 documented sightings of the nankeen night heron in New Zealand, nearly all of which have been of immature birds. The most intriguing sightings were made near Blenheim in 1958. Two obviously immature birds were observed between March and June. After this was reported, a young ornithologist claimed to have seen an adult with breeding plumes in January. The possibility that breeding took place cannot be excluded. Earlier attempts to introduce the bird failed, however.

The nankeen night heron favours the edges of sheltered swamps, rivers and inlets where there are trees and reed beds or similar tall ground vegetation. It is largely nocturnal, spending the day sleeping. Roost-sites recorded in New Zealand have been high in pine trees, macrocarpas, elms and walnuts. At night the birds feed in swampy areas of reeds or in shallow water, taking a wide range of fish, frogs, crustaceans and insects. Overseas they are reported to scavenge food scraps below the nesting colonies of other birds, and sometimes to plunder their nests, destroying eggs and young. M.J.W.

VAGRANT

OTHER NAME: *Rufous night heron.*

SIZE: *560 mm.*

DESCRIPTION
ADULT: *Sexes alike. In non-breeding plumage upper surfaces of back, wings and tail chestnut. Top of head and nape black. Throat and neck buff. Breast and belly cream. Facial skin pale green, surrounded by white feathers. Iris yellow. Bill short, stout and black. Legs and feet yellowish green. In breeding plumage up to 3 white plumes extend from back of head to well down back.* IMMATURE: *Generally brown, streaked or spotted with white or pale buff. Bill varies from yellow to grey with black ridge. Legs greener.*

MOULT
Not known.

VOICE
Harsh croak at night.

DISTRIBUTION
Permanent waters throughout Australia, New Guinea, the southwestern Pacific, Indonesia, and the Philippines.

RECOGNITION

Chestnut colouring with whitish breast and black cap. Short, heavy bill. Slow wing-beat.

The nankeen night heron usually nests in colonies, over or alongside water.

A small, stocky heron, the cattle egret favours open grassy fields or swampland where animals graze regularly.

Cattle Egret

Bubulcus ibis coromandus
(Boddaert, 1783)

MIGRANT

OTHER NAME: *Buff-backed heron.*

SIZE: *510 mm.*

DESCRIPTION
ADULT: *Sexes alike. In non-breeding season white with pale yellow wash on forecrown (apparently absent for several months after post-nuptial moult). Bill yellow. Iris pale gold-yellow. Facial skin greenish yellow. Legs greenish grey to dark grey. Feet black; soles yellow. In breeding season whole head, except chin and forehead, buff-orange. Buff-orange plumes develop on lower neck and back; neck and throat feathers lengthen and turn same colour. Immediately before laying, bill, iris, facial skin and legs red. Shortly after laying, bill, iris and facial skin become yellow, and legs change through yellow-orange to brownish yellow to slate.*
JUVENILE: *Like non-breeding adult but yellow on forecrown apparently slower to appear.*
NESTLING: *White down. Yellow iris. Bill and facial skin flesh or horn-coloured at hatching; greenish black after 5 to 10 days; and yellow from 2 or 3 months. Legs olive to yellowish green; black before fledging.*

MOULT
Not described for Australasian subspecies but full adult post-nuptial moult expected January or February to June or July; and partial pre-nuptial moult August to October. First-year birds probably assume breeding plumage October or November.

VOICE
Silent except at breeding colony.

DISTRIBUTION
Indian subcontinent, Sri Lanka, Burma, Thailand, Indochina, southern China, Japan, Java, the Philippines. Small numbers breed in Korea and possibly southern USSR. Breeding status uncertain in Borneo, Sumatra, Sulawesi, the Moluccas and Timor. Winter visitor to Malay Peninsula, the Philippines, and the Moluccas. Sedentary in equatorial regions; migratory elsewhere. Introduced to Australia about 1933, self-introduced birds soon followed; now found in north and along eastern seaboard. First recorded in New Zealand winter 1963. Now widely distributed each winter; main concentrations in western districts and mid-Canterbury.

CATTLE EGRETS FIRST APPEARED from Australia in the 1960s, both singly and in pairs. Bigger parties were noticed in 1972 and 1973, and by 1976 it was clear that a remarkable annual migration was developing. Now they come in hundreds every year.

During May cattle egrets are scattered across New Zealand, but by June or July they have gathered in fewer, larger flocks on their favoured farms, often near open bodies of fresh water. Rarely are they seen on the coast. They stay at least until mid-October. The main exodus back to New South Wales or southern Queensland takes place in November, though a few birds linger until mid-December. A few stay on through summer, apparently without breeding.

If cattle egrets take to breeding in New Zealand, they can be expected to nest in colonies in clumps of trees or shrubs, often in or beside fresh water, and with shags or other herons. The nest is an untidy mass of sticks in which three to five eggs are laid. These are white with a faint blue-green tinge and no gloss.

The cattle egret has a fundamental attachment to grazing animals. In many countries it follows at their feet to feed on the insects and other prey that are disturbed; and birds often perch on cattle to rest. In New Zealand the cattle egret feeds independently, but usually among or near a herd of cattle, or less commonly, a flock of sheep and, rarely, pigs or horses. Most New Zealand feeding sites have become traditional: flocks of egrets associate with the same paddocks and herds year after year, differing only in the numbers that return— while large areas of equally suitable farmland nearby are ignored. In this country, they are very wary of people.

Feeding cattle egrets move across pastures in a steady walk, interspersed with short runs. On dry pasture and in long grass, they snap prey from the plants and the air. On damp ground, they make shallow probes, and snatch prey from plants. Big flocks overseas advance in leapfrog fashion—birds at the rear fly to the front—but that style of feeding has not yet been seen in New Zealand. Seldom

seen here is a neck-swaying hunting method, which in other countries is thought to be for the capture of flies—a very fast-moving prey.

Cattle egrets seem to adapt to local and seasonal variations in food and eat a wide variety of creatures. Little information is available on food taken in New Zealand, but earthworms in wet pasture seem to make up the bulk of the diet. Flies, crickets, and ground insects are also taken, and one bird has been seen eating a mouse.

The cattle egret is a gregarious bird. It lives in loose flocks, mixed in sex and age and constantly changing in composition. It roosts in trees, over or near water or sometimes in reed beds. Flocks in New Zealand, however large, usually stay together. The feeding place is often within sight of the roost; in fact one flock roosted on the ground where it fed.

Although in Asia the cattle egret is said to be tame, in New Zealand it is remarkably wary. When disturbed, feeding birds, which may be rather scattered, will all take flight and come together as a single flock. Then they may fly deeper into the grazing herd or away towards their roost or to the edge of water. The flock's descent is often accompanied by violent sweeps and swerves, each bird going its own way, but all ending up as a tight flock after landing. B.D.H.

Australasian Bittern
Botaurus stellaris poiciloptilus (WAGLER, 1827)

NATIVE

OTHER NAMES: *Australian brown bittern, brown bittern, matuku-hurepo.*

SIZE: *710 mm.*

DESCRIPTION
ADULT: *Sexes alike. General plumage brown, mottled with golden buff on upper surface. Lower surface light buff streaked or flecked with dark brown. Head and nape brown with pale spots. Thin brown bars on side of neck and thighs. Iris yellow. Upper mandible dark brown; lower yellowish green. Facial skin pale green. Legs and feet pale green.*
IMMATURE: *Generally duller or paler than adult.*
CHICK: *Down pale grey and sparse.*

MOULT
Not known.

VOICE
Booming call by male to advertise territory and attract female, mostly heard evenings June to February; female's response less audible. Flight call by both sexes nasal kau, *heard mostly in autumn. Female utters soft, bubbling noise at nest.*

DISTRIBUTION
On densely vegetated wetlands throughout main islands and some bigger offshore islands, but no longer recorded on the Chatham Islands. Also New Caledonia, southeastern and southwestern Australia and Tasmania.

RECOGNITION

Mottled brown colouring; invariably in swampland habitat. Flight like heron: head tucked in, slow wing-beat.

AUSTRALASIAN BITTERNS ARE HEARD more often than they are seen. Booming territorial calls resound mournfully across swamplands at nightfall. But the birds are furtive by day. If disturbed, they turn their bills skyward and 'freeze'. Camouflaged by dappled brown plumage, they are almost impossible to discern among reeds and thickets of scrub. And although they appear to be gazing up, they are still on watch against ground-level dangers: their eyes are placed so that they retain horizontal vision while their heads are upturned.

This bittern lives only in densely vegetated wetlands—particularly those with shallow standing water that does not fluctuate much. It favours tracts overgrown with tall vegetation, giving cover and vantage points close to pools and channels. Rarely is it found near more open areas such as lakes and rivers. Brackish water is tolerated, in estuaries or lagoons where the sea breaks in occasionally, but bitterns avoid the sea coast.

Bitterns stalk in reed beds in much the same way as herons stalk in open water. They pick their way, often knee-deep in water, with a stealthy, high-stepping gait. Their diet is solely animals, including fish, eels, frogs and tadpoles, insects, worms, spiders, lizards, mice, rats and even birds. Frogs and mice may be impaled on the darting bill and eaten whole, but fish are usually caught between the mandibles and killed by shaking and biting before they are swallowed. One observer has described vividly a bittern's long battle to subdue a struggling, coiling 600 mm eel, which it then swallowed headfirst.

The male bittern's 'booming season' is extraordinarily long. It proclaims its territory to females and rival males from mid-winter to late summer. This suggests that it may mate more than once a season. Polygamy has been confirmed in a European subspecies. Pair-bonding among Australasian bitterns does not seem to last beyond mating; males have never been seen to help in nest construction, let alone the incubation of eggs or the care of the young.

Nests are usually large platforms in reed beds, formed by breaking down all reeds within reach until the platform is 250 to 300 mm above water level. Three to five—occasionally six—olive-brown eggs are laid at two-day intervals, and incubation takes 25 days. As the hatched chicks develop feathers they wander from the nest and usually occupy feeding platforms of flattened reeds nearby. Their food, regurgitated by the mother, is not necessarily predigested. One female was seen to deliver a fully undigested frog to its oldest offspring and increasingly digested frogs to the smaller young, until the last one received its food almost wholly digested. Seldom do all chicks survive. Those that do are fully fledged in about seven weeks, and they are believed to disperse very soon after.

Bitterns are solitary hunters and they also roost alone. In their separately established feeding territories they are active both in daylight and at night. Birds are rarely seen flying, although there is sometimes a conspicuous spiralling flight. This is probably associated with post-juvenile dispersal and the sorting out of territorial boundaries. Males are extremely aggressive towards one another: they fight both on the ground and in flight, attempting to jab or spear their opponents.

Feathers of the Australasian bittern are sought-after as trout flies. This caused the persecution of the species in the late nineteenth century. Imitation feathers are more frequently used now, but the bittern population has continued to decline as a result of widespread wetland drainage.

The official checklist of New Zealand birds considers the Australasian bittern to be a subspecies of *Botaurus stellaris*, the bittern of the old world. Many ornithologists do not agree and consider the bird from this region to be a separate species, *Botaurus poiciloptilus*. Nonetheless, all four species of *Botaurus*, although found in separate areas, are much alike and could be considered one superspecies.   M.J.W.

A solitary hunter, the Australian bittern stalks its prey in densely vegetated wetlands, especially those with extensive shallow standing water.

Glossy Ibis

Plegadis falcinellus (LINNAEUS, 1766)

VAGRANT

OTHER NAMES: *None.*

SIZE: *560 mm.*

DESCRIPTION
ADULT: *Sexes similar, but male's bill longer. Plumage reddish brown with dark greenish gloss, most obvious on upper wing, back and tail. Bird appears black from distance. Iris dark brown. Bill olive-brown, downcurved. Facial skin blue-green. Legs and feet brown.*
IMMATURE: *Duller brown than adult, lacking greenish gloss. Head and neck streaked white. Bill shorter, less curved.*

MOULT
Not known.

VOICE
Grunting among feeding flocks. Guttural 4-note flight call.

DISTRIBUTION
Widespread in tropical and inland southeastern Australia, straggling to New Zealand and Tasmania. Also found in Europe, Asia, Africa, North and Central America.

RECOGNITION

Dark colour. Downcurved bill. Flies with head, neck and legs extended, alternately flapping and gliding. Flocks fly in V formation.

The gregarious glossy ibis, an increasingly regular straggler to New Zealand.

ONLY FIVE SIGHTINGS of glossy ibises were made up to 1951. Then in 1953 two flocks—one of 24 birds, the other of 18—arrived in early summer and stayed for several months. Similar influxes took place in 1968 and 1975. In most other recent years individuals or smaller groups have been sighted, suggesting that New Zealand is an increasingly regular destination. The birds come at a time when most of those in Australia are nesting, though the breeding season varies with the availability of water. There is no evidence yet of their breeding in New Zealand.

In Australia and elsewhere they nest in colonies, often with other ibises and herons. Nests are usually low in trees that overhang or fringe wetlands. Rough assemblages of leafy branches or twigs are barely lined with vegetation. The birds have also been reported nesting in reed beds of trampled reeds.

Freshwater habitats are preferred—especially shallow lakes, swamps and flooded pastures. The glossy ibis can tolerate brackish water, but avoids it where possible. Probing water or mud with a rapid feeding style that has been likened to that of starlings, it takes all forms of aquatic animal life. Its New Zealand diet includes fish, small eels, frogs, tadpoles and insects, along with earthworms from pastures. The species is highly social, feeding and roosting in flocks year-round as well as nesting communally in Australia. If a bird is separated from its own flock, it will quickly join flocks of waders or other gregarious wetland species.   M.J.W.

The white ibis, a highly social bird, has been sighted in New Zealand in estuarine waters and at edges of large lakes.

White Ibis

Threskiornis molucca

(CUVIER, 1829)

VAGRANT

OTHER NAME: *Australian white ibis.*

SIZE: *730 mm.*

DESCRIPTION
ADULT: *Sexes similar, but male's bill longer. Overall dull white; with primaries and secondaries black-tipped and some secondaries plumed, giving impression of black tail when wings folded. Head and neck naked, black; with pale pink bands across back of head. Red skin patches below wing base and bastard wing. Iris dark brown. Bill black, long and downcurved. Upper legs pink; lower legs and feet purplish brown.*
IMMATURE: *Head and upper neck white-feathered. Bill shorter and straighter than adult.*

MOULT
Not known.

VOICE
Variety of grunts, sometimes in flight but mostly among feeding or roosting flocks.

DISTRIBUTION
Common in northern and eastern Australia, straggling to New Zealand and Tasmania. Also occurs in New Guinea and Indonesia.

RECOGNITION

White with black head, neck and rear. Downcurved bill. When flying alternates rapid flapping with gliding, with neck outstretched and long legs trailing.

INFLUXES OF WHITE IBISES to New Zealand usually follow prolonged Australian droughts. They were first recorded in 1925. Ten or more arrived at scattered localities in 1957. All were white-headed—apparently juveniles. Birds were seen in various places throughout the following five years. A similar-sized influx occurred in 1975, initially in North Auckland and Southland; birds were later seen in the Bay of Plenty and the Manawatu. There is no evidence of breeding in New Zealand.

Sightings in New Zealand have been in estuarine areas or at the edges of large lakes. The birds feed in water by moving their heads from side to side like spoonbills, at the same time probing the bottom. They eat a wide variety of freshwater crustaceans, worms, small fish, frogs and snails. Tough-shelled animals are held in one foot against a hard surface and smashed by blows of the bill. These birds also feed readily over wet grasslands or over mud, eating mainly worms and insects. They are highly social, feeding in big flocks in Australia and flying in characteristic V formations. Although New Zealand sightings have been few, the majority have been of more than one bird.   M.J.W.

Royal Spoonbill

Platalea leucorodia regia GOULD,1838

NATIVE

OTHER NAME: *Kotuku-ngutupapa.*

SIZE: *780 mm.*

DESCRIPTION
ADULT: *Sexes alike. In non-breeding plumage white. Iris red; eyelid and streaks above and below yellow. Bill black, spoon-shaped. Face naked: skin black with red patch on forehead. Legs and feet black. In breeding plumage long plumes from back of head sometimes raised as crest; and breast feathers may appear pale yellow.*
IMMATURE: *Similar to adult, but no forehead spot or yellow above and below eye; and primaries may have black or brown tips.*
CHICK: *White down, black face. Bill initially brown, darkens near fledging.*

MOULT
Not known.

VOICE
Low grunting, chew and cho calls at nest. Other sounds produced by bill-clapping.

DISTRIBUTION
Recorded from most major estuaries about the New Zealand coasts but mostly at the Manawatu River estuary; the northern harbours; and Hawke, Tasman and Golden Bays. Also occurs in Australia (some straggling to New Zealand), New Guinea and Indonesia.

RECOGNITION
White with black, spoon-shaped bill and black legs. Side-to-side feeding motion. Flies with outstretched neck and trailing legs.

A royal spoonbill broods its young on a shallow nest of sticks.

KNOWN TO THE MAORI as kotuku-ngutupapa, the royal spoonbill must have reached New Zealand from Australia many times before European settlement. It started breeding in New Zealand in the early 1940s. Juveniles were first recorded at the Ohau River mouth, Horowhenua, in 1944. In the summer of 1949–50, one breeding pair found sanctuary among the white heron colony at Okarito, south Westland, and from then the national population increased steadily to reach a peak of about 100 in 1972. Breeding then lapsed at Okarito and total numbers, including winter visitors from over the Tasman, fell to the forties by 1978. Breeding began the following year with a small colony on a sandbank in Wairau Lagoon, Marlborough.

Spoonbills are particularly sensitive to disturbance at nesting time: in Australia whole colonies have deserted their eggs after only a minor upset. This may have been what caused the birds to cease breeding at Okarito. But long before that happened, fewer and fewer young were being successfully raised. In the late 1950s the average was two chicks fledged from each nest; between 1960 and 1966 it was less than 1.5; and from 1967 to 1971 the average had fallen to less than one successful rearing per nest.

In New Zealand the royal spoonbill is almost exclusively an estuarine bird, though it is occasionally sighted on lagoons and freshwater lakes near the coast. The major wintering ground is the Manawatu River estuary. Birds are usually encountered feeding over mud flats at the water's edge, or resting at high-tide roosts among various other waders as well as terns and gulls. They are gregarious throughout the year, and seen more often in small groups than individually. But full flocks are seen only at roosts or during post-breeding dispersal flights. Once established at their winter grounds, birds tend to follow regular habits—they feed over the same sites each day, commuting between them at similar times. But unlike herons, they appear not to maintain separate feeding territories.

Spoonbills feed in shallow water in a highly characteristic way, sweeping their partly opened bills from side to side. Their food is presumably located by touch, for they feed in the dark as well as by day. Their New Zealand diet has not been identified conclusively, but small fish—especially flounders—are thought to be the main food fed to chicks. Crustaceans, molluscs and worms are probably also eaten. Birds in Australia have been seen picking insects off plants.

At Okarito breeding birds assemble at nesting sites about October. When pairing, both sexes perform conspicuously exaggerated bowing movements, with frequent bill-clapping. Nuptial plumes are raised and lowered, probably also as part of a pairing display, and mutual preening follows the establishment of a bond. Shallow nests of sticks are built almost immediately, high in trees above water. They are lined with grass or rushes. Two or three eggs—sometimes four—coloured white with light brown streaks or blotches, are laid at intervals of two or three days. Parents share the incubation, and young are seen in most nests by late November. Chicks fledge in about seven weeks, but even when they are on the wing they remain with their parents and are fed by them for several more weeks. They most likely follow their parents or other adults to the traditional wintering grounds. The age of first breeding is uncertain, but unlikely to be earlier than the fourth year. M.J.W.

Yellow-billed Spoonbill *Platalea flavipes* GOULD,1838

The yellow-billed spoonbill, endemic to Australia, has been recorded only once outside continental Australia— at Rangaunu Bay, North Auckland.

VAGRANT

OTHER NAMES: *None.*

SIZE: *890 mm.*

DESCRIPTION
ADULT: *Sexes alike. Non-breeding plumage white; with primaries and some secondaries black-tipped. Iris pale yellow. Bill yellow, spoon-shaped. Facial skin fleshy yellow with narrow black border. Legs and feet yellow. Breeding plumage similar with long feathers at base of neck; and facial skin light blue edged with black.*
IMMATURE: *Similar to adult but face lacks black border.*

THE ONLY YELLOW-BILLED SPOONBILL recorded in New Zealand was seen in August 1976, feeding with royal spoonbills and white ibises over shallow mud flats at Rangaunu Bay in North Auckland. It is endemic to Australia and with this one exception has not been found outside the continent—not even in Tasmania. Feeding methods and breeding patterns in Australia are like those of the royal spoonbill; these and other aspects of its character would presumably be similar in New Zealand, should it become a more frequent visitor. M.J.W.

MOULT
Not known.

VOICE
Low grunts. Single chhee call. Bill-clapping.

DISTRIBUTION
Widespread on Australian mainland *at swamps, dams, and river margins.*

RECOGNITION
Distinguished from royal spoonbill by yellow bill and legs.

Plumed Whistling Duck

Dendrocygna eytoni (EYTON,1838)

VAGRANT

OTHER NAMES: *Grass whistle duck, plumed tree-duck, Eyton's tree-duck.*

SIZE: *430 mm.*

DESCRIPTION
ADULT: *Sexes alike. Generally brown. Yellow edges on upper back feathers. Upper tail coverts buff. Rump and tail dark brown. Head, face and neck pale brown. Throat off-white. Breast chestnut with black bars. Abdomen pale buff. Yellow-buff plumes with black margins rising from flanks and curving up over settled wing. Wings short and rounded; brown above, paler below. Iris yellow. Bill pink, mottled with black. Legs and feet pink.*
IMMATURE: *Generally paler than adult, with breast banding less distinct.*

MOULT
Not known.

VOICE
Continuous twittering among flocks. Periodic short whistles. Wings also whistle in flight.

DISTRIBUTION
Northern and eastern Australia. Four sightings in New Zealand.

RECOGNITION

Wings shorter and rounder than in other ducks; wing-beat slower. In flight head low, shoulders look hunched and legs trail. On ground or in trees, long legs and erect stance. Flank plumes usually prominent.

Sightings of the plumed whistling duck usually follow drought in Australia.

TWELVE BIRDS SEEN NEAR GREYMOUTH in 1975 were the first plumed whistling ducks recorded in New Zealand since the 1890s. In Australia they inhabit open tropical grasslands, breeding in the wet season and living off green grasses. They move to permanent swamps and lagoons in the 'dry' and eat rushes. Their arrival in New Zealand is thought to follow severe drought.   M.J.W.

Mute Swan *Cygnus olor* (GMELIN,1789)

INTRODUCED FROM BRITAIN IN 1866 as an ornamental bird for parks and gardens, the mute or white swan has had some success in the wild. Breeding flocks in Canterbury and Hawke's Bay number fewer than 200 birds. However they are unlikely to extend their range, in the face of competition from the more numerous Australian black swan. The mute swan has always had a special relationship with man—it was declared a 'royal bird' in Tudor England, and remains principally a stately decoration on the ponds of municipal parks.

It is a strongly territorial bird, pugnaciously defending its feeding area and particularly its nest-site. Nests are placed as far apart as possible. On Lake Ellesmere breeding is confined to the Harts Creek wildlife refuge, the only area of the lake shore with extensive margins of raupo *Typha*. Space is limited there, however, and nests are built close together. But they are hidden from one another by dense stands of raupo, and there is little contact between neighbours.

Most birds start breeding in their third or fourth year, the females usually earlier than the males. Pairing takes place after elaborate courtship displays involving head and neck movements, and is for life. At Lake Ellesmere, most birds build their nests—massive floating mats of raupo leaves—in September. The clutch consists of four to 11 pale green-white eggs. The average clutch is five. Incubation, by the female only, takes about five weeks. Both adults guard the brood during the five months before they fledge.

No food studies have been made in New Zealand, but the tastes and requirements of mute swans in the wild are presumed to be much the same as those of the black swan. In Europe, where the bird is widespread, the diet consists mainly of aquatic plants, although birds also eat small animals, such as frogs, worms and fish.   M.J.W.

INTRODUCED

OTHER NAME: *White swan.*

SIZE: *1500 mm.*

DESCRIPTION
ADULT: *Sexes alike, female smaller. Plumage all-white. Bill orange; tip, edges and base black. Facial skin black, extending to eye. Fleshy black knob on forehead, enlarged in breeding male. Iris brown. Legs and feet black.*
IMMATURE: *Plumage greyish brown, and bill grey.*
CYGNET: *Down light grey. Bill and feet bluish grey. Some cygnets pure white, passing straight to white plumage of adult.*

MOULT
Non-breeders probably undergo main annual moult October to December; breeders a month or two later.

VOICE
Hisses, snorts and occasional quiet whistle.

DISTRIBUTION
Park ponds. Breeds in wild on Lake Ellesmere; wetlands and streams north of Christchurch; and some Hawke's Bay lakes. Straggles to Lake Wairarapa. Introduced to Australia, North America and South Africa.

RECOGNITION

Only white swan seen in New Zealand.

Declared a 'royal bird' in Tudor England, the mute swan was introduced as an ornamental species in 1866. In the breeding season the male defends the nest, usually a large mat of raupo leaves, with an angry hissing.

Throughout its history in New Zealand the black swan has been a prized game bird. A cyclonic storm in 1968 caused a major population decline.

Black Swan *Cygnus atratus* (LATHAM, 1790)

LAKE ELLESMERE IN CANTERBURY, before the *Wahine* storm of 1968, had so many black swans—perhaps 60 000—that numbers had to be controlled. Hunters were encouraged, and organised drives involved motor boats and 100 or more shooters at a time. Eggs, too, were collected in vast numbers: more than 200 000 were sold in eight years for confectionery manufacture and as food for racehorses. Then, the storm killed or crippled thousands of birds and tore up the lake weeds on which the survivors relied for food. The Ellesmere population crashed to 23 000 in the following season and has continued to decline. A count in 1980 recorded barely 7000 birds, few of them attempting to breed. The total New Zealand population in the early 1980s was about 60 000, with a further 3000 on Chatham Island.

Although introduced from Australia as a game bird in the 1860s, the black swan also probably reached New Zealand naturally at about the same time. Occasionally it may still do so. It prefers wide expanses of permanent fresh or brackish water for breeding. The main concentrations are at coastal lakes and lagoons around the South Island and in the North Island, in the Wairarapa and Hawke's Bay, and inland lakes in the Waikato and near Rotorua. The bird is also quick to exploit temporarily flooded swamplands and pastures, and non-breeders are found year-round on major estuaries and in some marine areas. The diet is almost exclusively vegetarian, consisting mainly of the leaves and shoots of aquatic plants. But where seasonally high water levels put lake weeds below reach, black swans annoy farmers by eating and fouling pasture grasses. About 5000 a year are currently shot as game, mostly in the North Island.

Nesting habits depend on the locality. Where the water level is more or less constant through winter and spring, and where aquatic plants are spread in a thin band around the water margin, pairs nest at widely spaced intervals. They are strongly territorial, defending hectares of feeding water as well as big areas of the swamp edge around their nesting sites. Where water levels fluctuate widely before a summer decline, and where food plants are patchy or distributed all over the wetland, black swans nest colonially. Nests are merely pecking distance apart, and only the immediate area is defended. Territorial birds have a regular July to October nesting season; the timing of colonial nesting depends on when the final decline in water level exposes traditional sites—never before September.

Only about one in five of New Zealand's black swans nests in any year, and no more than a third of the birds present at a breeding area attempt to nest. They heap available plant material—usually rushes—in piles of varied shape and size, shallowly depressed on top and lined with down. Three to 14—usually five or six—greenish white eggs are laid, mostly at daily intervals. Incubation, taking about five weeks, is by both parents. Cygnets are led to water within 24 hours of hatching. At territorial sites they are reared in family broods, but in colonies four or more broods may be reared collectively, apparently attended by only one pair of adults. The fledging period varies between localities, ranging from 95 to more than 140 days.

For most of their pre-breeding life, black swans seem to desert their birthplaces and frequent marine or estuarine habitats. They favour particular regions. Lake Ellesmere birds fly to coastal Otago and Southland; Lake Wairarapa birds disperse to the Marlborough Sounds and Farewell Spit; and Waikato birds make for the harbours of Northland. But when breeding age is attained, most return to where they were born and may remain there more or less permanently. Some live for at least 20 years.   M.J.W.

INTRODUCED

OTHER NAMES: *None.*

SIZE: *1300 mm.*

DESCRIPTION
ADULT: *Sexes alike, female smaller. General colour black but underparts slightly lighter. Back feathers often bordered greyish brown. Wing primaries and some secondaries white. Iris red. Bill red with tip and band near tip white. Legs dark grey. Occasional pale birds: most fawn, some almost white.*
IMMATURE: *At fledging all plumage mottled dull grey-brown. Bill dull grey, reddening in first year. Adult coloration after post-juvenile moult. Primary tips black for at least 2 years.*
CYGNET: *Down light grey. Iris grey-brown. Bill, legs and feet dark grey.*

MOULT
Non-breeders start complete body and wing moult in October; breeders later. Flightless for 4 weeks.

VOICE
High-pitched bugling in flight or among flocks on water. Loud hiss in defence of nest or young. Shrill whistle. Wings whistle in flight.

DISTRIBUTION
Widespread on lagoons and lakes. Non-breeders also found on estuaries and bays. Native of Australia, mainly non-tropical.

RECOGNITION
Black body with white wing tips. Long neck outstretched in flight. Wing-beat slow.

The only truly wild goose in New Zealand, the giant Canada goose presents a challenge to the game shooter. Flocks may damage crops and foul pastures.

Giant Canada Goose *Branta canadensis moffitti* ALDRICH, 1946

INTRODUCED

OTHER NAME: *Honker.*

SIZE: *1000 mm.*

DESCRIPTION
ADULT: *Sexes alike, but female smaller. Head and neck black. Cheek, chin and throat white. Back, wing coverts, secondaries and central flanks brown with pale edges forming bars. Primaries, tail and rump black. Upper tail coverts, vent and posterior flanks white. Breast and belly pale grey-brown to cream. Iris dark brown. Bill black. Feet dark grey.*
GOSLING: *At hatching head and neck bright yellow; crown olive; upper parts olive-brown; and underparts yellowish. Second down dirty grey.*

MOULT
Full moult begins in December.

VOICE
Trumpeted, guttural uh-whong, *second syllable higher-pitched. Gander's call loud and sustained; goose's shorter and staccato. Hiss when fighting or threatening.*

DISTRIBUTION
Mainly the eastern South Island. Stragglers and secondary introductions elsewhere. Native of North America.

RECOGNITION

Black and white contrast of head and cheek. Honking call.

NEW ZEALAND'S GIANT CANADA GEESE flourish only on high tussock grasslands in the South Island, and on a few coastal lakes and lagoons to the east. They are descendants of fewer than 40 birds that survived introduction in 1905 and 1920. Yet in spite of their restricted range, and the efforts of hunters, the peak annual population approaches 20000. Until the mid-1950s there were even more, eating or fouling so much farm pasture that the government had to order culling. Grasses and clovers seem to be the bird's main food. Cereals are also eaten in summer and autumn, especially waste grain after crops are harvested.

Lake Ellesmere in Canterbury is the most important assembly place for the geese, though hardly any breed there. About 4000 younger birds spend the flightless period of their summer moult at the lake—really a brackish lagoon—and breeding birds with their young arrive later to swell the wintering flock to about 10000. In September most return to breeding grounds in isolated headwater valleys of the major rivers flowing east from the Southern Alps—the Clarence, Waiau, Hurunui, Waimakariri, Rakaia, Rangitata, Waitaki and Clutha. The most notable coastal breeding ground is Lake Forsyth, just east of

Ellesmere. Birds sometimes wander to the west coast of the South Island but do not breed there. Nesting sites are not necessarily close to water; these wary birds place more importance in having a good view of any approaching danger.

Nests are made of grasses and lined with down and feathers from the female's breast. Laying starts about the third week of September and extends through October. The youngest females may lay as late as November, along with those re-laying after losing an early clutch. Two to 10 white eggs—the average is five—are laid at intervals of about a day. Incubation, by the female alone, takes a month and goslings follow their parents from the nest within a day of hatching. Broods are often combined and looked after by one pair of adults.

The young can fly at less than three months and in the autumn they accompany the adults to the coastal wintering places. Some families are still together on their springtime return to the nesting ground, but the previous year's young are chased off as soon as nesting starts. In November they wander from the breeding area and by December many have found their way back to the wintering ground to moult. The age of first breeding varies; most commonly it is three years, with males tending to be more advanced than females. A study of first-time breeders returning to the Waimakariri headwaters showed that many chose not to nest in the valley of their birth but went to another.

In New Zealand, perhaps because of inbreeding, only 75 per cent of eggs are fertile compared with 90 per cent on the North American prairies. Once fledged, however, the birds have a very low natural mortality—10 per cent or less per year—and can live to at least 25 years. Most deaths are by game shooting. Research at Lake Forsyth has indicated that juveniles are almost three times more likely to be shot than adults—and half of them die in their first year of life.

Giant Canadas are New Zealand's only truly wild geese. Isolated flocks of other types, mainly of greylag parentage, are descended from escaped domestic geese. Attempts have been made to establish the giant Canada species in the North Island, but it seems unlikely that big flocks will ever be seen outside the southern strongholds. The only permanent North Island breeding site known in the early 1980s was at a small coastal lake near Wairoa, northern Hawke's Bay, founded with pinioned birds introduced from Canterbury in 1970.   M.J.I.

Cape Barren Goose

Cereopsis novaehollandiae (LATHAM, 1801)

THIS UNUSUAL WATERFOWL has a long history of exploitation in Australia, particularly in the islands of Bass Strait near Tasmania, where it is still common. Sealing gangs lived off the birds and their eggs and, more recently, the geese were shot as agricultural pests because they ate grasses and seeds. Numbers are recovering and the present 8000 birds are protected and carefully managed. Captive-reared birds were introduced to New Zealand during the First World War, at Lake Hawea and Lake Wanaka in Central Otago. They bred successfully, but their descendants died out in the late 1940s. The most recent sightings, near Benmore in 1966 and in Fiordland in 1967, are considered to have been of stragglers from across the Tasman. Bones from an unknown New Zealand location, but now in the National Museum, testify to the presence of this bird in New Zealand in times past. The great similarity between Cape Barren geese and the extinct flightless geese that roamed New Zealand thousands of years ago suggest that the two forms evolved from a common ancestor.   M.J.W.

Once greatly exploited in Australia, the Cape Barren goose is now protected.

INTRODUCED

OTHER NAME: *Pig goose.*

SIZE: *850 mm.*

DESCRIPTION
ADULT: *Sexes alike, but female smaller. General colour grey. Head paler with white patch on crown.*

Scapulars and wing coverts spotted darker grey. Primaries and secondaries black-tipped. Tail and tail coverts black. Iris brown. Bill black but mostly covered by lime-green cere. Legs pink or red. Feet black.
DUCKLING: *Top of head, neck and back dark brown. Face grey with black-brown stripe through eye. Flank grey with dark brown band.*

Underparts grey. Bill black; green cere. Legs and feet dark grey-green.

MOULT
Once a year, after breeding.

VOICE
Low grunt by both sexes. High-pitched, multisyllabic honk by male. Very vocal in flight.

DISTRIBUTION
Islands off southern Australia, migrating to mainland in summer.

RECOGNITION
Grey colour, long legs. Head usually erect.

Chestnut-breasted shelducks, recently recorded vagrants from Australia, are grazers and feed on plants in shallow waters or on land.

Chestnut-breasted Shelduck *Tadorna tadornoides* (JARDINE & SELBY, 1928)

VAGRANT

OTHER NAMES: *Australian shelduck, mountain duck.*

SIZE: *650 mm.*

DESCRIPTION
MALE: *Head and neck black, often suffused with brown and tinged glossy green. Broad white ring at base of neck. Breast and mantle cinnamon brown. Back and scapulars black with fine yellow transverse lines. Rump and upper tail black. Belly dark brown with fine light brown lines. Undertail glossy black. Upper wing coverts white. Primaries black. Secondaries glossy green, with black base. Tertiaries chestnut. Iris dark brown. Bill black. Legs and feet dark grey. In eclipse plumage breast yellow-*

brown and neck-ring less well defined.
FEMALE: *Similar to male, but chest bright chestnut, and white ring round eye and base of bill.*
IMMATURE: *Similar to adult but duller. White on wing flecked with grey. Some white flecks between bill and eye.*
DUCKLING: *White when hatched with crown, neck and back brown. Wing brown with white band.*

MOULT
Adult pre-nuptial moult April to June, body feathers only. Complete post-nuptial moult in summer. Post-juvenile moult 2 or 3 months after fledging.

VOICE
Loud honk from male; more high-pitched call from female.

THE CHESTNUT-BREASTED SHELDUCK is principally a resident of south-eastern and western Australia where it inhabits large coastal brackish lakes, lowland lakes and ponds and billabongs. During dry spells it undertakes extensive seasonal migration.

When they are not breeding these birds often live in flocks of 1000 or more. By day they rest in loose groups at the water's edge; during the late afternoon they fly out noisily to feed. It is believed that, like most shelducks, the chestnut-breasted shelduck pairs for life, and mated pairs return to the same nest year after year.   M.J.W.

DISTRIBUTION
First recorded in New Zealand in December 1982 at Lake Ellesmere. Subsequently seen at Invercargill, the West Coast and at numerous localities throughout the North Island, indicating the presence of at least 20 birds. Individuals also seen on The Snares and on Enderby Island in the Auckland Islands.

RECOGNITION
Distinguished from similar paradise shelduck by white neck-ring; female also has white about eye and bill base.

Paradise Shelduck *Tadorna variegata* (GMELIN,1789)

FLIGHTLESS DURING ITS SUMMER MOULT period, the paradise shelduck has been exploited as food since the start of Polynesian settlement. Early European writers described Marlborough Maoris gathering as many as 5000 birds at a time, storing some for their own use and sending the rest to the Wellington market. Slaughter on that scale no longer occurs, but the species is classed as game in most districts and 8000 to 10000 are shot each season. The national population is estimated to be at least 130000 birds, about 60 per cent of them in the North Island. Thanks to liberations there, and intermittent protection in the South Island, numbers have recovered so well from a decline late in the nineteenth century that the bird is more widespread and numerous than at any time in its recent history.

The principal North Island habitat is grazed pasture. Breeding pairs centre their activities on stock ponds with an open aspect, while flocks tend to stay near larger bodies of water or on open grass flats. Birds are commonly found on wide gravel riverbeds in the South Island, and beside high country lakes. Small numbers may be seen along streams or on coastal flats, lakes and lagoons. On farmland the species is partial to young grass or clover shoots. Grains and seed-heads are also taken. Flocks can occasionally cause damage to newly sown pastures or crops, and farmers complain that droppings foul their grazing land. The birds also eat swamp and pond grasses, especially in the breeding season, and they take insects and earth-worms when available. On the coast, their diet is said to include crustaceans. Ducklings on ponds feed initially on aquatic insects, but obtain most of their food from grazing after about two weeks.

Paradise shelducks first breed in their second or third year, and pairs stay together for life. If one partner dies, the other remates quickly. Breeding pairs occupy and defend territories, spaced out over the available habitat, throughout the year—except for about two months spent at a communal moulting site. Non-breeding birds typically remain in large flocks. Females coming to maturity incite males to fight one another, and choose mates from among the more successful fighters. New pairs start to prospect for territories towards the end of the October-November breeding season. Nesting begins the following August. Nests are usually depressions in the ground, thickly overlaid with down and concealed under fallen logs, tree roots, buildings or stacks of timber or hay. But some birds nest in hollow logs, rock crevices, culverts or in holes up to 20 m high in trees.

Eight to 12 white, nearly elliptical eggs are laid at the rate of one a day. They are incubated for 30 to 32 days, by the female alone. She leaves the nest to feed for about one hour in every five or six during daylight. The male accompanies his mate back to the nest, but spends the rest of the incubation time waiting at the centre of the territory. He stands at the nest-site only when the eggs have hatched. Both parents lead the ducklings to water after they have been brooded in the nest for about 24 hours, and guard them throughout the fledging period of about eight weeks. Few eggs are laid after October, and nesting again after loss of a clutch is uncommon. Late-breeding pairs sometimes rear their young on the same ponds as earlier breeders, leading to a mistaken belief that the species breeds twice a season.

Banding of thousands of paradise shelducks during their flightless period has shown that in areas where they are hunted their average death rate is about 35 per cent a year and their average expectation of further life is only two years—though one adult is known to have lived for seven years after it was banded. Banding data also show that the species is remarkably sedentary. Over half of the banded birds shot were killed less than 30 km from their moulting site, and only five per cent were recovered more than 100 km away. But juvenile birds are more mobile: five months after fledging, some have been found more than 200 km from the birthplace. The movements of birds living on flat grasslands are greater than those of birds on hill country, where there is diversity of habitat within a smaller area.　　　M.J.W.

ENDEMIC

OTHER NAMES: *Paradise duck, pari, putangitangi.*

SIZE: *630 mm.*

DESCRIPTION
ADULT MALE: *Head and neck black. Breast and belly slightly lighter, flecked with pale yellow. Back and flank black and flecked. Rump and tail black; undertail chestnut. Upper and lower wing coverts white. Primaries black. Secondaries metallic green on exposed vane, forming speculum. Tertiaries rusty brown on outer vane, flecked grey-brown on inner. Iris, bill and legs black.*
ADULT FEMALE: *Head and neck white. Breast, belly, flanks and undertail bright chestnut. Back grey-black, heavily flecked with pale yellow. Rump and tail black. Wings, iris, bill, and legs as in male. In eclipse plumage, breast chestnut; belly and flank feathers black-tipped, interspersed with dark, heavily flecked feathers; overall appearance dark chestnut.*
JUVENILE: *Fledglings of both sexes resemble adult male, but female smaller and usually has white patch at bill base. Female assumes white head during post-juvenile moult; general body colour similar to male's throughout first year, but breast and belly appear dark chestnut.*
DUCKLING: *White when hatched with top of head brown and brown stripe from back of head to tail. Brown mark on flank and wings.*

MOULT
Post-juvenile moult 2 or 3 months after fledging. Adult pre-nuptial moult April to June, body feathers only. Post-nuptial moult of body, wing and tail feathers in summer. During post-nuptial moult flightless for 3 weeks and birds assemble in large flocks at traditional pond or lake sites.

VOICE
Persistently noisy. Piercing, monosyllabic flock call by both sexes. Numerous courtship and territorial calls, including distinctive female 'inciting call' of 2 syllables, second louder and higher-pitched. Male alarm call a goose-like honk.

DISTRIBUTION
Widespread except on Canterbury Plains. Concentrated in Northland, Poverty Bay-Hawke's Bay, Taihape-Wanganui, Nelson-Marlborough and Otago-Southland. Resides on larger offshore islands. Straggles to Chatham Islands and Lord Howe Island.

RECOGNITION
White upper wing patch in flight. Female has white head and neck; male appears black. High-pitched female alarm call; deep honking by male.

The female paradise shelduck, strikingly different from the male, is recognised by its white head and neck. In the North Island, the species prefers grazed pasture habitat; in the South Island, wide gravel riverbeds or high-country lakes.

The female mallard spends up to two or three weeks prospecting for a nest-site. Though sites are varied, they commonly provide overhead cover from predators.

Mallard *Anas platyrhynchos platyrhynchos* LINNAEUS, 1758

MALE MALLARD ENGAGE in behaviour, unique in the waterfowl world, that horrifies untrained observers. A few days after females begin incubation, the drakes leave their breeding partners and join up in gangs. Sometimes, if they come upon a lone female, all of them forcibly mate with it. A big group may take so long that the exhausted female drowns. But these gang rapes account for up to a fifth of all egg fertilisations, and females caring for broods are seldom attacked.

Mallard are the world's most successful dabbling ducks. They evolved in northern hemisphere habitats that were already dominated by agriculture, so they are at ease in farming environments. New Zealand flocks have expanded remarkably since the 1930s, when acclimatisation societies introduced American birds for breeding programmes and liberated their captive-reared progeny. Now they number about five million, making up at least 80 per cent of the total dabbling duck population, and are the mainstay of duck shooting as a sport. About one million are shot each season.

In many districts, particularly in the South Island grain-growing belt, the mallard has virtually taken over from the endemic grey duck. Habitats of the two species overlap, except that the mallard seems better adapted to exploit artificial stock ponds. It is commonly seen on salty or brackish water, but is relatively scarce in less densely populated areas and has been slow to take to inland rivers and streams, where the grey duck still predominates. Like all dabbling ducks, mallard have little use for deep waters, except to rest on or to take refuge from hunters.

Most mallard breed when one year old, having paired in June after elaborate mate-selection displays similar to those of the grey duck. Nest-sites may be under logs, haystacks or buildings or among tree roots, but are more commonly in rank pasture grasses or under bushes. The female pushes and wriggles, breaking down protruberances and rough grass to form a bowl. About 13 buff-green eggs are laid, one a day, soon after dawn. Incubation, by the female alone, usually takes 27 days. The male defends a water territory for the first few days, and the female leaves the nest to feed for two short periods each day. The breeding season is September to December, with a peak from late October to early November. Nesting occurs again if a clutch of eggs or a very young brood is lost. The female, which has sole charge, leads the ducklings to water within a few hours of hatching. They fledge in eight to 10 weeks.

Protein dominates the diet of ducklings and pre-breeding birds. Small aquatic invertebrates are preferred. Seeds of pond-edge plants and the fruits of many aquatic plants are also common foods. But some birds create a minor agricultural nuisance by singling out ripening grain crops. Pasture grasses are eaten when flooded, along with drowned worms and insects. Mallard take readily to city ponds and streams, often feeding from the hand. Probably no other waterfowl species is as tolerant of people, though as a game bird it is extremely wary, demanding good concealment, skilful calling and the most lifelike decoys.

In localities where hunting pressure is highest, banding records show that up to 35 per cent of birds are shot. Overall mortality in the first year is less than 55 per cent. The expectation of further life at the time of banding is 1.4 years. But birds that survive their first year live an average of nearly three more years. The oldest bird recovered so far was 14. The mallard's lower mortality rates and greater expectation of life, coupled with its larger clutches, give it a distinct biological advantage over the grey duck.

Because the two species are closely related and courtship behaviour similar, there is some cross-breeding in domestic flocks. Most hybrids result from pairings by grey drakes and female mallard; mallard drakes are normally rejected by female grey ducks. Hybrid plumages vary, but are generally intermediate between the species.   T.A.C.

INTRODUCED

OTHER NAMES: *None.*

SIZE: *580 mm.*

DESCRIPTION
ADULT MALE: *Head glossy green with white collar ring. Upper breast chestnut with finely streaked silvery grey underparts. Rump and tail coverts black. Tail grey and white with curled-up black central feathers. Wing grey with bright blue speculum and black-and-white trailing and leading bands. Iris dark brown. Bill yellowish green. Legs orange. In eclipse plumage, more like female, but face greyer and lighter; crown darker; upper parts and breast not streaked.*
ADULT FEMALE: *Upper body brown, streaked and spotted with lighter and sometimes blackish markings. Chin, throat and front of neck light buff. Crown, upper parts and upper breast more heavily marked. Irregular dark line through eye. Face flecked with fine black. Wing similar to male. Iris brown. Bill orange-brown or orange with black spots. Legs orange. Wide individual variation in tone and density of all markings.*
JUVENILE: *Similar to female and eclipse male but generally duller and less well marked.*

DUCKLING: *For 2 or 3 weeks blackish brown above with yellow face, underparts and sides; darker spots on back and wings; dark line through eyes; shorter dark lines or spots on ears.*

MOULT
Post-juvenile moult 2 or 3 months after fledging. Full adult moult in summer after breeding, females individually, males in flocks. Flightless for about 3 weeks.

VOICE
Female calls raucous quaaack, quaaack, quaaack; *male calls softer* raeb, raeb, raeb. *Both calls almost indistinguishable from grey duck.*

DISTRIBUTION
Widespread. Self-introduced to the Chatham Islands. Vagrant to subantarctic islands. Native of cold or temperate northern hemisphere.

RECOGNITION

Gaudy male plumage distinctive for most of year. Female's tones browner and more muted than grey duck. In flight, white bars conspicuous above and below blue speculum.

Grey Duck *Anas superciliosa superciliosa* GMELIN,1789

Though once numerous and widespread, the grey duck now persists most abundantly in wild wetland areas away from human interference.

UNTIL ABOUT 1960, grey ducks made up 95 per cent of New Zealand's dabbling duck population. Now, with the introduced mallard overwhelmingly dominant, they comprise less than 20 per cent. The estimated national population is one million. Average seasonal shooting harvests have fallen from 500000 to about 200000, and few hunters can achieve their daily limit bag.

Fresh water is the usual habitat, though birds are sometimes found on brackish or saline estuaries. They inhabit inland rivers and streams and even penetrate to alpine tarns. But in all instances the water is shallow. Food is taken by dabbling on or just under the surface, or by upending to dredge from the bottom. Ducklings and pre-nesting birds feed mostly on aquatic snails and other invertebrates. Towards the end of the breeding season the seeds of aquatic plants are eaten. Worms, and caterpillars are taken from wet pastures.

Most grey ducks breed at one year. They pair immediately after the shooting season—normally in mid-June. Birds commonly congregate on a pairing ground where the males perform an elaborate series of frenzied movements, and females incite the males of their choice to take part in vigorous pursuit flights. Pairs spend two or three weeks prospecting for a nest-site—perhaps a hole in a tree, but more commonly on the ground, in rank grass or tussock where overhead cover is available. Once a site is chosen each pair frequents a territory that may be kilometres away, spending all their time together there until the September to December breeding season.

The male accompanies its mate to the vicinity of the nest, but returns to a waiting place on the territory. After laying its eggs, normally one each morning, the female flies to the territory to feed. But when incubation starts, the female leaves the nest for only two brief periods a day. The male loses interest after about five days and goes off to look for solitary females.

About 10 creamy white eggs are laid. They are packed in down, and normally covered to retain warmth during the female's absences. Incubation takes 26 days. The young leave the nest within a few hours of the last-hatched drying off, and are promptly led to water to feed. But for the first fortnight they rarely spend more than an hour at a time on the water; feeding is alternated with spells of brooding ashore to restore warmth. Brooding ceases after about three weeks and the young fledge in eight to 10 weeks. They may stay in a group for a

further week or so but then they generally separate and join different groups in the area, later dispersing widely throughout the country.

Banding records indicate a first-year mortality rate of 66 per cent. Survivors of the first year have an expectation of two more, and one 14-year-old bird has been recovered. Sexes are equal in numbers at hatching, fledging and during the juvenile stage, but adult males seem to outnumber females about 53:47.

Grey ducks adapt readily to captivity though wild birds may take some years to settle before breeding. Birds have been exported to Europe since last century. They are found in some collections, particularly in Britain, but have not been very successful.   T.A.C.

ENDEMIC

OTHER NAME: *Parera.*

SIZE: *550 mm.*

DESCRIPTION
ADULT: *Sexes alike, but female slightly smaller. Top of head and back of neck dark brown. Face light cream with dark brown stripes from bill through eye to behind ear, and from gape across cheek. Throat cream. Body feathers dull brown with pale crescent edges; underparts lighter brown with paler edges. Speculum green with black borders and fine white bar on trailing edge. Underwing predominantly white. Iris reddish brown. Bill grey-green with black tip. Legs yellow-green.*
JUVENILE: *Like adult, but small notch in trailing edge of each tail feather for first 2 or 3 months.*
DUCKLING: *For first 2 weeks face yellow with dark lines through and under eye. Top of head, back of neck and back dark brown. Underparts, flanks and chest yellow with brown spots on back and rear edge of wing.*

MOULT
Gradual post-juvenile body moult, but no difference in appearance. Complete adult post-breeding moult, females individually, males collectively. Flightless for 3 weeks in mid to late summer.

VOICE
Female calls raucous quack, quack, quack *usually associated with feeding. Soft, drawn-out* quaaack *when disturbed or calling brood together. Similar but louder response to males flying over in hunting season. Male calls soft, drawn-out* raehb, *sometimes doubled to* raeb, raeb.

DISTRIBUTION
Widespread. Rare near people but numerous on wild wetlands. Related subspecies found in Australia, New Guinea and Indonesia.

RECOGNITION

Light throat and face above and below dark eye-stripe. In flight, overall dark appearance, green speculum.

Grey Teal *Anas gibberifrons gracilis* BULLER,1869

NATIVE

OTHER NAME: *Tete.*

SIZE: *430 mm.*

DESCRIPTION

ADULT: *Sexes alike. Top of head and back of neck dark brown, flecked with lighter brown. Throat, chin and side of head almost white. Back and flank feathers dark brown with pale brown edges. Primaries and tail feathers dark brown. Outer wing coverts, tips of inner coverts and secondaries white. Speculum glossy black with bluish sheen; with wing folded, it forms dark band edged on upper and lower surfaces with white band. Iris bright red. Bill and legs black.*
IMMATURE: *Slightly paler. Iris brown.*
DUCKLING: *Head, neck and back grey-brown. Dark brown stripes through and below eye.*

MOULT

Post-natal, post-juvenile and immature moults observed in young Australian birds, and pre-nuptial and post-nuptial moults in adults. No eclipse plumage detected.

Flightless for 3 weeks during post-nuptial moult.

VOICE

Rapid cuck-cuck-cuck *and muted* eep *to young. Loud, rapidly repeated* quack *by female.*

DISTRIBUTION

Scattered, never common. Highest concentrations in South Auckland, Waikato, Hawke's Bay and Otago, mostly below 300 m. Native to Australia, New Guinea and New Caledonia. Also found on Lord Howe and Macquarie Islands. Other subspecies occur in Indonesia, the Solomon and Andaman Islands.

RECOGNITION

Noticeably smaller than grey duck with paler face. In flight, distinguished from shoveler, mallard and grey duck by prominent white triangle on upper wing. From below, underwing has less white than other duck species. Fast wing-beat.

GREY TEAL ARE REMARKABLY MOBILE. A bird that was colour-marked at Mangere had flown 125 km by the following day, when it was unlucky enough to be shot. Hunting the species is prohibited, but many are killed by mistake for grey ducks or shovelers. Movements within New Zealand are apparently random, with birds dispersing in all directions. Rapid changes in numbers can occur at any time in any locality, though concentrations tend to build up in January, remaining high until June. But even when local populations seem fairly constant, their composition is changing as different individuals arrive and depart. The New Zealand population is also subject to periodic irruptions of birds from Australia, driven out by drought.

Shallow freshwater lakes, lagoons and swamps with extensive marginal cover are preferred, though birds are sometimes seen on salt or brackish water. They feed mostly at dawn and dusk, by dabbling on the surface to filter out insects and seeds, by dredging muddy bottoms, and by stripping seeds from overhanging plants. Occasionally they feed on land, but never far from the water. The composition of the grey teal's diet has not been studied in New Zealand. In Australia it varies with the locality: some birds feed almost entirely on seeds, while insects provide nearly a third of the diet of others.

Breeding probably occurs at one year, as is the case with most other dabbling ducks. It appears to be seasonal in New Zealand, but is spread over an extremely long period—as early as June or as late as January. Nest-sites include tree hollows, rabbit burrows and spots on the ground shielded by tussocks, sedges or rocks. Grey teal also take readily to nesting boxes. A clutch of five to nine cream eggs is laid at a rate of one a day, normally on a bare surface. The eggs, gradually covered with down, are incubated by the female alone. They hatch in 24 to 26 days. The drake helps to rear the ducklings, and it is thought that bonds between breeding pairs may last from season to season.

Banding records indicate an average annual mortality rate of about 50 per cent for adult grey teal. Of juveniles banded, 68 per cent died in the first year, 77 per cent by the end of the second and 85 per cent by the end of the fourth. The average expectation of further life for juveniles at banding is just under a year, but birds surviving their first year have an expectation of nearly three more. One grey teal is known to have lived for six years.

J.A.M.

Grey teal are highly mobile birds and are most commonly found in shallow freshwater lakes, lagoons and swamps with extensive marginal cover.

Brown Teal *Anas aucklandica* (GRAY, 1844)

ENDEMIC
Brown Teal
A.a. chlorotis GRAY, 1845.
Auckland Island Teal
A.a. aucklandica (GRAY, 1844).
Campbell Island Teal
A.a. nesiotis (FLEMING, 1935).

OTHER NAMES: *Pateke, brown duck, teal duck.*

SIZE: *480 mm.*

DESCRIPTION
Brown teal: *A number of partial albinos have been recorded, in both sexes, with whiter head and paler breast.*
ADULT MALE: *In breeding plumage head and face dark brown with metallic green sheen on crown and nape. Narrow white ring around eye; less distinct white band around front and sides of neck. Breast bright chestnut, paler towards belly. Each chest and upper abdomen feather has dark central spot, progressively bigger and more conspicuous towards back. Belly buff with central spots lightening towards tail. Flank feathers finely barred buff and dark brown. Undertail dark brown-black with prominent white patch on each side of base. Back dark brown with light tips and edges. Scapulars dark brown with broad pale edges; some barred black and brown with black on outer web. Upper wing brown. Speculum black with partial green sheen. Thin white lower wing-bar; cinnamon upper wing-bar not obvious. Underwing brown; coverts mottled brown and white. Tail and upper tail coverts black-brown with paler edges. Iris black. Bill bluish black. Legs and feet slate grey. In eclipse plumage loses green sheen, white eye-ring, white tail patches, flank barring and chestnut breast colour. Head and face blotchy brown. Breast dark brown with central spots giving mottled look.*
ADULT FEMALE: *Head, face and throat mottled brown. White half-ring sometimes below eye. Back, tail and upper tail coverts almost black with pale edges. Chest dull dark chestnut. Breast and belly pale with dark brown blotches. Flanks as in eclipse male. Wings, iris, bill and legs like male.*
IMMATURE: *Like adult female but generally darker with heavy black blotching on chest.*
DUCKLING: *Upper surface brown-black with small whitish spot at tail base. Undersurface pale brown. Head dark on top. Light stripe above eye; black stripe through eye.*

Auckland Island teal: *Smaller than brown teal and flightless.*
ADULT MALE: *Similar to brown teal. Green gloss on head faint. White eye-ring prominent. No neck ring. Breast dark brown. Belly brown with intermingling white feathers. Flanks brown with fine wavy buff lines. Back, wings and tail dark brown. Undertail black. Dull white spot at base of tail. Speculum on wing green edged with pale cinnamon and white. Iris dark brown. Legs, feet and bill dark brown. In eclipse plumage resembles female.*
ADULT FEMALE: *Similar to brown teal. Head purplish on crown, lacks gloss. Chin, throat and foreneck more mottled white than male. Belly feathers sepia edged white. No wavy lines on feathers; no tail spot. Otherwise as male.*

Campbell Island teal: *Smaller than Auckland Island teal and flightless.*
ADULT: *Head and neck sepia, darker on hind neck. Back and upper tail coverts sepia, with faint warm sepia edges. Undertail coverts warm sepia. Underparts umber without spots or wavy lines. Lower breast and belly feathers edged with light buff. Wings dark sepia with no speculum. Underwing coverts mottled buff and umber. Axillaries light buff with 2 centre sepia spots. Tail feathers dark sepia. Iris dark brown. Pale eye-ring. Legs medium brown. Feet blackish brown.*

MOULT
Brown teal: *Little known; timing of main annual moult apparently varies widely. Birds moult in flocks at roost-sites.*

Auckland Island teal: *Two annual body moults. Complete moult follows breeding season; birds remain on territories.*

Campbell Island teal: *Not known.*

VOICE
Female utters rapidly repeated quack; raucous growl in roost encounters; and coarse rasp in courtship. Male utters wheezy mn-yea; and bell-like burp in courtship.

DISTRIBUTION
Brown teal: *Great Barrier Island and Northland. Rare and isolated elsewhere.*

Auckland Island teal: *Disappointment, Adams, Rose, Ocean, Ewing, Enderby, French and Dundas Islands in the Auckland group.*

Campbell Island teal: *Dent Island.*

RECOGNITION
Small dark brown duck. Brown teal more elongated than scaup; wings cross high up on back. Auckland Island teal has conspicuously short wings. Campbell Island teal has black bill and runs rapidly along ground with body hunched and neck outstretched.

The outstanding feature of the brown teal is its gregariousness and, outside of the breeding season, these birds assemble in large flocks at traditional sites.

TOTAL PROTECTION SINCE 1921 has failed to arrest the decline of this once-common species. Swamp drainage, forest clearance and extensive shooting late last century were major factors in the South Island. But drastic reductions—in some cases complete disappearances—occurred in the North Island after 1920. These may have been linked with the near-extinction of wekas, which is usually blamed on an

The Auckland Island teal, which is largely nocturnal, occupies both stream and shoreline habitats.

fallen to fewer than 500 birds, concentrated in the Russell-Whangaruru and Kaeo-Kerikeri areas. Numbers seem to be stable only on Great Barrier Island, which probably has 600 to 1000 birds.

Brown teal are birds of heavily vegetated wetlands, preferably but not necessarily with some still or slow-flowing open water. Those in North Auckland have shown some adaptation to an agricultural environment by using partly overgrown stock ponds as breeding territories. On Great Barrier Island the favoured habitats are pastoral flats that are boggy for most of the year, with reeds and sedges in abundance and streams close by. Feeding usually starts at dusk and continues through the night. Insects, worms and snails are taken as well as shoots and succulent roots of vegetation. Birds have also been seen sieving mud at the bases of stream banks and nibbling the seed-heads of streamside vegetation. In coastal areas, where small marine crustaceans are presumably eaten, feeding is controlled by tidal rhythms rather than by a nocturnal cycle.

The species' ability to exploit marine or estuarine environments, though it is not primarily suited to them, must have assisted its ancient colonisation of Auckland and Campbell Islands. There it differentiated into two distinctive flightless races. The European introduction of cats and rats quickly led to their disappearance from the main islands. No more than 600 of the Auckland Island subspecies remain, on neighbouring islands in the group, and perhaps under 30 Campbell Island teal live on Dent Island. The teal is New Zealand's least-known bird and one of the world's rarest waterfowl.

Captive brown teal breed at one year, and birds in the wild probably do the same. Duckling broods have been seen on Great Barrier Island in all months except April and May, but the main breeding season is July to December with a peak in September to October. Island residents claim to have observed the same pairs breeding twice in one year. This has also happened in captivity. But as a rule it is unlikely in the wild.

Nest-sites located on Great Barrier Island have all been in sedge clumps close to creek edges, but newly hatched broods have been seen well away from creeks. Northland nest-sites have included long grass next to roadside ditches. A clutch of four to eight creamy brown eggs is laid in a bowl of grass, lined with down. Incubation, by the female alone, takes 27 to 30 days in captivity, and the young can fly 50 to 55 days after hatching. The male stays in the breeding territory as a guard, aggressive towards all other waterfowl.

Outside the breeding season brown teal are highly gregarious, assembling in big flocks at traditional sites and roosting communally. The importance of this social habit has contributed to the downfall of the species: in Northland wherever a roosting site has been destroyed, the number of birds in the area has declined. Hopes of saving the species rest in its ready adaptation to captivity.　　　M.J.W.

unidentified disease. Stewart Island remained a stronghold of brown teal until the 1950s, when cats became common; the birds disappeared from there in 1972.

Dwindling remnants of the mainland population are found in Fiordland, inland Bay of Plenty, the Waikato and at the tip of Coromandel Peninsula. A few birds in the Manawatu, and also on Kapiti Island, originated from liberations of captive-reared stock. Northland had a significant population until the 1960s but it has

Northern Shoveler

Anas clypeata LINNAEUS,1758

VAGRANT

OTHER NAMES: *None.*

SIZE: *500 mm.*

DESCRIPTION
ADULT MALE: *In breeding plumage head and neck glossy dark green. Back and rump blackish. Breast white, reaching up across back to form white upper mantle. Abdomen and flanks chestnut. Narrow white strip separating abdomen from black undertail, enlarging at sides to form conspicuous rump patch. Scapulars white, separating dark back from darkish folded wing. Upper wing pale blue; speculum green with white forward bar. Primaries dark. Underwing white. Iris yellow-orange. Bill dark grey, spatulate. Legs orange-red. In eclipse plumage resembles female and almost impossible to distinguish from New Zealand shoveler.*
ADULT FEMALE: *In breeding plumage head and body mottled brown; cinnamon-buff edging on some feathers may appear pinkish. Wing like male. Iris brown-yellow. Bill olive grey-brown. Legs orange-red.*

In eclipse plumage darker mottled brown, with pale feather edges. Head and neck almost grey.

VOICE
Male calls took, took, *loud and regularly spaced during courtship or when threatening, soft and rapid to mate in flight. Female quacks, usually 1 to 4 long descending notes followed by 3 to 9 shorter quacks of same pitch.*

DISTRIBUTION
Northern hemisphere species present throughout Europe, Asia and North America. Birds of the North American population occasionally pass into central Polynesia; New Zealand stragglers probably come from these birds.

RECOGNITION

Small fast-flying duck with obvious spoon-shaped bill and powder blue upper wing. Extremely difficult to distinguish from New Zealand shoveler.

The northern shoveler is an inhabitant of lowland shallow wetlands.

ONE MALE OF THIS SPECIES was shot in the Waikato in 1968, and another near Lake Horowhenua in 1969. Three other sightings were claimed in the 1970s. All these later birds were in full breeding plumage and seen at times when they have been in eclipse in the northern hemisphere. This suggests they had been in New Zealand long enough to adapt their moult cycle to the southern climate. But given the considerable variation in plumage of New Zealand shoveler drakes it is more likely that the birds were wrongly identified. Habitat and diet requirements of the species are essentially the same as those of the New Zealand shoveler.　　　M.J.W.

New Zealand Shoveler *Anas rhynchotis variegata* (GOULD, 1856)

ENDEMIC

OTHER NAMES: *Kuru whengi, spoonbill, spoonie.*

SIZE: *480 mm.*

DESCRIPTION
ADULT MALE: *Head bluish grey; black round base of bill, vertical white line in front of eye. Undersurface bright chestnut. Breast dark brown with white freckling; extent of white varies widely between birds. Prominent white patch on flank. Upper wing coverts pale blue; speculum green; coverts and speculum separated by triangular white bar. Underwing white. Rump and tail coverts black with green gloss. Iris red. Bill black, long with spatulate tip. Legs and feet bright orange. In eclipse plumage resembles female but flank patch remains.*
ADULT FEMALE: *Body plumage uniformly mottled brown. Wing like male. Legs and feet yellowish brown.*
JUVENILE: *Like adult female but duller with less conspicuous markings.*
DUCKLING: *Dark across top of head, back of neck, and back when hatched. Dark stripe through eye, small dark spot in front of eye, darkish line below ear. Cheeks, chest and underparts pale yellow. Legs blackish.*

MOULT
Juvenile body moult 2 or 3 months after fledging. Adult post-breeding moult from late January to mid-February; flightless for 3 weeks.

VOICE
Unusually quiet duck. When pairing, female gives muted quack, male soft took, took. Soft chatter in flight, not usually detectable.

DISTRIBUTION
Widespread on shallow wetlands but uncommon above 350 m. Different subspecies in eastern and southwestern Australia.

RECOGNITION

Sits lower than other ducks; head bigger and longer on short neck. Long, wedge-shaped bill and male's white flank distinctive. In flight, triangular white bar conspicuous between green speculum and blue coverts. Fastest-flying waterfowl; with jinking flight and whistling wings before landing.

SHOVELER ARE THE FIRST NEW ZEALAND ducks to have taken to the open ocean as a refuge from hunters. Swift and erratic flight also aids their survival, and there is no agricultural pressure for their control—they do not eat grain or pasture grasses. But the species responds readily to decoys and callers. About 30 000 are shot each season, out of an estimated national population of only 150 000 birds. Furthermore, the fertile, raupo-fringed lowland shallows that they prefer

remain under constant threat from drainage attempts.

Unlike other dabbling ducks, shoveler cannot supplement their diet by grazing on grass shoots or grains. The edges of their bills have fine growths—lamellae—through which only soft foods can be sieved. So they are almost exclusively protein feeders, taking small freshwater invertebrates and the seeds of fringing plants. Shoveler are sometimes found on flooded pastures, but only to feed on worms and insects.

Birds are sexually mature at one year, and commonly congregate for pairing in June. Flock sizes stay much the same until September, when egg-laying starts. Nest-sites are usually in rank pasture grass and invariably safe from flooding, though rarely more than 300 mm above the ground. About 11 oval, creamy white eggs, sometimes with a faint green-blue tinge, are laid. Incubation, by the female, takes 25 days. Broods, generally of four or five young, seldom appear before October or later than December. The female is usually responsible for rearing the ducklings, but males have been seen helping. Crèches of up to 50 young birds have been found with no adults attending. The young fledge about eight to 10 weeks after hatching.

Banding records indicate a juvenile mortality rate of 50 per cent, compared with an annual rate of 44 per cent for adults. Sexes are evenly divided among banded juveniles, but in pairing flocks the ratio is 60 males to 40 females. This imbalance is maintained from the start of the July to September pairing period, so it cannot be accounted for by the risks of nesting and egg-laying. Females apparently suffer higher adult mortality for some other reason. Birds on average live for one year after banding, but those surviving that year have an expectation of 1.8 more. The oldest bird so far recorded was nine.

The species is highly mobile. Many birds, banded during their summer moult and recovered in the autumn hunting season, have meanwhile traversed the length or breadth of the country. Individual moult sites are variable, but marked birds have used the same breeding sites in successive seasons. One such bird, reared in the Manawatu, spent part of its first year in Otago and Southland, 800 km away, and then returned to its original area to breed. Breeders have had little success with captive birds as habitats in which they can be confined offer a limited diet and are seldom suitable.   T.A.C.

Lowland coastal swamps are favourite haunts of the New Zealand shoveler. It prefers shallow, highly fertile wetlands, edged usually with raupo.

The blue duck is a river specialist: ducklings, for example, are hatched with disproportionately big feet which help them swim against strong currents.

Blue Duck *Hymenolaimus malacorhynchos* (GMELIN,1789)

BLUE DUCKS are uniquely specialised feeders in the white water of turbulent, fast-flowing mountain rivers where their diet of freshwater insects is especially abundant. Hatched with disproportionately big feet, ducklings are immediately capable of swimming against strong currents and jumping up onto rocks, logs or ledges. With some schooling near the shoreline, they quickly learn to dart between rocks to feed on insects in the downstream eddies. The parent birds are extremely attentive. The female feeds as close as possible to its brood while the drake—the most dutiful male of all duck species—moves from rock to rock keeping constant guard. Even so, duckling mortality is high, and the survival to fledging of two young from a brood signifies a highly successful season.

Populations may be further limited because juvenile birds do not disperse widely. They seem to move only up or down the watercourse on which they were reared, where territories may already be hard to find. Occasionally they are found at the heads of fiords and around the edges of mountain lakes, but river habitat is always nearby. Each breeding pair needs on average about one kilometre of river. In its favoured habitats in rivers of steep gradient the blue duck is far from rare. It is not, as sometimes thought, in imminent danger of extinction. But it can be classed as a threatened species because in many localities its habitat may be modified by small hydro-electric developments or poor catchment management.

Most feeding is carried out in shallow white water, with only the head and neck submerged as the bird expertly works its way among the downstream faces of rocks. In deeper water birds can feed by diving, staying under for up to 20 seconds. They may also feed by upending, or by picking adult insects from the water surface. Soft lateral flaps at the tip of the bill were once thought to serve as scrapers or clamps for feeding. It is more likely that they protect the bone of the bill from abrasion in contact with rocks.

Breeding birds maintain their pair-bond and territory year-round, and from year to year. Many moult before their ducklings have fledged, perhaps to ensure that they can fly again by the time the juveniles challenge for territory. Young birds attempt this within a few weeks of their first flight, either by squeezing in between the territories of established pairs or by competing with and displacing a resident adult. Those that fail feed furtively on the territories of two or three pairs, waiting for later opportunities. Even when successful in obtaining a territory these juveniles do not breed in their first year; the earliest recorded age of breeding is at the end of the second year.

Nesting may start as early as July or as late as December, but the peak is August to October. Sites include hollow logs, tree trunks, clumps of vegetation, rock clefts, cave ledges and even spaces under buildings. Most are close to a stream edge. Nests are simply heaped collections of all the sticks and grasses within reach, and contain little down. Eggs are creamy white and elliptical, and laid in clutches of four to nine. Incubation, by the female, has not been timed in the wild. Artificially incubated eggs have taken 31 or 32 days, indicating a longer period than for any other duck species. Captive-reared ducklings can fly 70 days after hatching, but a slower growth rate could be expected in the wild. Over half of each year's young are thought to die in their first year. Banding records are insufficient to estimate the adult mortality rate. One bird, banded as an adult, was still alive seven years later.

The species is particularly secretive in parts of its range. Birds tend to feed mostly at dawn and dusk, spending the rest of the day hidden under river banks, vegetation or log jams. Their coloration makes them difficult to see against backgrounds of broken or glistening water, rocks and logs. Camouflage, and such furtive behaviour, are hard to account for in an environment that could have had few significant predators before the arrival of humans and their introduced animals. M.J.W.

ENDEMIC

OTHER NAME: *Whio.*

SIZE: *530 mm.*

DESCRIPTION
ADULT: *Sexes alike. General body colour slate blue; with slight greenish gloss on top of head. Breast feathers spotted chestnut. Wings slate blue above and below; outer secondaries often narrowly bordered with white; inner secondaries and tertiaries have longitudinal black line on outer margin. Iris yellow. Bill pinkish white, with black flap at tip. Legs and toes pale grey, but black at joints; webs black.*
IMMATURE: *Like adult but chestnut breast spots fewer and darker; no head gloss; iris dark brown; and bill light grey.*
DUCKLING: *Top of head, neck and back dark grey with metallic green sheen. Breast and belly white. Undertail chestnut. Face white with dark stripes from bill through eye to back of head and from eye to crown. Wings black with white trailing edge. Dark stripe along back of thigh. Prominent spot at tail base: in male dark chestnut; in female fawn. Iris dark brown. Bill grey-blue with rosy tip and black flap. Legs and feet yellow-brown.*

MOULT
Full post-breeding moult: flightless

for about 6 weeks between December and May.

VOICE
Male gives high-pitched, wheezy whistle as territorial or advertisement call—Maori whio *is good representation. Also short* whi *whistle. Female utters long, low, grating note as threat or in response to human disturbance; also low-pitched, staccato rasping.*

DISTRIBUTION
Formerly widespread throughout North Island and most of South Island; now mainly restricted to forested mountains of the North and South Islands. Recorded throughout Kaimai, Raukumara, Huiarau, Kawhenua, Kaimanawa, Kaweka and Ruahine Ranges. Occasional reports from Tararua Mountains and inland North Taranaki (but not Mt Egmont). In the South Island in bush west of the Alps; the Tasman Mountains; and Fiordland. Also recently sighted in Richmond Range; headwaters of Clarence, Rakaia and Waimakariri Rivers; and in Catlins.

RECOGNITION

Slate or blue duck with pale bill. Sits on water with tail prominent, inclined upward.

Scaup *Aythya novaeseelandiae* (GMELIN, 1789)

ENDEMIC

OTHER NAMES: *New Zealand scaup, black teal, papango.*

SIZE: *400 mm.*

DESCRIPTION

ADULT MALE: *Upper surface black with green or purple sheen, particularly on head. Undersurface brownish black; lower breast and belly mottled with whitish brown. Upper wing black but secondaries have broad white bar in centre. Underwing mottled brownish white. Iris yellow. Bill blue-black. Legs and feet black.*

ADULT FEMALE: *Upper surface dark brown; rump almost black. Upper breast dark brown. Lower breast and belly mottled brownish white. Upper wing darker brown; white bar in centre of secondaries. Underwing mottled brownish white. White band at bill base, most conspicuous in breeding season. Iris brown. Bill brownish black. Legs and feet dark brown.*

IMMATURE: *Resembles female. Males*

colour up about 6 months after fledging.

DUCKLING: *Pale brown above, white below. Obscure whitish marks at wing and rump. Bill reddish brown. Legs light brown.*

MOULT

Flightless during full post-breeding moult. Timing and duration unknown.

VOICE

Muted quacking by female; series of soft whistles by male.

DISTRIBUTION

Northland; central and eastern North Island; high country lakes east of Southern Alps; lower lakes on the West Coast; Fiordland.

RECOGNITION

Small and dark with rounded profile on water. In flight, white upper wing-bar conspicuous. Flies, with rapid wing-beat, low over water.

BRILLIANT DIVING SKILLS set the scaup apart from all other endemic New Zealand ducks. It can probe lake depths of more than two metres for its animal food. Even ducklings, within a day of hatching, are reputed to dive up to one metre. Kicking slightly at the start of its descent, the scaup paddles to a feeding depth and maintains it by the gentle use of its big splayed feet, held out at a wide angle from the body. To ascend, it simply stops paddling and lifts its head. The feet acting as vanes, it shoots to the surface at an angle of about 45°. Wings are never used under water. Most dives last 15 to 20 seconds, but the bird is capable of staying down for well over half a minute.

Widespread until late last century, scaup were heavily exploited by hunters and severely affected by agricultural development. Now their range is restricted to the bigger, deeper lakes. Though unable to recolonise shallower wetlands, where dabbling ducks have tended to take over, scaup were quick to take advantage of hydro lakes on the Waikato River. But they do not inhabit flowing water, and do not seem to disperse widely.

Flocks or groups of this highly social species may be encountered at any time of year, with individuals showing no apparent aggression towards one another. At breeding time, the closeness of many nests gives the impression of a loose colony. Breeding starts at one or two years. Pairs are formed, for only one season, after elaborate male courtship displays. In the most obvious display the head is flung backwards to lie along the back with the bill pointing up. In another the body is extended flat on the water with the head and neck stretched towards the female, to the accompaniment of a soft, wheezy whistle. A different, high-pitched whistle of three or four notes is often heard 50 metres away. Another courtship call, usually *whe-whe*, is given with a display in which the neck takes an obvious double kink.

Nesting occurs late in the season—usually October to February. A bowl is made of broken reeds or grass, topped with down, in dense cover by the water's edge. A clutch of five to eight creamy white eggs is incubated by the female in 28 to 30 days. The drake stays close by: a solitary male, floating quietly near the shoreline in summer, is a good guide to the presence of an incubating female. Both parents take part in rearing the ducklings. Their fledging period in the wild has not been recorded.

Scaup take readily to captivity, keeping happily to themselves among other waterfowl in pond collections. Females are willing to nest in artificial structures, and can lay new clutches if their eggs are taken for mechanical incubation. One female at the Mount Bruce native bird reserve laid 26 eggs in a season. Birds reared at the reserve have thrived after liberation on lakes in Taranaki and the Wairarapa. This ease of breeding in captivity and re-adaptation to the wild seems to assure the future of the species. M.J.W.

The range of the scaup, once widely distributed, has been restricted by hunting last century and, more recently, by agricultural development of wetlands.

White-eyed Duck

Aythya australis australis

(EYTON, 1838)

VAGRANT

OTHER NAMES: *Karakahia, hard head, Australian white-eyed duck.*

SIZE: *480 mm.*

DESCRIPTION
ADULT MALE: *Head, throat, neck, back, rump and tail rich dark brown. Wing brown with reddish or chestnut tinge on upper coverts; outer primaries brown; other primaries white with brown tips; secondaries brown with broad white band. Breast dark brown suffused with red. Lower breast white mottled with brown. Belly dark brown. Undertail coverts white. Iris white. Bill black with slate blue bar at tip, and black nail. Legs and feet grey; webs slate.*
ADULT FEMALE: *Generally lighter than male with narrower and paler bar on bill. Iris brown.*
IMMATURE: *Similar to female but paler. White parts on underside more mottled. Iris hazel brown.*
DUCKLING: *Light brown above, suffused with pale yellow. Pale yellow below. Iris pale brown. Upper bill blue-grey; lower bill pale pink with blue edge. Legs and feet blue-grey.*

VOICE
Usually silent. Soft, harsh croak by female; soft, wheezy whistle by male.

DISTRIBUTION
Eastern and southwestern Australia. Vagrant to Indonesia, New Guinea, Pacific Islands and New Zealand.

RECOGNITION

Small, round profile on water. Brown colouring. White eye in male. White undertail and upper wing-bar conspicuous in flight.

Endemic to Australia, the white-eyed duck is a diving duck adapted to deeper, more permanent bodies of water.

WHITE-EYED DUCKS APPEARED in New Zealand in abundance in the 1860s and 1870s, but there is no record of their having bred. Sightings this century have been few, perhaps because they are becoming rare on the east coast of Australia. Nearly all sightings have been of flocks—the species is highly social—and all have been on lakes. Across the Tasman, however, birds also frequent swamps and rivers. They are nomads, extremely mobile in times of drought. As diving ducks, adapted to deeper waters, they fill a role equivalent to that of the scaup in New Zealand. Ever alert, they spring almost vertically from the water when disturbed and fly with a characteristically rapid wing-beat.

They obtain all their food from the water either by diving to the bottom of deep waters, dabbling on the surface or feeding on emergent vegetation at the edge. Most of their food is plant material such as seeds of aquatic grasses, and other submerged vegetation such as water millfoil. They also eat aquatic insects and their larvae, small shrimps and occasionally small fish.

White-eyed ducks breed in the Australian summer, depending on rainfall. The bowl-shaped nest of woven plants is built in reeds or bushes close to the water's edge. The female incubates the nine to 12 eggs for 25 days. Soon after hatching the ducklings are able to dive for their food.   M.J.W.

Wood Duck *Chenonetta jubata* (LATHAM, 1801)

FIVE SPECIMENS of the wood duck have been found in New Zealand, all of them in the South Island, and the most recent at Wairau Lagoon in 1979. The species feeds mainly on green herbage and seeds. In Australia flocks assemble about stock ponds or reservoirs and fly nightly to feeding areas. They cause occasional agricultural damage by feeding on green crops, particularly wheat.   M.J.W.

VAGRANT

OTHER NAME: *Maned duck.*

SIZE: *480 mm.*

DESCRIPTION
ADULT MALE: *Head and neck chocolate brown; with black feathers on back of neck. Back, tail coverts and tail black. Breast mottled brown and white. Belly black. Flanks and sides of breast grey with fine, closely spaced black lines. Upper wing coverts grey; speculum brilliant green, edged above and below with white. Underwing white. Iris brown. Bill, legs and feet olive-brown.*
ADULT FEMALE: *General colour mottled grey-brown. Head and neck pale brown. Whitish line above and below eye. Back, rump and tail black. Undertail white. Breast and flanks brown, each feather crossed with white band. Lower breast and belly white. Wing, iris, bill and legs as for male.*
IMMATURE: *Like adult female but paler.*

VOICE
Drawn-out, mournful mewing; call of male higher-pitched and shorter.

DISTRIBUTION
Eastern and western Australia; most numerous on southeastern slopes and tablelands.

RECOGNITION

Long legs, extended neck, goose-like head. In flight, large white patch obvious behind speculum on upper wing; black belly and undertail of male obvious when overhead. Slow wing-beat.

The wood duck, rare vagrant to New Zealand, occurs throughout Australia.

Australasian Harrier *Circus approximans* PEALE, 1848

NATIVE

OTHER NAMES: *Kahu, swamp harrier, marsh harrier.*

SIZE: *600 mm.*

DESCRIPTION

ADULT MALE: *Upper surface mainly dark brown. Edges of head and neck feathers tawny. Edges of wing coverts and scapulars pale rufous. Quills black, with outer webs silver. Upper tail coverts white barred with rufous. Tail silver-brown with dark brown bands and side feathers washed with rufous. Undersurface white streaked with rufous; leg paler and with narrower streaks. Under-wing and tail light fawn varied with grey. Axillaries pale rufous with darker bars. Cere and eye-ring yellow. Iris light brown to golden during second winter changing to pale yellow with thin black outer ring. Feet yellow; when breeding yellow-orange. Claws and bill blue-black.*

ADULT FEMALE: *Similar to male, but larger and underparts yellow-brown with broad streaks. Iris dark or mid-brown during second winter taking years longer than male to change to pale yellow with thin black outer ring.*

JUVENILE MALE: *Upper surface mainly dark brown. Hind neck varied white and rufous. Quills dark brown tipped pale tawny. Tail dark brown, very faintly banded with lighter brown and tawny tips. Upper tail coverts rufous and fawn at base. Undersurface rufous, with shafts of feathers black. Cere and eye-ring pale yellow, darkening in first breeding season. Feet yellow changing to dark yellow. Iris dark brown at fledging, becoming light brown or golden yellow with brown specks by end of first post-nuptial moult. After first post-nuptial moult complete wing-bars first appear, upper tail coverts white with brown spots and rufous edges; and banding on tail more conspicuous. Under surface becomes lighter with brown streaks.*

JUVENILE FEMALE: *As juvenile male but iris dark chocolate brown.*

NESTLING: *Thick buff-white down, darker above with white nape patch. Cere and feet pink changing to pale yellow.*

MOULT

Adult females moult from December to June; adult males from January to July. First post-nuptial moult from December to May. Juveniles undergo partial body moult 3 or 4 months after fledging.

VOICE

Generally silent outside breeding season. Plaintive kee-a, *short repeated* see-o *and quiet* chuck-chuck-chuck *from males. High-pitched* see-uh *from juveniles, and from females during courtship display, when attacked or asking for food. Loud sharp* chit-chit-chit *or* cheet *when threatened.*

DISTRIBUTION

The North and South Islands; Stewart Island and adjacent islets; Hen and Chickens; the Kermadec, Three Kings, Poor Knights, and Chatham Islands; Mokohinau and Kapiti Islands. Visits the Auckland and Campbell Islands and probably Macquarie Island. Also found in southeastern New Guinea; mainland Australia and Tasmania; New Caledonia; Vanuatu; Fiji; Tonga; and Îles de la Société, Loyauté and Wallis. Visits Norfolk and Lord Howe Islands and Samoa.

> ### RECOGNITION
> Slow sustained flight with alternate periods of flapping and gliding when flying low over swamplands and crops. Long wings form shallow V as birds soars on thermals. White upper tail coverts contrast strongly with dark back when flying. Long legs noticeable when perched.

WHEN THE AUSTRALASIAN HARRIER HUNTS, it flies slowly into the wind, alternately gliding and flapping up to nine metres above the vegetation. It quarters open country, such as swamps, sand dunes, ferns, tussock, grassland, farm drains, pond margins and crops—particularly where the vegetation is between a half and three metres high. It rarely chases small birds in flight and, generally, surprises animals on the ground or in shallow water. Often, in autumn and winter, it soars at heights of 50 to 200 m while searching for dead animals in farmland and at roadsides.

Mammals make up most of its prey. In the autumn it eats rabbits, hares, hedgehogs, possums, rats, mice and large insects. In the winter and spring, when large insects are not available and other live prey is scarce, the Australasian harrier eats carrion, including dead sheep. It returns to live prey in summer, especially introduced songbirds and their eggs, and to a lesser extent young rabbits, hares and hedgehogs. Game birds, frogs, fish and lizards are taken in small numbers throughout the year.

Distribution and abundance

Before the Maoris arrived, when most of the low country was heavily forested, there were probably few Australasian harriers in New Zealand. Then European settlers greatly increased both the open country that this bird prefers and the number of small mammals it feeds on, and the Australasian harrier flourished.

Yet there is evidence that since the early 1950s its population has declined. This is partly due to successful rabbit control. Swampland, where the Australasian harrier hunts, roosts and nests, has been drained and more intensive grazing has made grassland unsuitable for hunting. Also, this is one of the few unprotected native birds and, although there is no longer a bounty for its feet, farmers and sportsmen still slaughter it because they think that the Australasian harrier kills young lambs and game birds. Occasionally it does take feathered game and domestic poultry, but mostly it feeds on animals that people do not eat.

Despite widespread persecution, the Australasian harrier is still abundant and road counts indicate that there is an average of one bird for every 10 km in open country. Where the habitat is particularly favourable, there is one bird for every 50 ha in the breeding season and one for every 80 ha during the rest of the year.

Throughout the year, some non-breeding Australasian harriers roost communally in long grass or raupo. More roost together in autumn and winter in flocks that vary from 20 to more than 150 birds. Around dusk, they arrive at the roost alone, flying steadily and purposefully about 20 m above the ground. Before they land, they sometimes soar above the roost or preen themselves on prominent perches. At dawn, they leave to hunt, usually within four kilometres of the roost, but occasionally they travel as far as 12 km. In spring and summer, mated birds generally roost near the nest. They normally hunt alone, but in autumn and early winter, flocks of about 60 harriers have been seen in the day, usually in areas where people have poisoned rabbits. Sometimes females and juveniles hunt in pairs and trios.

During the breeding season, pairs defend a three dimensional territory of about 30 ha and 20 m high. They range over about nine square kilometres, which overlaps with the range of other pairs, but they tend to hunt a core area of three square kilometres.

The long breeding season begins in June when pairs soar together, chase each other and evict intruders from their territory. From July to September rival males mark out their territories by flying on either side of the boundary with their wings held at an exaggeratedly high angle and their bright yellow-orange tarsi thrust straight down. Usually this display ends when the males land silently on prominent perches in their respective territories.

Courtship and breeding

In one courtship flight, pairs of Australasian harriers soar with wings raised high and bent slightly back. This soaring display is often followed by an undulating flight with deep wing-beats. Later in the season both sexes, but more often the male, perform spectacular U-shaped dives of 25 to 100 m deep. With strong wing-beats, the bird dives steeply, then flips sideways or upwards and calls loudly. Sometimes, if the female is higher than the male, she follows him soaring slowly down. If she is lower she flips over and presents her claws to him as he dives close to her. Should she land, the male makes several short loops above her and then lands beside her. Occasionally several harriers dive together over their territories, suggesting that this may be a territorial display too.

When the birds are courting, the male takes food to a 'cock nest' that it has built in swampland some 50 m from where the female will build the breeding nest. The male raises its wings and calls the female to eat. In August and September the pair fly low over their territory.

The young of the Australasian harrier, hatched at different times, vary greatly in size. Older chicks take most of the food and will eat dead smaller chicks.

One bird lands while the other soars, then the roles are reversed. The male calls a short *see-o* about 10 times in a row when it lands. From this period until after the young have hatched the female spends most of its time in the pair's territory. Birds defend their territory by flying directly at intruders and attacking them if they do not retire immediately across the boundary or fly to a height of at least 20 m from where they are escorted across the boundary. When the male calls the female to feed at the nest or when it soars over their territory, it utters a short plaintive *kee-a*.

Females occasionally breed in their first year, but although one-year-old males defend territories they do not breed until they are two years old. The breeding nest is built in fern, toetoe, raupo or on a sedge, usually on or near the ground. Carrying material in both beak and claws, the female lines the nest with grass on a base of cabbage tree leaves, thistle stems, lupin branches, toetoe stems and flax leaves. The nest measures about 80 cm by 50 cm with the base of the cup 40 cm above ground or water level.

Between October and December the female lays, on alternate days, about four white, elliptical eggs and incubates them alone for 31 to 34 days. During incubation the male feeds the female, passing food to her in the air which she eats 20 to 100 m from the nest. Sometimes the female stops brooding, without deserting the young, as early as five days after the hatching of the first egg, so that the other eggs do not hatch. She remains within the territory, often perched on a prominent vantage point for long periods and only returns to the nest during wet weather or with food provided by the male. Usually the female does not begin hunting as regularly as the male until two to five weeks after the chicks hatch. A male may land at the nest and leave prey; many others never visit the nest however.

Leaving the nest

At two weeks the chicks clamber out of the nest and scatter widely in the surrounding vegetation, particularly if the nest-site is located in a standing crop. At seven days their wing quills protrude; at 21 days they are largely covered by feathers; and by 28 days the young are completely feathered.

Between one and three chicks fledge. They fly at about 45 days old, but for the next two weeks the fledglings remain within the parental territory. During this time the female does much of the hunting and sometimes the male is seen infrequently in the territory. The fledglings call shrilly and pursue the adults until they drop their prey, then the young try to catch it in mid-air. For the first four weeks after fledging the young harriers roost near the nest-site. During the day, they fly increasing distances from the territory—up to two kilometres. In late February and March the juveniles and then some of the adults leave the breeding grounds.

The Australasian harrier adapts readily to captivity and training, through the correct use of falconry techniques. But its extreme shyness at the nest and elaborate aerial courtship displays would probably make it a difficult bird to breed in captivity.   D.J.B-G.

Nankeen Kestrel *Falco cenchroides cenchroides* Vigors & Horsfield,1827

The nankeen kestrel favours open country, grassy plains and light woodland. The most common clutch size is five eggs.

VAGRANT

OTHER NAMES: *Australian windhover, hoverer, Australian kestrel.*

SIZE: *330 mm.*

DESCRIPTION
ADULT MALE: *Head pale blue-grey with narrow black streak above eye and black stripe from side of eye down side of throat. Feathers of upper parts rufous brown with dark centres. Primaries dark brown notched with white on inner ribs. Rump blue-grey. Tail blue-grey with black band and narrow buff tip. Underparts white or yellow-buff with narrow brown shaft lines on breast feathers. Cere and eye-ring yellow. Iris brown. Bill horn-colour with black tip. Legs yellow-orange.*
ADULT FEMALE: *As male but upper parts less rufous; head and rump pale brown; tail pale brown with broader black band and white tip.*

MOULT
Not known.

VOICE
Rapid kek-kek-kek-kek .... *Indrawn quavering* ee agh *followed by a few clucks. Slow* tek-tek-tek-tek.

DISTRIBUTION
Australia, Tasmania and New Guinea. Straggles to New Zealand from Australia and reported at Waimate, Kaipara, Portland Island, Castlepoint, Wellington, Masterton, West Oxford and Burnt Hill.

RECOGNITION

Small falcon with long, pointed wings and long tail. Underparts appear white. Either flies fast with flickering wings or soars on flat wings. Sometimes hovers in mid-air with head facing into wind and tail depressed.

FLYING SLOWER THAN the New Zealand falcon, the nankeen kestrel hunts over open country, grassy plains and light woodland. Mostly it preys on ground-living creatures, such as grasshoppers, crickets, beetles and other large insects, mice and other little mammals, and small lizards. On sighting its prey it hovers lower and lower in stages, then rapidly drops the last few metres onto its victim. Sometimes it snatches small birds on the wing.

In Australia the nankeen kestrel breeds between August and November. Generally no nest is built, and the eggs are placed in hollow trees, cave recesses, ledges of buildings, or the old nests of other species. Between three and seven eggs are laid.   P.M.M.

New Zealand Falcon *Falco novaeseelandiae* Gmelin,1788

THE NEW ZEALAND FALCON is an adaptable hunter. Sometimes, it stands on an overlooking perch waiting quietly for a chance to sally out and attack unwary prey. At other times, it soars for long periods until, spotting distant prey, it descends in a slanting dive. Almost invisible to its victim, the approaching falcon captures the animal easily. In the cooler parts of the day the falcon flies low over the ground or weaves rapidly through trees, surprising birds in the open.

A determined solitary predator, the falcon will chase Australian magpies, spur-winged plovers, New Zealand pigeons and skylarks for several minutes, even into houses. Adult males especially are nest robbers and may check starlings' nest-holes daily and snatch the young when they emerge. Insects taken on the wing are often released, only to be playfully recaptured. The falcon is strongly territorial and seemingly mainly sedentary, though less so in the winter when food is scarcer. It lives in most inland areas, especially in hill country and although it prefers open country it also nests in temperate rainforest. It rarely nests in settled or cultivated districts.

There are three types of New Zealand falcon, which so far have not been divided into subspecies. The bush falcon, with a population estimated at 400 to 900 pairs, inhabits the main mountain ranges of the North Island. In the South Island, it is found in the Paparoa Ranges, northeast to the Wairau River and the Nelson lakes and on the wooded northwestern side of the main divide. The eastern falcon is found mainly in the main ranges of the South Island from the Wairau River to the eastern side of Lake Te Anau, with an estimated population of 2000 to 3000 pairs. The southern falcon nests in Fiordland, at the Auckland Islands and probably on Stewart Island, with a total of up to 250 pairs estimated.

Eastern falcons hunt mainly birds, predominantly yellowhammers and greenfinches as well as some skylarks, New Zealand pipits, blackbirds, chaffinches, song thrushes, starlings and other songbirds. Occasionally they catch and eat larger birds such as Australian magpies, grey ducks, white-faced herons, domestic poultry, black-backed gulls, feral pigeons, spur-winged plovers, white-headed petrels and cattle egrets. Also, they often catch skinks, beetles, locusts and dragonflies as well as a few brown hares and rabbits. Bush falcons probably hunt mostly endemic forest birds such as New Zealand pigeons, tuis, kakas, parakeets, grey warblers and fantails. To aid digestion, falcons swallow smooth, pea-sized rangle stones.

From August to December falcons perform courtship flights. The male swoops at the female in mock attack, either when she is perched or in flight. Sometimes he carries food past her to entice her to chase him. Often such chases end near the future nest-site with the male presenting the food to the female. The male bows and bobs rapidly when he gives the female food and just before they mate.

They nest in a mere scrape under a rock on a steep slope, on a ledge on a bluff, on the ground under a log or branch, or among epiphytic growths in trees. Occasionally, they nest in hollow tree stumps or under overhanging bushes. At night they roost in guano-caked holes in bluffs. They first breed successfully at two years old and lay between mid-September and early December. The three eggs are slightly ovoid and blotched pink when fresh, turning to rusty mahogany. If the first clutch fails they lay a second 15 or 16 days later. After the female has laid, both parents defend the nest against intruders.

Incubation lasts 30 to 33 days, with the parents changing over every one to four hours. Usually the clutch hatches together. The female feeds and broods the young until they are about 10 days old. The chicks reach their full weight in 18 days. Males can fly by 32 days; females by 35 days. Males are fully fledged by 52 days; female birds a week later.

Since 1970 New Zealand falcons have had full legal protection but this has had little practical effect. Many falcons are still shot, either wantonly or for taking poultry. Such persecution prevents successful breeding in some areas but probably has little effect on the overall population. However, owing to biocides which affect breeding, and loss of habitat, the population is probably decreasing. New Zealand falcons have been used successfully for falconry and were bred in captivity for the first time in 1976. N.C.F.

ENDEMIC

OTHER NAMES: *Karearea, sparrowhawk, bush hawk, quail hawk, eastern falcon, southern falcon, bush falcon.*

SIZE: *450 mm.*

DESCRIPTION
ADULT MALE: *Crown, nape and back blue-black, barred on scapulars, wing coverts and tail coverts with rufous or grey. Sometimes, at back of head, 2 buff patches. Primaries black with broad white bars on inner webs. Secondaries black, barred with grey. Tail black with narrow interrupted white bars and buff tip. Cheek buff. Eyebrow and cheek stripe black. Throat tawny-white with narrow black lines. Crop and breast white or cream, streaked vertically with*
black. *Flanks barred horizontally black and cream. Belly cream, streaked with rufous. Undertail coverts rufous-cream. Thighs rufous with narrow brown streaks. Cere and eye-ring yellow. Bill black with base blue-grey. Legs yellow. Claws black.*
ADULT FEMALE: *Larger than male with less blue on crown and nape. Sometimes no barring on back and often darker underneath. Cere, eye-ring and legs yellow.*
IMMATURE: *Both sexes with upper parts black, with blue bloom, fading to dark brown. Some, especially males, barred above with buff and grey. Tail black, lightly barred with white. Eyebrow and cheek buff. Cheek stripe black. Throat cream with fine black streaks. Crop and breast blotched dark brown and tawny. Underparts dark brown or*
cream. *Belly cream with fine brown streaks. Undertail coverts dull brown or rufous. Thighs dull rufous brown, streaked with dark brown. Iris dark brown. Cere, eye-ring and legs olive green, sky blue or dull grey, changing to yellow after 9 months. Claws black.*
NESTLING: *White down replaced at about 11 days old by thick coat of woolly grey down. Feathers appear at 14 days. Bill and legs pink, becoming dull grey at about 10 days.*

MOULT
Adults moult between November and May. Some females begin moult during incubation, then stop while rearing young, and recommence in late summer. Often, breeding males begin after December. Juveniles moult between September and February.

VOICE
Rapid, piercing kek-kek-kek in territorial and courtship displays. Chittering during courtship. Chup when nesting. Squealing in disputes with other falcons. Whining whee-up when asking for food.

DISTRIBUTION
Bush falcon: *In the North Island confined to main ranges, very rare north of Auckland. Main breeding areas from East Cape to Tongariro and south to the Tararua Range. Also found at Mt Pirongia, Mt*
Egmont; *the Coromandel, Kaimai, Hunua, Puketoi, Rimutaka and North Taranaki Ranges; and the Aorangi Mountains. In the South Island breeds in the ranges, including the Paparoas; north and east to the Wairau River; the Nelson Lakes; and the wooded northwestern side of the main divide to Greymouth.*

Eastern falcon: *The main ranges of the South Island from Wairau River south to eastern Lake Te Anau. Also breeds in the Hundalee and Lowry Peaks Ranges; the Doctors Hills; North Rough Ridge; and the Kakanui Mountains. Breeds sparsely on the west coast between Greymouth and Jackson Bay.*

Southern falcon: *Fiordland, the Auckland Islands, and Stewart Island.*

The New Zealand falcon has also been recorded on the Hen and Chickens; Little Barrier, Great Barrier, Kapiti and D'Urville Islands. Straggles to the Campbell Islands.

RECOGNITION

Dark and powerful on the wing. More robust than nankeen kestrel. Seldom hovers although it soars and stops on wind for short spells. Faster wing-beat than harrier.

A New Zealand falcon at its nest, a simple scrape beneath projecting rock. The clutch, usually of three eggs, is laid between September and December.

The introduced chukar is a hardy, introduced game bird found mainly throughout the dry hill and mountain country of the eastern Southern Alps.

Chukar *Alectoris chukar* (J.E. GRAY, 1830)

THE CHUKAR—which obtained its name from its reverberating call of *chuck-chuck-chuck*—was first introduced successfully into New Zealand in 1926. These birds were Indian chukar from the southern Himalayas of India and Nepal. Six years later, Persian chukar were also imported and released. Now the two races have merged into an interbreeding population, which reached its peak in the late 1940s. Since then the number of chukar has declined as each year many birds die from poisoned carrots and swedes laid for rabbits.

This is a bird of dry hill and mountain country and, in the South Island, lives between a height of 235 and 1950 m. A hardy bird, it survives in snow, but tends to move to lower altitudes in winter, especially when the weather is severe. It frequents bare, rocky terrain with sparse vegetation, particularly on outcrops, ridges, bluffs and small valleys. Often, it seeks the warmth and dryness of sun-facing rocks. In the arid to semi-arid foothills of the Himalayas there is a rainfall of 250 mm a year or even less. In New Zealand, annual precipitation is much heavier and in Central Otago the chukar lives in mountain ranges with between 380 mm and 1520 mm rainfall.

The breeding season extends from September to January. Chukar first breed at one year. They are monogamous and birds from the same winter covey pair up in the spring. Such a covey is either a single brood or more often 50 to 150 birds from a number of broods. Often a pair travel far from the communal winter territory to take up a separate breeding territory. The aggressive male fights all other male chukar that enter his territory. He displays to the female with a waltzing dance, running at her and circling her with his neck extended and one wing lowered so that its tip scrapes the ground.

The female scratches a depression in the ground, either under a rock or well-hidden in scrub or weeds, and lines it with dry grass, roots, stems and, usually, some feathers. There it lays about 14 eggs. Sometimes as many as 24 eggs are found in the same nest, but such large clutches are probably the result of several hens laying in the same nest. The eggs are oval and strongly pointed, creamy white to pale café-au-lait and marked with brown, red or purple dots and streaks. The hen lays one egg a day with an occasional rest so that on average it lays 10 eggs in 13 days. Usually, the female incubates for 24 or 25 days and sits very tightly. After hatching, the female also usually cares for the brood. Occasionally the male incubates the eggs or leads a brood and, if the female lays two clutches, one parent rears each clutch. But in most cases, the male ignores the eggs and young, although it will defend the brood.

If weather permits, the precocious chicks leave the nest as soon as they are dry. During the first few days the parent will feign injury to lure away any intruders. The brood does not stay together for long and from the time chicks are three weeks of age, hens may merge broods, often into coveys of 30 to 50 chicks and several adults. Later these become the large wintering coveys. At two weeks old the chicks can fly short distances.

In New Zealand the chukar eats mainly the seeds and leaves of matagouri; tussock and weed seeds; rose seeds; and the flower-heads of various weeds. Near farmland, it takes waste grain from the ground in autumn and winter. The chicks feed first on insects and their larvae, gradually eating more and more plant food. Chukars swallow small stones and pebbles to grind down hard foods such as rose seeds. K.E.W.

INTRODUCED
Indian Chukar
A. c. chukar (J.E.GRAY, 1830).
Persian Chukar
A.c. koroviakovi ZARUDNY, 1914.

OTHER NAMES: *Chukor, chukar partridge.*

SIZE: *330 mm.*

DESCRIPTION
ADULT: *Sexes alike but male slightly larger. Upper surface ash grey, crown and shoulders tinged wine red. Wings brown. Cheeks, chin and throat white, tinged with buff, framed by distinct black line running from bill through eye and down side of neck to join on upper breast. Breast grey, tinged with brown. Flanks barred vertically with black, chestnut and white. Rest of underside buff. Iris brown, orange or red-brown. Bill red. Legs and feet pink to deep red.*
IMMATURE: *Upper surface striped sandy brown. Face pale. Belly dirty white. Breast spotted with yellow. Flanks marked with dark bands.*
CHICK: *Dense, soft down. Crown light brown and darkly speckled. Side of head and streak over eye cream. Black streak from eye to back of neck. Back black-brown with*

3 white, longitudinal stripes. Breast and belly off-white.

MOULT
Post-juvenile moult between fifth and 17th weeks. Complete moult after breeding.

VOICE
Loud resonant chuck-chuck-chuck, increasing in tempo and volume, heard mostly in the morning and evening from as far as 2 km. Chicks and young birds peep continuously to keep the brood together.

DISTRIBUTION
Eastern slopes of the Southern Alps. Native to India, Nepal, Iran and Pakistan. Also introduced into mainland United States and Hawaii.

RECOGNITION

Upright, fowl-like bird, the size of a pigeon. Predominantly grey with buff underside and conspicuous vertical flank bars. White throat and chin surrounded by black 'necklace'.

Grey Partridge *Perdix perdix* (LINNAEUS, 1758)

INTRODUCED

OTHER NAMES: *Common partridge, Hungarian partridge.*

SIZE: *300 mm.*

DESCRIPTION
ADULT MALE: *Head yellow-chestnut with spotted brown crown. Red bare skin behind eye, enlarged when breeding. Back barred and spotted brown. Buff bar along centre of median wing coverts. Tail rufous. Underparts and neck vermiculated and grey. Chestnut bands on flanks. Dark chestnut, horseshoe-shaped patch on lower breast. Bill horn-coloured to grey. Legs and feet grey.*
ADULT FEMALE: *Like male; slightly smaller. Grey eyebrow. Horseshoe on breast small or absent. Pale buff bars across median wing coverts.*
JUVENILE: *Uniformly brown with buff streaks on shafts and dark bars on wings. Bill dark horn. Legs and feet yellow to yellow-brown.*

CHICK: *Dense down. Head and back chestnut with black spots and lines. Underparts pale yellow-buff. Bill black to horn. Legs and feet yellow.*

MOULT
Juveniles moult from 4 or 5 weeks to 14 or 15 weeks; primaries moulted except outer 2. Complete adult moult after breeding, males ahead of females.

VOICE
Loud, hoarse chir-rick.

DISTRIBUTION
Widespread in temperate parts of Europe and Asia. Introduced into New Zealand and North America.

RECOGNITION
Pigeon-sized bird with chestnut head and throat. Short round tail. No crest.

OF ALL BIRDS THE PARTRIDGE lays the largest clutch. Usually 15 to 18 eggs, it can be as many as 28. After wintering in coveys of family groups with a few other birds, partridges pair and occupy a breeding territory in late winter or early spring. The paired birds are very devoted to each other and never part. They build a deep hemispheric nest on the ground in dense cover, such as under a hedge or amongst clover. The hen incubates the eggs for 25 days alone. After they hatch the cock shares in the brooding, care and defence of the chicks. The young birds grow rapidly, making their first short flights at about 11 days old and flying perfectly at 20 to 30 days.

During their first two or three weeks partridge chicks feed mainly on small insects, pupae and larvae. Gradually they change to the predominantly vegetarian diet of their parents, which includes weed seeds, especially *Polygonum*, waste grain, and some green vegetation, such as clover, grass, and beet leaves.

Originally from the vast Eurasian steppe, the grey partridge has been very successful in the rural landscape of western Europe with its many hedgerows and different crops. It has also adapted well to the prairie country of North America. Yet despite various attempts since the end of the last century, the grey partridge has not flourished in New Zealand. Small colonies of birds survive in Southland and Canterbury only.

K.E.W.

Attempts to introduce grey partridge late last century and early this century proved unsuccessful. Eggs imported in 1959 gave rise to today's small numbers.

ORDER GALLIFORMES pheasants, partridges and quails FAMILY PHASIANIDAE pheasants   157

Bobwhite Quail *Colinus virginianus* (LINNAEUS, 1758)

The bobwhite quail persists only in brushy, open country, farmland, and at roadsides in northern Hawke's Bay. Its nest is a grass-lined hollow.

INTRODUCED

OTHER NAMES: *Virginian quail, bob-white.*

SIZE: *230 mm.*

DESCRIPTION
ADULT MALE: *Crown and back of neck brown. Back spotted; mottled brown. Tail short and dark. Black stripe with white band above it from bill continuing round eye and down side and neck. White throat. Underside white with narrow wavy cross bars. Large longitudinal chestnut bars along flanks. Iris dark brown. Bill short and sturdy, black. Legs and feet yellow-grey to dark grey.*
ADULT FEMALE: *Slightly smaller than male. Plumage similar but throat buff.*
JUVENILE: *Head dusky grey. Back dull brown and spotted. Rump pale brown, feathers finely edged white. Tail grey with white mottling. Wing grey with mottled buff edges. Chin white or buff. Belly white. Feathers of rest of underside dull grey; white shaft streaks. Bill dusky brown or red-brown, paler at base. Legs pink.*

CHICK: *Warm chestnut down above with darker spots and lighter longitudinal stripes, head buff with black stripes behind eye and on crown and neck. Underside grey-buff with throat pale. Bill, legs and feet pink.*

MOULT
Chick moults into juvenile plumage after 3 or 4 weeks, then into first-winter adult plumage at 3 months. Adult has annual complete moult after breeding.

VOICE
Loud, clear whistle bob-white *or* poor-bob-white.

DISTRIBUTION
Small populations near Wairoa and Waikaremoana. Native to North and Central America.

RECOGNITION

Small red-brown quail with white, cross-barred underside. Black and white eye-stripes. White or buff throat.

A DISTINCTIVE WHISTLE of *bob-white* or *poor-bob-white*, often called from small trees or fence posts, gives this quail its common name. Other calls include the cock's crow and soft sounds from parents with chicks, as well as calls to assemble a scattered covey or to signal alarm.

Outside the breeding season the bobwhite quail lives in coveys. When these are flushed it flies fast and vigorously. The coveys separate into pairs when the birds breed. In a grass-lined hollow in the ground, they lay between 10 and 20, usually 15 or 16 eggs, which are very broad with one pointed end. Generally, incubation is by the female alone. After 23 days the chicks hatch and both parents share the brooding and rearing. The young feed mainly on insects and larvae. Adult quail are largely vegetarian and eat weed seeds, waste grain, berries, fruits and flower-heads, with insects in the summer.

From 1899 to 1902 some 1300 bobwhite quail were imported from America and liberated in many parts of the North and South Islands. At first the birds bred successfully, but after 1923 no further birds were sighted until 1952 when a small population was found northwest of Wairoa in the Raupapa Road area. Since then, bobwhite quail have been found at several localities around Waikaremoana in farmland, open bush and at roadsides. K.E.W.

Brown Quail *Synoicus ypsilophorus* (BOSC, 1792)

INTRODUCED

OTHER NAMES: *Australian quail, swamp quail, Tasmanian quail.*

SIZE: *180 mm.*

DESCRIPTION
ADULT MALE: *Head, forehead and crown brown with fine black spots and white spot in centre of crown. Feathers of neck and back dark brown with white shaft stripes and chestnut and black freckles. Wings brown, mottled with chestnut. Throat and cheeks buff-white to light brown. Neck and underside buff to brown, criss-crossed with fine, black, wavy bars. Feathers of underside have fine, white shaft stripes. Iris red. Bill blue to blue-horn. Legs and feet yellow to orange.*
ADULT FEMALE: *Slightly larger than male. Plumage very similar to male but appears darker as black spots and markings on back coarser and shaft stripes pale buff rather than white. Underside has less black.*
JUVENILE: *Resembles female but barred more coarsely on underside. Dark mottling on back and wings with black spots and bars.*
CHICK: *Dense, soft down. Head,* back and wings chestnut brown, spotted and barred with black. White line lengthwise on crown surrounded by chestnut. Black line from bill to crown. Black lines above and below eye. Breast and belly white.*

MOULT
Adults moult annually, after breeding.

VOICE
Loud drawn-out whistle tu-whee, *rising in pitch. Generally quiet.*

DISTRIBUTION
Northland, Three Kings Islands, South Auckland, King Country, Bay of Plenty, Rotorua-Taupo, Gisborne, Hawke's Bay, Taranaki, and the western Wellington coast. Widely distributed in Australia, Tasmania, Indonesia and New Guinea.

RECOGNITION

Small, roundish, brown quail. Short tail. Uniformly spotted. Transverse bars on underside. Yellow legs. Red iris.

The brown quail lives in breeding pairs from September to December, its nest carefully hidden in dense vegetation. Chicks remain with parents until winter.

THE BROWN QUAIL IS OFTEN seen sunning or sand bathing by the side of the road. This small, round bird lives in low-lying, often swampy areas, flat grassland or abandoned farmland covered in dense, coarse grass or thickets and scrub. Most of the year it forms small coveys, but during the breeding season, from September to December, it lives with its mate. Its nest is a lined depression in the ground, usually well hidden in dense vegetation. There it lays seven to 11 eggs that are round with a pointed end, dull white in colour and freckled with olive and light brown. The hen incubates for 20 or 21 days. The male guards the nest and helps look after the chicks. After they have fledged, the chicks usually remain with their parents during autumn and winter. The young quail feed first on insects and gradually change to a vegetable diet. Adult birds feed on grass and clover leaves and other green matter, weed seeds, waste grain and insects.

The brown quail was introduced by acclimatisation societies into many parts of New Zealand in the 1860s and 1870s. Despite a number of attempts to establish the brown quail in the South Island it does not breed there in the wild. The brown quail has been more successful in the North Island and it is common in Northland, South Auckland and Bay of Plenty. It also lives on the Three Kings Islands, though it is not known how the birds got there. They were first sighted in 1888, but it is unlikely that an acclimatisation society released them. Possibly the birds were blown across the sea from Northland or, although it is unlikely, the species could have been there already. K.E.W.

California Quail

Lophortyx californica brunnescens RIDGWAY, 1884

INTRODUCED

OTHER NAMES: *Californian quail, callie.*

SIZE: *250 mm.*

DESCRIPTION
ADULT MALE: *Back slate-brown. Short black plume curving forward from crown. Large black patch on face and throat, surrounded by white. Breast blue-grey. Underside pale buff with black marginal feathers giving black scaly pattern. White bars on flanks. Iris dark brown. Bill short and black. Legs and toes grey or black.*
ADULT FEMALE: *Slightly smaller than cock with more brown in coloration. Crest on crown shorter and straighter and black bib missing.*
JUVENILE: *Feathers tan with darker brown streaks and bars.*
CHICK: *Soft buff down, striped and streaked with brown and black longitudinal lines. Underside dull white with pale buff on breast, flanks and thighs.*

MOULT
Chick moults into juvenile plumage at 5 to 10 weeks, then into first-winter adult plumage at 16 to 18 weeks. Adult has complete annual moult after breeding seasons.

VOICE
Loud, often repeated call interpreted as Dick Vercoe *or* where are you?. *Frequently heard during hunting when coveys are split up, and by cock on its territory. Cock also calls loud* kurr. *Hen clucks for chicks.*

DISTRIBUTION
Widespread in the North Island and in north and east of the South Island. Also released in the Chatham Islands, Norfolk Island, King Island in Bass Strait, Hawaii, Argentina and central Chile. Native to California and Baja California.

Where it is common, the California quail is a popular game bird. Males guard the territory and the well-concealed nest.

RECOGNITION
Small, grey-blue game bird. Cock has forward-pointing crest on crown and black face. Hen browner with smaller crest and no black face. Often in trees.

SINCE IT WAS INTRODUCED successfully into New Zealand between 1862 and 1880 the California quail has been a popular game bird. It lives in open farm and scrub country where there are some bushes and trees for cover and roosting. Most of all, the California quail prefers marginal farmland with manuka scrub and fern, and—especially in the South Island—tussock grasslands with scrub-covered gullies and scattered bushes or trees. It occurs from sea level to an altitude of 1880 m, generally in places with between 500 and 1500 mm annual rainfall, although it also lives in areas of up to 2000 mm rainfall.

In autumn, family groups join up with other broods to form large coveys. Quail are instinctively social birds and there are major advantages to be derived from this flocking behaviour: the covey can locate food easily and alert guards can warn against predators.

In August and September fighting begins in the coveys and pairs separate gradually to take up their own territory in the neighbourhood. California quail are monogamous, and because there are more cocks than hens, the cock must defend his territory against unmated males. Because of the even New Zealand climate, the breeding season extends over several months. Egg-laying varies from year to year, depending on the weather, but generally it begins in September and October and continues to March. Most eggs hatch in November and December; in January or even February in late years. The nest is a rounded depression in the ground, lined with grass and stems, usually in long grass at the foot of a tree or shrub.

California quail lay an average of 14 eggs and sometimes as many as 22. If the first clutch is lost, the bird lays again, but second clutches average only eight or nine eggs. Both during laying and incubation the quail are very secretive and few nests are found. The eggs are pointed-oval and a warm creamy white colour, spotted, streaked and blotched with light golden brown. They lay one egg a day with several rest days before the clutch is complete. About 90 per cent of eggs hatch, but as with so many other ground-nesting game birds, nest losses are high. About one third of birds desert their nests because of discovery. Other nests are destroyed by farming and predators such as cats and ferrets.

Normally when the clutch is complete, the incubation period of 23 days begins. The hen incubates while the cock guards the territory and keeps a look-out for the hen when she is feeding off the nest. Sometimes, when the hen is killed, the cock takes over the incubation. The entire brood hatches within an hour or two. The embryonic chicks synchronise their development by a system of clicking sounds.

Within a few hours of hatching, as soon as they are dry, the down-clad chicks are ready to leave the nest with their parents. But in wet weather, the newly hatched young stay in the nest, warmed and protected by the hen, for up to a day. The cock remains in close attendance and during the following weeks assists in guarding and brooding the chicks. During the first day or two the chicks can survive by absorbing the yolk sac within them. As soon as warmth and sun allow, they are on the move in search of food. They eat small weed seeds as well as insects, their eggs and larvae. Gradually their diet changes to weed seeds with some insect matter and green material.

In a couple of weeks the chicks flutter off the ground and in three or four weeks they fly short distances. By the age of four months they approach the size and weight of their parents. After hatching, many chicks die. Only about half survive to independence. Usually 10 to 13 hatch, but after one week broods average nine or 10 chicks, by four weeks six chicks, and by nine or 10 weeks five. At this stage broods often combine to form larger coveys.

Quail feed mostly in the early morning and late afternoon. In cold weather and during the winter when less food is available, they feed more during the middle of the day. They eat mainly seeds, with some green material such as grasses, clovers, sorrel and broom. In the summer they eat insects too. When supplies are available, they feed on waste grain in stubble fields, fruits, berries, and even acorns. During autumn and winter rains the birds eat newly sprouted seeds. In hill country where there are small brooks and little pools quail seek water and drink daily, but they can survive in arid conditions without water if they eat succulent insects and green plants. K.E.W.

The ring-necked pheasant, the most common introduced pheasant, lives mainly in open farm country, but near cover.

Pheasant

Phasianus colchicus

LINNAEUS, 1758

INTRODUCED
Black-necked Pheasant
P.c. colchicus LINNAEUS, 1758
Ring-necked Pheasant
P.c. torquatus GMELIN, 1789
Mongolian Pheasant
P.c. mongolicus BRANDT, 1844

OTHER NAME: *Melanistic mutant pheasant.*

SIZE: *600-800 mm.*

DESCRIPTION
ADULT MALE: *Plumage varies according to subspecies and degree of hybridisation. Iris yellow to orange, surrounded by large patch of bare bright red skin which swells during courtship displays. Legs horny-grey to brown with spurs, longer and more pointed with age. Black-necked pheasant, a dark, heavy bird with black head and neck, copper body, purplish red back and rump with green gloss; wing coverts cinnamon brown. Ring-necked pheasant, lighter bird with white collar on sides of neck, white eyebrows, copper and golden mantle and pale slate-grey or bluish wing coverts. Mongolian pheasant most closely resembles black-necked but has wide white collar, white wing coverts and bright lemon iris. Melanistic mutant, often incorrectly given systematic name P.c. tenebrosus, is a mutation of the black-necked pheasant and has very dark metallic green plumage with breast and sides purplish blue.*
ADULT FEMALE: *Smaller than cock. Dull brown plumage, spotted, mottled and barred with black and brown. Throat pale. Iris brown. Bill horn. Legs and feet brown-grey.*
JUVENILE: *Drab, grey plumage at fifth week. From 20 weeks young cock looks like adult, but with shorter spurs.*
CHICK: *Closely covered with soft down. Upper parts red-brown and buff, spotted and barred with black. Underparts pale buff. Some chicks black-brown with white or cream throat and underparts.*

MOULT
Juvenile first-winter adult plumage by 20th week. Adult complete moult follows breeding season.

VOICE
In territorial display during breeding season, cock calls resonant, usually 3-syllable kor-r-rk. Also calls when flushed. Chuckling notes from both sexes. Hen clucks for chicks.

DISTRIBUTION
Widespread across Eurasia, from the Caucasus to Japan. Successfully introduced into most of Europe; North America; Hawaii; Rottnest Island in Western Australia; and King Island in Bass Strait. In New Zealand found mainly in Northland, Waikato, Taranaki, Bay of Plenty and Wairoa-Gisborne. Scattered populations found elsewhere in the North Island and in eastern coastal areas of the South Island.

WHEN THE PHEASANT was first introduced into New Zealand in the middle of the nineteenth century it was immediately successful. Today three subspecies of this game bird are found in the North Island and scattered along the eastern coastal strip of the South Island. The first birds, which arrived in 1842, were black-necked pheasants. This dark, heavy pheasant is distinguished by its black head and neck and its cinnamon brown wing coverts. Nine years later the ring-necked pheasant was brought from China. Now the most common wild pheasant in New Zealand, this bird has a white collar, distinct white eyebrows and pale grey or blue wing coverts. In 1923, the Mongolian pheasant was imported from England. Similar to the black-necked pheasant in appearance, this bird has a wide white collar and white wing coverts. A fourth colour type, known as the melanistic mutant pheasant, with very dark metallic green and purple-blue plumage, was introduced in 1938. Although this bird is sometimes classified as a separate race, it is in fact a mutation of the black-necked pheasant.

Behaviour

Pheasants are sedentary birds that must be able to satisfy all their needs within their home range. They require enough food all year round; cover in which to hide, roost and nest; water; grit; a crowing ground; and sand for bathing. Pheasants are found mainly in open farm country, usually where pasture or crops join scrub or scrub-covered gullies, and particularly in maize fields. They also occur in partly opened-up fern and manuka country and in lupin-covered sand dunes. In order to travel safely from one area to another pheasants need covered communication lanes, such as hedges, windbreaks, and scrub along roads and watercourses.

Pheasants are generally polygamous; each cock mates with several hens. Where pheasants are hunted heavily, such as in parts of western Europe and North America, one cock mates with up to 10 hens. But in New Zealand, cocks and hens occur in almost even numbers, except in the shooting season when between a third and half of the cocks are killed and some hens are shot accidentally. Two thirds of cocks have one hen, about a quarter have two hens and the rest three or four hens.

They breed for the first time when they are just under one year old. In spring the cock selects his breeding territory and defends it by crowing. This attracts one or more hens and he displays to them with his tail outspread and wing trailing. The hen chooses the nest-site within the cock's territory. In New Zealand the breeding season is very extended and nests with eggs have been found from late July until late March. Most nests however are established between October and December. Favourite nest-sites are in hayfields, scrub, road-sides, pasture and rough pasture, garden and crop areas, ditch and river banks, and swamps. The nest itself is simply a hollow scraped in the ground, lined with dry grass and other vegetation and is usually well hidden.

Raising young

In Europe the pheasant's clutch averages 12 eggs, but in New Zealand it is about nine. The hen alone incubates the olive-brown eggs, turning them on average once every hour, day and night. Usually the incubation period lasts 23 or 24 days, longer if the hen is disturbed much. The embryo breaks through the blunt end of the egg, cutting a ring with a special pipping tooth near the tip of its upper bill. The newly hatched chick weighs 23 g and has a yolk sac of reserve food to nourish it during its first one or two days. On hatching the chick is well-developed, active, with open eyes and strong legs and covered in dense down. It is able to leave the nest with its mother as soon as it is dry. It grows rapidly, especially its flight feathers, so that by the 12th day it is able to fly short distances. By the fifth week it is in the drab, grey juvenile plumage and at 20 weeks old, the young cock has the general appearance of an older or mature bird.

Up to two thirds of nests placed in scrub and pasture are successful. Of nests placed on roadsides, in gardens and crops fewer than half hatch. Many nests are ruined by farming: no fewer than three quarters of hayfield nests are destroyed by mowing and up to 60 per cent of these hens are killed or crippled. If the hen is not killed, she will in many cases make a new nest and lay a second but smaller clutch. Two thirds of surviving hens manage to rear a brood. Chick mortality is high, many die in the first month, and on average a hen will rear only three or four to maturity.

During their first weeks the chicks feed mainly on small soft insects, their larvae and pupae. Gradually they eat more and more green leaf material, seeds and berries. The diet of adult birds is varied, which is why the pheasant is successful in many areas. They feed on green leaf material, seeds, waste grain, fruits and berries, and insects such as crickets and grasshoppers. They also swallow small sharp pebbles for grinding hard seed, grain and mast feed in the gizzard. K.E.W.

Peafowl *Pavo cristatus* Linnaeus, 1758

The courtship dance of the peacock is one of the most spectacular of bird displays. First, the brilliantly coloured male raises its long, sweeping tail and stands with it fanned and erect. Then, with its wings drooped and quivering, the bird shivers violently as it struts and prances in front of its mate. But the drably plumaged hen appears unimpressed and mostly ignores this splendid performance.

Originally from India and Ceylon—where, in Hindu mythology, they are sacred—peafowl now decorate gardens, parks and zoos all over the world. The first shipment to New Zealand was landed at Wellington in 1843. In the 1860s and 1870s acclimatisation societies tried to establish them as game birds. Since then birds that have escaped from large gardens have boosted the numbers of feral peafowl.

Wild peafowl inhabit thickets and bushland in river valleys or near streams. They roost in trees, often near water, and live in small flocks that usually consist of a cock and his harem of three to five hens. In a nest-scrape in the ground the hen lays four to six broad eggs, pale cream to warm buff in colour, with thick and glossy shells, pitted with minute pores. She incubates these for 28 days. After breeding, the sexes split up into small flocks of adult males and hens with their broods. Peafowl are cautious birds that feed in the early morning and late afternoon, scratching the ground for berries, waste grain, leaves, shoots, flower buds, insects, larvae and worms. K.E.W.

INTRODUCED

OTHER NAMES: *Peacock, Indian peafowl.*

SIZE: *900–2300 mm.*

DESCRIPTION
ADULT MALE: *Head metallic blue and green with fan-shaped crest of wire-like feathers. Neck and breast brilliant glistening blue. Back bronze-green. Wings close-barred with black, buff and chestnut. Long tail bronze-green, with copper and purple black-centred discs.*

Underparts dark glossy-green. Undertail dark brown. Thighs buff. Iris dark brown. White patch of naked skin above, under and behind eye. Bill and legs horn-brown. Sharp spur above hind toe.
ADULT FEMALE: *Appreciably smaller than male and without sweeping tail. Upper parts brown and mottled. Flight feathers brown. Lower neck metallic green. Breast buff-brown with green gloss. Belly buff-white.*
JUVENILE: *Like adult female. Young cocks have chestnut primaries.*
CHICK: *Back down rufous. Underside pale buff. Wing dull chestnut mottled*

with brown. Brown spot across nape from eye to eye.

MOULT
Adult moults after breeding.

VOICE
Cock crows loud, harsh, trumpet-like may-awe, repeated several times. Short gasping scream cain-cain. Alarm call kok-kok *from hens leading chicks.*

DISTRIBUTION
Native to India and Ceylon. In the North Island along the Wanganui

River, Hawke's Bay, Mahia Peninsula, Gisborne, Waimarama, Wairoa and near Tutira.

RECOGNITION
Cock is large blue-green bird with long sweeping tail, erected and fanned in display. Fan-shaped crest on head. White cheeks. Hen smaller, brown and mottled, with shorter tail.

In a splendid courtship display the peacock, a polygamous bird, raises its long sweeping tail in a fan. It then struts and prances before the smaller hen.

Wild Turkey *Meleagris gallopavo* LINNAEUS,1758

A NATIVE OF THE AMERICAS, the turkey arrived in New Zealand as a domesticated bird from England. Inevitably, some of these farmyard turkeys escaped to form feral, self-maintaining populations.

In autumn and winter wild hen turkeys move about in flocks, but the old gobblers range alone. Then, in early spring the flocks break up and the birds form pairs. Calling their characteristic throaty gobble the older males fight off younger gobblers and attract hens. A successful male acquires a harem of up to four or five females. Each hen builds a leaf-lined nest, well-concealed on the ground, where it lays eight to 15 buff, spotted eggs over 12 to 20 days. Often only one mating is necessary for a hen turkey to produce a clutch of fertile eggs. During laying, the four-week incubation period, and the rearing of the brood, the hen turkey leads a solitary existence.

Turkeys eat mainly green plant material, grass and weed seeds, berries, fruits, waste grain and acorns. In the summer they supplement this vegetable diet with insects, especially grasshoppers, beetles and ants. At first, the chicks eat only insects. Turkeys also consume grit to grind hard foods such as acorns in the gizzard. K.E.W.

INTRODUCED

OTHER NAMES: *None.*

SIZE: *1000 mm.*

DESCRIPTION
ADULT MALE: *Plumage black, bronze and iridescent with pale wings and bronze-brown, barred tail. 'Beard' of elongated feathers on breast. Head naked, blue and red, varying with mood of bird. In displaying gobblers head red, with red wattles hanging below bill. Iris brown. Bill yellow-white tinged with red. Long, sturdy, grey or pink legs, with long, pointed spurs.*
ADULT FEMALE: *Like male but smaller, browner and with less iridescent plumage. Smaller wattles, no spurs, and no 'beard'.*
JUVENILE: *Smaller than adult. Plumage duller, no spurs, and 'beard' small or absent.*
CHICK: *Down cinnamon to brown, spotted with dark brown. Underside paler, straw yellow.*

MOULT
Complete adult moult late summer and partial pre-nuptial moult late winter.

VOICE
Throaty gobbling from males in courtship displays, territorial disputes and fights. Short alarm calls, put-put or pit. Female keeps brood together by clucking.

DISTRIBUTION
Small, isolated flocks in clearings, bushland edges and open farm country cutting into forest.

Wild turkeys, originally brought from England as domesticated birds, also persist in feral flocks in clearings, bush edges and open farm country.

The guineafowl, native to Africa, is a strongly gregarious bird which lives in open scrub country. It has bred with little success in New Zealand.

Guineafowl *Numida meleagris* (Linnaeus, 1758)

OUTSIDE THE BREEDING SEASON flocks of up to 20 or more guineafowl squeak noisily to one another. Once heard, there is no mistaking this raucous, far-carrying call. When disturbed, this wary game bird runs swiftly, but if flushed by hunters it takes to the air with much cackling and flies short distances. It lives in open scrubland, often near cultivated fields, and roosts in trees or rocky hills.

In spring, usually in October, the flocks break into pairs and scatter over a wide area. In grassy cover or under shrubs each pair lines a hollow in the ground. In this simple nest, between October and January, the female lays six to eight cream or off-white eggs, with thick shells, small dusky pore markings and fine speckles. Sometimes, much larger clutches of 20 or more eggs are found, but these are probably the result of several hens laying in the same nest. The hen most probably incubates alone for 24 or 25 days.

The food of the guineafowl is mainly vegetarian and consists of green grass, flower-heads, waste grain, fruits, berries, roots, bulbs and seeds. During the summer it eats a variety of insects and larvae. It swallows grit to grind hard seeds in its muscular stomach.

Early missionaries first brought the guineafowl to New Zealand. Later, acclimatisation societies liberated birds to establish the species for sport. But the guineafowl has bred with little success in the New Zealand bush. Those birds that are occasionally seen are as likely to be escapees from farms and aviaries as ones that were born in the wild. Today no truly wild, self-maintaining guineafowl populations are known in New Zealand.   K.E.W.

INTRODUCED

OTHER NAMES: *Pintado, helmeted guineafowl, crowned guineafowl, tufted guineafowl.*

SIZE: *630 mm.*

DESCRIPTION
ADULT: *Sexes alike. Very distinctive, plump game bird. Generally grey and densely covered with small, white dots. Head and most of neck bare with blue-grey skin. Blue-grey feathers on rest of neck. Bony red plate covering top of head with backwards-extending horny helmet. Cheeks white. Hanging wattles red. Wide collar of grey or brown on upper mantle and upper breast. Iris dark brown. Bill red, red-brown or horn-coloured. Legs and feet strong and dark brown.*
JUVENILE: *Similar to adult, but horny helmet shorter and rounder; bare face and neck grey-black; bill dark; and smaller dots on body.*
CHICK: *Covered in down on head, breast, underside and wings white to pale buff. Crown and back brown.*

Flanks and thighs buff-brown. Bill and feet pale yellow.

MOULT
Complete adult moult after breeding.

VOICE
Loud, squeaky cackling cry which carries far. Unmistakable call, as calling plays an important role in flocking behaviour of this noisy bird.

DISTRIBUTION
Native to Africa, south of Sahara, with small population persisting in Morocco. Released since European settlement throughout New Zealand. Established Northland, Waikato and Wanganui only.

RECOGNITION

Plump fowl-sized bird. Grey plumage with small, white dots. Head naked with horny helmet. White cheeks. Red wattles. Red bill.

There have been only two sightings of the brolga—one in south Auckland in 1947 and one in Westland in 1968. In Australia this stately bird is renowned for its spectacular courtship display. The dance is also performed outside the breeding season, perhaps to strengthen the pair-bond.

Brolga *Grus rubicunda* (PERRY, 1810)

BROLGAS ARE FAMED in Australia for their spectacular and fascinating courtship display. It is performed before and during the nesting season as well as outside the breeding season. When the dance is performed it serves the purpose of strengthening and maintaining the pair-bond. Brolgas, like other cranes, apparently mate for life.

According to a legend of the Australian aboriginal, the brolga was once a famous dancer, Buralga. When she spurned the attention of an evil magician, he became furious and changed her with a whirlwind cloud of dust into the elegant, dancing crane.

Brolgas dance in pairs or groups, the sexes facing one another. They stride forward towards one another, with wings lifted and half-open and all the while they are shaking, bobbing their heads up and down, now and then leaping into the air or stopping, throwing back their heads and trumpeting. Sometimes pieces of twig and grass are thrown into the air. The breeding season is extended and takes place from October to April during the tropical wet season. The nest is a large circular platform in or near swamplands; the eggs, usually two, are cream-coloured with brown and purple spots. The downy young are brooded and cared for by both parents.

Brolgas feed on tubers and roots of sedges and, in farmland, on potatoes. They also eat seeds, including cereals, green shoots, insects and other small and larger invertebrates. They feed in swamps, ponds and billabongs, wading in water up to their knees, and also spend much time digging up roots in dry swamps. Brolgas have exploited the many artificial dams and ponds built in northern Australia in recent years. They water at artesian bores and their adaptive feeding habits (eating green shoots of wheat, or potatoes) have led to conflict with farming interests. During the drier months they congregate in flocks of thousands. The usual habitat is swampland dominated by sedges.

Brolgas occur in the tropical, mainly coastal, regions of Australia and New Guinea. They are rarely seen outside their main range but vagrants are known from Coral Sea islands and New Zealand.   K.E.W.

VAGRANT

OTHER NAMES: *Australian crane, native companion.*

SIZE: *950–1250 mm.*

DESCRIPTION
Sexes alike, female slightly smaller. Generally pale grey, with primary wing feathers darker. Head naked, orange-red with green-grey crown; dewlap black; and ear coverts grey. Iris yellow. Bill greenish grey. Legs grey-black.

VOICE
Loud kawee-kree-kurr-kurr-kurr *on ground or flying. Pairs trumpet* garoooo, *often in unison, during courtship display.*

DISTRIBUTION
Northern and eastern Australia, mainly in tropical coastal regions; large flocks concentrate during drier months in rapidly evaporating wetlands; New Guinea.

RECOGNITION

Bigger than any other heron in New Zealand. Long legs, neck and bill. Red face. Neck stretched in flight, legs trail and long wings move in easy, narrow arch.

Banded Rail *Rallus philippensis* GRAY, 1843

IF ALARMED IN THE OPEN, the banded rail is unwilling to take to the air. It scampers for cover like a weka. Yet it is a most capable flier—the species' wide dispersal in the Pacific region is proof of that. There is also a contradiction in its choice of habitat. In spite of being shy and secretive, it persists in the midst of residential development in parts of Auckland and Northland. There it lives almost exclusively in mangrove marshes. South of the limit of mangrove growth, it is found in swamps dominated by reeds and sedges. Birds are usually seen only singly or in pairs, suggesting that the species is highly territorial.

Nests and chicks have been found in almost all months between August and March. Two broods are raised each year; the second nest starts when the chicks of the first are about a month old and independent. In Northland nests have been located in grass clumps beside mangrove forests, in roadside vegetation and in sedge clumps over salt marshes. Commonly, about five eggs, buff with purple, brown or grey spots, are laid. They are incubated in 18 days, probably by both parents. The young fledge in five or six weeks and seem to be evicted from the territory immediately: no family groups have been seen with other than unfledged chicks.

Land snails, worms, insects, fruits and seeds are eaten in swampland habitats. In estuarine areas birds have been observed taking a variety of mud flat molluscs and crustaceans, extracting worms from seagrass beds, and pecking at animals encrusted on mangrove trunks. In parts of Northland, banded rails forage in rubbish tips.

Closely related subspecies of the banded rail, found on the Chathams and Macquarie Island last century, are now extinct. A flightless Chatham Island rail, *Rallus modestus*, also extinct, almost certainly represented an earlier invasion of banded rail stock.   M.J.W.

ENDEMIC
Banded Rail
R.p. assimilis GRAY, 1843.

EXTINCT ENDEMIC
Dieffenbach's Rail
R.p. dieffenbachii GRAY, 1843.
Macquarie Island Rail
R.p. macquariensis HUTTON, 1879.
Chatham Island Rail
Rallus modestus HUTTON, 1872.

OTHER NAME: *Moho-pereru.*

SIZE: *310 mm (extinct species: 210 mm).*

DESCRIPTION
ADULT: *Sexes alike. Top of head dark brown. Chestnut band through eye to back of head; white streak above. Chin whitish. Throat and upper breast pale grey. Broad chestnut band across centre of breast; rest of undersurface striped black and white. Undertail striped reddish brown and black. Back and top of wing brown, spotted with black and white; underwing paler. Iris and bill reddish brown. Legs brown, sometimes pinkish. Partial albinos occur.*
IMMATURE: *Similar to adult but chestnut face band paler and less well developed; breast and undertail paler brown, almost buff.*
CHICK: *Down sooty black. Bill, legs and feet black.*

MOULT
Main moult January to April; flightless about one month.

VOICE
Calls most often heard at dusk. Creaky swit swit, *and high* quee quee *like rusty gate opening. At or near nest, low* kik-kik-kik *and low growl.*

DISTRIBUTION
Mainly in northern mangrove swamps from Northland to Bay of Plenty; regularly reported from Coromandel Peninsula, edges of Tauranga and Ohiwa Harbours; lower Waikato and Taupo; some northern offshore islands; Golden Bay, Nelson; Stewart Island and neighbouring islands. Different subspecies in Australia, New Guinea, Indonesia, the Philippines, and the southwest Pacific.

RECOGNITION

Prominent white streak over eye. Chestnut breast-band. Black and white striped belly. Bantam-sized—biggest of swamp rails.

Nests of the banded rail are usually matted layers of rush, with vegetation above pulled together in a rough canopy.

An Auckland Island rail captured on Adams Island has been the only live bird obtained for study. Typical of small rails, it moved with speed and stealth.

Auckland Island Rail *Rallus pectoralis muelleri* ROTHSCHILD,1893

THE ONLY LIVE Auckland Island rail obtained for study was captured on Adams Island in 1966 foraging in a garbage dump. (Rails were heard on Adams Island during World War II coast-watching expeditions but none were captured.) It was kept at the Mount Bruce native bird reserve for nine years, remaining shy, wary but alert throughout its confinement. It showed all the speed and stealth of movement typical of small rails. Nothing further of its biology was learned. Other birds were seen on Ewing Island in 1962. M.J.W.

ENDEMIC

OTHER NAMES: *None.*

SIZE: *210 mm.*

DESCRIPTION
ADULT: *Sexes alike. Crown chestnut streaked with black. Rest of upper surface dark chestnut streaked with brownish black. Cheeks, sides of neck and nape rich red-brown. Chin and throat whitish. Foreneck grey. Breast grey tinged with olive. Flank, belly and undertail black barred with white. Underwing grey. Primaries dark grey-brown. Iris brown. Bill dull pink with brown along ridge of culmen. Feet pinkish grey.*

MOULT
Not known.

VOICE
Kek, kek *in 2-note brackets. Sharp single* clink, *perhaps distress* call. *Deep grunt.*

DISTRIBUTION
Adams Island, probably also Ewing Island, in the Auckland group. Different subspecies in Australia and New Guinea.

RECOGNITION
Very similar to closely related Lewin's water rail of Australia but perhaps smaller with softer plumage.

Marsh Crake *Porzana pusilla affinis* (GRAY,1846)

The marsh crake, a secretive swampland bird, is heard rather than seen.

ENDEMIC

OTHER NAME: *Koitareke.*

SIZE: *180 mm.*

DESCRIPTION
ADULT: *Sexes alike. Top of head and neck brown mottled with black. Back, rump and upper wing brown with black and white streaks. Sides of head, throat, breast and upper abdomen blue-grey; throat paler. Lower abdomen, flanks and undertail barred black and white. Underwing brown mottled with white. First primary has narrow white line on outer margin. Iris red. Bill bright pale green, brown on culmen. Legs and toes yellowish olive; claws brown.*
IMMATURE: *Like adult but buff-brown where adult is blue-grey.*
CHICK: *Black with greenish sheen.*

MOULT
Not known.

VOICE
Trilling, purring and harsh krek-krek. Generally silent by day.

DISTRIBUTION
Poorly known. Sightings widespread and spasmodic, but more frequent in the South Island. Reported on Chatham Island, but present status uncertain. Different subspecies in Australia, New Guinea, Borneo, Asia, Europe and Africa.

RECOGNITION
Tiny rail. Brown back and grey chest easily distinguished from sooty appearance of spotless crake.

NOWHERE IN THE WORLD has the marsh crake been adequately studied. It is the most secretive of swampland birds, emerging at swamp margins only at night. All New Zealand sightings have been among thinner vegetation beside open water. Only four nests have been found. One, in Southland, located in rushes beside a farm pond, was a loose structure of stalks with a sparse canopy and contained seven ovoid, olive-brown eggs. Two nests have been located in the crowns of tussock sedges. Birds probably feed mainly on insects. M.J.W.

Spotless Crake _Porzana tabuensis plumbea_ (Gray, 1829)

NUMBERS OF SPARE NESTS, built for no apparent reason, have been found in the territory of every pair of spotless crakes observed in New Zealand. It was once supposed that they were used as roosts by birds that were not incubating, and later by the young. But studies have produced no evidence that the extra nests, though they may be maintained throughout the incubation period, are ever occupied. Much remains to be discovered about the habits of this furtive species.

Almost all sightings have been in swamps or marshy areas where tall—but not dense—overhead vegetation affords permanent cover. The only recorded exception is on the Poor Knights Islands, where birds roam over a dry forest floor. Lately, spotless crakes have been seen in marshy pockets of farmland. Their widespread colonisation of such disjointed habitats suggests that they are capable dispersers, though they are rarely seen in full flight. Usually they flap for short distances, with legs trailing. But they run at high speed and swim well.

Spotless crakes appear to be strongly territorial, responding quickly to tape-recorded purring calls at any time of year. They show particular aggression in spring, when birds have often been seen chasing one another. The breeding season seems to peak in September-October, but nests have been found in every month from August to January. They are usually constructed above ground in the crowns of clumps of sedges, rushes, ferns or grasses, some of which are woven into a bowl. Fragments of other nearby vegetation may sometimes be added, but there is no feather lining. There is frequently a canopy over the nest.

Eggs are creamy brown, heavily flecked with dark brown. A clutch of two to five (usually three) is laid. Incubation, by both parents, takes 19 to 23 days. Birds take turns at intervals of 30 to 90 minutes, their frequent changeovers accompanied by a variety of soft calls. Once on the nest, each bird tries to pull over surrounding vegetation to form a canopy, frequently altering the shape of the nest in the process.

The diet of the spotless crake in New Zealand is most likely insects such as grasshoppers, craneflies and caterpillars, though small seeds may also be eaten. Birds have been observed feeding among drift material at the edge of a river, taking items from beneath the surface of small pools, and foraging in short grass.   M.J.W.

NATIVE

OTHER NAMES: _Putoto, puweto._

SIZE: _200 mm._

DESCRIPTION
ADULT: _Sexes alike, with no seasonal variation. Back dull chocolate, appearing black unless seen in strong sunlight. Head and underparts leaden grey; chin paler; undertail coverts lightly barred with white. Outer web and edge of first primary may be whitish. Underwing mottled ashy brown and white. Iris red. Bill dark brown or black. Legs dull reddish brown._
IMMATURE: _Usually lighter than adult, duller with whitish mark on shoulder, dull white throat, light breast and abdomen._
CHICK: _Woolly black down with greenish sheen on head and back._

MOULT
Not known.

VOICE
Slightly nasal mook, _single or repeated, varying in pitch and loudness. Also bubbling sound and sharp, squeaky_ pit-pit _alarm call. At nest, high murmuring, strident purring, harsh_ harr _and_ mint-mint.

DISTRIBUTION
Widespread, more common in the North Island, but rarely seen. Also occurs in Australia. Different subspecies in Pacific Islands, New Guinea, and the Philippines.

> **RECOGNITION**
> Tiny rail, sooty coloured, seen at swamp edge.

Though common where swampland vegetation occurs, the spotless crake is seen rarely. Studies have given no clue as to why it habitually builds extra nests.

A western weka and chicks. Capable of breeding at a young age, wekas have a prolonged breeding season and often more than one brood is raised by a pair in a year. The clutch usually consists of four eggs, and the young remain with their parents for up to four months.

Weka *Gallirallus australis* (Sparrman, 1786)

THIS FLIGHTLESS BIRD has a remarkable homing instinct and is capable of traversing seemingly difficult terrain. A bird taken from Gisborne to Hawke's Bay walked 130 km home. Others, removed from Maud Island in the Marlborough Sounds to the mainland, swam over 900 m back to the island. Last century, when wekas were widely abundant, local populations were reported to appear and disappear abruptly and unaccountably. Birds today walk up to one kilometre to camp sites or picnic spots, where they glean scraps of food and sample bright objects such as spoons.

The natural diet of wekas in forests is predominantly fallen fruits and invertebrates. Lizards, snails and the eggs and young of birds are also taken. Wekas readily kill mice, rats and young rabbits, and two were seen killing a stoat. Birds on the coast forage for sandhoppers, shellfish and storm-cast food. On farmland they eat grasses and seeds, and in some districts they are blamed for pulling out seedlings and damaging vegetable crops such as tomatoes.

Agricultural development and the introduction of mammal predators largely accounted for a decline in weka populations late last century. But they remained abundant in many areas—only to vanish suddenly, between 1915 and 1925, from most of the North Island and parts of the South Island. A disease may have been responsible. Once hunted by Maoris for food, feathers and oil, wekas are now protected everywhere except the Chatham Islands.

Habitats vary from rocky shorelines, sand dunes, swamp margins, scrub and forest to alpine tussock grasslands and settled districts where gorse or hedges offer cover. Pairs maintain territories throughout the year, and may remain together for many years. One pair is known to have lived at least 18 years. Some start breeding early: one North Island pair nested at about nine months and succeeded in rearing a chick. Nesting has been recorded in every month of the year but the peak of the breeding season, in the North Island at least, seems to be July and August.

Nests are usually on the ground in dry, sheltered situations. Most are concealed in vegetation, but logs, rock overhangs, burrows and even outbuildings may be used. Most nests are made of grass and lined with finer grass or sometimes feathers, wool, hair and leaves. When grass is not available, twigs and moss are sometimes used. Ovoid eggs, creamy white to pinkish with scattered brown and pale purplish blotches, are laid in clutches of one to six. Incubation, shared by both parents, takes 25 to 27 days.

Though chicks are active within hours of hatching, they stay close to the nest for two to four days. Then they are brooded in the open.

Sometimes a brood is left in the sun or in a hiding place while both parents forage; they call the young when suitable food is found. Juveniles may remain in the family group for up to four months, but are often evicted from the territory sooner if re-nesting is attempted. Double brooding is common, some birds breeding three or even four times in one year.

Predation by wekas, especially on islands where they have been introduced, has severely affected other birds: in the Stewart Island area small petrels have suffered local extinctions. H.A.R. & A.J.B.

ENDEMIC
North Island Weka
G.a. greyi (BULLER, 1888).
Western Weka
G.a. australis (SPARRMAN, 1786).
Buff Weka
G.a. hectori (HUTTON, 1873).
Stewart Island Weka
G.a. scotti (OGILVIE-GRANT, 1905).

OTHER NAMES: *Woodhen, woodrail.*

SIZE: *530 mm.*

DESCRIPTION
ADULT: *Sexes alike, male larger.*
North Island weka: *Reddish on upper surfaces, flanks and rump. Head, neck, back and wing blotched with black. Quills black, banded with reddish brown. Tail feathers black, reddish at edge. Throat, foreneck, streak over eye, lower breast and abdomen slate, brownish on lower abdomen, with reddish brown band across breast of most birds. Undertail coverts black with*

reddish band. Iris red to reddish brown. Bill reddish brown, darker on ridge. Feet brown to reddish brown.

Western weka: *Two recognised colour phases and wide variety of intermediate forms. In chestnut phase, much like North Island weka, but darker on breast and lower abdomen. In black phase, upper surface brownish black, each feather edged with blackish chestnut. Quills brownish black with narrow chestnut bars, sometimes broken. Dark brown lores and line under eye. Grey of throat and streak over eye tinged with brown. Reddish band across chest blotched with brownish black. Patch on upper abdomen grey washed with brown. Rest of undersurface reddish brown, barred on flanks and undertail coverts with brownish black.*

Buff weka: *Yellowish buff upper surface, longitudinally spotted and blotched with brownish black and reddish tinge on head. Primaries and coverts chestnut, narrowly and*

irregularly barred with black and partly edged with buff. Tail feathers reddish with central and lateral black lines. Throat and streak over eye light grey; chin paler. Lores and band under eye reddish brown. Foreneck and breast tawny, shaded with brown. Abdomen ashy brown. Flanks and undertail coverts yellowish brown, narrowly barred with brownish black.

Stewart Island weka: *Chestnut phase like western weka with iris light chestnut and bill and feet pinkish brown. In black phase, paler than black western weka. Upper surface and breast feathers have large black centres and dark chestnut margins. Throat and abdomen dark brown. Bill, iris and feet darker than chestnut phase.*
IMMATURE: *Tones darker than adult in most birds, but buff weka lighter. Markings less distinct. Iris brown. Bill black.*
CHICK: *Most nestlings have brown-black down.*

MOULT
First-year birds moult early summer; breeding adults delay until brood almost independent. Body moult precedes loss of major wing and tail feathers by a few days. Total plumage replaced in 4 to 6 months.

VOICE
Shrill whistle, coo-eet, coo-eet, or wee-eek, wee-ee-eek, rising in pitch

and many times repeated, can be given by all birds over 7 months and often by pair in duet; most frequent at dawn or dusk. Resonating boomp, *given by territorial birds sometimes preceding main call but also while feeding or during disputes. High squeal in anxiety or chases. Low growls in courtship and mating.*

DISTRIBUTION
North Island weka: *Moderate numbers in Northland and Poverty Bay.*

Western weka: *Locally abundant northwest Nelson, the Marlborough Sounds, Buller and Grey Valleys, Fiordland.*

Buff weka: *Widespread and common on the Chatham Islands where it has been successfully introduced. Re-establishment attempted in Canterbury.*

Stewart Island weka: *Halfmoon Bay and some offshore islands.*

> **RECOGNITION**
>
> Big, flightless rail.
> Strong bill and feet.
> Rounded wings. Inquisitive.
> Walks with deliberate stride, tail flicking. Fast runner with neck outstretched parallel to ground.

The buff weka, introduced successfully to the Chatham Islands in 1905, was once abundant in low rainfall areas of the eastern South Island.

The productivity of the takahe, once considered extinct, is low and conservation of the species in the wild has become a major concern.

Takahe *Notornis mantelli* OWEN, 1848

ENDEMIC

OTHER NAMES: *Moho, pass bird.*

SIZE: *630 mm.*

DESCRIPTION
ADULT: *Sexes alike. Plumage loose with silky sheen. Head, neck, breast and abdomen iridescent indigo. Scapulars peacock blue, merging into metallic olive green on mantle. Back, rump, tail and wing coverts olive green. Undertail white. Primaries indigo, changing to charcoal brown towards base. Undersurface charcoal brown. Wing reduced in size; bony spur at carpal flexure. Iris brown. Bill red but becomes creamy pink at edges towards tip; frontal shield red. Legs and feet red.*
IMMATURE: *Slightly paler than adult. Mantle and back brownish. Primaries olive green. Iris dark brown. Bill, frontal shield and legs bluish grey.*
CHICK: *Down jet black. Upper bill black except for white strip; lower bill has white tip.*

MOULT
Partial juvenile moult of back and mantle, feathers brightening but still duller than adult. General post-nuptial moult of yearlings and adults starts mid-January, lasting through February and March.

VOICE
Pairs sing in duet, alternating different phrases. Contact or distress call oomp *when disturbed; rising* klowp *if contact lost.*

DISTRIBUTION
Murchison and Stuart Mountains, Fiordland National Park.

RECOGNITION

Superficially like pukeko but flightless, two or three times heavier and more robust with short, thick legs. Voice easily confused with weka but generally deeper and more resonant.

SUBFOSSIL AND MIDDEN REMAINS indicate that the takahe once lived throughout the North and South Islands. Yet by the time the Maori arrived in New Zealand the takahe was reduced in numbers and localised in its distribution. Only four specimens, all from Fiordland, were identified last century, then none at all until 1948. About 200 pairs were discovered in the Murchison Mountains and two neighbouring ranges rising from the western shores of Lake Te Anau. By 1980 the population had declined to about 120 birds, the majority in the Murchison Mountains.

Predation by stoats may have been partly to blame. But the major factor has been competition for food from red deer in the winter forest and the summer grassland habitats. On the alpine grasslands takahe feed on tussock shoots and the seeds of various tussocks and grasses. The forest diet in winter, when the tussock country is snowbound, is mainly the starch-rich underground rhizomes of a fern, *Hypolepus*

millefolium. Invading deer compete for the highly nutritious tussocks and, by depleting forest undergrowth, they make the soil more prone to freezing, preventing takahe from digging out fern rhizomes.

Takahe generally have a low reproductive rate. The earliest confirmed breeding is at three years. They raise only one brood a year and if the clutch or chicks are lost do not relay, except in tussock-seeding years. On average only two eggs are laid. Chick mortality is extremely high: many pairs that succeed in hatching broods lose them within two months. Poor nutrition is probably the main cause. Culling has reduced the deer population, however with the damage already done it takes only a few deer to prevent plant regeneration, particularly in the forests. Fertilisers have been applied to the tussock country, in the belief that increasing nutrient content of the plants will improve the takahe's breeding productivity. Little can be done to speed the regeneration of its wintering grounds.

Eggs are usually laid between mid-October and the end of December, though some have been found as late as mid-February. Nests are deep bowls of fine grasses and tussock shoots, built on well-drained sites overhung by tussock bowers that give shelter from snow as well as concealment. A typical nest has two entrances. Several trial nests are built in different localities—perhaps to help synchronise the male and female reproductive cycles—before the incubation nest is started. The eggs, buff with mauve and brown markings, are incubated by both parents. Chicks hatch in about 30 days and are quickly active, but remain close to the nest for a day or two. As they leave, further nests are built to shelter them at night.

The young are fed mainly on insects for the first two weeks, then gradually their diet becomes increasingly vegetarian. They continue to beg from their parents; some have been seen receiving food five months after hatching. Juveniles may remain with their parents for 18 months, but it is more usual for broods to disperse at one year. Adult pairs stay together through the year and into the next—if both survive. They are territorial while on the tussock country, holding the same areas in successive years. In winter their home ranges are apparently less well-defined.

Since 1958, 17 adults and six chicks from the Murchison Mountains have been taken to the Mount Bruce native bird reserve for captive breeding. Eggs laid up to 1971 were infertile. Ten chicks have hatched since then, four surviving to one year.   J.A.M.

Pukeko *Porphyrio porphyrio melanotus* (Temminck, 1820)

ESSENTIALLY A BIRD of the lowland swamps, the pukeko has expanded its range with the development of agriculture. Pastures and croplands in high-rainfall areas have become foraging grounds. At the same time, in some localities, old habitats have been reduced by drainage or reclamation. So while farmers and market gardeners argue that pukeko are pests, conservationists are worried by declining populations. Duck shooters join in the controversy with a claim that pukeko prey heavily on eggs and ducklings. Where the Wildlife Service recognises a serious agricultural problem, special off-season control permits are issued. Only about 600 birds a year are destroyed under such permits, compared with 50 000 to 80 000 shot in the hunting season. In some districts pukeko make up a third of the annual waterfowl bag—even though they present little challenge to shooters and are regarded as poor eating.

Soon after the hunting season, wintering flocks start to break up as pairs or groups of breeding birds move to nesting habitats. Nesting extends from August to February and sometimes longer, with a September to December peak. Bonds are established and maintained by bill-nibbling, mutual preening, mock mounting and occasionally by courtship feeding. Group pecking orders and territorial issues are settled by displays of aggression and submission and sometimes by fighting—usually with the feet rather than the most lethal weapon, the robust beak.

Nests are sited on debris or in vegetation, either surrounded by saturated ground or near still or slow-flowing water. Material is added as eggs are laid. If a flood threatens, building activity increases in an attempt to raise the nest-bowl—sometimes burying the eggs. They are ovoid and coloured buff with irregular blotches and smears of grey, brown and mauve. The usual clutch size is five or six. Most territories are occupied by three to six birds. Those in group territories sometimes share nests. Two or three broods are raised in a season; if eggs are destroyed, up to five replacement clutches may be laid. Incubation, shared by the sexes, takes about 24 days. It starts when a clutch is about half completed, so hatching is spaced over several days. Chicks are tended by both parents, or in group territories by certain dominant adults, sometimes with the help of older chicks or yearlings. The young can fly at about three months.

Flooding or dehydration of a breeding territory may force birds to move to a neutral feeding area, where rivalries are suspended and loose assemblies form. If eggs are being incubated during floods or droughts at least one bird usually stays behind while the others are transients, moving to and fro, from their territory to the feeding area. In some instances territories are deserted altogether; eggs and young chicks perish. Neutral areas are also occupied by yearlings driven from their birthplaces, and by birds of low social rank. Breeding birds spend time on neutral ground even when conditions in their territories are favourable. Breeding birds in a stable nesting habitat spend more time in their territories.

Pukeko are mainly vegetarian. They strip seeds from plants, slice or wrench off shoots, and use their beaks to unearth rhizomes and corms. Live animals, including small fish, birds and mammals, are also taken. They are actively stalked in the breeding season, when flesh makes up much of the diet of chicks. Larger dead animals are eaten as carrion. Tame pukeko, reared among ducks and fowls, eat their eggs and an occasional duckling, but wild birds rarely do so. Food is often eaten parrot-fashion, held in one foot. Some is dunked first in water—a habit also observed in takahe.

Banded birds have been found up to 240 km from their earlier point of capture, but most records indicate that the species is fairly sedentary. This applies especially to localities where an extensive habitat is available year-round—at Lake Ellesmere, for example. Some birds marked as chicks have remained where they were born for four years, and one banded bird was still in the same territory after seven years. Pukeko, like several other rail species, will return to a locality from which they are removed, and one relocated bird homed 97 km in eight days.   G.A.T.

NATIVE

OTHER NAMES: *Swamp hen, pakura, puke, pukaki.*

SIZE: *510 mm.*

DESCRIPTION
ADULT: *Sexes alike, female smaller. Upper parts sooty black, sometimes glossed with green or turquoise. Neck, throat, and chest purplish blue; chest and sides sometimes barred with turquoise. Belly and flanks black, tinged purplish blue. Undertail coverts white. Underwing glossy black; marginal coverts edged purplish blue; axillaries edged purplish blue and turquoise. Upper wing black with purplish blue on leading edge, outer edge of alula web and greater primary coverts. Tail rectrices black above with greenish gloss on edges; shiny black below. Iris red. Bill and frontal shield bright red. Legs brown-red. Albinos, part-albinos and purple-buff variations.*
IMMATURE: *Upper parts blackish brown, with traces of buff or light brown. Wings tinged blue. Chin pale brown. Foreneck, breast and sides blue; some feathers edged with tawny brown. Abdomen pale tawny brown. Rectrices with buff-edged tips. Undertail coverts creamy white. Iris brownish black to olive. Bill and frontal shield reddish black. Legs dark brown, tinged orange.*
CHICK: *Black. Iris dark slate. Bill greyish ivory, black-tipped, red at base. Legs dull flesh pink.*

MOULT
Complete post-nuptial moult. Flightless about one month.

VOICE
Mostly one-syllable monotones in repetitive series. Harsh screech most common. Also scream, high whine, low croon, nasal hum, grunt, click, cluck, sigh, bleat, soft purr and coo.

DISTRIBUTION
Widespread. Common Whangarei-Auckland-Waikato; Taranaki-Wanganui-Horowhenua. Other concentrations at Kaitaia, western Bay of Plenty, Wairoa, central Hawke's Bay, near Nelson, West Coast, Lake Ellesmere fringes, southern Otago, and Southland. Also Australia. Different subspecies in Africa, southern Europe, Asia, and some Pacific Islands.

RECOGNITION
Size of small hen. Red bill and frontal shield. White undertail coverts conspicuous when tail flicked. Fast runner, noisy through vegetation. Swims with head up, swaying back and forth. Runs over water before laboured take-off, legs dangling at first then projecting behind tail. When disturbed dives and progresses under water partly or fully submerged.

The pukeko may breed at one year. The nest material, scant at first, is progressively built up during incubation.

Dusky Moorhen

Gallinula tenebrosa

Gould, 1846

VAGRANT

OTHER NAMES: *None.*

SIZE: *350 mm.*

DESCRIPTION
ADULT: *Sexes alike. Generally grey-black with olive brown tone on back and shoulders, appearing iridescent green in strong light. White patches each side of tail. Underparts similar to general plumage but paler. Iris brown. Bill red with bright yellow tip; frontal shield orange-red. Legs green; knees sometimes reddish.*
IMMATURE: *Generally browner plumage than adult; bill and frontal shield tending yellow-green.*
CHICK: *Down almost jet black; bright red patch on bill.*

MOULT
During moult breeding plumage muted.

VOICE
In Australia, kurk; *mostly silent.*

DISTRIBUTION
Eastern and southwestern Australia (not Tasmania), New Guinea.

RECOGNITION
Similar in size to black-tailed native hen. Yellow bill tip. White at sides of tail.

The dusky moorhen, abundant throughout eastern Australia, has been sighted only once in New Zealand.

NEW ZEALAND'S ONLY SIGHTING of a dusky moorhen was in 1968 on Lake Hayes, Central Otago—where another bird from across the Tasman, the Australasian coot, was first found to be breeding. In its homeland, especially during droughts, the dusky moorhen is common on urban lakes and ponds. However its preference is for swamps where open water is interspersed with floating vegetation. On water it may feed by upending like a dabbling duck. It eats all kinds of vegetable matter, frogs from water margins, and insects on land. Nests in Australia are big platforms of aquatic vegetation at the bases of trees, usually among rushes but sometimes in rank pasture grasses.

Dusky moorhens, in Australia, breed from August to February. Pairs maintain a territory around the nest and defend it vigorously against other intruding moorhens. Within the territory they will have several roosting platforms. T.A.C.

The black-tailed water hen is nomadic in Australia, often moving great distances to newly flooded areas which have been dry for substantial periods.

Black-tailed Water Hen

Gallinula ventralis Gould, 1837

VAGRANT

OTHER NAME: *Black-tailed native hen.*

SIZE: *350 mm.*

DESCRIPTION
ADULT: *Sexes alike. Upper parts dark green-brown with iridescent green tinge, tending to black on head. Tail black, often held upright and fanned. Underparts dark green with slight blue tinge. White flecks on flanks. Iris yellow. Bill pea green above, red below. Legs brick red.*
IMMATURE: *Duller than adult.*
CHICK: *Black.*

MOULT
Not known.

VOICE
Usually silent; sharp cackle when alarmed.

DISTRIBUTION
Australia except for north; vagrant to Tasmania and New Zealand.

RECOGNITION
Two-toned bill. White spots along flanks. Brick red legs. Runs swiftly.

THIS RAIL SPECIES is totally nomadic in Australia, adjusting its movements and breeding cycle to the erratic availability of water. It breeds in loose colonies sometimes numbering hundreds. Nests are cups of plant matter, on or near the ground, and always close to water. The eggs are dark green with red, pink or purple blotches and small spots. The clutch size is usually about five. The chicks, typical of rail species, hatch as small, black, fluffy creatures.

The birds are capable of migrating great distances in times of drought, but only two have been convincingly reported in New Zealand. One was shot in Southland at Colack Bay in 1923; the other frequented the bed of the Tukituki River, Hawke's Bay, in 1957–58. T.A.C.

Australasian Coot *Fulica atra australis* GOULD,1845

NATIVE

OTHER NAMES: *None.*

SIZE: *380 mm.*

DESCRIPTION
ADULT: *Sexes alike. Top of head, neck and upper parts sooty black. Face and underparts dark grey. Rarely, thin white edge on shoulders and white flecks on undertail coverts. Outer primaries brownish. Iris red. Bill and frontal shield bluish white. Legs and feet steel grey; toes lobed.*
IMMATURE: *Upper parts paler than adult with brownish hue. Throat greyish white. Underparts pale grey. Bill and frontal shield greyish.*
CHICK: *Down dusky, black-flecked. Head orange-red. Bill crimson, tinged yellow, tipped white with black at extreme tip.*

MOULT
Little known, but flocks formed after breeding tend to moult together, at which time they become flightless.

VOICE
Harsh notes uttered singly or strung together; variously krark, kowk, kyik, kyok, kratack-krat-krat, kow-kow-kow, kok-kowk, kik-kowk.

DISTRIBUTION
Lakes in Auckland, Rotorua, central plateau, Wanganui, Hawke's Bay, Wairarapa, north and central Canterbury, Central Otago. Throughout Australia. Different subspecies also in New Guinea, Asia, Europe and North Africa.

RECOGNITION
White bill and frontal shield contrast with dark plumage. Patters across water before take-off.

RARE VAGRANTS UNTIL THE 1950s, Australasian coots were confirmed as New Zealand breeders in 1958, at Lake Hayes in Central Otago. Since then their range has expanded widely; the population is probably more than 1000 and could be twice that. They favour reed-bordered lakes, rather than the swamps frequented by other rails. At Lake Virginia in Wanganui, as on many municipal ponds in Australia, coots have become tame enough to compete with ducks for bread and grain, taking food almost from the hand. So far they have not been recorded in brackish or estuarine waters, but they can be expected to adopt such habitats as their numbers continue to increase.

Coots are thought to be capable of breeding at one year. Their season is most likely August to February, as in Australia. Nests at Lake Hayes are big bowls, lined with willow rootlets and raupo, in a tangle of willow roots with overhead willow cover. Floating nests have been reported in Australia.

Eggs are creamy white, uniformly dark-spotted, and oval, with distinctly contrasting blunt and pointed ends. The usual clutch size is between five and seven. Incubation, shared by both sexes, takes 22 days. Pairs may breed twice or even three times in a season, but there is some evidence that multiple brooding occurs less often as a lake's population increases; clutch sizes also decrease.

The diet of New Zealand coots has not been studied, but their feeding behaviour suggests that they are largely vegetarian. The proportion of animal matter found in Australian birds is so low that it is probably taken accidentally while attached to plants. Movements, too, remain to be studied: banding of birds had not been attempted by the early 1980s. However it is clear that the species is highly mobile. Extensive movements are triggered by drought or flood in Australia, where coots seem to travel at night to avoid aerial predators. They can sustain long flights, and can rest on land or water. T.A.C.

The numbers and range of the Australasian coot, which is the most aquatic of rails, have expanded greatly and the species is now well established.

South Island Pied Oystercatcher *Haematopus ostralegus finschi* Martens,1897

ENDEMIC

OTHER NAMES: *Torea, redbill.*

SIZE: *460 mm.*

DESCRIPTION
ADULT: *Male smaller than female, with shorter, redder bill. Head, neck, breast, upper back and tail black. Lower back, rump, upper tail coverts, flank and belly white. Tips of terminal upper tail coverts black. Upper wing black with broad white bar on secondaries and secondary coverts; usually 2 of inner secondaries entirely white; and white patches at base of primaries. Underwing coverts white with grey tips to primary coverts and black bases to carpometacarpal coverts. Eye-ring orange. Iris scarlet. Bill bright orange-red, often fading to yellow near tip. Legs coral pink. Colours more intense when breeding.*
IMMATURE: *In juvenile back feathers brown with buff edges; iris brown; and legs grey-pink. In second year bird, back darker; iris orange-red; and legs pink. In sub-adult or non-breeding bird iris dull red.*
NESTLING: *When hatched, upper down buff grey with dark brown vertical band on crown; line through eye; 2 roughly parallel stripes down back; and bar on thigh. Lower breast and belly white. At about 3 weeks flight and back feathers appear and at end of sixth week juvenile plumage complete. Eye-ring changes gradually from brown to yellow. Base of bill becomes orange.*

MOULT
Complete moult in late summer and autumn. Body moult in early spring. Juveniles moult flight feathers in summer.

VOICE
Piercing hu-eep *as alarm call. Quiet* kleep *in flight. In courtship and aggressive encounters chorus of high-pitched calls* kervee-kervee-kervee-kervee *often ending in short lower trill. Sharp* click *from adults to warn chicks of approaching predators.*

DISTRIBUTION
In the spring, breeds in the South Island east of the main ranges from Marlborough to Southland and sometimes along the west coast rivers. Summers and winters on

The South Island pied oystercatcher is a monogamous bird that may begin breeding at about three years old. The chicks are usually brooded in the nest scrape for one or two days while their yolk sacs are absorbed.

harbours, estuaries and sandy beaches from Parengarenga Harbour in the North Island to Paterson Inlet on Stewart Island.

RECOGNITION
Sharp boundary between black and white plumage and distinctive white bay at front of wing. In flight broad white band on upper wing extends towards tip and almost joins wedge of white on rump and lower back.

During the winter the South Island pied oystercatcher probes with its long powerful bill in estuaries, mud flats and sandy beaches, mainly catching and prising open bivalve molluscs such as cockles and pipis. It also takes a few polychaete worms, gastropods and chitons as well as the odd sea anemone, crab and small flounder. If the winter is particularly wet, flocks of birds forage for earthworms and insect larvae in sodden coastal fields. At the beginning of the breeding season, in late July and early August, the South Island pied oystercatcher migrates to the inland riverbeds and surrounding farmlands of the South Island. It feeds on arable land, including newly cultivated fields. In recent years the birds have also spread onto tussock grasslands, especially in the Mackenzie highlands.

Although the birds breed only on the South Island, they winter from the northern tip of the North Island to as far south as Stewart Island. Large flocks concentrate on major harbours and estuaries. In the North Island about 15 000 birds congregate at Kaipara Harbour, 25 000 at Manukau Harbour, 12 000 at Firth of Thames and 1600 at Kawhia Harbour. Large numbers also flock at Westhaven Inlet, Farewell Spit, Takaka and Motueka in the northern South Island, on the coasts of Otago and Southland in the pied south and the Heathcote-Avon estuary in the east. Adult birds tend to return to the same area each winter, but immatures wander. Birds that breed in the far south of the South Island usually winter in the South Island, but those that breed in the northern South Island winter in the North Island. However, not all South Island pied oystercatchers migrate inland for the summer; many non-breeders remain on the coast. Similarly,

although most birds return to the sea shore between November and April, some stay inland.

Because of its large and tasty breast muscles, the early Europeans regarded the South Island pied oystercatcher as a choice table bird. Consequently from about 1885 its numbers declined drastically until 1940, when the shooting of shorebirds was banned. Since then there has been a spectacular increase. In the Auckland harbours, for example, where only a few hundred wintered in the early 1940s, there are now many thousands. A conservative estimate of 49 000 in New Zealand in 1973 is now exceeded in some years in the Auckland harbours alone.

They are strictly monogamous and pairs remain together for life. Divorce is rare. If one bird dies during the breeding season the partner acquires a new mate quickly, which suggests that there are a number of unattached birds at the breeding grounds.

Egg-laying begins in late August and reaches a peak in September. Early clutches on riverbeds are commonly destroyed by heavy spring rains and flash floods. A second peak in laying in October is due largely to replacement clutches. The nest is a shallow scrape, often lined with a few twigs or pebbles, and placed on any slightly raised area with a good all-round view. First clutches usually contain three eggs, sometimes two. Replacement clutches are sometimes smaller, with one or two eggs. The eggs are laid two days apart and the eggs laid last tend to be the smallest. They are usually olive-grey, blotched with dark brown spots and waves.

Incubation is shared by both sexes; it begins after the penultimate egg is laid and takes 24 to 28 days. Often the female is reluctant to leave the nest near hatching time and may attack the male if he attempts to take over. The parents brood their offspring in the nest scrape for one or two days while the young resorb their yolk sacs. Then the chicks leave the nest and both parents feed them until they fledge at about six weeks old.

In the breeding season these birds defend their territories from other South Island pied oystercatchers with piping displays, fighting and aerial chases. At boundary disputes both members of a pair display to another pair, with occasionally other nearby pairs joining in. Sometimes, as many as 12 birds participate in these territorial displays. When a pair drives an intruder out of their territory they run toward it and stand side by side. With their tails depressed and fanned, their wings raised upwards and away from their bodies, they extend their necks forward and direct their bills down. A.B.

Variable Oystercatcher *Haematopus unicolor* Forster, 1844

ENDEMIC

OTHER NAMES: *Torea-pango, redbill.*

SIZE: *480 mm.*

DESCRIPTION

ADULT: *Male smaller with shorter redder bill. Three plumage phases: black, pied and intermediate. Black birds entirely black with wings less intensely black than contour feathers. Pied birds black with belly, flank, rump and tail coverts white; upper edge of rump patch mottled with black; band of mottled feathers between black and white plumage on breast; wing-bar on secondaries and secondary coverts white; inner webs* of primaries black with grey areas; outer webs of secondaries mainly white. Intermediate birds have variable amounts of white on wing-bar, rump and belly. In all birds eye-ring orange; iris scarlet; bill bright orange, often with yellow tip; and legs coral pink, sometimes with purple tinge.

IMMATURE: *In first-year bird upper feathers brown with buff edges; in black phase belly feathers have buff tips; iris brown; bill tip dusky; legs grey-pink. In second-year bird upper parts black; iris orange-red; legs pale pink.*

NESTLING: *Light grey to buff-brown down. Dark brown band on crown, line through eye, 2 stripes down back, and bar on thigh. Sometimes* Stewart Island and Otago chicks have dark brown heads. Northern chicks paler. Black phase chicks grey underneath; pied chicks white; and intermediate chicks white interspersed with grey. Flight and trunk feathers appear at about 3 weeks; juvenile plumage complete at about 6 weeks. Eye-ring brown changing to yellow near fledging. Iris brown.

MOULT
Not known.

VOICE
Alarm call hu-eep. *Quiet* kleep *in flight. In courtship and aggressive encounters chorus of* kervee-kervee-kervee-kervee *often ending in short lower trill. Sharp* click *from adults* to warn chicks of predators. Lower pitch than South Island pied oystercatcher in courtship and aggressive calls.

DISTRIBUTION
Scattered around the coasts of the 3 main islands.

RECOGNITION

Black and intermediate birds with bright orange bills. Pied birds have restricted area of white on wing and rump, smudgy boundary on breast, no white patch on shoulder.

IN FLOCKS OF UP TO 150 birds the variable oystercatcher lives scattered around the New Zealand coast. In the South Island it inhabits rocky shores and forages for limpets, mussels, gastropods and chitons that are too big for the slimmer-billed South Island pied oystercatcher. In the North Island it hunts beach and estuarine bivalves, only retreating to the rocks where the South Island pied oystercatcher is abundant. Although essentially a bird of the seashore, it also ventures into coastal fields after heavy rain to catch earthworms and insect larvae.

It occurs in three colour types: black, pied and an intermediate colouring that is a hybrid of the other two. In 1979 there were about 1300 black phase birds, 300 pied ones and 400 intermediates. There are few pied and hybrid birds in southern New Zealand, and in Stewart Island only black birds occur. The occasional pied or intermediate bird that wanders to the far south is invariably an immature bird. Young variable oystercatchers sometimes wander extensively before pairing and settling in one area. A chick banded at Waipu was sighted 15 months later at Eastbourne, 570 km away.

During the breeding season, from October to February, the winter flocks break into pairs which occupy territories around the seashore. Some birds defend a territory all year round. They are monogamous and divorce is rare. The birds defend their domains with piping displays, fights and aerial chases that are similar to those of the South Island pied oystercatcher.

They probably begin breeding at four years. Egg-laying extends from October to February with a peak in December. If the first clutch is lost they lay another later in the season. The nest scrape is unlined, or lined with shells, twigs or small stones. Usually it is sited on a sandy ridge with a good view around it. At other times, the birds nest on cliff ledges, on top of rocks, under shrubs and inside wooden boxes washed up on the shore. The usual clutch is three, but two eggs are common later in the season. The eggs are olive-grey with dark brown spots and waves, and tend to be darker when laid on rocks. Each egg is laid two days apart. Incubation begins with the laying of the penultimate egg. Both sexes incubate for about one to one and a half hours at a time. The eggs hatch after 26 to 29 days. The parents brood the chicks for one or two days. At six weeks the chicks fly. A.B.

Variable oystercatchers in black plumage. Black phase birds are more numerous than pied or hybrid birds, and increase in frequency southwards.

The population of the Chatham Island oystercatcher, a very rare species, totals only about 50 birds. They are typically found on rock platforms at low water.

Chatham Island Oystercatcher *Haematopus chathamensis* HARTERT, 1927

THE CHATHAM ISLAND OYSTERCATCHER forages on rocky coasts between the high and low water marks. Usually it feeds at low water on rock platforms which abound with limpets, chitons, mussels and small gastropods. Nests are located away from the waterline—higher up on the shore or among short vegetation.

The precise timing of the breeding season is not known, but most birds lay in October and November and probably the young fledge by the end of January. The male of one pair had dull sub-adult plumage, suggesting that it was a three year old breeding for the first time. The birds lay in scrapes lined with small stones or twigs. As there is little open ground on the smaller islands, these scrapes are often in unusual sites such as small caves, under large boulders, on cliff edges, among growths of *Mesembryanthemum* and at the base of small shrubs. Early clutches contain three eggs and later ones two. The eggs are olive-grey with fine dark brown spots and waves. Both sexes incubate for about 75 minutes at a time. The clutch takes about 48 to 72 hours to hatch; and the parents brood the young for one or two days.

Chatham Island oystercatchers are strongly territorial and drive out other birds of the same species with piping displays and occasionally by attacking them. Unattached birds are rarely seen so it is probably difficult for birds that lose their partners to mate again in the same season. In November 1970 an adult bird was found defending a territory that contained two unincubated eggs and an adult which had been dead for more than two weeks.   A.B.

ENDEMIC

OTHER NAME: *Redbill.*

SIZE: *480 mm.*

DESCRIPTION
ADULT: *Sexes alike but female larger. Head, neck, upper back, tail and breast black. Lower back, rump, upper tail coverts, flank and belly white. Between rump and lower back mottled feathers. Upper wing black with inner edge darker and white bar on secondaries and secondary coverts. Usually 3 of inner secondaries entirely white. Base of primaries patched with white. Lesser undercoverts mostly black. Primary undercoverts tipped with grey. Axillaries minutely spotted with grey. Eye-ring orange. Iris scarlet. Legs pink. Bill orange-red.*
IMMATURE: *In juvenile back feathers brown with buff edges; iris brown; bill tip dusky; legs grey-pink. In second-year bird back darker; iris orange-red; legs pale.*
NESTLING: *Buff grey down. Dark brown band on middle of crown, line*
through eye, 2 parallel stripes down middle of back bordered by ochre-buff, and bars on thighs continuing around rump.

MOULT
Not known.

VOICE
Alarm call piercing hu-eep. *Quiet* kleep *in flight. In courtship and aggressive encounters high-pitched chorus of* kervee-kervee-kervee-kervee, *often ending in short trill.*

DISTRIBUTION
About 50 birds concentrated on Rangatira and Mangere Islands.

Least Golden Plover *Pluvialis fulva* (GMELIN,1789)

MIGRANT

OTHER NAMES: *Pacific golden plover, Asiatic golden plover, lesser golden plover.*

SIZE: *250 mm.*

DESCRIPTION
ADULT: *In non-breeding plumage sexes alike. Upper parts dark brown, feathers with dull yellow edges. Forehead, eye-stripe, chin and throat whitish buff, often with yellowish tinge. Sides of head and neck yellowish buff, streaked brown. Breast buff-brown, feathers streaked and spotted darker, with dull yellow tips; grading into white with slight buff tinge on flanks, belly and undertail. Some brown streaks and yellowish brown wash on flanks. Wing dark brown, with narrow whitish edges to coverts. Faint partial wing stripe in flight. Axillaries and underwing coverts pale grey-brown with yellowish tinge. Iris dark brown. Bill short, straight, slender, black. Legs slate grey to dark grey. In breeding plumage upper parts, including lesser and median wing coverts, black-brown, spotted densely with golden yellow and sparsely with white. Rest of wing and underwing as in non-breeding plumage. Upper tail coverts barred yellow. Tail barred light and dark brown, with yellowish white spots. Broad white stripe from forehead extends above eye, down side of neck to side of breast. In male rest of underparts black with some white on thighs and sometimes on flanks. Undertail coverts mostly white, irregularly marked with black. In female black underparts of male slightly brownish black mixed with white or white-tipped feathers.*

JUVENILE: *Like non-breeding adult but feathers of upper surface spotted yellow and white; neck, breast and flanks darker buff-brown with strong golden tinge; and pale brown bars on flanks and belly. Yellow fades during migration.*

MOULT
Post-nuptial moult begins on breeding grounds and completed on wintering grounds. Birds reaching New Zealand in September and early October still in body moult. Later in October most in full non-breeding plumage. Wing moult after migration, usually November to February with peak about January. Pre-nuptial body moult February to May with peak in March. Post-juvenile moult in winter quarters September to January. First wing moult of immatures usually at end of first winter, July to November.

VOICE
Common flight call clear, shrill but melodious tuill, tu-li, too-weet, tya-lee, klew-wee, zhwee or whee-oo-wit. Generally silent on ground in non-breeding season.

DISTRIBUTION
Breeds in northern and northeastern Siberia and on west coast of Alaska. Winters from southern and eastern India, Sri Lanka, Burma, Thailand, Vietnam, Malaysia, Hainan, southern China, Taiwan, Japan, south to Indonesia, New Guinea, the Philippines, Micronesia, Melanesia, Polynesia, Australia, Tasmania, New Zealand, east to the Hawaiian and Line Islands, Îles Tuamotu and Marquises. Small numbers winter on coasts of Arabia and eastern Africa. Straggles to Europe, Greenland and North America.

RECOGNITION
Plump, medium-sized plover, with large-looking head. Overall appearance dark mottled buff-brown, with pale forehead, eye-stripe and belly. In flight rather long-winged and dark above. Distinguished from grey plover by smaller bill and buff or yellowish plumage; from New Zealand dotterel by erect stance and buff colour.

AT THE END OF AUGUST the first few least golden plovers arrive in New Zealand. Small numbers reach here during September, mainly in the far north, but the main build-up occurs in October and early November. At Parengarenga, this is often followed by a sharp drop in late November and December, with more birds arriving in January, although these could be golden plovers from other parts of New Zealand. In late March there is often another build-up of birds in the North Island before they leave in late March or early April. Very few golden plovers winter in New Zealand.

Because numbers vary from year to year, and the birds do not roost in one place, it is difficult to determine how many golden plovers visit New Zealand. During the 1950s and 1960s the numbers seemed to increase greatly, perhaps because swamp-land next to estuaries was converted to fallow and grassland. In 1977, at least 500 birds were in New Zealand and each year there are probably between 600 and 800 birds. As many as 350 birds have been seen at Parengarenga, 160 in Manukau Harbour, 240 at Firth of Thames, 150 in the harbours and lagoons of the Bay of Plenty, and 260 in the estuaries and lagoons of Southland. Regular flocks of 10 to 100 birds have been seen at the Kermadec Islands, Whangarei, Kaipara, Great Barrier Island, Gisborne, Napier, Manawatu estuary, Farewell Spit and Lake Ellesmere. Groups of fewer than 10 have been recorded at the Waitotara, Rangitikei, Porangahau, Wairoa, Ashley and probably Nelson estuaries, and at Chatham Island. They have also been seen at the Auckland Islands. They are rarely seen inland.

In Siberia and Alaska, the golden plover breeds on dry upland tundra. Whether on the coast or inland, it prefers a ground cover of lichens and mosses, into which its breeding plumage blends. In New Zealand, it lives mainly on tidal flats of harbours and estuaries, ranging inland up to several kilometres to fallow and short-grass fields.

A quiet bird in its winter quarters, it is often remarkably tame on some Pacific Islands, though rather wary in New Zealand. It migrates and winters in small flocks but in New Zealand is sometimes seen in groups of over 100 at high tide roosts or on *Salicornia* flats of the larger harbours and estuaries, often with turnstones. Its roosting habits are erratic, but sometimes it roosts in the same place, on ploughed or short-grass fields at spring tides, and well up on the shore, especially on *Salicornia* flats, at neap tides. On landing it holds its wings erect briefly, then folds them carefully. When alert, it stands very erect.

It feeds away from other species which are following the tideline, often strung out in a long line close to the edge of the salt marsh where its buff-brown colour blends into that of the firm sandy mud. Or it forages among *Salicornia* turf or on a *Zostera* flat among mangroves. It feeds in the typical plover way—making short runs with its back horizontal, stopping abruptly, standing erect and tipping forward to pick or snatch from the surface. It takes a wide range of animal food, especially insects and their larvae, including earwigs, moth and butterfly caterpillars, beetles, grasshoppers, ants, and flies, as well as spiders and plant seeds. On tidal flats, it also eats small crustaceans and molluscs. At the northern hemisphere breeding grounds, it eats dried blueberries and crowberries from the previous season.   B.D.H. & D.H.B.

The least golden plover feeds in loosely scattered groups and eats a wide range of animal food.

Grey Plover *Pluvialis squatarola* (LINNAEUS,1758)

In winter, the grey plover favours tidal mud flats and saltmarsh pools.

FROM AUGUST TO APRIL the grey plover is an occasional visitor to New Zealand. Usually it is seen on tidal mud flats, saltmarsh pools or sand flats, but unlike the least golden plover favours muddy conditions, feeding close to and often wading in the tideline or the margins of pools. Occasionally it travels inland to freshwater swamps or wet fields close to the coast. A wary plover, it often keeps to itself or congregates in small flocks. Its food includes worms (both aquatic and terrestrial), small molluscs and crustaceans as well as a wide range of water insects and their larvae.   B.D.H. & D.H.B.

STRAGGLER

OTHER NAME: *Black-bellied plover.*

SIZE: *280 mm.*

DESCRIPTION
ADULT: *In non-breeding plumage sexes alike. Upper surface mainly grey-brown. Feathers darker near edges and tipped with white. Primaries and their coverts blackish brown; white on inner webs of primaries and secondaries forms whitish wing stripe in flight. Upper tail coverts white with pale brown bars. Tail barred blackish brown and white. Forehead, eye-stripe, side of head and underparts white, side of head with dark brown streaks. Breast and flanks often with pale brown or grey wash and irregular brown streaks and mottling. Underwing white. Axillaries black. Iris brown. Bill short, stout, black. Legs dark grey. In breeding plumage upper surface mottled brownish black and white, white predominating on crown and nape. Upper tail coverts and tail as in non-breeding plumage. White of forehead extending over eye and down rear of cheek to broad white patch at side of breast. In male, cheek, side of neck and underparts from bill to belly black. Lower belly, underwing and undertail white. In female, upper surface darker and underparts brownish black with scattered white feathers.*
JUVENILE: *Similar to non-breeding adult but upper surface black-brown. Edges of feathers spotted with pale gold fading to cream except on back and rump. Tail washed golden. After migration, worn upper parts overall dark. Eye-stripe, side of head and neck thickly streaked with brown. Throat, breast and flanks pale buff with brown streaks and irregular bars.*

MOULT
Post-nuptial complete moult late July to December, with wing moult usually August to November. Pre-nuptial partial moult February to May. Juveniles moult into first-winter plumage October to January, with wing moult May to August.

VOICE
Flight call plaintive 3 syllables with middle syllable shorter and lower than other 2: tlee-oo-e, tee-oo-ee, pee-oo-wee, pee-er-ee *or* pee-a-weep.

DISTRIBUTION
Breeds in arctic North America and northern USSR south to limits of open tundra. Winters in America from southwestern British Columbia south to Galapagos Islands, the West Indies, Chile and southern Brazil; in Europe and Africa from the British Isles, the Mediterranean and the Persian Gulf to South Africa and Madagascar; in the Indo-Pacific region from India, Sri Lanka, Southeast Asia, the Philippines, Indonesia, south to Australia. Regular in small numbers in New Guinea. Stragglers to New Zealand seen at: Parengarenga, Kaipara and Manukau Harbours; Firth of Thames; Lake Grassmere; Farewell Spit; Southland; the Chatham and Kermadec Islands.

RECOGNITION
Distinguished from similar least golden plover by white upper tail coverts, whitish tail and whitish wing stripe, but above all by black axillaries. When seen with golden plover, distinctly larger, more robust; bill more robust and upper parts more grey and uniform.

Spur-winged Plover *Vanellus miles novaehollandiae* STEPHENS,1819

THE SPUR-WINGED PLOVER fearlessly defends its young. If a harrier approaches the chicks, the plover dives and screams at the aggressor. Sometimes both parents join in the chase. They swoop down on the harrier from above, side-swiping it with their wings and spurs. As one plover speeds past, calling raucously, its mate waits above ready to attack in turn. The harrier, for its part, takes spectacular avoiding action so that feathers seldom fly. As the harrier moves out of the air space above the plovers' territory, the plovers return to the ground. Then sometimes at this point, spur-winged plovers from a neighbouring territory take over the chase. Throughout September such dramatic confrontations are relatively common in Southland and Otago skies. Until the danger has passed the chicks 'freeze' and their plumage provides excellent camouflage, even in sparse cover.

From across the Tasman

This plover is a fairly recent addition to New Zealand's bird life. Two birds arrived in Invercargill from Australia in 1932. Two years later there were five birds, and by 1951 there were 100 within a 16 km radius of Invercargill. Numbers continued to increase until 1965. Since then they have remained fairly stable at about 1200 birds in this area. By 1965 they were firmly established throughout Southland and Otago as a breeding species and had colonised other parts of the South Island and Stewart Island.

In 1973 the first breeding birds were recorded in the North Island. By 1980 they were well established in the southern and eastern parts of the North Island, especially in Manawatu and Hawke's Bay, and single birds or small groups appeared in the far north, the Firth of Thames, at East Cape, the Volcanic Plateau and northern Taranaki. They populate new areas in two ways. Either they breed at the edges of an established breeding area or they travel to a previously unpopulated area. Most of these new arrivals are probably New

Zealand-bred birds, but some may be Australian vagrants.

Although it has now established itself in New Zealand's three main islands, the spur-winged plover is a sedentary bird that, once it has settled somewhere, lives within a range of three or four kilometres. It prefers wet swampy ground with short cover. Scattered rushes and sedges provide a broken pattern that camouflages both the incubating bird and chicks. It also inhabits pasture with a short cover of up to 13 cm, cultivated paddocks, grain-crop or hay stubble, new turnip crops and areas left fallow after turnip or choumoellier crops have been eaten down. Other places include stony or sandy river verges and riverbeds with sparse tussock cover, as well as gravel pits, estuaries, and sometimes coastal beaches. In Central Otago it is found in overgrown gold-dredge tailings, or in other dry stony places with sparse grass cover. In most cases there is water nearby. The spur-winged plover also needs good visibility and consequently is rarely found in narrow gullies. It lives at altitudes of up to 670 m.

Breeding activities

A pair usually stays together, and birds live for up to 12 years. If one bird dies or disappears, the other takes a new mate within a couple of weeks. They begin breeding at the end of their first year. In Southland pairs explore nesting territories in mid-April. Typically the nest-site is on slightly raised rough ground with a clear view, and surrounded by short cover, in a swampy place or with a wet area nearby. Preferably the location is free of grazing animals, particularly sheep.

Both adults build the nest. They hollow a shallow cup in the ground with a shuffling circular movement of their breasts. This they line sparsely with dead vegetation which they toss in from the perimeter. From June to November they lay three or four, rarely five, eggs. They are green-brown, heavily blotched with darker brown, and pyriform in shape. About 24 hours separates the laying of each egg and incubation does not usually begin until the clutch is complete. Both adults incubate for 30 or 31 days. Occasionally they turn the eggs with their bills and maybe their feet. They keep the nest very clean and remove egg shells after hatching. The bird that is not incubating feeds, preens and loafs 100 m or more away from the nest. Sometimes it flies away from the territory to flock with other spur-winged plovers.

Half the nests fail. Sheep trample some, and cultivation of the land destroys others. Predators, such as rats, pukekos and stoats, eat the eggs. Sometimes the nests are deserted for no apparent reason, but often the birds nest again 15 to 700 m away from the first. Approximately 70 per cent of eggs hatch.

The chicks leave the nest within a few hours and begin to feed in the nearby wet area almost immediately. Occasionally the brood travels 800 m from the nest-site within a few days of hatching, but usually the family remains on the original territory unless it is seriously disturbed. Small chicks have been seen crossing flowing streams several metres wide. In the first week the adults brood the chicks for much of the time if temperatures are low. Over half of chicks die in the first 14 days. About a quarter survive to fledging age, at seven or eight weeks.

Although most birds fly well by eight weeks, the chicks remain with their parents until they are seven or eight months old. Not until March or April do they begin to mingle with other family groups for part of the day. Many family groups are still together in June, but by July the families break up. In autumn and winter the birds may join flocks of up to more than 100 birds.

Autumn and winter are also the time for noisy displays, when groups of five or six birds strut and posture with necks extended, white breasts puffed, shoulders forward and spurs prominent. From a hill top or any slightly raised ground the birds sometimes march in a row, advancing and retreating, or they step around in solemn circles. Usually these displays are preceded by noisy aerobatics. They break up when the birds move off desultorily in ones and twos. In some way this behaviour is connected with mate selection and establishment of territory. Mated pairs of long standing also take part.

Not much is known about the spur-winged plover's diet. It eats large numbers of lepidopterous larvae and is often seen eating earthworms. Vegetable matter is probably also eaten, and sometimes it takes pebbles from road verges. It feeds in open country, both rough and cultivated, with a running and darting action. By its consumption of insect species which are agricultural pests, the spur-winged plover can be considered beneficial to man. It is a colourful and elegant addition to New Zealand's avifauna. M.L.B.

NATIVE

OTHER NAMES: *None.*

SIZE: *380 mm.*

DESCRIPTION
ADULT: *Crown, ear coverts, nape, hind neck and shoulder patch black. From hind neck to rump olive-brown. Primaries black, with brown* tips and white barbs at base. Primary coverts black, narrowly edged with white. First 10 secondaries black at tip, grey in middle and white at base. Remaining secondaries grey with white tips. Greater wing coverts olive-brown edged with white. Middle and lesser wing coverts olive-brown. Alula white and grey. Upper tail coverts white. Tail white with broad black band and narrow white tip. Base of forehead, cheek, chin, throat and undersurface white. Wattle from eye over forehead to base of bill and hanging below bill, yellow. Iris brown. Bill yellow tipped with horn or brown. Wing spurs yellow, tipped with dark brown or black. Legs and feet red with grey-black scale pattern.*
IMMATURE: *Crown speckled, later barred black and brown. Shoulder patch smaller and less prominent than adult. Back and wing coverts olive-brown barred and flecked with brown. Wattles small, putty-coloured and sometimes with lemon tinge. Bill and small wing spurs horn-coloured with brown tips. Legs and feet grey-red. Otherwise as adult.*
NESTLING: *Crown black, lightly flecked brown and buff. Narrow black band at nape above white collar. Upper surface and shoulder patch flecked black, brown and buff. Undersurface white. Small putty-coloured to lemon wattle in front of eye. Bill, legs and feet slate-blue to horn-coloured.*

MOULT
Not known.

VOICE
Loud rattling call repeated rapidly in flight, especially at night and when attacking predators. Also uttered on ground when people appear. Male calls soft repeated cluck when mating. Shrill scream when trapped or handled.

DISTRIBUTION
The 3 main islands. Australia and Tasmania.

RECOGNITION
Large plover about the size of an oystercatcher or magpie. Brown above and white below, with black on head and shoulders. Yellow bill and large yellow wattles. Red legs. Broad blunt-tipped wings. Flies with slow wing-beats.

The spur-winged plover, a colourful Australian species self-introduced during the 1930s, has spread successfully from Southland and Otago and is now established throughout New Zealand's three main islands.

Banded Dotterel *Charadrius bicinctus* Jardine & Selby, 1827

THE MOST ABUNDANT and widespread plover in New Zealand, the banded dotterel was once shot in large numbers until its protection in 1908. Recently it has benefited from increased feeding and breeding areas created by new farmland next to coasts, lakes and rivers.

Mostly it breeds inland on dry, open, well consolidated parts of shingle riverbeds and nearby ploughed or stony fields; in similar conditions near inland lakes; and also around the lakes, tussock plains and mountain tops of the Volcanic Plateau and on the unforested tops and gentler slopes of the mountains of Central Otago. On the coast it breeds just above the tideline on beaches, on open flats among dunes or on short pasture. It is particularly common on the riverbeds of Hawke's Bay, Manawatu, Marlborough, Canterbury, Otago and Southland. It is less widespread but abundant on the west coast of the South Island and in the North Island north of Manawatu and Hawke's Bay where, since the 1950s, the breeding population seems to have declined, perhaps owing to heavy use of pesticides and great increase of black-backed gulls. On the main island of the Chathams it breeds on the coast and inland on peat 'clears' and on marsh turf around lagoons.

Movement patterns

At the end of the breeding season, most banded dotterels migrate from inland to the coast, to the northern North Island and to Australia. Flocks begin to gather at estuaries, coastal farms, flats and airfields in late December, probably mainly local breeding birds. The main build-up develops in January, rising to a peak in late February. In the north, this peak extends to March, sometimes at Parengarenga Harbour even to as late as April and May.

In the South Island, the limited evidence suggests that, after an initial build-up, numbers on the coast remain stable, except in Southland. Therefore birds moving northward to wintering grounds at Farewell Spit, on Auckland and Northland harbours, or in Australia, may fly direct without stopping off in southern North Island districts. However, on northern harbours, an abrupt drop from a February-March peak to a much lower winter population in April-July is sometimes thought to be because the birds have left for Australia. It has been suggested that the main movement to Australia occurs from the South rather than the North Island, but the evidence for this is lacking and much further study is needed. Although January to March totals of well over 1000 have been recorded at Lake Ellesmere and regularly at Farewell Spit, there is no evidence of onward movement or a high proportion of juveniles.

During late autumn and winter, small flocks of ten to several hundred birds are widely distributed around the New Zealand coast from Stewart Island to the far north, including coastal farmland. They feed mainly on sand flats in estuaries. At high tide they roost in loose flocks on sand flats above the high tide line, or on salt marsh or fields behind the shore. They generally ignore the roosts used by other common waders. Some flocks winter on close-cropped farm pasture, on ploughed fields and on airfields, sometimes well inland.

Most return to their breeding grounds from mid-July onwards, many apparently travelling inland by night. At first, they form small restless flocks that display and call aggressively. Then, during August and September, pairs spread out on to separate territories.

At the nest-site

Banded dotterels nest at least 50 m apart. Inland they prefer the older, more stable parts of the riverbed that are unlikely to be flooded, where the stones are well cemented by sand and mat plants and where the food supply is better than on clean shingle. Often they choose level consolidated ground without shrubs and with a clear all-round view. They rarely nest in shingle hollows without an all-round view, and then it is usually a site with nearby stilts or oystercatchers that give early warning of predators.

After a period of shallow trial scrapes, the male deepens a chosen scrape between two and a half and four centimetres deep. It lines the scrape with fragments of plants and dung and with small stones, which it gathers from within a metre or so of the nest and throws backwards over its shoulder towards the nest. Then the male sits in the scrape and gathers in the material. Nests on clean shingle or away from rivers may have little or no lining. In the North Island, pumice fragments have also been recorded as nest lining.

The female lays two to four, usually three, eggs which are pyriform, and range in ground colour from pale grey through pale aqua-green to olive-green and olive-brown. They are marked with dark brown and black spots or blotches, often more heavily towards the blunt end. These are laid about two to five days (averaging three) apart.

The incubation period is 25 to 27 days from laying to hatching of

A banded dotterel at its nest. The eggs are incubated for 25 to 27 days.

ENDEMIC
Banded Dotterel
C.b. bicinctus JARDINE & SELBY, 1827.
Auckland Island Banded Dotterel
C.b. exilis FALLA, 1978

OTHER NAMES: *Pohowera, tuturiwhatu, double-banded plover.*

SIZE: *180 mm.*

DESCRIPTION
MALE: *In breeding plumage, upper parts brown, feathers with pale edges. Underparts white. Forehead white, tapering to narrow white line above and behind eye, sometimes also below eye. Forecrown black. Black line from bill to below eye, continuing as narrow edge to brown of cheek and neck, merging finally with thin black breast-band that forms collar across lower neck. Broad dark chestnut band across lower breast often has sharply defined vertical sides and tapers from upper edge to shoulder with less intense colour. A specimen in National Museum of New Zealand has the upper third of chestnut band black; there are no field records of this pattern. Bill short, slender, black. Legs pale green. Non-breeding plumage of both sexes nondescript and very variable. Upper parts brown lightly suffused with rufous. Black lines of forecrown, cheek, and neck absent. Breast-bands much reduced, blurred, shed during moult. Sometimes indistinct shoulder patches. Underparts seldom a clean clear white. Legs pale greenish brown or yellowish brown.*
FEMALE: *In breeding plumage, similar to male but less intensively coloured and averaging slightly smaller. Black lines on forecrown very narrow or brown. Line from bill to eye brown rather than black, and usually no black margin on cheek and neck. Chestnut band less rich and often narrower than in male, with indistinct edges.*
JUVENILE: *In first months, broad buffy edges to feathers give sandy, speckled or dappled look to upper parts, which have a warm buffy tone. No face or chest-bands. Buff wash prominent on face and neck, and sometimes irregular grey or buff wash on chest. Some juveniles have no buff. Instead, upper parts scalloped with white edges to feathers; eyebrow stripe white; underparts white except for mottled brown wash on chest or just single or double shoulder patches. After early*

months, both forms are apparently indistinguishable from adult non-breeding plumage.
NESTLING: *Upper parts grey and white; gold; gold and white; or intermediate. Thickly speckled with black. All these forms may be in the one brood. Wing has white trailing edge. Underparts white, sometimes with pale buff on breast.*

MOULT
Post-nuptial complete moult begins in adults before their chicks have fledged; proceeds rapidly once they have fledged. Most birds moult November to March. By mid-January many adults, especially females, hard to distinguish from many juveniles. Wings completely moulted before migration. Pre-nuptial body moult of adults begins in some birds late April to August.

VOICE
Loud high-pitched pit, *a warning call uttered singly or twice quickly. Lower-pitched abrupt chip-chip. Musical* tink *called rapidly in flight.* Peet *when alarmed;* chee-ree-a-ree, *accented on the second syllable, when males chase intruders from their territory. Soft crooning* kwereep *of rapidly rising pitch, by male during courtship. Drawn-out* weer *by adult during distraction display. Soft* chirp *by adult to chicks.*

DISTRIBUTION
Banded dotterel: *Breeding widespread, especially in South Island, North Island; the Chatham Islands; Great Barrier, Great Mercury, Kapiti, and Ruapuke Islands. After breeding major movement from inland to the east, to the northern North Island and Australia. Straggles probably regularly to Norfolk and Lord Howe Islands and Fiji; rarely to Vanuatu, New Caledonia, the Kermadec Islands, Auckland and possibly Campbell Islands.*

Auckland Island banded dotterel: *Confined to the Auckland Islands.*

RECOGNITION

Small fairly chunky plover, brown above and white below. In breeding plumage two breast-bands: narrow black upper band and broad chestnut lower band. Faint wing stripe in flight.

the last egg. Both sexes incubate, but the female spends by far the most time on the nest. Most birds lay between August and December, with a peak in late September and early October. Late nests probably result from lost first broods, as there is no evidence that the birds raise two broods. Sometimes the eggs from one clutch hatch on the same day; at other times, up to 48 hours between first and last eggs. The chicks leave the nest after several hours in fine weather, but after more than a day in bad weather. They feed independently in the territory, while the parents guard them. At five or six weeks old the chicks fledge. The parents remain with them in the territory until several days after fledging, when they join flocks.

Feeding and displays

The stomachs of five Australian birds were found to contain crustaceans, spiders, earwigs, plant bugs, ground beetles, water beetles, cockchafers, weevils, maggots and ants. Foods available for birds breeding in the Cass River, near Lake Tekapo, were mainly spiders, carabid beetles, caterpillars, and the fruits of such mat plants as creeping pohuehue *Muehlenbeckia axillaris*. In September and October they fed also on mayflies at the stream edges. During July and August, on mud and sand flats of the delta, the birds fed on tubificid worms and chironomid larvae; on earthworms and caterpillars in the pastures; and in riverbed riffles, on mayfly and caddis fly larvae.

The banded dotterel feeds in loose flocks, running and stopping at random over sand flats or sand and mud flats. On dry sand flats, it uses a rhythm of run-stop-look-step-peck, in which each run may disturb prey that the bird stops to see. On damp sand, where prey is less mobile, a rhythm of run-stop-peck is often used; on open wet sand or mud the bird either does the same or walks more slowly and probes. On saltmarsh flats and runnels the bird walks steadily and pecks as it finds prey among the vegetation. On wet pasture it pecks and probes. The birds respond to changes of habitat, and therefore food, caused by the ebbing tide, flooding, or rainfall. For example, at Lake Wainono on cold mornings birds fed at the water's edge on shore flies until the flies became active after sunrise, when they changed to saltmarsh feeding.

The displays of the banded dotterel are typical of plovers generally. When a bird with young chicks or hatching eggs is threatened by a predator it feigns injury. It runs across the path of the predator with the nearer wing drooped. This running display is sometimes followed by a spread-eagled posture, with the wings spread and flapping noisily on the ground, as the bird calls a loud *weer*.

When the birds are courting, the male scrapes a trial nest and calls *kwereep* from a hunched posture. As the female approaches, the calls stop and the male bows, tilting his body forward and jerking his head up and down at increasing speed. Often the birds mate after this display. The aggressive display of the male is a rapid run alternated with abrupt stops and upright jerks, with *che-ree-a-ree* calls. Rarely, and usually with young chicks, birds strike with wings and feet. Most often, the two birds run side by side, attacking at intervals. After a male has driven away an intruder, it flies in curves, circles and figures-of-eight with stiff wings making a far-carrying rhythmic clicking sound, accompanied by *che-ree-a-ree* calls. These display flights are also given to establish and maintain territory and as part of courtship.

Auckland Island banded dotterel

At the Auckland Islands, the mainland subspecies *Charadrius bicinctus bicinctus* is replaced by the Auckland Island banded dotterel *C. b. exilis*. In appearance it is very like the mainland race, but the upper parts are darker, a warmer more olive-brown with buffy tone, the feathers broadly edged buff-brown. As far as is known, the breeding plumage is less clearly defined: the black band is usually spotted with grey; the chestnut one with white. There are a few dark streaks on the front of the thigh. The most common call is a deep *pit*. Between August and October probably fewer than 200 of these birds breed on the open parts of tussock-covered tops on Auckland Island and Adams Island. The prime wintering habitat is Derry Castle Reef on Enderby Island.   B.D.H., D.H.B. & R.J.P.

Red-capped Dotterel *Charadrius alexandrinus ruficapillus* TEMMINCK, 1822

OVER THE LAST FORTY YEARS there have been several sightings of the red-capped dotterel in both the North and South Islands. A few birds have even raised young, sometimes by mating with banded dotterels. In Australia, red-capped dotterels nest on beaches and estuaries near the high-water mark and among dunes; in freshwater and brackish marshes; in flooded fields near the coast; and well inland on the edges of permanent salt lakes, lagoons and swamps. In New Zealand, they appear to breed only on shingle riverbeds in northern Canterbury up to 15 km inland, joining banded dotterels at the coast on sand, mud or shingle.

On the southeastern Australian coast, the breeding season extends from August to March, with a peak from September to December. Inland, and in the tropics, the birds may breed in any month. The nest is a simple depression in the open, unlined or thinly lined with small stones, pieces of shell or quartz, or wisps of seaweed or dry grass. Sometimes the nest is sheltered by tussock, reeds, or low bushes. The usual clutch is two oval to pyriform eggs, light grey to yellow-brown, sometimes with a greenish tone and overlaid with blackish freckles, spots, blotches, streaks and some light grey to lavender markings. The female incubates for about 18 days.

The red-capped dotterel feeds on the drier parts of sand and mud flats. It alternates rapid runs with abrupt stops and an upward jerk of the head. It pecks at and probes into the surface, generally avoiding wet mud or water, and probably eats a wide variety of invertebrates, including minute crustaceans, larvae, beetles and flies. On ocean beaches it often feeds close to the waves, darting after each receding wave for stranded food. It has a curious and distinctive flight that alternately shows its brown upper side and white underside.   D.H.B. & B.D.H.

The red-capped dotterel.

Red-kneed Dotterel *Erythrogonys cinctus* Gould, 1838

The red-kneed dotterel occurs around the muddy edges of inland swamps.

IN AUSTRALIA the red-kneed dotterel feeds in fine mud near the edges of freshwater and brackish swamps, lagoons and lakes. Flocks of up to 60 birds forage together, running rapidly back and forth in the shallow water or among bushes and clumps of plants. They peck and probe into the soft surface, searching for aquatic insects and their larvae. Or they wade up to belly depth and plunge their heads beneath the surface. In water of uneven depth they swim from shallow to shallow. When resting they sometimes stand motionless among plants or shrub branches in the water or beneath bushes.

On permanent waters this is a resident bird. Elsewhere it is strongly nomadic, appearing after rains at swamps and lakes that have been dry for years. In northern Australia it is commoner on the coast during the dry season, from about May to September, and in the interior during the wet, from November to March. In New Zealand the only record is of one bird, possibly an immature, seen at the Manawatu River estuary in March 1976. D.H.B. & B.D.H.

New Zealand Dotterel *Charadrius obscurus* (Gmelin, 1789)

THE NEW ZEALAND DOTTEREL breeds in two separate populations. Around 100 breeding pairs nest on Stewart Island and, at the other end of the country, about 1400 birds live in the northern part of the North Island.

In the North Island, the New Zealand dotterel usually breeds among sand dunes or on sand spits on the coast, less often on sand or gravel beaches, and sometimes on sandy estuarine islets and estuarine shellbanks. One pair has nested near Parengarenga on a low bare hill among scrub, and several pairs nested for several seasons at Firth of Thames in stony grass and maize-stubble fields. The New Zealand dotterel breeds from North Cape to Kawhia Harbour on the west coast and to the eastern Bay of Plenty on the east coast. It is abundant in Northland and on the Coromandel Peninsula. It also nests on offshore islands with sandy beaches such as Great Barrier, Waiheke, Ponui, Great Mercury and Motuhora Islands; the Cavalli Islands; and the Rurima Rocks. In recent years the odd bird has also been seen inland in Waikato, at Rotorua, on the coast at Gisborne, and in Taranaki, Manawatu, Wanganui and southern Wairarapa.

On Stewart Island the New Zealand dotterel breeds on exposed mountain tops and ridges from 500 to over 900 m high and often descends to the nearest tidal flats to feed. A few pairs nest in the dunes of Mason Bay. Outside the breeding season it lives on the coast. Many of the Stewart Island birds winter in Paterson Inlet; a few migrate to the Southland coast.

Breeding territories

Until the late nineteenth century, the New Zealand dotterel bred on mountain slopes, foothills and plains—but apparently not on the coast or riverbeds—of the eastern South Island. Like the Stewart Island birds, the South Island ones wintered on the shore, where they were shot for market. Few New Zealand dotterels have been seen inland in the South Island in recent years, but possibly a small breeding population still exists in the northern highlands of the South Island. Small flocks are regularly seen at Farewell Spit from January to May, and occasionally in September or October.

In the North Island, the birds start pairing in June and July. In one case the same birds paired for three successive seasons; in another for two. One female bred in its first year. The birds are strongly territorial on favoured beaches and usually the nests are well apart. On a typical stretch of Northland sandy beach strongly guarded territories are a half to three kilometres long. The nest is a bare depression or lined with only a few pieces of grass, weed or shell. Often it is beside a landmark such as a tuft of vegetation or a piece of driftwood. Nests on

In breeding plumage the New Zealand dotterel has variably reddish underparts.

estuarine sand and shell banks are often destroyed by spring tides or storms. In the Mason Bay dunes on Stewart Island, the birds nest in loose sand in the lee of marram grass. On the mountain tops, they nest in depressions in moss that are deep enough to stop the eggs blowing away in the frequent blizzards, usually in the lee of a rock or a thicket of prostrate manuka.

In both the North and Stewart Islands the normal clutch is three pyriform, buff or olive eggs, heavily blotched with black and dark brown. If the clutch is lost, the birds quickly make a new nest and lay

again. If the second clutch is lost, they sometimes lay yet again. Eggs buried by wind-blown sand are soon cleared. Laying extends from mid-September to mid-January, with a peak in October and November. Incubation lasts 28 to 32 days. Sitting is shared until the clutch is complete, but incubation by day is wholly by the female, which does not leave the nest to feed and is not fed by the male. The male remains at a distance and drives away intruders. Occasionally the male sits on the nest when the female has been disturbed by an intruder, and in one case the female then drove the male from the nest with a swooping dive. Some males have brood patches, but it is not known whether the male incubates while the female feeds at night.

The chicks leave the nest as soon as they are dry. The adults guard but do not feed the young. Usually the chicks move to the cover of vegetation until they fly. The fledging period is 29 to 51 days; the reasons for this wide variation are not known.

After breeding, some birds flock at major estuaries from February to April. These flocks contain both young and adults, but not all adults flock. In the region south of Auckland city, many birds wander locally in small parties throughout the year; others are sedentary. Why some birds flock, some wander, and others are sedentary is not known. Many flocking birds return to their breeding areas by early winter. In some localities, non-breeding birds and failed breeders outnumber the territorial pairs but seem to be tolerated by them.

When approached by a person or dog, another dotterel, or a bird such as an oystercatcher or gull, a New Zealand dotterel with eggs runs or flies noisily at the intruder, circling in the air with frequent *tsp-peep* calls. Birds draw an intruder away from young chicks by running in the low hunched posture of chicks, flying when it is safe to do so. If an intruder is persistent the dotterel feigns injury by trailing one wing and one leg, ruffling its feathers, drooping its tail and squealing. These displays are most intense when the eggs are close to hatching. One bird was seen dashing frantically about, even colliding with obstacles on the beach. When a New Zealand dotterel attacks other dotterels, it holds its head and body horizontal, puffs out its breast and flank feathers and rushes at its opponent, often calling *che-wee-wrrrr*.

Feeding preferences

It feeds by picking at the surface on ocean beaches on exposed wet sand, especially near stream mouths. As the tide rises it shifts to stream margins or the dry sand at the top of the beach or on flats among the dunes. Sometimes it forages in nearby fields where it remains feeding or resting well after other waders have left. In estuaries, it roosts on sandy spits, sandy or shelly islets, or on saltmarsh flats, typically in small loose groups not closely attached to another species. Usually it disperses widely to feed over the intertidal sand of a beach and even post-breeding flocks scatter in small parties to feed. Its food on wet sand and mud is molluscs and small crustaceans; on dry sand or short pasture, crickets, moths, other insects and sandhoppers.

Some authors group the New Zealand dotterel with the golden and grey plovers in the genus *Pluvialis*. But by structure, behaviour, and by its general and breeding habitat, it seems more likely to belong to the 'plains plover' group of *Charadrius,* which includes the large sand, oriental and black-fronted dotterels.   H.R.McK & B.D.H.

The nest of the New Zealand dotterel is a bare depression that may be lined with only a few bits of grass, weed or shell. The normal clutch is three eggs.

ENDEMIC

OTHER NAMES: *Tuturiwhatu pukunui, paturiwhata,* red-breasted dotterel.

SIZE: *270 mm.*

DESCRIPTION
ADULT: *All breeding plumages highly variable. In male upper feathers brown with dark brown shaft streaks and pale chestnut edges. Wing coverts grey-brown with pale chestnut or dull white edges. Flight feathers dark brown. Inner webs of inner primaries white, forming narrow wing stripe in flight. Innermost secondaries edged and tipped white. Central tail feathers dark brown; outer ones paler, ranging from white to buff with white tips. Forehead, eyebrow stripe, lores, chin and cheek dull white. Broad brown stripe from ear coverts to eye, sometimes extending narrowly towards bill. Underparts dull white, irregularly washed with chestnut brown to light red. Flank, lower*

belly and undertail coverts dull white. Bill almost as long as head, heavy, black. Legs grey to pale green-brown or yellow-brown. Female similar to male but usually edges of upper feathers less obviously chestnut; and underparts usually mainly white, with single reddish patch or light red wash on lower breast and belly. Some females as well coloured as males. In non-breeding plumage, sexes alike. Paler than in breeding plumage. Upper feathers brown, with whitish edges. Forehead, eyebrow stripe, most of lores and underparts white. Sometimes faint chestnut on underparts. Often partial band from side of neck to side of upper breast grey-brown, sometimes linked by scattered grey-brown speckles.
JUVENILE: *Similar to adult but more study needed. Paler brown above; cleaner white below. Rusty red flush on chicks reverts to white before they fly. Some develop partial grey-brown upper breast-band of many adults. Some immatures develop coloured underparts in first summer;*

most do not.
NESTLING: *Buff-white above, blotched and speckled with black. Forehead, side of face and underparts white, sometimes with rust wash on breast.*

MOULT
Little information available. Post-nuptial moult begins during incubation, so that body moult may occur from September to January. Non-breeding plumage seen mainly January to April or May. No information on wing moult. Pre-nuptial moult early May to August in the North Island; little known about South or Stewart Island birds. Post-juvenile moult unknown.

VOICE
Short penetrating trrt *or* prrp, *sharpening to* tirrit tirrit *in flight. On breeding territory, quiet* tsit *or* psit. *When approached by intruder* prrp *interspersed or replaced by high-pitched, liquid* tsp-peep *or* wheep *with sharply rising pitch. Plaintive squealing during*

distraction display. Che-wee-wrrrr *when chasing other dotterels.*

DISTRIBUTION
Breeds in the northern North Island and on Stewart Island; also on some offshore islands. Some birds winter on the Southland coast. A few may breed in the South Island highlands.

RECOGNITION

Large, thickset plover with large-looking head, large eye, and heavy black bill. Easily recognised in breeding plumage by varying amounts of chestnut on underparts and chestnut tone of brown upper parts. In non-breeding plumage, pale brown above and white below, often with traces of brown band on upper breast. Large sand dotterel smaller, more slender.

A quiet unhurried feeder, the ringed plover has the run-and-stop action typical of many plovers. There has been only one certain sighting in New Zealand.

Ringed Plover *Charadrius hiaticula* LINNAEUS,1758

TOWARDS THE END of the northern summer, many ringed plovers abandon their breeding grounds in the northern hemisphere to winter in the south. Birds of the subspecies *Charadrius hiaticula tundrae*, which nest in northern Scandinavia, Russia and Siberia, migrate to the coasts of Africa, the Persian Gulf, western India and the Maldive Islands. They migrate in groups of fewer than 12, sometimes even singly, and readily join flocks of other migrants. The occasional ringed plover that reaches Australasia is probably one of this subspecies that flew with a flock of tattlers, stints or other small waders. Records from India, Sri Lanka, Singapore, Australia, Fiji and New Zealand indicate that the ringed plover is a frequent wanderer. The one bird found in New Zealand—probably a young female—was seen at Firth of Thames from December 1970 to May 1971. Possibly a second ringed plover, apparently another juvenile, was also seen at Firth of Thames in November 1983.

During the northern winter, the ringed plover lives on sandy or muddy shores. A quiet, unhurried feeder, with the run-and-stop action typical of many plovers, it eats small crustaceans, molluscs, sandhoppers, worms, insects and their larvae. Tilting its body forward it snatches them from the surface. It feeds with other small waders. In Australia it mixes with Mongolian and red-capped dotterels, tattlers and stints. One New Zealand bird, however, chose to roost with wrybills, rather than banded dotterels.

B.D.H. & D.H.B.

VAGRANT

OTHER NAMES: *None.*

SIZE: *190 mm.*

DESCRIPTION

ADULT MALE: *Upper parts uniform dull brown. Primaries and secondaries blackish, largely white at base, producing with white-tipped coverts a clear but narrow white stripe in flight. Tail dark brown with black band near tip; white tip narrow or absent in centre and broadening outwards; outermost tail feathers white. Narrow black band across base of upper mandible, broadening to and below eye and across ear coverts. Ear coverts brown in non-breeding plumage. Forehead and narrow crescent beneath eye, white. Narrow orange eye-ring. Broad black band across forecrown. White patch from behind eye almost to nape. Chin and throat white, continuing back as white collar around hind neck. Across upper breast broad black band, widening at side of breast and narrowing around hind neck below white collar. Rest of underparts, including underwing, white. Bill short, orange (yellow or brown in winter) with black tip. Legs and feet orange-yellow (more yellow in winter), with slight web between outer and middle toes.*
ADULT FEMALE: *Like male but black markings of head and collar generally brown mixed with blackish and buff; forecrown often dull brown, without black band leaving complete white eyebrow stripe; breast-band narrower, black mixed with grey; eye-ring obscure, grey to yellowish; bill and legs less brightly coloured.*
JUVENILE: *Upper parts less uniform, feathers with dark bars near edges and light buff edges, giving buff tinge and slightly mottled head and scaly back. Dark bands of head, breast and collar brownish and not sharply defined. Whitish eyebrow stripe linked to white forehead. Breast-band narrower and often broken in centre. Bill blackish, with some yellow. Legs dull yellow.*

MOULT
Post-nuptial moult mostly after migration. In some birds, wing moult begins in October and is completed after migration; in others, delayed completely until after migration. Pre-nuptial body moult February and March. Post-juvenile moult August to January, with wing moult December to April.

VOICE
When disturbed, melodious, liquid rising too-ee, tu-li *or* coo-eep.

DISTRIBUTION
Breeds in Iceland, the Faroe Islands, the British Isles, northern Europe, Greenland, Canada, Russia and Siberia. Migrates south, straggling to New Zealand.

Mongolian Dotterel *Charadrius mongolus* PALLAS, 1776

STRAGGLER

OTHER NAMES: *Mongolian plover, lesser sand plover, short-billed sand plover.*

SIZE: *190 mm.*

DESCRIPTION
ADULT: *In non-breeding plumage very similar in appearance to large sand dotterel and banded dotterel. Smaller than large sand dotterel with darker plain grey-brown upper parts; lighter and greyer than banded dotterel. Narrow grey-brown band across breast, usually reduced to blunt-ended shoulder-tabs. Bill short, deep, black. Legs dark slate-grey, sometimes with greenish or yellowish tinge, darker than in large sand or banded dotterels. In breeding plumage, subspecies C. m. mongolus male very like large sand dotterel but more intensely coloured. Black lines of forehead narrower. Edge of forecrown, side of crown, hind neck and side of neck orange-buff, extending onto breast and flanks as a band about 4 cm broad. Some grey feathers also on sides. Black patch on ear coverts through and below eye to bill. Rest of underparts white. Female usually duller.*
JUVENILE: *Like non-breeding adult but upper feathers buff edged; buff wash on breast, becoming more grey-brown across upper edge and sides.*

FROM SEPTEMBER TO MAY the Mongolian dotterel is widespread along the coasts of Australia. In many years the occasional bird (or even two or three) straggles to New Zealand, most often to Manukau Harbour or Farewell Spit. It winters mainly on tidal mud flats and sheltered sandy flats, but also on rock flats, salt marshes and bare ground. A gregarious bird, it associates with other small to medium waders; in New Zealand, especially with the banded dotterel, wrybill and red-necked stint. It is rather tame, runs swiftly and, especially when alert, stands erect. There are several subspecies of the Mongolian dotterel. Those that reach Australasia are thought to be of the subspecies *Charadrius mongolus mongolus* which breeds in eastern and north-eastern Siberia.   B.D.H. & D.H.B.

Mongolian dotterels in breeding and non-breeding plumage.

MOULT
Little information available. Complete post-nuptial moult August to October, and is apparently rapid. Pre-nuptial moult begins in New Zealand February to May. Wintering birds generally remain in non-breeding plumage.

VOICE
Short clear pip-ip, drrit, krrik, twip or trik. Melodious kruit-kruit. Flock in flight calls continuous musical piping.

DISTRIBUTION
Two widely separated populations.

Southwestern population breeds in central Asia north of the Himalayas and winters on the coasts of the Persian Gulf, India, Sri Lanka, eastern Africa, islands of the Indian Ocean, the Malay Peninsula and western Indonesia. Northeastern population breeds in eastern and northeastern Siberia (not Mongolia) and winters in southeastern China, Hong Kong, Taiwan, Hainan, Indochinese countries, the Malay Peninsula, Micronesia, Indonesia south of Timor, the Philippines, New Guinea, the Solomon Islands, and Australia. Straggles to New Zealand and Norfolk Island.

RECOGNITION
In non-breeding plumage darker grey-brown above, with rather broad single shoulder tabs that sometimes extend high across breast to meet indistinctly in centre. Face and underparts white. Shorter bill, dark legs, erect posture and very rapid run may distinguish it from paler large sand dotterel. Darker around eye than similar banded dotterel.

Large Sand Dotterel *Charadrius leschenaultii* LESSON, 1826

The large sand dotterel is a rare migrant, seldom seen before October.

ALMOST EVERY YEAR, from about November to March, a few large sand dotterels winter in New Zealand. Singly, or in twos or threes, they have been recorded from the north of the North Island to the south of the South Island, but mostly at Firth of Thames. In the northern hemisphere they breed mainly in barren stony deserts and on high mountain plains. At their winter quarters they are rare inland and inhabit mud flats, sandy beaches and salt flats, especially the sandier parts of estuaries.

In New Zealand they are seen alone or with wrybills, banded dotterels, New Zealand dotterels, curlew sandpipers, red-necked stints, turnstones and golden plovers. They eat small crustaceans, molluscs, marine worms and insects. If disturbed when feeding, their flight is swift, low, and brief. After the danger has passed the birds often return to the same spot.   B.D.H. & D.H.B.

STRAGGLER

OTHER NAMES: *Greater sand plover, long-billed sand plover, Geoffroy's sand plover.*

SIZE: *220 mm.*

DESCRIPTION
ADULT: *In non-breeding plumage sexes alike. Upper parts light grey-brown with sandy tinge, feathers with narrow pale edges, especially wing coverts. Primaries and their coverts darker brown. In flight narrow white wing stripe, broadening on inner primaries. Tail grey-brown, darker in centre and near tip, narrowly tipped white; outermost feathers mostly white. Forehead and broad eyebrow stripe white. Grey-brown stripe from lores through and below eye, broadening behind eye and on side of neck, varying in extent and intensity according to state of moult but always dark about eye. Underparts and underwing white. Broad patch of grey to grey-brown wash extends from hind neck onto chest, often continuing as thin grey line across breast and meeting in centre. Eye large. Bill black, longer and heavier than that of Mongolian and banded dotterels. Legs usually grey. In breeding plumage upper parts warm brown, lightly washed with chestnut. Line across forecrown, side of crown, down side of neck and broadly across hind neck pale buff, slightly orange on forecrown, merging into broad band 15 to 40 mm deep of light orange-chestnut across upper breast. Chin, throat and rest of underparts white. Vertical black median stripe from bill to forehead. Large white patch on each side of forehead. Female usually duller without black line across forehead and vertical median stripe on face. Breast-band tawny buff and narrow, mixed with grey at sides of breast.*
JUVENILE: *Like non-breeding adult*

but upper feathers edged with buff and grey-brown shoulder tabs washed with buff.

MOULT
Little precise information available. Complete post-nuptial moult usually late June to September, occasionally later. Long-distance migrants may moult wings at wintering grounds. Some birds arrive in New Zealand in fading breeding plumage. Sometimes breeding plumage grown in February or March before leaving New Zealand. Juvenile may assume first-winter plumage by mid-August.

VOICE
Largely silent in winter quarters. Slowly repeated treep, trrt, or tir-rip. Quiet chirrirrip.

DISTRIBUTION
Breeding range not completely known. Breeds from Jordan, Syria and Turkey north to the southern Caspian Sea, eastwards across the southern USSR to Mongolia and probably northern Sinkiang. Possibly breeds in Arabia, Iran and on the Red Sea coast. Winters on the shores and islands of the Indian Ocean, the Persian Gulf, Madagascar, Indochina, the Philippines, New Guinea, Solomon Islands, Australia and, rarely, New Zealand.

RECOGNITION
Chunky plover distinctive in breeding plumage with chestnut breast-band, heavy black bill, and black-and-white face pattern. Larger than *mongolus*. In non-breeding plumage rather nondescript; hard to identify unless other species present for comparison. Always dark about eye. Seldom calls or bobs.

Oriental Dotterel *Charadrius veredus* GOULD, 1848

IN AUGUST THE FIRST ORIENTAL DOTTERELS arrive in northern Australia from their breeding grounds, but most arrive between early September and November. From October stragglers reach southeastern Australia and between November and March the occasional bird is seen in New Zealand. Usually only single birds are found here, but in December 1954 a flock of 10 was recorded in Firth of Thames.

In Mongolia the oriental dotterel breeds on stony plains, semi-desert hills and stony mountain terraces, sometimes far from water, and on the shores of bitter lakes. Its winter habitat in northern Australia is mainly inland black-soil plains including mud flats, claypans, airfields and open flats beside lakes and ponds. In New Zealand it has usually been found on estuaries, especially on dry mud or adjacent pasture.

It eats small insects, especially beetles, catching them with short quick runs and tilting its body forward to pick its prey from the ground. When uneasy it bobs its head. It runs and flies swiftly. Often solitary, it has also been seen in New Zealand with the least golden plover and the New Zealand dotterel. In Australia it also associates with pratincoles, the little whimbrel and the Mongolian dotterel.

Some authorities consider the oriental dotterel to be a subspecies of the Caspian plover *Charadrius asiaticus*. Recorded twice in northern Australia, the Caspian plover differs in its smaller size, proportionately shorter legs, darker upper parts on the male and a narrower black breast-band. In non-breeding plumage it is distinguished by its white rather than brown axillaries and underwing. B.D.H. & D.H.B.

The oriental dotterel is different in shape and stance from other dotterels.

STRAGGLER

OTHER NAMES: *Oriental plover, eastern sand plover, eastern long-legged sand plover.*

SIZE: *250 mm.*

DESCRIPTION
ADULT: *In non-breeding plumage sexes alike. Crown, mantle, back, rump, centre of tail and wing sandy brown with paler edges to fresh feathers. Hind neck paler than crown or mantle. Primaries and coverts dark brown; shaft of outer primary white. Tail darker towards tip, narrowly tipped with white, and outer web of outermost feather white. Broad eyebrow stripe, lores, chin, throat, and side of head cream or buff-white. Forehead cream or buff-white merging into brown on forecrown. Brown patch on ear coverts. Underparts dull white. Underwing and axillaries pale grey-brown. Broad breast-band pale buff-brown, slightly brighter in male. Bill short, straight, slender, black, but paler at base of lower mandible. Legs long for a plover, brown-yellow to dull yellow. In male breeding plumage, of third-year bird and older, upper parts and underwing as in non-breeding plumage. Head, neck, chin and throat white, except for grey-brown patch on hind-crown and ear coverts. Broad band (10–40 mm) across foreneck and breast rich dark chestnut, extending back onto side of breast, bordered below by broad black band. Belly and undertail white. Legs yellow. In second-year bird, crown, nape, hind neck and ear coverts grey-brown, paler on hind neck. Forehead, broad eyebrow stripe, lores, cheeks, chin and throat white. Breast-band less distinct and with black border reduced. Breeding plumage of female similar to second-year male on head and neck. Breast-band pale chestnut or buff-brown to grey-brown, with no black border.*
JUVENILE: *Like non-breeding adult*

but upper feathers broadly edged rufous-buff to pale buff, producing scalloped effect. Nape paler than rest of upper parts. Breast darker with rufous tinge.

MOULT
Little known. Post-nuptial moult probably begins in July and may be completed after migration. Wing moult begins on breeding grounds, is suspended, and completed after migration by October or November. Pre-nuptial body moult probably occurs mainly on wintering grounds. Post-juvenile body moult not known. Juvenile wing moult at end of first year. Immature males take 3 years to develop full adult plumage, which is unusual for plovers.

VOICE
Not recorded in New Zealand. Sharp piping klink. *Loud* chip-chip-chip. *Soft* tsip *or* tick.

DISTRIBUTION
Breeds in Mongolia, east to northwest Manchuria. Common only in Mongolia. Winters mainly in northern Australia. A few pass through or winter in the Malay Peninsula, the Philippines, southern Indonesia and New Guinea. Straggles to New Zealand— recorded at Firth of Thames, Parengarenga, Ninety Mile Beach, Ruakaka, Waipu, Kaipara and Manukau Harbours, Nelson, Lake Wainono, Greymouth and the Kermadec Islands.

RECOGNITION
Erect stance with head held high when not feeding. Nondescript in non-breeding plumage: plain buff-brown above, often with prominent paler edges to feathers, and off-white below with grey-brown breast-band. Folded wings extend beyond tail.

Black-fronted Dotterel *Charadrius melanops* VIEILLOT, 1818

BEFORE THE 1950S there were no records of the black-fronted dotterel in New Zealand. Now it is well established in both the North and the South Islands. It breeds in the southern half of the North Island south of the Rangitikei River in the west and the Esk River in the east. In the South Island small groups breed on the Wairau and Awatere Rivers in Marlborough; on the Opihi and Orari Rivers in Canterbury; and on Manuherikia River in Otago. The local abundance of the species depends closely on the availability of suitable feeding sites on the rivers during the breeding season. There are few records of birds breeding away from rivers; in spite of the numbers in the main breeding districts, remarkably few birds appear to straggle elsewhere. Possibly other small breeding populations exist, however, as this unobtrusive and sedentary species often goes undetected until it is firmly settled in a new area.

In Australia it is common and widely distributed, especially inland, but also in the extreme north of the Northern Territory and Queensland and inhabits the muddy edges of lagoons and swamps, dams, river pools and slow-moving waters. In the interior it may be found on any mud patch or waterhole on rivers and streams, and on muddy tracks and shallow ditches beside little-used roads. In New Zealand it lives on shingle riverbeds and feeds beside side channels, pools and backwaters with fine wet mud.

It picks its prey from the surface or probes its bill into the mud, feeding back and forth on the same stretch of mud for as long as it is wet. During droughts it forages among wet stones at the river's edge, especially at shallow riffles and where algal mats are stranded. Little is known about its food. Earwigs, grasshoppers, beetles and their larvae, weevils, caterpillars, ants, snails, and seeds have been recorded in Australia. In the New Zealand winter, feeding on earthworms and flies

has been seen, but its main foods are not known.

Its winter distribution differs little from that of the breeding season. When the rivers become too high or, as in Otago, are frozen, the birds move to muddy places nearby and return to the rivers when the waters fall again. They may feed at wheel tracks, in floodwater pools, cowshed effluent pits, sewage and abattoir settling ponds with a mud or sludge surface, and on coastal freshwater lagoons. They are rare on estuaries and never seen on beaches.

Courtship and breeding

The breeding season extends from September to March but varies according to district. The start of nesting depends on river conditions and few eggs are laid before rivers have settled to normal summer levels. The preferred site is the top of a shingle ridge or terrace within 10 to 30 m of a backwater or pool for feeding. Only one pair feeds at each pool so pairs are well spaced along a river. The shallow nest scrape is lined with tiny pebbles and perhaps a few scraps of wood, grass or sheep droppings.

The birds lay three eggs, sometimes two or four (and late in the season, sometimes one), loosely on the surface. The eggs are oval to pyriform, cream or stone, but so thickly marked with dark brown, light brown and grey speckles and fine irregular lines as to look khaki. They are laid about 24 hours apart. The incubation period needs further study; however both sexes share incubation, apparently for 25 to 28 days. The eggs of a clutch seem to hatch on the same day. The chicks keep together, guarded by one of the parents, at the feeding pool close to the nest-site. The other parent is usually well out of sight. Unless disturbed, the chicks fledge within the territory. The fledging period is not known but is 27 to 40 days in Otago. Freshly flying juveniles have

The black-fronted dotterel, a self-introduced species from Australia, was first recorded in 1954.

been seen in Wairarapa from late December to March.

Both on its breeding territory and among winter feeding flocks, an attacking bird sprints at an opponent with tightly compressed plumage, horizontal back and lowered head. The opponent may turn aside, flee, or spring into the air while the attacker sprints beneath. The attack may be followed by a leap-frog flutter over the opponent, or both may stand facing each other with head and tail down, mantle and scapular feathers raised, or in an erect stiff-legged posture, sometimes with wings slightly drooped. Attacks are often preceded by *ree-ree-ree* calls. In group confrontations, two to five birds—both adults and immatures—face inwards or slightly sideways and give loud *ree-ree-ree* calls followed by a long period of unmoving silence.

During courtship, the presumed male circles widely over its territory with stiff wing-beats, calling *rrrr-reep*. Before they mate one or both call *ree-ree-ree*. Then the male sprints towards the female, high-steps beside her and mounts her. Afterwards, they preen or move off to feed.

If an intruder approaches a bird on the nest, the sitting bird leaves the nest and runs or flies close to the water's edge and pretends to feed. Some stay on the nest and then explode into the air with a twittering alarm call and a flurry of wings. Generally, both birds stay away from the nest area until the intruder has gone, or one stands or crouches at a distance with its back turned and twists its head to watch; it may false-feed and false-brood as it gradually moves away. Before and during incubation, the bird stands with its back to the intruder, swaying the rear of its body slowly from side to side or, more often, depressing its tail and fanning it slowly open and shut, partly opening each wing alternately. In late incubation or during chick-rearing the bird stands or runs at a distance, uttering *pit* calls and bobbing its head; or it may fly past the intruder and then sprint away.   B.D.H. & D.H.B.

NATIVE

OTHER NAME: *Black-fronted plover.*

SIZE: *180 mm.*

DESCRIPTION

ADULT: *Sexes alike. Upper parts brown with chestnut tinge. Dark brown centres and light brown or whitish edges to feathers give dappled appearance to upper surface and vertical pale streaks to folded wing. Scapulars rich dark reddish chestnut, forming conspicuous longitudinal stripe between mantle and folded wing. Primaries and tips of secondaries black. Rest of secondaries white, forming in flight tapering white bar. Upper tail coverts reddish chestnut. Tail feathers blackish brown grading to black at end and narrowly white at tip; outermost tail feather white; next feather blackish with broad white tip that forms 'eye-spot' when displayed. Forehead black, extending as broad black band through eye and round base of hind neck. Triangular black patch from forehead onto crown. White band above black extends round nape, above eye onto side of forehead and sometimes forms tapering border to black crown stripe. Broad black Y-shaped chest-band tapers up to and across shoulder to link with black on side of neck. Underparts white with primaries and tips of secondaries dusky. Iris brown, eye with bright red ring. Bill bright orange-red with black tip. Legs and feet flesh pink. Claws black.*
JUVENILE: *When first fledged lacks black and white bands, chestnut scapulars and upper tail coverts, red bill and eye-ring. Upper feathers including tail coverts light brown, with dark brown edges, giving scaly effect. Crown lightly mottled with white. Forehead white. Greater wing coverts lack pale edges so folded wing lacks vertical pale streaks. Wing pattern in flight as adult. Central tail feathers have buff, occasionally bright yellow, tips. Bill brown. Legs light pinkish brown, claws brown. Several weeks after fledging, black bands appear, especially that through eye, but forehead remains white. Bill brown with darker tip and reddish base. In final stages, resembles adult plumage but black forehead, median crown stripe and chest-band may be mottled; scapulars indistinct or absent; and upper tail coverts may be brown or with chestnut tips. Often bill and eye-ring change last.*
NESTLING: *Upper parts tawny, sparingly speckled and blotched with black. Underparts white. Black along leading edge of wing and on lower back and tail forms border between upper and under surfaces. Broad black patches on centre of back. Band on hind neck white above and black below, the black extending to eye and sometimes to 2 black patches on upper forehead. Small black patch on lower forehead and another behind gape. Black on back of head often tapers indistinctly to rear or centre of crown. Bill dark grey. Legs pale flesh.*

MOULT
Adult moult not known. Post-juvenile body moult seems to begin soon after fledging, and moulting immatures seen November to July.

VOICE
Sharp high-pitched pit *or* pip. *Feeding flocks on winter gathering places call soft* chip, *which sounds like quiet chattering. Vigorous rippling* ree-ree-ree-ree-ree *used as aggressive call all year and to communicate with mate. Sharp shrill twittering alarm call when flushed suddenly. Rolling languid chirring* rrrr-reep, *apparently by male when flying in wide circles over breeding territory and occasionally on ground.*

DISTRIBUTION
Widely distributed and common throughout Australia, especially inland. Sedentary but nomadic in response to changes in water. One Indian record. First recorded in New Zealand in 1954. Found mainly in the southern half of the North Island. Small numbers in Marlborough, Canterbury, Otago and Southland.

RECOGNITION

Small slim dotterel with horizontal stance. Smaller than banded dotterel. Y-shaped black chest-band. Black-and-white pattern on head. Red bill with black tip. Red eye-ring. Dark chestnut shoulder stripe. In flight, conspicuous white wing patch and black primaries. Languid, slightly undulating flight, each wing-beat a deep flick.

New Zealand Shore Plover *Thinornis novaeseelandiae* (Gmelin, 1789)

The rare New Zealand shore plover, usually a sedentary bird, is now confined to South East Island.

ONCE FOUND ON MAINLAND New Zealand and all over the Chatham Islands, the New Zealand shore plover is now confined to South East Island in the Chathams. There the population has varied from about 70 pairs in 1937, to between 68 and 82 pairs in 1972-75 and to more than 100 birds now.

On the mainland the New Zealand shore plover lived on sandy beaches, especially near river mouths. With no sandy beaches on South East Island it inhabits salt-swept turf and herbaceous plants in bays between headlands. Shore plover also range over the rockshore platform and feed on small crustaceans found in tide pools.

Adult New Zealand shore plover are sedentary and rarely move away from their part of the coast. When not breeding they often roost and feed in small groups. By September most birds form pairs, although occasionally three birds are seen together. Each pair defends the area around its nest and even excludes other plovers from its feeding area. Territories range from 0.2 to one hectare in size.

The bulky nest is usually hidden in a hole or crevice among boulders, in a muttonbird burrow, hollow log or dense ground vegetation among buttressed tree roots. The birds lay from September to the end of the year. The eggs are usually olive brown with brown blotches, spots and lines all over them. Three-egg clutches are more common than two.   H.A.B.

Wrybill *Anarhynchus frontalis* Quoy & Gaimard, 1830

NO BIRD IN THE WORLD has a beak like the wrybill. The last third of its long bill turns to the bird's right at an angle of 15 to 22 degrees. The upper mandible is slightly broader than the lower one and overlaps it on the outer side of the curve. Inside the curve the two halves do not meet so that seen from the right, the bill has a spoon-like shape.

On the seashore and at the edge of estuaries the wrybill wades across the mud, sweeping its bill down and to the right. With this spooning motion it traps tiny crustaceans. Each movement causes some crustaceans to move and these are then captured by the next sweep. The wrybill then uses its bill to sieve the animals from the water. Feeding like this it makes as many as 100 feeding movements a minute. At a much slower rate—as few as 10 a minute—it stalks and grabs large polychaete worms and small crabs. It also probes in the mud for worms and small bivalves. On riverbeds it pecks and probes under and between stones, searching for aquatic insect larvae, small fish and eggs, as well as carabid beetles, dipterans and spiders.

It breeds between latitudes 42°S and 45°S in the South Island, mainly in the mid to upper reaches of sea-flowing shingle rivers and at deltas which feed into lakes. Its winter range lies almost entirely north of 38°S. In mid-winter about half the population is found on the western and southern coasts of Firth of Thames. Another thousand or so birds are located in Manukau Harbour, with 400 to 500 in Kaipara Harbour and smaller flocks in Tauranga, Whangarei, Houhora and Parengarenga Harbours. A few birds are found at some of the smaller estuaries, such as Ruakaka, Mangawhai, Whangateau, Tairua and the Tamaki at Auckland, and occasionally on sandy ocean beaches. Small flocks occur regularly at estuaries further south in the country, such as Porangahau, Muriwai, Manawatu, Lake Onohe and Nelson, and at some Southland coastal sites. Normally flocks spend most of the winter in one place. Birds that breed in the same area do not necessarily winter together.

The earliest fledging wrybills begin to leave their breeding places in late November and start to arrive in the north a month later. The adults and the rest of the fledglings move off in late January or February when breeding finishes. The return flight south begins in early August with the peak of departures in the middle of the month. Between five and ten per cent of non-breeders remain in the North Island while other yearlings migrate south in September and October. Breeding birds fly direct to the rivers, while non-breeders appear on coastal lagoons and rivermouths before moving up the rivers.

At its wintering grounds in the North Island the wrybill lives on mud flats. It feeds in soft silty mud with a surface film of water. During this season it is a highly gregarious bird and roosts in flocks away from other species. Close to Auckland city several hundred birds roost on an industrial reclamation site in an inlet of the Manukau Harbour, flying across the isthmus to feed in the Tamaki Estuary on the Pacific side. At Firth of Thames and south Manukau, flocks roost on shell banks or paddocks next to lowtide flats.

Birds within a flock are often aggressive to each other. One bird will run at another with its body flattened, giving a chirring sound. Usually the other bird runs away or jumps in the air. The wrybill flies with rapid wing-beats and flocks perform spectacular aerial displays, particularly just before moving south. Birds feeding on mud flats in winter can be distinguished at a distance by a steady movement involving a rapid twisting and dabbing motion of the head. Often when birds in a flock are disturbed they remain stationary or hop rather than fly away.

At the breeding grounds

When the flocks return south they disperse into breeding pairs. They nest on greywacke shingle riverbeds, which camouflages them well. They prefer areas free of plants and close to water, preferably on the high points of bare islands or banks. Often they nest at or near the previous site and pairs stay together from year to year. Each pair maintains a separate territory. Occasionally nests are as close as 40 m but usually they are separated by several hundred metres.

The birds perform various displays to establish their territory and expel intruders. Birds from adjacent territories move close together

along an invisible line between their two nests. Sometimes they circle each other or 'leapfrog'. Often, a resident bird drives out an intruder by running at it in a horizontal posture calling a chirring sound. The run ends either with a peck at the opponent or in an upright display in which the breast expands. A dominant bird intimidates another by crouching in a hollow and moving its head and bill as if trying to regurgitate. Or it attacks with its beak, wings and claws. Submissive birds crouch and turn away or bob up and down quickly. Sexual displays often involve these aggressive displays. Before mating the male runs with his body horizontal or 'goose-steps'. If the female is receptive, she crouches and the pair mate.

When chicks are threatened they 'freeze' in response to loud adult calls and are extremely difficult to locate. When aerial predators such as black-backed gulls are in the vicinity, an adult which is brooding chicks quickly moves away from its young. Lone birds bow with their heads close to the ground and their tails pointed to the sky as gulls fly overhead.

Birds attain adult breeding plumage in their first year but they do not breed until they are at least two. On the Rakaia River the first eggs are laid in late August or early September. The nest is a shallow scrape lined with several hundred small pebbles. During courtship the male hollows a sandy patch between the stones with its breast. It then flicks pebbles into it or carries them in its crop and regurgitates them.

The two eggs are pyriform, pale grey tinged with blue or green, and evenly peppered with minute dark brown and pale blotches, spots and lines. Occasionally they appear completely brown because of heavy blotching. They are laid about 48 hours apart and incubation begins at or just before the second egg is laid. Both sexes incubate, but mostly the female, usually for 30 or 31 days. The chicks hatch either together or up to 36 hours apart. The first remains in the nest until the second hatches, then both are led to a nearby backwater, riffle or other suitable feeding area. Though guarded by adults, the chicks gather all their own food. Fledging takes approximately 28 days, after which the chicks leave the parental area for short periods, before they move off the river in small groups. Normally the parents nest again and lay a second clutch shortly after the first brood fledges. 　　　　J.R.H.

The wrybill has a distinctive bill and is well camouflaged among the greywacke riverbed shingle where it breeds. The nest, initially formed in courtship by the male, is a shallow scrape lined with several hundred small pebbles.

Far-eastern Curlew *Numenius madagascariensis* (Linnaeus, 1766)

MIGRANT

OTHER NAMES: *Eastern curlew, long-billed curlew, Australian curlew.*

SIZE: *610 mm.*

DESCRIPTION
ADULT: *Sexes alike, female with longer bill on average. Upper parts dark brown, mottled with buff. Crown, nape streaked dark brown and buff. Tail, upper tail coverts barred dark brown and buff. Whitish stripe above eye; chin, throat white; sides of face, foreneck whitish, streaked brown. Other underparts pale dingy buff with long brown streaks—broadest on breast—and irregular brown bars. Axillaries, underwing heavily marked with dark and pale brown bars. Bill dark brown, pinkish at base of lower mandible, downcurved and up to 5 times as long as head. Iris brown. Legs bluish grey or slate.*
JUVENILE: *Upper parts with extensive buff-white edgings; underparts more finely streaked.*

MOULT
Post-nuptial complete moult, mainly August to October. Wing moult delayed until after migration, completed before March. Pre-nuptial body moult starts before departure from winter quarters, continues during migration, and is completed on breeding grounds.

VOICE
Loud repeated melancholy croo-lee *or* ker-lee *with second syllable rising in pitch, uttered in flight or on ground. Clear* whoip *and series of widely spaced* keep *notes in flight also recorded in New Zealand.*

DISTRIBUTION
Breeds in eastern and northeastern Siberia. In Australia, widely distributed on all coasts October to February, most abundantly in the east and south. Regular small summer flocks Parengarenga Harbour, probably Kaipara Harbour, Firth of Thames, Farewell Spit, Southland coastal lagoons. Smaller parties Kaituna, Kawhia, Manawatu estuary. Other birds from far north to Stewart Island. A few stay in winter.

The far-eastern curlew, its bill up to five times the length of its head.

SIGHTINGS OF FAR-EASTERN CURLEWS have increased steadily over the past 30 years, but the summer total in New Zealand probably still does not reach 100, compared with the thousands that migrate to Australia. The biggest flock seen was of 37 birds, at Farewell Spit, in 1962. Parties arrive on the Northland coast in August, and at the southernmost localities by September. Numbers continue to increase to November and sometimes December, and usually dwindle in March. Few birds are seen by April. Some winter over, however.

In the Soviet far east this species breeds on open marshes, bare boggy ground and floodplains. In wintering grounds it is almost exclusively a bird of open estuarine mud flats, which it probes deeply. A crab abundant in the mud, *Helice crassa*, is believed to be the main food. If several curlews are in one locality, they generally keep together and may roost apart from other species. But a single curlew may feed and roost with a flock of godwits or knots. If so, it is obvious by its size and bill length. B.D.H. & D.H.B.

Bristle-thighed Curlew *Numenius tahitiensis* (Gmelin, 1789)

The bristle-thighed curlew, a rare straggler to the Kermadec Islands, usually winters in central and eastern Polynesian islands.

VAGRANT

OTHER NAMES: *None.*

SIZE: *480 mm.*

DESCRIPTION
ADULT: *Sexes alike, female averaging larger. Two broad dark brown stripes on head, separated by light buff median stripe and bordered by light buff eyebrow stripe. Narrow dark brown line through eye. Hind neck light buff, streaked blackish brown. Upper parts dark brown, strongly marbled with rufous buff spots and notches. Lower back, rump almost uniform dark brown. Upper tail coverts uniform bright rufous buff or tawny; tail light rufous buff, barred brown. Primaries and coverts blackish with paler shafts; innermost primaries and secondaries spotted rufous buff. Sides of head and neck, lower throat, foreneck, upper breast pale rufous buff, streaked dark brown. Chin, upper throat, lower breast, abdomen, undertail coverts whitish. Underwing rufous buff, axillaries broadly barred and coverts heavily spotted dark brown. Bill pinkish brown grading to dark grey towards tip, long, downcurved. Iris brown. Legs light bluish grey. Shafts of thigh feathers and often of some belly feathers lengthened into white bristles, visible only at close quarters.*

MOULT
Little information available. Presumably similar to whimbrels, with wing-moult after migration.

VOICE
Drawn-out whistle, variously pee-ow, tee-a-wee, kiu-vee, *often given in flight.*

DISTRIBUTION
Breeds only in northern Alaskan upland tundra; winters mostly on islands of central and eastern Polynesia, straggling west to Japan and south to the Kermadec Islands. Migrations poorly documented, but southward migrations August and September.

ANNUAL MIGRATIONS NORMALLY bring the bristle-thighed curlew no closer to New Zealand than the Cook Islands. Three vagrants have been recorded in the Kermadec group however—one on Macauley Island in 1966 and two on Raoul Island in 1972. One of the latter was found dead; the other was in a party of Asiatic whimbrels.

When breeding, this bird is unwary and approachable, though it is aggressive to other wader species and often to those of its own species. It tends to spread out to feed. It feeds by probing in mud or in reef crevices, and breaks open molluscs and crabs by dashing them on a rock with a left-to-right swing of the bill. B.D.H. & D.H.B.

Whimbrel *Numenius phaeopus* (Linnaeus, 1758)

Two whimbrel subspecies visit New Zealand. The Asiatic form *Numenius phaeopus variegatus* is an annual migrant, though its numbers total well under 100. Birds start arriving early in September, in small parties or in ones and twos along with godwit flocks. Most return to their Siberian breeding grounds in March or April. Flocks sometimes include vagrants of *N.p. hudsonicus*, the American form seen almost every year since 1964.

Whimbrels in New Zealand usually frequent estuarine mud flats. They sometimes feed on sandy beaches, however, and roosting flocks often choose dunes or dry sand at the top of a beach. A flock of 19 Asiatic whimbrels and one American whimbrel were seen sunning in a depression among the sandhills of Farewell Spit; they lay with their bodies flat, necks stretched forward, wings spread and rumps exposed. Whimbrels in ones or twos, roosting among godwits, reveal themselves by their wariness. Their heads and necks are raised at the first sign of intrusion, and they take flight when other species around them are unperturbed.

Whimbrels feed by snatching at the surface or by deep probing. Their curved bills are especially suited to the slanting burrows of crabs and marine worms. The prey is grasped, perhaps with a twisting motion, pulled out, sometimes battered or shaken, raised high and swallowed with a backward toss of the head. Small molluscs are also taken and, on land, insects and their larvae.   B.D.H. & D.H.B.

MIGRANT
Asiatic Whimbrel
N.p. variegatus (Scopoli, 1786).

STRAGGLER
American Whimbrel
N.p. hudsonicus Latham, 1790.

OTHER NAMES: *Little curlew, eastern whimbrel (Asiatic); Hudsonian curlew (American).*

SIZE: *410 mm.*

DESCRIPTION
ADULT: *Subspecies very similar.*
Asiatic whimbrel:*Sexes alike, female averaging larger. Crown dark brown with narrow buff-white stripe down centre; broad buff-white stripe over eye; grey-brown stripe from bill to eye, continuing less distinctly to ear coverts; side of head, whole neck pale brown with darker streaks. Mantle, scapulars dark grey-brown, wing coverts paler; secondaries pale grey-brown notched with white; primaries blackish brown, barred white on inner webs. Lower back, rump white, thickly mottled with brown bars and spots; upper tail coverts whitish, barred brown. Tail grey-brown with broad dark-brown bars. Chin white; throat, foreneck, breast pale buff, thickly streaked dark brown. Sides of body, flanks pale buff with dark brown transverse bars. Abdomen, undertail coverts white; undertail coverts irregularly barred; axillaries, underwing white, heavily barred dark brown. Bill dark brown, pinkish at base, downcurved, twice as long as head. Iris brown. Legs light bluish or greenish grey.*

American whimbrel: *Lower back, rump and upper tail coverts the same dark grey-brown, with pale feather edges, as the mantle and scapulars. Underparts darker, more buff brown especially on sides and flanks. Ground colour of axillaries and underwing sandy buff rather than whitish, broadly barred dark brown.*

MOULT
Little known. Post-nuptial complete moult presumably starts July to August with body feathers and extends to January; wing moult after migration. Pre-nuptial partial moult February to May.

VOICE
Rapid, musical, even tetti-tetti-tetti-ter *or* titti-titti-titti-tit, *usually in flight.*

DISTRIBUTION
Asiatic whimbrel breeds in northeastern Siberia, winters commonly from southeastern China and Southeast Asia through to Australia. American whimbrel breeds in Alaska and northwest Canada, winters on Pacific coasts from southern California southwards to Peru and Chile. Regular small summer flocks of Asiatic whimbrels, sometimes including 1 or 2 American whimbrels, at Whangarei, Kaipara, Manukau and Ohiwa Harbours, Firth of Thames, Farewell Spit; some birds attached to godwit flocks at other coastal locations. A few winter over.

RECOGNITION

Size and general colouring of Asiatic whimbrel resembles godwit, but darker with downcurved bill and striped crown.

The Asiatic whimbrel is distinguished from the American whimbrel by its pale back and rump.

Little Whimbrel · Numenius minutus GOULD,1841

IN MOST YEARS at least one little whimbrel is identified in New Zealand. However, it may be present, unnoticed, in greater numbers; and some birds have probably wintered over instead of returning to Siberia. In New Zealand the little whimbrel is usually found alone but it has been seen in association with least golden plovers, New Zealand dotterels and pied stilts, mostly on coastal mud flats —usually the drier or more sparsely vegetated parts —as well as pools and saltmarshes. Birds studied in Australia ate insects and seeds.

The little whimbrel is considered by some authorities to be a subspecies of its close relative, the almost extinct Eskimo curlew *Numenius borealis*, which used to breed in vast numbers in far northern Canada and winter in South America. For this reason the little whimbrel is sometimes classified as *Numenius borealis minutus*.　　　B.D.H. & D.H.B.

STRAGGLER

OTHER NAMES: *Little curlew, pygmy curlew.*

SIZE: *330 mm.*

DESCRIPTION
ADULT: *Sexes alike, female averaging larger. Upper surface blackish brown mottled with buff spots and feather margins. Crown blackish with pale buff stripe through centre and buff stripe over eye. Wing blackish brown, secondaries paler; coverts edged buff, except on leading edge. Feathers of lower back, rump, upper tail coverts blackish brown, mottled and tipped whitish. Tail brownish grey with narrow blackish bars. Chin, throat whitish. Sides of face, foreneck, breast light buff with brown streaks on breast, especially at sides. Abdomen, undertail whitish. Underwing pale buff with dark brown bars. Bill blackish brown,* *flesh pink at base, slender, less downcurved than whimbrel's, 1½ times as long as head. Iris brown. Legs blue-grey.*
JUVENILE: *Buff spots and edges on feathers of upper parts paler and so more contrasting with dark brown of feather centres than in adults.*

MOULT
Little is known. Post-nuptial body moult mostly before migration; completed, together with wing and tail moult, after migration. Pre-nuptial body moult apparently completed by mid-April. Juvenile body moult partly before migration and partly on wintering grounds.

VOICE
Soft musical te-te-te *among feeding flocks. When flushed, harsh* klee-klee-klee, tchoo-tchoo-tchoo *or* weep...weep *in slow succession, repeated after pause.*

DISTRIBUTION
Breeding range not well known. Breeds in mountainous regions of central and eastern Siberia and believed also to breed elsewhere in same general area. Winters in northern Australia. Straggles irregularly to New Zealand.

RECOGNITION
Smaller than whimbrel, crown much less prominently striped, bill shorter, less curved. Size and colouring of least golden plover but distinguished by bill, slim striped head, long neck, blackish primaries, longer legs, erect stance. In flight, upper surface uniformly brown but flight feathers and leading edge blackish.

An irregular straggler, the little whimbrel is recorded mainly in coastal areas, on mud flats and tidal pools.

Asiatic Black-tailed Godwit · Limosa limosa melanuroides GOULD,1846

THE FIRST BLACK-TAILED GODWIT recorded in New Zealand stayed by the Firth of Thames from August 1952 to January 1956. A male, it adopted a southern hemisphere moult cycle and did not associate with other birds arriving later. At least one or two birds have been recorded in most years since, mostly beside harbours and estuaries, and two have been recorded at the Auckland Islands. The biggest parties seen—up to six birds—were in Firth of Thames. Sightings are generally made from October to March. Birds seen as early as August or as late as May were probably wintering over. The species may associate with the bar-tailed godwit but is often found alone or with pied stilts on pools or sodden pastures away from tidal flats. It will feed in deeper water than the bar-tailed godwit, with its head fully submerged.

The habitat of the eastern race is known only from open marshy areas of grass and moss with small bushes. It winters on tidal mud flats and also favours the mud and salt marsh of estuaries, creeks among mangroves and, less often, inland marshes and muddy shores of lakes. Though mainly coastal in New Zealand, the species has been recorded 30 km inland at Lake Wairarapa.　　　B.D.H. & D.H.B.

The Asiatic black-tailed godwit, a frequent straggler to New Zealand, is often found on pools or sodden pastures, alone or with pied stilts.

STRAGGLER

OTHER NAME: *Eastern black-tailed godwit.*

SIZE: *380 mm.*

DESCRIPTION
ADULT: *In non-breeding plumage sexes alike, female averaging larger. Upper parts brown-grey grading to blackish brown on lower back, rump. Upper tail coverts and base of tail white; tips of central coverts and rest of tail black; tail narrowly and indistinctly tipped white. Primaries, secondaries and coverts blackish brown; tips of greater coverts white; bases of secondaries white, increasing inwards forming broad wing stripe. Chin, eyebrow stripe whitish. Head, neck, throat, breast, flanks light brown-grey. Abdomen, undertail coverts white. Axillaries white, underwing white with black margins. Bill pinkish grading to blackish at tip, brown along culmen ridge, long, straight or slightly upcurved towards tip. Iris dark brown. Legs slate grey, often with greenish tinge. In breeding plumage male has rufous chestnut head, neck, upper breast and flanks; feathers of mantle and scapulars blackish brown with broad chestnut edges and scattered white tips; broad brown or black transverse bars on breast and flanks, fewer on belly and undertail. Eyebrow stripe indistinct or absent. Bill bright orange-yellow grading to black at tip. Female* *breeding plumage variable—similar to male but head, mantle and scapulars as in non-breeding plumage but with chestnut feather-edges; underparts paler, mixed with grey and white, fewer brown bars.*
JUVENILE: *Similar to non-breeding adult but dark brown above, feathers edged pale buff; head, neck, breast grey, tinged rufous.*

VOICE
Sometimes quiet kuk *or* kik *when feeding; loud* wicka-wicka-wicka *or* kip-kip-kip *in flight. Generally silent on wintering grounds.*

DISTRIBUTION
Breeding range probably from northwestern Mongolia eastwards through northwestern Manchuria to Sea of Okhotsk. Winters from eastern India, parts of Southeast Asia to New Guinea, northern Australia and New Zealand.

RECOGNITION
Slim, greyish godwit with straight or near-straight bill. Proportionately longer legs than other godwits, with feet projecting noticeably beyond tail; white underwing; white wing stripe and bold black and white tail bands conspicuous in flight.

Hudsonian Godwit *Limosa haemastica* (Linnaeus, 1758)

STRAGGLER

OTHER NAME: *American black-tailed godwit.*

SIZE: *380 mm.*

DESCRIPTION

ADULT: *Sexes alike in non-breeding plumage, female averaging larger. Like Asiatic black-tailed godwit but wing stripe narrower, less sharply defined, white band across upper tail coverts narrower, axillaries and underwing blackish. Bill slightly but distinctly upcurved towards tip. Legs light bluish grey. In breeding plumage, male's head and neck grey-brown with buff or rufous tinge and blackish shaft streaks, broadest on crown. Clear whitish stripe over eye;* dark line from bill to eye. Feathers of mantle, scapulars black with whitish edges and reddish spots and notches. Lower back, rump, tail, upper wing as in non-breeding. Chin whitish. Throat to undertail deep chestnut with blackish streaks on throat and foreneck and blackish transverse bars on rest of underparts, most heavily on flanks and undertail, sometimes absent from centre of breast. Basal half of bill becomes yellow, then bright orange during courtship period. Breeding female's upper parts duller; underparts irregularly barred blackish, chestnut and white, largely brown and white on flanks. Bill flesh pink with purplish tinge on basal half.*
JUVENILE: *Darker above than non-breeding adult, feathers with buff* edges and tail narrowly tipped buff. Crown heavily streaked blackish. Throat, foreneck, breast pale grey with pale buff wash extending to rest of underparts. Abdomen white.*

MOULT
Post-nuptial complete moult starts with body moult in July; wing moult delayed until September–December on wintering grounds. Pre-nuptial partial moult starts early March on wintering grounds. Post-juvenile body moult probably begins in October. First wing moult end of first northern summer.

VOICE
Low ta-it *or* ta-wit *in flight; sometimes sharp* kit-kee. *Generally silent in wintering grounds.*

DISTRIBUTION
Breeds mainly in central northern Canada, perhaps Alaska; most birds winter in South America.

HUDSONIAN GODWITS SEEN in New Zealand, in ones or twos nearly every year, are of uncertain origin. They may represent a small population breeding in Alaska. Some birds, mainly younger ones, may be caught up in the southwestern movement of bar-tailed godwits from the same region. Birds from the major breeding ranges, farther east in Canada, migrate to remote coasts of southern Chile, Argentina and south to the Falkland Islands. The species has not yet been recorded in Australia, neither has it been recorded anywhere between North America and New Zealand.

Until 1940 the Hudsonian godwit was recorded only at Lake Ellesmere. Since then it has appeared at most of the harbours and estuaries frequented by other migratory wading birds. The most favoured localities have been Manukau Harbour, the Manawatu River estuary and Southland. Birds are seen mainly from October to March—occasionally late September or April—but single birds have wintered over. The New Zealand habitats and habits of the species, and presumably its diet, are similar to those of other godwits. It is usually seen with bar-tailed godwit flocks. B.D.H. & D.H.B.

The Hudsonian godwit is a frequent straggler to New Zealand, seen mainly from October to March. It is thought that, after breeding, it passes in a narrow path down the west coast of Hudson Bay directly to South America and its wintering grounds, which are located mainly in the far south.

Eastern Bar-tailed Godwit *Limosa lapponica baueri* NAUMANN, 1836

BAR-TAILED GODWITS start to arrive in New Zealand in conspicuous numbers in the second half of September. The influx occurs simultaneously at many localities, suggesting that most birds return directly to traditional wintering grounds. But others work their way south: small parties can be seen in October, moving along sandy coasts of the Manawatu and Canterbury. Local midsummer populations fluctuate, presumably as a reflection of breeding success. The most favoured localities seem to be Kaipara (with a maximum of 12 000 birds), Manukau (23 000), Firth of Thames (17 000) and Farewell Spit

(19 000). The birds are regular visitors to the Chatham Islands. Departure, mainly in the second half of March, seems to be direct although there is often a February build-up at Auckland harbours and some movement up the Northland peninsula. Birds seen after March are mainly non-breeders, few of them showing reddened plumage.

Close flocks are formed in flight, often in company with knots. Just before alighting a flock may split apart, its members side-slipping erratically, then landing and running together with an excited chattering. The big flocks that build up before the return migration are

markedly restless, making frequent swirling, spiralling flights. Feeding birds form looser groups. They probe deeply into intertidal mud flats or wet sand, often with a side-to-side levering action, in search of crustaceans, molluscs or worms. Birds roost characteristically on sandbanks, shellbanks and spits that are surrounded by water at high tide, but salt marshes and coastal paddocks are also used. They move out to feed as the tide falls, advancing with the tideline, and only much later flying to disperse over the exposed flats. Birds on inland roosts may wait until the feeding flats are well exposed.   B.D.H. & D.H.B.

MIGRANT

OTHER NAMES: *Kuaka, Pacific godwit.*

SIZE: *400 mm.*

DESCRIPTION
ADULT: *In non-breeding plumage, sexes alike but female markedly bigger with longer bill. Upper parts pale grey-brown, the feathers with dark shaft streaks and whitish margins, particularly prominent on scapulars and wing coverts. Lower back, rump, upper tail coverts white, thickly spotted and barred brown. Tail brown, barred white. Primaries and coverts dark brown. Side of head and neck pale grey-brown, the feathers with darker shaft streaks; speckled and darker on lores, ear coverts. Broad, whitish eyebrow stripe. Underparts dull white; foreneck, breast pale grey-brown, the feathers with narrow dark shaft streaks; sides of breast, flanks, undertail irregularly and indistinctly barred grey-brown. Axillaries, underwing white, heavily barred brown. Bill flesh pink on basal half, grading to blackish at tip, slightly upcurved, twice as long as head in female, 1½ times in male. Iris dark brown. Legs dark greenish grey. In breeding plumage, male's head, neck, underparts reddish chestnut; eyebrow stripe paler; breast and belly darker; crown, nape, sides of head, neck, breast streaked blackish brown; flanks with a few indistinct brown bars. Feathers of mantle, scapulars blackish brown, notched and tipped chestnut and white. Bars on rump and upper tail coverts brown tinged chestnut. Breeding plumage of female much paler with wide individual variation.*
JUVENILE: *Similar to non-breeding adult but darker above, the feathers with pale buff edges, fading to white;*

underparts tinged buff, especially on foreneck, breast, flanks, which are more heavily streaked than in adult.

MOULT
Post-nuptial complete moult of adults July to October, with wing moult presumably delayed until after migration. Nuptial reddening prominent February to March. Post-juvenile body moult September to April.

VOICE
Both when flushed and in normal flight, clear but not loud, or harsh double call, variously ku-wit, kewit, kirruc, trrik, krick, *and more excited, shrill* kew-kew *or* krick-krick. *Quiet, rapid* kit-kit-kit-kit *or* wick-wick-wick-wick *among flock in flight. Generally fairly silent on wintering grounds.*

DISTRIBUTION
Breeds in northeastern Siberia, west-central and northern Alaska. Winters also in southern China, Taiwan, Philippines, Borneo, Moluccas, New Guinea and Australia. Estimated 70 000 each summer at North Island harbours and estuaries, 30 000 in South Island and Stewart Island; about 10 000 winter over. Regular in Chatham Islands; straggler to subantarctic islands.

RECOGNITION
Long-legged, with long, slightly but visibly upcurved bill. Mottled dull brown and white above in non-breeding plumage, dull white below with breast and flanks washed, mottled or streaked pale grey-brown. In flight, wing stripe faint.

A regular migrant to all three main islands, the visiting population of the eastern bar-tailed godwit has been cautiously estimated at 100 000. The birds commonly feed in loose groups on firm, wet, exposed mud flats.

Upland Sandpiper

Bartramia longicauda (BECHSTEIN,1812)

VAGRANT

OTHER NAMES: *Upland plover, Bartram's sandpiper.*

SIZE: *300 mm.*

DESCRIPTION
ADULT: *Sexes alike. Forehead and crown dark brown streaked with buff. Nape and hind neck buffy, narrowly streaked dark brown. Mantle and scapulars dark brown with distinct pale buff edges, scapulars with blackish bars. Wings grey-brown, coverts edged with buff and barred blackish. Back, rump and upper tail coverts blackish brown; outer webs of outermost tail coverts whitish. Underparts dull creamy white, more warmly buff on the breast. Sides of head and neck, and foreneck, strongly streaked blackish brown. Bill black, straight and slender. Legs yellowish.*

MOULT
Post-nuptial complete moult of

adults August to January, with body moult first and wing moult delayed until December to January after migration.*

VOICE
Rapid, bubbling, even-pitched kip-ip-ip-ip-ip *alarm call.*

DISTRIBUTION
Breeds in parts of Alaska, Canada and United States. Winters on the pampas of southern South America. Casual in Greenland, Europe, Malta; South Shetland and Tristan da Cunha Islands.

> **RECOGNITION**
> Short, straight or slightly downcurved bill. Plumage reminiscent of small whimbrel. Tail extends well beyond tips of folded wings. Stands erect with long slender neck, small-looking head.

The upland sandpiper, recorded once in New Zealand at Manukau Harbour.

AN ELEGANT SANDPIPER, formerly abundant on the North American prairies, the upland sandpiper has been recorded once in Australia (in 1848) and once in New Zealand—in 1967, at a high-tide roost on a marshy field beside the southern Manukau Harbour.

Excessive hunting severely reduced the population in the North American habitat in the late nineteenth and early twentieth centuries. There, the preferred habitat remains the inland prairies and large open grassy fields. The upland sandpiper nests in long rank grass or crops and feeds on short pasture or ploughed land. The habitat of the New Zealand sighting was not typical.   B.D.H. & D.H.B.

Lesser Yellowlegs *Tringa flavipes* (GMELIN,1789)

The lesser yellowlegs favours the sheltered areas of shallow water margins.

VAGRANT

OTHER NAME: *Yellowshank.*

SIZE: *270 mm.*

DESCRIPTION
ADULT: *Sexes alike. In non-breeding plumage, upper surface light grey-brown, the feathers with darker shaft streaks and pale edges; scapulars and wing coverts often also notched dark brown and white, giving speckled effect. Upper tail coverts white. Tail white with dark brown bars. Primaries and coverts blackish brown, secondaries dark grey-brown. Broad whitish eyebrow stripes meet over bill base. Grey-brown line from bill to eye; eyelids white. Ear coverts, cheeks white, finely streaked grey-brown. Other underparts white; sides of neck, lower throat, upper breast lightly streaked and spotted grey-brown, darker on sides of breast; light brown bars on flank and undertail. Axillaries, underwing white with grey-brown bars. Bill black, brownish at base, slightly longer than head, straight, slender except at base. Iris brown. Legs long, bright yellow to yellowish orange in breeding season. In breeding plumage, crown, nape, hind neck streaked blackish brown and white; mantle, scapulars, wing coverts*

blackish with white notches. Rest of wing, back, rump and tail as in non-breeding plumage. Streaks and bars of underparts darker, heavier.*
JUVENILE: *Notches of upper surface buff, fading to whitish; general tone of upper parts browner and darker. First winter plumage like adult but buff-edged wing coverts remain.*

MOULT
Adult post-nuptial complete moult mainly August to September with wing moult delayed until after migration. Pre-nuptial body moult February to April. Post-juvenile body moult September to January.

VOICE
Fairly silent outside breeding season. Single or double call in flight, variously described kit-to, yew-yew, wheu-wheu, wheep-wheep, ti-tu.

DISTRIBUTION
Breeds in Alaska and Canada. Winters in small numbers from southern United States through to Chile and Argentina; Straits of Magellan and Falkland Islands; Galapagos Islands. Nine or 10 records in New Zealand.

> **RECOGNITION**
> Slim sandpiper, longish-billed, long yellow legs. Greyish above with white mottling, white below with streaked chest. In flight, no wing stripe; tail looks white; white patch on upper tail coverts does not extend past rear edge of wing; feet trail behind tail.

NINE OR TEN LESSER YELLOWLEGS have been recorded in New Zealand in the past 20 years, frequenting the quiet muddy margins of estuaries or coastal lagoons between October and April. All were seen singly, usually in association with pied stilts and sometimes also with curlew sandpipers, banded dotterels and bar-tailed godwits. The species feeds mainly on insects and larvae found on or in water. These birds walk gracefully with a firm and often rapid stride, wading in water up to their bellies, with necks stretched forward and bills angled to jab at the surface or plunge below. On mud they snatch at the surface—seldom probing. Head-bobbing, with the neck upstretched and tail lowered, is frequent, especially when the birds are mildly alarmed.   B.D.H. & D.H.B.

Marsh Sandpiper *Tringa stagnatilis* (Bechstein, 1803)

VAGRANT

OTHER NAME: *Little greenshank.*

SIZE: *250 mm.*

DESCRIPTION
ADULT: *Sexes alike, female averaging slightly larger. In non-breeding plumage, upper surface grey-brown, the feathers with narrow white margins and some dark shaft streaks. Wing coverts grey-brown with white margins; primaries blackish. Back, rump, upper tail coverts white. Tail whitish with irregular grey-brown transverse bars. Forehead, forecrown, eyebrow stripe, lores, all underparts, underwing white; fine brown streaks on sides of neck and breast. Bill dark brown, green-grey at base, slightly longer than head, straight, very slender, tapering to fine point. Iris dark brown. Legs greenish grey or olive, long, fine. In breeding plumage, forehead and crown spotted brown; mantle and scapular feathers have blackish brown centres; sides of head and neck heavily streaked brown; chin, throat lightly spotted, breast heavily spotted brown; flanks, undertail irregularly barred brown.*
JUVENILE: *Upper parts dark brown, feathers with buff margins or spots. Mostly lost at post-juvenile moult. Underparts white.*

MOULT
Adult post-nuptial complete moult extends to October in most birds; wing moult of some suspended until after migration. Pre-nuptial body moult of adults December to April. Post-juvenile body moult August to November but some brown feathers retained on upper parts; outer primaries of some birds renewed January to May but wing moult of most occurs from June onwards.

VOICE
Single or repeated tee-oo, tew *or* tchew, *less loud and rich than greenshank. Also sharp, rapidly repeated* chewk, tchick *or* tchip.

The marsh sandpiper often feeds by waving its bill back and forth in shallow water, usually alongside pied stilts.

DISTRIBUTION
Main population breeds throughout grassy steppes of central Europe; eastern population in parts of Manchuria. Winters in equatorial to southern Africa, and from eastern Mediterranean through to Southeast Asia and Australia.

ALWAYS ASSOCIATED WITH PIED STILTS in New Zealand, the marsh sandpiper feeds like a smaller, daintier and livelier version of its companions. It tilts up its rear as it picks and probes in mud or in water up to its belly. Sometimes it sweeps its straight, slender bill from side to side, and it may dart through shallow water in pursuit of prey. Aquatic insects and their larvae comprise most of the northern hemisphere diet. Not much is known of its winter diet, but small crustaceans and water snails are important.

Birds recorded in New Zealand, on 11 occasions since 1959, have frequented coastal lagoons and estuarine pools. Except for four at Maketu, Bay of Plenty, in 1970, and four at Lake Ellesmere in 1981–82, the other nine sightings have been of single birds. Most were seen between January and May, but one bird wintered over at Manukau Harbour in 1969, one wintered over in Firth of Thames in 1980 and 1981, and perhaps another in 1963. Observations have been widespread in the North Island but, apart from Ellesmere, only one in South Island, at Westport in 1968.   B.D.H. & D.H.B.

Common Sandpiper *Tringa hypoleucos* Linnaeus, 1758

The common sandpiper.

STRAGGLER

OTHER NAMES: *None.*

SIZE: *200 mm.*

DESCRIPTION
ADULT: *Sexes alike, female averaging slightly larger. In non-breeding plumage, forehead to tail dark grey-brown with olive wash apparent in sunlight; feathers with darker brown shaft streaks and with bars near tips. Nape paler. Sides of* back, rump white. Outermost tail coverts white on edges; tail edged and tipped white. Primaries, secondaries brown. Leading edge of wing white. Tips of greater coverts, bases of secondaries white, forming broad wing stripe in flight. White eyebrow stripe and ring round eye; dark grey-brown line from bill to eye. Sides of head, neck, breast pale grey-brown, darker on breast. Chin, throat, sides of breast, other underparts, axillaries, underwing white. Bill dark brown, straight, slightly longer than head. Iris brown. Legs dull green or light greenish grey, sometimes yellowish green; fairly short. In breeding plumage, slight bronze-green gloss to upper parts; shaft streaks and bars blackish. Eye-stripe, sides of head and neck, chin, throat, upper breast, sides of breast greyish brown, streaked dark brown.*
JUVENILE: *Upper parts brown with buff tips and dark bars near tips, especially on wing coverts. Slight buff wash on sides of neck, breast.*

MOULT
Adult post-nuptial complete moult starts July; many birds moult during migration or in winter quarters, July to September. Wing moult delayed from September to March, often coinciding with onset of pre-nuptial body moult, February to May.*

VOICE
Shrill piping twee-wee-wee *or* tee-tee-tee *alarm call, uttered rapidly with last notes briefer and lower than first.*

DISTRIBUTION
Breeds through most of the Palaearctic region south of the Arctic Circle. Winters in tropical and southern Africa and from Mediterranean basin, Arabian countries, through India and Pakistan to Southeast Asia, New Guinea and Australia.

THE NAME 'common' given to this sandpiper reflects its abundance in Europe—it is rarely seen in New Zealand. Single birds have been recorded between late spring and mid-autumn at Rangaunu Bay, Kerikeri, Kaipara Harbour, Waiapu River, Manukau Harbour, Firth of Thames, New Plymouth, Waikanae, and Westhaven Inlet.

In winter quarters the common sandpiper prefers running to still waters. Its widely ranging habitat includes the banks of rivers and streams, canals, dams and ponds, roadside gutters and puddles. On the coast it prefers rocky beaches, mangrove inlets and the tidal parts of rivers, and will perch on logs, jetties and moored boats. At the water's edge it is always in motion, its head bobbing incessantly, or pausing with its tail and rear jerking up and down like a pipit. The diet consists of a wide range of insects—mainly aquatic—along with small molluscs, crustaceans and worms. Birds feed by picking, not probing, at the water's edge.   B.D.H. & D.H.B.

Wandering Tattler *Tringa incana* (GMELIN,1789)

VAGRANT

OTHER NAMES: *American tattler, American grey-rumped sandpiper, Alaskan tattler.*

SIZE: *280 mm.*

DESCRIPTION

ADULT: *Sexes alike, female averaging slightly larger. In non-breeding plumage, uniform dark grey from crown to tail; fresh feathers with narrow white edges. Primaries, coverts blackish. Whitish eyebrow stripe extends to forehead; slate grey stripe from bill to eye. Sides of head and neck white with indistinct grey* streaks. *Pale grey wash on foreneck, breast, sides of body; rest of underparts white. Axillaries, underwing white with dark grey spots and bars. Bill blackish, grading to yellowish at base, straight, stout, slightly longer than head; broad nasal groove runs two thirds of length. Iris brown. Legs yellow. In breeding plumage, grey of crown extends on to forehead; throat, sides of head, neck more heavily streaked; rest of underparts heavily barred dark grey or blackish, often looking blackish overall with white bars.* JUVENILE: *Buffish white edges and spots on scapulars, wing coverts; grey wash of breast and flanks* mottled with white.

MOULT

Adult post-nuptial complete moult August to January; wing moult October to February after migration. Pre-nuptial body moult March to April. Post-juvenile body moult September to January, outer primaries January to August.

VOICE

Clear, sweet whistle or rippling trill of 6 to 10 notes at increasing speed. Often double or single peet-weet.

DISTRIBUTION

Breeds in extreme northeastern Siberia, Alaska and northwestern Canada. Winters mainly in Pacific Islands, also northeastern Australia, American Pacific coast.

RECOGNITION

Dark grey above, white below, pale grey wash on breast. Longish yellow legs. Stout, straight bill. In flight, no wing stripe, no white on back or rump. Wings flick, stiffly arched, below horizontal on short flights.

THE TATTLER HAS THE USUAL head-wagging walk and tilted feeding style of many *Tringa* sandpipers, but it is more likely to be seen on rocky shores, where it picks and probes among seaweed and barnacles. On beaches and protected mud flats, it feeds at low tide or on the incoming tide, dodging waves. Resting at high tide, it often perches on partly submerged stakes, driftwood, rocks or jetties.

The wandering tattler breeds on gravel beds of mountain streams above the timber line. Its winter quarters are the coasts of islands and reefs and include coral and estuarine mud flats and tidal riverbanks up to several kilometres inland.

Conclusive records of the wandering tattler in New Zealand are scarce because some identifications are based on hearing calls rather than on close examination. Various unidentified tattlers may well have been of this species. The first record was of two birds collected at Portland Island, off Mahia Peninsula, in 1883. Except for two more seen at Kaikoura in 1976, and a flock of seven in the Kermadecs in 1974, all other sightings have been of single birds. There is no certain record of birds having wintered here.   B.D.H. & D.H.B.

The wandering tattler tends to feed alone, at low or incoming tides. It feeds upon a variety of molluscs, worms, crustaceans and flies.

Siberian Tattler

Tringa brevipes

(VIEILLOT, 1816)

STRAGGLER

OTHER NAMES: *Grey-tailed tattler, grey-rumped tattler, grey-rumped sandpiper.*

SIZE: *250 mm.*

DESCRIPTION
ADULT: *Very similar to wandering tattler but, in the hand, distinguished in all plumages by length of nasal groove, which extends halfway to tip of bill; also averaging smaller and less robust, with lighter grey upper parts. Feathers of rump and upper tail coverts with narrow white edges, producing in fresh plumage 2 or more distinct white cross-bars; often not visible in the field. Axillaries and underwing grey. In breeding plumage, barring of underparts less dense.*

MOULT
Adult post-nuptial complete moult July to January, wing moult delayed until after migration. Pre-nuptial body moult from March onwards.

VOICE
Sharp, high-pitched too-weet *or* troo-weet, *often with second syllable higher, in flight.*

DISTRIBUTION
Breeds in mountainous northeastern Siberia. Winters mainly in Southeast Asia, western Pacific, New Guinea, northern and eastern Australia.

The Siberian tattler breeds mainly above the treeline in remote mountain country of northeastern Siberia.

SIBERIAN TATTLERS HAVE been seen in New Zealand in most recent years, usually singly and not totalling more than 10 a year; however a party of 18 seen at Mahia may have been of this species. Most birds are identified mainly by their call. Though seen with greatest frequency in the far north, birds have occurred in coastal localities, as far as Southland. They have wintered over at Kawhia, Gisborne, Kaikoura, Aramoana (Dunedin) and Awarua Bay. Sheltered mud-flat harbours and rocky coasts, especially near the mouths of streams, are the most favoured habitats. The diet in New Zealand has not been analysed, but a bird observed for six months at Waikanae, near Wellington, took small fish, crabs, sand hoppers and sea lice, usually in about 30 mm of water at the river's edge or round the lagoon.   B.D.H. & D.H.B.

RECOGNITION

White-barred upper tail coverts sometimes visible. Distinguished, in breeding plumage, from similar wandering tattler by white belly and undertail. Nasal groove length is only wholly reliable comparison. Typical calls are distinctive, but both species have other calls.

Greenshank

Tringa nebularia (GUNNERUS, 1767)

STRAGGLER

OTHER NAMES: *None.*

SIZE: *330 mm.*

DESCRIPTION
ADULT: *Sexes alike. In non-breeding plumage, crown and nape pale grey with grey-brown streaks. Other upper parts grey brown, feathers darker near edges with narrow white margins and darker shaft streaks. Primaries, coverts blackish brown. Back, rump, upper tail coverts white; tail white or greyish with grey-brown transverse bars. Forehead to above eye, sides of head and all underparts white; sides of neck and breast finely streaked or spotted brown. Underwing white with irregular brown bars. Bill blackish, paler at base (often grey-green), stout at base, 1½ times as long as head, slightly upcurved. Legs pale olive green, long. In breeding plumage, forehead, crown and nape heavily streaked brown. Mantle, scapulars, wing coverts irregular mixture of feathers, dark brown with white or grey edges and grey-brown with blackish margins and white tips. Lower throat, upper breast, flanks heavily spotted and barred dark brown.*
JUVENILE: *Forehead, crown, nape streaked brown; mantle, scapulars dark brown, wing coverts paler; light buff margins on all feathers. Sides of face, neck heavily streaked brown; sides of breast, flanks spotted brown.*

MOULT
Adult post-nuptial complete moult June to November; wing moult may be suspended in long-distance migrants. Pre-nuptial moult January to May. Post-juvenile body moult August to March; outer primaries sometimes moulted February to May by long-distance migrants, otherwise late in first winter. Breeding plumage not assumed in first winter.

VOICE
Ringing tyew-tyew-tyew *or* chew-chew-chew *in groups of 2 to 6, frequently 3, when alarmed or in flight.*

DISTRIBUTION
Breeds in forests south of the Arctic Circle in Scotland and Eurasia from Scandinavia eastward to Kamchatka. Winters in Mediterranean, Africa, South and Southeast Asia, Australia.

RECOGNITION

Slightly smaller, slimmer than male bar-tailed godwit, bigger and heavier than marsh sandpiper. Strongly grey about head and neck with prominent white of forehead reaching eye; narrow whitish ring around eye. In flight, inverted white V from tail on to back and loud, ringing call are distinctive.

The greenshank eats a wide range of aquatic animals, even small frogs.

A MOST AGILE FEEDER, the greenshank patrols the muddy margins of pools and lakes in a brisk walk, head nodding, and tips over much like a stilt to prod, probe and dart at crustaceans, marine worms, aquatic insects or fish. Often it runs rapidly after fleeing fish. It may wade up to its belly—sometimes with its head partly submerged and its bill sweeping from side to side—or it may even swim. Birds generally keep to themselves or in small parties, but in New Zealand they are almost always associated with pied stilts.

Greenshanks have been recorded in most years since 1952—usually single birds among stilts, but parties of up to four have collected. The species is most frequently seen at Parengarenga, south Manukau Harbour, Farewell Spit, Lake Ellesmere and the Southland coast. Habitats are widespread, and include open, muddy pools, and marshy inlets, but rarely tidal mud flats. Sightings are mainly between October and March. Single birds have wintered in several years in the Manukau locality, the Manawatu estuary, Washdyke Lagoon (Otago) and possibly Farewell Spit.   B.D.H. & D.H.B.

Terek Sandpiper *Xenus cinereus* (Gueldenstaedt, 1774)

RESTLESSLY ACTIVE, dashing about in the shallows, the terek sandpiper bobs while feeding, standing with its rear bobbing vigorously. It feeds by dabbing at and probing soft mud, sometimes probing deeply—almost to its eyes. But in spite of the distinct upward curve of its bill, reminiscent of an avocet, it seldom uses the scooping action of that bird. Crabs, beetles, small molluscs, flies and their larvae have been noted in the winter diet. One bird at Lake Ellesmere was seen sweeping its bill sideways through short grass, as if to stir up insects.

Numbers in New Zealand are tiny, though visits are fairly regular. Rarely are more than six birds recorded in any year, and the biggest group ever seen was six in the Firth of Thames. Several birds have overwintered there and at Whangarei, and one at Motueka. However, the species is most commonly seen between October and April—occasionally September or May. It favours mangrove swamps, tidal creeks, estuarine mud flats, coastal lagoons and saltmarsh pools where shallow water covers mud, in localities scattered from the far north to Southland. Birds are often found feeding or resting among wrybills; otherwise they may be loosely associated with banded dotterels, pied stilts or sometimes least golden plovers.

The terek is undoubtedly a close relative of *Tringa* sandpipers, and some authorities include it in that genus. When this is done, the name *Tringa terek* LATHAM, 1790 must be used.

B.D.H. & D.H.B.

MIGRANT

OTHER NAME: *Avocet sandpiper.*

SIZE: *230 mm.*

DESCRIPTION

ADULT: *Sexes alike, female averaging larger. In non-breeding plumage, upper parts including rump and tail light brown-grey, the feathers with narrow darker shaft streaks except on nape. Outermost tail feathers usually whitish. Sides of back, rump, upper tail coverts white. Primaries, coverts, dark brown; rest of wing brown-grey, darker on coverts. Secondaries broadly tipped white. Forehead, broad eye-stripe, lores, sides of face and neck, lower throat white,* faintly streaked grey. Grey wash on sides of breast. Other underparts, axillaries, underwing white. Bill black or dark brown, paler at base, often yellowish or dull orange; 1½ times as long as head, broad at base but narrowing before half length; distinctly upcurved. Iris brown. Legs dull yellow to bright orange-yellow; fairly short; feet partly webbed. In breeding plumage, broad blackish shaft streaks on forehead crown, nape, mantle and especially scapulars. Some short scapulars black-brown, forming dark line down each side of back. Upper tail coverts barred and edged brown. Whitish eye-ring. Sides of face and neck, lower throat, sides of breast whitish, distinctly streaked brown.*

JUVENILE: *Upper parts browner, the* feathers edged buff, including tail, wing coverts. Lower throat, breast with light buff wash, faintly streaked.*

MOULT

Adult post-nuptial complete moult August to January; wing moult usually starts September to October but is suspended and finishes December to January. Pre-nuptial body moult February to May. Post-juvenile body moult September to January; outer primaries may be moulted during first northern winter or delayed until after first summer.

VOICE

Melodious trill weeta-weeta-weet *in flight; also 3-note titter* tee-tee-tee, pi-pi-pi *or* wee-he-he.*

DISTRIBUTION

Breeds mainly south of Arctic Circle from Finland to Siberia. Most birds winter from Persian Gulf to East Africa, South and Southeast Asia, New Guinea, Australia.

RECOGNITION

Slim, restless; uniform grey above, dark at bend of folded wing, white below. Short yellow or orange legs; long, dark, upturned bill. In flight, prominent white rear wing edge, whitish sides of tail. Larger than sharp-tailed and curlew sandpipers.

The terek sandpiper favours coastal habitats with soft mud and a shallow covering of water. It is rarely found inland.

A tame bird, the turnstone is the most animated of the shore-feeding waders. It feeds busily in small scattered groups, inspecting every object and crevice.

Turnstone *Arenaria interpres* (LINNAEUS, 1758)

MIGRANT

OTHER NAME: *Ruddy turnstone.*

SIZE: *230 mm.*

DESCRIPTION
ADULT: *Sexes alike in non-breeding plumage. Upper parts dull dark grey-brown, feathers with blackish centres and paler brown edges. Lower back, rump white, smaller upper tail coverts black, forming transverse crescent behind large oval white patch; longer upper tail coverts and most of tail white, broad black band near white tip of tail. Wing dark brown with white patch of lesser coverts close to body near leading edge; broad white wing stripe formed by tips of outer scapulars and greater coverts, almost whole of secondaries and bases of inner primaries; primaries and coverts blackish. Head brown, streaked white, sometimes paler on forehead,* lores, cheeks and rear of eyebrow stripe. Chin, throat white. Blackish breast-band forming double loop, with line extending from each loop across side of neck. Rest of underparts, including axillaries and underwing, white. Bill black, short, conical, tapering to point. Iris dark brown. Legs orange-yellow to dull orange-red, short, stout. Male in breeding plumage has predominantly white head, crown and upper nape streaked black, nape and hind neck slightly mottled brown and buff. Small black patch each side of nape. Mantle black and rufous patches forming tortoiseshell appearance. Extensions of black breast-band run across each side of neck, nearly meeting behind, and up over cheeks to eye then forward to base of upper bill, also along sides of throat to lower bill. Legs bright orange-red. Female has much darker crown, less rufous on upper parts, narrower black face bands, white areas of* forehead and lores reduced and tinged buff.
JUVENILE: *Like non-breeding adult but upper surface blackish brown, distinctly tipped and edged pale buff; slight buff tinge about head, breast; breast-band brownish. Legs brownish yellow or dull orange.*

MOULT
Adult post-nuptial moult July to October; body plumage mostly moulted on breeding grounds and during migration. Pre-nuptial partial moult mainly February to March. Post-juvenile body moult August to November; first winter plumage retained, without wing moult, probably until complete moult July to August.

VOICE
Rattling kitititit *common in flight and when flushed; clear, more melodious* kewk, kee-oo *or* kuiti *in flight or when greatly alarmed.*

DISTRIBUTION
Breeds on Arctic coasts from Ellesmere Island eastward across Europe and Asia to eastern Alaska. Winters widely on Atlantic coasts of Europe and Africa and in South and Southeast Asia, Pacific Islands, New Guinea, Australia. Many New Zealand harbours, estuaries, coastal lagoons; Kermadec, Chatham and Auckland Islands, straggling to Campbell and Antipodes Islands.

RECOGNITION

Small, plump and stocky, short-necked, short-legged. Blackish above, white below, heavy black double loop on breast. Short, stout, chisel-shaped bill. Orange legs. In flight, bold black and white pattern on wings, back, tail. Juvenile duller, more buff.

A FAIRLY TAME SPECIES, the turnstone feeds busily in small scattered groups. On rocky shores it investigates every object and crevice. On beaches it dashes out between waves to dab at wet sand and examine stranded debris. Pebbles, shells, seaweed and pieces of wood are flipped over with a flick of the bill and a toss of the head. Heavier material is shifted—perhaps only enough to see if there is food below—by wedging the sturdy bill underneath, bracing the short legs and pushing upward with the head and breast. Some birds even team up to move objects too massive for one alone.

Barnacles and molluscs are opened by sharp downward blows of the bill. Crabs, caught in the open or taken from their burrows, are flipped over and similarly struck. A study at Farewell Spit showed that more than 90 per cent of birds neglected the seaward shore, preferring sheltered flats on the Golden Bay side. They followed the falling tide on to saltmarsh and *Zostera* eelgrass beds, and with the rising tide they took crabs on the open sand. Birds at high tide at Parengarenga, Northland, often feed in short pasture or ploughed fields, presumably on insects, while other species are resting. They often toss aside cowdung pats.

Turnstones in New Zealand seem to be constantly on the move in small parties. The total wintering population is probably in the range of 4000 to 6000. More than half of these frequent the Northland and Auckland harbours, Farewell Spit and the Southland coastal lagoons, but smaller numbers occur at many estuaries and lagoons elsewhere. Migrants start arriving in late August, but the main build-up in major localities comes in the second half of September and continues throughout October. Birds regroup in big flocks in the second half of March and April.
B.D.H. & D.H.B.

Snipe *Coenocorypha aucklandica* (GRAY, 1845)

The Chatham Island snipe is the smallest of the snipe subspecies, its chief food worms and grubs. It prods for insect larvae with its long sensitive bill.

POSSIBLY EXTINCT
Stewart Island Snipe
C.a. iredalei (ROTHSCHILD, 1921).

ENDEMIC
Chatham Island Snipe
C.a. pusilla (BULLER, 1869).
Snares Island Snipe
C.a. huegeli (TRISTRAM, 1893).
Antipodes Island Snipe
C.a. meinertzhagenae (ROTHSCHILD, 1927).
Auckland Island Snipe
C.a. aucklandica (GRAY, 1845).

OTHER NAMES: *None.*

SIZE: *230 mm (except Chatham Island Snipe: 200 mm).*

DESCRIPTION
ADULT: *Sexes alike.*
Chatham Island snipe: *Top of head striped black and medium brown to reddish brown, rest of upper surface brown to reddish brown, mottled with black, feathers margined with buff. Wing and tail quills brown. Sides of head buff to off-white, spotted dark brown; dark line from gape to eye. Chin buff to off-white.*

Foreneck, upper breast, sides of body buff, heavily blotched brown. Feet pale brown.

Stewart Island snipe: *Throat spotted, lower abdomen and flanks barred. Markings bolder above and below. Upper surface marked irregularly with chestnut and black; some feather margins off-white, standing out against darker plumage.*

Snares Island snipe: *Undersurface barred dark brown throughout. Bill greyish brown but base of lower mandible yellowish. Feet greyish brown.*

Antipodes Island snipe: *Flanks barred, plumage darker overall with pale parts yellowish.*

Auckland Island snipe: *Only flanks are barred; plumage lighter overall. Feet brownish yellow.*
IMMATURE: *Dark blotches less developed. Feet bluish grey.*
CHICK: *Reddish or dark brown above; blackish line on head. Bill, feet slate.*

MOULT
Not known.

VOICE
Soft, low keerk *or* kurk *quickly repeated, often working up to series of sharp whistles,* queeyoo.

DISTRIBUTION
Common South East and Mangere Islands (Chathams), North East and Broughton Islands (Snares), Antipodes Island and Bollons Island (Antipodes). Also smaller Auckland Islands. Stewart Island subspecies last seen South Cape Islands in 1964.

RECOGNITION
Compact; long bill, short legs. Shy. Flight short, fast, erratic. Only snipe-like bird on outlying islands of New Zealand.

SNIPE FOUND ON SOME of New Zealand's outer islands are named for their resemblance to the migratory *Gallinago* species of the northern hemisphere. Along with a similar appearance they have the fast, weaving flight that makes true snipe a popular challenge to shooters. But *Coenocorypha aucklandica* does not migrate, and its remote strongholds are safe from most human interference. Long-isolated populations have differentiated into five known subspecies—one, the Stewart Island snipe, is presumed to have died out since the 1960s.

Damper areas of grassland, tussock, scrub or forest are favoured as habitats. Snipe probe soft humus for insects and their larvae. They nest on or near the ground, in cups or on heaps of finer vegetation. Breeding takes place in late spring or early summer. Limited observations suggest that eggs are laid in clutches of two or three and incubated by both sexes. In the case of Snares Islands studies, no parent was seen with more than one chick. H.A.B.

Japanese Snipe
Gallinago hardwickii (GRAY,1831)

VAGRANT

OTHER NAMES: *Australian snipe, Latham's snipe, longbill.*

SIZE: *330 mm.*

DESCRIPTION
ADULT: *Sexes alike. Crown with black stripe either side of pale median strip; pale line over eye; upper surface buff, heavily mottled in brown and black; central tail feathers pale chesnut with white tips, outer feathers narrow and mostly buff-white. Primaries dark brown with whitish tips. Throat, sides of face whitish; dark brown line from bill through eye; front and sides of neck reddish buff barred with brown. Upper breast light brown flecked with black; sides of body barred black-brown and white; underparts pale grey or buff. Bill olive-brown to olive, darkening at tip; long, straight. Iris brown. Legs olive grey-brown.*

MOULT
Not known.

VOICE
Sharp arrk *or* krek *when flushed.*

DISTRIBUTION
Breeds in Japan. Normally winters in eastern Australia and Tasmania.

RECOGNITION

Compact, smaller than godwit or stilt, long dark straight bill, short legs, buff upper parts heavily mottled brown-black. In flight, no wing stripe or pale rump discernible.

The Japanese snipe is a secretive and inconspicuous bird of coastal wetlands.

THE JAPANESE SNIPE is a furtive, wary bird of swamps and wet grasslands, where it probes for worms, aquatic insects and their larvae. It is inconspicuous unless flushed, when it gives a loud cry and makes a swift, erratic flight. It was first recorded at Arch Hill, Auckland, in 1898, and then at Castlecliff, Wanganui, in 1914. Sightings of this rare vagrant have been recorded at Taieri Beach (1941 and 1969), Ahuriri Lagoon (1952) and probably at Otaki (1972), and Coopers Lagoon and Lake Ellesmere (1973). H.A.B.

Knot *Calidris canutus* (LINNAEUS,1758)

THOUSANDS OF KNOTS EAT, rest and fly together in dense masses. Flocks in flight twist and turn like swirling smoke clouds. On the ground, they feed with remarkable co-ordination, running, slowing, turning this way and that almost in unison. They pick and probe busily with their bills held vertically, making several jabs before moving on. In New Zealand, though flocks often roost and fly with bar-tailed godwits they separate out in flight and to feed. Single birds and small groups sometimes associate with other small species.

On their Arctic breeding grounds, they feed on the seeds, buds and shoots of grasses, sedges and willows before the thaw and take oligochaete worms and fly larvae and on the coast, small crustaceans and molluscs, worms and beetles. In their winter quarters they eat mainly crustaceans, annelid worms and insects. Small molluscs, however, are thought to be the staple food. B.D.H. & D.H.B.

MIGRANT

OTHER NAMES: *Huahou, lesser knot, red knot.*

SIZE: *250 mm.*

DESCRIPTION
ADULT: *Sexes alike in non-breeding plumage. Upper surface light brownish grey, feathers with narrow darker shaft streaks and pale edges. Upper tail coverts white, crossed by irregular dark brown bars. Tail brownish grey. Primaries blackish brown; tips of greater coverts, bases of primaries and secondaries white, forming narrow stripe along most of wing in flight. Eyebrow stripe from base of bill white, finely streaked brown-grey. Brownish grey stripe on lores from bill to eye. Side of head and underparts white, with fine brownish grey streaks on ear coverts, side of head and neck and on throat; freckles on breast, and some arrowhead or boomerang markings on sides of body. Underwing white with some brownish grey bars. Bill brownish black, about as long as head, stout, straight and tapering. Iris brown. Legs dark greenish grey. In breeding plumage, male's crown black, feathers with rufous edges. Nape and hind neck grey with narrow black streaks. Mantle and scapulars black, feathers with chestnut and white edges. Lower back grey-brown, feathers white-tipped. Pale areas of face, chin, throat and undersurface rufous; undertail coverts white, with a few dark freckles. Bill black. Female like male, but has white rather than rufous edges predominant on upper surface, and scattered white feathers on rufous underparts.*
JUVENILE: *Upper surface brownish, feathers with blackish marks near white or cream edges. Tail feathers edged with buff. Underparts like non-breeding adult but buffish white, somewhat darker on breast and flanks. Legs pale greenish grey.*

MOULT
Insufficiently known but probably complete adult post-nuptial moult late June to October, usually during migration except for wings.

VOICE
Generally silent in winter quarters. Normal call hoarse, low-pitched knut *or* kloot. *When alarmed, more liquid* whit-wit *or* too-it-wit. *Continuous low chittering from packed high-tide flocks.*

DISTRIBUTION
Breeds in widely separated populations in Arctic North America, Greenland, Spitsbergen and 3 areas of northern Siberia. Recorded on all Australian coasts, most commonly in the east. Widespread throughout New Zealand September to early April on harbours, estuaries and coastal lagoons. The largest flocks (from 3000 to 27 000) favour Houhora, Kaipara and Manukau Harbours, Firth of Thames and Farewell Spit. Between 100 and 1000 birds regularly at Rangaunu Bay, Whangarei Harbour, upper Waitemata Harbour, Manawatu River estuary, Southland estuaries and lagoons and on Chatham Island. Numbers fluctuate greatly from year to year and month to month. Large wintering numbers and lack of migration data between the Arctic and Australasia support theory that complete breeding populations move to New Zealand, revealing the year's breeding success.

RECOGNITION

Plump, short-legged, with straight bill looking barely longer than head. Non-breeding plumage, grey above, white below; in flight narrow wing stripe and rump and tail uniformly grey and paler than the back. Differs from larger great knot by almost uniform crown, distinct eye-stripe, grey-looking rump and tail, and different voice.

A knot, a dumpy wader with short legs, is surrounded by godwits.

Great Knot *Calidris tenuirostris* (Horsfield, 1821)

THE GREAT KNOT BREEDS in the northern hemisphere on flat mountain tops among scanty vegetation or loose lichen-covered stones. It is a regular and common visitor to parts of New Guinea, especially the southwest, and to Australian coasts, mainly in the Northern Territory. A few great knots have been seen in New Zealand between September and April at larger natural harbours or estuaries in the North Island. It is gregarious, groups keeping together or with other waders, mainly the knot but also the least golden plover and sharp-tailed sandpiper. If seen alone it is hard to distinguish from a knot. There is little information available about its habits and none about its diet, though the latter is probably similar to, but larger than, that of the knot.

B.D.H. & D.H.B.

STRAGGLER

OTHER NAMES: *Greater knot, eastern (Asiatic) knot, great sandpiper.*

SIZE: *290 mm.*

DESCRIPTION
ADULT: *Sexes alike. In non-breeding plumage upper parts pale grey-brown, feathers of crown, nape, hind neck and mantle with fairly broad dark brown shaft stripes. Eyebrow stripe indistinct or lacking. Upper tail coverts white, lightly spotted with black. Tail grey-brown. Primaries and their coverts blackish. Secondaries grey-brown. Greater coverts tipped white, forming indistinct narrow white wing stripe in flight. Axillaries white with pale brown streaks. Side of face and underparts white. Light grey-brown streaks on side of face and neck. Small dark grey-brown spots on foreneck, breast, and flanks. Bill stout, fairly long, straight, sometimes with slightly downcurved tip, brownish black. Legs fairly short, dark olive-grey. In breeding plumage head and hind neck black, feathers with white edges, looking striped. Mantle blackish brown, feathers with white edges. Scapulars and smaller wing coverts black with white edges and large chestnut patches near tips. Tail and wing as in non-breeding plumage. Side of head and underparts white. Side of face and neck streaked brown. Throat, foreneck, breast, and flanks with blackish brown patches. Breast looks almost totally black. A few blackish streaks on undertail coverts.*
JUVENILE: *Rather like breeding adult but without chestnut on scapulars, much darker above than non-breeding adult. Upper surface blackish brown, feathers with pale buff edges; primaries and tail with narrow white tips. Breast with slight buff tinge. Dense light-brown spots on breast and flanks.*

MOULT
Little information available. Many birds seen in Australasia in transitional or immature dark plumage. One bird seen in New Zealand in breeding plumage in mid-April. Birds recorded in China in July and August in breeding plumage. Adult wing moult September to December. First wing moult of immatures after first (northern) summer.

VOICE
Given variously as double-noted whistle nyut-nyut; queet-queet *like black-tailed godwit; and low* chucker-chucker-chucker.

DISTRIBUTION
Breeds in northeastern USSR. Probably rather small population. Winters on coasts of eastern India, Burma, Thailand, Malaysia, the Philippines, Micronesia, Indonesia (especially Borneo), New Guinea and Australia. Straggles to the Persian Gulf, Alaska and New Zealand. Times of migration little known. First birds leave USSR in early August, with main passage in first half of September. Near Darwin, birds occur all year and birds in breeding plumage seen in August. Few Queensland records before November. Australian birds apparently leave in March. Migration probably rapid and birds believed to reach breeding grounds in second half of May.

Somewhat larger than the knot, the great knot is distinguished by its longer bill with a slightly downcurved tip.

Pectoral Sandpiper

Calidris melanotos (Vieillot, 1819)

The pectoral sandpiper, seen each year in small numbers.

IN THE BREEDING SEASON the male pectoral sandpiper, like the sharp-tailed, develops a pair of throat pouches that it inflates to golfball size. With these it utters deep, resonant but musical booming notes while it displays on the ground or in the air.

It breeds on grassy tundra, especially wet tundra with drier hummocks and ridges. In winter, it usually inhabits wet grassland and the edges of lakes and lagoons in South America. The few birds that migrate to Australasia are mainly found on coastal lagoons and estuarine marshes where there is ample short vegetation. It eats a wide range of insects (especially flies and their larvae), worms, small crustaceans and molluscs.   B.D.H. & D.H.B.

MIGRANT

OTHER NAMES: *None.*

SIZE: *220 mm.*

DESCRIPTION
ADULT: *Sexes alike, female averaging smaller. Very similar to sharp-tailed sandpiper but markings of upper surface dark brown rather than blackish and, in breeding plumage, lacking the reddish brown tone of the sharp-tailed. Crown buff-brown, boldly streaked dark brown; sometimes with warmer tone but not chestnut or rufous. Chin white.*

Neck, throat and breast buff-brown, heavily and distinctly streaked dark brown, forming a dark pectoral band which ends abruptly against the white of flanks and abdomen. Streaks on flanks few and indistinct. Bill dark, yellowish at the base, becoming bright yellow at base in breeding plumage. Legs greenish yellow to brownish yellow, becoming dull or bright yellow in breeding plumage.
JUVENILE: *Similar to adult but edges of feathers of upper parts more buff and, on chest, wash more buff and streaking less distinct. Whitish edges of scapulars form pale line down each side of back.*

MOULT
Post-nuptial complete moult of adults mostly delayed until after migration, September to February. Pre-nuptial body moult February to May. Post-juvenile body moult after migration, with wing moult delayed until second summer.

VOICE
Usually silent in winter. When flushed, clear, husky call uttered once, twice or repeated: trrit, prrrt, trrerp, kriek or kreek.

DISTRIBUTION
Breeds on Arctic tundra of Siberia, Alaska and Canada. Winters in southern South America. Birds reaching Australasia presumably caught up with migrating sharp-tailed and other sandpipers. In Australia, recorded as rare in all states, but probably overlooked among sharp-tailed and curlew sandpipers. In New Zealand, small number recorded annually but seldom more than 20. Recorded late September to early April, mainly October to March. Birds in breeding plumage noted in April and one as early as late January. Only one record of overwintering, 2 birds at Lake Ellesmere in 1982.

Baird's Sandpiper *Calidris bairdii* (Coues, 1861)

VAGRANT

OTHER NAMES: *None.*

SIZE: *190 mm.*

DESCRIPTION
ADULT: *Sexes alike, females averaging slightly larger. In non-breeding plumage upper parts grey-brown, feathers of mantle and scapulars with narrow pale buff margins and darker shaft streaks. Crown and nape indistinctly streaked darker grey-brown. Upper wing grey-brown, coverts with pale buff margins; secondaries and primaries darker grey-brown, secondaries with white tips. Rump, upper tail coverts and tail dark grey-brown. Outer tail coverts and tail lighter brown. Side of face and neck, breast and upper flanks buff-brown, often with indistinct dark streaks. Eyebrow stripe buff, prominent mainly in front of eye. Chin, throat, axillaries, underwing and belly white. Bill rather short (almost as long as head), straight, fairly slender, black. Legs fairly short, black or greenish black. In breeding plumage upper parts blackish brown, feathers of mantle and scapulars with broad pale buff and bright buff edges, producing striking scaly appearance on back. Dark streaks on crown. Streaks on hind neck so fine as to make it look overall grey. Breast and sides of head and neck prominently buff with narrow darker streaks. Wing and rest of underparts as in non-breeding plumage.*
JUVENILE: *Upper feathers blackish, with broad whitish or pale buff edges, emphasising scaly appearance of back. Wing coverts grey-brown with whitish or buff tips and edges. Underparts as in adult non-breeding plumage.*

MOULT
Post-nuptial complete moult may begin August but occurs mainly

September to October, with wing moult delayed until after migration, October to March. Pre-nuptial body moult mainly February to April. Post-juvenile body moult completed by October but some juvenile wing coverts retained in first winter. Juvenile wing moult varies: some do not moult in first year, others moult outer primaries only.

VOICE
High-pitched vibrating or twittering prreet or kreep. One bird studied closely in Victoria called trilled krreep-krreep-krreep-krreep.

DISTRIBUTION
Breeds in extreme northeastern U.S.S.R.; on islands in the Bering Strait; Alaska and Canada east to Ellesmere and Baffin Islands and northwestern Greenland. Winters mainly in western and southern South America. Straggles to the Falkland Islands, western Europe, the British Isles, Australia (2 records), New Zealand (several records), Hawaii, Galapagos Islands, the Kuril Islands, Sakhalin and Japan. Southward migration begins late July but occurs mainly in August and September. Most leave wintering grounds by early March and reach breeding grounds late May to early June.

A Baird's sandpiper, a vagrant to New Zealand, on its nest in the Yukon.

BAIRD'S SANDPIPER breeds on drier parts of the Arctic tundra, on ridges, flats, and rocky slopes both inland and on the coast. At its winter quarters in South America it prefers sheltered sparsely vegetated flats near lakes, ponds, and lagoons, but away from the water's edge. However, one bird in inland Victoria fed in shallow lakeshore water, often up to its belly. The few birds that reach Australia and New Zealand are presumably caught up in the migration streams of other species that fly over eastern Asia.

Baird's sandpiper is rather tame. It feeds by picking and snatching from the surface of the drier parts of muddy places with a low-crouched stance and often with a run-and-stop manner. A bird observed in Victoria picked from the surface of the water or from dead vegetation at the water's edge, at times working over a small area energetically and methodically. The species associates readily with other small sandpipers, especially red-necked stints.

At its summer quarters and on migration, it eats insects, mainly the larvae of sandflies, sawflies, crane flies and mosquitoes. It also feeds on amphipods, crustaceans, weevils, grasshoppers, ground beetles, leeches, spiders and algae.   B.D.H. & D.H.B.

Sharp-tailed Sandpiper *Calidris acuminata* (HORSFIELD, 1821)

MIGRANT

OTHER NAME: *Siberian pectoral sandpiper.*

SIZE: *220 mm.*

DESCRIPTION
ADULT: *Sexes alike, female averaging smaller. In non-breeding plumage upper surface grey-brown, streaked and striped blackish. Feathers of scapulars, mantle and back blackish with broad brownish edges. Crown has distinctive chestnut or reddish tinge, with blackish streaks, narrower on nape. Rump, central tail coverts and tail blackish. Sides of back, rump and tail coverts white. Sides of tail grey-brown, forming dark centre line in flight contrasting with oval white patch on each side. Wing feathers grey-brown with pale edges. Eyebrow stripe, sides of head and neck, breast and flanks whitish or with light grey-brown wash, usually with fine darker streaks on sides of head, neck and breast. Chin, belly, underwing and undertail white. Bill blackish with base of lower mandible brownish, as long as or slightly longer than head, fairly deep at base, tapering from below, with slight downward curve at tip. Legs olive-green to yellowish green. Breeding plumage similar to non-breeding adult but blackish feathers with contrasting chestnut edges make upper parts look overall rich reddish brown. Breast and side of neck with rufous tinge, heavily marked with dark brown spots and bars and with distinctive crescents or V-shaped marks, especially on side of breast and on flanks. Male has distensible paired throat-sacs on breeding grounds.*
JUVENILE: *Crown bright chestnut, streaked black, contrasting strongly with broad whitish eyebrow stripe. Upper parts blackish-brown, feathers edged chestnut and whitish buff. Chest and flanks with buff wash, finely streaked on chest, forming a pale gorget contrasting with white chin and breast.*

MOULT
Post-nuptial moult probably August to November, with wing moult delayed until after migration. In Western Australia, wing moult recorded early October to mid-January. Pre-nuptial body moult February to May. By late March and early April, birds in New Zealand may be richly marked above and have prominent spots and crescents on breast and flanks. Post-juvenile moult into first-winter plumage October to January, with outer primaries of most birds moulted December to March.

VOICE
Usually silent in winter quarters but, when flushed, calls soft but sharp single or repeated note: twee, chwee, wheep, pleep, whit, krip or chew.

DISTRIBUTION
Breeding range not well known and few nests have been found. Known from arctic Siberia from delta of Lena River eastward to delta of Kolyma River. Main wintering area Australia, especially in southeast. Winters in small numbers in Micronesian islands; the Moluccas; Timor; New Guinea; New Caledonia; Kiribati, the Solomon and Phoenix Islands; New Zealand; and west coast of North America. Straggles to Tonga, Fiji, Norfolk Island and Chatham Island. Arrives in northern Australia mainly in September. Most birds leave Australia in March and April and, *passing through eastern Asia, arrive on breeding grounds by late May or early June. Few birds overwinter. In New Zealand, 100 to 200 visit annually, well scattered in small flocks of up to 40 birds. Much local movement. A few birds may arrive in August but main influx usually begins in second half of September, increases during October and early November to a summer peak in December and January. Main flocking occurs late March or early April, after which numbers drop rapidly. A few may linger to late April, occasionally early May. Birds rarely overwinter. Straggles to The Snares.*

RECOGNITION
A brown trim-looking sandpiper. Boldly mottled and streaked above, the dark feathers with whitish-buff edges giving a scaly effect; crown chestnut, and varying amount of grey or buffy wash and darker streaks on breast. In flight, no wing stripe. Legs greenish rather than yellowish.

DESPITE ITS NAME, the tail of the sharp-tailed sandpiper is wedge-shaped. It is the individual tail feathers which are pointed. This bird breeds, as far as is known, on moss and lichen tundra interspersed with moist hollows and shrub-covered hummocks. In winter, it prefers shallow open swampland, whether fresh, salt or brackish, with sparse low vegetation.

It tends to keep to itself, accompanied perhaps by pectoral sandpipers. On tidal mud flats, it may associate with knots, curlew sandpipers or red-necked stints, favouring wet mud well back from the tideline. Sometimes it roosts at high tide with other waders on spits or fields. At Parengarenga Harbour it is usually seen around pools on *Salicornia* flats, sometimes bathing as a flock in shallow water or feeding in a line on exposed tidal mud. When approached, it remains motionless if in vegetation or flushes with a zig-zag flight which steadies to a swift direct flight.

Two displays have been noted in Australasia among feeding and roosting birds. One is a semi-erect posture, with the feathers of the back and throat raised, the wings stiffly drooped, and sometimes the tail held vertical, fanned and vibrated sideways. The other is similar, but with the wings raised and arched. In this display the bird jerks its wings, head and tail up and down. These displays may lead one into the other, with two birds chasing each other, sometimes the roles reversing or a third bird intervening.

It is a quiet unhurried feeder that is not easily disturbed. Little is known of its diet. Birds collected on the Pribilof Islands in the Bering Sea had been feeding largely on flies and their larvae. It also takes crustaceans, molluscs, caddis flies and beetles.　　B.D.H. & D.H.B.

Up to 200 sharp-tailed sandpipers visit annually in small flocks. Their name is derived from their pointed tail feathers.

Dunlin *Calidris alpina* (LINNAEUS,1758)

THE DUNLIN FEEDS in wet mud, often at the edge of the tide, or by pools on mud flats or by salt marshes. Sometimes it wades into shallow water. It hunts with its shoulders hunched, head and bill lowered and held forward. It walks briskly, tapping and probing at the surface until it detects food, then probes deeply. It sometimes paddles and jumps to disturb prey. On its breeding grounds, it eats mainly aquatic insect larvae and small molluscs. In winter, it takes marine polychaete worms, small crustaceans and molluscs, insects and their larvae.

It breeds on wet marshes or grassy and mossy tundra, often by lake shores or where grass and sedge are dotted with lakes and ponds and intersected by tidal river channels. In its winter quarters, it is mainly a bird of intertidal mud flats, saltmarsh runnels and coastal lagoons. In New Zealand, it is seen at high-tide roosts next to tidal mud flats.

It is strongly gregarious and seldom alone. It flies and roosts in tight flocks. In Australia, it associates with curlew and sharp-tailed sandpipers and red-necked stints; in New Zealand, with curlew sandpipers, wrybills and New Zealand dotterels. B.D.H. & D.H.B.

The dunlin is seen mostly at high-tide roosts adjacent to tidal mud flats.

STRAGGLER

OTHER NAMES: *Red-backed sandpiper, black-bellied sandpiper.*

SIZE: *200 mm.*

DESCRIPTION
This description is of the eastern subspecies C. a. sakhalina.
ADULT: *Sexes alike, female averaging larger. In non-breeding plumage upper surface, including rump, plain brownish grey, paler on nape and darker on crown, feathers with blurred brownish shaft streaks and narrow whitish edges. Upper tail coverts and central tail feathers brownish black. Outermost tail coverts white. Outer tail feathers brownish grey. Central pair of tail feathers longer than rest. Wing coverts darker than back, with whitish edges. Primaries dark grey-brown. Inner primaries and* secondaries with white bases, forming narrow wing stripe in flight. Whitish eyebrow stripe indistinct. Brownish about and behind eye. White narrowly between bill and eye, and on all underparts. Neck and upper breast pale grey, with blurred darker streaks, sometimes also on flanks. Bill slightly longer than head, tapering to tip, usually downcurved, black. Legs black or greenish black. In breeding plumage crown black, feathers broadly edged orange-chestnut, giving streaked appearance. Rest of head and nape grey-brown streaked blackish. Dark line from bill to eye. Feathers of mantle and scapulars black, broadly edged rich orange-chestnut. Chin and throat white. Neck and upper breast white streaked with black. Lower breast and fore-part of abdomen black.*
JUVENILE: *Similar on upper surface to breeding adult. Head and neck buff with blackish streaks. Wing and tail coverts with buff edges. Upper* breast grey or buff, with blurred dark streaks. Rest of underparts white, with scattered dark spots on lower breast and sides.*

MOULT
In Alaska, post-nuptial moult of C. a. sakhalina mid-June to late September before migration. Pre-nuptial body moult starts mid-February to March on wintering grounds and is completed by mid-April to early May. Post-juvenile body moult starts late July to early August and first winter plumage worn until first pre-nuptial moult starts in March.

VOICE
Generally silent in winter quarters. When flushed, rather shrill nasal treep, teerp or preep.

DISTRIBUTION
Breeding range almost circumpolar, with a gap north of Hudson Bay, in Canada, and in western Greenland. Birds reaching Australasia probably those that winter in eastern Asia and breed in northeastern Siberia and northern Alaska (subspecies sakhalina). Recorded in New Zealand at Manukau Harbour, Kaipara Harbour, and Firth of Thames.*

RECOGNITION

In non-breeding plumage, grey and white sandpiper. Differs from curlew sandpiper by shorter straighter bill, heavier at base; indistinct eye-stripe; voice; pattern of black central and white outer rump and tail; plump-bodied, shorter-necked, shorter-legged appearance; at rest, characteristic hunched posture, often with bill drooped.

White-rumped Sandpiper *Calidris fuscicollis* (VIEILLOT,1819)

STRAGGLER

OTHER NAME: *Bonaparte's sandpiper.*

SIZE: *190 mm.*

DESCRIPTION
ADULT: *Sexes alike, female averaging slightly larger. In non-breeding plumage upper parts uniform grey-brown, back and wings darker and with white tips on wing coverts. No distinct wing stripe. Tail brown, central feathers darker. Upper tail coverts and lower edges of rump and back white, forming white crescent across base of tail. Eye-stripe white, streaked grey. Dark stripe from bill through and below eye. Sides of face and neck white, streaked grey. Rest of underparts white, but breast and upper flanks with grey wash and irregular darker streaks. Bill short (almost as long as head), straight, fairly slender, black, sometimes paler at base of lower mandible. Legs blackish. In breeding plumage crown light rusty red streaked blackish; nape paler. Mantle and scapulars blackish brown, feathers with broad rusty red margins. Dark line from bill through eye with rusty red tinge, especially on ear coverts. Wing, tail, and pattern across base of tail as in non-breeding plumage. Breast and upper flanks whitish with broad dark streaks, broadest on chest and sides of breast, irregular on flanks. Rest of underparts, forehead, eye-stripe, chin and throat white.*

THE WHITE-RUMPED SANDPIPER, a rather tame bird, snatches food from the surface or probes rapidly, thrusting the full length of its bill into soft mud or mud covered by very shallow water. It eats a wide variety of small animal matter, especially the larvae and pupae of aquatic insects, small molluscs, blood-worms, leeches, crustaceans and annelid worms. It also takes the seeds of plants.

It breeds on grassy or mossy tundra. In its winter quarters it inhabits tidal mud flats but mostly lagoons on the coast or inland. It is gregarious and occurs in small groups to large flocks, often with other sandpipers. The birds that straggled to Australia associated with red-capped dotterels, red-necked stints, curlew sandpipers and sharp-tailed sandpipers. The New Zealand birds roosted near turnstones, red-necked stints, knots and sharp-tailed sandpipers. B.D.H. & D.H.B.

The white-rumped sandpiper, a small gregarious bird.

JUVENILE: *Upper parts dark brown to blackish, feathers with chestnut, whitish and buff margins, giving warm tinge. Wing coverts brown with whitish and buff margins. Underparts white; grey wash on breast and flanks tinged with buff.*

MOULT
Post-nuptial complete moult of adults August to October, with wing moult delayed until after migration, November to March. Pre-nuptial body moult about March. Post-juvenile body moult September to October, sometimes to November.

VOICE
Thin high-pitched call like the squeak of a mouse, pipit or swallow: jeet-jeet, tsick-tsick.*

DISTRIBUTION
Breeds on Arctic coasts and islands of North America from Alaska to Hudson Bay. Winters chiefly in southern South America east of the Andes. About one million birds move south July to October. Unrecorded between Alaska and Australasia. Northward migration begins early March, reaching breeding grounds early June. Two Australian records near Melbourne: one, apparently juvenile, November 1973 to February 1974; the other January to February 1977. Two New Zealand records: 2 birds in Manukau Harbour, December 1969; and one at Parengarenga in March 1971.*

RECOGNITION

In non-breeding plumage, small grey and white sandpiper with white rump. Tips of folded wings extend well beyond tail, giving elongated appearance. Similar to winter curlew sandpiper, but smaller, shorter legged and shorter necked, with short straight bill and narrower unmarked white crescent across tail.

Curlew Sandpiper

Calidris ferruginea (PONTOPPIDAN, 1763)

IN NEW ZEALAND, the curlew sandpiper is a bird of estuaries, brackish pools and coastal lagoons. It breeds on coastal Arctic tundra, where it also lives on heaths and low ground near rivers.

It feeds among other waders; in New Zealand and Australia especially with red-necked stints. It usually roosts with flocks of wrybills in the Auckland district and with banded dotterels or knots elsewhere. It forages mainly at the water's edge or just into the water, mostly by probing deeply or jabbing with its bill. The stomachs of 58 birds collected in Tasmania contained soft insect larvae, small hard-shelled molluscs, and seeds; also polychaete worms up to 80 mm long, apparently swallowed whole, and crustaceans.   B.D.H. & D.H.B.

The curlew sandpiper commonly feeds among other waders at the water's edge.

MIGRANT

OTHER NAME: *Curlew stint.*

SIZE: *220 mm.*

DESCRIPTION
ADULT: *In non-breeding plumage sexes alike, female averaging slightly larger, especially in bill length. Upper parts, including tail, plain grey-brown, lighter on nape, feathers with darker shaft-streaks and whitish edges. Wings darker grey-brown, feathers with white tips. Greater coverts with white tips, forming narrow wing stripe in flight. Upper tail coverts, side of rump and lower back white. Forehead, eyebrow stripe, side of head and neck, and all underparts white, with varying amounts of greyish wash and fine brownish streaks on neck and breast. Bill dark, long, slender, tapering, downcurved. Legs dull black. In breeding male upper surface bright chestnut, feathers of mantle and scapulars with black centres and white tips. Crown streaked blackish. White upper tail coverts with a few dark bars. Sides of head, neck and most of undersurface rich chestnut-red, sparsely barred with black, especially on flanks, feathers with white edges. Underwing, chin and undertail whitish; varying amounts of white on flanks. In breeding female chestnut areas paler; dark bars and spots more numerous on undersurface; more white on belly.*
JUVENILE: *Similar to non-breeding adult but darker brown above, mantle and scapulars blackish brown with buff, cream and a few chestnut feather edges. Wing coverts with pale buff edges. Sides of head and neck with grey streaks. Throat, breast and flanks buffy and streaked. In first winter buff-edged wing coverts remain.*

MOULT
Post-nuptial moult July to December. Wing moult varies: either September to February or else begun August, suspended, and finished November to March. Pre-nuptial body moult February to May. Juveniles moult into adult winter plumage September to December.

Juvenile wing moult varies and occurs during nothern winter. Some adults reaching New Zealand in September show traces of breeding colour. Some begin to redden in New Zealand in January and are in full plumage by late March. Few birds have fully moulted, however, before they leave.

VOICE
Clear liquid chirrip *or* chirririp. *Low musical twitter from feeding flock.*

DISTRIBUTION
Breeding confined largely to northern Siberia. Winters in Africa, Madagascar, islands of the Indian Ocean, Iraq, India, Sri Lanka, Bangladesh, Burma, southern Thailand, Hainan, Vietnam, Kampuchea, Malaysia, the Philippines, Indonesia, New Guinea, Australia and New Zealand. Australasian migrants probably fly through China. Starts to arrive in Australia late August, building up to a peak that in December may include flocks of 500 to 1000. Especially numerous on South Australian and Victorian coasts, where over 60 000 were counted in February 1983. Leaves in late March and early April. A few, mainly immatures, overwinter. In New Zealand, arrives from early September and builds up in some northern localities to flocks of 30 to 50 during October. Departs in March and April, some lingering to May. A few immatures overwinter. New Zealand population unlikely to have exceeded 150 in any year.

> **RECOGNITION**
>
> Slim sandpiper with slender, long, downcurved bill and fairly long black legs. Narrow white wing stripe in flight and distinctive white upper tail coverts. Larger than broad-billed and western sandpipers, whose bills are downcurved at tip only. Upper surface greyer than banded dotterel and sharp-tailed sandpiper.

Western Sandpiper *Calidris mauri* (CABANIS, 1857)

The western sandpiper is a rare vagrant, mainly to northern New Zealand.

THE WESTERN SANDPIPER DARTS about picking and dabbling at the surface of the wet sand of beaches or the wet mud of saltmarsh pools. It tends to feed at the edge of the receding tide, starting as soon as the ebb begins. The New Zealand birds were seen feeding and roosting with red-necked stints and roosting with bar-tailed godwits. On migration and in winter, the western sandpiper lives on beaches, coastal marshes, and especially wet, tidal, mud flats. It breeds in coastal tundra, nesting on drier knolls and hillsides.

The western sandpiper can be distinguished only with great care from the semipalmated sandpiper (*Calidris pusilla*) of North America. This bird is not recorded in Australasia. Over recent years a number of observers believe they have seen the latter species but have been unable to prove so. The semipalmated sandpiper generally has a shorter bill that is not downcurved. The western sandpiper tends to hold the bill pointing downwards, even in flight, and it may retain scapulars with bright rufous edging.   B.D.H. & D.H.B.

VAGRANT

OTHER NAMES: *None.*

SIZE: *170 mm.*

DESCRIPTION
ADULT: *Sexes alike, female averaging slightly larger. In non-breeding plumage upper parts plain brownish grey, feathers with darker shaft-streaks and narrow whitish edges. Scattered breeding plumage feathers with bright rufous edges often retained, especially on scapulars. Flight feathers darker brownish grey. Face, narrow eyebrow stripe and underparts white. Chest faintly streaked greyish or dusky, mainly on sides. Bill slightly longer than head, dark, broad at base and tapering to slightly expanded and noticeably drooped tip. Legs dark olive but usually appear black. Partial webbing between bases of toes. In breeding plumage upper surface, especially hind crown, ear coverts, mantle and scapulars bright rufous, streaked with black. Lower scapulars and back feathers with black centres and rufous or tawny edges. Wing and tail brown-grey, tail darker in centre. Broad white eyebrow stripe; rufous brown stripe from bill to eye, broadening to patch behind eye. Forehead and neck white, streaked dark grey. Chin, underwing, and rest of underparts white, breast heavily spotted and streaked dark brown. Part of flanks with dark brown triangular marks.*
JUVENILE: *Dull blackish brown above, with feathers of back, scapulars, and wing coverts edged bright reddish chestnut, whitish and bright buff. Forehead, eyebrow stripe white. Underparts white. Breast with pale buff wash; finely streaked.*

MOULT
Post-nuptial complete moult July to September or later. Wing moult July to October in short-distance migrants but postponed until after migration, October to February, in long-distance migrants. Pre-nuptial body moult March and April. Post-juvenile body moult mostly completed by October.

VOICE
Rather thin squeaky cheep *or* jeep.

DISTRIBUTION
Breeds in northeastern USSR, only on Cukotskij Peninsula; Alaska; and on St Lawrence and Munivak Islands. Winters on Pacific coasts to Peru, on Atlantic coasts to Venezuela. One record in Australia; 7 in New Zealand: North Island and Farewell Spit.

> **RECOGNITION**
>
> In non-breeding plumage small, white-faced, grey and white sandpiper. Differs from stints by long black bill with drooped tip and slightly longer legs. Differs from Baird's sandpiper by smaller size, different bill, and lack of buff on face and chest; from broad-billed sandpiper by slighter bill, black legs, and lack of head stripes.

Red-necked Stint *Calidris ruficollis* (PALLAS,1776)

NEW ZEALAND is at the end of the red-necked stint's range. This wader was regarded as rare here before the 1940s; now up to 300 to 400 visit each year. Yet this is very few considering the ample habitat available.

It is thought to breed on both dry and wet grassy tundra with or without willow scrub. At its winter quarters it is common mainly on tidal mud flats, also sea beaches, Pacific island reefs, the edges of coastal lagoons, paddy fields, and salt and freshwater swamps close to the coast. In New Zealand it mainly feeds in the wet mud of large tidal flats of harbours, estuaries and tidal lagoons.

It is highly gregarious and generally roosts, flies and feeds in dense flocks. It readily associates with other small to medium-sized species: in Australia usually with sharp-tailed and curlew sandpipers and red-capped dotterels; in New Zealand usually with wrybills and banded dotterels. Flocks scatter to feed but not far apart. When disturbed, red-necked stints fly close together, swiftly and directly at first, then turning and twisting in unison.

They feed primarily on areas of mud and sand that have a film of moisture, both where the tide falls and at the edges of non-tidal lagoons, where they also wade up to 20 mm deep. They feed eagerly, with legs flexed and bodies low to the ground, running about with mouse-like rushes, their bills working busily up and down like sewing machines. They take most of their food by snatching and jabbing at the surface; in shallow water they also probe. One Tasmanian study showed that important foods were small crustaceans, larvae and pupae of flies, the gastropod mollusc *Assiminea*, and various plant fragments and seeds.   B.D.H. & D.H.B.

MIGRANT

OTHER NAMES: *Rufous-necked sandpiper, eastern little stint.*

SIZE: *150 mm.*

DESCRIPTION
ADULT: *Sexes alike. In non-breeding plumage upper surface pale grey with slight brownish tinge, feathers of crown, mantle and scapulars with fine dark shaft streaks. Wing coverts grey-brown, with narrow dark shaft streaks and whitish edges; greater coverts with white tips, forming narrow but distinct wing stripe in flight. Primaries, primary coverts and secondaries dark grey-brown; primaries with white shafts. Rump, central upper tail coverts and centre tail black. Outer tail coverts white; outer tail feathers pale brownish grey. Forehead, broad eyebrow stripe, side of head and underparts, including underwing, white. Lores, ear coverts and side of chest greyish. Bill shorter than head, straight, stout, black. Legs black. In breeding plumage feathers of crown, mantle and scapulars blackish brown with rich chestnut-red edges. Nape paler. Wing and tail as in non-breeding plumage. Scapulars with white tips, giving spotted effect. Sides of head and neck, throat, foreneck and upper breast rich chestnut-red. Forehead and chin whitish. Little or no eyebrow stripe. Rest of underparts and underwing white but a few large brown spots on sides of breast and flanks.*
JUVENILE: *Upper surface blackish brown, feathers edged pale buff or chestnut. Wing coverts grey-brown, edged cream and pale buff. Forehead, forecrown and eyebrow stripe white. Lores and ear coverts greyish. Underparts white. Sides of neck and breast with buff-grey wash and some fine brown streaks, sometimes with wash extending across breast.*

MOULT
Some birds begin post-nuptial body moult in late June or early July and finish during migration in mid-August. Others begin up to late July and then suspend moult until after migration. Many reaching Australia and New Zealand in late September and October still show some breeding plumage. Adult wing moult occurs after migration, with birds wintering in northern parts of the range moulting August to December, and those in southern parts moulting September to March. Pre-nuptial body moult begins on wintering grounds. In New Zealand, is noticeable on some in second half of February, is prominent during March, and many of those that have not left in April are in good colour. Post-juvenile body moult may begin during migration but occurs mainly on wintering grounds, lasting even through to April. Breeding plumage not assumed until second (northern) summer but some overwintering birds acquire scattering of rufous feathers on neck and shoulders. Birds overwintering in New Zealand occasionally show some red.

VOICE
Rather quiet in winter quarters. Large feeding flocks twitter quietly among themselves, short pit, pip, *or* chit. *Flight call is thin high-pitched* chit-chit-chit *or* week-week-week. *Alarm call is louder* teet-teet-teet *or* krrit.

DISTRIBUTION
Known to breed in Siberia on Tajmyr Peninsula and from Lena River delta east to Tiksi Bay; also Alaska. Winters on coasts of southeastern China, Hainan, Taiwan, southern Japan, Burma, Thailand, the Andaman and Nicobar Islands, Kampuchea, Vietnam, the Philippines, Micronesia, Kiribati, the Bismarck Archipelago, Solomon Islands, Malaysia, Indonesia, New Guinea, Australia and New Zealand. Straggles to Fiji and Norfolk Island. Migrates largely through East Asian coasts; leaves USSR from late July onwards. Arrives back late April to mid-June. In Australia, common on coasts of all states September to early May, especially in the southeast. In New Zealand occurs widely in small flocks. In some years, many migrants have arrived by late September. Most arrive in October and November. Most leave in late March to mid-April but some linger to the end of April, in some years even to early May.

The smallest wader to visit New Zealand regularly, the red-necked stint generally roosts and feeds in dense flocks.

RECOGNITION
By far the smallest wader visiting New Zealand regularly. Grey and white, lack of breast markings, short, straight bill and black legs distinctive of non-breeding plumage. Immatures similar but much darker above, often with fairly dark, streaked breast.

Sanderling · *Calidris alba* (Pallas, 1764)

When feeding, the sanderling holds its body horizontal and moves its legs so fast that it has been likened to a clockwork toy. On white sand beaches it rushes in and out of the wave line, following each backwash and jabbing rapidly. It also picks among vegetation washed ashore and probes the sand with its bill tip partly open. In New Zealand it hunts on open sandy beaches and estuarine and mud-flat pools, catching amphipods, small crustaceans and molluscs, marine worms and insects.

It associates readily with other small waders such as banded dotterels and wrybills, although it generally keeps somewhat apart. When disturbed it flies rapidly and direct, and lands abruptly.

The sanderling nests on barren stony tundra not far from the sea. At these Arctic breeding grounds it eats small plant buds before the thaw, and then insect larvae in shallow pools.

Past records include four birds in the South Island up to 1938: one at Waikanae in 1930, and five at Parengarenga in April 1950 and February 1951. During and since the 1960s it has been recorded more often at various localities: Parengarenga, Rangaunu Bay, Coromandel Peninsula, Manukau Harbour, Firth of Thames, Maketu (five in 1967), Manawatu estuary, Farewell Spit, Lake Ellesmere and Southland coastal lagoons. Up to five birds are reported regularly in Southland each year.

B.D.H. & D.H.B.

STRAGGLER

OTHER NAMES: *None.*

SIZE: *200 mm.*

DESCRIPTION

ADULT: *In non-breeding plumage sexes alike, female averaging slightly larger. Upper parts pale grey, feathers with darker shaft streaks and, on back, broad white margins. Crown and nape very pale with light streaks. Face, broad eyebrow stripe and underparts, white. Slight grey wash on side of breast. Rump, central tail coverts and central tail feathers blackish grey, contrasting in flight with white outer tail coverts and brownish grey outer tail. Primaries and their coverts blackish; rest of wing lighter. Much of secondaries and their coverts white, forming broad white wing stripe in flight. Lesser coverts on leading surface of wing blackish, especially near body, producing dark patch at angle of folded wing. Iris brown. Bill short, straight, black. Legs black, lacking hind toe. In breeding plumage sexes differ slightly. In male, head, neck, throat, upper breast, mantle and scapulars light rufous; feathers of crown and nape with broad black shaft-streaks; feathers of mantle and scapulars with black patches and narrow white or grey tips; feathers of neck and breast with black streaks, spots, bars, and white tips. Rufous upper breast contrasts with white of rest of undersurface. Wing coverts grey with paler margins. In female, upper parts greyer, rufous of head and chest paler than male. Throat sometimes white.*

JUVENILE: *Crown, mantle and scapular feathers blackish brown with buff or white spots. Wing coverts blackish brown with broad buff spots. Upper tail coverts blackish with tawny tips, forming streaked and barred rump pattern. Buff wash on upper breast.*

MOULT

Post-nuptial complete moult of adults July to October with wing moult August to October in medium-distance migrants and October to February in long-distance migrants. Pre-nuptial body moult March to May. Post-juvenile body moult September to December with wing moult January to July. In New Zealand, sanderlings seen in March and April and one in January were starting to change colour; generally December to February birds in non-breeding plumage.

VOICE

Generally silent in winter quarters but when flushed calls shrill liquid wick-wick, twick twick *or soft* twick.

DISTRIBUTION

Breeds on Arctic islands of Canada, Greenland, Spitsbergen and northern USSR. Winters widely, mainly on coasts, as far south as southern South America, Africa and Australia. Main Pacific wintering area is Australia where widespread September to April, though not abundant, on ocean beaches and reefs. In New Zealand, a few are recorded each year, mainly December to March, on coasts of the North and South Islands.

RECOGNITION

Plump sandpiper. In non-breeding plumage pale grey above and white below. Looks rather like an oversized stint but with broad white wing stripe, white-edged back feathers, proportionately longer bill.

Small, pale waders, sanderlings feed on the seashore, darting after food in the sand as the waves recede and probing with their bill tips partly open.

Eastern Broad-billed Sandpiper *Limicola falcinellus sibirica* Dresser, 1876

DESCRIPTION

ADULT: *Sexes alike, female averaging larger. In non-breeding plumage crown, nape, hind neck, mantle and scapulars pale brown-grey, feathers with darker shaft streaks and narrow white edges. Back, rump, upper tail coverts and central tail feathers blackish brown, feathers with narrow white edges. Sides of rump and tail coverts white, outer tail feathers grey, producing flight pattern of white with narrow dark central stripe. Broad eyebrow stripe white; roughly parallel, a second, narrow white stripe joins it slightly forward of eye and runs back on to hind crown. Narrow brown-grey band between these white stripes, and broader dark band in mid-crown tapers forward to bill. Grey band from lores through eye to ear coverts. Breast and side of neck white, lightly streaked or speckled dark grey. Chin, throat and rest of underparts white. Wing coverts brownish grey; white tips on greater coverts form faint wing stripe in flight. Flight feathers and primary coverts dark grey-brown. Iris brown. Bill blackish, deep, slightly longer than head, downcurved at tip; when seen from above, broad, widening slightly in middle and tapering at tip. Legs short, dull greenish brown to greenish grey. In breeding plumage crown, mantle, scapulars and back black, feathers edged yellowish chestnut, producing longitudinal stripes. Nape and hind neck buff, streaked blackish brown. White head stripes as in non-breeding plumage, but second white stripe much less distinct. Dark brown line from bill through eye to ear coverts. Sides of head and neck, chin, throat, upper breast and flanks white with light chestnut wash, heavily streaked and spotted with dark brown. Rest of underparts white. Wing and tail as in non-breeding plumage but central tail feathers edged with chestnut.*

JUVENILE: *Upper parts, and dark line through eye, like breeding adult. Wing coverts with broad buff edges. Underparts like non-breeding adult but suffused with buff or dull brown on sides of face and neck, upper breast and flanks.*

MOULT

Little information available. Post-nuptial complete moult of western race August to October; wing moult late August to December. Pre-nuptial body moult of the western race February to April. Juvenile body moult into first-winter plumage September to January, with outer primaries moulted March to April. In Siberia, non-breeding adults of eastern race may begin body moult mid-July and breeding adults late the same month.

An inconspicuous bird, the eastern broad-billed sandpiper has noticeably short legs and a long heavy bill.

VOICE

Flight note low chr-r-r-reet *or* chrrreep, *less musical than* chirrip *of curlew sandpiper.* Chirrup-chip-chip *recorded when taking flight; also described as trilling* purrr.

DISTRIBUTION

Breeding range poorly known. Western race breeds in Scandinavia and northwest Russia, wintering in eastern Mediterranean, the Red Sea, Aden, Persian Gulf, India, Sri Lanka and possibly eastern Africa. Eastern race breeds in Arctic Siberia and winters in small numbers on the coasts of eastern India, Burma, Thailand, the Malay Peninsula, Vietnam, Hainan, southeastern China, Taiwan, the Philippines, Indonesia and New Guinea. In Australia, winters mainly in north, also Cairns from mid-August to early May. Sometimes reaches southeastern and Western Australia. Recorded in New Zealand at Parengarenga Harbour, February to March 1970; Manukau Harbour, December 1963; Firth of Thames, January to March 1960, May and October to December 1964, February 1968, November 1970; Lake Ellesmere, December 1962. All were single birds except for 2 in February 1968.

RECOGNITION

Slightly larger than red-necked stint; smaller than sharp-tailed and curlew sandpipers and wrybill. In non-breeding plumage like a stint but usually with snipe-like head pattern; long, heavy bill, downcurved near tip; and double eye-stripe on each side of head. Brown-grey above with mottled look; white below with grey-streaked breast.

THE BROAD-BILLED SANDPIPER is easily overlooked. At its northern breeding grounds it is skulking and inconspicuous. At its winter quarters it is usually quiet, and generally alone or in small groups. Yet in Vietnam, Malaya and parts of Burma it is sociable and appears in large numbers, sometimes mixed with other species. In Japan it migrates with dunlins and red-necked stints. In Australia it sometimes associates with red-necked stints.

It breeds in bogs and morasses. On migration and during winter it remains near the coast, especially at the muddy edges of tidal creeks and saltwater lagoons, sometimes on open muddy shores and estuaries. In India and Burma it favours the muddy areas of tidal flats; near Darwin the soft mud on the seaward side of mangroves. In New Zealand mostly single birds have been recorded, on high-tide roosts among wrybills and on a lake shore.

It feeds with its bill held vertically, probing vigorously up and down, sometimes inserting the full length of its bill and submerging its head. Occasionally it feeds by pecking at the surface; food includes beetles and their larvae, molluscs, worms, gastropods, small crustaceans and the seeds of aquatic plants.

The eastern race *sibirica*, which occurs in New Zealand, differs from the nominate *falcinellus* by being larger on average, paler and more greyish in its non-breeding plumage, and more reddish above in its breeding plumage. The two races overlap in eastern India, in their winter range.

B.D.H. & D.H.B.

Red-necked Avocet *Recurvirostra novaehollandiae* Vieillot, 1816

The red-necked avocet, a stilt-like wader with a long upcurved bill.

THE RED-NECKED AVOCET FEEDS in shallow water, sweeping its long upturned bill from side to side and swaying its whole body in time with this movement. Often it wades up to its belly and continues sweeping with its head submerged. With its webbed feet it swims well and sometimes feeds out of its depth by upending like a duck, so that its rear end looks like a fisherman's float bobbing on the surface. Its food is small aquatic animals including insects, molluscs and crustaceans. Its flight is leisurely, with its legs trailing behind. During the 1850s and 1860s the species was reported widely in New Zealand but not proved to breed. The only confirmed records this century are of one bird shot at Lake Ellesmere in 1912 and one seen at Orowaiti Lagoon, Westport, from February 1968 to 1970.   B.D.H. & D.H.B.

Pied Stilt *Himantopus himantopus leucocephalus* Gould, 1837

OVER THE LAST 100 YEARS, as forests have been turned to farmland, the pied stilt has greatly increased its range in New Zealand. From July to February it breeds in open areas on swamps, lagoons, flooded fields, riverbeds, estuaries and salt marshes. It avoids trees but sometimes nests among tall rushes and sedges if there is a good supply of food. At the end of the breeding season inland birds migrate to the coast. Hundreds and even thousands of birds flock at northern harbours such as Kaipara and Manukau. Smaller flocks winter in estuaries and lagoons as far south as Invercargill. Many young non-breeding birds remain at these winter feeding grounds during the following summer. Although a common bird in mainland New Zealand, the pied stilt is rare on Stewart Island and the Chatham Islands.

Autumn and winter flocks feed on tidal flats and shallow muddy lagoons. At high tide they forage in swamps, lake edges and the lower reaches of rivers. In the North Island especially, large numbers feed on flooded pasture. They walk through shallow water pecking at the surface or plunging their heads underneath. In soft mud they scythe or probe with their bills. They eat mainly water insects, but also crustaceans, at coastal lagoons and earthworms in sodden fields. Within this diet pied stilts often specialise for long periods: for example on certain crustaceans at coastal lagoons, and on earthworms and scarabid larvae in damp fields. They are opportunist feeders; when food is abundant there is less than a metre between each bird, but when food is scarce they defend large feeding territories. They feed throughout the day and sometimes at night, but mainly in the early morning and late afternoon. Usually they fly across deep channels in rivers and lagoons; occasionally they swim.

They first breed at two or three years, rarely one year. Birds in the north begin breeding before those in the south; and birds in the lowlands before those in the high country. The first clutches are laid in July near Auckland; in August in lowland Canterbury, Otago and Southland; and in late September and October in inland Canterbury and central Otago. If food is abundant and the weather is mild, nesting may be up to two months earlier than usual. On the other hand if food is very scarce the birds may not breed.

They nest in small colonies, usually of between five and 15 pairs. Nests are well apart, preferably on an island or plant in a shallow swamp. Other nesting sites are islands and banks of shingle riverbeds; islands in flooded fields; and muddy or grassed edges of ponds, estuaries and streams. The nests are always close to, and usually

surrounded by, water. The type of nest depends on the available plants, and ranges from a mere scrape in shingle or grass to a large platform of grasses, sedges, rushes, roots and small branches.

During the weeks leading up to egg-laying the pair mate several times a day. The female stands with her head, neck and bill stretched forward and downward. The male approaches and walks back and forth behind the female splashing his bill in the water and preening himself. He then jumps on her back and sinks slowly down with his wings stretched in the air. Afterwards the male jumps down and walks

Common throughout most open wetland areas, the pied stilt is unmistakable: a slim black and white wader with very long reddish legs and a yapping call.

forward with the female, their bills crossed. This is usually followed by slow feeding or by preening.

The birds usually lay one clutch of four pyriform to oval eggs, brown-buff to olive in colour and heavily marked with brown-black blotches, spots and streaks. Replacement clutches often have three eggs only. Both parents incubate, changing over 10 to 20 times a day for 24 or 25 days. The eggs hatch together and, if the weather is fine, the chicks leave the nest within a few hours. At first, the young stilts forage close together, but after about a week they separate. One parent guards the chicks while the other forages up to a kilometre away. Sometimes, the family party moves to new feeding grounds and

is disbanded a few weeks after the chicks fledge at four to five weeks.

Pied stilts defend their feeding or nesting territories from other stilts by running or flying towards the intruder. Usually the interloper retreats, but if it does not leave, a confrontation results with much calling, hovering with rapid wing-beats, and chasing, both on the ground and in the air. In most cases it results in the intruder flying off. When aerial predators such as harriers approach, several stilts attack until the predator leaves. Injury feigning is the usual display in response to ground predators. The birds group together, feign flightlessness and utter calls of distress. False-brooding and direct attacks, such as dive-bombing, are also used.   R.J.P

A black stilt (right) and a hybrid stilt at a nesting site surrounded by water. The black stilt is now one of the rarest wader species in the world.

Black Stilt *Himantopus novaezealandiae* Gould, 1764

DURING THE NINETEENTH CENTURY black stilts were fairly common in New Zealand. By 1900, however, they were rare on the North Island and by the 1940s breeding was restricted to South Canterbury and Otago. Now only 40 to 50 birds breed in inland river valleys of South Canterbury and North Otago. In the autumn family parties and pairs move to tarns and river deltas around Lakes Tekapo, Pukaki, Ohau and Benmore. About 10 per cent of birds winter at North Island harbours such as Kawhia and Firth of Thames. Occasionally single birds are sighted on the Canterbury coast.

Black stilts forage in shallow water on shingle riverbeds, streams, swamps and tarns. In winter, they forage on rivers and river deltas. Those few birds that migrate to the coast forage in muddy lagoons, estuaries and harbours.

Black stilts feed throughout the day and sometimes at night. At streams, rivers and rivermouths they walk through the water, pecking or probing for animals (particularly mayfly and caddis fly larvae) that live at the bottom. Sometimes they flip over stones to expose insects. They also prey on small fish and insects such as emerging mayflies that drift on the surface. At tarns and swamps black stilts feed on insects and their larvae, such as waterboatmen, backswimmers and damselflies, as well as gastropods. Sometimes they swish through surface mud to catch worms or the larvae of midges. They also forage in open, damp, grassy areas where they probe for earthworms and grass grubs (*Costelytra zealandica*).

Black stilts begin breeding at two or three years of age. Usually they nest in isolated pairs and defend their territories from other stilts. Some pairs nest within 100 m of other pairs or even in loose colonies of pied stilts. The nest is a depression in shingle or grass lined with grasses, twigs or riverbed debris. Usually it is placed near water on a flat or gently sloping bank or island. At swamps and tarns some nests are built on waterside plants while others are mounds of grasses and algae built up above the surrounding water. In September or October (earlier than local pied stilts) the birds lay four brown eggs tinged with green and streaked and blotched with brown-black. If the first clutch is lost, they lay another.

Both parents incubate the eggs, changing over every hour (less frequently at night), for 25 days. Within a few hours of hatching the chicks leave the nest and forage in very shallow water nearby. Before the young fledge at six to eight weeks the family may move several kilometres to new feeding grounds where any pied stilts are chased away. Family groups continue to defend feeding territories throughout the winter. In August and September the parents expel the young stilts from the family unit.

The decline of black stilts was probably caused by introduced predators and habitat destruction. Nests and young are very susceptible to predation by feral cats, polecats and Norway rats. Vulnerable features of this species include nesting in areas and at times of high predator densities, solitary nesting, poor reactions to predators, and the long fledgling period. The consequently low level of population recruitment contributes to the formation of mixed pair-bonds of pied x black stilt or hybrid x black stilt.

R.J.P.

ENDEMIC

OTHER NAME: *Kaki.*

SIZE: *380 mm.*

DESCRIPTION
ADULT: *Sexes similar. Upper parts black, with green gloss mainly on wing. Underparts brownish black. Forehead, face and parts of belly sometimes paler, especially in female. Iris crimson. Bill black. Feet bright pink. Claws red. Hybrids of black and pied stilts are mainly black above with white head and white markings on tail; throat white; variable black band on foreneck and breast; black markings on flanks and sides; belly mainly white; undertail black and white.*
JUVENILE: *At fledging mainly dark above and white below. Iris dark. Bill black, pink towards base. Legs pale pink. From fledging grey-black blotches and streaks develop on flank. These extend over flank and most of side, with dark band extending to cloacal region. In July, crown and hind neck develop grey-black blotches which extend over foreneck. Area between blotches becomes dark grey. By September blotching and darkening extends to breast and sides. By October plumage is predominantly black with extensive white mottling mainly on underparts. Bill black. Legs pink. Adult plumage attained at 14 to 20 months.*
NESTLING: *Forehead pale brown. Upper parts buff or pale brown blotched and streaked with black horizontal lines. Horizontal black line from base of upper mandible through eye to hind neck. Undersurface white or off-white, with grey-black thighs. Bill black-brown. Upper leg dark brown-grey. Lower leg and toes pale blue-grey. Soles orange.*

MOULT
Moults twice annually: an incomplete pre-nuptial moult from July to September, during which the remiges and rectrices are retained; and a complete post-nuptial moult from December to April. In mid-January most adults are in wing moult.

VOICE
Single high-pitched yapping note repeated several times when alarmed. Softer low-pitched calls during courtship, nest-building and incubation. Juvenile calls quiet high-pitched kip.

DISTRIBUTION
Wetlands of inland South Canterbury and North Otago. A few birds winter in northern harbours.

RECOGNITION

Adults distinguished from black oystercatcher by narrow black bill and very long legs. Immatures distinguished from pied stilts by pale or mottled hind neck.

Grey Phalarope

Phalaropus fulicarius (Linnaeus,1758)

VAGRANT

OTHER NAME: *Red phalarope.*

SIZE: *200 mm.*

DESCRIPTION
ADULT: *Sexes alike, female averaging larger. In non-breeding plumage, head, neck and underparts, including underwing, white. Blackish patch on hind crown, becoming dark grey on central nape. Blackish patch from lores to ear coverts. Mantle, scapulars, back and rump light bluish grey, feathers with narrow white edges and darker shaft streaks. Sides of back, rump and upper tail coverts white. Tail feathers brown-grey with white edges and pale rufous tips. Wings darker grey: primaries dark grey-brown with white shafts; secondaries dark grey-brown with white bases forming narrow wing stripe in flight. Side of breast blue-grey with a few grey feathers on flank. Bill slightly shorter than head, straight, deep, broad, dark brownish black and yellow or brownish yellow at base. Legs and feet brownish with yellowish swimming lobes. In breeding plumage female brighter than male. Upper parts brownish black, feathers edged with yellow, rufous or creamy buff. Tail dark grey-brown in centre, lighter toward sides, feathers edged and tipped rufous-buff. Wings as in non-breeding plumage. Head and usually chin slate grey. White patch from lores to ear coverts and sometimes around upper nape. Throat, sometimes chin, neck and underparts rich chestnut, mixed with slate grey on hind neck. Underwing white. Bill yellow with dark tip. Legs brownish, feet with yellowish lobes.*
JUVENILE: *Forehead light buff or white. Feathers from crown to tail dark brown with tawny or buff-brown edges. Eye-stripe, lores, cheeks, chin, foreneck, breast and flank washed brownish buff. Rest of underparts white.*

MOULT
Complete post-nuptial moult July to mid-September. Wing moult August to November. Pre-nuptial moult March to May. Juvenile body moult August to September, occasionally later. First wing moult at end of first northern summer.

VOICE
Low twit, tweet, zip *singly or in short series.* Choo kit *when feeding.*

DISTRIBUTION
Breeds in arctic North America, Greenland, Iceland, Novaja Zemlja and Siberia. Winters off the coasts of western South America and western Africa, and apparently in the North Pacific. Casual New Zealand and Australia.

Very mobile, the grey phalarope floats lightly on water like a gull or duck.

WHEN PHALAROPES BREED the usual roles of the sexes are reversed. The female, which is slightly larger and more brightly coloured, displays, and selects the nest-site. The male builds the nest, incubates, and rears the brood; the female helps only occasionally.

After breeding, the grey phalarope winters at sea, far from the coast. It comes to land only occasionally, either after a gale or as a vagrant. It is well adapted to marine life with dense undersurface plumage, lobed toes and webbed feet. Very mobile on the water, it swims erratically with frequent changes in direction to jab here and there at surface prey. The grey phalarope is unapproachable at sea, where it flies off swiftly, low to the waves. Often it spins gracefully on the spot. On land, the grey phalarope feeds like a sandpiper; it is restless and active, pecking rapidly. Over the last hundred years four birds have been recorded in New Zealand (the most recent at Kaituna Lagoon, Bay of Plenty, late June 1977) and one in Australia. All were seen on lakes or coastal lagoons. At sea the grey phalarope probably eats mainly plankton; also tiny fish, jellyfish and crustaceans and sometimes forages in the wake of whales. At its breeding grounds in the Arctic it feeds on crustaceans, molluscs, insects and their larvae, spiders, worms, algae and moss.   B.D.H. & D.H.B.

A red-necked phalarope in partial breeding plumage only.

Red-necked Phalarope

Phalaropus lobatus (Linnaeus,1758)

THE RED-NECKED PHALAROPE winters at sea, further inshore than its relative the grey phalarope; migrating flocks gather, for example, in some wide bays in North America and Japan. From March onwards it returns north where it nests in open tundra and forest clearings and eats molluscs, crustaceans, beetles, waterboatmen and the larvae of mosquitoes, midges and other insects. Several birds have straggled to Australia in recent years. Of the three New Zealand records, a male in non-breeding plumage was shot at Lake Ellesmere in 1929, a female in breeding plumage was collected at Wanganui in April 1935, and a bird in non-breeding plumage was seen at Washdyke Lagoon, Timaru, in March 1961.   B.D.H. & D.H.B.

VAGRANT

OTHER NAME: *Northern phalarope.*

SIZE: *190 mm.*

DESCRIPTION
ADULT: *Female averaging slightly larger. In non-breeding plumage sexes alike. Upper parts blue-grey, the feathers with broad white edges and tips when fresh, giving scaly appearance. Tail dark grey. Wings grey-brown: primaries blackish with white shafts and coverts black. Broad white tips of greater coverts and white bases of secondaries form white wing stripe in flight; secondaries tipped with white. Head, neck and underparts white. Crown and centre of nape dark grey. Blackish patch from eye to ear coverts. Side of breast has blue-grey wash. Flank has some grey feathers.*
Bill slightly longer than head, straight, slender, tapering, black. Legs blackish or slate-grey. Webs and lobes yellowish. In breeding plumage of female, head, mantle, scapulars, wing coverts, and hind neck slate-grey, the feathers tipped with white when fresh. On side of mantle and outer edge of scapulars bold rufous or tawny buff stripe. Tail and wing as in non-breeding plumage. Small white patch above and below eye. Chin and throat white, encircled by crescent of reddish chestnut from behind eyes broadly down sides of neck and on to upper breast. Side of breast slate-grey, mottled white, extending on to upper breast. Rest of underparts white with streaks and patches of brownish slate on flanks and under-tail coverts. Bill black. In male, dark areas of head and upper surface brown-grey; feathers of mantle and scapulars broadly edged with rufous-buff and tipped with white; mantle stripes less prominent; and chestnut neck-crescent less bright and extensive, sometimes almost absent.
JUVENILE: *Like adult non-breeding plumage but upper parts, including crown and nape, dark brown; feathers of mantle and tail broadly edged with warm buff; light grey-brown or buff wash on breast and flanks; and legs bluish to yellowish grey.*

MOULT
Post-nuptial complete moult July to October, sometimes to January. Wing moult in winter quarters. Pre-nuptial body moult February to June. Juvenile body moult September and October.

VOICE
Whit *or* weet. *When alarmed,* chik *or* chek *singly or in rapid series.*

DISTRIBUTION
Breeds in the Arctic. Winters off the coasts of Peru, Argentina and western Africa; in the western Indian Ocean, the western Pacific and the South China Sea. Casual in New Zealand and Australia.

Oriental Pratincole *Glareola maldivarum* J.R. FORSTER,1795

IN THE HEAT OF THE DAY the oriental pratincole is sluggish. It merely sits or stands and, even when disturbed, does not fly far. It feeds in the cooler morning and evening, soaring to a great height in pursuit of flying insects, which are trapped in its wide gape. Sometimes it feeds on the ground, running swiftly with its back horizontal.

An occasional visitor to New Zealand, it has been found on or near the coast, from the Kermadec Islands to Stewart Island. Its main wintering grounds are in northern Australia. There flocks of 30 to 40 and sometimes thousands of birds live on dry open places such as grassland plains, airfields and claypans, often but not always close to water. The species breeds in Asia on open flat land covered sparsely with low grass, especially on sunbaked mud flats in marshes, river deltas, valleys and lakeshores. In southern Asia it also nests in burnt-over rice fields and grasslands, even in sand dunes. B.D.H. & D.H.B.

VAGRANT

OTHER NAMES: *Eastern pratincole, eastern collared pratincole, swallow-plover.*

SIZE: *230 mm.*

DESCRIPTION
ADULT: *In breeding plumage, upper surface from forehead to rump and wing coverts smoky brown with olive tinge; slightly paler and faintly rufous on hind neck. Primaries and outer secondaries blackish grading to brown on inner secondaries. Upper tail coverts white. Tail black, white at base; deeply forked with outermost feather 1½ times as long as central feathers. Lores black in male, dark brown in female. Chin and throat pale buff or rufous, enclosed by narrow black necklace running from above gape and below eye, sometimes with slight white inner border. Upper breast and side of breast smoky brown, grading to pale rufous on lower breast and flanks and to white on belly and undertail coverts. Axillaries and underwing coverts bright chestnut-red, blackish near wing edge. Bill short, broad, deep at base, strongly arched on top, and gape wide; black, blood red at gape. Legs short, russet brown to grey-black. In non-breeding plumage throat is buff, mottled and streaked with brown, necklace stripe broken and streaky, even absent. Lores brown.*
JUVENILE: *As adult but lores smoky brown; throat streaked with brown: necklace absent; and breast dark, mottled dark brown and buff. In first-winter plumage, as non-breeding adult.*

MOULT
No study available.

VOICE
Harsh chitter. Soft plover-like to-wheet to-wheet as it rises. Loud chik, chik-chik, or tar-rak, occasionally a loud chet or cherrr. Flock call churr-ah.

DISTRIBUTION
Breeds in Pakistan, India, Bangladesh, Sri Lanka, Southeast Asia, Mongolia, China and southeast USSR. Winters mainly in northern Australia from Point Cloates in the west across to northern Queensland; also Southeast Asia, Taiwan, Philippines and Indonesia. In New Zealand, several stragglers often in non-typical habitat.

RECOGNITION
Mainly brown with pale throat encircled by black necklace. Short legs and long narrow wings extending beyond tail when folded. Slow buoyant flight. When feeding in flight, flies high, wheeling, twisting, and swooping.

The oriental pratincole nests throughout much of the Asian region. In flight, with its forked tail and long pointed wings, it looks like a swallow or tern.

The displays and calls of the south polar skua, which is a fish-eating and scavenging bird, are very similar to those of the southern great skua.

South Polar Skua *Stercorarius maccormicki* SAUNDERS, 1893

DURING THE SEVERE ANTARCTIC WINTER this skua deserts its southern breeding grounds and ranges throughout the world's oceans. One chick banded in Antarctica in February was seen five months later in Greenland. Some birds, especially immatures, fly around the Pacific Ocean, first north to Japan, then east to Alaska and south past British Columbia. Four birds have been sighted in New Zealand, all between January and April.

Banding shows that young skuas mate for life and return to the breeding area of their birth. They continue to breed in the same territory year after year and often nest in the same scoop. They lay two eggs and incubation begins with the first egg so that the chicks hatch in sequence. Both eggs are incubated against two brood patches on the breast, held side by side off the ground by the feet and webs. Very few pairs of chicks are raised in southern populations. Most mortality occurs when the younger chick is chased from the nest by the older one soon after hatching; others die through starvation, blizzards and predation by skuas. An eight-year study of a colony showed that only 27–29 per cent of fledged chicks survived. Survival of breeding birds was very high at 97 per cent, and their life expectancy, though not fully determined, is more than 20 years.

South polar skuas primarily hunt fish that shoal near the surface. They also scavenge at seal, penguin and petrel colonies, taking eggs and young chicks lost from the nest, dead and starving chicks and krill spilt at chick-feeding. Some breeding pairs make no attempt to exploit these food sources within a territory and feed on fish throughout the summer, 'protecting' penguin colonies from non-breeding flocks. Other skuas have developed skills as predators of penguin eggs and chicks, pursuing complex strategies and showing great determination in their attacks on nesting adults. They have considerable difficulty in killing older chicks and do not use their clawed feet as talons. Skuas show evidence of being superbly adapted fish-eating birds which secondarily exploit penguin colonies. E.C.Y.

CIRCUMPOLAR

OTHER NAMES: *McCormick's skua, Antarctic skua.*

SIZE: *530 mm.*

DESCRIPTION
Three plumage phases: light, intermediate and dark. In light and intermediate phase head, neck, nape and underparts light contrasting strongly with black wings. Sometimes collar or mane of silky golden feathers. In dark phase head, neck and underparts dark brown to black, but lighter than back, wings and tail. In all phases iris brown; feet black; and bill grey to black with black tip. IMMATURE: Head, nape and underparts pale to medium grey. Back, scapulars, wings and tail dark slate.

MOULT
Complete moult in non-breeding season, possibly followed by partial second moult in spring. Some lightening through wear or bleaching during breeding season.

VOICE
Similar to southern great skua. Long call as part of display. Alarm call high-pitched, repetitive screech. Attack call of higher intensity.

DISTRIBUTION
Breeds on ice-free islands and coasts of Antarctica; the Antarctic Peninsula; and the South Shetland and South Orkney Islands. Range increasing recently through Scotia Arc islands. Migrates into northern oceans. Rare vagrant on mainland New Zealand.

RECOGNITION

Darker and bulkier than immature Dominican gull, with white wing flashes. Smaller than southern skua, with slender bill tapering to long non-bulbous nail. Light phase birds unmistakable, with contrasting black wings. Dark phase birds, hard to separate from southern great and pomarine skuas.

Southern Great Skua *Stercorarius skua lonnbergi* (MATHEWS, 1912)

NATIVE

OTHER NAMES: *Hakoakoa, southern skua, brown skua, subantarctic skua.*

SIZE: *630 mm.*

DESCRIPTION
ADULT: *Sexes alike but male slightly smaller. Dark brown plumage, with wings darker than back. Head and neck sometimes much paler. Varying amounts of lighter streaks or blotches. Prominent white band at base of flight feathers. Iris brown. Bill and legs black. Bill massive,* blunt and strongly hooked at the tip.
IMMATURE: *Plumage, except for white wing flashes, darker and more uniform than adult.*
NESTLING: *New Zealand nestling brown down; elsewhere grey-brown, with buff tips. Bill dark grey to black. Grey legs.*

MOULT
During breeding season.

VOICE
Long call as part of display. Alarm call high-pitched, repetitive screech. Attack call of higher intensity. Sometimes brisk quack notes during aerial chases. Mew call by male during courtship feeding. Soft feeding call to attract chick from nest for feeding. Squeaking during scoop building.

DISTRIBUTION
Around the subantarctic and Antarctic, but not on Antarctic mainland. In the New Zealand region breeds on The Snares; the Auckland, Solander, Antipodes and Chatham Islands; Campbell and Macquarie Islands; islands off Stewart Island; in southern Fiordland; and possibly also on the Bounty and Balleny Islands.

The southern great skua is a powerful bird, often fiercely aggressive. In local populations nesting territories may be held by three adults instead of pairs.

A POWERFUL AND BELLIGERENT BIRD, the southern great skua—like all skuas—defends its eggs and young ferociously. Attacks on human intruders are sometimes so fierce that the person is forced to leave the field. The bird sweeps past at great speed, knocking the intruder's head with its wings and feet. It attacks from all sides and if threatened with a hand or stick, returns silently from behind.

A skua that enters another's territory is dealt with in a similar fashion. Sometimes, the attacking bird simply rushes or flies towards an opponent and tries to peck it. A fight is avoided or ended when one bird runs or flies from the area.

When threatened by another skua, a bird on the ground may extend its neck and point its bill up or down, or open its bill wide without making a sound. In competitive situations it walks with a stiff-legged gait quite unlike its normal walk. An incubating skua threatened by another bird curves its neck, ruffles its feathers and points its head and bill to the ground or tucks it into its breast. Sometimes it calls stifled long notes. In a territorial display, the skua raises its wings to display the white flashes, extends its neck and head, and utters a long call.

When a bird in flight spies another on the ground intruding upon its territory, it flies towards it with rapidly beating wings, smacks it with its webbed feet, then soars up and swoops down again. As the swoop develops the attacked skua presses itself down onto the ground. Once the swoop has passed it lifts itself up and utters a long call before resettling for the next swoop. This species appears to have no appeasement displays to reduce or mitigate attacks.

The main habitat of this bird is the open water of the southern oceans. It breeds on exposed coastal areas or clear uplands within sight of the sea, from forested temperate islands to barren antarctic ones. The population in the New Zealand region has been estimated at several thousand birds, with about 100 breeding pairs on the Chatham Islands and 'great numbers' on islands off Stewart Island. Birds from the southern end of the range migrate northwards for the winter, but they usually stay in the southern hemisphere. They are rarely seen near the New Zealand mainland, except in the far south.

Territory and breeding

Throughout the breeding season, from about September to late February, the southern great skua is strongly territorial with the same breeding areas held by pairs over many seasons. Away from the territory it is gregarious and forms large flocks when fishing.

During the breeding season, skuas eat whatever is available. At the beginning of the season they eat dead seal pups. Later they scavenge and prey on penguin eggs and chicks, and on the eggs, chicks and adults of different petrel species. Some birds have strong individual preferences. One pair will concentrate on penguin eggs, a neighbour on petrels. Introduced animals such as rabbits and lambs are also eaten. Little is known about winter feeding habits.

This skua probably breeds first at four to five years, but this depends on the availability of nesting territories. Eggs are laid from September onwards in the New Zealand region but progressively later further south so that laying does not begin until mid-December in the southernmost populations. In the New Zealand and Indian Ocean regions some territories are held by three adults.

The pair arrive separately at the territory at the start of the summer. The male feeds the female during the whole of the period before laying and throughout incubation. The female also scavenges for herself if food is available nearby. In many pairs, the male is a reluctant feeder at first and the female becomes so frenzied and aggressive that the male can scarcely regurgitate the food. The female dances, chases and circles as the male twists and turns away. Similar behaviour is seen by feeding parents in response to the pecking of hungry chicks.

The nesting period

Nests are selected and built during 'squeaking ceremonies', in which the male calls the female and the two birds squeak together with lowered bills before the female settles and begins shuffling and scraping to form a nest in the ground. This is a scoop on mosses and lichens, in soil, moraine or shingle, occasionally lined scantily with vegetation. Sometimes several scoops are made before egg-laying, but the same scoop may be used for several years.

The two eggs are laid about two days apart. One clutch is laid each year. Both birds incubate for about 30 days. The chicks leave the nest within 24 hours of hatching but they are usually brooded by the parents through the first week and less frequently during the second week. From then on they wander throughout the territory. Chicks begin flying on New Zealand islands in late December and January. Chicks studied on Signy Island began to fly at about 60 days old but stayed on the territory for a further three to four weeks before leaving the island in the second or third week of March. One parent stayed with the chicks until they left the island. Over three seasons on Signy Island 59 per cent of eggs survived to fledging. Adults probably live 20 to 30 years.   E.C.Y.

Pomarine Skua *Stercorarius pomarinus* (TEMMINCK, 1815)

MIGRANT

OTHER NAMES: *Pomatorhine skua, pomarine jaeger.*

SIZE: *700 mm.*

DESCRIPTION
ADULT: *Two colour phases, light and dark. In light form well-defined black cap to below bill. Neck yellow. Rest of upper parts dark grey-brown. Chin, upper breast, flank and belly white, with dark narrow band across neck. Wing and tail black-brown, with white flash at base of outer primaries. In dark form most of body uniform brown-black. In northern winter 2 forms similar with new feathers in light phase barred brown and white on neck and back and overall pigmentation more subdued. Bill yellow-brown, tipped with black. Legs and feet black and grey.*
IMMATURE: *Generally brown, with feathers tipped rufous or buff.*

Underparts brown, barred with buff or buff-white.

MOULT
Body moult February to April and August to January. Wing and tail moult October to April.

VOICE
Long call with wing raising as in great skuas.

DISTRIBUTION
Breeds entirely within the Arctic Circle. Regular summer migrant to New Zealand.

RECOGNITION

In breeding plumage elongated and twisted central tail feathers form blunt 'spoon'. Pale birds easily confused with Arctic skua but have larger wing flashes.

A pomarine skua, regular migrant in the New Zealand region during summer.

IN THE ARCTIC CIRCLE breeding pomarine skuas eat lemmings and other small rodents. When a bird sights a rodent from the air or from a roost, it flies to the ground, runs after the rodent and grabs it with its bill. If the rodent is lucky enough to escape into its burrow, the skua pursues it by ripping off the plants that roof the tunnel. Pomarine skuas are so dependent on lemmings that they breed only when these animals are abundant.

Each pair of pomarine skuas controls a large territory in swampy coastal tundra. In the middle of the northern summer the female lays two eggs in an unlined scrape in slightly raised ground. A few days after they hatch, the chicks leave the nest and wander over the territory. At five to six weeks the young birds fly.

In September, after the young have fledged, the birds migrate south. The main wintering grounds are at sea off the west coast of Africa and the eastern coast of Australia, and birds regularly reach New Zealand. Often, groups of 40 to 50 birds follow ships at sea. The return flight north begins in April so that by June all breeding birds are back on their Arctic nesting grounds.   E.C.Y.

Arctic Skua
Stercorarius parasiticus
(Linnaeus, 1758)

MIGRANT

OTHER NAME: *Parasitic jaeger.*

SIZE: *600 mm.*

DESCRIPTION
ADULT: *Two colour phases. In summer plumage, crown of light form black; collar yellow; upper parts sooty brown with white patch at base of primaries when wing extended; and underparts white with sooty band across breast. In dark form, dark brown above and below with small wing patch. In winter plumage, pale form has neck, throat and breast barred and mottled brown, with white bars on back, flank and tail coverts. Dark form winter plumage similar to that of summer. Iris brown. Bill black-brown with tip black. Legs and feet black.*
IMMATURE: *Varies from nearly uniform dark brown to black mottling on buff, with head and neck yellow-brown with dark streaks.*

MOULT
Body moult January to April and October to December. Wing and tail feathers November to April.

VOICE
Long call without raising wings. Alarm call short and descending.

DISTRIBUTION
Circumpolar. Breeds in Northern Europe, Asia and America, but generally further south than pomarine or long-tailed skua. Range extending recently into temperate areas. Winters in southern temperate oceans.

An Arctic skua of the dark colour form on its nest, generally a shallow scoop, in the northern hemisphere.

FROM AUGUST, when the young start flying, until the following April, small numbers of Arctic skua winter around northern New Zealand and off the coasts of southeastern and Western Australia. They feed in these seas by harrying gulls and terns, forcing them to disgorge their food. During the northern summer they breed on open spaces inland, on coastal flats and islands from the Arctic to as far south as northern Scotland. Each pair occupies its own territory on moorland, tundra or shingle. In an unlined, shallow scoop the female lays two eggs. The breeding birds eat a range of food from small mammals and insects to other birds, their eggs and young.   E.C.Y.

RECOGNITION
Similar in size to red-billed gull, but lighter with more slender wings. Two long, straight feathers projecting from tail distinct from broad, twisted feathers of pomarine skua or long flexible streamers of long-tailed skua. Wing flash. Flight buoyant.

Long-tailed Skua
Stercorarius longicaudus VIEILLOT, 1819

NOT MUCH IS KNOWN about the range of the long-tailed skua. It is away from its Arctic breeding grounds from August to May. During this period, however, few birds have been sighted north of the tropics. There have been many observations of birds off the coasts of South America, and so this region is most likely their major wintering area.

At sea it dives into the water to catch fish and forces gulls and terns to disgorge their food; but it is less piratical than other skuas. During the breeding season it holds very large territories, up to 1.0 km² in area, in which it hunts lemmings, voles and shrews. Flying 15 to 50 m above the ground it stops and hovers, looking for prey. When it spots a rodent it dives swiftly and kills the animal by pecking. It also eats birds, insects and berries.

When food is plentiful the birds lay two eggs; if food is scarce they lay none at all. Breeding is dependent on abundance of small rodents. The supply of food also governs the size of the eggs, the closeness of the nests, and the fledging period. The birds nest on the ground on tundra and alpine heath above the timber line, sometimes far inland. They defend their territories with ritualised aerial displays.   E.C.Y.

A long-tailed skua in breeding plumage, with strikingly tapered tail feathers.

STRAGGLER

OTHER NAME: *Long-tailed jaeger.*

SIZE: *550 mm.*

DESCRIPTION
ADULT: *Sexes similar. In breeding plumage, crown and nape dark brown. Throat, neck and breast white or grey with yellowish tinge; belly, undertail and coverts pale grey; upper parts brownish grey; wings and tail blackish brown. Iris dark brown. Bill black. Legs slate grey. Feet and webs black. In non-breeding plumage crown brown-black, feathers very narrowly tipped with dull white. Wings and tail as in summer. Side of head and throat, and upper breast mottled and spotted with dark brown. Broad band of dark brown on upper breast. Lower breast and belly white; tail coverts and flanks streaked and barred with dark brown. Dark form occurs rarely.*
IMMATURE: *Head and back dark brown. Neck usually grey-buff streaked with brown. Side of head and neck streaked with brown and grey-buff. Tail and wings brown-black with some white. Upper breast brown. Rest of underparts white, usually barred with dark brown.*

MOULT
Into breeding plumage in spring; into winter plumage in October.

VOICE
Long calls, short and descending alarm calls.

DISTRIBUTION
Circumpolar in high Arctic, generally north of Arctic Circle; breeding in Northern Europe, Siberia, Alaska, Canadian arctic islands, Greenland and Spitsbergen (not Iceland or other Atlantic islands). Winters off coasts of South America. Straggles to New Zealand.

RECOGNITION
Lighter and smaller even than white-fronted tern. In breeding plumage long flexible tail feathers tapering to narrow point. In winter plumage difficult to distinguish in flight from pomarine and Arctic skuas. Flies gracefully and hovers frequently. White marking along outer primary feather.

Dominican Gull *Larus dominicanus* LICHTENSTEIN,1823

THE DOMINICAN GULL adapts its diet to its environment. Over water it takes algae and plunge-dives for echinoderms, molluscs, and surface fish. It breaks the shells of molluscs by dropping them onto the ground from a height. On land it picks grasses and other plants, and hunts live animals such as worms, crustaceans, insects, amphibia, small reptiles and mammals, young birds and their eggs. It eats offal, carrion, and scavenges noisily over rubbish tips. Those parts of this varied diet that it cannot digest it regurgitates as rounded pellets.

The New Zealand population has increased this century and this gull is now widely known, especially in coastal towns and cities where it scavenges for food; flocks move daily between roosts and refuse tips near airports and are hazardous to aircraft. In the country it inhabits farmland, inlets, estuaries, rocky and sandy sea shores, wide shallow rivers, lakes and even mountain tarns. These gulls are mostly sedentary, but more are moving to urban areas.

Usually, the Dominican gull breeds in colonies; sometimes it breeds alone. Each pair occupies a territory which one bird always defends. Some birds may breed in their third year, but most begin in their fourth. Courtship displays occur from April onwards, and pairs first occupy the colony during daylight in July. The nest is built mostly by the male from local plants and oddments. The site varies from open pasture, beaches, rock ledges, weathered lava, rushes and small shrubs, to beneath overhanging rocks. Most nests have little or no shelter.

The one, two or three oval eggs are basically green or grey, with brown spots and streaks. They are laid two or three days apart between mid-October and January. The birds may lay a second clutch if the first is unsuccessful. The parents share incubation from about the laying of the second egg.

The parents brood their offspring fairly constantly for three or four days, then sporadically. The chicks move out of the nest at two or three days, but usually stay in their territories. The young swim at two weeks and fledge at seven, though wisps of down may still persist. Rats, stoats, ferrets and floods kill some eggs and chicks.

Non-breeders form a 'club' at the edge of the colony, while at any one time up to a third of the breeding birds leave the colony to feed, bathe and rest. Between breeding seasons the birds flock together. Adults begin to desert the colonies in January.

Displays include the courtship display in which the birds utter a long call, adopt the upright and face-away postures, give the mew call, choke, and toss their heads. Feeding of the female by the male, or mating, follows. There are also aggressive displays that include fighting with wing blows and pecks, especially to the head, that are sometimes fatal. When predators approach, the birds chatter anxiously and, in breeding colonies, charge screaming. The Dominican gull lives at least 28 years. It has been kept in captivity. R.A.F.

NATIVE

OTHER NAMES: *Karoro, southern black-backed gull, kelp gull.*

SIZE: *600 mm.*

DESCRIPTION

ADULT: *Sexes alike, but male larger. Mantle black but edges of wing white. Rest of plumage white. Gape and eyelid bright orange. Iris grey. Bill yellow to orange-yellow, with deep orange or red spot on lower mandible. Legs and feet yellow to pale orange. Colours, other than plumage, more intense during breeding.*

IMMATURE: *Sexes alike. First juvenile plumage dark brown. Head, neck and underparts mottled with buff and white. Mantle feathers mottled and edged with buff. Wing and tail feathers dark brown with buff edges (except for primaries). Base of tail barred with white. Gape white. Eyelid grey. Iris, legs and feet brown. Bill black. In second year, head, neck and upper chest spotted with brown. Mantle black mixed with brown. Primaries dark brown. Secondaries and scapulars tipped with white. Tail dark brown with white bars. Underparts mainly white. Eyelid yellow. Iris grey-brown. Bill pale yellow, often with black band at tip of lower mandible. Gape cream-yellow. Legs and feet blue-brown. Third-year bird like adult, but often with brown mottling on head, neck and upper breast, and eyelid, beak, legs and feet paler. Full adult plumage usually achieved in fourth year.*

NESTLING: *Down lead grey above with darker spotting on head. Chest and lower wing down grey with white tips. Iris, legs and feet dark brown. Bill black.*

MOULT

Complete adult moult January to August. Partial moult August to October.

VOICE

Characteristic long call. Separate calls for contact, mating, alarm and attack, and others for both pairing and aggression.

DISTRIBUTION

South America, southern Africa, Madagascar, Australia, Lord Howe and southern ocean islands. Common on mainland New Zealand, the Campbell, Chatham, Auckland, Antipodes and Bounty Islands. Strays to the Kermadec Islands.

RECOGNITION

Largest and only black-backed gull.

The growing population of Dominican gulls indicates their successful adaptation to scavenging, and is directly related to the growth in human population.

The red-billed gull, predominantly a coastal species, is abundant on the eastern coasts of the North and South Islands. It feeds in flocks, mainly inshore.

Red-billed Gull *Larus novaehollandiae scopulinus* Forster, 1844

THE RED-BILLED GULL is one of the commonest gulls on the New Zealand coast; it rarely lives inland. Breeding colonies are found mainly on the eastern coasts of the North and South Islands. On outlying islands, the species has been reported at Campbell, Snares, Auckland and Chatham Islands. Around the mainland dense colonies nest in the open on barren stacks and islands; on the Chathams and in the Subantarctic the nests are concealed, and located in small groups or singly.

The main food during the breeding season is planktonic crustaceans, although some earthworms, kelp-fly larvae and fish larvae are also eaten. They feed inshore on foraging trips that last about two hours. Flocks of several thousand gulls swarm at locally abundant food sources.

Outside the breeding season the diet is more varied. Some birds continue to feed at sea, some forage along the shore for marine invertebrates, and others eat refuse. Large numbers of red-billed gulls scavenge at sewage outfalls, rubbish dumps, parks, playing fields, river banks and fishing ports. On arable land they follow the plough, and on wet pastures they forage for earthworms. They have also been observed eating taupata and puka berries.

Red-billed gulls harass other birds and attempt to force white-fronted terns, gannets, oystercatchers, shags and even other red-billed gulls to drop food they are carrying. They force young shags to disgorge food their parents have just fed them. Some specialise in nest-robbing, preying on eggs of white-fronted terns and neighbouring red-billed gulls.

Until the early 1970s the New Zealand population was increasing, apparently because of an abundance of winter food—in the form of offal from freezing and fish processing works, and rubbish from garbage dumps. After legislation was passed to limit the discharge of offal into the sea the number of red-billed gulls declined.

The breeding season extends from July to January. Many gulls breed at the natal colony; once they have bred at one site they often return, usually with the same partner. From late July onwards the birds defend the nest-site. They spend more and more time there; until 12 days before laying the nest-site is seldom left undefended. The gulls display aggressively, but rarely fight. The first sites claimed are the central or elevated parts of the colony. Gulls which arrive late are forced to take up territories on lower ground or on the edge of the colony. They are capable of breeding at two years.

Egg-laying occurs over an extremely long period. At Kaikoura it extends from early October to the end of December. On subantarctic Campbell Island nesting commences approximately a month later than on the mainland. Nest-building begins about two to three weeks before egg-laying. The nest is frequently constructed of seaweed, sticks and grasses. Though both sexes share nest construction, most of the material is collected by the male. The normal clutch is two eggs.

Both sexes share incubation, and the eggs hatch 24 to 27 days after being laid. Chicks remain in the vicinity of the nest and are seldom left unattended. Any that wander onto an adjacent territory are attacked or even killed by other adults.

Interbreeding between red-billed gulls and black-billed gulls has been recorded at Lake Rotorua. The hybrids have proved to be fertile and have bred with red-billed gulls.

The birds begin to leave the colony in mid-January. Banded adult gulls from Kaikoura sometimes wander as far away as Invercargill and Auckland, but most remain within about 380 km of their colony. Juveniles tend to disperse slightly further than adults.   J.A.M.

ENDEMIC

OTHER NAMES: *Silver gull, tarapunga, akiaki, mackerel gull, jackie.*

SIZE: *370 mm.*

DESCRIPTION
ADULT: *Sexes similar, although male slightly larger with stouter and slightly longer bill. Almost completely white. Mantle, back, wing coverts and underwing coverts pale grey. Primaries mainly black with white tips. First and second primaries black with white patch or mirror near end. Third to sixth primaries white with black tips. Rest of wing grey. Iris white. Bill, eyelids and feet scarlet in breeding season; duller during rest of year.*
IMMATURE: *Similar to adult but brown patches on secondaries. Buff tips to feathers of mantle and secondaries dull brown-black. Much less white on primaries than in adult. Iris dark brown. Bill, legs and eye-ring dark brown.*

DISTRIBUTION
Coasts and offshore islands of the North and South Islands; The Snares; the Chatham, Auckland and Campbell Islands; subspecies present in mainland Australia, Tasmania, New Caledonia, South Africa, and the Indian Ocean.

RECOGNITION
In flight white flash on black wing tip. Heavier and stouter, with shorter, thicker bill than the black-billed gull.

Black-billed Gull *Larus bulleri* HUTTON,1871

DURING THE SUMMER over 75 000 pairs of black-billed gulls breed in Southland on shingle islands and at the shores of lakes and rivers. They also breed in large colonies in Otago and Canterbury. A few nest in the North Island. In the winter many birds migrate to the coast, especially to the southern shores of the North Island.

They feed in open country, on lakes and rivers, and at city parks and playing fields. Their diet includes insects, small freshwater fish and, on the coast, shoreline and shallow water, invertebrates. In cities and towns they sometimes eat refuse, but to a lesser extent than the other New Zealand gulls. They catch earthworms from wet pasture land and by following the plough. Often these are fed to the young. They are competent aerial insect feeders, and while standing on the ground snap up passing flies. They catch surface aquatic animals while swimming, and also by hovering and dipping, although they seldom immerse more than their heads or necks. When feeding in flocks over schools of small fish they attract other gulls. Such concerted attacks confuse the fish, making capture easier.

Middens show that the Maori ate black-billed gulls. In European times these birds have increased as land has been turned to agriculture, making insects and worms available at ploughing time. With more arable land, the numbers of insect pests have exploded. Black-billed gulls eat these and help to control them.

They breed first at two years old. Courtship displays begin in August while the birds are still at the coast. Food-begging bouts between pairs lead to regurgitation feeding and mating. By mid-September most mature birds are at the breeding sites. There, flocks swoop and soar noisily. Often the birds settle in the same nest-site as the previous year. In early October nest-building begins and the birds lay soon after. Silent 'dreads' or 'panics', when all the birds suddenly take wing, circle, and noisily drop back to the ground, are common at this time of the year, and again just before the gullery is deserted.

The nest is a deep depression of rootlets and small sticks, neatly lined with grass. The clutch is usually two eggs, which vary in colour from pale grey, pale olive-green, to pale blue. Usually they are blotched with dark and light brown.

Both sexes incubate for 20 to 24 days. The eggs are never left unattended. Within 24 hours of hatching the family abandons the nest. Both parents brood, feed, and defend the chicks during this nomadic period. They feed the young by regurgitating food onto the ground. Older chicks sometimes take food directly from their parents' bills. Groups of young birds congregate into crèches defended by a few adults. This system enables most of the parents to forage for the young. Birds returning with food wander through the group until they find their own chicks. If alarmed the whole group of chicks takes to the water forming a tightly packed raft, the attendant adults swimming with them or hovering overhead. When the alarm is over, the adults shepherd the young ashore. The chicks fly at 26 days. Immediately both adults and young disperse in mixed flocks, often to the coast.

When a predator threatens the colony the gulls gang together. They swoop at the intruder calling harshly and loudly. Sometimes they strike it with their feet or bills. Human intruders, however, are hardly ever struck; the attacking bird soars out of the swoop about 30 cm above the person.   L.G.

ENDEMIC

OTHER NAME: *Buller's gull.*

SIZE: *370 mm.*

DESCRIPTION
ADULT: *Sexes alike, but male larger. Head, neck, underparts, and tail white. Mantle, scapulars, upper and underwing coverts, and secondaries pearl grey. Two outermost primaries white with black edges, subterminal black bar and white tip. Rest of primaries gradually fade to grey with no black on leading edge. Iris white. From June to January eyelid red. Bill black. Gape orange-red. Legs mostly black, with some pale orange or red showing, especially on toes. Webs and toenails black. From February to June eyelid black. Bill, legs and feet black and dull red or orange.*
IMMATURE: *Similar to adult except buff feather tips on crown, ear, nape, back, scapulars and upper wing coverts. Brown on head and back lost by wear, usually by 6 months. More black on primaries especially on outermost ones. Brown patches on secondaries. Tail white, sometimes with traces of black. Eyelid black. Iris brown-black. Bill flesh pink, with tip grey-black and gape pale pink. Legs flesh pink with black tinge on webs and feet. Toenails black.*

NESTLING: *Light buff down, sometimes almost pink, spotted with black. Undersurface white. Bill and feet, pale flesh pink. Tip of bill grey-black.*

MOULT
Not known.

VOICE
Higher pitched and more penetrating than that of red-billed gull. Anxiety and warning calls kek-kek. *Anti-predator call loud* kaark *while swooping. Aggressive calls* kear *and* kwow. *Long call* kar. *Soft gurgling* churr *in courtship, nest-showing and relief.* Ur-ur-ur *while mating.* Psee *when begging for food.*

DISTRIBUTION
Breeds on riverbeds and lakes, mainly in South Island. Many birds winter on the coasts of the North and South Island. Straggles to Stewart Island and The Snares.

RECOGNITION
Two outer wing primaries mainly white with small black border and black area near tip. Long slender bill. Fine slender lines, especially of the wings.

The black-billed gull is essentially an inland gull. Of the three New Zealand gulls it is the most specialised feeder and the least likely to scavenge.

White-winged Black Tern *Chlidonias leucopterus* (Temminck, 1815)

A flock of white-winged black terns at Lake Nakuru, Kenya. In New Zealand the species prefers the muddy lagoons, lakes and estuaries of coastal areas.

THERE IS ONLY one record of the white-winged black tern breeding in New Zealand. In the summer of 1973–74 a pair nested in South Canterbury. Usually this tern is a migrant from its breeding grounds in the northern hemisphere. From early summer to late autumn single birds, pairs or small flocks live on the coasts of both main islands, and occasionally inland.

By the shore it prefers shallow muddy lagoons, lakes and estuaries. It also feeds in streams, wet pasture and mangroves near the coast, but it avoids harbours and open seashore, although it sometimes feeds out at sea. Inland, shallow pools, muddy streams and especially shingle riverbeds are also areas for foraging.

In Europe this tern breeds in colonies. The nest is a floating mass of reeds or other plants. Between late May and June it lays about three pale brown to brown-green eggs, which are heavily blotched with brown-black. Both parents share incubation. Chicks leave the nest within a few days of hatching, but their parents continue to feed them.

The pair which bred in New Zealand first nested in December, with black-fronted terns at a river mouth. The three eggs were in a shingle scrape and were subsequently lost, but the birds built another nest, this time of marram grass. In January it contained a single egg from which a chick hatched in early February. When it was only a few days old, one of the parents guarded it while the other collected lagoon insects to feed the chick about every 10 to 15 minutes.

A gregarious bird, the white-winged black tern is territorial at its nest and chases away intruders, whether of its own or other species. Inland in the South Island it shows a marked affinity for the black-fronted tern, flying over their colonies in soaring displays. Non-breeding birds regularly settle among flocks of waders and other terns.

The white-winged tern feeds mainly in flight, taking aquatic insects from or above the water surface. In coastal areas of New Zealand, dipterans which dwell on the surface of pools or mud flats are important prey. The birds spend hours on the wing, flying swiftly and buoyantly with agile dips to the water's surface. Most prey are taken while the bird is flying into the wind. It also feeds on land or in shallow water by walking around on mud flats, snapping up flies. Sometimes it catches small fish, tadpoles and other small vertebrates. R.J.P.

MIGRANT

OTHER NAME: *White-winged marsh tern.*

SIZE: *230 mm.*

DESCRIPTION
ADULT: *Sexes alike. In breeding plumage head, neck, body and scapulars black. Tail white. Primaries pale grey; secondaries darker grey. Upper wing coverts mainly white. Underwing grey with black coverts. Axillaries black. Bill red-black. Legs bright red to red-black. In non-breeding plumage upper parts pale grey; underparts white. Forehead and forecrown white. Rest of crown and nape white with black speckling. Small black spot in front of eye. Ear coverts black. In some birds head all-white. Most birds seen in New Zealand in early pre-nuptial moult. Narrow black median line from crown extends as club-shaped line to nape. Ear coverts linked to crown by vertical black line. Hind neck white. Mantle, rump and tail pale grey; sometimes with broad dark band on upper mantle. Wings pale grey, with small black patch and narrow dark band behind white leading edge. Underparts white. Iris dark brown. Bill and legs black with red tinge.*
JUVENILE: *Similar to non-breeding adult but mantle dark brown; crown darker; solid black line links crown to ear coverts; rump white; tail darker grey with brown terminal band; bill black-brown; legs red-brown.*
NESTLING: *Upper parts rich buff, blotched and streaked with black.*

Fewer black markings on underparts. Broad white circle surrounds eye.

MOULT
Birds that breed in the northern hemisphere moult into breeding plumage December to June and into non-breeding plumage June to December. Birds that breed in New Zealand moult into breeding plumage by August or early September, and post-nuptial body moult begins in January.

VOICE
Relatively quiet outside breeding season. Sometimes calls sharp keet or keevit. Defends nest-site with rasping graack or graack-grak.

DISTRIBUTION
Breeds in eastern Europe, Asia; one record in New Zealand. Winters in New Zealand, Southeast Asia, Malaysia, Indonesia, Australia and Africa.

RECOGNITION

In breeding plumage contrasting pattern of black head and body with white tail. In non-breeding plumage separated from black-fronted tern by white underparts and forewing. Differs from whiskered tern by black U-shaped band from eye to eye around hind crown, and tail not as deeply forked. Buoyant and leisurely flight.

Whiskered Tern

Chlidonias hybrida (PALLAS, 1811)

THE WHISKERED TERN is a bird of lakes, swamps, rivers, lagoons and brackish waters, mainly inland but also close to the coast. It is rare on marine waters except in shallow sheltered bays in the Northern Territory of Australia and Java.

It flies slowly into the wind several metres above the water. Usually it dips to take food from on or just above the surface, but sometimes it dives lightly and thrusts its head under water. When there is no wind it circles haphazardly and stalls with its tail fanned. On the ground it walks readily and often stands erect, like a gull. Its food is mainly dragonflies, flies and beetles; also grasshoppers, butterflies, moths, flying ants, centipedes, water-beetles, worms, insect larvae and eggs, tadpoles, small fish and frogs, freshwater shrimps and crayfish.

In Australia, this tern is partly sedentary and, especially after breeding, partly nomadic and partly migratory. A gregarious bird that is seldom seen alone, it breeds in colonies in swamps, mainly from September to December. Its nest is a fragile pile of grass or rushes, floating on water or anchored to plants. There have been several sightings of the whiskered tern in New Zealand since 1975, mostly between the months of May and October, on Lake Horowhenua and the lower Waikato River; one bird in breeding plumage was observed in March 1980, at Tuakau. B.D.H.

The whiskered tern is not a marine bird, but favours inland swamps, lagoons and lakes. Since 1975, there have been several New Zealand sightings.

VAGRANT

OTHER NAME: *Marsh tern.*

SIZE: *250 mm.*

DESCRIPTION
ADULT: *Sexes alike, with bill of male averaging larger. In breeding plumage upper parts from hind neck to wings and tail pale grey and outer primaries darker grey. Head from bill to nape black. Chin, throat and side of head and neck white, grading to slate grey on lower breast and belly, darkest on belly. Axillaries, underwing and undertail white. Iris dark brown. Bill and legs wine red. In non-breeding plumage upper parts* *from hind neck to tail paler grey. Underparts dull white. Primaries darker grey. Head white; crown streaked with rows of black spots that merge into blackish nape. Black on ear coverts extends to lores and back to nape. When the head is erect, the compressed nape forms black arc from eye to eye around nape. Bill dark red-brown. Legs dark red-brown to blackish.*
JUVENILE: *Similar to non-breeding adult but back and wing coverts look dark brown as feathers tipped with dark brown and edged with buff; brown band near tip of tail; cap on head mixed with brown; forehead and forecrown white. Sub-adult birds retain some brown-tipped feathers.*

MOULT
No precise information available. In Australia, into non-breeding plumage March to April; into breeding plumage August to September.

VOICE
Generally silent except when breeding. Feeding birds sometimes call harsh reedy kitt *or* ki-kitt. *Alarm call* kreek-kreek.

DISTRIBUTION
Breeds in Africa, Madagascar, Europe, Iraq, southern U.S.S.R, northern India, China and Australia. Straggles to Tasmania and New Zealand.

A nesting gull-billed tern warns off intruders with a harsh alarm call.

Gull-billed Tern

Gelochelidon nilotica macrotarsa (GOULD, 1837)

STRAGGLER

OTHER NAME: *Long-legged tern.*

SIZE: *430 mm.*

DESCRIPTION
ADULT: *Sexes alike, the female slightly smaller. In breeding plumage forehead extending below eye to nape glossy black. Rest of upper parts pale grey except for white tail, and primaries appear darker towards the tips from a dark line along inner webs. Underparts white. Iris dark brown. Legs and heavy bill black. In non-breeding plumage forehead white. Crown to nape white with brown streaking. Lores white, speckled black. Dark grey around and behind eye. Strong contrast between dark primaries and pale wings.*
JUVENILE: *Like non-breeding adult,* *but feathers of upper parts tipped or edged with buff, and those of mantle, upper scapulars, tail, and greater wing coverts marked with brown near tips. Legs dark brown.*
IMMATURE: *First-year bird similar to non-breeding adult but head more heavily marked with black and legs dark brown. Second-year bird has white crown and black streak from bill through eye.*

MOULT
Complete post-nuptial moult during 3-month period after breeding, merging into second moult which extends over 6 months. First-year birds moult about 2 months later than adults.

VOICE
A repeated kuh-wuk *or* ka-huk *and harsh* che-ah *and* za-za-za. *Other calls are a repeated* kayweek, tirruck, *and* kerr. *Stuttering, rattling, and buzzing noises denote alarm or hostility.*

DISTRIBUTION
Australia, especially in north and east, and New Guinea. Straggles to New Zealand.

GULL-BILLED TERNS live in most parts of the world. The Australian subspecies wanders across open country from the seashore to inland plains; then, between September and March, hundreds flock and breed together at lakes and swamps. Intruders at these breeding colonies are mobbed by noisy terns. A succession of birds swoops onto the outsider, frequently delivering pecks before rejoining the flock. All New Zealand records are coastal, from Invercargill to Auckland; and only adult birds have been sighted, mainly on the west coast in May. This coincides with the main post-breeding movement in Australia. Often the gull-billed tern roosts with other terns, gulls and waders.

It feeds generally in small flocks, hawking in a leisurely manner over water or open country, and eats insects, small crabs, fish (including small eels), small reptiles (especially lizards), young birds and small mammals. The gull-billed tern usually takes food from the ground or water surface. On sighting prey it fans its tail and glides swiftly down with the bill held vertically. It grabs the animal and then quickly regains its original height. Usually only the bill tip appears to touch the ground or water. When fishing, this tern rarely dives or takes fish from below the surface. J.S.

The clutch of the Caspian tern usually consists of two or three eggs. For the first five to 10 days, chicks are guarded by either parent and fed fresh fish.

Caspian Tern *Hydroprogne caspia* (PALLAS,1770)

AT THE MOST, 3500 Caspian terns live in New Zealand. A species of shallow coastal waters, it is most often seen on wide sandy beaches and the sand spits and mud flats of estuaries, sheltered harbours and coastal lakes. It follows the major rivers of both main islands for considerable distances, reaching the lakes of the Volcanic Plateau and the eastern foothills of the Southern Alps. Sometimes it is seen along rocky coastlines. Breeding is predominantly on sandy beaches and spits usually exposed to the open sea and often close to the high tide mark. The main nesting colonies are close to sheltered areas of relatively shallow salt or brackish water.

The majority of New Zealand birds breed in long established colonies in the northern half of the North Island. Some of the better known of these colonies are those in Whangarei Harbour and at South Kaipara Head in Northland, and near Whangapoua on the Coromandel Peninsula. Some breed in the southern half of the North Island and there are several long established colonies in Nelson and Marlborough. A colony in the Invercargill estuary marks the southern end of its range. Elsewhere individual pairs and small groups occasionally nest in suitable coastal areas, inland on braided river-beds, and sometimes on lake shores.

At the end of the breeding season Caspian terns disperse from their nesting areas. Birds from the northern North Island tend to stay within 100 km of the colony and winter in harbours such as Manukau and Firth of Thames. Birds from the southern colonies tend to travel northwards. At least some of the South Island birds winter in the north of the North Island.

Caspian terns nest in colonies varying from 20 to 200 pairs, usually in association with (but tending to be aloof from) other terns and gulls. Breeding birds return to their nesting areas in late August and September; the first clutches are laid between late September and early November. If the initial clutch is lost most pairs promptly lay another. Some lay a third time when this is necessary. When a whole colony loses its eggs at the same time the birds re-nest up to several hundred metres away. The nest is merely a shallow unlined hollow in sand or shingle about 25 cm in diameter. The bird forms this depression by resting on its breast and paddling with its feet. Nests are often positioned on very exposed windswept sites or alongside driftwood or stunted vegetation which provide a little shelter.

Incubation is shared by both birds and takes 20 to 22 days. One of the parents guards the chicks for the first five to 10 days. After a few days the young are led away to an adjacent and usually more sheltered site. They are fed fresh fish from the start, which are offered whole, direct from the adult's bill. Well-grown young can run considerable distances and if pressed will take to water when approached by people. They fledge at 30 to 35 days old.

Caspian terns feed mainly on surface swimming fish such as yellow-eyed mullet and piper, up to 20 cm in length, as well as a variety of other fish including small trout and flounder. They usually fly at around five to 10 m above the surface of the water with their bills pointed downwards. When they sight a suitable fish they hover for a few seconds then plunge into the water at a steep angle, often completely submerging themselves. If successful they sometimes sit on the surface for a short while.

C.N.C.

NATIVE

OTHER NAME: *Taranui.*

SIZE: *510 mm.*

DESCRIPTION
ADULT: *Sexes similar. Forehead, cap to below eye and nape black in summer, but streaked with white in winter, appearing lightest on forehead and darkest around and below eye. Upper parts mainly ash grey. Primaries silver grey with part of inner webs dark grey, appearing black from below in flight. Underparts, back of neck, rump and tail white. Iris dark brown. Bill stout, bright red, dusky towards tip which is yellow. Legs and feet black.*
IMMATURE: *Similar in appearance to adults in winter plumage. Juvenile plumage differs in that markings on head more extensive and dark brown; upper parts mottled brown with feathers edged with buff-white; and bill, legs and feet dull orange. Dark mottling lost during first autumn moult when upper parts become dull grey. Streaking on head and duller grey of upper parts persist into following summer. Progressive reddening of bill and darkening of legs and feet with age.*
NESTLING: *Down soft and long with fine hair-like tips. Upper parts vary from buff to grey with brown mottling on back. Underparts white*
with throat light grey. Bill, legs and feet dull orange.

MOULT
Adults have 2 complete moults each year: pre-nuptial moult July to September; post-nuptial moult February to June. Juvenile and winter plumages of first-year birds apparently moulted at around same time as adult summer and winter plumages respectively.

VOICE
In flight, especially at nesting colonies, harsh karh-kaa and scolding yakketi-yak. Repeated kuk-kuk-kuk at intruder which becomes raucous kaah-kaah. Shrill squeals and whistles from young.

DISTRIBUTION
Coasts, rivers and lakes of the North and South Islands and many inshore islands. Discontinuous distribution through temperate zones of Africa, Europe, Asia, Australia and North America.

RECOGNITION

Very large thickset tern with slight crest and large conspicuous red or orange bill. Dark cap and primaries. Shallow forked tail.

Black-fronted Tern *Sterna albostriata* (GRAY, 1845)

BLACK-FRONTED TERNS RARELY venture far from water. During spring and summer, from August onwards, they breed on shingle riverbeds. Pairs or flocks of up to 150 fly over lakes, tarns and farm dams. They often visit fields near rivers, especially those which have been freshly ploughed or are under irrigation. In the winter a few remain inland but most migrate to the coast between December and April. They live in harbours, river mouths or estuaries where they roost on tidal flats, sand bars or bare islands. They have been recorded at sea, though usually within 10 km of the coast.

They breed in small colonies, usually of fewer than 40 nests. Between August and November—and even as late as Janaury—the birds perform aerial courtship displays. In one display a tern, usually holding an animal such as a fish, earthworm or skink, glides for a few seconds with its wings held in a V. One to three other terns glide after it with their wings held horizontally. Another aerial display, the high flight, sometimes involves all the adults in a flock. First two or three birds initiate a spiral ascent. Then others follow until they are about 50 to 150 m above the ground where they glide in a horizontal circle for five to 30 minutes.

Black-fronted terns lay from mid-October to late November, sometimes into January. The nest is merely a hollow in the shingle, often lined with twigs, and generally protected from northwesterlies by boulders. The two eggs are ovoid, pointed, and dark grey with large light and dark blotches of brown or olive green. They are laid on separate days and hatch separately. The parents share the incubation period of about 23 days, changing over every 15 to 60 minutes.

The chicks leave the nest within 24 hours of the last egg hatching, but they remain nearby for a further one to three days. From then on they roam over the shingle, often away from the colony. They swim well. Holding food crosswise in their bills, the parents feed the young several times each hour during daylight.

One month after hatching the young terns fledge and begin foraging for themselves. The parents cease feeding the juveniles by mid-January. The success rate from breeding is low: in late December there are 10 adults to each juvenile. Flooding destroys many eggs and sheep trample some nests. Mustelids and possibly cats eat eggs. The birds pluckily defend their nests, darting down at the intruder and calling harshly as they swoop past its head.

Inland, the black-fronted tern eats mainly water insects. Groups of up to 70 birds fly within two metres of the river surface and pluck prey from the water. Usually only the bird's bill touches the water and it does not stop flying. It also plunge-dives with open wings to catch fish up to 10 cm long. Earthworms and grass grub larvae are the main prey from farmland, and a wide variety of aerial and terrestrial insects, especially beetles, are also taken. On shingle, it takes skinks and cicadas, and along the coast planktonic crustaceans.   C.L.

Migratory within New Zealand, the black-fronted tern breeds in small colonies along the shingle-bed rivers of the South Island, east of the Southern Alps.

ENDEMIC

OTHER NAME: *Tara.*

SIZE: *300 mm.*

DESCRIPTION
ADULT: *Sexes alike. In breeding plumage crown from bill to nape and surrounding eye black, bordered below by thin white line. Rump, upper and undertail coverts white. Wings and rest of body slate grey, paler below. Darker tips to primaries; dark leading edge and prominent white shaft to outermost primary. Tail feathers pale grey with darker tips. Underwing pale grey. Iris black. Bill and feet bright orange. In non-breeding plumage head pale grey with black feathers forming rough U round eyes and base of nape. Light scattering of* black feathers on rest of the head visible at close quarters. Bill orange, sometimes darker.
IMMATURE: *Body plumage as adult. Crown grey mottled with black. Nape and ear coverts black. Chin white. Median wing coverts pale brown; greater and lesser wing coverts slate grey. Flight and tail feathers pale or mid-brown. Primaries and tail feathers with darker tips. Bill usually very dark brown and reddish at base. Feet bright orange.*
JUVENILE: *Crown and nape greyish brown mottled with black. Lores and ear coverts black. Lesser wing coverts and feathers of mantle and back brown, darker towards tips but margined with yellow, giving upper surface mottled appearance. Throat, foreneck, upper and undertail coverts white. Rest of underparts grey.*

Greater and median wing coverts pale brown. Flight, tail feathers and feet as in immature plumage. Bill very dark brown, reddish at base. Feet bright orange.
NESTLING: *Covered with long down. Upper surface grey-brown or pale olive-green, with dark speckling. Dark patch on lores and cheeks not back beyond eye or forward to bill. Throat dark but not mottled. Rest of undersurface white. Bill dark yellow with black tip. Feet bright orange.*

MOULT
Breeding plumage June to late November. Complete post-nuptial moult mid-December to early May. Non-breeding plumage February to late April. Post-juvenile moult 4 to 8 months after fledging. Immature moults into breeding plumage in March of second year.

VOICE
Feeding flocks call repetitive kit *or* kit-kit. *Birds feeding alone usually quiet but utter extended* ki-ki-kew *or* ki-ki-ki-kew *if others try to feed nearby. Also calls during aerial courtship displays.*

DISTRIBUTION
Breeds along shingle-bed rivers east of the Southern Alps and near Blenheim. Winters on the coasts of the 3 main islands. Recorded from The Snares and Chatham Islands.

RECOGNITION

Grey body. Prominent white rump in flight. Black cap in summer plumage. Orange feet and bill.

The Antarctic tern is virtually non-migratory, with some birds remaining close to the breeding islands, even in winter.

Antarctic Tern *Sterna vittata bethunei* BULLER, 1896

THE ANTARCTIC TERN FEEDS close inshore. Either alone or in a flock it flies slowly above the sea, occasionally hovering before dropping into the water. Briefly, and almost totally, it submerges. Sometimes it hunts low over the water, with a rapid flight, and plunges at the surface. It defends good feeding grounds from other terns. Mostly it eats fish, but one bird collected was found to have a stomach full of sea lice; another was seen to eat a few insects.

From about February to November Antarctic terns flock together. Young terns remain in flocks during the summer, but breeding adults form pairs. The two birds fly together, the male carrying a fish across its bill. They land briefly at several places before the male offers the fish to the female. Then they look for a suitable nest-site—each bird tests several places by pressing its breast on the ground, while scraping with its feet. When a site is selected the immediate area is defended vigorously until the end of breeding.

To some extent the Antarctic tern adapts its breeding habits to local conditions. On some islands it breeds in colonies, but at The Snares, where fur seals and Hooker's sea lions occupy the land suitable for colonial nesting, the terns nest alone. Nest-sites are usually on cliff ledges overlooking the sea or on tops of rocks a short distance inland. On Tristan da Cunha, after the introduction of rats, Antarctic terns abandoned nesting on sandy beaches for the safety of inaccessible ledges. Sometimes red-billed gulls nest in the same area. The nest itself is a shallow scrape in peat or vegetation, sometimes lined with a thin layer of leaves.

The breeding cycle varies from island to island. At The Snares egg-laying occurs in late October and November, while on Campbell Island eggs were seen from late November to late January. The normal clutch is one elongate and buff-olive egg with brown and black blotches. Two-egg clutches hatch about two days apart.

Both adults share incubation for 24 or 25 days. They defend the nest and drive off intruders with fierce dives and bill clicking. They brood the chicks for two days before abandoning the nest for nearby open vegetation. Both parents feed the chicks at irregular intervals. When the adult returns from the sea it gives a short call and the chick appears. On The Snares four chicks fledged between 27 and 32 days after hatching. The parents continue to feed the young for at least three days after fledging. Both parents and chicks leave the breeding area after the young have fledged. However, in the northern part of

their range (for example, The Snares), they remain in the coastal waters surrounding the breeding islands throughout the year. Further south, birds are absent from the breeding islands from April to October.

On many islands, southern skuas kill Antarctic terns. Yet at The Snares skuas breed within 50 m of the terns and predation has not been recorded. Bad weather accounts for many deaths, especially when the chicks are young.   P.M.S.

ENDEMIC

OTHER NAMES: *None.*

SIZE: *400 mm.*

DESCRIPTION
ADULT: *Sexes similar. Forehead, lores, crown and nape black, with broad white streak from gape to ear coverts. Upper surface pale grey, with outer web of outermost primary black. Tail coverts and tail white, with outer web of outermost feather washed with pale grey. Undersurface grey-white. Undertail coverts white. Bill and feet red. Iris brown. In eclipse plumage forehead, lores and undersurface white. Crown streaked with white. Bill and feet dull red or reddish black.*
IMMATURE: *Like adult in eclipse plumage, except side and back of crown black. Bill and feet black.*
JUVENILE: *Top of head white with black and brown streaking. Upper surface grey, strongly barred with black and washed with buff. Undersurface and rump white, finely barred with black and brown. Bill and feet black.*
NESTLING: *Cryptically patterned. Upper surface buff, blotched with brown and black. Undersurface brown, with belly brownish white. Bill and feet reddish black.*

MOULT
Complete moult probably begins

February or March. Body and head moult from September to December. Juvenile moults back feathers in March and into immature plumage at beginning of next breeding season.

VOICE
Shrill and high pitched. Short call before landing at nest-site. Bill clicking at intruders.

DISTRIBUTION
Breeds on islets in Port Pegasus, Stewart Island; Big South Cape and Solomon Islands; The Snares; and the Auckland, Campbell, Bounty and Antipodes Islands. Related subspecies breed on South Georgia; Îles Crozet, Kerguélen, Amsterdam and Saint-Paul; Stag, Marion, Heard and Macquarie Islands; the South Orkney and South Shetland Islands; and Tristan da Cunha.

RECOGNITION

In flight white tail and rump contrast with grey body. In breeding plumage red bill and feet. Forked tail extends slightly beyond wing tips when standing. Distinguished from Arctic tern by longer leg; darker outer webs of outer tail feathers; and shorter tail streamers.

Crested Tern *Sterna bergii cristata* STEPHENS, 1826

VAGRANT

OTHER NAMES: *Swift tern, greater crested tern.*

SIZE: *470 mm.*

DESCRIPTION
ADULT: *Sexes alike, but female slightly smaller. In breeding plumage forehead white. Crown to nape feathers erectile, black with white speckling, extending to below eye. Hind neck white. Rest of upper parts medium slate grey. Primaries silvery, darker at base of outer webs and along length of inner webs next to shafts. Secondaries white, with grey on outer webs increasing towards innermost feathers. Tail feathers pale grey, with white inner webs on outer feathers and outermost pair almost white. Underparts white,* including axillaries and underwing coverts. Iris brown. Bill yellow, with green tinge at base. Feet black. In non-breeding plumage black on head restricted to back, with some black-streaked or white-edged black feathers on crown.
IMMATURE: *Like adult but black on head replaced to variable extent by dark brown with white spots; variable amount of buff or brown on side of neck, upper back and wing coverts. Flight and tail feathers as in juvenile.*
JUVENILE: *Upper parts white heavily mottled with dark brown. Feathers of crown have brown central bands; rest of upper feathers have brown tips. Primaries dark brown, inner half of inner webs white except towards tips. Secondaries brown to ash grey with broad white tips. Rest of wing feathers dark brown with* white tips. Base of scapulars grey; base of median coverts white. Carpal bend and marginal coverts white. Lesser coverts brown. Tail feathers grey at base, browner towards apex and tipped with white. Bill greener and feet browner than adult.

MOULT
Little information available. Birds breeding between September and December in eastern Australia undergo post-nuptial moult during March and April and pre-nuptial moult in August.

VOICE
Alarm calls wep-wep, kree-kree, kirrick, kur-ruk, kyark and numerous variants. Deeper korr indicates excitement. Kirrah in mating display. Flocking call krow. Thin whistle from immatures.

DISTRIBUTION
Coasts and islands of the East and South China Seas, the Philippines, Indonesia, Australia, Tasmania, and the South Pacific as far east as Îles Tuamotu. Straggles to New Zealand.

RECOGNITION

Large size, dark upper parts and long yellow bill. White hind neck contrasts with dark mantle. At rest wing tips project beyond tail. Distinguished from lesser crested tern by yellow bill and in breeding plumage by broad white forehead. Thinner, yellow bill and deeply forked tail separate it from Caspian tern.

FOR SO LARGE A BIRD, the crested tern's flight is graceful, with long easy wing-beats. Flocks fly up in spirals and tumble down with great agility; pairs zigzag through the air together. When a flying bird drops its prey, it often recaptures it on the wing.

The crested tern feeds close to the shore. Pointing its bill straight downwards it flies about six metres above the water. Occasionally, when the bird sights food, it hovers and plunges vertically, but usually glides at a shallow angle, with its tail fanned, and takes prey from near the surface. After fishing, the bird circles to regain height, then resumes travelling parallel to the shore. Its diet is almost entirely fish, with some crabs, baby turtles and turtles' eggs.

A bird of the coast, the crested tern only penetrates far inland along the larger rivers. It lives on coastal reefs, lagoons, bays, harbours and estuaries, as well as salt and freshwater lakes and swamps. The bird will float on the water, but prefers to perch on posts, ships' masts or floating logs. It bathes in shallow water and dries out on land. Crested terns roost on land with other terns and gulls.

The birds breed in colonies on islands. The season occurs between September and December in southern and eastern Australia; between February and June in the north; and during both periods in the west. Birds in southeastern Australia disperse up to several hundred kilometres after breeding; one travelled over 1600 km. At least eight birds are recorded from New Zealand—from Raoul Island, the east and west coast of North Island, and south to Farewell Spit. Adults in both summer and winter plumage and immatures have all been recorded, mostly between January and April.   J.S.

Crested terns breed mostly on offshore islands in compact colonies. They prefer some vegetation as shelter from prevailing winds.

Fairy Tern *Sterna nereis* (Gould, 1843)

AT THE TURN OF THE century the fairy tern was a common bird along the coasts of both main islands. It also bred inland on some South Island riverbeds. Today it is rare. There are probably fewer than 10 pairs breeding in New Zealand; all have established north of Auckland near Mangawhai and Ruakaka, over a large area of open sandhills and often with a river or lake nearby. This tern is seldom seen and readily deserts its nest when people approach. Occasionally a bird is observed in Kaipara or Manukau Harbours or in Firth of Thames.

A noisy, active species, it flies high with a rapid twisting flight. In the summer it forms pairs; in the winter it congregates in flocks. During nesting it is aggressive and readily defecates on intruders. When fishing it climbs into the air, hovering back and forth over the water until it spots its prey. Usually it hunts singly, often in flocks of other species. Its food is mainly small fish with some gastropods, crustaceans and plants.

Before nesting one bird pursues another in flight with a fish in its bill. The male, holding a fish, crouches behind different females in a resting flock. When a female crouches the male raises its head, tail and wings and rhythmically turns its head from side to side. It then mounts the female. Before the male dismounts, the female seizes the fish and flies off, with the male in pursuit.

Fairy terns usually breed in isolation, sometimes in company with white-fronted terns. This contrasts with colonial nesting in Australia. The nest is merely a scooped-out hollow in the sand. One nest was reported surrounded by shell fragments, collected by the birds, which camouflaged the eggs and prevented sand blowing over the nest. The two ovoid eggs are a pale stone colour with dark brown blotches, and they are usually laid in November. Both sexes share in incubation which lasts about 18 days. At nest relief, one bird feeds the other

before taking over incubation. When first hatched, the chicks remain in the nest but later they shelter nearby in seaweed or other cover. When disturbed they 'freeze' with head and neck held straight. Young laid in November fly by late January. Once they are able to fly, fairy terns flock together, leave the breeding grounds and do not return until about August.

P.W.S.

NATIVE

OTHER NAME: *Tara-iti.*

SIZE: *250 mm.*

DESCRIPTION
ADULT: *Sexes alike. In breeding plumage upper parts pale grey, with forehead white and crown and nape black. Black band extending forward from eye, but not reaching bill. Tail forked, with outer feathers pale grey, inner tail feathers white. Underparts white. Bill entirely yellow. Legs orange. In non-breeding plumage head white mottled with black. Tip of bill black.*
IMMATURE: *Forehead and crown pale grey mottled with brownish black. Upper surface silvery grey mixed with white, many feathers with dark brown tips. Wing coverts grey-brown. Undersurface white. Bill and legs dark.*
NESTLING: *Mottled buff down lined with black above and white below.*

MOULT
Not known.

VOICE
Occasional high-pitched, rasping zwit *when feeding.* Tee-tee *followed by* zwit *when nesting area threatened.*

DISTRIBUTION
Northern coasts of the North Island, mainland Australia, Tasmania and New Caledonia.

RECOGNITION

Smallest tern breeding in New Zealand. In breeding plumage distinguished from little tern by orange feet, entirely yellow bill, and black stripe in front of eye that does not extend to base of bill. In flight appears all-white with black cap.

Fairy terns are now rare in New Zealand and nest in isolation among sand dunes, usually with a river or lake nearby.

Arctic Tern

Sterna paradisaea PONTOPPIDAN, 1763

FROM ARCTIC AND TEMPERATE regions of Asia, northern Europe and North America, the Arctic tern migrates south, down the eastern sides of the Atlantic and Pacific Oceans as far south as the Antarctic pack ice. Neither New Zealand nor Australia are on its migration routes, but stragglers and wind-blown birds have reached both countries. The few sightings in mainland New Zealand have been mainly on the west coast of the North Island. Usually they arrive in the southern autumn during their northward migration. Some adults in breeding plumage are seen, but most are in non-breeding or immature plumage. The Arctic tern has also been reported on the Auckland and Campbell Islands as well as on Macquarie Island. Possibly it is a regular visitor to these places. In the southern hemisphere it eats mainly krill with some fish and kelp-dwelling amphipods.   M.H.P.

The Arctic tern, which breeds in the northern hemisphere, migrates annually to the Antarctic.

STRAGGLER

OTHER NAMES: *None.*

SIZE: *380 mm.*

DESCRIPTION
ADULT: *Sexes alike. In breeding plumage forehead, crown and nape black, contrasting with white band on side of head. Mantle and back dark grey. Rump and tail feathers white except outer web of outer tail feathers dark grey. Ends of primaries pale grey. Iris brown. Bill, legs and feet red. In non-breeding plumage forehead white. Crown white*
streaked with black. Back pale grey. Tail white. Wing grey. Underparts white. Bill and legs black.
IMMATURE: *Similar to adult in winter plumage, but wings and tail as for juvenile.*
JUVENILE: *Forehead and crown grey with black margin. Back and wings pale grey mottled with buff and brown. Rump and tail white, with outer webs of tail feathers dark grey. Undersurface white, with side of breast brown. Bill red with black tip. Feet red.*
NESTLING: *Forehead, lores and throat black. Upper parts buff or pale grey spotted with black. Underparts white.*

MOULT
Adults moult twice a year. Complete moult begins September, during migration; growth completed while birds in Antarctica. Partial moult of head and body occurs February to March. Juvenile moults into immature plumage in first winter. Moults into adult non-breeding plumage in following summer.

VOICE
Low drawn-out kei-kirk with downward inflection. Kik-kik-kik when fishing and as contact call during migration. High-pitched keee-yah, rising in pitch, when anxious or uneasy.

DISTRIBUTION
Breeds in the northern hemisphere. Straggles to New Zealand.

RECOGNITION
Very short legs noticeable when perched. In breeding plumage tail deeply forked with long streamers. In non-breeding plumage differs from Antarctic tern by black bill and feet, white underparts and sometimes patchy brown mantle and wings. Flies straight with frequent dives.

Eastern Little Tern *Sterna albifrons sinensis* GMELIN, 1789

MIGRANT

OTHER NAMES: *Little tern, Asiatic little tern, sea-swallow, white-shafted ternlet, black-lored tern.*

SIZE: *250 mm.*

DESCRIPTION
ADULT: *Sexes similar. In breeding plumage pale grey above and white below. Crown, nape and stripe from eye to bill black. Forehead white, extending as a recess above and back beyond the eye forming an acute angle. Outermost 2 or 3 primaries have black outer web and broad black line on inner web next to shaft; shafts of outer primaries white. Tail grey, forked, with short streamers. Iris brown. Bill yellow with black tip. Legs and feet orange-yellow. In non-breeding plumage forehead pale grey or speckled black and white. Black of crown restricted to band around nape from eye to eye. Some black in front of eye. Tail short and without streamers. Bill black, occasionally yellow at base. Feet dull yellow to dark brown.*
IMMATURE: *Plumage similar to non-breeding adult, but with crown white and nape dark grey. In first plumage mantle and upper wing coverts mottled black, turning dark grey within a*
month of flight, then grey, leaving dark grey leading edge on inner wing. Outer tail feathers white, others grey. Bill black-brown. Feet dark brown.*

MOULT
Arrives in New Zealand in immature or non-breeding plumage October-November. Assumes breeding plumage between February and April.

VOICE
Short, high-pitched kweek *or rasping* zweek *may be an alarm note. Urgent* peep-peep-peep *often repeated while hovering. Lively* chi-chi-chi *or excited chittering accompanies what seems to be pair-formation or courtship flights.*

DISTRIBUTION
Migrant to New Zealand. Breeds eastern and southern Asia, Philippines, New Guinea, southern and western Australia.

RECOGNITION
Identified in breeding plumage by pale yellow bill with black tip; white stripe above and back beyond eye, and black tapering stripe from eye to bill.

Visiting eastern little terns are believed to be from breeding populations in Japan, Korea and Australia. They nest in colonies on sand or shingle beaches.

THE EASTERN LITTLE TERN is seen regularly in the large northern harbours, such as Kaipara, Manukau and Firth of Thames, where it roosts among flocks of wading birds, especially wrybills. It forages along the tideline, particularly near creek mouths. Hovering above waders standing in shallows, the tern dives for small fish.

Each year since the later 1950s the eastern little tern has arrived in New Zealand from October onwards. Most birds appear between January and March in flocks of fewer than 20, though one flock of 88 was counted. It has been recorded as far south as Stewart Island, but usually it remains in the northern North Island. The birds that arrive

in October and November probably breed in Japan and Korea. Those that arrive later in the year could be from breeding populations in Australia. A few winter in New Zealand. Other subspecies breed in Europe, Africa and North America.

In autumn, eastern little terns occasionally fly in pairs and take part in what seem to be courtship flights. The two birds fly to a height of a hundred metres or so, circle each other and call loudly. At the top of this upward spiral, the birds plunge into a dive, twisting and turning in unison, and finally come to rest at the roost site. In Australia, before this display, the birds present fish to each other.   R.G.P. & F.C.K.

White-fronted Tern *Sterna striata* (Gmelin, 1789)

THE WHITE-FRONTED TERN EATS fish, such as yellow-eyed mullet, piper, anchovy, pilchard, yellow-belly flounder, sand fish and small shrimp. It hunts in coastal waters or a few kilometres out to sea, either in large mixed flocks or small groups. When feeding in flocks, which can include gannets, fluttering and flesh-footed shearwaters, as well as red-billed and black-backed gulls, it flies into the wind, close to the surface. It dips down and picks its prey from the water. As the bird gains height it swallows the fish.

When fishing on its own or in small groups the white-fronted tern flies high above the water. On sighting a fish it either hovers momentarily, then descends step by step; or it plunges directly into the water and submerges completely for a few seconds. It seldom alights on the water, except to bathe.

Arctic skuas steal food from white-fronted terns. The skuas pursue the terns and force them to drop their catch. Often the skua seizes and swallows the fish before it hits the water. Red-billed gulls also try to rob food from white-fronted terns, but with little success: the terns are too dexterous.

Mating and breeding

White-fronted terns start breeding in their third summer and known-age birds have reached more than 20 years of age. They tend to return to the site where they were born and, once mated, keep their partner for several years, maybe for life. However, breeding behaviour is capricious and some breeding sites are abandoned for no obvious reason. Sometimes they visit nest-sites as early as August, but usually the breeding season can extend from late October to February and the young normally fly by early December.

The birds nest on sandy beaches, low-lying banks of shell or shingle, rocky islets, steep cliffs, deserted barges and wave screens, often within reach of heavy showers of spray. The nest is merely a hollow depression in sand or among plants. After incubation begins, the sitting bird often adds material to the nest. Sometimes white-fronted terns use nests vacated by gulls when associated with their colonies.

An unmated male attracts the attention of a female by flying over the flock, carrying a fish and calling. If after a time no female is attracted, the male settles and eats the fish. In another display two or more birds spiral higher and higher with rapid short wing-beats. The hind bird passes the lead bird, stretches its head forward and goes into a zig-zag glide. The pair mate at the nest-site or at the roost.

The clutch is one or two ovoid eggs which vary in colour from pale green-blue to dark brown, with spots of all shapes and sizes. Panic flights are common if the birds are disturbed at this stage, especially around dusk when the whole or part of a flock rises. The eggs are laid two to five days apart and the second egg is smaller. Both sexes share incubation for about 23 days and both parents brood the newly hatched chicks for four to six days. From then on one adult guards the young or the chicks form a crèche. It is either loose and strung over a wide area or a tightly packed mass which readily takes to water.

The parent recognises its chick first by voice and secondly by sight.

The chick fledges at 29 to 35 days after hatching. Only one fledges; if two eggs hatch the smaller bird dies from starvation and cold. The fledgling follows its parents away from the nesting colonies to nearby beaches. Some three months after leaving the colony the parents still feed their young. A high degree of skill is needed for hunting success, and the young need a considerable amount of time to perfect their skills and exploit scarce food. At this time the birds also form mixed-age flocks of adults, immatures, and fledglings, the former far outnumbering the others. In the following months they disperse: some cross the Tasman Sea to Australia, while others remain in New Zealand, possibly migrating to the north.

This is the most common New Zealand tern and once it was abundant around the coast. The Maoris ate its eggs; but the Europeans introduced other predators, such as stoats, dogs, rats and mustelids. Red-billed gulls walk calmly between incubating and brooding terns, searching for uncovered eggs. The terns threaten the gulls by 'gakkering', which consists of pointing their bills in the direction of the intruder, stretching their necks forward and ruffling their plumage. They do not actually attack the intruder. Spring tides with strong winds kill many eggs and chicks. Winter storms kill many birds, especially in Australian waters.

Today this bird is protected, but people disturb it during the breeding season. Beaches have become accessible to leisure vehicles; offshore islands and stacks are visited by pleasure boats. Indirectly, the increased number of gulls compete with the terns for nesting sites. The white-fronted tern moves to less suitable sites, often with greater distances to travel to adequate food sources.   A.MacC.

ENDEMIC

OTHER NAMES: *Tara, sea-swallow, kahawai bird, black cap, grenadier, swallowtail, noddy, tikkitak.*

SIZE: *420 mm.*

DESCRIPTION
ADULT: *Sexes alike, but females tend to be smaller. In breeding plumage forehead and lores white. Crown and nape black. Rest of upper parts pearl grey. Underparts white. Outer web of first primary brown-black. Tail white, long and deeply forked, streamers extending beyond folded wing tips. Iris black. Bill black with white tip. Legs vary from black to rusty orange. In pre-nuptial plumage often salmon pink flush on breast. Eclipse plumage lacks lustre; black cap smaller: white on forecrown more extensive; and mid-crown mottled.*

IMMATURE: *Similar to adult. No tail streamers. Outer primaries have narrow black band edging shaft. High white forehead and mottled crown. Middle and lesser wing coverts sometimes show traces of light brown mottling.*
FLEDGLING: *Upper parts barred and mottled ash grey. Nape and crown streaked with black, white and buff. Dark patches in front and behind eye. Hind neck dull white.*
NESTLING: *Down varies in colour. Upper parts off-white to dark brown-grey. Sometimes spotted on head. Underparts white. Legs flesh-coloured.*

MOULT
Full breeding plumage recorded as early as mid-winter. Complete post-nuptial moult begins when chicks are young and continues after birds have left breeding colonies. Post-juvenile moult in first winter. Sub-adults remain in eclipse plumage over first breeding season.

VOICE
Varied vocabulary, most vocal prior to and during breeding season. Single short zeat, tsit or zitt when feeding. Contact call crik, krra, grrik or kraek. Muffled krrrr or kgrrra when carrying fish. Rasping yawn as alarm call. Short high-pitched pit twit when leaving flock. Other calls include crooning; throaty growl when chasing off another white-fronted tern; and mating and begging calls. High-pitched trill from fledglings.

DISTRIBUTION
Breeds on the coasts of the main islands; the Chatham and Auckland Islands. Ranges to the Snares and the Campbell Islands. Some, especially young birds, winter in southeastern Australia and Tasmania. A few recently bred in Bass Strait.

RECOGNITION

Medium-sized tern. Buoyant and graceful on the wing. White band of feathers separates black cap from black bill.

White-fronted terns breed only in New Zealand and its vicinity, their nest often a mere depression in sand or rocks.

Sooty Tern
Sterna fuscata
(LINNAEUS, 1766)

NATIVE

OTHER NAMES: *Wideawake tern, whale bird, egg bird.*

SIZE: *450 mm.*

DESCRIPTION
ADULT: *Sexes similar. Upper parts brown-black, except for white forehead and white recess above eye. Black stripe narrows from eye to beak. White leading edge to wing shows clearly in flight. Tail dark above, with outer edges of streamers white. Underparts white, though undersurface of primaries and secondaries grey-white with white shafts. Iris brown. Bill and legs black with slight red tinge.*
IMMATURE: *As adult, but speckled buff or white on upper parts; and some dark flecking on breast.*
NESTLING: *Upper parts dark brown with feathers of mantle, scapulars, wing coverts and upper tail coverts narrowly tipped with white, forming prominent pale bar and crescent markings. Throat grey. Rest of underparts dark brown, paler on belly. Bill brown. Feet flesh-coloured.*

MOULT
Complete moult between breeding seasons.

VOICE
Wideawake, wek-wek-wek, wuk-wuk-wuk. Wruk *alarm or threat note. Deep growl when a neighbour encroaches on another's territory. Drawn-out growl* scra-are *from nesting birds when a person walks past. Harsh scream in the air.*

DISTRIBUTION
Tropical and subtropical zones of the Atlantic, Indian and Pacific Oceans. In New Zealand breeds on the Kermadec Islands. (During 1966–67 expedition, 40 000 pairs estimated to be breeding in 2 colonies on Raoul Island.)

RECOGNITION

Black upper parts, white forehead and underparts. Black band from eye to bill. Long deeply forked tail.

A sooty tern breeding on the Kermadec Islands. The most oceanic of terns, it is often found many days from land.

THE SOOTY TERN is the most oceanic of all terns; it ranges over most tropical and subtropical seas and comes to land only to breed. It eats small fish, cephalopods and crustaceans and depends on larger fish to drive them to the surface. In their efforts to escape their fish predators minnows jump out of the water, only to be caught by the terns. Sooty terns feed by hovering over the water and swooping to the surface. They rarely dive as their plumage would soon become waterlogged. The preponderance of squid fed to nestlings at some colonies indicates that the adults feed at dawn and dusk and perhaps at night. Their food is scattered widely and the terns cover large areas in search of it. Their flight is buoyant and undulating and they are capable of soaring to great heights in updrafts on motionless wings.

The terns are first heard back at the Kermadecs during the second half of August, but it is not until about mid-September that they begin landing at the breeding sites. Initially they arrive in the evening and at night, then in October they settle in the daytime. In 1966–67 at least 170 000 birds bred on the Kermadec Islands. But at one colony on Raoul Island the number of chicks fell from 8500 in 1966–67 to 3000 in 1978. If this decline were the result of predation the sooty tern might soon disappear from the island as a breeding species.

Most eggs are laid between mid-October and the end of December. By mid-February some chicks are flying and the colonies are deserted by the end of April. On Raoul Island the nest is an unlined depression in bare sand or among sand and low vegetation. Elsewhere the birds lay on coral, gravel, rocky slopes or ledges. In crowded colonies nests are within 500 mm of each other. The single egg is ovoid or elongate-ovoid and usually white with a pink tinge, marked with spots and blotches of dark brown, chestnut and ash-grey.

Incubation lasts 26 to 30 days. Both sexes incubate, changing over every one to six days. They brood the chicks for about a week. After a few days the young are capable of sheltering from hot sunshine, rain and wind. Sometimes they form a crèche and move about the nesting area. Sooty tern chicks are able to survive long periods on very little food, but grow quickly when well fed. Unlike most terns, the adult regurgitates food to its chick. The chicks are feathered by about 30 days old, but they stay in the colony up to 70 days. Introduced rats and cats destroy many eggs and chicks on Raoul Island. High seas wash away many nests and in some seasons numerous chicks die of starvation. At some breeding sites, sooty terns lay again after their first clutch has been destroyed.

This species congregates in large numbers, both to feed and breed. Over the breeding site pairs perform a high speed, synchronised, zigzag flight interspersed with slow wing-beats. On the ground they display by raising their wings into a sharp V over their backs, with their heads thrust horizontally forward. In a very common display, often associated with changing over at the nest, one bird circles another. Both droop their wings, arch their necks and turn their heads slightly away from each other, presenting their black napes. R.G.P.

The white-capped noddy builds its nest in the forks of trees, with twigs, leaves and litter from the bush floor. The nest is cemented with faeces.

White-capped Noddy *Anous minutus* BOIE,1844

NATIVE

OTHER NAMES: *Black noddy, lesser noddy, titerack.*

SIZE: *340 mm.*

DESCRIPTION
ADULT: *Sexes similar. Forehead and crown silvery white. Rest of plumage various shades of sooty black: the wings darkest; the tail brownish.*

Lores and band through eye and throat jet black. White arc above and below eye. Iris brown. Bill slender, black. Legs light or medium brown. Feet dark brown. Tail slightly forked, third and fourth feathers from outside longest.
IMMATURE: *Forehead and crown white. Lores black. Primaries black. Rest of plumage dark brown.*
NESTLING: *Sooty brown, paler below, with forehead white and crown grey.*

MOULT
Not known.

VOICE
Harsh staccato rattle; sharp care *or* kerr; kik-kirrik. *Juveniles beg with piercing, hissing* see-ew.

DISTRIBUTION
Tropical and subtropical Atlantic and Pacific Oceans. In New Zealand breeds at the Kermadec

Islands and straggles to the North and South Islands.

> **RECOGNITION**
> Dark tern-like bird with obvious white crown. Longer more slender bill than common noddy.

AT THE BEGINNING of the breeding season the male white-capped noddy feeds his mate. He sidles along a branch towards the female, bobbing his head slightly and calling. He then caresses her head, neck and beak with his beak. The female responds with a guttural rattle while bobbing her head up and down. She holds her beak wide open and takes regurgitated fish from the male by putting her beak across his widely open gape.

At the Kermadec Islands laying begins in October and most young are on the wing by March. The birds breed in colonies, nesting in the forks of trees. On Macauley Island, where trees are absent, they nest on rock ledges and in caves. On the Meyer Islets the nest takes several weeks to build and is a flat platform of twigs, leaves, litter from the bush floor, and occasionally seaweed, cemented with faeces.

The one ovoid egg is cream with blotches of purplish red. Both parents share the incubation period of 36 days. When they change over each bird nibbles the bill of the other. There is a high failure rate: of 12 marked nests, five were deserted during building, four lost eggs, one hatched, and the others were still being incubated after six weeks, so presumably contained dead eggs.

Observations of one chick showed that it was brooded continuously for the first three days. By the fourth day it was becoming active and for the next three weeks the parent squatted nearby to guard it (rather than brooding it). It flew for the first time at 52 days of age, but continued to roost at the nest at night.

The chick was fed by regurgitation. While the chick was very young, the regurgitated fluid was thin and oily. As the chick got older, the fluid became thicker. The chick approached the adult from the side to obtain food from the very back of the parent's tongue.

White-capped noddies do not migrate; they roost on their nesting islands throughout the year. Roosting birds adopt a 'sunbathing' posture: the tail and one wing are spread and the head is on one side. Most of the adult birds leave for the open sea in the early morning and return just before dark. Immature birds also disappear during the day, but return at night to be fed by the parents. These noddies mostly eat small fish, molluscs and plankton taken at the surface, although sometimes they dive for food. They feed in flocks away from the shore.

On open, bare patches of ground, noddies — possibly immatures — form 'clubs'. They sun themselves and attempt to mate.   M.H.P.

Common Noddy *Anous stolidus* (Linnaeus, 1758)

THE COMMON NODDY has not been seen in New Zealand this century. It ranges throughout the tropical and subtropical waters of the Indian, Pacific and Atlantic Oceans. Perhaps it is surprising that it does not reach New Zealand as it nests in the South Atlantic at Tristan da Cunha on the same latitude as Auckland. Its breeding grounds nearest to New Zealand are on Lord Howe and Norfolk Islands. The diet consists of fish, cuttlefish, molluscs and plankton.   M.H.P.

VAGRANT

OTHER NAMES: *Greater noddy, noddy tern, gogo, brown noddy.*

SIZE: *390 mm.*

DESCRIPTION
ADULT: *Sexes similar. Forehead white. Crown pale grey, shading gradually into darker grey neck. Lores black. Rest of plumage dull brown-black, with wing tips and tail darker than rest of body. In flight, primaries darker than rest of wing. Black rim around eye; white arc above and below it. Iris dark brown. Bill black. Legs and feet brown-black. Webs yellow. Tail heavily pointed or wedge-shaped, often notched at the tip.*
IMMATURE: *Similar to adult but*
lighter brown and lacking well-defined cap.

MOULT
Wings and tail moulted during breeding, December to March.

VOICE
Harsh kar-r-rk, kwok-kwok *or* eyak.

DISTRIBUTION
The Indian, Pacific and Atlantic Oceans. Rare straggler to New Zealand.

> **RECOGNITION**
> A dark brown tern with greyish-white cap and long, wedge-shaped tail.

The common noddy breeds on tropical islands and coral cays where it builds its nest—on the ground or on a low shrub—of seaweeds, sticks and leaves.

Grey Ternlet *Procelsterna cerulea* (Bennett, 1840)

THE GREY TERNLET BREEDS in loose colonies on the coasts of Pacific islands. It lays in a cliff crevice or under plants or boulders. The nest is bare but sheltered from the sun. The one egg is oval, white, with small dark and light blotches. At the Kermadec Islands the birds start laying in August and the last chicks fledge in January.

The incubation period is not known. The chick hatches with its eyes open and is soon active. For the first three days the parents brood it all the time. From then on they leave it unattended for increasing periods. At eight days the chick is still downy but its pin feathers show through. At 25 days it has more feathers than down and wanders about the nest-site. At about 31 days it starts to fly and by 42 days it has lost all of its down. However, the parents continue to feed the young ternlet for

considerable periods before full independence. Chicks of all ages are fed by regurgitation. The chick approaches the parent from the side and appears to induce regurgitation by pecking the adult's legs and feet. Chicks take food from the back of the adult's tongue.

In one aerial display the birds hover in the wind and weave a criss-cross pattern in unison across each other's flight path. In another, a single bird hovers directly in front of its incubating mate; with its wings and tail at an acute angle, it executes a series of dipping U-shaped flights.

Grey ternlets eat small fish and crustaceans picked up at the surface. They feed in flocks of up to 500 close to shore. Occasionally they are seen off northern New Zealand.   M.H.P.

NATIVE

OTHER NAMES: *Grey noddy, blue-grey noddy, little blue petrel, blue billy.*

SIZE: *280 mm.*

DESCRIPTION
ADULT: *Head and underparts grey-white. Upper surface and undertail coverts ash grey, darker on wing. Underwing coverts white. Short white line behind eye; black line in front of it. Iris black. Bill slender, short, black. Legs long, black. Feet black with yellow webs.*
IMMATURE: *Dark slate grey, with wings darker.*
NESTLING: *Pale grey above; white below.*

MOULT
Not known.

VOICE
Noisy screams in flight. Purring cror-r-r-r *on ground.*

DISTRIBUTION
The central and South Pacific. Breeding places include the Kermadec Islands, Bay of Plenty, Norfolk and Lord Howe Islands.

> **RECOGNITION**
> Small grey bird with long legs and large feet. Tail slightly forked with pointed feathers.

In recent years, flocks of grey ternlets have been seen more frequently in New Zealand's coastal waters.

White Tern *Gygis alba* (Sparrman, 1786)

The white tern does not build a nest, but balances its egg in a depression on the branch or trunk of a tree. At Raoul Island, in the Kermadecs, it usually lays in pohutukawa trees, often far above the ground. The single elliptical egg, blunt at both ends, is white or pale grey with light and dark blotches all over it. Often the birds breed alone, but occasionally two or three pairs nest on the same tree on different branches. The breeding season extends from early September to April. Birds on Norfolk Island are reported to fly about in groups of three during the breeding season.

Once hatched, the chick grips the wood tightly with its large hooked claws. It remains on the branch until it fledges. At first it eats small fish brought by its parents. When fully feathered it fishes with its parents during the day and returns to the branch at night. Feeding white terns flutter over the water, taking fish and crustaceans from the surface without submerging themselves. When disturbed by an observer they often hover close above the person's head, buzzing.

There are five records of white terns which have straggled to the New Zealand mainland: at Waipu, 1883; at Ettrick in Otago, 1945; at Bethell's Beach, Auckland, 1960; Pakotai, Northland, 1964; and most recently at Palmerston North in 1972. M.H.P.

NATIVE

OTHER NAMES: *White noddy, fairy tern, love tern, Pacific tern.*

SIZE: *310 mm.*

DESCRIPTION
ADULT: *White all over except for narrow black ring around eye. Wings and tail almost translucent. Shafts of primaries and rectrices brown. Iris dark brown. Bill straight, broad at base and pointed sharply, black with blue base. Upper legs black. Lower legs and toes light grey-blue. Webs yellow. Claws black.*
IMMATURE: *Similar to adult, except for black spot behind eye; and feathers of nape, back, scapulars, inner secondaries and wing coverts tipped with rusty brown.*
NESTLING: *Grey-brown with top of head and two broad stripes down*

back black. Breast light grey. Belly white. Bill very short, grey. Feet light yellow-red.

MOULT
Not known.

VOICE
Guttural heech-heech.

DISTRIBUTION
Throughout tropical and subtropical regions of the Indian and Pacific Oceans. Breeding places include Raoul, Norfolk and Lord Howe Islands. Five records of stragglers to the New Zealand mainland.

RECOGNITION

All-white tern with black eye-ring and short, slightly forked tail.

The white tern is a rare straggler to mainland New Zealand. It breeds at the Kermadec Islands, particularly on Raoul Island, where it arrives in early September and leaves by the end of April. Apart from a narrow black eye-ring, the adult bird is completely white; it can be distinguished also by its short, slightly forked tail.

The feral pigeon is a descendant of introduced domestic varieties which have subsequently become wild. The plumage of these birds is highly variable.

Feral Pigeon *Columba livia* Gmelin,1789

DOMESTIC PIGEONS—descendants of the wild rock pigeon of the northern hemisphere—first arrived in New Zealand with the early European settlers. Since then, many birds have reverted to the wild to form the basis of a large feral population, and they now live in cities throughout New Zealand. Pigeons flock in parks where people feed them, and nest on the ledges of tall buildings. They inhabit wharfs and goods yards where grain is spilt. In country districts they roost and breed on rocky outcrops and under bridges.

Feral pigeons are highly gregarious and only defend the area just around the nest. City feral pigeons roost and feed in the same areas, but country birds sometimes have to travel several kilometres between roosts and feeding places. They commute in tight fast-flying flocks. Several of these flocks meet on rich feeding grounds such as a recently harvested grain crop. In city parks, feral pigeons are usually tame and readily take food from people. Rural feral pigeons, on the other hand, are often wary, doubtless because of periodic shooting. The crops of several New Zealand feral pigeons were found to contain peas, barley and maize and, less commonly, clover, ryecorn, broad beans, worms, slugs and snails.

Normally their flight starts with a noisy flapping of wings as the birds gain height and speed. From then on their passage is swift with rapid wing-beats. Sometimes flocks sweep low over water or flat land. Displaying birds fly with slow wing-beats interspersed with glides, with wings held high. On the ground feral pigeons walk briskly. During courtship the male bows and circles the female with his neck arched and throat swollen.

Some feral pigeons breed when only six months old. They secure a nest-site and defend it throughout the year, mainly by threat displays but sometimes by striking the opponent with a wing. They lay throughout the year, with a peak in spring and summer and a low in March. The nest is often simply a depression in a modest pile of straw and faeces. Often they are little more than pecking distance apart. One nest, taken from a building in Wellington, was composed almost entirely of pieces of wire.

Usually the clutch is two white eggs. Both parents incubate for about 18 days but the male generally sits for short periods only. Both parents also feed the chicks: at first on 'pigeon milk', a regurgitated

cheesy substance, and later with grain softened in the parent's crop. At four weeks the young fledge. They spend another week or so in the colony before foraging with the adults. Females sometimes lay another clutch, usually in another nest, while still feeding well-grown young.

Many people consider feral pigeons a nuisance. Faeces and nest material disfigure buildings, block gutters and make footpaths messy. The birds also carry diseases, such as psittacosis, which can be transmitted to humans. In rural areas large flocks of feral pigeons sometimes eat newly sown cereals or peas. They have also been blamed for eating ripening seed peas, and barley grain fed to sheep in winter. With limited success, farmers in New Zealand have attempted to reduce feral pigeons by occasional shooting or poisoning with phosphorus or strychnine.   P.C.B.

INTRODUCED

OTHER NAMES: *Rock pigeon, rock dove.*

SIZE: *330 mm.*

DESCRIPTION
ADULT: *Sexes alike. Plumage varies. Crown, side of head, chin and lower rump dark blue-grey. Throat, upper breast, side of neck, nape and upper mantle metallic green or purple. Lower mantle, back, upper rump, belly and underwing pale blue-grey, with grey-white around vent. Tail dark grey with broad band of black. Primaries brown-grey; secondaries paler. Black bands on secondaries and greater coverts form 2 black bars on wing. Rest of coverts grey. Some birds much darker; some mainly red-brown; others almost white. Iris orange-red with yellow inner ring. Bill slate; cere white. Legs and feet dull red.*
JUVENILE: *Like adult, but darker and browner without metallic sheen on*

neck and breast. Chin and gape bare.
NESTLING: *Sparse yellow down. Bill purple with white tip. Legs grey-flesh.*

MOULT
Not studied in New Zealand.

VOICE
Displaying male calls characteristic rippling coo of 3 or 4 notes, such as oor-roo-cooo.

DISTRIBUTION
Europe, northern Africa and western Asia. Domestic varieties introduced into all countries, including New Zealand.

RECOGNITION

Plump, medium-sized bird with rather small head and short legs. Plumage varies from grey to red-brown to mainly white. Walks briskly.

Although traditionally a forest dweller, the New Zealand pigeon now occurs in a variety of habitats. It is totally herbivorous and feeds alone.

New Zealand Pigeon *Hemiphaga novaeseelandiae* (GMELIN,1789)

BEFORE EUROPEANS ARRIVED the Maoris killed many pigeons for food. They snared or speared the birds and preserved them in their own fat. They also used the feathers for making cloaks. In 1882, at Opawa, Rawiri Kahia and his people snared 8000 birds in a single strip of miro bush about three kilometres long and almost a kilometre wide. Even so, the pigeon was abundant throughout New Zealand. Numbers declined after European settlement as the pigeon's forest habitat was destroyed and even more birds were shot for sport and the table.

The first restrictions on hunting were passed as early as 1864. This had little effect and it was not until total protection was granted in 1921 that the decline of the New Zealand pigeon was arrested. Since then, despite illegal poaching, numbers have increased and are probably still increasing in many areas. Traditionally a forest dweller, this pigeon is now common throughout most of the country although it is absent from most of the dry tussock land of Central Otago, Canterbury and Marlborough and from above the bush line. It is also absent from farmland that has been completely cleared of forest.

It reaches its greatest numbers in mature podocarp forest mixed with hardwood, especially where there is plenty of miro. It is rare in pure beech forest. An adaptable bird, it also lives in many areas far from forest. Even exotic shrubs, such as broom and elderberry, support substantial pigeon populations, provided there are taller trees for nesting and roosting. Pine plantations provide no food, but they are often used by pigeons for nesting, overnight roosting and resting during the heat of the day. The New Zealand pigeon is also found in some towns and cities, especially if the cities are not too densely populated and have ample parks, gardens and remnant patches of second-growth native forest. New Zealand pigeons usually show no concern when feeding only a few metres from passers-by, and nests have been found above footpaths and close to busy city streets.

The New Zealand pigeon breeds at any time of the year, but especially between October and January. Its nest is a shallow platform of intertwined twigs. There is no lining to the nest and the incubating bird and egg are often visible through the gaps in the twigs. Either one or more branches support the nest or it rests on several lighter twigs. The nest is continually added to as incubation proceeds. The sitting bird leaves the nest, breaks off a twig, returns to sit in the nest and carefully incorporates the twig. Sometimes its mate brings a twig for the sitting bird to place. Nests are built in a wide range of trees and shrubs, generally among dense foliage or overhanging lianas. Nests are usually placed between two to six metres, and sometimes up to 20 m, above ground.

Mating is preceded by a bowing display. The male moves to a branch beside the female. He places his bill under the top of his wing, shakes his bill vigorously and faces the front again. He repeats this up to four times. Generally the male then places his bill down on his breast and bobs his entire body up and down. The female crouches on the perch, the male mounts, and mating takes about three seconds. The male flaps his wings to maintain balance. After the male dismounts, both birds preen.

Nesting, roosting and feeding

The female lays one smooth, white oval egg. If this is lost it may lay another in the same nest. It takes 10 or 11 weeks from laying till the young bird leaves the nest, an unusually long time for pigeons. The incubation period of 29 or 30 days is shared by both parents. Sometimes the sitting bird leaves the nest when the mate arrives in a nearby tree, while at other times they indulge in a lengthy changeover procedure which may take five minutes. When this happens the arriving bird pecks gently at the back of the neck and head of the sitting bird or each bird pecks the bill, head and neck of the other. Both birds sit on the nest together until this is over and one bird leaves. Usually the original incubating bird leaves but sometimes it refuses.

Initially, the chick is fed on a creamy protein-rich liquid known as 'pigeon milk' which the parent secretes from the walls of the crop. This is gradually replaced by regurgitated fruit. The chick places its bill inside the parent's bill and the birds sway and bob their heads for about seven seconds. The young pigeon fledges at 40 to 45 days.

When roosting or resting during the day, the New Zealand pigeon draws in its head, and puffs out its feathers a little. On cold clear mornings, birds often move onto a sunny perch before they feed. They have no uniform daily feeding routine. Feeding tends to increase gradually through the day and reaches a mid to late afternoon peak which is more pronounced in winter. On average, pigeons devote a mere quarter of their daylight hours to feeding. This is remarkably low for a totally herbivorous bird.

Unlike many pigeons, the New Zealand pigeon feeds and roosts alone. Flock feeding is rare. During winter, single birds or pairs defend feeding territories. Over the summer, territories break down but the birds continue to display aggressively. In one such display a roosting bird takes off and flaps to gain speed, then soars upwards into a steep stall with wings and tail spread wide, falls back and continues in the same direction or returns to the original perch. This flight is often the response to another pigeon flying close to the roosting bird. These flights are seen as early as August but reach their peak in February to April. They are also part of the courtship display.

New Zealand pigeons sometimes shower in light rain. With a firm grip on a branch, the bird rolls over to allow the rain to fall on its undersurface. After a few minutes the bird rolls over on the other side.

Although harriers never pursue New Zealand pigeons, the presence of a hawk disturbs them considerably. A feeding or roosting bird generally flies from its perch, circles around and then returns to its original position, or goes to roost in a tall tree. If other New Zealand pigeons are present in the area, they fly around in a flock. New Zealand falcons are known pigeon predators.

This herbivorous bird eats a wide range of plants. It prefers fruit but eats leaves and flowers when fruit is unavailable. Over the winter, leaves provide more of its food until by spring and early summer, they form almost the entire diet. New Zealand pigeons obtain a small amount of food from ferns and seedlings by walking over the forest floor. Outside of forest areas, New Zealand pigeons have readily adapted to eating a wide range of both native and introduced plant species. In these areas fruit is only available in late summer and autumn and forms less than 25 per cent of the entire diet.

The New Zealand pigeon plays a vital role in the ecology of the forest. It is mobile, has a distensible gape which allows large fruits to be swallowed whole, and little abrasion of the seed occurs in its gizzard. These factors combine to make the pigeon an ideal agent for dispersing seeds. At the same time it perpetuates its own food species. The larger fruited podocarps—notably miro and matai—as well as the hardwood species of karaka, tawa and taraire are almost totally dependent on the pigeon for dispersal.

The Chatham Island pigeon

At the Chatham Islands the New Zealand pigeon *Hemiphaga novae-seelandiae novaeseelandiae* is replaced by the Chatham Island pigeon *H. n. chathamensis*. This subspecies is larger than the mainland race, has greyer upper parts and breast and a heavier bill. It is easily identified as it is the only pigeon on these islands. Once abundant, it had all but disappeared by the turn of the century. A few birds survive on Pitt Island and the main Chatham Island, where they inhabit lowland, coastal forests.   P.D. & R.B.M.

ENDEMIC
New Zealand Pigeon
H.n. novaeseelandiae
(GMELIN, 1789).
Chatham Island Pigeon
H.n. chathamensis
(ROTHSCHILD, 1891).

OTHER NAMES: *Kereru, kuku, kukupa.*

SIZE: *510 mm.*

DESCRIPTION
ADULT: *Sexes alike. Head, throat and upper breast metallic green with gold reflections. Nape, mantle, back, scapulars and upper wing coverts purple with coppery green sheen. Lower back, greater wing coverts, primaries and secondaries metallic grey-green. Tail brown-black with green lustre. Underside of tail grey. Lower breast, belly, feathered upper legs and undertail coverts white. Iris dark red. Bill crimson, slightly yellow towards tip. Feet dark red. Claws black. H.n. chathamensis has purple head and breast with bronze and green reflections, pale grey lower back, bronze-green undertail coverts.*
IMMATURE: *Similar to adult but head, neck and upper breast dull grey-green rather than bright golden green. Iris and bill dull red.*
NESTLING: *Sparsely covered with yellow-brown down. Undersurface and area around eye bare. Iris brown. Bill and feet grey-brown.*

MOULT
Not known.

VOICE
Usually silent but some 5 distinct calls. Soft oooo when feeding or resting, sometimes ending on higher pitch, sometimes trailing off.

DISTRIBUTION
New Zealand pigeon: *The 3 main islands; some offshore islands.*

Chatham Island pigeon: *Pitt and Chatham Islands.*

RECOGNITION

White breast, 'shoulder straps' and belly. Differs from feral pigeon by coppery green head and neck, red bill and large size. Noisy whistling wing-beats.

The rare Chatham Island pigeon is larger than the mainland race and performs spectacular aerial displays.

Barbary Dove
Streptopelia risoria LINNAEUS,1758

INTRODUCED

OTHER NAMES: *Ring dove, ringed turtle dove, domestic collared dove, Java dove.*

SIZE: *280 mm.*

DESCRIPTION
ADULT: *Sexes alike. Overall colour creamy buff. Distinctive black collar round back of neck. Iris red. Bill black. Feet purplish red.*
IMMATURE: *Paler than adult with no neck band. Iris, bill and feet greyish.*

MOULT
Not known.

VOICE
Mellow cu-cru *or* cu-cu-cu. *Also a more high-pitched note.*

DISTRIBUTION
Introduced to North Island.

THIS NATURALLY TAME and confiding dove is a recent introduction to New Zealand. The first birds were released in gardens and parks at Masterton about 1970. The Barbary dove lays two white eggs in a shallow platform of twigs and incubates them for 14 days. In the wild its food is seeds, fruits and scraps, taken from the ground. However to ensure survival of colonies elsewhere than in New Zealand, birds are sometimes artificially fed, and young bred in captivity may be released to make up the numbers killed by predators.   E.G.T.

The Barbary dove, distinguished by its predominantly creamy-buff plumage.

Spotted Dove *Streptopelia chinensis tigrina* (TEMMINCK,1810)

IN NEW ZEALAND the spotted dove is found only in and around the city of Auckland. The original stock is believed to be from escaped cage birds. Since then deliberate introductions have boosted this small feral population.

In Auckland it lives where trees and shrubs are abundant, especially in parks and older, established gardens. It gathers much of its food from the ground, including seeds, fruits, insects and refuse. The breeding season is long, with peaks in spring and autumn. The bird builds a fragile platform in a tree well above the ground and lays two white eggs. Its flight, which is strong, level and direct, may include soaring manoeuvres similar to those of the New Zealand pigeon. After gaining height, the bird drops on spread wings in a shallow glide.   E.G.T.

INTRODUCED

OTHER NAMES: *Malay spotted dove, laceneck dove, spotted turtledove.*

SIZE: *300 mm.*

DESCRIPTION
ADULT: *Sexes alike. Head pale grey, pinkish at back. Black and white chequered patch on nape and side of neck, each feather divided and spotted at tip with white. Remaining upper parts grey-brown with dark brown shaft stripes to scapulars and wing coverts. Wing quills black-brown. Outer primary coverts pale grey on outer webs. Tail dark brown, the 3 outer feathers on each side broadly tipped with white. Underparts grey-pink, shading to white on chin and lower belly. Undertail coverts white. Iris orange to pink-yellow. Bill black-brown. Feet dull red.*
IMMATURE: *Head pale grey. Body brown above with dark brown shaft stripes on scapulars and wing coverts, and grey outer webs on outer primary coverts. Outer tail quills tipped with white. Underparts yellow-brown. Bill dark brown. Feet brown-red.*

MOULT
Not recorded in New Zealand.

VOICE
Cu-cru-cu, cu-cru-cu-cuc, cu-cu-cru-cuc, cu-cru-cuc, cu-cru *and other variations.*

DISTRIBUTION
Number of subspecies extend from East Bengal through Southeast Asia to Indonesia. Introduced in Australia and various Pacific Islands; New Zealand.

The spotted dove, introduced to Auckland from southern Asia, is found wherever trees and shrubs are abundant.

Sulphur-crested Cockatoo

Cacatua galerita (LATHAM, 1790)

DURING THE BREEDING SEASON this noisy and conspicuous bird usually lives in pairs or small family parties. The rest of the year it congregates in flocks of up to hundreds of birds. While most of the flock feeds on the ground, a few individuals perch in trees nearby. When an intruder approaches these sentries screech loudly and the flock flies away. The flight of the sulphur-crested cockatoo is a series of rapid, shallow wing-beats interspersed with glides. It flies at a considerable height, gliding down to trees in wide, sweeping circles on broad, rounded wings.

Soon after sunrise the flock flies to a nearby watering place to drink. From there it flies, often particularly long distances, to the feeding ground, where it remains for the day. Towards dusk it returns to the roost, where with much screeching it squabbles over perching sites.

The sulphur-crested cockatoo forages in native forest and adjacent farmland. In Australia it feeds on the seeds of grasses and herbaceous plants, fruits, berries, nuts, grains, flowers, leaf buds, bulbous roots, and insects and their larvae. A pest in cereal-growing districts, it digs up newly-sown seed and raids ripening crops. It also damages haystacks and bagged grain stacked in paddocks. To some extent the bird compensates for this by eating weed seeds.

Arrivals in New Zealand

Sulphur-crested cockatoos arrived in New Zealand as cage birds from Australia. Since about 1920 some have escaped and others have been released. Possibly this feral population is occasionally boosted with wind-blown stragglers from Australia. Such a bird may have arrived in May 1959 when after three days of strong westerlies a sulphur-crested cockatoo was seen at the southern head of Kaipara Harbour, so tired it would fly only downwind. In New Zealand the species' largest colonies are in the watersheds of the Turakina and Rangitikei Rivers near Wanganui, where a population of about 400 birds was estimated in 1962, and also between the lower Waikato and Raglan Rivers where a flock of about 200 birds was seen in 1964.

Little is known about its breeding habits in New Zealand. At Hunterville in January birds were seen entering and leaving a nest hole high up in a kahikatea tree. Presumably the cockatoos were incubating eggs or else brooding young nestlings. Another nest was found on top of a pile of hay bales under the roof of a barn. In Australia, the nest is usually in a hollow limb or hole high up in a large tree. It also nests in cliff holes. On a layer of decayed wood-dust lining the bottom of the hole, the female lays two or three white, elliptical eggs. Both sexes incubate the eggs which hatch after about 30 days. The nestlings leave the nest at about 40 days old.

When giving his courtship display, the male struts along a branch towards the female. With crest raised he bobs and sways his head in a figure-of-eight movement, calling soft, chattering notes. Mutual preening and bill-touching follow. R.G.P.

Outside the breeding season, the sulphur-crested cockatoo congregates in huge flocks.

INTRODUCED

OTHER NAME: *White cockatoo.*

SIZE: *500 mm.*

DESCRIPTION
ADULT: *General plumage white. Ear coverts and base of cheek and throat feathers pale yellow. Narrow forward-curving crest yellow. Underside of flight and tail feathers* strongly washed with yellow. Naked eye-ring white or tinged with blue. Iris dark brown in male; red-brown in female. Bill grey-black. Legs dark grey.
IMMATURE: *Similar to adult. Very young bird has faint tinge of grey on crown, back and wing. Iris brown.*

MOULT
Moult of feral population in New Zealand is unrecorded. Captive sulphur-crested cockatoos undergo a complete post-nuptial moult, which is typical of parrots in general.

VOICE
Contact call in flight is harsh, raucous screech with slight upward inflection. Alarm call is succession of abrupt guttural screeches. Roosting, preening and feeding accompanied by occasional squawk or shrill, piping whistle.

DISTRIBUTION
The western North Island. Also in Australia, Indonesia and New Guinea.

RECOGNITION

Large white parrot with raucous screech in flight.

Kakapo *Strigops habroptilus* GRAY,1845

ENDEMIC

OTHER NAMES: *Tarapo, tarepo, owl parrot, ground parrot, night parrot.*

SIZE: *630 mm.*

DESCRIPTION
ADULT MALE: *Upper parts mainly yellowish green, barred and mottled with dark brownish grey or black. Colour tones and intensity of barring vary. Emerald blue sheen often on crown, nape and mantle. Primaries, secondaries and tail brown-grey barred or mottled with pale yellow. Tail often well-worn at tip. Face, throat and front grey, yellowish grey or brownish grey. Often conspicuous grey or brownish grey ear patch. Indistinct yellow eyebrow stripe to above ear patch. Breast and flanks yellowish green streaked with yellow and finely barred with mid-brownish grey to dark grey. Belly and undertail coverts yellow streaked with pale green and weakly barred or streaked with pale brown-grey. Iris dark chocolate brown with naked grey eye-ring. Broad bulbous upper mandible blue-grey with tip and cutting edge ivory. Lower mandible ivory, and with throat, often heavily stained tobacco brown. Bulbous cere blue-grey with pale grey bloom. Nostrils large and crescent-shaped. Legs and feet massive, smooth-scaled, fleshy and blue-grey with cream soles.*
ADULT FEMALE: *Closely resembles male, but smaller, with finer and less domed head; narrower and proportionately longer bill; smaller cere blue-grey, generally without pale grey bloom; smaller, oblong nostrils; more slender, pale pink-grey legs and feet; and proportionately longer tail. Plumage similar to male and varies between individuals. In general tonings more subtle, with less yellow; and barring and mottling on underparts paler. Last 4 or 5 cm of inner vanes of outer primaries lack barring or mottling present in male. Breeding females have large well-developed brood patch of bare skin on belly.*
JUVENILE: *Closely resembles adult in size and colour. Generally dull olive green with less yellow than adult. Barring on upper parts finer and darker than in adult. Barring on*

The rare kakapo, by weight the largest of all parrots, is flightless.

underparts tends to be pale and indistinct. During first year at least, tail and wings comparatively short. Bill shorter, and with more pronounced curve near tip than in adult. Fledglings with 3 poorly developed longitudinal struts beneath lower mandible. Face pale grey with prominent dark grey ear patch. Indistinct broad pale yellow or

cream breast-band. Eye-ring paler grey than in adult. Primary wing feathers narrower than those of adult and pointed at tips. Docile but often vocal when handled.
NESTLING: *Long white down, replaced within first month by long grey down, pale on head and darker on body. Iris pale brown. Bill rich chocolate brown. Feet and legs pale*

grey. Contour feathers appear first on back at about 6 weeks and first primary quills appear soon after. Fully feathered at 9 or 10 weeks when fledging occurs.

MOULT
Appears to be protracted and complete moult may not occur every year. Male begins soon after booming ends and often in heavy moult during winter and early spring. Breeding female begins about June after young fledge. In non-breeding years both sexes may begin moult in late summer. Contour feathers of head and body moult first, followed by wings and tail.

VOICE
Seldom calls, except during courtship or booming season when male's characteristic low-frequency, resonant boom given from its court, normally at night. Also during courtship season sustained screech-crowing from one male. Aggressive territorial defence call scrark. *High-frequency, metallic, nasal* ching *from both sexes. Also very soft humming and bill-clicking during visual displays from a court. Throughout the year brief isolated grunts and squeals; hoarse hisses and screeches; duck-like* warks; *and donkey-like brays. When handled male generally silent, but female and juvenile utter low, complaining, vibrant croaks.*

DISTRIBUTION
Fewer than 25 birds on Stewart Island. Very small (fewer than 10 birds), scattered, all-male population in Fiordland. Introduced to Little Barrier Island.

'ONE OF THE MOST WONDERFUL, PERHAPS, OF ALL LIVING BIRDS', is how the kakapo is described in Buller's *A History of the Birds of New Zealand*, published in 1888. By weight, the largest of all parrots, the male weighs up to 3.4 kg. Massive legs and feet, rounded wings and a relatively short, slightly decurved tail emphasise its bulk. Compressed against its face is a broad pale bill. Its plumage is soft and yellow-green, with a conspicuous facial disc of sensory hair-like feathers. It is the only parrot with a rudimentary keel to the sternum and with five well developed ridges along the underside of its lower mandible.

Although the kakapo cannot fly its wings are not useless: it spreads them to help break its fall when occasionally it jumps a few metres at a steep downward angle; and it uses them constantly for balance and support, especially when climbing. They are also used constantly in courtship display. Except during courtship, when males call and display together, both sexes are solitary. Each bird generally keeps several hundred metres away from its neighbours. It walks with its body held horizontally and its head close to the ground.

A steadily diminishing habitat

The kakapo is rarely seen: a nocturnal bird, it roosts in dense cover by day. Its plumage blends with the foliage so well that even at very close quarters it is almost invisible. When threatened it freezes. The kakapo is now confined to a few remote areas, yet it once ranged throughout the three main islands and possibly the Chatham Islands. Even at the time of first European contact its range had contracted considerably. However it still inhabited parts of the central North Island and was

abundant in the Nelson district, on the west coast and in Fiordland. It lived in the Marlborough Sounds as late as 1879. The reasons for its pre-European decline are not known, but the impact of Polynesian settlement, particularly that of the rat or kiore *Rattus exulans* and Polynesian dog, kuri, which accompanied them, is probably responsible. The Europeans brought the stoat *Mustela putorius* and the ship rat *Rattus rattus*. These two mammals, in particular the stoat, account for much of the kakapo's rapid decline in the late nineteenth and early twentieth centuries. Now it has gone from the North Island and, but for a very small scattered all-male population in Fiordland, it is extinct in the South Island. A small breeding population persists on Stewart Island, but this too is endangered.

The kakapo is uniquely vulnerable to predation by mammalian carnivores, especially during breeding: it is the only flightless lek bird; it is ground-nesting, with helpless young that are cared for by a sole guardian; and the young are left alone for long periods at night. Further, it has a particularly slow reproductive rate.

Because the Fiordland population is beyond recovery, between 1974 and 1981 nine birds were released on predator-free Maud Island in Pelorus Sound. During the summer of 1981–82 booming, or mating, calls were heard on Maud, proving that relocated birds are capable of achieving breeding condition. Then, in June 1982, following the discovery of a stoat on the island, the surviving four birds (two males and two females) were moved to Little Barrier Island, New Zealand's largest predator-free offshore island. During 1982, 22 birds (nine females and 13 males) were released there. Only one is known to have died and the remainder appear to have settled in well.

In 1977 kakapo were rediscovered on Stewart Island in a remote locality east of the Tin Range. Until recently between 100 and 200 individuals may have been present, however feral cats kill up to 60 per cent of the birds each year. Now only three females and 10 males are known to survive on Stewart Island, although undoubtedly a few others are present.

Considering its failure to survive on the two main islands, perhaps it is surprising that the kakapo will tolerate a broad range of environmental and climatic conditions. Once it ranged from sea level to the uppermost limits of woody vegetation in rolling to extremely steep country. It lived in lowland and upland forests and scrubland at all altitudes but, like many species, preferred the forest edge, where food is more varied. The birds occurred in areas of very high rainfall as well as those of low rainfall. They will tolerate cold subalpine winters as well as the high summer temperatures of some lowland areas. In the south of Stewart Island, gales and icy squalls are frequent, temperatures cool and sunshine hours few.

With the exception of three birds near Doubtful Sound, all kakapo found recently in Fiordland have been in the Milford catchment. Invariably they have inhabited the subalpine zone 700 to 1200 m above sea level—where they have ranged from the upper margins of beech forest, through the subalpine scrub zone to the tussock and herb fields. When feeding, kakapo prefer areas of regenerating vegetation, such as the banks of streams, old slip-faces, subalpine terraces, areas of wind-thrown trees, or old avalanche debris where food species are more abundant and varied. Such rich feeding areas were termed 'kakapo gardens' by early writers.

On Stewart Island the birds occupy damp rolling to hilly peatlands 100 m to 400 m above sea level. The environment is harsh and the variety of plants is limited. Kakapo released on Maud Island adapted well to dry hilly pasture, bracken, scrub and coastal forest. They ranged from the shoreline to the 400 m summit.

The kakapo is the only New Zealand bird—and also the only parrot, as well as the only flightless bird—known to exhibit lek behaviour. A lek or arena mating system is one in which there is no permanent pair-bond between the sexes and males establish a mating station that has no connection with feeding or nesting. A female visits a male solely for mating. The males are sexually active and display on arenas for very long periods, whereas females make only brief visits. This skewed sex ratio, in favour of males, on an arena is a feature of a lek mating system.

Each male kakapo excavates and maintains one or more shallow depressions or bowls 30 to 60 cm in diameter and five to 20 cm deep, linked by tracks 30 to 60 cm wide. Wherever possible, the bird sites these bowls against the base of an overhanging bank, rock face or tree trunk, which acts as a sound reflector. Generally, such a track and bowl system, or 'court', is in a commanding position. It may extend for 50 m or more along a ridge crest, or occupy an area up to 20 m in diameter on a hilltop. Kakapo appear to be unique among lek birds in maintaining tracks within their courts. Since they are flightless, tracks are essential if booming from more than one part of the court is to be achieved. Courts of neighbouring birds are between 15 and several hundred metres apart. Groups of up to 50 associated courts or 'arenas' sometimes extend over several square kilometres.

Performing at the mating arena

From the bowls within their courts males perform a variety of displays, postures and calls, the best-known of which is the booming call. They do not boom every year, but at intervals of one to four years, generally every two years. The booming season lasts for two to three months, beginning between late November and early January. This low-frequency, resonant call can be heard up to five kilometres from the bird. Usually booming occurs at night and lasts six to eight hours. In foggy weather it may continue for up to 17 hours.

Another call heard at night during the booming season is a relatively high-frequency, metallic, nasal *ching* which both sexes appear to utter. Sometimes males alternate between booming and *ching* sequences. Several times a bird believed to have been a female has been heard exchanging *ching* calls with a male while approaching his track and bowl system. Possibly this call guides the female to the male once she has heard and been attracted to the general area by the booming call.

Males on courts have elaborate displays. They rock from side to side while walking backwards, slowly raising and lowering their fully extended wings. They keep their courts meticulously clean. The floor of the bowl is cleared of all debris and often carefully grubbed; the connecting tracks are often cleared of debris, and flanking vegetation is clipped well back. Displaying males whet their bills and carry twigs, leaves and lichens.

Nesting only takes place in those years when booming occurs and booming takes place only in summer. Usually, but not always, either all the males of a region boom, or none boom. Yet birds of different regions do not necessarily boom together. It seems likely that the erratic booming and breeding cycle of the kakapo is regulated by the availability of food.

The age at which kakapo begin to breed is not known, but is probably at least five or six years. The nest is built within a female's traditional home-range which is about 60 ha in area, and may be either close by or some distance from an arena. The nest is a scrape on the ground under tussock or other cover, or in a shallow natural cavity such as under the roots of a tree, which may be enlarged by the female. Some nests found last century were in burrows, but probably these were made by kiwis or petrels. The nest is sometimes lined sparsely with tussock blades, leaves, powdered wood and a few feathers. The nesting female has a well-developed brood patch.

Two to five, but generally three, ovoid, finely granulated, white eggs are laid in January or February. The female alone tends the nest. The incubation period is not known but young chicks have been recorded between February and May. There are indications that intervals of several days may elapse between the laying of each egg, and that incubation may commence after the laying of the first egg. Thus, chicks of different ages and sizes would occur in the same nest. The young are hatched blind and helpless and are brooded by the female for about the first two weeks.

Kakapo nestlings feed exclusively upon vegetable matter regurgitated by the female directly into the bill. During the initial two or three weeks following hatching the chicks are fed about every six hours day and night, but the female apparently gathers food only after dark. When the chicks are about three weeks old the female roosts away from the nest by day, generally within about 100 m; it visits the nest to feed the young, usually twice during the night.

Apparently, only one or two chicks normally survive to fledge at nine or 10 weeks. Nestlings are vocal from an early age and become increasingly active. After leaving the nest, young from one Stewart Island nest remained within 40 m of their nest for at least a further month during which time they foraged for themselves to an increasing extent, while continuing to receive food by regurgitation from the female. Nothing is known of their subsequent dispersal other than the fact that one nestling banded on Stewart Island in June 1981 was recovered in May 1982 living alone six kilometres from its nest-site.

Diet and feeding methods

Recent studies confirm that the kakapo is indeed entirely herbivorous, eating a broad range of fruits, seeds, leaves, stems and roots from a wide variety of plant species. Forest trees, scrub, tussock, herbs, ferns, mosses and lichens are also browsed. The kakapo is nevertheless a selective feeder, not only in its seasonal exploitation of specific food species, but also in its selection of individual plants within a species. A particular tree, shrub or tussock plant is often selected and browsed while neighbouring individuals of the same species are ignored.

The kakapo's method of feeding is unusual and possibly unique. The powerful bill is adapted for crushing and grinding foods. The lower mandible forms an efficient grinder against a finely grooved pad in the upper mandible. Foods are crushed and ground and, with few exceptions, only very finely masticated material and juices are taken in. Possibly as a consequence the gizzard is small and degenerate.

Foliage is generally browsed while attached to the plant, grasses and tussock blades being consumed from the tip downwards. Berries are normally pulped; however in certain species seeds are deliberately not crushed but are swallowed whole and pass through the bird intact. As in most parrots, the feet are used skilfully to hold foods to the bill during feeding. The bill is used as a grubber in digging for palatable roots or tubers.

Its feeding habits bear certain similarities to those of the Australian brush-tailed possum with which it now shares its remaining natural habitats: both browse at night on the ground as well as in the foliage of shrubs and trees, exploiting identical species at the same seasons.

Fibrous material is ejected in the form of characteristic, tightly compressed, kidney-shaped pellets known as 'chews'. These may be attached to the plant or, more often, are to be found on the ground beneath. These soon bleach to a pale straw colour and may remain intact for many months. Such a characteristic feeding sign provides one of the few means by which field parties may determine the whereabouts of kakapo. D.V.M.

Kaka *Nestor meridionalis* (GMELIN, 1788)

EARLY EUROPEAN SETTLERS found the kaka abundant in forested parts of the North and South Islands. In the middle of the nineteenth century it reached almost plague proportions in parts of Otago. In pre-European times it even lived in considerable numbers on the Chatham Islands. It was an important bird to the Maori who killed it for its flesh and its feathers. They used a tame bird to decoy the kakas when they fed on the flowering rata. Today its distribution follows the larger remaining areas of native forest and consequently its numbers are limited. Kakas live in unbroken tracts of beech, or podocarp mixed with hardwood. They prefer low and mid-altitude forest, where they flock above the canopy and feed mainly in the upper tier.

The diet of the kaka is varied. It eats many insects and their larvae, in particular the young of wood-boring beetles. The kaka takes these from the ground, from logs and from trees. It uses its powerful beak to tear off loose bark, break up decaying wood and even extract larvae from live wood. It also eats many kinds of seeds and succulent fruits, such as miro, kahikatea, matai, puriri, poroporo and tawa.

The kaka turns and moves constantly as it peers and stretches under and over the vegetation, using its beak to steady itself. With its foot it holds fruit or flowers up to its bill. It obtains the seeds of the kauri by opening the cone. It has a brush tongue to take nectar from flowers. When on the ground the bird hops more than it walks.

To some extent, perhaps, the kaka is nocturnal. It calls frequently at night and is generally more active in early morning and late evening or on dull overcast days. At these times it feeds in noisy flocks calling and flying over the forest to various feeding localities. During the day, the kaka is less sociable. Individuals feed silently, the only indication of their presence being the steady fall of pieces of wood torn off as the bird searches for grubs.

Usually it nests in a hollow tree, preferably one on a warm, north-facing slope. The entrance hole can be at any height but often it is three to six metres above the ground with the nest down inside the tree. At any time between September and March it lays up to five white eggs in the dry powder and chips in the tree. The most common clutch size is four eggs, with two chicks raised and fledged.

The breeding season is long. The female incubates the clutch for about 24 days and leaves the nest for brief intervals only, mostly in the morning and evening. She is regularly fed by the male. Both parents feed the nestlings for nine or 10 weeks and may leave them for long period during the day. The male plays a greater part in their care after fledging.

The future of the kaka on the mainland, and in particular on the North Island, is not secure. Introduced mammalian predators, as well as the destruction of much of its habitat, threaten this species. Numbers are only high on islands such as Great Barrier where there are no stoats. But it is difficult to assess the current population. Kakas could be long-lived—one bird in captivity lived for at least 20 years—and their mobility and noisiness could give the impression of more birds than there really are.   K.T.M.

ENDEMIC
North Island Kaka
N.m. septentrionalis LORENZ, 1896.
South Island Kaka
N. m. meridionalis (GMELIN, 1788).

OTHER NAMES: *Brown parrot, bush parrot; kaka-kura, kaka-kereru, kaka-korako, kaka-pipiwarauroa (Maori names, given to colour variants rare or unknown in today's reduced populations).*

SIZE: *450 mm.*

DESCRIPTION
ADULT: *Sexes alike, except male sometimes brighter and bill is longer and more arched. Colour variants in both subspecies (apparently quite frequent when kaka were abundant, but now rare or unknown): most commonly change of brown and green of back to white, cream, yellow, red, or a mixture of normal colours with yellow and red.*
North Island kaka: *Forehead grey. Crown to hind neck feathers brown-grey edged with dark brown. Lower hind neck feathers crimson, edged with dark brown, forming collar. Rest of upper feathers olive-brown with dark brown tips. Inner webs of wing quills notched with pink. Lower rump and upper tail coverts crimson. Inner webs of tail feathers stained and notched with red. Facial disc behind eye red-orange; and below eye crimson with brown edges to feathers. Breast feathers grey-brown with dark brown edges. Belly feathers and undertail coverts crimson, centred and some faintly barred with brown. Underwing coverts and axillaries bright red barred with brown. Iris dark brown. Bill slate black; cere yellow. Feet slate black.*

South Island kaka: *Similar to North Island kaka but larger with more vivid green and red plumage. Forehead and crown almost white with grey or green tinge and faintly bordered with pale green. Nape feathers pale green, edged with yellowish brown. Hind neck crimson variegated with yellow and brown. Back and wings brown-green. Some of mantle feathers and wing coverts with red border and all except quills edged with black-brown. Rump and upper tail coverts crimson barred with black-brown. Tail brown-green, terminal portion dark brown and tip red-brown. Below eye red with white streaks. Underwing coverts and axillaries scarlet. Bill dark grey. Feet blue-grey.*

NESTLING: *In North Island kaka down white, short on underparts, and abdomen bare; bill whitish grey; cere pale yellow; feet dull pale grey. In South Island kaka down grey; upper mandible black; most of lower mandible and nostrils lemon yellow; nostrils grey. Down replaced by adult plumage with no intermediate juvenile stage.*

MOULT
Not known.

VOICE
Loud harsh grating call most common but loud quavering whistle on descending note, ringing melodious whistle u-wiia *and* hoo-ya, *and straight whistle all heard as parties fly above and through trees. Low-volume sounds while feeding, during courtship and by nest. Soft musical song from female by nest.*

DISTRIBUTION
North Island kaka: *Low to moderate numbers in forests of the Mamaku plateau; northwest and west of Lake Taupo; and the Urewera region. Elsewhere rare or in very low numbers from Northland to the ranges north and east of Wellington. Sometimes seen in towns and even cities during winter. Moderate to high numbers on Great Barrier, Little Barrier, Mayor and Kapiti Islands and present on some smaller forested offshore islands.*

South Island kaka: *Low to moderate numbers in continuous native forest, from northwest Nelson along and west of the ranges to Fiordland. Rare east of main forested regions, but occasionally recorded from unexpected localities. Moderate to high numbers on Stewart Island and forested offshore islands.*

Gradually diminishing areas of native forest form the habitat of the kaka, a species under threat on the mainland.

Kea *Nestor notabilis* GOULD, 1856

ENDEMIC

OTHER NAMES: *None.*

SIZE: *460 mm.*

DESCRIPTION

ADULT: *Sexes alike, except male larger with longer and more outward curving upper mandible. Head and hind neck green. Breast and undersurface slightly lighter. Back and wings brighter green. Quills blue on outer webs and elsewhere dark brown blotched with lemon yellow. Underwing coverts and axillaries scarlet. Rump and upper tail coverts dark red. Tail blue-green with dark brown band near tip. Iris dark brown. Bill and legs dark brown to black. In summer some adult females have bright orange-yellow in mouth at join of mandibles and at rear of lower mandible; conspicuous light-brown wing patch when viewed from above and in flight.*
JUVENILE: *Immediately after fledging crown and nape light olive-yellow. Nostrils grey. About nostrils and lower mandible bright orange-yellow. Legs light grey. Within 2 months crown fades and feet darken and become dirty. Yellow by beak gradually fades over 2 years or more. When soaked by heavy rain plumage brown.*

MOULT
Not known.

VOICE
Noisy keaa *delivered mainly in flight; variety of softer and conversational calls.*

DISTRIBUTION
Along the Southern Alps from Golden Bay to near Puysegur Point. Abundant in native forest on western side of mountains. Much less common east of the main divide where forest less extensive. In mountains above the Aorere Valley; in the mineral belt near the Dun Mountain; in the Pelorus Mountains; and in the Seaward Kaikoura Range. Seen in southern Tararua Range, North Island.

RECOGNITION
Olive-green above and below, scarlet underwing, dark red rump. More slender bill than kaka. In forest most reliably distinguished by large amount of green plumage.

The kea, most abundant in native forests west of the Southern Alps, often scavenges at human settlements.

FLOCKS OF KEAS SCAVENGE around human settlements in the Southern Alps. At tourist centres and ski huts these inquisitive and comic birds are a great attraction. At farm houses they are a nuisance.

Shepherds, in particular, dislike the kea. Soon after pastoral farming was established in New Zealand keas were discovered killing sheep, and for a hundred years large numbers of keas were legally slaughtered. Yet often large losses that should have been expected in alpine regions were blamed on the keas. Though evidence shows that they feed on carrion, and rogue birds do take live mammals, they seldom kill sheep and in 1970 the kea was granted partial protection.

Many travellers on foot through kea country fail to notice them. They live from altitudes of 2000 m to sea level. Almost all nests are in forest but the birds seem to need areas above the timber line for feeding. Where the land is steep, keas can be seen both at a low altitude and, nearby, a kilometre away at a high altitude. In conditions of storm or heavy and extensive snowfall they wander 20 or 30 km beyond their normal range.

Keas are probably older than three years before they breed. Often the nest is built over several years. These are frequently sited on the ground, under a lateral moraine boulder, within the forest, or near an open patch of ground and with a wide outlook from tree tops by the nest. The nest itself is built loosely of foliose lichens, old man's beard

Usnea barbata, twigs and leaves. One nest found in 1958 was still being added to and had not yet been used in 1965.

From watching birds in captivity the cock begins to feed a hen in the autumn. They mate in mid-winter, always at nightfall or soon afterwards, and on a branch. A week or more before laying the hen spends much time on the nest and lays a clutch of usually two or three eggs. She incubates for 23 or 24 days and the young hatch over several days. The nestlings remain in the nest for nine to 12 weeks or longer.

Before the chicks fledge the cock guards the entrance to the nest. One chick escapes, flies and is soon hiding and fossicking in the underscrub 10 to 20 m from the nest. The parents guard in the trees above, while the other nestlings remain in the nest for a few more days. The cock usually feeds the fledglings. In captivity male chicks are fed for two months out of the nest and females for five months.

Most cocks are monogamous, but some have several mates—one or two hens nesting, several building, and perhaps one feeding the cock. Later the second group of hens looks after and plays with the fledglings. One hen fledged with chicks in April, and was again with chicks the next December.

Banding shows that the mean annual mortality rate of keas older than one year is 36.8 per cent. One hen banded as an adult in 1956 was still alive 15 years later.   J.R.J.

Eastern Rosella

Platycercus eximius

(SHAW,1792)

INTRODUCED

OTHER NAME: *Rosella.*

SIZE: *330 mm.*

DESCRIPTION
ADULT: *Sexes similar, but female duller with less red on head and breast. Head, neck and breast red. Cheeks and throat white. Upper abdomen yellow merging into yellow-green on lower abdomen. Vent and undertail coverts red. Undertail pale blue. Feathers of lower nape, back and secondary coverts black with broad yellow-green edges. Primaries and primary coverts dark blue with dark brown inner webs. Shoulder pastel blue. Secondaries yellow-green with dark brown inner webs. Narrow white median band on underwing. Rump and upper tail coverts green tinged with yellow. Two central tail feathers blue-green, rest pale blue tipped with white. Iris dark brown. Bill grey-white. Feet grey-brown.*
IMMATURE: *Similar to adult female but nape and hind crown green.*
NESTLING: *Initially blind and naked or with sparse dorsal down.*

MOULT
In autumn and winter, immature birds acquire more red feathers on hind crown and nape, but first complete moult usually begun at 7 to 10 months old. Renewal of primaries from centre outwards usually takes 3 to 5 months; full adult plumage completed at about 12 months old. Subsequent complete moults at yearly intervals, generally at end of breeding season.

VOICE
Loud, ringing kwink, *sometimes as single note, but usually repeated on ascending scale. Metallic piping note repeated twice. Loud* chitty-chew. *Strident shrill screech when alarmed. Feeding usually accompanied by quiet chattering. All call notes higher than those of crimson rosella.*

DISTRIBUTION
Eastern and southeastern Australia and Tasmania. Small population established in the Dunedin area since about 1910. By the 1970s another population, probably originally from escaped cage birds, strongly established throughout Auckland, Northland and the far north, extending into west Waikato as far south as Kawhia and Te Kuiti and east to the Coromandel Peninsula. Also in the Wellington-Hutt Valley region, established in 1960s from cage escapees, later colonised the foothills of the Tararua Range, to Eketahuna in the east and Otaki in the west. Sightings from New Plymouth, Taupo, Gisborne, Tiritea and Banks Peninsula.

> ### RECOGNITION
>
> Very distinctively coloured parrot with loud carrying call and swift undulating flight. Larger, more brightly coloured than native parakeets. Distinguished from slightly larger crimson rosella by white cheek patches, scalloped yellow-green back, pale green rump and yellow and green belly.

The female eastern rosella (right) has duller head and breast feathers than the male. Birds form pairs in early spring.

IN NEW ZEALAND, as in their native Australia, eastern rosellas prefer lightly timbered and open habitats, including orchards. They are often found in pine forests. In Northland and near Wellington they live in dense native forest. Usually they occur in pairs or small family groups, but where they are plentiful they may form large flocks after the breeding season until early spring. They have a strong, swift, undulating flight low to the ground that finishes with upward glides to land in trees. Long-distance flights are generally level and at a considerable height.

They spend much of their time feeding upon a wide range of seeds, berries, fruits and blossoms in trees, as well as fallen seeds and grains. Occasionally they take insects. In New Zealand they cause minor damage to crops, especially to citrus fruits in Northland, but also to kiwi fruit, tomatoes and pip and stone fruit. If further established, the species could be a pest in major fruit-growing regions.

In early spring the flocks break up and the birds form pairs. The displaying male droops its wings, squares its shoulders and fluffs up its breast feathers and upper tail coverts. It moves its fanned tail from side to side while bowing slightly or holding the head high and tilted back. At the same time the bird chatters continuously.

The breeding cycle has not been studied in New Zealand. In Australia it lasts from August to January. The nest is usually situated in a hollow limb or hole in a living or dead tree, fencepost, stump, fallen log or even in a rabbit burrow. The nest itself is a shallow bowl of decayed wood dust. The female lays usually five or six white, oval eggs and incubates them solely for about 22 days. Both parents feed the young until they fledge at about 30 days old. Usually, they remain with their parents for several months after fledging. They are generally long-lived birds, and one Australian adult banded in 1961 was still alive in 1970.   H.A.R.

Crimson Rosella *Platycercus elegans* (GMELIN,1788)

THE CRIMSON ROSELLA is a colourful—if rare—addition to New Zealand's bird life. It was first seen about 1910 near Dunedin but none have been recorded from that area for over 30 years. Then, in 1963, crimson rosellas, probably cage escapees, became established in the Wellington area. They have since bred successfully. Two birds were also recorded from the Tararua foothills near Eketahuna in 1971. In Australia they are forest birds found in tableland not far from the coast. They also live on the outskirts of towns and cities and in orchards, but generally are not common in open or lightly wooded areas. In Wellington, they inhabit parks, reserves and well-timbered suburbs.

Its breeding habits have yet to be studied in New Zealand. In Australia, the breeding season extends from late August to February. The nest is usually a shallow bowl of decayed wood dust in a hollow limb or hole in a tree. The female lays about five white, oval eggs, and incubates for about 21 days. The young fledge after about five weeks and generally remain with their parents for several months longer.

Crimson rosellas are usually seen in pairs or small family groups; but in parts of Australia, where they are plentiful, immatures flock in autumn and winter while adults remain in pairs or small parties.

Crimson rosellas feed on a wide variety of grass, shrub and tree seeds, fruits, nuts, flowers, shoots, nectar and insects. The numbers of this richly coloured bird are very low and the range most restricted. Should they become common, however, they are likely to become a pest in major fruit-growing districts. H.A.R.

INTRODUCED

OTHER NAMES: *Red lory, red lowry.*

SIZE: *360 mm.*

DESCRIPTION
ADULT: *Sexes alike, but male larger with broader head and heavier bill. Head, breast, abdomen and undertail coverts dark crimson. Cheek patches and throat violet-blue. Feathers on lower nape, back and secondary wing coverts black, broadly edged with crimson. Primaries and their coverts with dark blue outer webs and dark brown inner webs. Shoulder pale violet-blue. Secondaries with crimson outer webs and black inner webs. Underwing coverts dark blue. Rump and upper tail coverts dark crimson. Central tail feathers blue, washed with green; side feathers with violet-blue bases, broad pale blue edges and white tips. Iris dark brown. Bill grey-horn with slate cere. Legs and feet dark grey-brown.*
IMMATURE: *Forehead, crown, upper breast, thighs and undertail coverts crimson red. Rest of head, nape and underparts dull olive green. Cheeks and throat violet-blue. Back and wing-coverts grey, broadly edged with olive green. Rump pale olive-green.*
NESTLING: *Initially blind and naked or with sparse dorsal down.*

MOULT
On leaving nest young birds usually olive-green with few red feathers. In autumn and winter immature birds gradually acquire more red feathers, especially on head, underparts and rump. Adult plumage generally attained at about 16 months.

VOICE
Low-pitched kweek-kweek-kweek, *middle note on a lower scale. Alarm call is quick series of shrill, short or 2-note metallic screeches. Feeding usually accompanied by quiet chattering. All call notes of deeper tone than those of eastern rosella.*

DISTRIBUTION
Northern Queensland, eastern and southeastern Australia. Introduced to Norfolk Island and New Zealand.

RECOGNITION

Brilliant crimson parrot with loud carrying call and swift undulating flight.

The crimson rosella occurs in New Zealand in very low numbers and is most often seen in pairs or small family groups.

Orange-fronted Parakeet *Cyanoramphus malherbi* (SOUANCÉ,1857)

SINCE EUROPEAN SETTLEMENT the orange-fronted parakeet has never been as common as the other New Zealand parakeets. But there were numerous sightings from various parts of the South Island during the nineteenth century and specimens were obtained from Hen and Little Barrier Islands in the 1880s. This century it has also been recorded on Stewart Island. In recent years, however, it has only been found near the Hope River in North Canterbury.

Because it is so rare, little is known about this bird. It lives from subalpine scrub to near sea level, although most recent records are from beech forest at elevations below 800 m. Recent field observations in North Canterbury indicate that buds, flowers, young leaves, seeds and scale insects are commonly eaten. The orange-fronted parakeet was kept as a cage bird in the nineteenth century. In 1883 a pair kept in France produced a brood of four. There is a clutch of three broadly elliptic eggs, reputed to be of this species, in the Canterbury Museum. The nest of a pair of orange-fronted parakeets was found in a hole in the trunk of a beech tree, near the Hope River in November 1982. It contained four eggs.

Most birds seen in the wild have been associated with parties or flocks of yellow-crowned parakeets. Orange-fronted parakeets appear to be quieter and less bold. They can mate successfully with yellow-crowned parakeets and some authorities believe them to be of the same species. But if this is the case it does not explain why the orange-fronted parakeet is now so rare whereas the yellow-crowned parakeet is still common in many localities. No orange-fronted birds have been seen this century on offshore islands where the yellow-crowned species is still abundant; nor have they been recorded from the many breeds of yellow-crowned parakeets reared in aviaries over the years. Captive breeding of orange-fronted parakeets is now under way in an attempt to clarify the bird's taxonomic status and to study further the structural differences between the two species. R.H.T.

ENDEMIC

OTHER NAME: *Alpine parakeet.*

SIZE: *220 mm.*

DESCRIPTION
ADULT: *Sexes alike, but female smaller. General plumage dull green, with underparts paler. Orange frontal band extends to eyes. Upper forehead and crown to just behind eye pale yellow. Orange patch on side of rump. Alula, primary coverts, and outer webs of inner half of primaries violet blue. Iris orange-red. Bill pale blue-grey at base, black at tip. Legs and feet grey-brown.*
JUVENILE: *Similar to adult, but with shorter tail and less distinct frontal band. Iris pale reddish brown.*
NESTLING: *Grey down. Iris dark.*

Bill pale pinkish horn. Legs and feet pinkish grey.

MOULT
As in other Cyanoramphus *parakeets.*

VOICE
Very similar to yellow-crowned parakeet, but softer.

DISTRIBUTION
Probably now in the South Island only.

RECOGNITION

Orange frontal band and pale yellow crown. Duller green than yellow-crowned parakeet.

Red-crowned Parakeet *Cyanoramphus novaezelandiae* (SPARRMAN, 1787)

The Kermadec parakeet, confined solely to islands of the Kermadec group.

THERE ARE FOUR SUBSPECIES of the red-crowned parakeet in New Zealand: the New Zealand red-crowned parakeet *Cyanoramphus novaezelandiae novaezelandiae*, the Kermadec parakeet *C.n. cyanurus*, the Chatham Island red-crowned parakeet *C.n. chathamensis*, and Reischek's parakeet *C.n. hochstetteri*. Elsewhere, there are separate subspecies on Norfolk Island and in New Caledonia, and two other subspecies, the Lord Howe Island parakeet and the Macquarie Island parakeet, became extinct before the end of the last century.

The New Zealand red-crowned parakeet was once widely distributed on the North and South Islands. It was so common during the 1870s and 1880s that it was a serious pest of crops, orchards and gardens. However introduced rats, stoats and other predators slaughtered many birds and now parakeets are scarce on the two main islands. It breeds successfully in captivity and, recently, aviary-bred birds have been released in the Wairarapa, the Waitakere Ranges, and on Tiritiri and Cuvier Islands.

It inhabits forests, scrublands, and open areas. Usually it is found more at forest edges and at lower altitudes than its relative, the yellow-crowned parakeet. Hollow branches of tree trunks are favourite nest-sites but it also uses holes in cliffs or among rocks, burrows in the ground or densely matted vegetation. Nests in decaying trees are often lined only with powdered wood, but sometimes feathers, moss, grass stems, tree fern scales and small amounts of other dry plant material are used. Often the same nest-site is used year after year.

Birds in captivity begin breeding when less than one year old. In the wild the timing of the breeding season depends on the availability of food: most eggs are laid in October, November or December. About five broadly elliptical, white eggs are laid over one or two days. The female incubates for about 20 days from the laying of the second egg. The male brings her food and assists with the feeding of the nestlings. He usually transfers regurgitated food to the female but when the female is away from the nest he directly feeds the chicks. All the young leave the nest at about the same time, five to six weeks after hatching, when the younger ones in a large brood will be noticeably less developed. Both parents continue to feed the chicks for about another week. Occasionally, as on Auckland Island, the New Zealand red-crowned parakeet breeds with the yellow-crowned parakeet.

Pairs sometimes remain together throughout the year but territorial behaviour has not been recorded. The birds flock to abundant food sources at any season and, on islands with limited fresh water, they congregate at springs and seepages to drink and bathe. They eat many kinds of seeds, berries, fruits, buds, flowers and shoots, as well as invertebrates, and nectar.

The island subspecies

Over 10 000 Kermadec parakeets were estimated to live on Macauley Island in 1980. Smaller populations also inhabit Curtis, Meyer, Napier, Dayrell and Chanter Islands. They were abundant on Raoul Island in 1836 but exterminated there by wild cats, probably before 1854. Birds are known to disperse to Raoul Island, where parakeet feathers disgorged by cats have been found, but the species is unable to re-establish itself there. Most eggs are laid in October and November. Numerous family parties of about four young were seen on the Meyer Islands in later December. Kermadec parakeets feed mainly upon seeds, berries and other vegetation. When goats were killed on Macauley Island the birds fed upon their carcasses. They have also been seen feeding on seaweeds and small limpets.

The Chatham Island red-crowned parakeet lives at forest margins, bush patches, scrublands and open areas. On South East Island in

ENDEMIC
Kermadec Parakeet
C.n. cyanurus SALVADORI, 1891.
New Zealand Red-crowned Parakeet
C.n. novaezelandiae (SPARRMAN, 1787).
Chatham Island Red-crowned Parakeet
C.n. chathamensis OLIVER, 1930.
Reischek's Parakeet
C.n. hochstetteri (REISCHEK, 1889).

OTHER NAMES: *Kakariki, New Zealand parakeet, Antipodes red-crowned parakeet.*

SIZE: *280 mm.*

DESCRIPTION
ADULT: *Sexes alike, but female smaller. General plumage bright green: emerald on face; yellowish green on underparts. Forehead and crown to just behind eye, band from forehead to eye, and patch immediately behind eye, all crimson red. Red patch on side of rump. Alula, primary coverts and outer webs of inner half of primaries violet blue. Tail feathers generally green above and grey below. Iris red. Bill pale blue-grey at base, black at tip. Legs and feet greyish brown. Occasionally green replaced by yellow. In Kermadec parakeet more blue on flight feathers; underparts greener; and tail blue-green. In Chatham Island red-crowned parakeet underparts yellower; side of head emerald green; and feet flesh grey to dark grey. In Reischek's parakeet plumage yellower; flight feathers greenish blue; and iris yellow-red.*
JUVENILE: *Similar to adult but with shorter tail; pinkish tinge to base of bill when newly fledged, dull green plumage and less distinct red on head; and iris pale reddish brown.*
NESTLING: *Light grey down. Eyes open at about 10 days. Feathers appear after 3 weeks. Coloured feathers on forehead visible at about 4 weeks. Iris dark. Bill pinkish horn. Legs and feet pinkish grey.*

MOULT
Adult moults soon after breeding.

VOICE
Large variety of calls and conversational notes. Flight call is loud rapid chatter ki-ki-ki-ki-ki. Similar, but quieter and more interrupted chatter while perching. Also soft tu-tu-tu-tu, pretty dick, twenty-eight or tee-pee-wee. Begging call of fledged young similar to Antipodes Island parakeet.

DISTRIBUTION
New Zealand red-crowned parakeet: *Now scarce on the 2 main islands: only recent records from large bush remnants in Northland and the Waitakere, Coromandel, Hauhungaroa, Tararua, Rimutaka, Nelson and Fiordland Ranges. Widespread on Stewart Island and many smaller islands, including Three Kings, Poor Knights, Hen and Chickens; Sail Rock; Little and Great Barrier Islands; Arid, Mokohinau, Mercury, Aldermen and Kapiti Islands; and Enderby, Rose and Adams Islands in the Auckland Islands.*

Kermadec parakeet: *Confined to the Kermadec Islands, with population of about 100 on Meyer Islands, and smaller Napier, Dayrell and the Chanters islets.*

Chatham Island red-crowned parakeet: *Small numbers on Chatham and Pitt Islands. Plentiful on South East Island. Lower numbers also on Mangere and Little Mangere Islands, where it has hybridised with rare Chatham Island yellow-crowned parakeet.*

Reischek's parakeet: *Antipodes and Bollons Island and smaller islets of the Antipodes Islands.*

RECOGNITION

Red forehead and crown, and red patch behind eye.

November 1976 these birds were common around the coast and at clearings and forest edges. Their numbers were markedly lower inside the thickly regenerating forest. The recent opening up of the forest cap on Little Mangere Island has allowed this species to become established there within the last decade.

It has an extended breeding season and most eggs are laid between October and December. The average clutch is six. Sometimes it breeds with the rare Chatham Island yellow-crowned parakeet. Resultant hybrids have an orange upper edge to the red crown or a completely orange crown and a reddish orange patch behind the eye. It is far less sedentary than the Chatham Island yellow-crowned parakeet and much more often seen in flight over open habitats. During October and November it eats mainly leaves and shoots, flowers, seeds, and small amounts of nectar, invertebrates and fruit on South East and Mangere Islands. From March to May more seeds are eaten but leaves and shoots are still the main items of diet. Small grits of volcanic glass have been found in the crops of birds collected on Mangere Island.

Reischek's parakeet occurs on all parts of the Antipodes and Bollons Islands but is most common on the more open parts of the elevated central plateau and in coastal areas with low vegetation and penguin colonies. It nests in tunnels about 40 cm deep in the crowns of tall *Poa litorosa* tussocks or clumps of *Polystichum* fern. The nest cavity is lined with small cut pieces of tussock or fern. It breeds from December to February. Captive birds lay about five eggs.

These birds are capable of strong flight and flock to a good food source. Reischek's parakeet is relatively fearless of man but when alarmed takes to the wing, calling as it flies. It feeds most intensively during mid-morning and later afternoon. On fine days when not feeding it spends considerable time basking and preening, perched in the lee of sheltering vegetation. It bathes regularly in shallow pools. Birds are less active in wet and windy weather. At night they roost above ground in thick tussock or fern.

R.H.T.

Though the red-crowned parakeet was once widely distributed, predators such as rats and stoats have severely limited its numbers on the mainland.

Antipodes Island Parakeet *Cyanoramphus unicolor* (Lear, 1831)

THERE IS USUALLY PLENTY of evidence that Antipodes Island parakeets have been feeding nearby. The birds discard piles of crushed and twisted leaves, each still attached to an unchewed tip. With their bills they cut lengths of tussock or sedge up to 20 cm long, then, holding the leaf in one foot, they chew towards the tip. A single bird can chew more than 15 lengths in a minute. As well as leaves, Antipodes Island parakeets eat seeds, berries, flowers and dead penguins and petrels.

They feed most intensively during mid-morning and before dusk, and often remain in one place for long periods. They can fly well, but when feeding they walk and climb through the vegetation. They are relatively fearless and if approached quietly will remain feeding less than two metres from an observer. Sometimes they are attracted by human activity and climb over tents, pecking at seams and ropes. When alarmed they become furtive and silent or give only a short call before disappearing into thick vegetation. They roost at night in burrows or tunnels under thick vegetation. They do not flock.

Antipodes Island parakeets live in greatest numbers in areas of tall dense tussock or sedge, especially on steep slopes and along water courses. They nest in well-drained burrows in fibrous peat beneath vegetation or in the thick matted bases of tall tussocks. Often burrows are over one metre deep. During the breeding season the males are well-spaced and relatively sedentary whereas the females have overlapping home ranges.

The breeding season lasts from November to January. Probably they begin breeding at one year old. Captive birds lay about five elliptical white eggs. The incubation period is about 28 days in captivity and the male helps feed the nestlings. He transfers regurgitated food to the female and also frequently enters the nest. Fledglings are fed by both parents for at least one week, at the end of which they are flying strongly. At Antipodes Island, broods of from one to three newly fledged young were seen being fed by adults during the first two weeks of February 1969.

The Antipodes Island parakeet has adapted readily to captivity and bred successfully at Mt Bruce Reserve since 1969. Captured wild birds are at first susceptible to respiratory infection, and display an obvious fondness for block salt, perhaps because they eat considerable amounts of salt in the wild. Matings with red-crowned parakeets in aviaries have resulted in hybrid young; these are unknown in the wild. Two of 38 birds banded at Antipodes Island in 1969 were recaptured 10 years later close to where they were first marked.   R.H.T.

ENDEMIC

OTHER NAME: *Antipodes green parakeet.*

SIZE: *310 mm.*

DESCRIPTION
ADULT: *Sexes alike but female smaller. Yellowish green, much paler on underparts. Crown and face bright emerald green. Alula, primary coverts and outer webs of inner half of primaries violet-blue. Tail feathers dark green with yellowish green edges. Iris varies from brown-red, red-orange, bright orange, pale orange to yellow. Bill pale blue-grey at base; black at tip. Legs and feet light pinkish grey to greyish brown. Sometimes irregular yellow markings on back, rump, wings and tail.*
JUVENILE: *Like adult but with shorter tail; pinkish tinge to base of bill when newly fledged and iris brown or reddish brown.*
NESTLING: *Grey down. Iris dark. Bill pale pinkish horn. Legs and feet pinkish grey.*

MOULT
January and February, following breeding.

VOICE
Large variety of calls similar to, but lower pitched than red-crowned parakeet. When locating other parakeets pretty dick. *Contact call soft, deep querulous* twenty-eight. *Danger call varies from soft clucking to loud high-pitched chatter. Fledged young beg with high-pitched rapid* aw-dit-dit aw-dit-dit-dit.

DISTRIBUTION
Antipodes and Bollons Islands and some of the smaller islets nearby.

RECOGNITION

Only New Zealand parakeet with entirely green head. Considerably larger and with heavier bill than other New Zealand parakeets.

The Antipodes Island parakeet is most abundant in areas of tall dense tussock or sedge. It nests in deep burrows.

After a decline throughout the mainland earlier this century, the yellow-crowned parakeet can now be observed regularly in the larger forest tracts.

Yellow-crowned Parakeet *Cyanoramphus auriceps* (KUHL,1820)

THIS IS YET ANOTHER New Zealand bird that has suffered from the destruction of native forest. Once common throughout the three main islands, the yellow-crowned parakeet declined considerably in the first part of this century. It appears to be on the increase again, but is still largely absent from the area north of Auckland.

It prefers mixed podocarp forest. On offshore islands where the red-crowned parakeet also occurs it favours taller unbroken forest and scrub; the red-crowned parakeet generally lives in more open areas with low vegetation.

On the main islands, pairs or small groups usually feed in the forest canopy or on the outer branches and leaves of shrubs, and (very infrequently) on or near the ground. However on offshore islands where there are no introduced predators the yellow-crowned parakeet commonly feeds on the forest floor. It eats a wide range of invertebrates, buds, shoots, flowers and seeds, including those of beech and podocarp. Its diet is similar to that of the red-crowned parakeet, but with a higher proportion of invertebrates. Early observers recorded that the yellow-crowned parakeet often followed flocks of whiteheads in the North Island and yellowheads in the South Island.

The breeding season depends on the availability of food. It can extend over most of the year. Young birds have been seen from July until April, but most eggs are laid between October and December. The nest is often in a natural hole in a living or dead tree. In captivity the birds begin breeding at less than one year. The clutch of elliptical white eggs varies from five to nine. The female, fed by the male, incubates for about 20 days. In three nests at Stewart Island the young were fed on tender shoots and buds. Chicks leave the nest at five or six weeks and continue to be fed by both parents for a further week or so.

Yellow-crowned parakeets have been kept and bred in captivity in New Zealand and overseas. They can successfully mate with red-crowned parakeets, both in cages and in the wild.

At the Chathams, the nominate subspecies *Cyanoramphus auriceps auriceps* is replaced by the larger Chatham Island yellow-crowned parakeet *C.a. forbesi*. In this race the crimson frontal band does not reach the eye and the outer webs of the flight feathers are green-blue. Its voice is higher pitched than that of its neighbour, the Chatham Island red-crowned parakeet, and the male calls a distinctive squeaking *keek-keek-keek-keek* during boundary chases.

Few birds of this subspecies remain. On Pitt and Mangere Islands it disappeared with the forests. With the regeneration of the bush it has since returned to Mangere and in 1980 there were 20 to 30 birds. However, on Little Mangere Island the population had declined to eight pairs in 1976 and it continues to fall.

The Chatham Island yellow-crowned parakeet is usually seen singly or in pairs. It stays near its nesting areas throughout the year and, during the breeding season on Little Mangere, aggressively defends its boundaries by calling loudly and flying after intruders. It lays over a long period from October to March and recently fledged birds have been seen as late as May. Its food varies somewhat depending on what is available. On Little Mangere invertebrates are an important food but on Mangere it eats more leaves and seeds. On both islands birds feed among litter on the forest floor.   R.H.T.

ENDEMIC
Yellow-crowned Parakeet
C.a. auriceps (KUHL, 1820).
Chatham Island Yellow-crowned Parakeet
C.a. forbesi ROTHSCHILD, 1893.

OTHER NAMES: *Kakariki, Forbes' parakeet.*

SIZE: *250 mm.*

DESCRIPTION
ADULT: *Sexes alike, but female smaller. General plumage bright green, yellower underneath. Crimson frontal band above bill. Golden yellow crown to just behind eye. Red patch on side of rump. Alula, primary coverts and outer webs of inner half of primaries violet blue. Tail feathers generally dark green above and grey below. Iris orange-red. Bill pale blue-grey at base and black at tip. Legs and feet grey-brown. Occasionally green plumage partly or entirely replaced with yellow.*
JUVENILE: *Similar to adult, but with shorter tail and less distinct colours on head. Iris pale reddish brown.*
NESTLING: *Similar to red-crowned parakeet.*

MOULT
Soon after breeding season.

VOICE
Same calls as red-crowned parakeet, but higher pitched and weaker.

DISTRIBUTION
Yellow-crowned parakeet:
Larger forest tracts in the North and South Islands. Also on Three Kings, Hen and Chickens, Little and Great Barrier, Kapiti, Inner and Outer Chetwode, Titi, Big and Little Solander, Codfish, Auckland and Adams Islands; Stewart Island and surrounding smaller islands.

Chatham Island yellow-crowned parakeet: *Mangere and Little Mangere Islands.*

RECOGNITION

Yellow-crowned parakeet has crimson red frontal band, no red behind eye, and golden yellow crown. Smaller than red-crowned parakeet. In Chatham Island subspecies narrower crimson red frontal band does not reach eyes.

Fan-tailed Cuckoo

Cuculus pyrrhophanus prionurus LICHTENSTEIN, 1823

THE ONLY FAN-TAILED CUCKOO recorded in New Zealand was killed by a cat, near Christchurch, in June 1960. This species bears many similarities to the brush cuckoo *Cuculus variolosus*, but can be distinguished by its larger size, longer tail and yellow eye-ring, as well as its shorter call. Any future sightings should be examined critically.

The fan-tailed cuckoo is common in Australia, particularly in the east. A forest and woodland bird, it perches on exposed branches. When it lands it fans and tilts its tail. On the ground it hops and feeds on caterpillars and other insects. Like other cuckoos, this species is parasitic, and 50 different species have been recorded as hosts. Eggs are laid from August to December, mainly in the dome-shaped nests of small birds and occasionally in open cup-shaped nests. After the young bird has fledged, an adult may sometimes be seen near it. With an undulating flight the cuckoo moves south in spring and summer, then returns north in winter.   J.M.C.

VAGRANT

OTHER NAME: *Ash-coloured cuckoo.*

SIZE: *250 mm.*

DESCRIPTION
ADULT: *Sexes similar, but female slightly duller below. Dark blue-grey above. Wings brownish with white patch near bend of wing. Tail dark grey with prominent white notches on both webs of each feather. Face and chin grey. Rest of underparts dull rufous, with belly paler. Iris dark brown with prominent yellow eye-ring of bare skin. Bill black. Legs yellow-brown; soles of feet yellow.*
IMMATURE: *Upper parts dull olive-brown, rufous edges to feathers. Tail black with rufous notches. Underparts mottled olive-brown and grey.*

MOULT
Not known.

VOICE
Fast trill of descending notes lasting about 2 seconds, repeated 4 or 5 times, described as a 'drowsy summer sound of plaintive quality'— although also heard at night in spring.

DISTRIBUTION
Common in Australia, particularly in the east.

> **RECOGNITION**
>
> Dark blue-grey above and rufous below. Barred tail. Yellow eye-ring.

There is only one New Zealand record of the fan-tailed cuckoo, which is a woodland bird very similar to the brush cuckoo.

Pallid Cuckoo *Cuculus pallidus* (LATHAM, 1801)

The pallid cuckoo, in flight, may easily be mistaken for a hawk.

VAGRANT

OTHER NAMES: *Storm bird, brainfever bird.*

SIZE: *300 mm.*

DESCRIPTION
ADULT: *Sexes similar, except female streaked brown above. Upper surface greyish brown, with small white patch on nape. Wing coverts edged with white. Wing quills dark grey-brown with leading edge white near bend of wing and inner webs barred with white. Tail black, both webs barred with white or buff. Undersurface ash-grey with buff tinges and faint barring on flanks. Iris dark brown. Eyelid yellow. Bill brownish black above; dark olive-brown. Legs greenish grey.*
IMMATURE: *Much chestnut brown or buff streaking and mottling, the feathers edged widely with white. Barring on breast. Full plumage not reached until fourth year, though females may breed in first year.*

MOULT
Not known.

VOICE
Male calls series of rapid melancholy notes with rising inflection for up to several hours at a time. Female utters harsh kyeer.

DISTRIBUTION
Throughout Australia and Tasmania. Straggles to the Moluccas, New Guinea and rarely to New Zealand.

> **RECOGNITION**
>
> Only slim, all-grey cuckoo with pale underparts and long broad tail in southwest Pacific.

THE FLIGHT OF THE PALLID CUCKOO is swift but undulating so that, like several other cuckoos, it could easily be mistaken for a hawk. It raises its tail as it lands and often sits on fence posts. One bird approached quite close when someone answered its whistle, and it frequently accompanied the person by flying from post to post as he walked along the road. Although usually solitary it gathers in flocks before migrating. It swoops to the ground to feed on grasshoppers, beetles, earthworms and, especially, hairy caterpillars. Although a woodland bird, it is also seen or more often heard in open country.

In Australia the pallid cuckoo lays its egg from September to January in the open nest of any of at least 80 species of small perching birds. Its movements in Australia are rather complex, however it probably travels mainly south and west in summer and north and inland in winter.   J.M.C.

Oriental Cuckoo *Cuculus saturatus* BLYTH, 1843

OTHER NAMES: *Himalayan cuckoo, hawk cuckoo.*

SIZE: *330 mm.*

DESCRIPTION
ADULT: *Sexes alike. Upper surface dove grey, lighter on head. Wings dark brown, inner webs of outer primaries barred white. Tail slaty black, spotted and tipped with white. Throat and breast pale grey. Rest of underparts white, closely barred brownish black. Iris brown. Eyelid yellow. Bill brown-black above; olive-brown below. Gape orange. Legs and feet yellow. Sometimes much rufous present.*
IMMATURE: *Upper surface dark rufous, barred black, with pale tips to feathers. Tail tipped with white. Underparts browner than adult with bars up to neck. Iris paler.*

MOULT
Not known.

VOICE
Five or 6 piercing notes of even pitch described as hi-hi-hi-hi-hi *or* hoo-hoo-hoo-hoo-hoo.

DISTRIBUTION
Breeds from northeastern Europe to China and Japan. Winters in northern and northeastern Australia. Straggles to New Zealand.

RECOGNITION

Dove-grey above and lighter below, strongly barred with dark brown.

The oriental cuckoo, a shy retiring bird, is distinguished from the pallid cuckoo by its barred underparts.

ITS LONG WINGS and tail and swift, direct flight give the oriental cuckoo the alternative name of hawk cuckoo. After breeding in the northern hemisphere in the nests of fly-catchers and leaf-warblers it migrates south, reaching Australia mainly between November and April. Occasionally it wanders further afield to New Zealand where most sightings are from the west of the two main islands, from Northland to Codfish Island off Stewart Island.

In Australia it is shy, retiring and solitary. It lives in dense forest, usually near the coast and mangroves. Its food consists of insects, especially ants, beetles, caterpillars and stick insects. In New Zealand it has been seen with wings outspread flopping down to a garden to take worms and green—but not brown—cicadas.   J.M.C.

Channel-billed Cuckoo *Scythrops novaehollandiae* LATHAM, 1790

OTHER NAMES: *Storm bird, flood-bird.*

SIZE: *610 mm.*

DESCRIPTION
ADULT: *Head and neck pale grey. Rest of upper surface dark olive-grey, feathers of back and wings with broad brownish black ends; wing coverts with buff edges. Quills dark brown, edged with buff. Tail pale olive-grey, barred black and white on inner webs with black band on both webs near tips. Underparts greyish white with dark brown barring on thighs and undertail coverts, fainter on belly. Iris red. Bill yellowish horn. Bare skin of lores and eyelids scarlet. Legs and feet grey.*
IMMATURE: *Head and neck pale buff. Rest of upper feathers grey with buff tips. Face, throat and breast paler. Belly and thighs white. Iris brown. Bill red-brown. Legs dark grey.*

MOULT
Not known.

VOICE
Loud raucous cry of several syllables, the first longer, the others quickening and dropping in pitch, often uttered in flight and at night.

DISTRIBUTION
Breeds in northern and eastern Australia to south of Sydney. Recorded in Tasmania. Migrates to islands north of Australia. One New Zealand record.

Viewed from below, the channel-billed cuckoo resembles a flying cross. It is most common in northern Australia.

WITH SLOWLY FLAPPING WINGS the channel-billed cuckoo—a fairly common breeding bird in Australia—flies above the forest, calling loudly. From below it looks like a flying cross. Usually a solitary bird, it lives among tall trees, especially where there are figs. It lays in the open cup-shaped nests of large birds such as the pied currawong, the magpie and the crow. As well as figs, it eats other fruits, berries, insects and birds' eggs and young.   J.M.C.

RECOGNITION

Large grey bird, darker on wings. Long broad tail with black bar near tip. Huge toucan-like bill.

Shining Cuckoo

Chrysococcyx lucidus lucidus (GMELIN, 1788)

ENDEMIC

OTHER NAMES: *Pipiwharauroa, bronze cuckoo, whistler.*

SIZE: *160 mm.*

DESCRIPTION

ADULT MALE: *Crown, mantle, scapulars, wing and upper tail coverts metallic green with bronze sheen from certain angles. Feathers on forehead have white bases with bronze-green tips, giving flecked appearance. Quills dark brown, with all but 3 outermost of 10 primaries having white patch on base of inner web which from below shows as white bar on wing. Eighth longest primary sometimes shows traces of russet. Secondaries nearer body show increasing amounts of green on upper surface. Tail bronze-green, each feather with dark brown bar. Outermost feathers broadly barred with white on inner web and spotted with white at base of narrower outer web. White spots on tips of inner webs of second to fifth feathers. In some cases obscure russet spots on inner webs of fourth feathers. Face, underbody and underwing coverts white, each feather barred with bronze-green, wider on belly. Iris red-brown. Bill thin in profile and slightly downcurved, rather broad at base, with upper mandible slightly overlapping lower one. Bill black with base half of lower mandible brownish. Feet black with yellowish soles.*
ADULT FEMALE: *Similar to male, but lacks white bases of forehead feathers; has purplish bronze bloom on head and mantle; and russet spots on inner webs of fourth tail feathers larger and more conspicuous.*
IMMATURE: *Similar to adult male, but lacks white bases of forehead feathers; face and neck not as clearly barred; belly almost white at first; russet spots on inner web of fourth tail feathers of females—and some males—replaced by white; and base of lower mandible yellowish brown.*

MOULT
Not known.

VOICE
Plaintive but pleasing silvery song is series of rapidly repeated upward slurs of 2 notes coo-ee. Number of slurs recorded varies from 7 to 176. Usually followed by 1 or 2 downward notes tsee-oo, also often uttered on their own, especially at night in flight. Chattering or trilling phrase heard when birds chasing. Full song often heard at night. Not known if both sexes or immature birds sing.

On the North and South Islands, the shining cuckoo lays its eggs in the small pendulous nest of the grey warbler.

First notes exceedingly faint so that songster appears to be getting closer. High pitch inaudible to some people. Song heard from September or October and rarely after January. Calls of song thrush or starling sometimes mistaken for shining cuckoo.

DISTRIBUTION
Breeds on the 3 main islands and the Chatham Islands. Recorded on the Kermadec Islands, The Snares, and Macquarie Island, but not on Auckland or Campbell Islands. Winters in the Solomon Islands and the Bismarck Archipelago. Straggles to, and may breed in, eastern Australia, Norfolk and Lord Howe Islands. Related subspecies found in Australia, New Guinea, New Caledonia and Vanuatu.

RECOGNITION

Slim sparrow-sized bird. Upper surface shining metallic green with copper or bronze tones. Undersurface white, strongly barred with golden green. Bill black, thin in profile, rather broad from below and slightly downcurved. Stance rather horizontal and sings in full view. Flight swift, direct and only slightly undulating.

LIKE MANY OTHER CUCKOOS, the shining cuckoo neither builds a nest nor rears its young: on the two main islands it lays in the nests of the grey warbler and in the Chathams in the nests of the Chatham Island warbler. The warbler rears one clutch before the cuckoo arrives but is victimised with later broods. The nest is small and pendulous with a side opening, and there is no evidence as to how the cuckoo inserts an egg. Either it squeezes into the nest from the front and then forces a way out through the back or it hangs onto the porch-like opening and extrudes the egg into the nest. Observers have watched unsuccessfully for many hours to confirm this, however evidence of the bird carrying its egg to the nest, and of removing warblers' eggs, is unsatisfactory.

The shining cuckoo probably begins breeding in its second year and is adept at finding warblers at the right stage of their breeding cycle. It is not known how many eggs the cuckoo lays as it lays only one in each nest, but one female had two large eggs in its oviduct and two more in the ovary. The eggs are elliptical, dull olive green, greenish or bluish white to dark greenish brown, unlike the smaller eggs of the grey warbler, which are white with red-brown spots.

The cuckoo lays from November to January. The warbler incubates the egg for about 12 days and broods it for a similar period. The young cuckoo grows rapidly and tramples or pushes out the warbler eggs or chicks. It is then fed exclusively by its foster parents. After leaving the nest, often damaging it, the chick is fed for up to four weeks. It ranges widely, following a well-defined route, through trees and shrubs, leading its foster parents through territories other than their own. It cries incessantly for food and utters single notes at the rate of about 160 a minute all day long without a moment's break. Then at roosting time the young cuckoo suddenly ceases begging and flies away, leaving its foster parents.

The shining cuckoo breeds wherever the grey warbler or the Chatham Island warbler are found. It lives in native forest, pine forest, wooded farmland and suburban gardens, and is particularly fond of willow trees along watercourses. Although vast areas of forest were turned to pasture last century both the shining cuckoo and the grey warbler are numerous, because they have adapted to settled districts.

Migration and feeding preferences

Apart from the occasional bird that stays for the winter, shining cuckoos are in New Zealand from late September to late March. They stop singing in January, so probably adults leave first, followed by young of the year. Some individual birds appear to show consistent arrival and departure dates at the same locality from year to year. Others vary considerably. Although there are August records, birds start arriving in numbers from the Solomon Islands and the Bismarck Archipelago in the last week of September and most have reached New Zealand by the first week in October.

The route they follow is not clear. Adults have been found in eastern Australia in September and October; immatures have been found there in February and March. It seems likely that birds leaving New Zealand follow a different route from their spring migration. Perhaps on leaving their winter quarters many, if not most, birds make their way down the eastern Australian coast before flying across the Tasman Sea to New Zealand. Immature birds leaving New Zealand may travel the same route in reverse while adults make a more or less direct flight of some 3000 km over the Pacific Ocean. Whereas trade winds could be of some assistance on the northward flight in January and February, many depressions in September and October would be likely to produce an easterly wind drift.

The diet of the shining cuckoo consists almost entirely of insects and their larvae. It is particularly partial to the hairy caterpillar of the magpie moth *Deilmera annulata* which is avoided by other birds. It collects a number of larvae in its bill and munches them for a considerable time until the food is compressed from them; they then eject the skins. Sometimes they swallow the whole larvae, as pellets of the skins of these larvae have been found beneath feeding birds. Other favourite caterpillars are those which feed on the kowhai and cruciferous plants; and crane flies comprised the bulk of the insect matter found in one bird's crop. It also eats scale insects and plum and pear slugs. Adults have been seen sucking warbler's and other eggs away from nests. Young shining cuckoos have been reared in captivity on pear slugs, as well as pieces of raw meat, worms, slaters, caterpillars and cicadas.

Normally a solitary bird, the shining cuckoo flocks in small numbers between mid-November and mid-January. They chase and display excitedly, waving or flicking their wings while uttering trilling notes and apparently sometimes offering food to one another. Such 'parliaments', as they have been called, have been observed at all hours of daylight, lasting usually five to 10 minutes but also up to nearly two hours. Numbers involved may be from four to 12 and one gathering in March or April of 250 to 300 birds may have been a pre-migration gathering.

Many birds, unfortunately, are killed by cats, presumably while feeding near the ground. They frequently stun or even kill themselves by flying into windows, particularly those under verandahs. Perhaps the birds mistake them for flyways through the shrubs. Stunned birds usually quickly recover. J.M.C.

Long-tailed Cuckoo
Eudynamys taitensis (SPARRMAN, 1787)

BECAUSE OF ITS PREDATORY habits the long-tailed cuckoo is heartily disliked by other birds. It is often mobbed by them and sometimes put to flight. Most of its food consists of insects, but it frequently takes eggs and young from nests. Sometimes it kills adult birds as large as sparrows, bellbirds and thrushes. It is also fond of lizards and creeps 'like a snake' among stones while they bask in the sun.

Largely a bird of the forest, particularly the canopy, it also lives in pine plantations in the central North Island and in second-growth bush, scrub and cultivated land, including suburban gardens. Usually alone, it ranges far by day and by night. In its winter quarters it lives in lowland forests, gardens and coconut plantations, where it constantly moves from tree to tree.

It lays in the nests of other small birds and takes no part in the rearing of its young. Favourite hosts are the whitehead in the North Island and the yellowhead and brown creeper in the South Island. Several other birds are victimised too, perhaps when its favourite species are not available. There are reports of it carrying the egg into a nest with its bill, but this has never been reliably observed, and probably it lays directly into the nest. No eggs or chicks of the host survive: if the adult cuckoo does not take them, the rapidly growing cuckoo chick pushes them out or squashes them. The female lays one egg in each nest in November and December. It is white or very pale pink, slightly darker at the larger end and blotched purplish brown, more sparingly at the smaller end. Young cuckoos are seen in January and February.

The long-tailed cuckoo arrives in New Zealand from early October and leaves again chiefly in February and March, although there are numerous April, and occasional later, records. Some birds, probably immatures, remain at their wintering islands in the Pacific and the species is found throughout the year in the Kermadec Islands. The migration route is not known but birds probably cover their winter range by 'island hopping', with some non-stop flights of up to 3000 km. J.M.C.

Not normally a gregarious bird, the long-tailed cuckoo ranges alone through its forest habitat.

ENDEMIC

OTHER NAMES: *Koekoea, kohoperoa, screecher, screamer.*

SIZE: *400 mm.*

DESCRIPTION
ADULT: *Sexes alike. Crown and nape dark brown streaked with rufous. Back, scapulars and wing coverts dark brown with rufous bars; wing coverts with small white spots near tips. Wing quills and tail dark brown, strongly barred with rufous; tail feathers tipped with broad white spots which wear rapidly. Lores and eyebrow stripe light rufous or white. Underparts creamy white with dark* brown and rufous longitudinal streaks, but barred on undertail coverts. Iris dull yellow. Bill heavy and slightly downcurved, with upper mandible longer and hooked. Bill brown above; paler below. Feet greenish yellow with rather conspicuous yellow soles.
IMMATURE: *Similar to adult but lighter parts suffused with rich ochre, darker on underparts where dark brown longitudinal streaks not as prominent and appear more as spots. Back, scapulars and wing coverts spotted rather than barred, white or pale ochre. Tail shorter.*

MOULT
Not known.

VOICE
Harsh, long, drawn-out screech with rising inflection, often repeated every few seconds. Frequently uttered in flight, sometimes as bird flies in wide circles and probably heard more often at night than in day. Other rapid short notes.

DISTRIBUTION
Breeds in the North, South and Stewart Islands; on offshore islands; and on the Chatham, Auckland and Kermadec Islands. Winters from the Solomon, Caroline and Marshall Islands in the west and north to the Îles Marquises in the east, though chiefly north of New Zealand from Fiji to Îles Tuamotu. Recorded on New Caledonia, Lord Howe and Norfolk Islands but not Australia.

Australian Barn Owl *Tyto alba delicatula* (GOULD,1837)

THE AUSTRALIAN BARN OWL HUNTS by flying close to the ground or by listening for prey from a low perch. Suddenly the owl drops or dives onto its victim, grasping it with its claws and swiftly crushing the head in its bill. It snatches small birds from their roosting places or flushes them out by beating its wings on bushes. Once captured, the victim is either devoured immediately or carried a short distance to a more sheltered position before being swallowed whole.

Indigestible parts of prey, such as bones, hair and feathers, are regurgitated as pellets. Of 275 such pellets collected in southern Victoria, all but six contained only the remains of small mammals, in particular the introduced house mouse. It also eats small birds and night-flying insects, especially beetles, moths and scarabaeid beetles.

It hunts mainly in the evening and at night, but occasionally in daylight on winter afternoons or when feeding young. Its flight is almost noiseless and typically is a series of slow flaps with alternating glides and occasional short spells of clumsy hovering.

The Australian barn owl is usually found singly or in pairs. Generally it roosts by day in tree hollows or, if these are not available, in outbuildings, caves, rock crevices, thick foliage and even down wells. When disturbed while roosting it flies only a short distance, usually pursued by other birds, before perching in trees. But if the owl is unable to escape it changes from its usual bolt upright, slender-looking stance to a crouched position, with wings spread and feathers erect. It sways from side to side, moves its head in a circular motion, snaps its bill and hisses.

In Australia it is found in virtually all habitats, including grasslands with stands of timber, islets and islands, suburbs, cities and around farms where there are plenty of trees. R.G.P.

VAGRANT

OTHER NAMES: *Barn owl, delicate owl, lesser masked owl, screech owl, white owl.*

SIZE: *340 mm.*

DESCRIPTION
ADULT: *Sexes similar. Upper parts ash grey, with numerous fine, dark lines. Pale grey spot with dark spot immediately below it near each feather tip. Wing coverts have irregular patches of buff and white. Tail pale buff with 4 brown bands and fine flecks. Heart-shaped facial patch white, edged with pale brown above and dark brown below. Undersurface white with scattered brown flecks at tips of some feathers. Legs slender with feathers on lower legs usually reduced to sparse bristles. Iris dark brown. Bill ivory. Toes pale yellow-brown to brown; claws dark brown.*
IMMATURE: *Similar to adult.*

MOULT
Not known.

VOICE
Calls infrequently. Main call is loud drawn-out rasping screech. Courtship call of male at nest is shrill repetitive twittering. When disturbed at roost or nest, makes hissing and rasping noises and snaps bill.

DISTRIBUTION
Throughout mainland Australia and Tasmania in all habitats, particularly in open wooded country; also found in the Solomon Islands. Related subspecies found in Eurasia, Africa, Madagascar, North and South America, New Guinea, Indonesia and southwestern Pacific islands. Four specimens found in New Zealand, 3 in Westland and 1 in Auckland.

RECOGNITION
Large owl with prominent white, heart-shaped facial disc. Ash-grey above and white below. Sometimes hunts in daylight.

Three barn owl nestlings peer out from their nest in a tree hole. In Australia barn owls are found in most habitats.

The plaintive call of the morepork is a distinctive night sound in the New Zealand bush.

Morepork
Ninox novaeseelandiae novaeseelandiae
(GMELIN, 1788)

ENDEMIC

OTHER NAMES: *Ruru, New Zealand owl, boobook owl.*

SIZE: 290 mm.

DESCRIPTION
ADULT: *Sexes alike, but female generally slightly bigger. Plumage varies greatly. Head, back, scapulars and wing coverts brownish grey to dusky brown. Sometimes white to cinnamon brown flecks or radiating stripes on head, neck—forming collar—and back. Flecks on wing coverts and scapulars often large. Primaries dark brownish grey with obscure pale bars and 4 or 5 white to fawn flecks on outer web. Secondaries and tail feathers like primaries but without flecks. Facial disc greyish white with prominent white or cinnamon brows. Underside dark chocolate brown to deep rufous with white, buff or umber flecks, sometimes numerous and forming stripes. Large white flecks on underwing give distinct black-and-white striped pattern when wings open. Underwing coverts pale yellow brown to dark rufous. Undertail coverts from dull white with dark brown spots to rufous brown with white spots. Tarsus feathered, rufous to pale yellow brown. Toes yellow or yellow-brown; claws dark. Iris bright yellow. Bill varies from dark brown with white or yellow ridge on upper mandible to mainly yellow with dark cutting edges.*
NESTLING: *First down grey to white. Second down long, dark brown above with a few buff spots; and mottled buff and brown below.*

MOULT
Not known.

VOICE
More-pork, boo-book, quor-coo *or* ru-ru, *sometimes repeated in quick succession. Variations such as more-pork-pork quite common. Shrill, vibrating* cree-cree, *mainly heard in breeding season. Subdued grunting or cooing associated with courtship and mating. Calls throughout night, but mostly during first hours after dusk. Occasionally calls during day, particularly on dull days and in breeding season.*

DISTRIBUTION
Widely distributed throughout forests of 3 main islands from sea level up to bush line. Also small woods and wind belts of rural areas; parks and gardens of suburban areas; and exotic pine forests. Most larger, bush-covered offshore islands, including the Three Kings, Cavalli and Mercury Islands; Hen and Chickens; Mokohinau, Cuvier, Mayor, Kapiti, Stephens, and Great and Little Barrier Islands; and Codfish and other islands off Stewart Island. Related subspecies in Australia; New Guinea; Timor; Norfolk and Lord Howe Islands.

RECOGNITION

Characteristic *more-pork* call. Distinguished from little owl by bigger size and darker and browner plumage. Noiseless flight. Only owl living in New Zealand forests.

THE MOREPORK HAS ADAPTED well to the deforestation of New Zealand. Originally a bird of the native forest, especially of lowland podocarp and hardwood, now it also lives in man-made habitats, such as parks and pine plantations. However, in some open parts of the South Island it has been displaced by the introduced little owl. Because of this and the lack of large forests, the morepork is not common east of the Southern Alps and is absent from large parts of Canterbury and Otago.

Where moreporks still breed they live in pairs occupying territories throughout the year. Two pairs in a study area near Wellington had adjacent territories of at least 3.5 and 5.3 ha respectively. While generally sedentary, some birds move around, especially in winter, even to islands where they are not normally seen.

Some birds use the same roost over a long period; others choose a new one frequently. Though day roosts usually have overhead cover, the roost can be in any of a number of trees, with or without side cover and at any height above ground. The bird does not leave the roost during the day unless it is unduly disturbed, but it may fly off in the early hours of dusk long before actual nightfall.

The breeding season starts with an increase in calling activity, usually in the second half of August, and first mating has been recorded on 1 September. When one partner disappears it is usually replaced by another bird. Nest-sites are most commonly in tree-hollows, but also in thick clusters of epiphytes, cabbage trees, piles of pine needles in tree-forks, caves or even burrows in riverbanks. In the Mackenzie country moreporks have bred on the ground in the shelter of loose boulders. One morepork used a nest box. The nest itself is merely a depression formed in the material found at the site. The normal clutch is two, dull white, almost spherical eggs. Laying begins in early October and reaches a peak in November. The second egg usually follows two days after the first. Incubation starts with the first egg and lasts 30 or 31 days. Only the female seems to incubate; it is fed by the male on the nest. The chicks fledge after about 34 days. Until the young are feathered, the female stays in the nest throughout the day and leaves at night only for short hunting excursions.

Insects are the morepork's most important food. It hunts a variety of species, depending on what is available, but eats wetas throughout the year. It frequently hunts flying insects attracted to lights, catching them with its talons or its beak. Spiders, lizards, birds, rats and mice are also eaten. Any small or medium-sized bird is taken as prey and a short-tailed bat was found in a morepork nest on an island off Stewart Island. When eating large prey such as mice and rats, it holds the animal in one foot or stands on it with both feet and tears off pieces. Chicks are mainly fed on birds and, to a lesser degree, insects. While they are still small, the prey is offered by the parents in small pieces but, later, whole birds may be deposited in the nest. CH.I.

A little owl brings food to its chicks gathered at the nest entrance. Insects such as moths, earwigs, beetles and spiders form the bulk of its diet.

Little Owl *Athene noctua* (SCOPOLI, 1769)

THE LITTLE OWL WAS INTRODUCED into New Zealand between 1906 and 1910; the first shipment was delivered to Otago from Germany. It was hoped that the bird would control small passerines in orchards, but studies since then have shown that other birds do not form the largest part of its diet. It is primarily insectivorous and eats mainly earwigs, beetles, spiders, moths, snails and worms. Larger prey includes frogs, lizards and mice.

Little owls are ground feeders and do not usually take their food on the wing. Larger prey is dismembered on feeding tables or larders, the entire body consumed over several days. The indigestible parts are regurgitated as pellets. Much hunting takes place along roadsides, and the birds are frequently seen perched on fence posts, hedges, buildings, telegraph posts and trees in farm country. Little owls live in open agricultural or pastoral country and prefer areas near towns or with barns, outbuildings and clumps of trees. Occasionally they spread out into wasteland, rocky places and scrubby foothills. They do not invade forest but will hunt along the edges.

Some nesting sites are used year after year but little owls normally make use of holes in trees and old buildings; banks and cliffs; rabbit holes and hay stacks. The average clutch size is three eggs which are laid in October at intervals of two days. Incubation lasts 28 days and is solely by the female, who is reluctant to leave until the chicks are one week old. About a month after hatching the chicks come to the hole entrance, then a week later—while still downy—they fly short distances, sheltering in nearby cavities. Both parents continue to feed them for some weeks.

The little owl is not purely nocturnal and when approached performs a characteristic, comical bobbing display, often rotating its head. Because the large eyes are unable to move much in their sockets, this display is necessary for judging distances.   P.M.M.

INTRODUCED

OTHER NAMES: *German owl, brown owl.*

SIZE: *230 mm.*

DESCRIPTION
ADULT: *Sexes alike, but female slightly larger. Head brown, with triangular spots of white. Upper parts dark brown, mottled with oval white spots. Primaries brown, barred with paler brown. Upper tail coverts brown, barred with buff. Tail brown, with 4 bands and tip pale buff. Underparts white with heavy dark brown streaks. Side of face, chin and throat white with dark brown band across throat and darker circles set around eyes, coming together at beak. Iris, bill and feet yellow.*
IMMATURE: *Similar to adult, but facial disc brown apart from small amount of white at outer edges of eyes. Plumage fluffy and markings not quite as distinct.*
NESTLING: *Covered with white down.*

MOULT
Not known.

VOICE
Clear, high-pitched kiew, *heard most frequently during autumn and winter. Also strong* kiewick. *During breeding season slower, more mewing note, a modification of* kiew *call. When disturbed, both chicks and adults hiss and clatter their beaks. Wheezy snore from chicks when adult approaches nest.*

DISTRIBUTION
From England, western Europe and North Africa to northern Asia and the Pacific. Introduced to New Zealand. Common and widespread in the South Island east of main divide in area of lower rainfall. Abundant from mid-Canterbury to Foveaux Strait, and extending range into north Canterbury, Nelson, Marlborough, Westland, and southern Fiordland. Self-introduced to Stewart Island. Unconfirmed reports from Wellington Province.

RECOGNITION

Small squat owl with low forehead and flat-topped head. Distinguished from morepork by white face, brown band across throat and white undersurface with brown stripes. Flight is silent, low, rapid and undulating, giving it the appearance of bouncing along.

Spine-tailed Swift *Hirundapus caudacutus caudacutis* (LATHAM, 1801)

EACH YEAR SMALL FLOCKS of spine-tailed swifts and, on one occasion, a flock of about 60 birds, visit New Zealand. They have been seen from the North Island to The Snares and, occasionally, on Campbell and Macquarie Islands. They do not stay long. Most sightings have been near the coast, where they wheel about cliffs or circle islands or isolated hills.

Several exhausted stragglers have been picked up as beach-wrecks.

They feed in the air and in fine weather fly very high. Precise details of their insect diet in New Zealand are wanting. Flocks, apparently feeding, have been seen sweeping over forested slopes as well as round cliffs and bluffs. Heavy weather forces them to fly low. R.B.S.

To cling to vertical surfaces, the spine-tailed swift grips with its claws and is propped by its needle-tipped tail.

STRAGGLER

OTHER NAME: *White-throated needle-tailed swift.*

SIZE: *200 mm.*

DESCRIPTION
ADULT: *Sexes alike, but male marginally larger. Forehead white. Top and sides of head metallic green tinged with brown. Black space in front of eye. Back, scapulars and rump brown. Wings and tail metallic green with purple reflections. Chin, throat, undertail coverts and rear flank white. Breast and belly brownish black. Tail short and square with 10 stiff, virtually invisible, projecting spines. Iris dark brown. Bill black. Legs and feet purple-pink.*
IMMATURE: *First-winter birds resemble adults, except that undertail coverts usually tipped with black.*

MOULT
Not known.

VOICE
Faint high-pitched twittering.

DISTRIBUTION
Breeds in eastern Asia north to Mongolia, Manchuria, Kamchatka and northern Japan. Winters in eastern Australia and Tasmania. Straggles to New Zealand.

RECOGNITION

Long powerful sweptback wings, short square tail and white patch on lower belly and flanks.

Fork-tailed Swift *Apus pacificus pacificus* (LATHAM, 1801)

BETWEEN SEPTEMBER and April fork-tailed swifts reach Australia and New Guinea. Some birds may drift to New Zealand, particularly during stormy and humid weather caused by northern low pressure systems. They are seen usually on the west or south coasts. Fork-tailed swifts eat insects taken on the wing at varying heights, according to the prevailing weather conditions. R.B.S.

VAGRANT

OTHER NAME: *White-rumped swift.*

SIZE: *180 mm.*

DESCRIPTION
ADULT: *Sexes alike. Upper parts blackish brown with greenish gloss, except for white band across rump. Chin and throat white. Rest of*

underparts brown with scalloped appearance caused by feathers having grey edges and black bars. Tail deeply forked. Iris brown. Bill and legs black. Feet pink.

MOULT
Not known.

VOICE
Shrill excited twittering.

DISTRIBUTION
Breeds across eastern Asia to central

China, Korea and Japan and north almost to the Arctic Circle. Migrates to New Guinea and Australia. In New Zealand usually seen on the west coast and in Southland.

RECOGNITION

Long slender wings; deeply forked tail; and in low flight, white rump.

New Zealand Kingfisher   *Halcyon sancta vagans* (LESSON, 1830)

THE NEW ZEALAND KINGFISHER perches in a prominent place and waits until prey appears on the ground or in the foliage. Typical perches are bare branches, posts, fences, power and telephone lines, especially those overlooking pasture, and cultivated land and water. On open mud flats, it perches on any elevated object such as driftwood, a stake, a rock, or even a stone only a few centimetres above the ground. Sometimes, it merely sits at the high-tide line. A common sight wherever telephone lines cross tidal mud flats is a string of kingfishers patiently sitting along a length of wire.

When it sees food, the bird suddenly darts with a direct descending flight, snatches its victim (usually without landing), and immediately turns and flies straight back to its perch, carrying the prey crosswise in its bill. Larger animals are battered against the perch, several times if a crab or insect, many times if a bony animal such as a lizard, small bird, or mouse. Food is swallowed whole and indigestible parts regurgitated later as pellets. It takes tadpoles by dipping at the water's surface, or dives to take small fish and freshwater crayfish.

The food of the New Zealand kingfisher includes smaller vertebrates and a wide range of large invertebrates, according to season and locality. On tidal estuaries, small crabs are its main diet. In open country, it eats many earthworms, lizards and cicadas. Inland, freshwater crayfish and tadpoles are also important. In all habitats it catches insects such as wetas, stick insects, dragonflies, wasps, beetles and spiders. Larger prey includes mice and small birds, especially silvereyes. Sometimes it takes small fish. There are several records of kingfishers robbing other bird species of earthworms.

The New Zealand kingfisher lives in a very wide range of habitats. In the north, it breeds in open country on the coast or close to it, wherever it can find nesting sites in banks or rotting trees adjacent to water. Its greatest densities are at tidal estuaries and mangrove swamps. It also breeds extensively inland along river and stream edges; in open country with scattered trees; by lake shores; along forest margins; and well into forests, both native and exotic, where it feeds mainly in the canopy. It is least common in beech forest parts of the ranges. In winter, it is a bird of open habitat, mainly farmland with or without woody vegetation, tidal mud flats and mangrove swamps.

The breeding season extends from September to March, and nesting and laying generally occur from September to January. Young are in the nest mainly in January and February. A second brood is sometimes raised.

The nest is a tunnel. In the north it is most often excavated in a clay bank beside a beach or tidal inlet, in a river or stream bank, or in a roadside or farm track cutting. On farmland and beside rivers and lakes, nests are in decaying willows, cabbage trees, kahikateas, willow, pine, and macrocarpa stumps, and in the soil held by the roots of blown-over trees. On coasts, nests are in knot-holes in trees such as pohutukawa, kohekohe and puriri.

To start the tunnel, the bird sits on a branch slightly above and several metres from the chosen site and then flies straight at it, neck outstretched, and strikes it with its bill-tip. This performance is repeated until the hole is deep enough to perch in and the rest is pecked out. Several holes may be started and abandoned before one is completed. The same site may be used in successive years. The tunnel is 10 to 23 cm long, and slopes slightly upward to a chamber about 20 cm in diameter. There is no nest lining.

The broad, white eggs, usually five in a clutch, are apparently laid on successive days. They are incubated for about 19 days, apparently mostly by the female. The young probably hatch together and fledge at 26 days old. Both adults feed the young at 10 to 30 minute intervals, the size of food gradually increasing. After two weeks, the chicks come to the tunnel entrance to take food. Two or three chicks usually survive and stay with the adults for at least several weeks.   B.D.H.

ENDEMIC

OTHER NAMES: *Kotare, sacred kingfisher.*

SIZE: *240 mm.*

DESCRIPTION
ADULT MALE: *Crown deep green, grading at sides to ultramarine. Forehead deep green, often flecked with buff. Lores deep reddish buff, becoming pale above eye. Broad black band from gape through and below eye to encircle nape. Broad pale to deep buff collar across hind neck. Mantle and scapulars deep green; upper border of mantle black. Back, rump, upper tail coverts, upper wing coverts ultramarine. Tail brown, washed blue. Primaries brown, with outer webs bright cobalt blue. Secondaries brown, with outer webs ultramarine. Chin and throat pale buff to white. Rest of underparts, including underwing coverts, pale to deep buff. Feathers of flanks and breast often have brown tips, forming indistinct breast-band. Iris brown. Legs dark brown. Bill long, broad, rounded on top, black; whitish on underside and sides of lower mandible; sometimes wholly black. In the Kermadec Islands upper parts brighter green and blue, less washed with brown and olive; underparts paler; and brown feather tips usually absent.*
ADULT FEMALE: *Similar to male except ultramarine and cobalt areas less bright and green areas more olive.*
IMMATURE: *Like juvenile but brown markings of collar and underparts*
less pronounced; upper parts increasingly green; and buff edges of wing coverts become narrow or absent with wear.*
JUVENILE: *Crown, mantle and scapulars dark brown. Blue areas duller than in adult. Breast heavily marked with broad brown feather tips. Wing coverts scalloped by broad buff feather edges and tips. Bill and tail short in early weeks.*
NESTLING: *Naked when hatched. By 2 weeks covered with spiky feather-sheaths which show colour of juvenile.*

MOULT
Adult has complete post-nuptial moult. Post-juvenile body moult produces immature (first-winter) plumage, which does not change until complete moult after first summer. Limited New Zealand records show adult wing moult from late January to March, tail moult and sometimes wing moult extending to as late as May.

VOICE
Repeated penetrating kek-kek-kek-kek *heard at any time of year but mostly from September to January, just before and during breeding season. Generally silent in winter and while feeding. Pairs on territory utter various calls: repeated* krree-krree-krree *with rising inflection;* krrr-krrr-krrr *and quieter* ksss-ksss-ksss, *both uttered often during displays and chases between pairs; loud screech in the presence of danger; harsh scream as bird swoops to attack mammal intruder; and*
peculiar whirring as bird flies at hole it is starting to form for a nest. Chicks in nest utter strident rasping sound while adults absent.*

DISTRIBUTION
Breeds throughout the North, South and Stewart Islands. Also off-lying islands, especially in the north; and the Kermadec Islands. Greatest densities in the northern North Island and Great Barrier Island. In southern North Island, more abundant inland than on coast. In the South Island, thinly but widely distributed: in Nelson and Marlborough well inland to the Nelson lakes and high-altitude ranges; in the west south to Fiordland; rare inland in Otago and Southland. In winter, bulk of population, especially that of forests and high country, moves to low-altitude farmland and coasts. In Southland, from April to September, widely scattered singly on inland farmland, where absent in summer.

> ### RECOGNITION
> Small dumpy bird with large bill and short legs. Rather drab when perched, but colourful in flight, especially from behind in sunlight. Often prominent on power or telephone wires, sitting motionless except for rhythmical raising and lowering of tail. Repeated *kek* call in summer months.

The New Zealand kingfisher eats a variety of animals. Recorded at one nest were lizards, freshwater crayfish, mice, grey warblers, riflemen and a silvereye.

Kookaburra *Dacelo novaeguineae* (HERMANN, 1783)

INTRODUCED

OTHER NAMES: *Laughing kookaburra, laughing jackass, great brown kingfisher.*

SIZE: *450 mm.*

DESCRIPTION
ADULT MALE: *Head and underparts off-white, feathers of crown and face long and erectile. Centre of crown strongly streaked with brown. Forehead mottled with brown. Broad off-white band from over each eye joins on nape. Below this, dark-brown band passes from lores through eye to hind neck. Below this again, broad off-white collar from side of neck usually joins on hind neck. Upper surface and wings dark brown; greater wing coverts broadly tipped with pale blue; and base of primaries white, forming white flash on each wing in flight. Rump varies from chestnut, with black bars, sometimes tinged with blue, to bright sky blue. Upper tail coverts and tail chestnut with black cross-bars. Tail feathers, except 2 central ones, broadly tipped with white. Underparts often freckled with brown feather margins. Iris grey-brown. Bill shorter than head, wide, deep: upper mandible black; lower mandible dull cream or horn. Legs grey.*
ADULT FEMALE: *Like male but rump always chestnut with black bars, rarely with faint blue tinge; and off-white band above eye usually heavily mottled with brown.*
JUVENILE: *For 2 months after fledging, like adult female, but forehead and band above eye even more heavily mottled and breast mottled brown; rump always brown; tail and bill short; bill black. After 2 months indistinguishable from adult female.*
NESTLING: *Hatches naked. Eyes not fully open until 14 to 17 days. After a week, pin feathers start to appear. Fully feathered at 30 to 39 days.*

MOULT
In Victoria, post-nuptial complete moult of adult lasts about 3 months between December and April. First moult of young bird occurs in January to April of second year, at age 12 to 14 months, and is complete. Moult sequence: tail, body, head and wings, flight feathers.

VOICE
Loud boisterous koo-hoo-hoo-hoo-hoo-hoo-ha-ha-ha-ha-ha-ha uttered in undisciplined chorus by family or breeding group, groups in neighbouring territories singing in turn. Heard mostly at dawn and dusk, all year round but least when moulting from January to March and most in territory-adjustment period in July and August. Functions to declare territory and cement family bond. Social calls within family group include chuckle contact call; abrupt repeated chuck in breeding period; hoarse low-pitched squawk as submissive food-begging call, uttered by all birds in breeding period; aggressive cackle that precedes attack; and kooaa, warning of danger.

DISTRIBUTION
Eastern and southern Australia; Tasmania and southwestern Western Australia (introduced); on Kawau Island and on adjacent north Auckland mainland between Cape Rodney and the Whangaparaoa Peninsula. Stragglers, possibly from Australia, reach other parts of New Zealand.

KOOKABURRAS WERE INTRODUCED in small numbers in the 1860s and 1870s. Released in Nelson, Otago and Wellington, they did not establish. Today, however, a small stable population persists from birds liberated on Kawau Island in the early 1860s.

They are long-lived birds—in Australia, one bird banded as an adult was caught over 12 years later; and probably the birds can live much longer. As a result of this longevity the birth rate is low. Each year about one third of adults do not breed.

Breeding pairs stay together and occupy the same territory all year, year after year. Most young remain with their parents and help with

The kookaburra is twice the size of the New Zealand kingfisher.

territory defence, incubation, and care of young, sometimes for four years or more. In family groups, which vary in size from three to six birds, the position of a bird is acquired as a result of bill-grappling tussles. Each sex has a separate hierarchy, with older birds dominant and the breeding pair dominating all. Apparently the subordinate position of the non-breeders suppresses their breeding drive until one of the breeding pair or a neighbouring bird dies.

The breeding season is long: egg-laying to fledgling independence takes 15 to 19 weeks. In Australia the nest is usually in a hole in a tree trunk or branch or excavated in a termite nest in a tree. Occasionally it is in a creek bank or cliff or in a hole in a building. The bird perches about eight metres away before entering and after leaving the nest. Often the nest-site is close to the territorial boundary. In Australia egg-laying starts between September and November, with a peak in late September. The two to four white eggs are each laid at least a day apart. Incubation begins with the first egg and lasts about 23 days. All members of a family incubate, but one of the breeding pair is the main incubator and the others take short spells only. For about a quarter of the time the eggs are unattended.

The chicks remain in the nest for about 33 to 39 days. They are fed for eight to 13 weeks after fledging, depending on when adult moult starts. Consequently the young of groups are often fed longer than the young of pairs. Sometimes, pairs in family groups rear a second brood, while the non-breeders of the groups care for the first brood. Of a sample of 51 eggs, 66 per cent hatched but only 50 per cent produced fledglings. Those cared for longer by non-breeders survived better. After the first year, the survival rate is high.

Foods and displays

The New Zealand habitat and foods of the kookaburra have not been clearly described. In Australia it lives in woodlands and open forest. It is rare in open farmland, but occurs in rural towns. It eats anything—usually smaller than itself—that moves, especially on the ground. This diet consists mainly of worms, snails, a wide range of insects, freshwater crayfish, frogs, lizards and snakes; and sometimes its food includes small birds, rats and mice. The kookaburra feeds within its territory. Sitting rigid on a prominent branch or post, with its bill pointing down, it suddenly swoops. It kills large prey by bashing it on the perch, and softens bony prey by running it through its bill. Indigestible matter is regurgitated in pellets.

It calls with its bill pointing upwards, and raises and lowers its tail. As well as singing, territorial display involves single birds from each group flying between a special perch and a display hole or scar while the rest of the group sings. Displaying birds remain in sight of each other. This display may develop into two birds chasing high over the trees in a wide circle, the pursuer becoming the pursued whenever the boundary is crossed. Invading birds may be physically attacked and beaten about the head and breast with the bill.

When afraid, the kookaburra remains still, with its bill open and its head feathers raised. When an eagle is overhead, it holds its body rigidly upright with its head and bill pointing straight up. Courtship display is limited to courtship feeding, which may begin a month before egg-laying, and nest-showing, in which the pair visit holes together while the male cleans them out.   B.D.H.

A large dumpy bird, the broad-billed roller is usually seen alone or in small groups. Immature or juvenile birds occasionally reach New Zealand's west coast.

Broad-billed Roller *Eurystomus orientalis pacificus* (LATHAM, 1801)

THE COURTSHIP DISPLAY of the broad-billed roller is a spectacular rolling and tumbling flight. Outside the mating period its flight is strong and buoyant with slow wing-beats as it swoops and turns in pursuit of prey. Dropping from a perch to take an insect the bird will circle back with an upward swoop. Large flying insects, such as beetles, locusts, grasshoppers, cicadas, shield bugs, moths, wasps and swarming termites are the roller's main source of food. It also takes insects, and occasionally lizards, from the ground. Rollers flock to grass and other fires to feast on the insects flushed out by the flames.

Generally the bird hunts at dawn and dusk, when it flies to and fro at treetop level, calling loudly. During the day it habitually perches on the same exposed perch and takes to flight only if easy prey presents itself. In hot weather a bird may descend to the ground, spread its wings, lift its head and tail, and open its bill. It will maintain this posture for several minutes, perhaps to cool itself.

Immature or juvenile birds, either alone or in small groups, occasionally reach New Zealand's west coast. All sightings have been between December and May, when birds that breed in Australia are migrating northwards. Migrating broad-billed rollers reach considerable heights: one struck an aircraft at 2600 m and two corpses were found on a New Guinea glacier at 4500 m. J.S.

VAGRANT

OTHER NAME: *Dollar bird.*

SIZE: *290 mm.*

DESCRIPTION
ADULT: *Sexes similar, although female slightly duller than male. Crown to upper back, including side of head and neck, dark brown; feathers of upper back narrowly edged with blue. Lower back to upper tail coverts and base of tail dull greenish blue, tail feathers shading to deep ultramarine. Undertail blue at base, outer half blackish. Scapulars and innermost secondaries brown edged with blue. Secondary coverts turquoise. Alula,* primary coverts and outer webs of remaining flight feathers deep ultramarine, inner webs blackish. Pale, silvery blue, circular patch extends from first to eighth primary. Underwing coverts pale blue. Flight feathers blackish below, bluer at base. Circular blue patch also on underwing. Lores and feathers around eye black. Eye-ring red. Feathers of throat and neck purplish blue with light blue shafts. Breast bluish green. Rest of underparts pale blue. Iris dark brown. Bill red, with upper mandible black and slightly hooked at tip. Gape yellow. Legs red.*
IMMATURE: *Duller than adult and generally dull grey-brown. Eye-ring pink. Throat washed with green. Wing and tail feathers blacker. Blue areas of adult, particularly underparts, greener. Bill varies from dark brown, usually with some yellow along edge of lower mandible, to yellow or orange. Gape yellow. Legs yellowish or pinkish brown.*
JUVENILE: *Similar to immature. Bill black initially, becoming yellow, at least along edge of lower mandible. Gape lime green. Legs dull brown.*

MOULT
Little known.

VOICE
Loud, raucous, repeated kak *uttered both in flight and when perched,* more so in late evening and in dull weather. Also described as chattering, a grating chuckle, a rough repeated* treek, *and harsh croaking. During nesting also gives single, drawn-out, scolding alarm notes.*

DISTRIBUTION
Eastern India and Nepal to Manchuria; islands of the southwest Pacific from the Andamans to Australia, and from Japan to the Solomon Islands. Northern and eastern Australia. Most Australian birds winter in New Guinea, the Moluccas, Sulawesi, and the Bismarck Archipelago. A few birds winter in northern Australia. Straggles to Tasmania and New Zealand.

RECOGNITION

Heavily built, short legged, short-necked bird, with large head, flattened on crown. Usually seen sitting upright on an exposed perch. At rest appears mainly brown, with red bill and legs and blue throat. In flight blue in wings and tail, and silvery patch on wing become visible. Heavy, swooping flight on broad wings. Harsh voice.

Rifleman *Acanthisitta chloris* (Sparrman, 1787)

THE RIFLEMAN IS AN INSECTIVORE. It eats a wide variety of species, with a large proportion of moths and caterpillars, as well as crane flies, small wetas, spiders and harvestmen. It collects food from the trunks and branches of larger trees. With its slim beak it extracts spiders and wetas from crevices and folds of bark, and picks moths off the surface. The bird kills them by hitting them against the trunk or branch. It flies with quick flicks of its wings as it works its way up a tree. The short tail provides no support, but its feet and large thigh muscles enable it to cling upside down under branches. It also takes insects from the foliage of the canopy, although on windy days it feeds lower down the shrub layer.

Riflemen are seldom still and never remain in one position for more than a couple of seconds. Their wings continually flicker as they 'about turn' on slender twigs or spiral up a tree trunk, probing into bark crevices and under leaves. They seldom seem to fly any distance; their flight is usually short and direct, from the canopy of one tree into the next or to the base of an adjacent trunk.

Primarily a bird of mature native forest, in many areas the rifleman is the most common bird from the valley floor to the tree line. Although most common in beech forest, it also lives in podocarp-broadleaf forest, some second growth native forest such as kanuka, and even some older pine plantations. It thrives best in exotic forest if a native shrub layer is also present.

Riflemen breed in their first year. They rear two broods each season and lay again if any clutches are destroyed. Fledglings banded in January have been found building nests in August of the same year, and laying their first eggs in September.

The nest is in a hole, usually in a tree trunk. Such holes vary in size and shape, but the birds appear to prefer those at least 12 cm deep and 10 cm wide. Often the nest is well above the ground, although nests have been found in fence posts and among rocks on the ground. The height of nesting sites is influenced by the age and type of forest. The older the trees the greater the number of cavities.

Around Dunedin nest building begins in early August. As many as five nests may be started before one is chosen. The nest is completely enclosed. An entrance tunnel about five centimetres long and no wider than three centimetres, leads to the top of the egg chamber. Nesting material is collected from the forest floor and is mostly litter such as twigs, leaf skeletons, pine needles and shreds of bark. The fine rhizomes of ferns are often used in kanuka forest. A mat of litter is placed on the bottom of the cavity and the nest is loosely woven above this. An interval of several weeks may lapse before the chamber is lined with feathers gleaned from the forest floor.

Breeding behaviour

The first eggs are laid during September. The average clutch is four, the ovoid, white eggs laid about 48 hours apart. Laying usually occurs soon after dawn. Incubation, which begins once the last egg is laid, is shared by both sexes which sit on the eggs for about 20 minutes at a time. The eggs hatch at 20 or 21 days. The nestlings are entirely dependent on their parents for food. The first feathers emerge about the tenth day and the chicks fledge at about four weeks old. Both adults feed the nestlings on insects. The female appears to take over the greater share of feeding as the young approach fledging. However, once the chicks have fledged the male takes over.

Riflemen often begin building the second nest before the first brood has left its nest. They do not use the same nest twice although they will use an artificial nest box again if there is no alternative or if the box is cleared out and moved.

Fledglings remain in the adult territory for about three weeks, sometimes longer. Occasionally first brood chicks help their parents feed the chicks of the second brood. In Fiordland, polygamy is common but it has not been reported from other localities. Riflemen observed near Dunedin generally paired for life. They stayed together throughout the year and occupied the same territory.

Little has been recorded of displays. Wing quivering, trilling, and bill snapping have been seen at confrontations between neighbouring pairs. This display is also performed by adults when their nestlings are disturbed. Squawks from the nestlings incite the adults to attack both nestlings and observer. At such times the adults even alight briefly on the head and arms of the observer.

Banding shows that 14 per cent of chicks leaving the nest survive for at least one year. Two banded males survived for six years. The greatest distance travelled by any of the banded birds was less than one kilometre. Banding also showed that if one of the pair died the survivor either moved and established a territory with another mate nearby, or remained in the same territory until another bird of the opposite sex arrived. R.S.G. & P.D.G.

A forest bird, the South Island rifleman feeds upon a variety of insects. Much of its food is collected from the trunks and branches of trees.

ENDEMIC
South Island Rifleman
A.c. chloris (SPARRMAN, 1787).
North Island Rifleman
A.c. granti MATHEWS & IREDALE, 1913.

OTHER NAME: *Titipounamu.*

SIZE: *80 mm.*

DESCRIPTION
South Island rifleman
ADULT MALE: *Forehead and crown greyish brown merging on nape and hind neck to bright green. Back bright grass green. Rump yellow-green. Tail black, with off-white tip. Eyebrow stripe white. Ear coverts brownish grey. Chin, breast and belly white, merging into cream and lemon yellow on flanks. Primary and secondary quills dark brown, with outer vanes tinged green, changing to yellow towards base of each feather and forming conspicuous yellow stripe just below black upper wing coverts. Innermost secondary has white patch on outer vane. Underwing coverts white. Bill black or dark brown at tip, lightening to ochre about base. Tarsus and toes dark brown; soles yellow.*
ADULT FEMALE: *Forehead and crown dark grey-brown flecked and streaked with ochre-brown. Streaks may extend down hind neck and onto back before merging into more uniform olive-brown of back. Rump yellow. Tail black, tipped with off-white. Eyebrow stripe white. Ear coverts grey-brown. Chin, breast and belly white. Flanks cream-yellow. Wing primaries and secondaries dark brown. Leading vanes fringed with green-brown which broadens and changes to ochre and finally yellow at base of vane, forming yellow stripe across wing below dark brown-black upper wing coverts. Underwing coverts white. Bill and feet similar to adult male.*
JUVENILE: *Fledglings resemble parents of same sex except streaked pattern of head and neck more pronounced on juvenile female and also present on juvenile male.*

North Island rifleman
ADULT MALE: *Yellowish green above. Pale buff below. Rump and flanks yellowish green. Quills green on outer web; brown on inner edge. Wing coverts black. Yellow bar below coverts, with white spot behind this. Faint dark eye-stripe and pale eyebrow streak. Iris black. Bill dark, slender, slightly upturned. Tail very*

short, black, tipped with dingy brown. Legs and toes long and slender, dark brown with black claws.
ADULT FEMALE: *Top of head, hind neck, upper back and lesser wing coverts olive-yellow streaked with dark brown. Lower back and rump as male but lacking dark streaks. Otherwise similar to male although slightly larger.*
JUVENILE: *Similar to adult female with upper surface from crown to lower back streaked with dark brown. Male young tend to have more green on back while juvenile females retain a dusky colour. Upper breast darker than in adult and spotted with brown.*

MOULT
Not known.

VOICE
South Island race calls tsit, tsit, *frequently repeated. When confrontation between pairs or when chicks disturbed at nest, adult gives more drawn out* tsitrrrrr *trill. North Island race calls high-pitched* sipt, sipt *or excited* tutut-tutut *as nest approached.*

DISTRIBUTION
Most common New Zealand wren.
South Island rifleman: *Widespread throughout forests of the South, Stewart and Codfish Islands.*
North Island rifleman: *Larger tracts of native bush in the North Island but not north of the Coromandel Peninsula. Abundant in the Rimutaka and Tararua Ranges; and from Mount Egmont east to centre of island, the Ureweras and the Raukumara Range. Recorded from Rotorua north through the Kaimai Range. Present in isolated patches of bush in the Wairarapa; common on Little Barrier Island; and occasionally reported from Great Barrier Island.*

Bush Wren *Xenicus longipes* (GMELIN,1789)

THIS TINY, INCONSPICUOUS BIRD may be extinct; there have been no authenticated records for over 10 years. Since European settlement it has never been common outside the mountain forests of the South Island and islands off southwest Stewart Island. Because it breeds and forages close to the ground, its numbers have been depleted by introduced predators, such as cats, mustelids, and rats. A few birds may survive in the densely forested areas of the Ureweras, in mountain regions of the South Island, or on Stewart Island.

On the main islands bush wrens were found mostly in dense mountain forest, usually beech forest at high altitude but as far as the subalpine scrub zone. It also lived in lower damp beech and podocarp forests, especially in Fiordland. On smaller islands, Stead's bush wren was found in coastal forest or scrub.

Stead's bush wren has been observed feeding moths, flies and daddy-long-legs spiders to its chicks. It feeds on the branches and leaves of trees, in low vegetation, and among litter on the forest floor. On Solomon Island, robins forced it to feed on or near the ground. It moves swiftly and furtively while searching for food among plants on the ground or around the base of trees. In the South Island the bush wren is chiefly arboreal. It runs quickly along branches and makes short purposeful flights between branches, unlike the rifleman, which spends much time feeding on tree trunks.

During the breeding season on Solomon Island, Stead's bush wren was territorial. At other times of the year single birds, pairs, or small family parties have been recorded. Once, at least a dozen birds were seen feeding along the branches of withy willows.

Most information about the breeding habits of bush wrens comes from Stead's bush wren. Eggs have been found in November and December. The nest is often low to the ground, among the roots of standing or upturned trees, in a low hole or the fork of a tree, in a notch in a fallen log, among a clump of fern, or in a hole such as an old petrel burrow. The nest is more or less spherical, with a small side entrance near the top; it is built of moss, fern rootlets and leaves and lined with feathers. The clutch is two, occasionally three, white eggs. Neither incubation nor the fledgling period is known, but both parents incubate and feed the young. Nests studied on Solomon Island quickly became damp, so the parents frequently replaced damp feathers with fresh dry ones.

H.A.R. & A.B. (2)

ENDEMIC
South Island Bush Wren
X.l. longipes (GMELIN, 1789).
North Island Bush Wren
X.l. stokesii GRAY, 1862.
Stead's Bush Wren
X.l. variabilis STEAD, 1936.

OTHER NAMES: *Matuhituhi, green wren, Tom Thumb bird.*

SIZE: *90 mm.*

DESCRIPTION
ADULT: *3 subspecies recognised on basis of colour.*
South Island bush wren: *Top of head, hind neck, and side of face dark purplish-brown. Rest of upper surface dark green, tinged with yellow, with tail darker olive green. Near bend of wing lemon yellow patch bordered behind by deep brown patch. Outer webs of quills olive green; inner webs brown. Prominent eyebrow streak white or very pale buff. Chin and throat greyish white. Breast, belly and vent ash grey. Underwing coverts pale yellow. Sides and undertail coverts yellowish green. Bill and iris brownish black.*

Legs slaty black, sometimes pale. Feet pale brown.

North Island bush wren: *Similar to South Island subspecies, but side of neck and chest shining slate blue, tinged with green in certain lights; and patch of pure yellow on yellowish green flanks.*

Stead's bush wren: *Plumage varies from green to brown, but usually head and neck brown with scaly appearance, sometimes extending down back. Rest of upper surface brownish green, greener on rump. Usually prominent eyebrow streak from bill to nape grey-white, but sometimes absent. Darker spot in front of eye. Ear coverts brown, slightly lighter than crown. Breast, belly and vent slate grey with faint brown tinge. Side of body green, slightly lighter than back. Underwing coverts green with yellow tinge.*
IMMATURE: *Duller than adult. Top of head, hind neck, and side of face dark purplish brown. Upper back purplish olive; lower back olive brown. Tail olive green. Wing coverts, except primary coverts, and outer webs of quills olive brown. Primary coverts deep brown with lemon yellow patch near bend of wing. Prominent eyebrow streak white. Undersurface purplish grey. Underwing coverts lemon yellow. Flanks and undertail coverts yellowish olive. Bill black. Legs and toes pale yellow.*

MOULT
Not known.

VOICE
Weak, but lively, subdued trill. Stead's bush wren calls faint rasping sound. Loud cheep or seep when alarmed or excited. Flight call a rapid succession of merging cheeps, like whirring call of rock wren.

DISTRIBUTION
South Island bush wren: *Once common, but by 1950s rare, with most records from Fiordland, although a few from further north and in South Canterbury. Last authenticated records from Arthur's Pass in January 1966 and Moss Pass, Nelson Lakes National Park, in January 1968.*

North Island bush wren: *Once widespread, but now rare. Recorded from Waikaremoana-Urewera area; Mount Egmont; upper Waitotara Valley; and Makuri Gorge. Not reported since 1955.*

Stead's bush wren: *Possibly on Stewart and Kaimohu Islands. Not reported since 1972.*

> **RECOGNITION**
> Typical wren, with very short tail, rounded wings, and long legs and toes. Appreciably larger than rifleman, with prominent white eyebrow streak, brown head and hind neck, and distinctive grey breast and belly. Distinguished from rock wren by heavier build, grey breast and belly, absence of buff spots on secondaries, and shorter hind claw.

Like other bush wrens, the Stead's bush wren may be extinct; there have been no authenticated sightings since the 1970s.

Rock Wren *Xenicus gilviventris* PELZELN, 1867

A male rock wren, in the species' characteristic habitat of rocks and boulders.

ENDEMIC

OTHER NAMES: *None.*

SIZE: *90 mm.*

DESCRIPTION
ADULT: *Female generally duller than male, with less distinct markings. Olive brown above with darker green rump. Dark brown patch on outer wing edge. Grey-brown below with yellowish flanks. Cream stripe above eye. Bill and eye blackish brown. Feet pale brown.*
IMMATURE: *Forehead purplish brown. White streak above eye. Rest of upper surface brown tinged with yellowish green. Rump and tail more green. Dark brown spot on wing, with buff spots on secondaries. Flanks and lower body dull yellow.*

MOULT
Little known, but one Fiordland bird in last stages of moult in mid-April.

VOICE
Three notes, the first accentuated. Similar to call of rifleman but repeated less often. Also single shrill zipt.

DISTRIBUTION
Fairly common along central mountain chain of the South Island from Nelson to Fiordland. Usually occurs above bush line from 900 to 2500 m, but in Fiordland found at lower altitudes in subalpine scrub.

RECOGNITION

Distinguished from other New Zealand wrens by large feet and long claw on hind toe. Dwarfed only by rifleman. Characteristic bobbing and bowing movement on ground.

EUROPEAN EXPLORERS DISCOVERED the rock wren in the Southern Alps in the 1860s. The Maoris have no name for the bird and even now it has little contact with people. Consequently, it is usually unafraid of human observers and during the breeding season readily accepts feathers for nest building. Its remote habitat has not been threatened by man, and the species' future seems secure. Introduced predators such as stoats and rats may yet be a problem however.

Fallen and jumbled rock, often covered with scrub, form an ideal habitat. Crevices among the boulders provide both nesting sites and shelter during bad weather. The bird also feeds and shelters in subalpine scrub. During the harsh alpine winter it remains under the blanket of snow, feeding in the air spaces between boulders and scrub.

The rock wren spends most of its time hopping and flitting through boulders in search of food. Large feet and a long claw on its hind toe help it cling to rocks. Its flight is weak, and usually only five or six metres are covered in one stretch, although the wren can fly further than this. It has a most unusual habit of bobbing up and down on the spot. It also bows forwards at the hips, keeping its legs straight. The significance of this movement is not clear but it may be a display against intruders or a form of displacement activity when the bird becomes tense. It also flicks its wings.

The nest of roots, snow grass, twigs and leaves is usually built in a sheltered rock crevice. It is bulky and rounded with an entrance hole on the side. Feathers are much sought after both for constructing and lining the nest. A clutch of from two to five white ovoid eggs is laid between September and October. Incubation and fledging periods are unknown, but both parents incubate and feed the young. The adults return with food once or twice an hour. Worn nest feathers are regularly replaced with soft, downy ones and inedible food scraps are cleared away. The parents carry away and eat faecal sacs.

Some ornithologists believe a separate subspecies, *Xenicus gilviventris rineyi*, exists in Fiordland south of the Hollyford river. Fiordland males have brighter green upper parts and yellower sides than other rock wrens, but females everywhere look the same.   P.W.S.

The plumage of the female rock wren is usually duller than that of the male, with less distinct markings. It lays from two to five eggs in spring.

The sustained warbling song of the skylark is often delivered when the bird is hovering high in the air and nearly out of sight.

Skylark *Alauda arvensis arvensis* LINNAEUS, 1758

EARLY EUROPEAN SETTLERS yearned for the skylark's delightful, warbling flight song. Consequently in the second half of the nineteenth century, skylarks were imported and liberated on the three main islands and the Chathams. Now they live in open country, such as farmland, sand dunes, and tussock grasslands. They also inhabit subalpine herbfields, but avoid forests and thick scrub. Occasionally, they are kept in aviaries.

Skylarks usually lay from the last week of September to the third week of January. The nest, apparently built by the female alone, is invariably on the ground. It is little more than a depression—often a hoof mark—neatly lined with dry grass to form a cup up to about 10 cm in diameter. It is often well concealed by standing grass. The number of eggs varies from two to five. Laid a day apart, they are greyish white, sometimes with a greenish tinge and thickly blotched all over with brown. In Britain only the female incubates; this lasts 11 days. Both parents, however, share in feeding the chicks which leave the nest after nine or 10 days. They fledge after a further 10 days. Two or three broods may be reared in a season.

The skylark is territorial in the breeding season but gathers in loose flocks in autumn, especially at higher altitudes. On the ground, it moves by walking, usually with its legs flexed and its belly low, and crouches when uneasy. It enjoys dust baths, for example at the edge of unsealed roads. It roosts on the ground, often with little cover. Sexual display involves the male circling the female with his wings drooped and his crest raised. For her part the female quivers her wings.

The skylark eats a wide variety of seeds and invertebrates, as well as grit. A 1934 newspaper report complained of skylarks uprooting 'about 5000 young tobacco plants'. In recent years skylarks have been seen eating tomato seedlings and newly planted cabbages, but complaints by farmers of damage to crops have become less frequent. In Britain, skylarks sometimes damage sugar beet seedlings and similar damage has been noted in experimental crops of sugar beet and fodder beet in New Zealand.

In Europe skylarks are migratory. Only 30 skylarks had been banded in New Zealand up to March 1974 and these have yielded no significant recoveries. A skylark banded in Czechoslovakia lived at least eight years and nine months.

Sometimes hedgehogs eat skylark eggs, but other, possibly more important, causes of mortality in New Zealand are poisoned grain, stoats, falcons, unseasonable snow and, perhaps, disease.　P.C.B.

INTRODUCED

OTHER NAMES: *None.*

SIZE: *180 mm.*

DESCRIPTION
ADULT: *Sexes alike. Upper surface buff-brown heavily streaked with black-brown, especially on crown (where some feathers form slight crest), back and mantle. Wing quills dark brown. Outer primaries narrowly edged with pale brown or greyish white. Inner primaries and secondaries have conspicuous greyish white tips and rufous borders to outer vanes. All wing coverts dark brown fringed and tipped with buff. Tail feathers dark brown with narrow pale edges, but 2 outer pairs partly white. Side of head buff, flecked with dark brown. Throat pale buff, sparsely flecked with dark brown. Upper breast dark buff, strongly streaked with black-brown. Lower breast, belly and undertail coverts pale yellowish or greyish white. Flanks pale brown with a few elongated darker streaks. Axillaries and underwing coverts greyish buff. Iris brown. Upper mandible dark brownish horn; lower mandible paler. Legs and feet yellowish brown. During winter, upper parts gradually darken as pale tips and feather edges are reduced by abrasion; at same time underparts become whiter. Black, albino, creamy white and yellowish white birds reported.*
JUVENILE: *First winter and summer, like adult. Upper parts dark brown, each feather tipped with pale buff with dark brown subterminal line or mark. Underparts as adult, but throat with scarcely any spots; and streaks on upper breast paler and more drop-shaped. Wing and tail feathers brown, narrowly fringed with buff. Outer tail feathers like adult.*
NESTLING: *Down very pale straw, long and plentiful.*

MOULT
In Southland, adult skylarks moult in late January. Juveniles replace all wing and tail feathers before first winter.

VOICE
Liquid chirrup often given in flight. Vigorous warbling song lasting several minutes, usually while bird hovers, but occasionally from post or ground. Heard in all months, though mostly from August to January; rarely in February and March.

DISTRIBUTION
From the British Isles and northern Europe east to the Urals and south to central France, Switzerland, Austria and, in Russia, to about Kharkov. Successfully introduced to Vancouver Island in Canada, southeastern Australia and New Zealand. Now very common in open country from North Cape to Stewart Island. Breeds at the Chatham Islands and occasionally reaches The Snares and the Kermadec and Auckland Islands. Other races occur in eastern Asia, Afghanistan, Iran, southeastern and southern Europe and North Africa.

Tree martins often feed on the wing above large trees, or dive swallow-fashion to take insects from water surfaces, pasture, scrub and ploughed fields.

Australian Tree Martin *Hylochelidon nigricans nigricans* (VIEILLOT, 1817)

THE AUSTRALIAN TREE MARTIN, although a frequent straggler to New Zealand, has not established itself here. From time to time flocks of up to 35 birds arrive from Australia, and they have been sighted throughout the year—most frequently in autumn and early winter, when birds from southern Australia migrate north. The only record—though unsubstantiated—of tree martins nesting and hatching young was in 1893, in a mill near Oamaru.

A bird of open country, in New Zealand the martin feeds in the canopies of trees such as gums and ratas; over pools, lakes, rivers and estuaries; and over pasture, ploughed fields, stubble, and low scrub. The bird's diet consists mainly of insects. Flies, wasps, beetles, bugs and spiders are taken on the wing or from the water's surface.

In Australia, martins usually nest in small holes in large, often dead, trees. Occasionally nests are made in the nooks and crevices of cliffs, or buildings and other man-made structures. If the entrance to a nest chamber is overly large it may be partially blocked with mud, or the birds may build a cup resembling that of the welcome swallow. Dead leaves, feathers and grass are the common materials used to line the nest, where four eggs are laid between July and January.

During the breeding season the tree martin tends to form loose nesting colonies, with several nests in one tree or within a small area. Outside the breeding season they form large flocks and mix freely with welcome swallows and fairy martins *Hylochelidon ariel*. In New Zealand, vagrants often associate with welcome swallows, although one bird was observed being frequently chased by this companion.   H.A.R.

STRAGGLER

OTHER NAMES: *Tree martin, tree swallow.*

SIZE: *140 mm.*

DESCRIPTION
ADULT: *Sexes alike. Pale brick-red frontal band across forehead extends back towards top of eye. Upper forehead, crown, nape, side of neck, back and wing coverts steel blue-black. Rump dull white, tinged with sandy buff, with darker shaft streaks to most feathers. Upper tail coverts dusky brown with paler margins. Quills and tail dark brown. Tail only slightly forked. Feathers in front and below eye sooty black. Ear coverts smoky brown. Cheeks, chin and throat dull white with buff tinge, with dark shaft streaks to feathers. Breast and belly dull white with pale rufous tinge, especially on flanks. Undertail coverts tinged with chestnut brown. Iris dark brown. Bill black, short and flattened, wide at base. Legs and feet blackish brown.*
IMMATURE: *Similar to adult.*

MOULT
Not known.

VOICE
Call note uttered in flight or from perch is clear tsweet. *Usually quiet twittering chatter.*

DISTRIBUTION
Australia, Tasmania, New Guinea, Timor, the Moluccas, and the Aru Islands. In autumn migrates northwards from southern areas and returns in early spring. Straggles to the North and South Islands; The Snares; and the Kermadec Islands.

RECOGNITION

Typical swallow in its feeding habits: hawking insects around trees or over rivers and lakes. Distinguished from welcome swallow by white rump contrasting with steel blue upper parts, shallow forked tail, and less red on face, especially under bill.

Welcome Swallow *Hirundo tahitica neoxena* GOULD,1852

SINCE THE MID-1950s the population of welcome swallows in New Zealand has exploded and spread southwards from the far north. The species is still expanding, especially in the central North Island and the South Island. Unlike their Australian relatives, the New Zealand birds have no obvious migratory habits, although autumn and winter flocks are frequently seen in areas such as Southland, where little or no regular breeding occurs. This is more likely to be in response to food supplies than a migratory movement.

The birds are commonly found near rivers, lakes, estuaries, drains and farm ponds, especially in flat to rolling farmland. Flocks occasionally forage over dry areas such as sand dunes and crop fields.

Welcome swallows eat only insects, gathering food as they fly with a characteristic fast, flitting movement. Droppings from nest-sites have included remains of midges, blowflies, small beetles and moths.

Pairs begin prospecting for suitable nest-sites in early August. Before they begin building the nest the mating birds perform high-level chasing flights or slow, almost hovering, flights with much tail fanning. The pair often sit close together on a perch uttering a crooning twitter and, occasionally, rub bills. The male feeds the female, either perched at her side or by hovering just in front of her.

Both sexes build the nest, a mud cup strengthened with straw and lined with compacted straw, rootlets, small leaves, hair and wool. Loosely arranged feathers form the nest's final lining. The mud cup is generally attached to a rough vertical surface, although it may be placed on a horizontal or sloping ledge. One nest has been found suspended from a hook of wire protruding under a bridge. The size and shape of the nest varies considerably, depending on the situation. In New Zealand most nests are found under small bridges and culverts. Others are on buildings, boats, jetties, water tanks and other artificial sites. Occasionally they are built in natural sites such as caves or rock outcrops. There is often more than one occupied nest at a site.

The three to five blunt oval eggs are white, with a pale pink tinge and variably flecked with brown or reddish brown. They are laid a day apart, usually about one hour after sunrise.

Incubation lasts 15 to 18 days. It is not known if the male helps, but both parents remain near the nest for most of the time. They both feed the chicks, more frequently in the morning and evening. After 17 to 23 days, the young swallows fledge. The new fledglings return to the nest to roost for several days and are dependent on their parents for about three weeks, even though re-nesting may have begun. Egg-laying continues until February, and two or three broods are raised each year. One set of observations has shown that only 54 per cent of eggs hatched, but that 89 per cent of the young chicks fledged. Most losses were due to falling nests, flooding and human interference. Other predators such as rats and mynas are likely to interfere with more accessible nests.

From late December, young and old swallows may form flocks of up to 500 birds. These birds move away from breeding sites to areas of plentiful food. Flocking continues through autumn and winter, breaking up for breeding in early spring.   H.A.R.

NATIVE

OTHER NAME: *Swallow.*

SIZE: *150 mm.*

DESCRIPTION
ADULT: *Sexes alike. upper parts metallic blue-black. Black tapering* stripe from eye to base of bill separates bright rust brown of forehead and forecrown from slightly paler throat, foreneck and upper breast. Primary coverts and quills blackish brown, quills edged with buff. Some inner secondaries have whitish tips. Tail deeply forked, blackish brown, slightly glossy on upper surface. Small white wedges towards tips on inner webs of all but central and outermost tail feathers, visible when tail spread. Some inner secondaries may have whitish tips. Underparts pale greyish white with brown tinge on side of body and underwing coverts. Iris dark brown. Bill black, short and flattened, wide at base. Legs black, small, with long toes and claws.
IMMATURE: *Duller than adult with shorter, forked tail without elongated outer feathers.*
NESTLING: *Naked when hatched. Eyes open after 3 or 4 days. Covered with down by 1 week. Feathers appear by 10 days.*

MOULT
Little information available. Moulting adults recorded from early March to mid-July.

VOICE
Short tswit *in flight and occasionally from perch, often repeated rapidly as twittering chatter. This maintains contact, especially when parties congregate around good food supply. Alarm note sharper and louder* twsee *or* sweert *or occasionally* tit-swe, *with accent on second syllable. Song is soft, irregular mixture of squeaky twitters and trills, often called while perching.*

DISTRIBUTION
The 3 main islands; Great Barrier Island; the Auckland, Chatham and Kermadec Islands. From southern Australia, including Tasmania, north to Cape York and Western Australia. Uncommon in central Australia.

RECOGNITION
Small, slender, streamlined bird with rounded head, long pointed wings and deeply forked tail. Swift and irregular flight, often skimming low over the surface. Distinguished from the Australian tree martin by dark rump and deeply forked tail.

Welcome swallows may raise up to three broods each year in the strong mud and straw nest built by both parents.

The New Zealand pipit builds its nest on the ground, usually concealed in dense grass or low scrub. Two or three broods may be reared in the same nest.

Pipit *Anthus novaeseelandiae* (GMELIN,1789)

ENDEMIC
New Zealand Pipit
A.n. novaeseelandiae (GMELIN,1789).
Auckland Islands Pipit
A.n. aucklandicus GRAY,1862.
Antipodes Pipit
A.n. steindachneri REISCHEK,1889.

OTHER NAMES: *Pihoihoi, groundlark, native lark.*

SIZE: *190 mm.*

DESCRIPTION
ADULT: *Sexes alike. Upper surface brown, feathers centred with dark brown. Quills and tail feathers dark brown, edged with yellowish brown; 2 outer tail feathers on each side white, with brown inner edges. Greater coverts and inner secondaries broadly margined with brownish yellow-white. Eyebrow streak narrow, white. Dark line through eye. Throat and foreneck white. Side of face, side of neck, and breast brownish yellow-white, mottled with dark brown. Iris dark brown. Bill dark brown; base of lower mandible horn colour. Feet yellowish brown. Colour varieties range from creamy white to partial albinos, pure albinos and one specimen that combined elements of both albinism and melanism.*
IMMATURE: *Similar to adult, but crescent-shaped warm buff feathers on upper surface and distinct dark streaks on upper breast.*

MOULT
Not known.

VOICE
High-pitched scree *or rasping drawn-out* zuee, *also described as* tirr-eep, cheeet *or* peeet. *In spring, male repeatedly calls* pi-pit *from prominent perch and sometimes gives trilling song* tsew-tser weet-tsir. *Male may also call briefer* tzu-weet, *from perch or when descending in short display flight.*

DISTRIBUTION
Many subspecies recognised from Turkestan to Siberia to China, Indo-Malaya and Australia; central and eastern Africa. Throughout New Zealand mainland; on most coastal islands; the Auckland, Antipodes, Chatham and Campbell Islands. Straggles to the Kermadec Islands and The Snares.

RECOGNITION

Walks with dipping motion or runs. Rarely hops. When walking or standing flicks up tail spasmodically. More slender than skylark, with longer and finer bill, comparatively longer tail, shorter and more curved hind claw and no head crest. Swift undulating flight; does not soar.

PIPITS INHABIT ALL KINDS of open country from sea level to rocky mountain tops, including fernland, low scrub, tussocklands, cut-over forests, riverbeds, sand dunes, coastal rocks, rougher farmland and roadsides. They generally avoid improved pasture, however. It is one New Zealand bird which initially benefited from European settlement. The clearing of the forests considerably expanded its range, but this has since been offset by the refinement of pasture, land and road development, introduced predators and accidental poisoning.

Pipits flock around logging and sawmilling operations to catch insects and grubs as they fall from the logs. They also enter milking shed yards to pick ticks from cattle and the floor. Pipits usually feed on the ground, but will sometimes take insects, their major source of food, on the wing. The birds mostly eat beetles, wasps, ants, flies, cicadas and insect larvae. Grass grubs, earthworms, small snails and seeds, especially those of clover, grasses and thistle are also eaten.

During the breeding season the small flocks of pipits disperse as the birds form mating pairs. Displays are limited, but in spring the male may call repeatedly from a prominent perch and perform a short U-shaped flight in which it calls a short trilling song as it descends in short glides with its wings and tail lifted.

The breeding season extends from September to the end of February, with a peak from October to January. Some birds build nests as early as mid-August. They nest on the ground up to 1600 m above sea level. The nest is usually well concealed and sheltered by grass, low scrub or other plants which frequently overhang and almost totally enclose it. The nest is usually a deep cup of woven grass or similar material, with a substantial inner lining of finer grass, moss or lichen. Pipits rear two or three broods each year, sometimes using the same nest twice.

The three, four or five eggs are ovoid to elliptical and pale cream, heavily blotched with brown or purplish brown and grey. The female incubates for about 14 days during which time she may be fed by the male. On hatching the chicks are blind and naked. Both parents care for them, feeding them every five to 10 minutes. The young fledge at about 15 days old.

At the Auckland Islands a different subspecies of pipit is found. The Auckland Islands pipit *Anthus novaeseelandiae aucklandicus* has a stouter bill, more yellowish brown colouring and an obscure eyebrow streak. It is very tame and widespread from the seashore to the upper tussocklands. On the shore it feeds around intertidal rocks and seaweed lying along the high tide mark.

The Antipodes pipit *A.n. steindachneri* is a duller yellow than its Auckland Islands relative. It is plentiful at the Antipodes Islands and widespread from the shore to the upper tussocklands and is found along rocky streambeds, on fresh land-slips, rocky outcrops and at old albatross nests. On the shore it associates with parakeets in penguin colonies, where there is an abundance of insects feeding on the waste and carcasses. The Antipodes pipit prefers to feed in open areas, and its diet consists of small moths, other insects, and crustaceans, as well as small berries.

Some authorities believe two other subspecies exist: the Chatham Islands pipit *A.n. chathamensis*, which is abundant throughout the Chathams group, and *A.n. reischek* which has been found at Taupo, in the Waikato and on the Kermadec Islands.   A.S.G.

Black-faced Cuckoo-shrike Coracina novaehollandiae (GMELIN, 1789)

OTHER NAMES: *Large cuckoo-shrike, blue jay, shufflewing, summer bird.*

SIZE: *330 mm.*

DESCRIPTION
ADULT: *Sexes alike. Upper parts from crown to tail coverts pale grey, with lighter edges to back feathers. Forehead, throat and side of head to above eye and ear coverts black with greenish gloss, shading to grey on upper breast. Breast, flanks and thighs grey. Belly and undertail coverts white. Central tail feathers brownish grey, blacker towards tips with narrow white tips. Rest of tail feathers black, washed with grey towards base and broadly tipped with white. Outermost tail feathers edged with white. Undertail greyish brown, broadly tipped with white. Wing feathers pale grey with lighter edges. Alula black. Primary coverts and primaries black, edged with pale grey. Secondaries with black inner webs. Underwing coverts, axillaries and inner webs of primaries white. Rest of underwing brownish grey. Iris dark brown. Bill and legs black.*
IMMATURE: *Like adult except only black on body is stripe from lores to*
ear coverts; forehead, cheeks, chin, and throat grey with darker markings, often appearing as bars; grey of breast, flanks and thighs has lighter barring; tail dark brown, tipped and edged with white; and black of alula and primary wing coverts replaced by dark brown. Bill black, with base of lower mandible brown.
JUVENILE: *Similar to immature, but with whiter underparts. One female had horn-coloured bill, flesh-coloured legs and light blue eye.*

MOULT
Moults once a year. Spends at least one year in immature plumage. Juvenile collected at beginning of November had almost completed moult.

VOICE
Short, soft purring uttered mainly in flight, repeated several times, variously described as churring, jarring, croaking, and rolling. Also chereer-chereer *at rest; harsh, aggressive scolding in defence of territory; and piping or flute-like notes.*

DISTRIBUTION
India and South China to the Bismarck and Louisiade
Archipelagos in the east and to Tasmania in the south. Australian birds winter mainly in north and central Australia, and from New Guinea to the Bismarck Archipelago. At least 15 records from New Zealand, from Invercargill in the south to North Kaipara Heads in the north. Most sightings coastal; the majority from the west. Mainly immatures arriving between January and June, with
April probably commonest month, coinciding with main autumn migration in Australia.

RECOGNITION
Pale grey bird, often appearing bluish, with a longish tail, long pointed wings and black mask.

THE FLIGHT OF THE BLACK-FACED cuckoo-shrike is strong, direct and undulating. It alternately flaps and glides. When searching for food on the ground it hovers, especially if there are no suitable perches. When it lands it shuffles its wings and flicks them alternately several times before finally folding them. An exaggerated version of this, accompanied by loud calls, is part of the mating display.

Most of the bird's food is taken from the foliage of tall trees. It also catches flying insects on the wing, by swooping down from an exposed perch. Less often, it hunts from the ground. The cuckoo-shrike's diet consists mainly of caterpillars and other soft bodied insects and their larvae. It also eats fruit and other plant material, sometimes to the detriment of orchards and vineyards.

In Australia the black-faced cuckoo-shrike occurs in a greater variety of habitat than any other Australian bird, from semi-desert to open forest. It prefers the taller species of trees, usually eucalypts, in savannah and lightly wooded country. In Southeast Asia it occurs at altitudes of up to 2000 m in open forest and forest edge.   J.S.

The black-faced cuckoo-shrike attends a tree-fork nest in its native habitat in Australia. Nestlings will outgrow the small nest before they fledge.

White-winged Triller *Lalage sueurii tricolor* (SWAINSON, 1825)

GARDENS IN THE DUNEDIN suburb Macandrew Bay played host to the only white-winged triller known to have visited New Zealand. The male bird was first sighted on the Otago Peninsula in February 1969, at around the same time a number of other vagrant species arrived from Australia. It was in its breeding plumage of glossy greenish black feathers over the nape and back. In Australia the triller is common throughout the country, mainly in open grasslands scattered with bushes or trees. It also inhabits some pine forest, riverine forest and saltbush areas.

The male is active, noisy and strongly territorial in the breeding season, even though several pairs may nest in close proximity. The rich trilling of the New Zealand visitor was heard in the early morning from February to April. The bird sang and fed in the same places at the same times each day, and sunbathed on branches, with its head, back and rump feathers erect and its tail turned towards the sun, as if to expose the skin to sunlight. In contrast to the male, the female is quiet and inconspicuous. It is particularly difficult to discern on the ground, where the birds spend much of their time feeding around low vegetation, fallen wood and rocks.

The triller's diet consists mainly of medium to large insects and their larvae. A bird often knocks its prey on a twig or the ground before swallowing. Flying insects, especially swarming termites, are sometimes taken on the wing, although the triller seems unable to hover. Some seeds and fruits are also consumed.　　　　J.S.

VAGRANT

OTHER NAMES: *White-shouldered caterpillar-eater, peewee-lark.*

SIZE: *200 mm.*

DESCRIPTION
ADULT MALE: *In breeding plumage head to below eye, nape and upper back glossy greenish black, feathers grey at base. Lower back, rump and tail coverts grey. Tail feathers black with white tips and narrow white edges. Wing feathers black edged with white, especially inner webs of inner secondaries. Coverts largely white, forming white 'shoulder' patch. Underparts and underwing white, with outer webs of wing quills blackish. Iris dark brown. Bill and legs black. Non-breeding plumage similar to breeding plumage, except* crown to upper back brown, occasionally with a few black feathers; breast and flanks tinged with buff and with indistinct, pale grey markings; wing coverts edged with buff; and remaining tail and wing feathers with broader white edges.

ADULT FEMALE: *Similar to male in non-breeding plumage but all black on upper parts replaced by brown, including wings and tail; and eyebrow stripe dull white above short, darker eye-stripe.*

JUVENILE: *Upper parts brown, with darker crown, paler eyebrow stripe and paler rump, feathers edged with white giving barred appearance. Underparts, including underwing, white with dark streaks grading to pure white on belly. Undertail brown. Iris black. Bill black, the lower mandible yellow. Legs pale grey.*

IMMATURE: *Similar to adult female except whiter edges to wing feathers, particularly tips of primary coverts.*

MOULT
Two moults each year: July to November into summer plumage; February and March complete moult into winter plumage.

VOICE
Rich vigorous song of chi-chi-chi, ditch-ditch-ditch or joey-joey-joey and variations, throughout breeding season. Also much repeated call of oo-ee and aggressive tret-tret by male when defending territory. Female much quieter than male.

DISTRIBUTION
New Guinea and Australia. Some birds migrate to southern Australia between August and October, and return north between December and April. One New Zealand record of an adult male in breeding plumage from the Otago peninsula between February and June 1969.

RECOGNITION
Male in summer is conspicuous pied bird, black above with grey rump and white wing shoulder, and white below. Female predominantly brown with lighter eyebrow stripe and rump, and lighter below. Winter male distinguished from these by blacker wings and tail.

The striking pied breeding plumage of the male, and its high-pitched trilling song, identified the sole white-winged triller recorded in New Zealand.

The hedgesparrow, once described as 'the one bird against which no word of complaint has ever been raised', still enjoys a favourable reputation.

Hedgesparrow *Prunella modularis occidentalis* (HARTERT, 1910)

THE LONG BREEDING SEASON of the hedgesparrow—from early September to January—allows the birds to raise two or three broods each year. The female builds a cup of twigs, moss and dry grass which it lines with hair, wool or moss and occasionally with feathers or tree-fern scales. The nest is usually well-concealed in a thick hedge, bush or tangle of creepers, often close to the ground, and takes from three to seven days to build.

There may be a delay of up to seven days between the completion of the nest and the appearance of the first egg. The clutch usually contains four deep blue eggs, laid a day apart. The last egg occasionally appears more than a day after the others. The female incubates alone for 11 or 12 days. After hatching the young remain in the nest for about 12 days, taking food from both parents.

Hedgesparrows rarely move far from cover in gardens, orchards, thickets or scrub. They are apparently territorial, or at least not gregarious, throughout the year. Sexual displays involve chasing, quivering the wings and tail, and pecking at the female's cloaca by the male.

The birds feed mainly on the ground on beetles, spiders, flies, ants, seeds and, less often, on cockroaches, earthworms and aphids. They are vulnerable to poisoned grain put out for house sparrows.   P.C.B.

INTRODUCED

OTHER NAME: *Dunnock.*

SIZE: *140 mm.*

DESCRIPTION
ADULT MALE: *Crown and hind neck dark grey finely streaked with dark brown. Mantle and scapulars more brownish with dark-tipped feathers, giving streaked appearance. Lower back and rump uniform brown. Primaries and secondaries blackish brown with rufous brown edges to outer webs. Primary coverts dull black with pale brown outer edges. Greater wing coverts blackish brown with rufous edges and pale buff tips; median coverts similar, but with*

indistinct pale tips. Tail dark brown. Ear coverts brown with pale streaks. Throat and breast dark slate grey, with narrow brown tips to breast feathers when fresh, shading into greyish white on belly. Undertail coverts brown with pale buff edges and tips. Iris brown. Bill dark brown. Feet orange brown.
ADULT FEMALE: *Like male but breast feathers have wider buffish brown tips giving breast slightly browner appearance.*
JUVENILE: *Like adult female, except feathers of nape and side of neck conspicuously fringed with pale buff; breast yellowish buff, streaked with black-brown; and greater and median wing coverts have larger buff tips.*
NESTLING: *Down black, fairly long. Inside of mouth bright orange with 2 black spots on tongue spurs; externally, flanges whitish pink.*

MOULT
Two moults each year. Adult full moult late summer to early autumn. Subsequent abrasion causes upper parts to become more striped and breast feathers to lose their brown tips. Juvenile moults at same time as adult, but retains old primaries, primary coverts and all but innermost secondaries and greater coverts.

VOICE
Call a shrill, piping tseep. *Song a high-pitched jerky warble,* weeso, sissi-weeso, sissi-weeso, sissi-weeso *lasting a few seconds and repeated several times in fairly quick succession, usually from the top of a bush or hedge. Sings from April to January.*

DISTRIBUTION
The British Isles and Europe east to Turkey, the Caucasus and northern Iran. Introduced to New Zealand several times between 1867 and 1882 and now common throughout the 3 main islands. Also breeds on the Chatham, Campbell and Antipodes Islands. Recorded on the Auckland Islands and The Snares.

RECOGNITION

Small, nondescript, brownish bird with a slender bill. Lighter and daintier than female house sparrow. Usually seen skulking beside cover, singing from an elevated perch or making short flights from one bush to another. Usually solitary or in pairs.

Fernbird   *Bowdleria punctata* (QUOY & GAIMARD, 1830)

ENDEMIC
North Island Fernbird
B.p. vealeae KEMP, 1912.
South Island Fernbird
B.p. punctata (QUOY & GAIMARD, 1830).
Codfish Island Fernbird
B.p. wilsoni STEAD, 1936.
Stewart Island Fernbird
B.p. stewartiana OLIVER, 1930.
Snares Fernbird
B.p. caudata (BULLER, 1894).

EXTINCT
Chatham Island Fernbird
B.p. rufescens (BULLER, 1869).

OTHER NAMES: *Swamp thrush, grass bird, matata.*

SIZE: *180 mm.*

DESCRIPTION
ADULT: *Sexes alike. In North Island fernbird and South Island fernbird upper surface golden brown with broad longitudinal dark brown streaks; crown feathers dark brown, edged with rufous tint; eyebrow streak white; tail feathers dark brown with golden brown edges; undersurface white with brownish black spots, except on lower belly, spots increasing in size from chin towards belly and larger on South Island race; bill and legs grey brown. Stewart Island fernbird richer, more lustrous golden brown on upper surface with more distinctive markings. Codfish fernbird much darker than other forms with upper and lower surfaces much more densely spotted with brownish black. Snares fernbird larger than mainland forms; more uniform light cinnamon brown plumage; and brownish black streaks on upper surface less pronounced. In all forms, tail feathers may be worn and in some birds even shafts have broken.*
FLEDGLING: *Snares fernbird plumage darker and duller than adult. On leaving nest young have short, squared tails. By end of second week off nest soft yellow lining at gape almost entirely lost, but still very little spotting on underparts which are white with hint of palest brown. Four weeks after nest desertion spots well-defined only along sides of lower throat and upper breast. By 5 weeks tail full length and crown feathers starting to turn slightly chestnut. After 7 to 8 weeks young bird looks like adult, except for marginally shorter bill.*

MOULT
Snares adults moult for 5 or 6 weeks in late February and early March, after breeding.

VOICE
Short, metallic sounding calls, such as utick, tcherp, zrup, tchick *and* tee-oo. *Contact calls sometimes sound as if only one bird is calling, as female responds very rapidly to her mate. Territorial call of male is monotonous repetition of one note, at times lasting well over 15 minutes. During border disputes opposing males utter very rapid series of clicks between their usual* utick *or* tcherp *cries. Sometimes female produces same calls if it encounters a strange female on its territory.*

DISTRIBUTION
North Island fernbird: *The North Island from Parengarenga to Cape Palliser. Also Great Barrier Islands; the Alderman and Three Kings Islands.*

South Island fernbird: *The South Island from Cape Farewell to Foveaux Strait. Rare or absent in most parts of Canterbury, Marlborough and Otago. Most plentiful along the west coast from Nelson to South Westland. Abundant on Open Bay Islands.*

Codfish fernbird: *Codfish Island.*

Stewart Island fernbird: *Stewart and nearby islands.*

Snares fernbird: *Abundant on North East and Broughton Islands in The Snares. Possibly also on Daption Rocks and Alert Stack as well as other vegetated stacks close offshore.*

RECOGNITION

Differs from all other New Zealand birds by golden brown and black streaked upper parts; white front spotted with black; long straggling tail; reluctance to fly; and stealthy manner of slipping easily through dense ground cover of open areas.

THE FLIGHT OF THE FERNBIRD is weak, generally consisting of short fluttering trips or laboured direct flights close to vegetation. Flights of more than 100 m are exceptional.

On The Snares and islands off Stewart Island, fernbirds live in coastal tussock meadows and in *Oleari* and *Senecio* shrub forest, the floor of which comprises mainly bare peat, burrowed densely by nesting petrels. Elsewhere, fernbirds prefer dense ground vegetation standing about a metre high and combined with emergent shrubbery. They inhabit wind-shorn manuka, rata, tussock, flax and pakihi swamp, gorse and kie-kie thickets, bracken, umbrella fern, and raupo and rushes bordering mangrove swamps and tidal inlets.

Dense rushes conceal the tightly twined nest of a North Island fernbird.

Most of the information about fernbird breeding habits comes from observations of the Snares fernbird. It breeds at one year of age and tends to pair for life. Territories are established in late September to early October, and eggs are laid from mid-October or early November until the third week of February. Most nests are set close to the ground and have been found in the base of ferns, the crown or base of tussocks, in cutty grass, *Muehlenbeckia* shrubs, rushes, and occasionally at The Snares in hollow *Olearia* trunks. The most elaborate nests have ring-shaped bases to keep the bowl above water-soaked ground and a hood built on the side facing into the prevailing wind.

At The Snares, nests are almost exclusively made of the long needle shaped leaves of *Poa astonii* tussock, woven neatly into a cup and lined with varying amounts of seabird feathers. In North Auckland nests are made of dried rush grass lined with feathers. Both adults build, completing the nest in three days if fine weather prevails. Nests are built from ground level to two metres above the ground and are about 70 mm in diameter on the inside and about 66 mm deep.

The female lays a day or two after completing the nest, usually at one day intervals, early in the day. The two to four eggs are ovoid and mauve-pink, the first in each clutch heavily flecked with mauve-brown to purple-brown especially around the broader end. Each successive egg is paler than its predecessor. The birds lay one or two clutches, the first from mid-October to the third week of January, with replacement clutches from the third week in December to the third week of February. Both parents incubate the eggs and care for the young. The eggs of Snares fernbirds hatch about 16 days after laying and within 24 hours of each other. The only incubation record for other fernbirds is 12 or 13 days for the North Island race. The naked, newly hatched young are brooded constantly. After their fourth day, the Snares young are brooded progressively less often, until by the eleventh day they are almost entirely feathered and hardly brooded at all. Parents feed the chicks mainly during early morning and late afternoon.

Snares chicks fledge at 20 or 21 days old whereas South Island fernbird young fledge at 12 or 13 days. For the first day, they hide in cover near the nest, but as they grow older, the fledglings follow their parents on foraging trips. About 20 days after leaving the nest the young eat food they have caught themselves. They are independent about 15 days later. It takes some 10 weeks to raise one brood and the birds do not attempt to breed again or moult until their young are independent. Territorial maintenance declines in late February, but pairs tend to stay together until the next breeding season.

At The Snares, fernbirds eat arthropods, spiders, orthoptera, weevils, carabids and other beetles, mites, tipulids, kelp flies, blowflies and other diptera, moths, aphids and harvestmen. They forage among fronds of kelp, around seals, in penguin colonies, along cliff faces, on boulder and shingle beaches, in tussocks, *Hebe* shrubbery, leaf litter, shearwater burrows, among trees, and on top of the *Olearia* canopy. They seek their prey by digging; lifting leaves and other loose material; ripping off loose bark; burrowing through and under leaf litter and ground foliage; lunging at flies buzzing by; and investigating all other sites likely to harbour arthropods.   H.A.B.

Except during the early part of its breeding cycle, the brown creeper is a social bird. It can be seen in flocks of up to 50 birds, often with other species.

Brown Creeper *Finschia novaeseelandiae* (GMELIN,1789)

OFTEN CLINGING UPSIDE DOWN to small branches which bend under its weight, the brown creeper forages in the forest canopy, forcing its way through foliage and dislodging the insects on which it feeds. The bird occasionally feeds in the lower storey and also probes for insects under loose bark. In autumn its diet is supplemented with the fruits found in its habitat of native or exotic forest from sea level to alpine scrub.

In lowland forests during the non-breeding season juveniles form small flocks, while adults remain within their territories. At higher altitudes both adults and juveniles may form much larger flocks and associate with grey warblers, fantails, silvereyes, yellow-breasted tits, yellowheads and chaffinches.

The breeding season extends from late September to early February. The female alone builds a deeply cupped nest of bark strips, moss, lichens and leaf skeletons, held together by cobwebs and lined with grass and a few feathers. The nest is frequently placed in the dense foliage of the canopy or occasionally in a dense bush or vine of the understorey. The bird lays two to four eggs at one day intervals. These are white, light pink or dark pink with reddish brown or purple markings concentrated at the blunt end.

The female incubates for 17 to 21 days, often fed by the male away from the nest. Both sexes feed the young which fledge in 18 to 20 days. After the young leave the nest, they join the adults in moving about the territory as a family group. One or both parents continue to feed them for up to two months. When the young are completely independent, they form sibling flocks which remain together throughout the winter inside or outside the parental territory. Pairs may successfully raise two broods during a breeding season. Up to four nesting attempts can be made in one season if a brood fails because of predators, infertility of eggs or desertion. In the South Island, the brown creeper is the main host of the long-tailed cuckoo.   J.B.C.

ENDEMIC

OTHER NAME: *Pipipi.*

SIZE: *130 mm.*

DESCRIPTION
ADULT: *Sexes similar, although male slightly larger. Forehead, crown, lower back, rump and tail rufous, most intense on rump and tail, and gradually merging into grey-brown of back and nape. Ear coverts and side of neck pure grey. Wings dark brown. Grey face and buff underparts separated by sharp line well below eye. Pale buff stripe just behind eye. All but middle 2 tail feathers have dark brown spot one third from tip which form distinctive dark band when tail spread. Iris hazel brown. Bill, legs and feet light brown with claws slightly lighter.*
JUVENILE: *Similar to adult except legs and feet darker brown.*
NESTLINGS: *First down grey-brown, present on top of head, and along back and wings. Skin, pink at hatching, turns light orange. Inside of mouth bright yellow. At fledging bird is fully feathered, although tail feathers shorter than in adult.*

MOULT
Moulting of wing and tail feathers has been observed in late February and March.

VOICE
Song of male is 2 to 4 seconds long and composed of 5 to 14 notes, last of which is highest in pitch. Songs often repeated and coupled together with a trill or several harsh call notes. When singing throat and crown feathers are erected and tail is flicked. Female song lasts less than one second and is composed of 4 to 9 notes. The last note is prolonged and highest in pitch. Call notes include begging calls; the low intensive twittering of social contact calls; flocking calls, described as hoarse dee or repeated chattering dee; *short high-pitched call repeated during flight; and alarm calls similar to flocking calls but more intense.*

DISTRIBUTION
South Island, Stewart Island and their nearer outlying islands.

Whiteheads are active feeders. They hover to catch insects, glean them from leaves and twigs, and—if necessary—hang upside down in their search for food.

Whitehead *Mohoua albicilla* (LESSON, 1830)

ENDEMIC

OTHER NAME: *Popokatea.*

SIZE: *150 mm.*

DESCRIPTION
ADULT MALE: *Head, nape, neck, breast, middle of belly and undertail coverts white, faintly tinged with brown, especially on body. Side of body and flanks pale wine brown. Upper surface wine brown, paler on upper wing coverts. Quills dark brown; outer webs of primaries edged with grey and inner webs with yellowish white. Upper tail coverts and tail pale yellowish brown. Iris, bill, legs and toes black, with paler soles and brown claws.*
ADULT FEMALE: *Similar to adult male, but slightly smaller and nape and crown tinged with brown.*
IMMATURE: *Similar to adult female, but underparts washed with grey.*

MOULT
Complete moult shortly after breeding season, between January and April.

VOICE
Contact note is single cheet, chip *or* zit, *occasionally* ter-cheet. *In alarm*

call it becomes harsher and louder chirrt *and, when very excited, becomes rapidly repeated* chee-chee-chee-chee. *Male utters single* swerre. *Male sings bell-like trill of 6 rapid notes, with trills separated by soft clear whistling and piping. Song also described as clear canary-like notes, interspersed with harsher* viu, viu, viu-zir, zir, zir. *During nesting female occasionally gives harsh chattering* tche-tche ch-ch-ch-ch.

DISTRIBUTION
Formerly abundant throughout all bush areas of North Island, now in moderate numbers only in forested areas south of Mt Pirongia and Te Aroha, including Mt Egmont and the axial mountain system from East Cape to Cook Strait. Plentiful on Little Barrier and Kapiti Islands. Small numbers on Arid Island, off Great Barrier Island.

RECOGNITION
Mainly confined to canopy foliage. Whitish head and underparts with yellowish brown tail.

OUTSIDE THE BREEDING SEASON whiteheads are very social birds. In summer, small family parties and flocks of up to 10 birds are common. In autumn loose flocks of up to 70 birds form, and work through the forest searching for food. These large flocks are composed of smaller restless, noisy, inquisitive groups. The flocks remain together throughout winter and increase in size as the season progresses. Other birds, including silvereyes, fantails and warblers, often associate with whitehead flocks, perhaps taking advantage of the insects they disturb. In spring, the flocks break up into pairs and small breeding groups which move towards lighter forest and scrub to breed.

Whiteheads generally inhabit larger tracts of native forest and scrub, at altitudes of up to 1400 m. They prefer to breed in beech forest and manuka scrub, but sometimes move into adjacent podocarp forest in winter, and can live in small isolated patches of woodland and even in exotic pine plantations on the Volcanic Plateau.

The birds eat a wide variety of insects, as well as seeds and fruit, throughout all vegetation levels from ground to canopy. Although they catch some insects while hovering, most are gleaned from leaves, twigs and branches. Sometimes the birds hang upside down to feed and very occasionally catch flying insects. They use their bills to flake off fragments of bark and break up dead wood, and their feet to draw

foliage within reach and hold large insects while they dismember them.

Polygamy is quite common, with three or four birds sometimes at the nest. All assist in feeding the young, but little is known about their contribution to egg-laying and incubation or the ages and sexes of the birds involved. Whiteheads are not strongly territorial and allow others to come near their nests.

In one courtship display two males flank one female on a sunlit branch. With drooped and quivering wings and widespread, fan-like tail, each male slowly advances towards the female. At the same time the males bow and raise their tails and call a quiet twittering chatter.

The nest is a compact cup of fine dry leaves, twigs, leaf skeletons, small rootlets, thin strips of bark, lichen and moss. This is bound together with cobwebs and lined with feathers, hair, wool, punga scales, bark and moss. It measures about 120 mm in diameter, and 75 mm deep, with an egg chamber about 50 mm in diameter and 30 mm deep. On Kapiti and Little Barrier Islands most nests are in the centre or tops of low-growing, small leaved trees or shrubs between one and four metres above the ground. On the mainland nests have been recorded in thick scrubby bushes, pines, the crowns of tree ferns and, in one case, in the crown of a rata 25 m above ground level. Usually the nest is securely supported in a fork, but occasionally it hangs from light twigs or branches

Nesting activities

The two to four eggs are rounded and vary in colour from white to deep pink, but most are white, minutely speckled or marbled with yellowish to reddish brown, with the markings denser towards the larger end. Eggs within a clutch can vary considerably, perhaps because they have been laid by different birds.

It usually takes about four days to build the nest, sometimes up to a fortnight, then a couple of days pass before the female starts laying. She lays daily and remains on or near the nest throughout the laying period, but full incubation does not begin until after the final egg is laid. Both male and female incubate at some nests, but at others, where more than two birds are involved, it is done mostly or wholly by the females. The incubation period is approximately 17 days.

The young are initially naked, but a covering of blue-grey down grows by the third day. Eyes open and wing feathers appear by one week, and by 12 days they have grown full feathers. Brooding continues until the chicks are at least a fortnight old. All parents assist in feeding the young. At one nest attended by three adults, four-day old chicks were fed at intervals of 15 to 20 minutes. At 12 days the two chicks were each fed four times in a 45-minute period. Fledging occurs at 16 or 17 days, but the young remain dependent on the parents for several more days and remain in family parties for a couple of weeks.

The whitehead is the main host of the long-tailed cuckoo in the North Island. The cuckoo's arrival coincides with the beginning of the whitehead's breeding season, and parasitism of nests has been recorded as late as January.   H.A.R.

Yellowhead *Mohoua ochrocephala* (GMELIN,1789)

WHILE SEARCHING FOR FOOD in the forest canopy yellowheads pass quickly through the branches, thoroughly inspecting each leaf and twig from all angles, including upside down, and prying into small cracks and crevices. They also feed in the lichen, moss and crevices on the trunks of beech trees. As they climb trees they press their tails against the trunk which wears down the tail feathers until they look like spines. They often search for food in litter, occasionally on the ground, but usually in the fork of a tree, where they grip the bark with one foot and scratch with the other, like domestic fowl.

Beetles and their larvae, moths, caterpillars, bugs, wetas and spiders form the greatest part of their diet. It was thought that yellowheads lived solely on such invertebrates until a flock of eight was observed eating the ripe orange fruit of the bush lily *Astelia fragrans*.

In late summer these social birds congregate in small family parties and flocks which remain together throughout winter, or combine to form larger flocks, occasionally joined by parakeets. Flocks generally keep to the upper parts of trees, but sometimes they flock down in an inquisitive manner, or to mob a predator.

Once plentiful throughout the forest of the South Island, D'Urville Island and possibly Stewart Island, yellowheads are now restricted to large tracts of native forest. They prefer beech forest and generally keep to the canopy and subcanopy.

The breeding season

Flocks break up into pairs or trios in spring to breed; eggs are laid from October to February, but mostly in November or December. Yellowheads are sometimes polygamous and often nests have two females sharing the incubation evenly. Although males help feed the young, they are not thought to help incubate.

Early in the breeding season, the female solicits food from the male by fluttering her wings quickly while crouching in front of him. He occasionally regurgitates, but more usually feeds her with whole food items held in his bill. Courtship feeding appears to end after the clutch is complete and incubation has begun.

During observation of one nest it appeared that the site was selected by the male. He repeatedly flew backwards and forwards between his mate and the nest hole until she had investigated and accepted it. Within a few days the female bird was observed carrying nesting material to the site.

Before mating one male landed beside the female and waved his wings slowly back and forth at the rate of about three flaps a second. With every sixth or seventh flap he leant across and sharply pecked the female on the back of the head. After five or six pecks the female crouched and the pair mated.

At a nest where two females incubated, the relieving bird arrived with a moth or grub, entered the cavity and offered it to the sitting hen. After the incubating bird accepted the food it stepped aside and waited until the relieving bird had settled onto the eggs before flying out. When a male appeared with food, at intervals of about 30 minutes, it chirped softly. This brought the incubating female off the nest to accept the food.

The nest is often high in the canopy, usually more than six metres above the forest floor. It is almost invariably in a dry hole, often in a rotten stump, dead or dying tree, but sometimes in a live tree. The birds prefer cavities with an entrance hole 7 to 12 cm in diameter that opens into the bottom of the chamber, so that there is a hollow dome extending up inside the trunk. The nest is a cup of moss, rootlets, twigs, leaves and spiders' webs, with a lining of feathers and fine grass or *Carex*. Two open nests in manuka and beech trees have been recorded. One was built of twigs, rootlets, moss and wool, and had an untidy outside. The other was built of moss, grass and wool, with a few feathers intermixed.

The two to four round eggs are a uniform pinkish white to reddish cream, minutely and faintly freckled with pale reddish brown. Variations include one egg of a warm salmon colour; others have been a faint unfreckled brown.

Initially the hen spends considerable periods away from the nest, but she sits for longer periods as incubation progresses. At one nest the female incubated for spells of about 30 minutes and the male fed her at or near the nest. Another female left the nest to feed only three or four times a day, but stayed off the nest for an hour or more. In one clutch, belonging to a polygamous group, the females changed over about every 15 to 20 minutes near the end of incubation, so that the eggs were continuously incubated.

The young hatch naked after about 21 days. At first they are black, but by one week they are covered with blue-grey down. For the first five or six days after hatching all the adults feed the chicks by regurgitation; later they feed the nestlings a variety of insects. The young fledge at 17 or 18 days old but depend on the parents for several days and stay in small family groups for some time.

The yellowhead is a host of the long-tailed cuckoo.   H.A.R.

ENDEMIC

OTHER NAMES: *Mohoua, mohoua houa, bush canary.*

SIZE: *150 mm.*

DESCRIPTION
ADULT MALE: *Head, nape, breast, upper belly and sides of body bright canary yellow. Wing coverts, back and upper tail coverts yellowish brown, with olive tinge on back. Quills brown with yellow margins. Tail dark olive-yellow. Lower belly greyish white. Thighs and flanks pale brown. Undertail coverts yellow. Iris black. Bill and feet black; claws dark brown.*
ADULT FEMALE: *Similar to male, but duller, especially on nape.*
IMMATURE: *Yellow plumage tinged with olive-brown, especially on crown and nape.*

MOULT
Not known.

VOICE
Loud, penetrating call of 6 to 8 rapidly repeated notes described as a trill or a rapid shivering rattle with many variations, particularly during breeding season. Female calls lukaart, lukaart *a few days before and after eggs hatch. Song is variable number of fluid, musical notes which sometimes ends in guttural* curr *or in long trill of rapid staccato notes. Alarm call is harsh scolding note.*

DISTRIBUTION
Now restricted with a patchy distribution in the main axial range of the South Island from the Bryant and Richmond Ranges near Nelson to Puysegur Point. Commonly recorded in the Arthur's Pass region and parts of Fiordland, especially in the Routeburn-Hollyford-Eglinton area. A few birds live in the Catlins State Forest and other parts of eastern Otago and Southland.

RECOGNITION
Bright canary-yellow head, nape and breast, with tail a darker olive yellow.

The yellowhead's tail feathers are worn down to spiny shafts as it forages for food on tree trunks.

Grey Warbler *Gerygone igata* (Quoy & Gaimard, 1830)

ACCORDING TO MAORI FOLKLORE, the melodic, rambling song of the grey warbler heralded spring, the time of planting. The proverb '*i hea koe i te tangihanga o te riroriro?*' ('where were you when the grey warbler sang?') was used to shame a lazy or careless person who had not cultivated food. The Maori also believed that the position of the nest foretold the coming season's winds: the higher the nest, the calmer the weather would be.

The grey warbler lives in a wide range of habitats, from sea level to 1500 m, and is one of the few native songbirds to have remained common during European colonisation. It needs small shrubs for nesting and is found in most types of native forest, although it seems to prefer scrub. It also occurs in coastal sand dunes, swamps, mangroves, riverbeds and in the subalpine zone. It is equally at home in pine plantations, farmland, parks and gardens.

Adult grey warblers are sedentary. They tend to remain paired outside the breeding season and, although they are less territorial in autumn and winter, they forage in the same areas that they defended in spring and summer. The life expectancy of breeding adults is about five years.

The birds build a covered, hanging nest with a small circular entrance at one side—the Chatham Island warbler is the only other New Zealand bird to build such a nest. It is elongated and tapered, about seven centimetres wide and 14 cm long, although extra material trailing from the bottom may form a 'beard' as long as the nest itself. The entrance is about three centimetres in diameter and is usually surmounted by a small hood or porch. A framework of stout material, such as rootlets and grass, is filled out with fine moss and bound together with cobwebs. Twigs, leaves, wool, strips of bark and pieces of lichen are also used. The lining is formed by feathers or soft plant material such as thistledown.

The nest is always attached above and, while many hang freely, others are secured at the side and below. Often the birds nest in manuka or gorse within three metres of the ground. The female takes about a week to build the nest on her own, but longer at the start of the season. The first material is attached to a twig and extended downwards to form a loose column. The entrance is formed at an early stage and the central cavity enlarged from within.

The breeding season usually extends from August to January. The first nests are built in August, and the first eggs are laid later that month or in September. The first young fledge in October, and the laying of second clutches is under way by early November. The last young fledge in January.

The eggs, usually four, are ovoid and white, with a pinkish hue when fresh, and a variable amount of reddish brown spotting. They are laid at 48 hour intervals.

Only the female incubates, and the male does not feed her. The interval between laying and hatching of the last egg is 17 to 21 days. The nestling period is 15 to 19 days. Both parents feed the young for up to five weeks after they fledge, although they are capable of catching and eating their own prey after about two and a half weeks. The male plays the greater role in caring for the first brood of fledglings while the female prepares the second nest.

About half the second clutch may be parasitised by the shining cuckoo, which lays a single egg in the warbler's nest. The number of eggs in the nest does not change, because the cuckoo removes a warbler's egg. A few days after hatching, the cuckoo nestling evicts the warbler's eggs or young and is reared alone by its foster parents.

The grey warbler eats invertebrates, particularly spiders, beetles and caterpillars. It obtains most of its food from live foliage and hovers momentarily in mid-air to glean food from otherwise inaccessible leaves. It often carries its prey to a stout branch and, facing downwards if the branch slopes, holds the food in its bill and thoroughly beats it before swallowing. In autumn and winter grey warblers forage in mixed flocks with whiteheads, brown creepers, fantails, silvereyes and, occasionally, pied tits and chaffinches.   B.J.G.

ENDEMIC

OTHER NAMES: *Riroriro, teetotum.*

SIZE: *110 mm.*

DESCRIPTION
ADULT: *Sexes alike. Head, back and rump dark grey, tinged with olive, especially towards posterior. Throat, breast and flanks pale grey. Belly and cloacal region white. Undersurfaces tinged with yellow, especially towards posterior and* along sides and flanks. Wings grey, almost black above, paler below. Outer vanes of flight feathers edged above with olive. Edge of wing streaked with white close to insertion of first flight feathers. Tail rounded, dark grey, almost black, though paler underneath and at base. Tail feathers, except central pair, have subterminal white spot. Tail feathers may be edged with olive, especially at base. Side of head may be tinged with yellow, or have pale, faint eyebrow stripe. Iris bright red. Bill thin and pointed, black. Legs long and thin, black. Claws black. Soles pale grey.
IMMATURE: *Plumage paler than adult, and tail shorter at first. Pale yellow ring may surround eye. Iris brown.*
NESTLING: *Skin pink or grey. White down, mainly on upper parts of head, body and wings. Bill pink, black at tip. Sides of gape white at hatching; later bright yellow. Legs and claws pink at first.*

MOULT
Adults and young of the year moult from January to March, immediately after the breeding season.

VOICE
Male song loud, tuneful, wavering. This is sometimes extended or ended abruptly, but it continues uninterrupted during movement and flight. Singing occurs throughout the year, more so in September and October and less so in January and May. Female and juvenile occasionally give quiet sub-songs. Other calls include rapidly repeated twitter when agitated.

DISTRIBUTION
Common throughout the 3 main islands and many offshore islands. Reaches the Three Kings Islands in the north, and occasionally visits The Snares.

Grey warblers tend to feed year-round in the same restricted locality as their spring and summer breeding territory.

Chatham Island Warbler *Gerygone albofrontata* GRAY,1844

A small porch projects above the entrance to the hanging nest of a Chatham Island warbler.

THE CHATHAM ISLAND WARBLER has not adapted to human settlement and lives only in native bush. In the southwest of Chatham Island it prefers marginal forest, tall scrub and *Dracophyllum* forest; on South East Island it inhabits open patches and tracts of coastal *Olearia* forest.

The birds breed from September to January, and most eggs are laid in October and early November. A pair probably rears two broods each season.

The warbler's nest is a neat enclosed pendant, occasionally with a 'beard'. The entrance, which is at the side near the top, has a projecting porch. This entrance may face any direction, but usually looks towards a gap in the vegetation which allows the birds to approach and depart easily. The nest is about 15 cm long, seven centimetres wide and eight centimetres deep, the entrance about three centimetres in diameter. The site varies from close to the ground up to 12 m. Usually it is in a tangle of vines and branches, but often, especially in *Dracophyllum* forest, it hangs from a limb in the open. The nest, made of rootlets, mosses, leaves, bark, grass stems, spider egg-cases and cobwebs, is lined with feathers.

The three or four ovoid eggs are pinkish white with reddish-brown blotches and spots. The female incubates and broods the chicks, but the male often visits and helps feed the young and, in the latter stages, may take full charge of feeding the brood.

Fledglings stay near the nest for a couple of days, even though they can fly reasonably well. They tend to remain as a tight group and are shepherded and fed by their parents for several weeks after leaving the nest. In some cases the parents feed independently, each looking after one or two chicks.

During the breeding season Chatham Island warblers are strongly territorial. The male sings loudly and chases intruders in fast direct flights. In one chase between two warblers in early February, the two birds landed and the attacking bird, which was almost certainly an adult male, displayed its prominently expanded eyebrow stripe. The other bird faced down and away, and held its wings approximately half opened, presumably as a submissive posture. Parents form family groups with newly fledged juveniles, but by December, when adults are busy with a second brood, groups of up to 12 juveniles and the odd adult band together.

The Chatham Island warbler eats a wide range of invertebrates including flies, beetles, caterpillars, moths, cicadas, bugs and spiders. It collects these from many sources, but gleans most of its food from leaves and crevices, especially in trunks and branches of *Olearia* and *Dracophyllum*. Some food is taken while hovering. On Chatham Island, where there are mammalian predators, it does not feed on the ground.   H.A.R.

ENDEMIC

OTHER NAMES: *None.*

SIZE: *120 mm.*

DESCRIPTION
ADULT MALE: *Forehead, eyebrow stripe to behind ear coverts, cheeks, throat, breast and belly white. Thin brownish olive line extending from near gape, through eye and ear coverts. Crown, nape, side of neck and back olive-brown. Rump olive green. Tail coverts cinnamon. Tail feathers brownish-grey with cream band or patch; obscure band of dusky brown above patches. Tail feather tips drab brown. Primaries and secondaries brownish grey with outer webs buff-yellow. Underwing coverts white. Flanks, thighs and vent pale olive-yellow. Undertail coverts cream. Iris red. Bill black. Feet blackish brown.*

ADULT FEMALE: *Forehead, crown, nape, side of neck and back brownish olive except for some white or cream-coloured feathers at base of bill. Rump olive green. Tail coverts cinnamon. Tail and wings as in male. Narrow eyebrow stripe dull white. Underparts dull white tinged with cream, especially around throat which is sometimes pale straw yellow. Flanks, thighs and undertail coverts pale straw yellow. Iris red. Bill black. Feet blackish-brown.*
JUVENILE: *Forehead, crown, nape, side of neck, back and rump olive-grey. Upper tail coverts cinnamon. Tail as in adult. Wings similar to adult except outer webs green-yellow. Obscure eyebrow stripe white. Pale yellow eye-ring. Breast and belly dull white tinged with cream. Chin, cheeks, flanks, thighs, vent and undertail coverts pale straw yellow. Iris brown. Bill dusky brown with dull pink base. Feet dull pink.*

NESTLING: *Initially naked except for white down on upper parts. By 1 week feathers begin to emerge. Fully feathered by 2 weeks.*

MOULT
Little information available. Adults probably moult once a year in January and February, after the breeding season. Birds in immature plumage and moulting primaries seen late November or early December may be 12 month old birds, attending their first adult plumage.

VOICE
In breeding season, rapid 4 or 5 note phrase, with second note markedly higher than first, and other 2 or 3 on descending scale, repeated several times, sometimes monotonously. Outside breeding season fairly quiet with only short snatches of song. Only male gives full song; females and

independent juveniles occasionally utter weak bursts of song.

DISTRIBUTION
Endemic to the Chatham Islands. Moderately common in the south of Chatham Island, but extremely rare in the north. Abundant on South East Island and present on Pitt, Mangere, Little Mangere and Houruakopara Islands, and on the Star Keys.

Fantail *Rhipidura fuliginosa* (Sparrman, 1787)

ENDEMIC

North Island Fantail
R.f. placabilis Bangs, 1921.
South Island Fantail
R.f. fuliginosa (Sparrman, 1787).
Chatham Island Fantail
R.f. penitus Bangs, 1911.

OTHER NAMES: *Piwakawaka, pied fantail, black fantail.*

SIZE: *160 mm.*

DESCRIPTION

ADULT: *In pied phase, female smaller and duller. In South Island fantail, forehead, lores and band through eye sooty black. White streak above eye. Crown, nape and side of face dark greyish black. Back and wings dark olive brown, with 2 lines of tawny-white spots formed by pale tips of greater and middle secondary coverts. Inner secondaries edged with tawny white. Central tail feathers brownish black with white shafts and tips. Second to fifth tail feathers white, with outer parts of each outer web brownish black above. Outer tail feathers greyish white. Chin and throat greyish white above band of blackish grey on upper breast. Lower breast and belly yellowish rufous. Undersurface of outer tail almost clear white, sometimes tinged with tawny. Bill and iris black. Feet blackish brown. North Island fantail* similar to South Island fantail, but slightly paler; with only tip of central tail feathers white; and undertail darker. Chatham Island fantail similar to South Island fantail, but black edges on outer webs of second to fifth tail feathers narrower and separated from shaft by broad white strip; broad white tips on central tail feathers; and undertail almost pure white except for central and outermost feathers. Black phase occurs in 12 to 25 per cent of South Island fantails, less than one per cent of North Island fantails. Does not occur in Chatham Island fantails. Head and neck greyish black, with small spot of white behind ear. Back and wing coverts black, tinged with rusty brown. Quills dark brown. Tail black. Undersurface from lower breast to tail chocolate brown. Bill black, with base of lower mandible sometimes pale. White ear spot varies in size, and in some males extends below eye.*

FLEDGLING: *In pied phase like adult, but eyebrow stripe tawny; upper contour feathers tipped with brownish grey; terminal spots of greater and middle secondary coverts large and fawn-coloured; tail short, black cheek band absent and white throat undeveloped; beak and legs horn-coloured, not black.*

MOULT

Breeding pairs moult in summer after final brood is independent. At Stewart Island in March, parents were still associating with last brood while replacing tail feathers.

VOICE

During the breeding season, when flying to nest with building material or food, utters monotonous, regularly repeated single contact note tweet, *to which sitting bird or chicks react with excited movements. Same call used throughout year to keep feeding birds in contact. Throughout most of year, especially spring and summer, male calls chattering song of regular rhythm* tweet-a-tweet-a-tweeta... *which becomes pleasant high-pitched ecstatic song as bird displays.*

DISTRIBUTION

North Island fantail: *Common throughout the North Island; Hen and Chickens; Mokohinau, Mayor, Kapiti, and Little and Great Barrier Islands; and the Three Kings Islands. Flocks of hundreds of birds winter in lowlands and lake basins, while others remain in central uplands. Uncommon above 900 m on Mt Ruapehu and Mt Egmont in midsummer.*

South Island fantail: *Common throughout most of the South Island, Stewart Island and close offshore islands. Absent from unforested parts of Marlborough, Canterbury, Otago and Southland. Recently colonised The Snares. Adults with flying young move from highlands to lowlands in autumn, forming flocks of several hundred birds in valleys or plains.*

Chatham Island fantail:
Abundant on Chatham, Pitt and South East Islands.

North Island fantails often nest close to water and are commonly seen in gardens bathing under a sprinkler.

THE FRIENDLY FANTAIL is one of the best-known of New Zealand's indigenous birds. It has adapted particularly well to farms, gardens and parks where it is welcomed for its attacks on insects. By colonising man-made habitats the fantail may now be more abundant than when New Zealand was completely forested. It lives almost anywhere where there are trees, including coastal scrub, introduced plantations and shrubberies, and ranges up to mountain forest in summer.

It begins breeding in its first year and raises three or four broods. In the South Island the breeding season extends from September to about January. In the North Island it starts about a month earlier.

The nest is firmly attached to the outer branches or twigs of small trees, shrubs or tree-fern fronds. Often it is near a stream, between three and ten metres above the ground. It is compact, circular and open, with a wide edge and small central cup, and is composed of grass, moss, twigs, bark and rootlets, bound together with cobwebs and lined with hair or fibre, especially tree-fern fibre. Often there is an untidy tail hanging below.

Both sexes build the nest, incubate the eggs and feed the young. The three or four eggs are ovoid and white with small light brown blotches all over, but especially around the larger end. Incubation takes 15 days; fledging a further 15 days. The newly hatched young are almost naked and both parents take turns to cover them. The parents usually begin building the next nest while still feeding the flying young. The same nest is rarely used twice.

During the breeding season, fantails are territorial, snapping their bills at any intruding birds. Early broods may remain briefly near the parental territory but later they wander extensively to join other family groups which move to lake or stream edges where flying insects abound in midsummer.

Fantails are fond of water and enjoy bathing in shallow pools, waterfalls or spray from a garden hose. In summer they often enter houses and clear rooms of small insects. Sometimes they posture aggressively in front of their reflections in mirrors or window panes.

The males display freely, whether stimulated by their mates or by other males, most of the year. They droop their wings and fan their tails, so that they seem larger than normal, as they strut and pose and fly out from their perches in aerial acrobatics. When travelling with food or nest material, they fly directly, their tails folded and held horizontally.

Fantails begin feeding at dawn and continue well into dusk. They eat only insects, which they capture mostly on the wing. From perches in the canopy or at the edge of a clearing they fly out into hovering swarms of small insects and grab them with deft acrobatic movements. Each capture is marked by an audible snap of the bill and a beak-full of insects does not hinder further attacks. Over ponds, where swarming insects abound in summer, fantails sometimes swoop continuously, following their prey higher above the water as the sun sets. Occasionally they have been observed foraging among litter on the forest floor.   C.A.F.

Black Robin *Petroica traversi* (BULLER,1872)

THE BLACK ROBIN is one of the rarest birds in the world. Once it lived on Pitt, Mangere and Little Mangere Islands. Cats exterminated the species on Mangere and Pitt Islands, so that by the turn of the century only about 25 pairs remained. The degradation and reduction of forest on Little Mangere Island, coupled with the black robin's low breeding rate, caused its numbers to decline even further. To save the species from extinction, the seven birds surviving in 1976 and 1977 were moved to the larger Mangere Island. Birds and eggs were transferred to South East Island in 1982 and 1983.

The black robin breeds, roosts and feeds in woody vegetation. On Little Mangere Island it also lived on very steep slopes in vegetation less than one metre tall. However, these areas are abandoned when level areas with taller trees are available.

The species prefers to breed in cavities in hollow trees or long stumps buried in vine tangles. In territories which do not contain such sites nests have been located in a wide variety of places, including exposed and poorly supported branches. The nest is constructed of various plant fibres and lined with the feathers of other birds. Sometimes a blackbird's nest is used as a base. The female does all the work of nest building, incubation, and brooding, while the male attends her with food and song. The sitting female captures his attention when the eggs are hatching by vigorous displays which include asymmetrical wing flapping. Adult birds rarely show more than alarm when the nest or young are approached.

Two eggs are generally laid, though the clutch can vary from one to three eggs. They are ovoid and creamy white with purplish brown spots and blotches. The breeding season on Little Mangere Island was unexpectedly late and short. This was probably a response to the poor habitat rather than a characteristic of the species. Most clutches are laid from October to November. Second clutches are successfully raised if nestlings or fledglings die, however second nests are rare after successful first broods. The young robin fledges between the third week of November and the third week of January. Survival after fledging is higher for early broods.

Incubation takes from 17 to 19 days, and fledging occurs after 20 to 23 days. Both parents feed the nestlings and one or both continue feeding the young for at least four weeks after they leave the nest. The young are capable of weak flight at or close to fledging.

Black robins live all year as pairs or as bachelor males in territories. Nevertheless, birds often wander into neighbouring territories until discovered and driven off. In winter and spring, the male patrols its area, singing from prominent perches; at other seasons it often gives a range of calls. Females drive intruding females away, but boundary disputes most often involve males. These disputes are characterised by loud calls and a few simple postures rather than the mainly silent and highly visual displays of the South Island robin. Instead of crest feather displays, as in other robins and tits, black robin pairs perform chases which often end in mounting.

The black robin hunts with frequent short flights between low perches, with brief bouts of hopping on the ground, or by taking prey off bark surfaces. Since its transfer to new localities it now feeds mostly on the ground. Sometimes it hops a short way into the entrance of a petrel burrow. Normally the litter is not scratched or turned over during foraging, but prey is occasionally captured from leaf surfaces. It eats a broad range of invertebrates.

Fortunately this species is long-lived, with 10 to 12 year old birds being recorded. Following transfer to Mangere Island the numbers dropped to a total population of five individuals.

An intensive management and cross-fostering programme was started in 1980 to boost productivity. Initially first clutches were transferred to Chatham Island warblers, but the robin chicks died at 10 days. Accordingly the warblers were used as incubators and the hatched chicks returned to the robins. At the end of the 1980-81 season four robins were raised as a result of the management, whereas only one would have resulted without intervention.

Since then the Chatham Island tit has proved to be a more successful foster parent, and the population has been spread between two islands following the introduction of birds to South East Island in January 1983. Black robins normally breed at two years old. In 1983 the first successfully fostered chick, a male fostered by Chatham Island tits, bred successfully with a two year old female reared by robins. By December 1983 the total population stood at five adults and two juveniles on Mangere Island; three adults and eight juveniles on South East Island. J.A.D.F. & D.V.M.

ENDEMIC

OTHER NAME: *Chatham Island robin.*

SIZE: *150 mm.*

DESCRIPTION
ADULT: *Sexes alike, but female usually slightly smaller. Entire plumage black to blackish-brown, a few feathers fading with wear. Iris dark brown. Bill black. Legs and feet blackish brown; soles generally dull grey, but yellow in some birds.*
IMMATURE: *Slight streaking on crown and neck up to February or early March, then indistinguishable from adult.*
FLEDGLING: *Similar to adult, but crown, neck and scapulars faintly streaked.*
NESTLING: *Down dark grey; skin flesh-coloured.*

MOULT
Bachelor males and pairs that fail to raise young begin moult in December. Breeding birds begin moult in January or early February and complete it well into March.

VOICE
Beautiful song of pure tone notes forming 5 to 13 syllables. Differs from the warble of tits and the longer and more complex song of mainland robins. Heard frequently during breeding season and also from June, but not in autumn. Non-breeding birds do not sing in summer. Female sometimes sings brief phrases when feeding young. Also, short series of descending notes frequently called, especially in summer and autumn; simple call of one syllable, heard at fairly regular intervals, especially while foraging; also chucks, squeaks, harsh sounds and complex sounds.

DISTRIBUTION
Mangere Island and South East Island in the Chatham Islands.

RECOGNITION
All-black robin; confined to the Chatham Islands.

From 1977 to 1983 intensive Wildlife Service management raised the rare black robin's numbers from nine to 18.

The North Island robin population began to decline before European settlement, but in recent years numbers have stabilised and spread into pine forests.

Robin *Petroica australis* (SPARRMAN, 1788)

THE ROBIN VARIES its hunting methods according to habitat, season and the type of prey available. It hunts mainly on or near the ground among leaf litter, but searching at higher levels occurs especially during summer. The other major hunting technique is swooping from horizontal and vertical perches. Food includes earthworms, large moths, caterpillars, grubs, spiders, wetas, stick insects and winged insects, including large cicadas. It also takes prey too small to identify at a distance, and occasionally eats berries. It catches flies from under, and occasionally above, the forest canopy. When hopping in leaf litter, and sometimes while perched on branches, the robin rapidly vibrates a foot and sometimes also flicks its wing tips and tail. The catching of surplus food is common.

The robin lives in manuka and kanuka scrub and forest, beech, podocarp, and mixed beech and podocarp forest. In the North Island, it has also spread to pine plantations. In general, it avoids steep slopes, although it tolerates them on small islands. In rugged mainland areas it is often confined to gullies or ridge tops. The bird may use grazed vegetation where principal cover is provided by trees, cropped grasses or tussock grasses. Because it does not like large treeless areas it has limited ability to disperse between isolated forest patches or islands. However, it has been observed in gardens in Otago and in a formal garden in the Seaward Kaikoura Mountains.

South Island robins normally breed first between eight and 12 months, occasionally as early as four and a half months. On Outer Chetwode Island, however, some pairs did not begin breeding until their third spring, about 22 months after hatching.

Most nest-sites are against trunks, branch forks or in clusters of branches in bushes or tree crowns, such as at the base of palm branches. Nests in the tops of tree ferns are often tipped over by the rapidly growing vegetation. The nest-site varies in height from 45 cm to at least 11 m above ground. Building materials vary with availability, but the birds prefer moss, small twigs, bark, fine dry grass, dead leaves and lichens. The size of the inner cup expands as the chicks grow. Up to half the nests are built in, or on top of, old blackbird, song thrush or tui nests. If these bases are in good condition, the robin will often do no more than lightly reline the cup. Robins never use a nest twice in the same season; but the few that survive to the next season are occasionally used again. The female does all the work of nest building and the male, singing phrases of song as he approaches, carries food to her. One to four days are spent in building, and the clutch is begun after an interval of several days.

Raising the brood

In most years at Kaikoura the first clutches are laid from mid-July and the last in late December. On Chetwode Island, where population density is very high, the bulk of the population does not begin laying until September and stops by November. At Kaikoura and in Queen Charlotte Sound robins usually lay three eggs, but on Poutama and Pohowaitai Islands they normally lay two.

Robins raise three broods in a season from three or four nests at Kaikoura and in Queen Charlotte Sound, but on the mainland most pairs lose two or more nests, and consequently raise only one or two broods. On Stewart Island robins rarely breed more than once each year. If the nest is destroyed, the birds replace the nest and clutch in just over a week. The ovoid eggs are creamy white or greyish cream, with light brown, grey or purplish brown, fine, close spots or blotches which are sometimes concentrated at the larger end.

Hatching commonly occurs after about 18 days of incubation and usually all the eggs hatch within a few hours of each other, except in larger clutches. At hatching time, the female suddenly refuses to fly from her nest as the male approaches with food. Instead, she begins a rotating and rocking motion while vigorously flapping one wing and

ENDEMIC
North Island Robin
P.a. longipes (LESSON, 1828).
South Island Robin
P.a. australis (SPARRMAN, 1788).
Stewart Island Robin
P.a. rakiura FLEMING, 1950.

OTHER NAMES: *Bush robin, toutouwai.*

SIZE: *180 mm.*

DESCRIPTION
ADULT MALE: *In South Island robin white spot over bill; head, neck and side of body sooty grey; quills and tail smoky black, with obscure white bar on wing; breast yellow; belly yellowish white; undertail coverts white; iris black; bill and feet brownish black; soles yellow. North Island robin similar to South Island robin, except upper surface slate grey with streaky appearance from white shaft lines; cheek, throat and upper breast grey, mottled with white; lower breast, middle of belly and undertail coverts white; feet pale yellowish brown, with yellow soles. Stewart Island robin smaller than South Island robin, with darker upper parts and white breast.*
ADULT FEMALE: *South Island robin smaller than male, with more brown on upper surface and generally less yellow on underparts. North Island robin browner and paler than male, with mottled neck.*
IMMATURE: *South Island robin initially similar to adult female, but with pronounced shaft lines on crown, nape and scapulars. At first, lower breast and belly white. By late spring immatures from early nests similar to adults and only distinguished by numerous shaft lines.*
NESTLING: *In South Island robin down dark grey and skin flesh-coloured.*

MOULT
South Island bachelor males begin moult in December. Breeding pairs moult later, depending on stage of breeding. By end of January some adults have nearly completed moult while others have just begun. Most young of the year become indistinguishable from adults by February or early March.

VOICE
Loud chucks singly or in a downscale series that start in rapid succession and finish slowly; squeaks from nestlings; harsh begging sounds from young and females. Song is series of phrases, each of identical syllables, uttered in fixed sequence, often continuing for 10 to 20 minutes at a time. Song heard throughout day in any month. Unpaired males regularly sing until they mate. Short segments or phrases of song given by male and female before feeding older nestlings and juveniles, and by males prior to feeding female. Adult also sings when leaving nest. Juvenile sometimes sings sub-song.

DISTRIBUTION
South Island robin: *Throughout the island but abundance irregular and varies considerably with locality, habitat and altitude. Some populations of pairs widely scattered in continuous forest. In other areas small pockets of several pairs are widely separated by unoccupied forest or other vegetation. Continuous mainland populations of greater size appear to exist, and along the lower Kowhai River at Kaikoura there are sometimes more than 100 adults. Dispersal of young occurs from late spring, with a few birds still moving in winter. Adults rarely move far.*

North Island robin: *Kapiti and Little Barrier Islands; the central Taupo-Rotorua district; and near Otaki. No longer present in coastal areas.*

Stewart Island robin: *Isolated and disconnected populations on Stewart Island. Abundant only in large patches of manuka between Freshwater Landing and Mason Bay. Abundant on small islands including Green, Motonui, Jacky Lee, Poutama and Tamaitemioka Islands.*

then the other. When the male lands on the nest rim she stands, exposing the tiny begging young which the male and sometimes the female then feed. From then on, the male concentrates his efforts on feeding the nestlings, with help from the female. Nestlings fledge at about 18 days and parental care continues for four to seven weeks.

The female normally nests again, long before the young are able to hunt for themselves, about one or two weeks after fledging. Near to hatching of the new clutch, the female may attack earlier juveniles, but the male continues to feed them until the female brings his attention to the new nestlings. The age of independence varies because the male will continue feeding the fledglings if the next clutch fails to hatch.

Predators and defences

Mustelids kill many young robins. Ship rats and kiore destroy some nests and sometimes mice attack eggs and nestlings. On the mainland, opossums occasionally blunder onto and squash nests, possibly eating the contents, and cats may destroy a few low nests. On mammal-free islands, moreporks and possibly New Zealand falcons account for small losses.

Adult robins tend to be sedentary, living as pairs or as bachelor males in territories of varying size. Paired birds do not regularly sing or patrol, but they do defend territorial boundaries. There are some beautiful puffing and wing-lifting displays specific to border disputes. However, a certain amount of trespassing occurs in dense vegetation, and robins regularly cross territories to bathe in pools. The system also tends to break down during the post-breeding moult as independent young begin to settle. Territories are re-established after the moult, from March onwards.

The tameness of the robin has endeared it to many people, and has led to speculation that it should be easy prey to introduced predators. Its reaction time, however, is exceptionally fast, and it recognises and treats predators with alarm. Robins follow cattle and humans to take advantage of the invertebrates that they stir up. They fall prey only when surprised in dense cover or on nests or night roosts. Cyanide baits and traps put out for opossums kill many robins.   J.A.D.F.

Stewart Island robins are most abundant with small territories on small offshore islands.

The yellow-breasted tit often bears two broods in a season. The male attends the first nestlings while the female prepares the second nest.

Tit *Petroica macrocephala* (Gmelin, 1789)

TITS ARE MAINLY BIRDS of the forest that eat insects, such as moths, flies, beetles, bugs and their larvae. They also catch millipedes, spiders and earthworms. From perches a metre or two above ground level, they fly down to grab their prey from the forest floor or from tree trunks and stumps. They also forage in newly ploughed soil and sometimes catch flying insects on the wing. At Gouland Downs tits have been observed dunking food in a creek before feeding it to their young. Some tits gather round people to glean the food exposed by trampers' boots or by an axe-man's blow.

The yellow-breasted tit lives mainly in native podocarp broadleaf or mixed forest, second growth and coastal scrub, but also in exotic pine woods and deciduous plantations. It begins breeding in its first year and pairs tend to remain together throughout the year. Territorial

singing and ritual courtship feeding begin by September. Males fiercely chase away intruders.

Tits nest in forks of branches, in knot holes or cliff ledges, generally where the nest is protected on several sides and sometimes from above. The nest, large for such a small bird, is spherical or conical, with a deep crater-shaped cup. It is made of moss, leaves, rootlets, grass, bark and cobwebs, and lined with feathers. The female builds it while the cock accompanies and occasionally feeds her.

The three to five eggs, laid between 22 September and December, are ovoid and white, with small light brown and grey spots and blotches. Incubation lasts 15 or 16 days and the chicks fledge after about 19 days. The pair often rears two broods in quick succession, the female building a second nest while the cock looks after the first

ENDEMIC
Pied Tit
P.m. toitoi (LESSON, 1828).
Yellow-breasted Tit
P.m. macrocephala (GMELIN, 1789).
Chatham Island Tit
P.m. chathamensis FLEMING, 1950.
Black Tit
P.m. dannefaerdi (ROTHSCHILD, 1894).
Auckland Island Tit
P.m. marrineri (MATHEWS & IREDALE, 1913).

OTHER NAMES: *Ngiru-ngiru, piropiro, South Island tit, Maui-potiki, North Island tit or tomtit, white-breasted tit or tomtit, Snares tit, Snares Island robin.*

SIZE: *130 mm.*

DESCRIPTION
ADULT MALE:
Yellow-breasted tit: *Crown, back, scapulars, rump, upper tail coverts, sides of head, lores, ear coverts, throat, uppermost breast and gape bristles black with slight gloss, with bases of feathers slate grey, and bases of shafts white; small white frontal spot separated from culmen by broken line of small black*

feathers; flight feathers black, edged with brownish black, crossed by sickle-shaped white bar; lesser, median and greater coverts black, with white tips on some secondary major coverts; underwing deep mouse grey with triangular white bar; axillaries and lining coverts white; lesser undercoverts black, some with whitish tips; tail black, outer 3 feathers with oblique white bar; breast orange immediately below black neck, grading into yellow on mid-breast and ivory yellow on flanks and undertail coverts; iris dark brown; bill black, brownish at base; feet dark brown; soles yellow.
Pied tit: *Similar to yellow-breasted tit, but lower breast, flanks, belly, undertail coverts and thighs white with grey-black bases to feathers.*
Chatham Island tit: *Slightly larger than yellow-breasted tit, with longer legs.*
Auckland Island tit: *Larger than yellow-breasted tit, with paler breast; lower flanks peppered with grey subterminal feather bands; undertail coverts black with faint whitish tips; secondaries seldom tipped with white; and white tail bars often enlarged into spots.*

Black tits abound at The Snares.

Black tit: *Glossy black, bases of feathers grey with light shafts. Wing and tail brownish black; iris black; bill black, with angle of gape pink; legs brownish black; ankle and toes pink; claws blackish.*

ADULT FEMALE:
Yellow-breasted tit: *Crown, back, scapulars and rump brownish grey, bases of feathers grey and bases of shafts whitish; some rump feathers with dark olive-buff tips; lores, cheeks and ear coverts brownish olive mottled with olive-buff; frontal spot light*

olive buff, smaller than in male; flight feathers blackish brown, paler on inner webs, with bar as in male but pale ochre-buff to whitish; upper wing coverts blackish brown; undercoverts and axillaries whitish; lesser undercoverts mottled white and brown; tail blackish brown with oblique bar as in male; throat, breast and belly yellow, washed faintly with buff grading to brown on neck; undertail coverts buff; iris dark brown; bill brownish black, paler at base; feet dark brown; soles yellow.
Pied tit: *Similar to yellow-breasted tit, but upper parts more olive brown; and throat whitish, washed with buff on chest, grading into brown on sides.*
Chatham Island tit: *Upper parts warmer in tone, larger frontal spot outlined above by narrow brownish black band; and throat, breast and belly cream. A rare variant has blackish throat as in male.*
Auckland Island tit: *Similar to male but upper parts dull black; tail coverts tipped with buff; throat black; breast and belly white or ivory yellow; and wing and tail as in male, occasionally with white tips to secondaries.*

brood. When the second brood demands attention from both parents, or when moulting begins in January, the adults chase their young away. Sometimes tits are hosts to the long-tailed cuckoo.

Some yellow-breasted tits migrate to lowland forest in the autumn, but others remain on their territories throughout the year. They will join other small birds to mob a morepork or long-tailed cuckoo.

The pied tit lives in kauri, podocarp, mixed hardwood and beech forest, tall kanuka coastal forest and scrub, and forest clearings, as well as exotic pine plantations.

It begins nesting late in August. The earliest egg date is 20 September and the latest date for young still in the nest is 21 February. Various nest-sites have been discovered. These include a hole in a riverside bank, against the wall of a deserted building, in a mass of fallen manuka twigs, on an overhung shelf on a dead tree, in a hole in a hinau trunk, among the roots of an uprooted beech tree, in the fibrous fur of a Japanese fan palm, in a hole in green moss on a dead sapling, on the broken stump of a tall kanuka and of a punga, and more open positions on kaikomako, pigeon-wood and toatoa, and in forks of young *Pinus* trees. The nests have been at an average of two metres above the ground. Tits take quite readily to nest boxes erected against tree trunks in native forest.

The two to five eggs are creamy white and flecked with yellowish brown spots concentrated at the larger end. The female incubates for 15 or 16 days, leaving the nest frequently when called by the male, who brings insects for her at intervals of about 15 minutes. She flutters her wings like a fledgling when she receives the food. Both parents feed the young, the male sometimes presenting his catch to the female to feed them. After 17 or 18 days, the young fledge and the parents continue to feed them for at least 10 days after they leave the nest.

Variations in habitat

The Chatham Island tit lives in low coastal indigenous forest and scrub. No detailed studies of breeding have been undertaken but, according to one November report, a nest under construction was located one and a half metres from the ground, in *Muehlenbeckia* vine covering an old fence. In late December most pairs had families of two to four flying young. The reoccupation of Mangere Island and sporadic occurrences on Little Mangere indicate that Chatham Island tits undertake quite extensive dispersal movements, perhaps seasonally.

The Auckland Island tit inhabits scrub and littoral rata and *Olearia* forest, nearby open turf, tussock grassland, and coastal rocks. It nests in rock crevices or ledges and in hollow tree trunks, generally sheltered from above, a metre or two above ground level. It breeds at about 11 months. Territorial song and display become intense in July and August. Nest building begins in the latter half of August, laying a month later, but most eggs are laid in October and November. Second broods are likely and flying young are conspicuous in January. The three eggs are laid about a day apart.

In the coastal forest and scrub of the Auckland Island, tits are encountered in pairs throughout the year in the lower parts, but become scarce above 150 m (less in winter) and are absent from the highest scrub. They forage on the rocky shore, on the forest floor, and in adjacent sward and tussock grassland, commonly darting from a watching perch to take insect food on the ground or on tree trunks. As the male fledglings' plumage becomes more like that of adults they are attacked and chased by their own parents, while female fledglings are still being fed. Incipient sexual behaviour, noted in every autumn and winter month, intensifies in July.

The black tit lives mainly in *Olearia lyalli* scrub, but extends into coastal tussock and rocks. Territories are only half or one third the dimension of mainland territories. The three ovoid eggs are white with small brown and grey spots, sometimes covering the whole surface, but always more densely at the larger end. Different pairs observed in late November and early December were in all stages—building, incubating, with downy young and flying young. C.A.F.

The pied tit's nest is a sheltered deep cup lined with bark and feathers.

Black tit: *Similar to male, but slightly less glossy.*

FLEDGLING MALE:
Yellow-breasted tit: *Crown, nape and scapulars, back, rump dull brownish black; frontal spot smaller than in adult; upper tail coverts tipped with pale buff; wing and tail as in adult; throat dull brownish black with pale feather shafts; and breast buff-yellow grading into maize yellow and to whitish at belly, front mottled with bands of brownish grey.*

Pied tit: *Crown and back of head brownish black with faint brownish grey shaft streaks; frontal spot small; sides of head, lores and ear coverts brownish black with brownish grey centres to feathers, giving mottled appearance; upper breast cream with brown tips, forming indistinct band across chest; lower breast white with faint brownish grey pepperings; and wing and tail as in adult.*

Chatham Island tit: *Upper parts dull brownish black with light fuscous shafts and feathers with faint ochre-buff tips; frontal spot small, white; wings and tail as in adult; throat brownish grey, mottled with white; and undersurface white.*

Auckland Island tit: *Differs from adult in light shaft lines on head; brownish grey tips to upper feathers; smaller frontal spot; breast peppered with black; but no peppering on belly.*

Black tit: *Dull black, with slight gloss on back; crown, throat and breast feathers with pale grey shaft streaks; and flank feathers dull black with brownish grey tips.*

FLEDGLING FEMALE:
Yellow-breasted tit: *Similar to adult female, but with light shafts on brownish grey crown and nape, less conspicuous towards rump; frontal spot virtually absent; cheeks brownish grey, with light mottling; throat mottled brownish grey and buff; breast light buff, washed and mottled with brown; belly light buff with ochre tinge towards flanks and undertail coverts.*

Pied tit: *Frontal spot very small; upper parts warmer in tone than in adult, with pale ochre-buff shaft streaks; throat and breast washed with brown and ochre-buff, forming indefinite band.*

Chatham Island tit: *Similar to adult but upper parts brown with light buff shafts; wing-bar more buff-*

coloured; throat white, peppered with brown; breast and belly white, washed with pale buff and flecked on flanks and across breast; thighs and undertail coverts pinkish buff.

Auckland Island tit: *Upper surface dull blackish brown with light shafts; frontal spot small; lores and neck black with lighter centres to feathers; breast ivory yellow mottled with greyish olive; wing and tail as in adult.*

Black tit: *Similar to male fledgling, but flanks more extensively tipped with brownish grey and buff.*

MOULT
Probably in late summer after breeding.

VOICE
High-pitched see-see-see *is call note used for contact. Territorial song, heard most of year, is high warbling whistle* ti-oly-oly-ho *or* yodi yodi yodi, *uttered by male from high perches. Female calls soft* see, *but when excited utters whispered warble similar to male's song.*

DISTRIBUTION
Yellow-breasted tit: *South*
Island, Stewart Island and offshore islands, including D'Urville, Pickersgill, Resolution, Codfish and South Cape Islands.

Pied tit: *North Island, Hen and Chickens, Kapiti, Little and Great Barrier Islands.*

Chatham Island tit: *Chatham, Pitt, South East, Mangere and, occasionally, Little Mangere Island.*

Auckland Island tit: *Enderby, Ewing, Rose, Ocean, Adams and main Auckland Island.*

Black tit: *Main Snares and Broughton Islands.*

RECOGNITION

Distinctive song often leads observer towards singing male; bird then silently approaches observer. Large head. Except in black tit, white or cream-yellow breast contrasting with jet upper parts; white forehead spot; and, in flight, striking white wing and tail pattern.

Satin Flycatcher *Myiagra cyanoleuca* Vieillot, 1818

The female satin flycatcher attends its neat cobweb-covered nest.

THE SATIN FLYCATCHER migrates along the mountain ranges of eastern Australia. The single New Zealand record is possibly a bird which became lost during the crossing of Bass Strait. Less probably, it may have landed on a ship and received an assisted passage across the Tasman Sea.　　　　　　　　　　　A.B. (2)

VAGRANT

OTHER NAMES: *None.*

SIZE: *160 mm.*

DESCRIPTION
ADULT MALE: *Upper parts, throat and breast glossy blue-black. Belly white. Bill black, broad and short with 5 stiff bristles on each side of gape. Iris, legs and feet black.*
ADULT FEMALE: *Head and nape dark blue-grey, merging to dark brown on back and wings. Throat and breast bright rust red, sharply defined from dull white belly. Tail dark brown with narrow white outer edges. Iris, bill, legs and feet as male.*
IMMATURE: *As adult female.*

MOULT
Not known.

VOICE
Loud piping whistle chuee-chuee. *Rasping frog-like note,* queeark, *also given.*

DISTRIBUTION
From eastern Queensland migrates to southeastern Australia and Tasmania in October, returning in March. One New Zealand record, a female found near Gisborne in June 1963.

RECOGNITION

Feathers at rear of crown slightly raised and form distinct crest when calling or excited. Shivers tail constantly when perched, showing white edges.

Song Thrush *Turdus philomelos clarkei* Hartert, 1909

INTRODUCED

OTHER NAME: *Mavis.*

SIZE: *230 mm.*

DESCRIPTION
ADULT: *Sexes alike. Upper surface uniform warm olive brown except for inconspicuous blackish tips to primary coverts and yellowish buff tips to greater and median wing coverts. Lores and narrow line over eye buff. Chin and throat buffy white, throat flecked with brownish black. Breast rich yellowish buff heavily marked with elongated brownish black spots, each feather having wedge-shaped dark mark at tip. Upper belly white with brownish black spots, smaller and fewer than on breast. Lower belly and vent white. Undertail coverts greyish white with inconspicuous brown edges. Flanks pale brown, streaked with darker brown. Underwing coverts rich yellowish buff. Iris brown. Bill dark brown, but yellow near base of lower mandible. Feet yellowish brown. Albinos and partial albinos occur.*
JUVENILE: *Like adult but feathers of head, neck, mantle and wing coverts streaked with pale buff, especially conspicuous on mantle and wing coverts; feathers of mantle have narrow dark tips; smaller spots on breast; and lower breast and belly often washed with yellowish buff.*
NESTLING: *Presumably as in Britain, with fairly long golden buff down; inside of mouth golden yellow without spots; and flanges outside pale yellow.*

MOULT
Adults undergo complete moult January to March, when they become secretive. Juveniles replace body feathers at this time, but retain wing and tail feathers, primary coverts and outermost greater coverts.

VOICE
Song, usually delivered from elevated perch, is loud and clear with wide variety of separate phrases, each repeated several times. Occasionally mimics. Song period May to December, though heard occasionally in other months, especially in early January and in April. Alarm note sharp chip. *Also scolding chatter.*

DISTRIBUTION
The British Isles, Europe east across western Siberia to north-western Lake Baikal; and Turkey east to Iran. Migrants reach north Africa. Introduced to Australia and New Zealand. Ranges to Lord Howe, Norfolk and Macquarie Islands; The Snares; the Kermadec, Chatham, Antipodes, Auckland and Campbell Islands.

RECOGNITION

Olive brown upper surface paler than female blackbird. Spotted breast and white belly. Rich yellowish buff underwing.

FIRST INTRODUCED IN THE 1860s, the song thrush is now one of the most common New Zealand birds, and is found from North Cape to Stewart Island, as well as on most outlying islands. It lives in gardens, orchards, hedgerows, plantations, scrubland and native forest from sea level to 1200 m in the North Island and to 1000 m in the South Island. However, unlike the blackbird, it is scarce in large tracts of forest. It is occasionally kept in aviaries.

It defends its territory from April onwards, usually by threat displays and singing, occasionally by vigorous fighting. The main period of laying is from August to December but, in the North Island, a few birds occasionally lay in May, June or July. The nest, built by the female alone, is similar to the blackbird's, but tends to be a little smaller with a deeper cup. It is easily distinguished by the smooth lining of rotten wood, mud or dung, mixed with saliva. The song thrush builds this nest in a shrub, tree or hedge, often only one to five metres from the ground. It usually takes seven to 13 days to build and sometimes the eggs are laid before the lining is properly dry. At other times there is a gap of four to seven days between completion of the nest and laying of the first egg.

The eggs, laid on successive days, usually number three or four and are blue with a few small black spots. Incubation is usually by the female alone and takes 12 or 13 days. The young are fed by both parents until they leave the nest about 14 days after hatching. Unsuccessful clutches are soon replaced, usually in a new nest. Up to three successful broods can probably be raised in a season.

The song thrush feeds on earthworms, snails, a wide variety of insects and, to a lesser extent, wild and cultivated fruits. Mostly, it takes its food from the ground. When hunting worms it hops or runs forward a metre or so then remains motionless; if it detects no prey it moves forward again. A worm is swiftly seized and tugged from the ground. Birds collecting food for their young often hold several worms in their bills while continuing to search for more. Song thrushes often carry garden snails to a special stone or other hard object against which they bash the snail until the shell breaks and the animal can be shaken free and swallowed.

The effectiveness of song thrushes in controlling snails and harmful insects has not been established, but people widely appreciate the birds for their singing and relative tameness. On the other hand, orchardists believe song thrushes are responsible for eating strawberries, raspberries, grapes, cherries, apples, boysenberries, pears, plums, currants, peaches and tomatoes.　　　　　　　　P.C.B.

Song thrush young can fly from the nest about 14 days after hatching.

Blackbird *Turdus merula merula* LINNAEUS,1758

The yellow bill and eye-ring are the only touches of colour on the male blackbird, which is otherwise all black.

THE UBIQUITOUS BLACKBIRD lives in plantations, gardens, orchards, scrub and native forest, usually close to cover, from sea level up to at least 1500 m. Abundant from North Cape to Stewart Island, it was unknown in New Zealand before the second half of the nineteenth century. In the 1860s and 1870s acclimatisation societies liberated birds on the three main islands, and by the late 1920s their range had extended to the Chatham, Auckland and Kermadec Islands. The blackbird also survives in captivity—in Europe, a caged bird lived 20 years.

The nest, normally built by the female alone, is a substantial cup-like structure of twigs, moss, dry grass and roots, firmly bound together with mud and humus and lined with dry grass and leaf skeletons. Early nests take eight days or more to build, but later in the season, nests can be completed within three days. It is usually well-hidden in a leafy tree, shrub or hedge, but occasionally birds nest on rock ledges or in sheds. Most nests are firmly held in a fork or on a substantial branch at a height of one to ten metres, rarely at ground level.

Eggs are laid from late August to late December, about a month later near Lake Rotoiti at 600 m. The clutch usually contains three or four elongate, ovoid eggs, bluish green or greenish brown and closely blotched with reddish brown. Incubation, usually by the female alone, begins before all eggs are laid and takes 13 or 14 days. Both parents feed the young which leave the nest about 14 days after hatching. Failed clutches are quickly replaced in new nests and at least two successful broods can be reared in a season. Occasionally the same nest is used twice. One bird built five nests, laid 21 eggs and reared one chick. In the following year it laid 22 eggs in six clutches and fledged six chicks, using one nest four times. Between 14 and 30 per cent of eggs survive to become fledged young. Important causes of nest failure in New Zealand are human disturbance and predation by rats and stoats.

Male blackbirds establish territories in April and defend them, by occasional fighting and more frequent threat displays and song, till December. Females often chase away other females and will occasionally fight them. Territorial behaviour is most intense just before nesting and declines when the eggs hatch. A common threat posture involves lowering the head, stretching out the neck, drooping the wings and erecting the rump feathers. The tail may be held high and fanned, or drooped to the ground and fanned. The bird approaches an antagonist with running or mincing steps, never by hopping. Occasionally a male picks up a twig in its bill and rushes at an opponent.

Territorial defence occasionally extends to a blackbird attacking its own image reflected from a surface such as a window or the chrome fitting of a car. Territorial defence breaks down after the breeding season and in summer groups of 20 or more blackbirds, mainly young, gather together to exploit locally abundant food. Blackbirds living in native forest are more wary and elusive than elsewhere, their numbers often underestimated.

The blackbird eats a wide variety of wild and cultivated fruits as well as many invertebrates. It feeds mainly on the ground, especially under the shade of bushes or on short grass with cover nearby, but also high in trees when fruit is ripening. Occasionally it hunts for marine organisms along the shoreline. In its search for insects, it flicks aside leaves and other debris with its bill. When hunting earthworms, it usually hops a short distance and then remains motionless. Worms, when found, are quickly seized, pulled from the ground and eaten. The bird then continues its advance with frequent pauses. Blackbirds sometimes rob song thrushes of worms they have caught.

Orchardists list blackbirds more frequently than any other species for damaging a wide variety of fruit, and their spreading of seeds from fleshy-fruited weeds such as blackberry, boxthorn, barberry and elderberry creates a minor nuisance on farmland. Although blackbirds eat harmful insects such as the grassgrub it is unlikely that they take enough to be an effective control.

Banding shows that blackbirds rarely range more than a few kilometres from where they hatch, but one is known to have moved 90 km.   P.C.B.

Silvereye *Zosterops lateralis lateralis* (LATHAM, 1801)

NATIVE

OTHER NAMES: *White-eye, waxeye, blightbird, tauhou.*

SIZE: *120 mm.*

DESCRIPTION

ADULT: *Crown, nape and rump green. Back grey. Ring of small white feathers around eye. Lesser, median and greater wing coverts green. Primary coverts dark grey edged with green. Primaries and secondaries very dark grey tinged green on outer edges. Tail feathers dark grey with outer edges green except for outermost feathers. Throat pale yellowish green. Breast grey. Belly white. Undertail coverts tinged yellowish green. Flanks rich reddish brown, paler in female. Iris variable,* grey-brown to brick red. Bill mainly very dark grey (sometimes nearly black), but lower mandible pale grey, dark at tip. Legs pale grey. In some birds whole of undersurface cream or very pale yellow. White and yellow birds also recorded.*

MOULT

Complete moult between late January and early May and partial moult during August and September.

VOICE

Flocking call cli cli cli *or plaintive* cree, *both uttered more quickly by birds in flight or about to fly. Grating or nasal* swang *when kingfisher, owl or cat approaches nest.* Swang di di di di di *when flushed from nest. Warbling song performed by male in spring and* autumn, usually from concealed site within tree or bush. Consists of sequence of rather subdued trills, warbles and slurs, not unlike blackbird's sub-song but usually including 1 or 2 of silvereye's call notes. Challenge song given by male, especially in spring and early summer, usually from conspicuous perch, consists of rapid, rather jerky succession of high-pitched notes. Whisper song, audible from only a few metres, consists of whispered trills given by both members of a sexually excited pair and is accompanied by displays involving tail spreading, wing fluttering, quivering and preening.*

DISTRIBUTION

Mainland Australia, Tasmania, Norfolk Island and Tahiti. Common throughout the North, South and Stewart Islands. Seems scarcer in Southland and on northern offshore islands. Occurs on The Snares; and the Kermadec, Chatham, Auckland and Campbell Islands. Straggles to Macquarie Island.*

SILVEREYES WERE NOTICED in New Zealand as early as 1832, but they did not arrive in large numbers until 1856. The Maori had never seen this bird before and gave it the name of tauhou, meaning stranger. From 1862, when some silvereyes remained in the North Island to breed, colonisation of New Zealand was rapid.

Silvereyes may have always lived in small numbers on the South Island, but it is more likely that the dramatic increase from 1856 onwards was due to an influx from Australia. Although a non-stop crossing of the Tasman Sea (a journey of at least 1500 km) is a remarkable feat for such a small bird, such flights are possible for a migratory species, especially if assisted by a westerly gale. The birds may also have been helped by resting on a passing ship.

Silvereyes now live almost anywhere from sea level to at least 1200 m if a few trees or bushes are present. They are common in orchards, gardens, pine plantations, scrub and native forest. Feeding flocks have been recorded in North Auckland mangrove swamps. Winter flocks often visit suburban gardens.

First year birds take their mates from the winter flocks. Once established, pairs sometimes stay together from one year to another. Mated birds roost close together and preen each other.

The main onset of nest building is in early October. Both sexes share the building of a very delicate, cup-shaped structure with an inside diameter of about five centimetres. It is usually slung between slender twigs and hangs freely below. Common nesting materials are moss, fine grass, rootlets, fibres, hairs (especially horse hair), wool and spider webs. Some nests include lichen, thistledown or an occasional feather or two. Most are about two metres from the ground among the outermost twigs of trees, shrubs and vines. The period between starting the nest and laying the first egg varies from three to 13 days.

Most eggs are laid between October and December. The eggs, usually three, are pale blue and without markings; they are laid one each day until the clutch is complete. Incubation begins after the laying of the second egg and is shared by both parents.

The eggs hatch after about 11 days. Both parents brood and feed the chicks and remove their faeces, some of which they swallow. The adults feed unfeathered young about every 12 minutes. Later, the parents leave the chicks uncovered except in strong sun or rain. All the young birds leave together, about 10 days after the last egg hatches. The family stays intact for a further two or three weeks. Between 47 and 60 days after laying, the female produces a second clutch.

Territorial and feeding behaviour

When the last brood has fledged, the birds stop defending their breeding territories. By April most birds have moulted and are foraging in flocks. A complex peck order between individuals exists within the winter flocks, with males dominating females. Aggressive behaviour involves wing fluttering, showing the white underwing coverts and brown flanks, and beak clattering. A ritualised gesture often occurs when individuals of the same flock feed, bathe or perch close together. The aggressor points its beak at its opponent's body, but without actually touching the feathers. When threats fail, the birds attack and peck vigorously.

During winter some Tasmanian birds migrate to the Australian mainland, even flying as far north as Brisbane. Evidence suggests that a northward migration may also occur in New Zealand.

Silvereyes feed on nectar, fruit and insects. At bird tables they take bread, fat, syrup and cooked meat. The tip of the silvereye's tongue has four fibrous parts which may be an adaptation to nectar feeding. The main sources of nectar in native forest near Wellington have been rewarewa, kie-kie and rata. When nectar supplies cease during autumn and winter the silvereyes move away, probably to suburban gardens where they feed heavily on nectar from winter-flowering shrubs. Caterpillars and spiders are the most frequently eaten invertebrates in the forest throughout the year. Fruit seeds have also been found in most droppings from January to August. Silvereyes also eat many cultivated fruits. They occasionally attack large insects such as katydids or stick insects. At the Chatham Islands, large numbers of silvereyes were seen feeding on sandhoppers along the shoreline.

The birds are a nuisance to home gardeners and orchardists when they peck ripening fruits, particularly soft-skinned varieties such as grapes and figs. Large flocks occur mainly in winter, however, when most fruits are already harvested and, in any event, silvereyes often feed from fruit already damaged by other birds. Many of the fruits eaten by silvereyes have small seeds which remain viable after passing through the bird. Some of these seeds are desirable native species, but others are troublesome weeds.

The name blightbird was bestowed on silvereyes when they first appeared in New Zealand, because they fed on woolly aphis which was then infesting apple trees. They have also cleared plants of green-fly and other pests.

Despite their small size and comparatively recent arrival in New Zealand, silvereyes were taken by the Maori for food. They erected two vertical poles about one and a half metres high, and across the tops of these fixed a horizontal stick. Below this they hung a cord, to which a few live birds were tied by their bills. The fluttering of the captives attracted other silvereyes which were struck down with a rod wielded by the fowler hidden in a light shelter below.   P.C.B.

After breeding, silvereyes forage in flocks with a complex hierarchy.

Stitchbird

Notiomystis cincta

(Du Bus,1839)

ENDEMIC

OTHER NAME: *Hihi.*

SIZE: *190 mm.*

DESCRIPTION

ADULT MALE: *Head, neck, upper back and upper breast black. Tuft of white feathers behind eye. Back olive brown. Upper wings and tail brown with olive brown outer webs. White wing-bar (base of secondaries and their coverts). Lesser wing coverts and thin upper margin of breast yellow. Underparts pale greyish brown with some pale yellow flecking. Underwings and tail dark with yellow-brown edges.*
ADULT FEMALE: *Olive brown above. Pale grey-brown below with some streaking of dark and buff-yellow on breast. Faint white spot on side of head. White wing-bar as in male continuing to light yellow band on lesser wing coverts.*
JUVENILE: *Similar to adult female.*
NESTLING: *Yellow gape similar to bellbird and tui. Bill and legs dark grey-brown.*

MOULT

Adult males appear to moult in January (earlier than females) and become secretive at this time. Juveniles moult into adult plumage in autumn.

VOICE

Common call was believed to bear a resemblance to the word 'stitch', hence its name. Stit-tch or a thin whistled tsee *used by both sexes as counter calls between neighbours or members of a pair. Adult male has an emphatic 3-note whistle and a low warbling song of up to 3 minutes duration. Song and whistle given most frequently in December and January. Juveniles keep up persistent* sit *call. Alarm call, similar to that of bellbird, given when mobbing predators and to attract other birds.*

The male stitchbird, a monogamous bird, chases and sings over its territory early in the breeding season.

THE STITCHBIRD EATS NECTAR throughout the year, mainly from the flowers of rata, puriri, pohutakawa, flax, fuchsia, kohekohe, rewarewa, and *Alseuosmia*. It also eats the soft berries of mahoe, most *Coprosmas, Pseudopanax, Myrsine* and many other fruits, especially in late summer and autumn when nectar-bearing flowers are less common. Small invertebrates are taken in considerable quantities, usually by gleaning branches and leaves. Like the bellbird, the male takes more nectar and fruit than the female, which eats more insects. This pattern varies seasonally. Like bellbirds and tui, stitchbirds are important pollinators and also spread seeds of small shrubby species.

On Little Barrier Island stitchbirds are found at all altitudes and in all forest types. They prefer a dense understorey, especially where flowering and fruiting plants are common, and forage in coastal flax when these are in flower.

The birds usually nest in holes in trees between two and 20 m from the ground. The female builds an open nest of sticks and rootlets lined with finer material, including tree fern scales and feathers. The same nest-site may be used year after year. Nesting is usually from October to January. The female lays about four white eggs and incubates them alone. She leaves the nest for short intervals, presumably to feed on nectar nearby. The male often visits the nest area and sings. Both sexes feed the nestlings, although at one late nest—possibly a second brood—only the female fed the nestlings. After leaving the nest, fledglings tend to remain together. They can feed themselves, but also frequently give begging calls to prompt feeding by the parents.

Observations suggest that stitchbirds are monogamous, and chasing and singing by males early in the breeding season may indicate territorial behaviour. They are generally thought to be more sedentary than other honeyeaters, though they may travel to local nectar or fruit sources, and are often found feeding in association with whiteheads, presumably taking insects too large for these smaller birds.

The Maori took stitchbirds for food until early European times and the feathers, especially those from the yellow upper breast margin, were treasured for making cloaks.

J.L.C.

RECOGNITION

Small bush bird of similar size to bellbird. Male has black head, white ear patch and yellow bar on breast. Both sexes have white wing-bar and upwardly tilted tail. Distinctive song and calls are often first sign of presence.

DISTRIBUTION

Large numbers on Little Barrier Island. Until early European settlement, common throughout the North Island and Great Barrier Island. By 1885 extremely rare on the mainland. Recently introduced to Hen, Cuvier and Kapiti Islands; breeding on Hen Islands.

Young stitchbirds of both sexes have similar colouring to the adult female.

Bellbird *Anthornis melanura* (SPARRMAN,1786)

THE BELLBIRD TAKES ITS NAME from the clear bell-like notes of its song. Soon after leaving the nest, the young bellbird learns to sing by copying the songs of its parents or those of neighbouring adults of the same sex. By the following breeding season it can sing perfectly.

Bellbirds are strictly monogamous and pairs remain together for several years. They court in winter when the male sings in front of the female. During this display the male holds its body almost vertical and hovers or flies slowly upwards making a loud whirring noise with its wings. After mating, the pair stay constantly together and often duet.

Each pair remains in its range, although there is considerable overlap of adjacent ranges. Birds sing and countersing to space themselves in relation to each other. They move outside their ranges to feed at concentrated nectar sources. At such food areas, bellbirds interact vigorously with much displaying, chasing and singing. There is usually a hierarchy, with males dominating females and residents dominating neighbours and non-residents. During the breeding season a resident female may dominate incoming males.

Bellbirds live in native forest, forest remnants and scrub, as well as exotic forest, orchards and gardens, especially where these are near native forest. This species is more common in mixed lowland forest than in beech forest.

The breeding season

They can breed at one year old. The onset of breeding varies with locality and weather, but is usually between September and early January. The nest is built mainly by the female, usually near a flowering tree and anywhere from ground level to 15 m high. It may be placed in any position, but typically it is well hidden in or below an entanglement of vine or creeper, or among the dead or growing fronds of a tree fern. It is loosely constructed of twigs and fern fibre and lined with moss, fine grass or, more often, feathers or wool.

The three or four eggs are laid at daily intervals. They vary from pink-white to deep pink and most are blotched and spotted with pink. Incubation is by the female only. The male sometimes feeds her, but she also regularly leaves the nest to feed. She may sing on the nest. Incubation and fledging both take about 14 days. The young are fed mostly by the female who also removes shell and faecal sacs. At some

nests the male may do almost as much as the female, whereas at others the male does little.

On leaving the nest, the young remain together and are fed by their parents for a further 10 to 14 days while they slowly learn to feed themselves. Nestlings and fledglings are fed invertebrates, especially insects and arachnids, as well as fruits and nectar. Re-nesting after loss of clutch or brood is common.

Bellbirds are tenacious defenders of their nests and the female physically attacks any intruder near her eggs or young. To distract a predator she falls to the ground and flaps away through the undergrowth. The male appears in response to his mate's alarm calls and sings near the nest. Males occasionally visit the nests of neighbouring pairs.

Bellbirds eat nectar from many native and introduced plants. They take soft berries during late summer and autumn, when nectar-bearing flowers are less common. They catch small invertebrates, especially insects and arachnids, in considerable quantities, most commonly by gleaning trunks, branches and leaves, but also by hawking. Female bellbirds take more insects and less nectar than males, probably because male bellbirds exclude females from many nectar sites. Except at concentrated nectar sources, feeding bellbirds are usually silent.

Bellbirds play an important part in the ecology of the forest as they pollinate many plants and also spread seeds, especially those of the smaller shrubs.

J.L.C. & M.E.D.

ENDEMIC
Three Kings Bellbird
A.m. obscura FALLA, 1948.
Bellbird
A.m. melanura (SPARRMAN, 1786).
Chatham Island Bellbird
A.m. melanocephala GRAY, 1843.

OTHER NAMES: *Korimako, makomako, mockie.*

SIZE: *200 mm.*

DESCRIPTION
ADULT MALE: *Predominantly olive green changing to yellowish on belly and sides of body. Parts of head, especially forehead, crown and sides, glossed with iridescent purple. Wing and tail quills brownish black. Line of yellow feathers near angle of closed wing. Undertail coverts pale yellow. Iris red. Slightly curved bill black. Legs grey-black; claws brown. Tongue brush-like. Ninth primary terminates in a spur.*
ADULT FEMALE: *Smaller than male, with duller olive-brown plumage. Narrow white stripe from gape passing below eye. Faint purple gloss on forehead and crown. Line of feathers near angle of each wing and undertail coverts pale yellow. Wing and tail quills brownish black. Iris brown. Bill, legs, claws and tongue as in male. During breeding season breast greyer because of wear from incubation. Ninth primary similar to male. Partial and full albinos of both sexes recorded.*
JUVENILE: *Similar to adult female but with more uniform grey-brown plumage. Juveniles lack the spur on the ninth primary.*
NESTLING: *Born naked but gradually covered with grey down. Bright yellow gape.*

MOULT
All ages moult during late summer and autumn when immatures assume adult plumage. In some areas, immatures may moult into a first year plumage that differs slightly from adults.

VOICE
Song varies with locality although basic pattern similar. Male sings with body feathers fluffed and neck outstretched. It has 3 distinct songs. Dawn song usually has 2 to 6 pure frequency bell-type notes, occasionally interspersed with quieter
notes. This is monotonously repeated, usually for 10 to 40 minutes, at any time of day, but especially at dawn and more often in breeding season. Adjacent males may sing in unison. Full song varies and includes bell-type notes as well as mixed frequency chonks, clonks, harsh jarrs and quiet notes. Males give long choruses where ranges overlap, especially at rich food sources. Part or all of full song given at any time of day and often used for countersinging between neighbours. Heard less often in breeding season. Quiet song used during vertical hovering display and audible only within 10 m. Female sings relatively pure frequency song of 7 to 15 notes, prefixed by several 'titters'. Females countersing against each other and duet with their mates. Also, staccato call when alarmed and when mobbing predators such as the morepork; this serves to attract other birds. Occasionally alarm call given while feeding, especially during heavy rain, and often heard at dusk, perhaps to bring pairs together for roosting. Nestlings and fledglings utter relatively high-frequency begging calls, usually when parents nearby.*

DISTRIBUTION
Three Kings bellbird: *Most common bird on the Three Kings Islands.*

Bellbird: *In the North Island, common in larger forested areas from Raglan, Coromandel and East Cape southwards. Common throughout the South Island, Stewart Island, most off-lying islands and the Auckland Islands. Migrates to lower altitudes during winter, especially in the South Island. Local moves made to abundant nectar and fruit supplies. Males move more than females.*

Chatham Island bellbird: *Probably extinct.*

RECOGNITION
Vigorous movements; slender proportions, with a distinctively arched bill and shallow fork in tail. Located by characteristic bell-like song. Flight often noisy.

Young male bellbirds learn their distinctive bell-like song from nearby adult birds. Neighbouring males will often sing in near perfect unison.

Tui *Prosthemadera novaeseelandiae* (Gmelin, 1788)

ENDEMIC
Tui
P.n. novaeseelandiae
(Gmelin, 1788).
Chatham Island Tui
P.n. chathamensis Hartet, 1928.

OTHER NAME: *Parson bird.*

SIZE: *300 mm.*

DESCRIPTION
ADULT: *Sexes alike, with female slightly smaller. Mainly iridescent green with dark bluish purple reflections, appearing black at a distance. Back and sides of neck ornamented with white-shafted filamentous feathers which curl forwards on sides of neck. Back and wing coverts brown with bronze reflections. White wing-bar. White double throat tuft of curled feathers. Belly and sides reddish brown. Iris dark brown. Curved bill, legs and feet black. Partial and full albinos recorded. Eighth primary slotted, presumably for production of wing noise. Slotting more pronounced in males than females.*
IMMATURE: *Slaty black, except wing and tail quills which have metallic green outer webs. Greyish patch on throat and neck. White wing-bar. White throat tuft from about 6 weeks. Lacks wing slots.*
FLEDGLING: *Similar to immature but with more grey around neck and eye and bright yellow gape.*

MOULT
After breeding during late summer and autumn.

VOICE
Song varies with locality and season but typically contains relatively pure frequency bell-like notes; harsher clonks, rattles, wheezes, chuckles and clicks; and quiet squeaks. Covers wide frequency range, with higher-frequency notes inaudible to human ears. Often confused with bellbird. Both male and female sing, but male more vociferous. Mimics many noises, from human speech, whistles and pig squeals to other birds. Alarm calls extremely guttural and include beak clicking. Chicks and fledglings give high-frequency begging calls.

DISTRIBUTION
Tui: *The 3 main islands; the*

The tui's voice has greater range and variability than the bellbird's, which it can mimic perfectly. The two birds' songs are often confused, but in parts of the tui's range where bellbirds are not present bell-like notes are rare.

Auckland, Kermadec and most offshore islands.

Chatham Island tui: *The Chatham Islands.*

RECOGNITION
Curved black bill and dark plumage contrast with white of throat patch, neck frill and wing-bar. Flight is rapid, often noisy and undulating, with white wing-bar apparent. Performs aerial acrobatics, often plunging down from a height with closed wings.

THE TUI IS RENOWNED for its variable songs. It sings from high in trees, where it perches with its body feathers fluffed and its tongue partly extended. It is the first bird to sing in the morning and the last to finish at night, beginning before dawn and not stopping until after dusk. On moonlit nights, it may continue singing.

Though fairly common in forests, it avoids pure beech forest. It also lives in suburban gardens and exotic vegetation, especially where these are next to native forest. The tui flies considerable distances to concentrated food sources. In some areas, such as offshore islands, it is present only for the breeding season. In other areas, such as suburban gardens, it feeds in greater numbers outside the breeding season.

Tuis appear to be monogamous, although there is one record of a male with two mates. Courtship involves chasing round and round the nest area after the male has fed the female. The pair also duet. Each pair remains in a territory defended by the male. He vigorously chases trespassers away with much beak-clicking and wing-rustling. Most territories have emergent trees around the border which the male uses as song posts. The male also makes near-vertical dives above its territory, with loud wing-rustling or whirring and singing. Such dives are also given in other areas and so may be personal advertisement displays rather than just territorial displays.

The birds usually nest in a fork or outer branch of the canopy or subcanopy, although they also nest nearer the ground in the crown of tree ferns, or even in shrubs. The nest is usually an open-weaved, bulky structure of twigs and sticks, with a sparse lining of leaves, tree fern scales and moss. The female builds most of the nest and

constructs several, usually close together, before laying in one.

Nesting starts as early as September but is more common from November to January. The usual clutch is three or four elliptical eggs that are white or pink, with reddish brown specks or blotches. Clutches of one and two eggs occur sometimes.

The female incubates while the male sings from nearby trees, performs aerial displays and infrequently feeds the female, who may sing from the nest. Incubation time is normally about 14 days and the nestlings are fed in the nest for about a further 11 days. Both parents usually feed the nestlings, although the female generally does most of the feeding, as well as cleaning the nest. On leaving the nest, the young remain together for a further 10 to 20 days while their parents feed them invertebrates, especially stick insects and arachnids, but also fruit and nectar.

Tuis strongly defend their nests against human intruders. The female flies and sings in tight circles. Landing near the intruder and uttering alarm calls, it clicks its beak at the same time and gives broken wing displays. The male also appears and sings from a nearby tree.

Some birds visit their territories throughout the year, but most leave after the young become independent. These birds then move (often considerable distances) to new food supplies as old ones are depleted. At communal feeding areas, such as kowhai or pohutukawa trees, hierarchies are common and one bird may defend a flowering tree or other food source against all other birds. Tuis tend to be extremely pugnacious and often chase all birds away from a food source. They persistently mob long-tailed cuckoos.

Feeding activities

The birds eat nectar, fruit and invertebrates, especially large insects such as cicadas and stick insects. They take invertebrates by gleaning leaves, branches and trunks, as well as by hawking. They feed in the canopy and subcanopy for much of the time. Nectar is the most common food in winter and early spring, but they eat both nectar and invertebrates during the breeding season and take fruit when this is readily available in autumn. Some birds commute long distances, even on a daily basis, in order to obtain nectar.

The Maori kept tuis in cages, taught them to talk, used their feathers to adorn cloaks, and took them for food. Like bellbirds, tuis play an important part in the ecology of the forest by pollinating plants and disseminating seeds. Nevertheless, their attraction to fruit brings the birds to gardens and orchards where they may cause minor damage. The tui can be attracted quite easily to artificial food sources such as sugar-water.
J.L.C., A.S. & M.E.D.

Red Wattle Bird *Anthochaera carunculata carunculata* (WHITE, 1790)

WITH ITS HEAD THROWN well back this aggressive bird utters a harsh call. In Australia it lives in open forest, woodland and urban parks and gardens, especially in winter. It feeds actively in tree foliage on a wide range of insects and their larvae and spiders. It eats nectar from eucalypts, banksias and a wide range of garden flowers including coral trees, fuchsias and snapdragons.   B.D.H.

VAGRANT

OTHER NAME: *Wattled honeyeater.*

SIZE: *340 mm.*

DESCRIPTION
ADULT: *Sexes look alike, female usually smaller with smaller wattles. Forehead and crown blackish brown. Rest of upper parts dark grey-brown, feathers with whitish shaft-streaks; whitish edges to feathers of wing and tail; broad white tip to tail. Triangular silver patch below eye broadening on to ear coverts and cheek. Small pinkish red wattle hangs behind each ear-patch. Chin brown. Underparts including underwing grey-brown, streaked white. Belly bright yellow. Iris red. Bill almost as long as head, slightly downcurved, black. Legs pinkish.*
JUVENILE: *Like adult but without wattles and silver cheek patches.*

MOULT
Not known.

VOICE
Variety of loud harsh calls uttered in all seasons. Abrupt kwock kwock kwock *in flight.*

DISTRIBUTION
Southwestern and southeastern Australia as far north as southern Queensland. Nomadic, and in places migratory. Common in suburban gardens. Two New Zealand records: one at Matakana, east coast of North Auckland, about 1865, and one in tall scrub at Rahotu, Taranaki, in 1882. One doubtful sight record at Motupiko, south of Nelson, in early 1930s.

The noisy and aggressive red wattle bird is one of the most common honeyeaters seen in suburban gardens across the southern part of mainland Australia.

Yellowhammers undergo seasonal changes in appearance which result from the gradual abrasion of their feather tips. This then exposes the underlying colours.

Yellowhammer *Emberiza citrinella caliginosa* CLANCEY,1940

INTRODUCED

OTHER NAME: *Yellow bunting.*

SIZE: *160 mm.*

DESCRIPTION
ADULT MALE: *Forehead, crown and nape yellow, streaked with dark brown, especially on nape. Lower neck and upper back yellowish brown. Rest of back and mantle brown, heavily streaked with black. Rump and upper tail coverts chestnut. Underparts yellow except for chestnut brown across breast, chestnut broader at sides. Sides of head yellow, streaked with blackish brown. Flanks pale brownish chestnut with elongated streaks of dark brown. Primaries and primary coverts dull black, with narrow greenish yellow leading edge. Secondaries similar except for inner ones which have broad brown edges along outer vanes. Greater wing coverts dull black with broad brown edges along outer vanes. Median coverts dull black with brown tips. Lesser wing coverts yellowish brown. Underwing dark grey except for yellow coverts and axillaries. Tail feathers brownish black, central pair browner with narrow pale edges and 2 outer pairs with conspicuous wedges of white on terminal part of inner vane. Iris brown. Bill pale horn with ridge dull black. Feet pale brown.*
ADULT FEMALE: *Like male except head and throat heavily streaked; breast pale yellow streaked with brown; and underparts paler.*
FIRST YEAR: *Male like adult female, but brighter yellow and breast and flanks chestnut rather than brown. Female like adult but hardly any yellow on crown; breast browner,*
and belly paler yellow.
JUVENILE: *Male like first-winter female but browner and more streaked; less chestnut on rump, pale yellow underparts; tips of median and greater coverts paler, divided by dark brown. Female greyer with even less yellow on crown and underparts.*
NESTLING: *Down smoky grey, fairly long and plentiful. Inside of mouth pink; flanges outside yellow.*

MOULT
Not yet studied in New Zealand, but probably complete moult February to April.

VOICE
Call note single tink *or, especially in winter flocks, more liquid* twitip. *Song consists of high-pitched* chitty, *repeated several times, followed by prolonged* swee. *Main song period October to February. Songs heard early and late in season usually lack final* swee. *Soft, tuneful warbling heard in May from birds in flocks.*

DISTRIBUTION
The British Isles, Europe and Asia from Siberia to Syria and Iraq. Introduced to New Zealand several times between 1862 and 1871. Now very common on farmland from North Cape to Southland, scarce in Fiordland and Stewart Island. Present on the Chatham and Kermadec Islands. Straggles to Lord Howe Island; The Snares; and Campbell Island.

RECOGNITION

Chestnut rump. Yellow head and underparts. Longish tail.

MANY FARMERS AND GARDENERS dislike yellowhammers because they eat newly sown seeds. The birds were particularly troublesome in the North Island around the turn of the century when pasture was being established. There was a price on yellowhammer heads and the birds were slaughtered as pests. County councils bought their eggs by the thousand. Such massacres have stopped and, although damage to newly sown crops is still reported from time to time, the losses are rarely serious. As well as seeds, yellowhammers eat insects, such as caterpillars, beetles, flies and spiders.

They are mainly birds of open country, especially farmland, but in winter are also found in city parks and gardens. They are common in sand dunes on the west coast of the North Island. The birds sometimes live in open areas in and around exotic pine forests and, more rarely, in subalpine scrub and tussock, to about 1600 m in the Southern Alps.

Yellowhammers usually lay between the third week of November and the first week of January. The nest is normally on or close to the ground in a clump of thick vegetation such as bracken, blackberry, thistles or tall grass. More rarely, nests are sited in trees, and two have been found in old thrushes' nests. The nest consists mostly of dry grass, but sometimes it includes rootlets, moss, hair, or feathers, especially in the lining.

The three or four eggs, laid a day apart, are pinkish white and marked all over with a fine scribbling of dark brown lines and some paler spots. Incubation, mainly by the female, takes about 13 days. Both parents share the feeding of the young. The fledglings leave the nest 12 or 13 days after hatching. Yellowhammers usually rear two broods each year.

They are territorial birds in the breeding season but gregarious in winter when flocks of up to a hundred or more are seen, especially where hay has been put out for stock. They mainly feed on the ground and hop when searching for food on bare ground or short pasture. The flight of the yellowhammer varies. Often it is undulating with momentary closing of the wings.

Courtship displays have not been studied in New Zealand. In Britain, the male chases the female early in the breeding season and, later, parades around the female with his crest raised, tail spread, and open bill pointing upwards. Injury feigning at the nest has been recorded occasionally in Britain.   P.C.B.

Cirl Bunting *Emberiza cirlus cirlus* LINNAEUS, 1766

THE CIRL BUNTING is the rarest of New Zealand's introduced song-birds. It lives mainly in farmland with hedgerows, or in scattered scrub on slopes up to 750 m. Sometimes it occurs in coastal scrub.

In Marlborough cirl buntings live in groups of from two to four, although one flock consisted of six males and five females. The male seems to remain near its territory throughout the year and, from August on, advertises its presence by singing frequently from conspicuous perches. Occasionally, rival males fight. First the two birds utter excited rattling calls then fly vertically to a height of about five metres, face to face and almost touching, then they drop away in different directions.

Cirl buntings are thought to lay from about November to February. They nest in bushes and small trees from one to three metres above the ground. The female builds a nest mainly of grass, lined with hair. Some nests appear to be built on the remains of other birds' nests such as those of greenfinches, song thrushes or blackbirds.

The two to four eggs are bluish or greenish, with blackish streaks and hairlines. The female incubates, and is fed on the nest by the male. The young hatch after about 12 days. Both parents feed the chicks which, in Britain, fledge after about another 12 days.

One New Zealand bird was observed feeding on barley grass seeds. Adults feed their young on caterpillars and moths. Cirl buntings sometimes feed with yellowhammers.　　　　　　　　　　　P.C.B.

INTRODUCED

OTHER NAMES: *None.*

SIZE: *160 mm.*

DESCRIPTION
ADULT MALE: *Forehead and crown dull olive green, strongly streaked with black; hind neck similar but with few or no streaks. Mantle and scapulars chestnut, fringed with greyish buff and streaked with black. Lower back and rump olive brown. Upper tail coverts olive brown with black shafts. Black line through eye and yellow streaks above and below eye. Chin and upper throat black, finely flecked with buff. Lower throat yellow. Breast dull olive green, fringed below with chestnut and tipped with buff, the chestnut area broad at side of breast but narrow across centre. Belly and undertail coverts pale yellow, the latter with dark shafts. Flanks buff with darker streaks. Primaries and outer secondaries brownish black, with narrow greenish yellow leading edges. Outer vanes of inner secondaries broadly margined and tipped with chestnut brown. Primary coverts like primaries. Greater coverts blackish brown, broadly edged with chestnut. Median coverts dull black, edged with buff. Lesser coverts greyish green; underwing dark grey shading into yellow along leading edge. Axillaries yellow. Tail feathers, blackish brown, narrowly edged with greyish brown, white wedges on inner vanes of 2 outermost pairs. Abrasion gradually intensifies colours. Iris brown. Upper mandible dark horn; lower bluish. Legs and feet reddish brown.*
ADULT FEMALE: *Upper surface as in male except crown and nape brown and more streaked; mantle mainly olive brown, streaked with black; and yellow eye streaks less conspicuous. Throat and breast yellowish buff with black streaks. Belly and undertail coverts pale yellow, the latter streaked brown. Wings and tail as in male except that edges of inner secondaries and greater coverts buff rather than chestnut. With abrasion, brown of crown and rump becomes greyish, and buff of breast greyish yellow.*
FIRST WINTER AND SUMMER: *Like adult bird.*
JUVENILE: *Like adult female, but feathers of upper surface broadly margined with buff and tips of wing coverts duller.*
NESTLING: *Long and plentiful grey-brown down. Inside of mouth pink, no spots. External flanges pale yellow.*

MOULT
Not yet studied in New Zealand, but probably complete moult February to April, and partial moult (limited to ear coverts and yellow feathers above and below eye) September to October.

VOICE
Call note in Britain is thin zit *or* sip, *sometimes run together in flight to form sibilant* sissi-sissi-sip. *Two other calls recorded in New Zealand: very high-pitched* see *when just perched; and quiet chatter between adults and flying young. Clicking or rattling song delivered, up to 9 times a minute, from tree or power line. Another song, heard much less often, is like that of a yellowhammer, but without the terminal* swee. *Main song period in Marlborough from October to April.*

DISTRIBUTION
From southern Britain south to northwest Africa, and through Yugoslavia and Greece to Turkey. Introduced to New Zealand in 1871. Eastern and southern parts of the North Island; also Farewell Spit; Nelson; the eastern coast from northern Marlborough to South Canterbury; the Mackenzie Country; and Central Otago.

RECOGNITION

Male has black chin, yellow throat and olive green breast. Female has strongly streaked breast. More compact build and olive brown rump distinguish it from the yellowhammer.

The male cirl bunting, distinguished by a chestnut mantle and strong white lines above and below the eye, contributes to the nestling's diet of insects.

Numerous over a wide range of habitats, but less common at higher altitudes, the colourful chaffinch rarely conflicts seriously with human interests.

Chaffinch *Fringilla coelebs gengleri* KLEINSCHMIDT,1909

INTRODUCED

OTHER NAMES: *None.*

SIZE: *150 mm.*

DESCRIPTION
ADULT MALE: *Forehead black. Crown, nape and side of neck slate blue. Mantle chestnut. Lower back and rump yellowish green. Upper tail coverts grey. Two central tail feathers dark grey, rest black with white wedges on 2 outer feathers on each side. Primaries and secondaries dull black. All but outer primaries and inner secondaries have white bases, narrow greenish yellow outer edges and broad white edges to inner webs. Primary coverts black. Greater wing coverts black with broad white tips. Median wing coverts white. Lesser wing coverts white, but some grey. Side of head, throat, breast and flanks rich pinkish brown, paler on lower breast and flanks. Centre of belly and undertail coverts white. Axillaries white. Underwing coverts greyish white. Iris brown. Bill lead blue with dark tip. Feet brown.*
ADULT FEMALE: *Forehead, crown, nape and mantle brown. Rump pale green. Tail and wings as in male. Underparts pale brown, darker on upper breast than belly. Bill and feet brown.*
FIRST WINTER: *Like adult.*
JUVENILE: *Like adult female but rump brownish green and underparts paler. Mantle of male tinged chestnut brown.*
NESTLING: *Down pale, smoke grey, long and plentiful. Inside of mouth carmine, but hard palate orange; no tongue-spots. External flanges white.*

MOULT
Not yet studied in New Zealand, but probably once a year after breeding. In Britain moult lasts about 70 days. Greyish or buff tips worn away during winter to reveal brighter colours

below. Juveniles moult about the same time as adults, replacing body feathers and wing coverts but not wing and tail quills or primary coverts.

VOICE
Call note metallic pink pink. *Flight note soft* tsip. *Plaintive* wheet *given by male in summer. Song is short and loud, consisting of several short notes followed by terminal flourish:* chip chip chip tell tell tell cherry-erry-erry tissi cheweeo *often repeated several times within a minute, usually from a tree or other elevated perch. Sings from July to January but songs early and late in season usually lack terminal flourish. In Britain, female occasionally sings simplified song during breeding season. Individual and local differences in song.*

DISTRUBUTION
Europe, north almost to tree limit, south to North Africa and Iran, east into Siberia and west to the Canaries, Azores, Madeira and Cape Verde Islands. Most northeastern birds winter in the southwest. Introduced to New Zealand on several occasions between 1862 and 1877. Now one of the commonest and most widely distributed birds throughout 3 main islands. Found on most inshore islands; The Snares, Auckland, Campbell and Chatham Islands.

RECOGNITION

Sparrow-sized bird with undulating flight. Conspicuous white shoulder patch and wing-bar, and white on outer tail feathers. Seen closely, male has rich pinkish brown breast. Characteristic *pink pink* call and loud rattling song.

When chaffinches breed in Britain, the male first establishes his territory and advertises his possession by singing vigorously. He is soon joined by a female and, as the pair court and select a nest-site, dominance switches from the male to the female. They mate over a period of about 10 days between the early stages of nest building and the onset of incubation. The male's courtship displays include short moth flights, headlong chases and a crouching lop-sided posture in which he presents himself side-on to the female with his wing raised to expose his brightly coloured flanks.

The female builds the nest and takes from three to 18 days to complete it; older birds tend to build more quickly than young ones, especially if they are replacing a nest which has been destroyed. The nest is a compact structure of moss and dry grass, sometimes with wool, fibres, rootlets and cobwebs. The outside is usually decorated with lichen and the deep cup is lined with hair or feathers. It is firmly supported, usually in a fork of a branch, but occasionally between the main stem and a side branch. Over half of nests are in manuka, matagouri, pines, willows or gorse. The height varies from a little under one metre to about 18 m from the ground.

In New Zealand chaffinches lay between mid-September and late January, mostly between October and December. Nests completed early in the season occasionally remain empty for up to four weeks before the first egg appears. The eggs are greyish blue—occasionally pink—with purplish blotches which often have darker spots within them. Normally three to five eggs are laid on separate days. The female incubates alone for about 11 to 15 days.

The clutch hatches within two days. The female broods the newly hatched chicks and also feeds them, sometimes with help from the male. The parents eat the faeces of the young during the first two or three days and carry them away after this. The chicks leave the nest between 10 and 16 days after hatching. Their behaviour after the fledging period has not been studied in New Zealand. In Britain, however, both parents continue feeding the young for about three weeks after the fledglings leave the nest. There, chaffinches rarely attempt a second brood, although they replace failed nests.

Territorial defence wanes after the young become independent and the birds become inconspicuous during the moult. If both parents survive until the following year, they probably pair again, although during the winter there is no obvious bond between them.

Feeding chaffinches move over the ground with short quick steps as they search for fallen seed. They frequently hawk for flying insects over streams. Surprisingly little is known about the diet of chaffinches in New Zealand, although they have been seen eating insects, fruit, seeds, aphids, white butterfly caterpillars and grain. They gather pine seeds from the ground and extract seeds from newly opened cones by pulling the seed wing until it comes away from the scales of the cone, with the seed still attached. They do not swallow the seeds whole but break the hard shell and grind the fleshy part of the seed. P.C.B.

CHAFFINCHES ARE EQUALLY AT HOME in city parks and gardens, farmland hedgerows and wood lots, orchards, scrublands, pine forests, and native bush from sea level to subalpine scrub. In winter, flocks are most commonly seen on stubble and short pasture, especially where hay has been fed to stock.

Greenfinch *Carduelis chloris chloris* (LINNAEUS,1758)

INTRODUCED

OTHER NAME: *Green linnet.*

SIZE: *150 mm.*

DESCRIPTION

ADULT MALE: *Head and back dull olive green. Rump brighter yellowish green. Primaries and secondaries brownish black, with leading edges of primaries bright yellow except near tips. Median wing coverts greenish yellow. Greater wing coverts grey. Tail slightly forked, central feathers brownish black, others bright yellow with broad blackish brown tips. Breast yellowish green shading into yellow on belly. Flanks olive grey. Underwing dark grey with bright yellow leading edge. Undertail mainly yellow with dark grey areas at centre and broadly across tip. Upper surface becomes greener and underparts yellower as abrasion of pale feather tips exposes brighter colours below. Iris brown. Bill brown above, pale horn below. Feet reddish brown.*

ADULT FEMALE: *Like male, but much browner and with much less yellow on wings and tail.*

FIRST WINTER: *Usually retains some juvenile outer greater wing coverts (with faded tips). Has less colour on large outer feather of alula and this feather also lacks grey tip present in adults.*

JUVENILE: *Predominantly streaky brown, even on rump, but outer edges of primaries and bases of outer tail feathers yellow (much more so in males than females).*

NESTLING: *Long, greyish white down. Inside of mouth deep pink, no spots. Outside of gape yellowish white.*

MOULT

Not studied in detail in New Zealand, but probably adult has full moult after breeding. Juvenile undergoes partial moult at about same time. Subsequent abrasion of feather tips exposes underlying colours. In Britain, adults take about 12 weeks to replace feathers and moulting birds are in the population for about 25 weeks each year.

VOICE

Usual note, uttered chiefly on the wing, is rapid twitter chichichichichit. *Other notes are repeated* teu teu *and canary-like* tsooeet. *In spring and summer male utters persistent, drawn-out* tswee. *Song is variable elaboration of call notes* chichichichichit-teu-teu-teu-teu, *delivered from perch or during special display flight.*

DISTRIBUTION

Western Eurasia from about 65°N in Scandinavia and 60°N in Russia south to northwest Africa and Israel, and from Ireland east to the Urals and northern Iran. An isolated population in the highlands of Turkestan. Introduced to southeastern Australia, New Zealand and the Azores. Now widespread and numerous in New Zealand, especially on farmland, from North Cape to Stewart Island. Present on the Chatham Islands and Norfolk Island. Straggles to Campbell and Raoul Islands.

RECOGNITION

Predominantly green with bright yellow on wings and tail. Green rump of female distinguishes it from female or juvenile house sparrow.

FARMERS AND THE GREENFINCH have long been enemies. The birds eat fruit buds and ripening grain, although they seem rarely to cause serious damage nowadays.

Greenfinches studied in Hawke's Bay ate mainly seeds and a few insects such as weevils, but not enough to control pests. They sometimes fed sawfly larvae to nestlings. The most common seeds taken were maize, redroot, fodder radish, chickweed, storksbill, *Caprifoliaceae,* boxthorn, wild turnip and peas. The seeds of Scotch thistles and of *Pinus radiata* were major summer foods of greenfinches in coastal Manawatu. The birds pull apart small fruits such as rose hips, crab apples and cotoneaster berries to obtain the seeds inside.

Greenfinches prefer farmland, orchards and large gardens. They also live around the edges of pine plantations, in forest clearings, and other places where trees or tall shrubs occur close to farmland or seeding weeds. They tend to avoid high altitudes, treeless areas and unbroken stands of scrub and native forest. With other finches and house sparrows, they frequent cereal crops, stubble, weedy patches and short pasture, particularly where hay has been spread. They also occur in sand dune vegetation and, especially in winter, in open areas near the high tide line of harbours and estuaries.

They are sociable birds, especially in winter. They often use a communal roost, feed in flocks and confine their territories to the immediate vicinity of their nests. Winter flocks are sometimes very large: in July 1976 over 10000 greenfinches were seen feeding on scattered linseed around a Dunedin seed processing factory.

The birds pair in early spring before the winter flocks break up. During the winter males dominate females, but once the birds form pairs, this is gradually reversed. During pair formation the male often threatens and chases his mate and uses a special 'sleeked wings-raised' posture. In a less aggressive display the male points his bill upwards and lowers his wings showing the yellow on his rump, wings and tail.

Greenfinches in New Zealand normally lay between the second week of October and the end of January. The nest is usually placed in a fork towards the top of a bush or small tree or near the extremity of a spreading branch from a larger tree, with an average height of about three metres. Most nests are in conifers, gorse and manuka. The nest is a slightly untidy structure of twigs, moss, wool, dry grass and rootlets, lined with soft material such as wool, feathers, fine roots, moss, hair or occasionally down from the catkins of willows or poplars.

In Europe the birds build in spates of 10 to 40 minutes during which several lots of material are brought and fixed, usually by the female. Each spate may be followed by hours or even days when nothing is added. The time taken to complete the nest varies from a few days to two weeks or more, early nests often taking longer to build than later ones. Completed nests may remain empty for up to three weeks at the start of the breeding season.

The four or five eggs, normally laid on successive days, are pale bluish white with scattered spots and blotches of brown, mostly at the larger end. The female incubates alone and the male feeds her on the nest. This probably takes place for 12 or 13 days, but precise incubation periods have not been recorded in New Zealand.

The young are fed by both parents and receive the food, mostly seeds, by regurgitation. Nine-day-old chicks in one nest were fed once every half hour. Scanty New Zealand records indicate a nestling period of 13 or 14 days but in Europe the young usually leave the nest on the 14th or 15th day.

Most banded birds have been recovered near where they were banded, but one was recovered up to 380 km away across Cook Strait. In Europe, greenfinches have been recovered 12 years six months after banding. Greenfinches are occasionally kept in aviaries in New Zealand.   P.C.B.

A male greenfinch feeds its brooding young. Nestlings are fed by both parents on a diet consisting mostly of seeds.

Winged thistles and other weeds provide much of the goldfinch's diet of seeds, and down from the thistle is used by the bird to line its delicate nest.

Goldfinch *Carduelis carduelis britannica* (HARTERT, 1903)

WITH ITS BRIGHT PLUMAGE, and cheerful song, the goldfinch is a popular cage bird; in the wild, it is common in orchards and farmland. Large flocks gather on patches of seeding *Poa annua*, stands of seeding thistles, and other weeds. In the Auckland district, large winter flocks sometimes form on beds of *Salicornia* near the high tide mark in harbours and estuaries. They avoid large areas of forest and scrub.

The winter flocks usually number 50 to 500 birds, although flocks of 1000 to 2500 and even one of 15 000 have been recorded. Goldfinches roost together, and sometimes breed in loose colonies: in Hawke's Bay 10 nests were once counted in a clump of 30 fruit trees.

The bird moves between feeding places with a light and undulating flight. When feeding, it flutters lightly from one plant to another or hangs upside down as it extracts seeds from the heads of thistles or other tall weeds. It also feeds on short pasture. Sometimes a flock advances over the ground in a rolling fashion with birds continually fluttering over the flock from rear to front. A soft twittering comes from feeding flocks with occasional harsh notes and threat displays. Sometimes a bird reaches down with its bill to pull up a pendant birch or alder catkin. It then uses a foot to clamp the catkin against the branch on which it stands, leaving its bill free for pecking.

Goldfinches eat mainly weed seeds, but they occasionally catch small insects, especially for their young. Strawberry growers dislike goldfinches because they peck the seeds from the outside of the ripening fruit, which allows fungi to infect the berries.

They pair in early September shortly before the winter flocks break up. Courting males expand their wings to display their yellow patches. Most clutches are started between mid-November and late January.

The nest, built by the female with the male accompanying her, is a delicate cup of fine twigs, grasses, moss, wool and spider webs. The inside of the cup, which measures about 60 mm in diameter and 30 mm deep, is lined with thistledown or other soft material. It is usually placed in a fork of slender branches towards the outside or top of a tree about two or three metres from the ground. Goldfinches nest in a wide variety of trees, but particularly peach trees.

The three to six eggs are bluish white with reddish brown spots, especially at the larger end. With rare exceptions, the female lays one per day, usually early in the morning. She incubates alone for about 13 days, beginning after the second egg has been laid. The male feeds her on the nest by regurgitation.

The eggs normally hatch within less than 24 hours of each other. Females disturbed as the eggs are hatching may attempt to distract intruders by fluttering over the ground as though with a broken wing. The female broods the young almost continuously for the first few days, but rarely after the eighth day. At first the male feeds only the female which in turn feeds the young, but later the male feeds the

young himself. The parents carry away or swallow the faeces of small young, but faeces of older chicks are left to accumulate around the rim of the nest. The young remain in the nest for about 14 days, increasing their weight at hatching by almost 12 g. After leaving the nest their parents feed them for a further two or three weeks.

The long breeding period allows time for two or even three broods to be reared in a season and most goldfinches in New Zealand probably attempt at least two broods. In Europe, banded goldfinches have lived at least eight years.

P.C.B.

INTRODUCED

OTHER NAME: *Goldie.*

SIZE: *120 mm.*

DESCRIPTION

ADULT: *Sexes alike. Line round base of bill black. Conspicuous bright red mask covers forehead, front of crown, cheeks, chin and upper throat. Side of head behind eye white. Centre of crown black, extending onto nape and down side of neck behind white area. Back brown, paler on rump. Outer primary black. Remaining primaries and secondaries black towards outer edges with white tips and bright golden yellow towards centre on leading edges and white towards centre on trailing edges. Lesser and median wing coverts and primary coverts black. Greater wing coverts yellow forming, with yellow on primaries and secondaries, very large and conspicuous golden yellow wing-bar. Tail feathers mainly black, 2 outer ones with conspicuous subterminal white patches, and the rest with white tips. Throat, belly, undertail coverts, underwing coverts and axillaries white. Breast and flanks brown. Iris dark brown. Bill pinkish white at base, black at tip. Feet reddish brown. Partial albino recorded.*
JUVENILE: *Like adult except body plumage streaky and head greyish buff.*
NESTLING: *Down darkish grey, medium length. Tongue and floor of mouth crimson; roof of mouth dark lilac. Outside of flanges cream.*

MOULT
Not yet studied in New Zealand, but probably has complete moult after breeding. In Britain moult takes about 11 weeks. Subsequent changes in plumage due to abrasion: back of head becomes browner; mantle greyer; underparts whiter; and white tips of wing and tail feathers gradually wear off. Juvenile moults at about the same time as adult and replaces body feathers, wing coverts and innermost secondaries. Goldfinches hatched early in season in Europe occasionally replace all feathers.

VOICE
Call note is constantly uttered tswitt-witt-witt. *Aggressive note a grating* geez. *Song is pleasing liquid twittering elaboration of call notes, usually from tree or on wing. Song period October to January.*

DISTRIBUTION
The British Isles, Europe, northwestern Africa and western Asia. Introduced to mainland Australia, Tasmania, New Zealand, Argentina and Bermuda.

RECOGNITION

Small, brightly coloured finch easily recognised by conspicuous bar of bright golden yellow across upper wing and, except in juveniles, by bright red facial mask and black crown, with white on side of head and neck.

Redpoll *Carduelis flammea cabaret* (MULLER,1776)

INTRODUCED

OTHER NAME: *Lesser redpoll.*

SIZE: *120 mm.*

DESCRIPTION

ADULT MALE: *Narrow blackish area above bill. Rest of forehead and crown dark red. Rump pink. Rest of upper surface brown with darker streaks, paler on lower back. Greater and median wing coverts have broad buff tips which make indistinct pale wing-bars. Primaries and tail feathers dark brown. Secondaries brown, narrowly edged with pale buff. Chin black. Throat, cheeks and breast pinkish red. Belly, flanks, undertail coverts and underwing coverts greyish white. Intensity and extent of pink on rump and underparts varies. With wear, upper parts become less tawny and more streaked with greyish white, and pink on rump and breast becomes brighter and more extensive. Iris dark brown. Bill dark brown with sides yellow. Feet brown.*
ADULT FEMALE: *Like male but red duller and confined to forehead; and black chin often more extensive.*
JUVENILE: *Like adult female but without red crown and black chin; and with more dark streaks on throat and breast. Red crown appears after autumn moult and male develops trace of pink on rump.*
NESTLING: *Down darkish grey and fairly long. Inside of mouth red, with 2 small pale spots on palate. Outside, gape flanges yellow with extreme base red.*

MOULT

Not studied in New Zealand but British birds have complete moult March to April. Plumage redder in summer as edges and tips of feathers wear. Juvenile replaces body feathers and wing coverts in February and March. Moult takes about 8 weeks.

VOICE

Flight call metallic twitter chich-ich-ich-ich. Alarm call plaintive tsooeet. Song short rippling trill, often preceded by flight call, and given either in flight or from perch.

DISTRIBUTION

The British Isles, Europe, Asia and America. Introduced to New Zealand several times between 1862 and 1875. Now occurs from North Cape to Stewart Island. Common in higher altitude central and southern parts of the North Island, but more frequent in the South Island. Ranges to Lord Howe, Raoul and Macquarie Islands; The Snares; and the Antipodes, Chatham, Auckland and Campbell Islands.

RECOGNITION

Small, predominantly brown and rather shy. Relatively common on hill country farms and scrublands; occasionally in suburban gardens and orchards. Pink breast of male unmistakable when seen closely in good light, but red crown of female easily overlooked. When disturbed, usually takes to the air and often circles high overhead, calling.

TO FRUIT GROWERS redpolls are a pest. The birds destroy the buds of apricots and peaches, and peck the seeds from ripening strawberries. In Central Otago damage to apricot buds begins in spring as the buds swell. The birds alight on branches and move along them, systematically pecking every bud. They peck off all or part of the bud's protective sheath, often damaging or removing the ovary, but eat very little of the blossom. This pecking behaviour is not understood as the bird's main food in orchards is weed seeds. They also remove seeds from ripening strawberries. This results in minute holes through which bacteria or fungi enter and decay the berries.

Redpolls are sociable birds and in winter feed together in flocks of up to 250. Even in the breeding season several adults may feed together away from the immediate area of their nests. They also roost communally in winter. In Britain the roost changes as one feeding area is exhausted and the birds move to a richer one. In New Zealand, many redpolls wintering in the high country of Central Otago apparently become short of food early in September and descend to orchards and other cultivated land on the valley floors.

They are generally more common in higher altitudes up to 1500 m. They inhabit coastal sand dunes, hill country scrub, pine plantations, forest edges and subalpine scrub.

In New Zealand redpolls eat seeds, including those of rushes, grasses, dock, fat hen and thistle, as well as gall-forming insects on willow leaves, aphids and the buds of fruit trees. Like other cardueline finches, they feed their young on seeds.

Pair formation begins in late winter while the birds are still in flocks. Several pairs may nest in close proximity, with each pair defending a small territory around its nest. Nests for second broods may be far from those in which first broods are reared. Most nests with eggs have been found between 1 November and 15 January.

The nest, normally built by the female, but with the male in attendance, is small and compact. It is made of grass, twigs, wool, moss and rootlets, and is often lined with feathers, sometimes with fluff from willow or poplar catkins and occasionally with wool or hair. The nest is often in small bushes such as gorse, matagouri or lupin, but may also be in taller trees such as willows. It is usually about two metres from the ground in a fork, sometimes close to the trunk, but often on the outer branches.

The three to six eggs are laid on successive days, usually in the morning. They are bluish green, spotted and blotched with pale purple-brown, with a few spots and streaks of dark reddish brown. The female begins incubating when the clutch is complete, or nearly so. This takes about 11 days and the male feeds her on the nest. Both sexes feed the chicks which remain in the nest for 12 to 15 days. The parents continue to feed the young for a week or so after they leave the nest.

Redpolls live up to eight years. They are sometimes kept in aviaries in New Zealand but lose their red colour after the first moult.   P.C.B.

The red of some redpolls may vary from orange with scattered yellow feathers to a bluish red which is almost purple.

House Sparrow

Passer domesticus domesticus (LINNAEUS,1758)

The abundant house sparrow is possibly New Zealand's greatest bird nuisance.

INTRODUCED

OTHER NAMES: *Spadger, English sparrow.*

SIZE: *140 mm.*

DESCRIPTION
ADULT MALE: *In winter, forehead, crown and nape uniform dark grey. Mantle rich reddish brown streaked with black, with feather tips brown on one side of shaft and black on the other. Rump greyish brown. Tail blackish brown. Conspicuous chestnut streak behind eye broadens on side of neck and forms band across upper back where, in fresh-plumaged birds, partly concealed by grey feather tips. Upper surface of wings predominantly reddish brown streaked with black, but median coverts broadly tipped with white, forming white wing-bar. Primaries and secondaries blackish brown with paler reddish brown outer edges, especially on secondaries. Lores and line under eye black with often a few white flecks above and behind eye. Ear coverts and side of neck greyish white. Chin, throat and upper breast black but, in freshly plumaged birds, black bib on upper breast partly hidden by greyish feather tips. Lower breast, flanks and undertail coverts dull grey. Belly greyish white. Axillaries white. Bill brown above, pinkish horn below, yellowish near gape. Feet pale reddish brown. In summer, abrasion of greyish edges of feathers increases size and distinctness of black bib on upper breast, and also of chestnut areas of upper back and sides of neck. Bill becomes jet black before breeding; some males have black bills in May; nearly all have them by September.*
ADULT FEMALE: *In winter, upper parts pale uniform brown, but mantle and wings streaked with black. Median coverts with buff tips which form inconspicuous pale wing-bar. Tail dark brown. Pale buff streak behind eye. Breast, flanks and undertail coverts dull grey. Throat and belly greyish white. Underwing grey. Bill brown above, pinkish horn below, gape yellowish. Feet brown. In summer, streaking of mantle slightly more conspicuous due to abrasion of feather tips; and little if any yellow remains on bills of breeding birds.*
Albino, more commonly partial

albino, buff and cinnamon-coloured birds of both sexes and males with chestnut in otherwise black bibs recorded.
FIRST WINTER: *Like adults.*
JUVENILE: *Like adult female, but mantle, wings and tail usually paler.*
NESTLING: *No down. External flanges of bill pale yellow.*

MOULT
Both adults and juveniles undergo full moult between January and mid-May, though replacement of last primaries may occasionally extend into June. Moult lasts approximately 80 days. During winter and spring pale tips of feathers wear to expose darker colours below.

VOICE
Series of garrulous chirps, becoming a chatter when several birds chase or roost. Five main sounds: loud chee-ip, cheep or chissip; hard rattling twitter when excited; less metallic twitter; teu teu, sometimes as alarm note; low husky chreek and chirreek, often as flight note.

DISTRIBUTION
Europe, North Africa and Asia to north of Japan, and southeast through Iran, Pakistan, India, Sri Lanka and Burma. Successfully introduced to North America, South America, Hawaii, New Caledonia, New Zealand, Australia, Java, islands in the Indian Ocean and southern Africa. Liberated in New Zealand in 1860s by acclimatisation societies. Now present on the 3 main islands. Abundant in agricultural areas and absent only from higher parts of main axial ranges and from dense forests lacking human habitations. Ranges to Norfolk Island, The Snares and the Chatham Islands. Recorded on Antipodes Island.

RECOGNITION
Chestnut shoulder bars and black breast patch make the male unmistakable. Female browner than hedgesparrow and also distinguished by pale eye-stripe, streaked mantle, generally heavy build and relatively massive bill.

HOUSE SPARROWS WERE BROUGHT to New Zealand to help control the insects that were devastating the crops of early colonists. However, the birds increased rapidly and caused so much damage to the crops they were supposed to protect that a Small Birds Nuisance Act was passed in 1882, only 15 years after the first liberations. In 1908 the Injurious Birds Act allowed the wholesale destruction of the birds and their eggs. Despite bounties on the heads of house sparrows, the species not only survived, but thrived, and today is considered New Zealand's most troublesome bird. By far the most serious damage is to cereal crops. In Hawke's Bay in 1970 house sparrows removed, on average, five per cent of the grain from standing crops of wheat and barley. In some crops the loss rose as high as 20 per cent. The sparrows also take seeds at sowing time and nip the shoots from seedling peas, lettuce and beet. Damage to fruit occurs, but to a much lesser extent. The birds nip buds and blossom from apricots, peaches, apples and nectarines, and eat grapes, cherries, peaches and strawberries.

House sparrows contaminate human food in factories, warehouses and cafeterias; foul seats and footpaths under communal roosts in parks; block ventilators with nesting material; and drop faeces and nesting material on goods stored in warehouses. The birds also share the food of poultry and other domestic animals, and fly from one farm to another, becoming potential spreaders of parasites and diseases. It is not surprising that sparrows continue to be trapped and poisoned in substantial numbers.

The birds occur around human habitations throughout New Zealand, and are especially abundant in towns and in grain-growing and pig and poultry-raising areas. Some birds live away from man, for instance in coastal sand dune country, and small numbers are found on a few off-lying islands.

Provided they can acquire a suitable nest-site, house sparrows usually begin breeding when about a year old. Laying begins in September and ends in January. One pair raises three broods each year, rarely four. Although they occasionally change mates between broods, and readily accept a new mate after the loss of an earlier one, the same individuals usually breed together in successive years.

The nest, built mainly by the male, is a bulky, domed structure with a side entrance. It consists mostly of dry grass lined with feathers or other soft material. The nest can take from two to nine days or more to build and is often finished long before laying begins. Nesting material is carried to nest-sites at almost any time of the year, particularly by males. House sparrows prefer to nest in a hole in a tree, building, cliff or creeper-covered wall. They readily occupy artificial nest boxes if they are fairly high from the ground. In warmer overseas climates they also nest in the tops of tall trees.

The eggs, usually three or four, are laid one a day in the early morning. They are ovoid and usually greyish white, spotted and streaked with brown. All the eggs of the same clutch tend to be similar (except that the last egg laid has fewer markings), but different clutches can vary quite markedly. Incubation starts with the second last egg and lasts from 10 to 15 days. It is shared by both sexes but the male lacks a brood pouch and only the female incubates at night. With rare exceptions, the eggs of a clutch hatch within two days of each other, often on the same day. The young, which are fed by both parents, leave the nest about 15 days after hatching.

Territorial and feeding behaviour

House sparrows are gregarious. They feed in flocks that vary in size from a dozen to several hundred birds and have communal roosts usually in dense trees or hedges, but occasionally in deciduous trees. They tend to return to favoured roosts in successive years and are not easily frightened from them. Territorial behaviour is largely confined to the immediate vicinity of the nest which both sexes defend against other sparrows. Even so, the birds often nest in groups close together in the same tree or hedge.

House sparrows have several well-marked displays. A threatening male faces its opponent with its bill slightly open. The striking plumage of its head and throat is further emphasised by rotating its wings to show the white wing-bars. Young begging for food, males trying to attract females to a nest-site and females inviting coition crouch with their necks drawn in and wings slightly drooped. A common form of sexual display involves several males vigorously and noisily chasing a female. This may occur at any time of the year, but is very much more frequent in spring, with a peak in September, just before breeding starts.

Although house sparrows feed mainly on the ground, they also take seeds from standing crops, and buds and young foliage from tall trees. In pursuit of human-produced food, they readily enter hospitals, cafeterias, food-processing factories, poultry runs, stables and piggeries to take such foods as bread, sugar and fat.

House sparrows collected in Hawke's Bay between January and June one year ate mainly wheat in summer and maize, redroot and matt amaranth in winter. Some of the grain was obtained from stubble rather than standing crops. Adults ate a few arthropods and these formed the bulk of the food given to young nestlings, but chicks older than 11 days were fed mainly peas and wheat.   P.C.B.

Starling

Sturnus vulgaris vulgaris LINNAEUS, 1758

INTRODUCED

OTHER NAMES: *None.*

SIZE: *210 mm.*

DESCRIPTION

ADULT MALE: *In autumn, whole plumage blackish with green and purple sheen, except for brownish underwing. Feathers of upper parts with buff tips, those of underparts with white tips. Iridescent purple on nape, mantle and upper breast. Elsewhere, sheen predominantly green, but bluish on flanks. Belly and undertail coverts dull black. Primaries blackish brown with narrow buff leading edge and, except for 2 outer primaries, faint subterminal spot; secondaries and coverts with wider buff edges enclosing iridescent green near edges and black at tips. Tail feathers blackish brown, narrowly edged with buff. Axillaries and underwing coverts brown, edged and tipped with pale buff. Feathers of throat and breast long, tapering and pointed. Bill brownish black. Legs and feet reddish brown. Iris dark brown. In spring, whole bird darker and more glossy, especially on crown and underparts. Bill becomes yellow, and mandible blue at base.*

ADULT FEMALE: *Like male but body feathers shorter, rather broader, not so sharply pointed and buff and white tips larger, making female more spotted than male. Iridescent colours not so brilliant. Iris brown, with yellow or orange outer ring. When bill yellow, base of lower mandible pale yellow or pinkish white.*

JUVENILE: *Upper parts uniform greyish brown. Chin and throat greyish white, flecked with brown. Breast and flanks brown. Belly brown, streaked greyish white. Primaries and secondaries brown with buff outer margins. Tail brown. Bill brownish black.*

FIRST AUTUMN: *Like adult but body feathers broader, less pointed, buff and white tips larger and rounder giving very spotted appearance.*

FIRST SPRING: *Spots wear off, but not so much as in adult; iridescent colours less bright. Secondaries and coverts have less sheen.*

NESTLING: *Down greyish white, fairly long and plentiful. Inside of mouth bright yellow, no spots; outside flanges pale lemon yellow.*

MOULT

Heavily spotted autumn plumage acquired after complete moult beginning late December or early January. Breeding plumage develops by gradual wearing of buff and white tips from feathers. Juvenile plumage completely moulted January to March.

VOICE

Song heard throughout the year, though less often and more subdued from late December to early March. Consists of medley of throaty warbling, clicking and gurgling notes, often incorporating imitations of other birds. Usually sings from a tree, building or other elevated perch, often near nest-site. Alarm calls short and sharp. Young have harsh call note. Roosting flocks twitter until dark or even later if near street lights.

DISTRIBUTION

The Azores, the British Isles and continental Europe from about 71°N in Norway (60°N in Russia) south to France (except along the Mediterranean), Italy and southeastern Europe, and east to the Urals. Migrates as far south as the Mediterranean, North Africa, Turkey and Iran. Introduced to North America, South Africa, Australia and New Zealand. Now common from North Cape to Stewart Island. Recorded from Lord Howe, Norfolk and Macquarie Islands; The Snares; and the Kermadec, Chatham, Auckland, Antipodes and Campbell Islands.

RECOGNITION

Compact black bird with pointed wings and short tail. Walks with quick jerky step.

Starlings can create a serious hazard to aircraft by flocking near runways.

ACCLIMATISATION SOCIETIES, doggedly determined to find a New Zealand home for the starling, released groups of from three to 85 birds in Auckland, Wellington, Nelson, Canterbury and Otago between 1862 and 1883, The starlings flourished and, once their populations had stabilised, the increase in numbers was astounding. According to one report, the starling population of Napier—just four recently released birds in 1875—increased with a presumed influx of birds from surrounding districts to hundreds of thousands by 1886. Starlings have been more successful than any other species in establishing themselves on outlying islands.

Mainly birds of open pasture, starlings are also common in city parks and gardens, in orchards, along roadsides, and on coastal cliffs. Sometimes they feed along sandy or rocky shores, in lupin scrub on sand dunes or in tall berry-bearing trees along forest margins. They tend to avoid tall grass and unbroken areas of scrub.

At the nest-site

Many females breed in their first year, although others wait until they are two or three years old. Males rarely breed until they are two or more years old, perhaps because they must acquire and successfully defend a suitable nest-site before being able to attract a mate. Pairs that have bred successfully in one year frequently breed together again in successive years. Starlings commonly visit their nest-sites each morning and evening throughout the year to maintain ownership.

In most parts of New Zealand the first eggs appear during the second or third week of October. In the same district nearly all the birds that are going to lay do so within a week of each other. Failed clutches are replaced and, in years when laying starts early, true second clutches are common and sometimes successful. Few if any eggs are laid after mid-December.

The nest is usually built in a hole in a tree, bank, cliff or man-made structure, but occasionally in a less stable site such as a large clump of pampas or a thick entanglement of twigs and needles in a pine tree. If space permits, the nest is a cup-shaped depression, often lined with feathers, fragments of paper or cellophane, in a bulky surround of dry grass, leaves, pine needles and moss. Small nest cavities may be almost devoid of nesting materials but large ones, such as chimneys, may be packed full. In cities nests are commonly responsible for blocking gutters and ventilator shafts. Starlings quite often carry material to their nests in autumn, late winter and early spring, but most nests are built about two weeks before laying. Starlings readily accept nest boxes.

The eggs vary in colour from pale blue to almost white but the shade tends to be uniform within a clutch. The clutch size varies from one to eight but four or five eggs are usual and three and six not uncommon. Larger clutches are often due to two females using the same nest. Incubation begins with the laying of the last egg and is shared by both birds during the day, but only the female incubates at night. The first egg usually hatches on the eleventh day after the clutch is complete; the others hatch over the following 24 hours.

At first the chicks are brooded almost continuously by either parent during the day, but only by the female at night. She ceases to brood them at night once they are from five to 10 days old. Both parents feed the chicks and, even after the young leave the nest at 18 to 24 days old, they are accompanied and often fed by one or other parent (usually the male) for a further five to seven days, or even longer towards the end of the breeding season.

At its nest-site the male often displays by singing while standing erect on its perch. It points its bill skywards and stiffly flaps its wings. Competition for nest-sites is often acute. Fighting and chasing, especially by males, is frequent.

When the first broods fledge the young gather in flocks of 20 to 50. After the breeding season the birds form larger flocks and roost communally. As winter approaches, smaller roosts are abandoned and the birds congregate at a few very large ones, often on small islands. Some races in Europe are strongly migratory, but there is no evidence of migration among starlings in New Zealand.

Starlings travel 15 to 30 km each morning and evening between feeding and roosting areas, and normally feed in flocks which, outside the breeding season, may contain several hundred or even a thousand or more birds. They usually gather food from the ground, often by probing, especially in short pastures or newly-cut stubble. They take fruit from trees and caterpillars from lupin scrub in coastal sand dunes. They also feed along roadsides, at the tide line, around piggeries and poultry runs and in suburban parks and gardens. They may hawk for flying insects but frequently take nectar from flax and pohutukawa.

Starlings break the shells of garden snails to obtain the food inside. The bird carries its snail to the nearby road where, with a sideways motion of the bill, the mollusc is vigorously 'wiped' on the road until the shell breaks. Starlings locate underground prey by thrusting their closed bills into the soil and then partly withdrawing and opening their bills to widen the hole, which is then examined for exposed prey. Starlings feed mainly on insects, earthworms and spiders, but also take small snails, millipedes, centipedes, seeds (including grain) and fruit. The diet of nestlings is similar to that of adults, except that small nestlings are fed with more soft-bodied foods.   P.C.B.

Indian Myna *Acridotheres tristis* (Linnaeus, 1766)

INDIAN MYNAS ARE MOST common by roadsides and around houses, where scavenging is at its easiest. The birds also live in large numbers around intensively cultivated smallholdings, piggeries, poultry runs and rubbish dumps; in remoter areas they are found near farm buildings, work camps and roadside picnic areas. The birds thrive and breed in captivity, but one colony established on the uninhabited Poor Knights Islands has also shown the myna's ability to survive well away from humans.

The birds feed mostly on the ground eating a wide variety of fruits and invertebrates. They take milk and mash at piggeries and poultry farms, and scraps at rubbish dumps. They seize earthworms, caterpillars and grubs turned up by ploughing. With partly open bills they probe into grass and leaf litter. On roads they eat insects killed by cars and scraps thrown out by motorists.

Many mynas pair when they are less than a year old and a few one-year-olds manage to breed. The majority, however, fail to rear any young in their first season and unsuccessful breeding by one-year-olds is often followed by a change of mates. Pairs that have bred successfully normally remain together for life and keep the same territory.

Laying usually begins during the first half of November and may continue into early March, though the breeding season varies from year to year. Two clutches are often laid—in November and January—and normally the same nest is used for both.

The nest is usually in a hole in a building, tree, or bank. Both sexes build a cup of dry grass, twigs and leaves lined with a few feathers and fragments of paper or plastic.

The eggs, commonly three or four, are greenish blue and elliptical. They are laid on successive days, usually early in the morning. The male assists with incubation, but only the female has a brood patch. She spends much more time on the nest than the male, and is always on it at night. The incubation period is 13 or 14 days and begins before the clutch is complete. After hatching the chicks are fed in the nest by both parents for about 25 days, and outside the nest for about three weeks after leaving it.

Except when incubating, mynas spend the night at large communal roosts, some of which are occupied all year round. Permanent roosts, often containing hundreds of mynas, are usually in close-growing trees and may be shared with large numbers of starlings or house sparrows. Outside the breeding season, birds that have held territories the previous year leave the roost in the morning and fly direct to their old territories which may be two or three kilometres away. Birds without territories often sit about in small flocks in the early morning

before dispersing to feed, and usually gather together again, often on roadsides, before returning to the roost.

As the breeding season approaches, mynas begin to defend their territories more vigorously, and frequently destroy the eggs or young of any starlings in the vicinity. Some mynas leave the winter roost at this time and establish small, temporary roosts nearer their territories.

Mynas are widely disliked because they eat fruit and poultry foods, block ventilators and downpipes with their nests, and carry fowl mites. There are also reports of mynas destroying the eggs or young of other species, such as blackbirds and welcome swallows, and driving away the adults. But there is no clear evidence that they seriously affect the numbers of these species, except perhaps very locally. Orchardists and market gardeners blame mynas for eating a wide range of cultivated fruits.

P.C.B.

INTRODUCED

OTHER NAMES: *Common myna, minah, mynah.*

SIZE: *240 mm.*

DESCRIPTION
ADULT: *Sexes alike, although female has brood patch when breeding. Forehead, crown, nape and side of head glossy black; feathers of crown and nape elongated and partly erectile. Neck, back, mantle and rump wine-brown. Lesser, median and greater wing coverts brown. Primary coverts white. Primaries blackish brown on outer half, white on inner half. Secondaries dark brown. Tail feathers blackish brown, with white tips sometimes lost by abrasion. Throat and upper breast black. Lower breast and flanks brown. Belly, undertail coverts and underwing coverts white. Conspicuous patch of bright yellow skin below and behind eye. Iris brownish with distinct white flecks. Bill and legs yellow.*
JUVENILE: *Like adult, except head dark bown; tail feathers lack white tips; and bill pale yellow, streaked with dark grey. Bare skin below eye whitish for first 2 weeks after*

leaving nest, and iris uniform grey, gradually changing to white-flecked brown iris of adult.
NESTLING: *Down grey. Inside of mouth paler than in starling nestling.*

MOULT
Both adults and juveniles undergo full moult during summer or early autumn; afterwards, juveniles indistinguishable from adults. Non-breeding birds begin moult in December; breeding birds start a month or more later.

VOICE
Described as 'rapid sequence of calls like ahCHOOkee ahCHOOkee ahCHOOkee . . .' and 'rowdy medley of notes, raucous, gurgling, chattering, even bell-like, in rapid sequence'. These calls help to maintain pair-bonds (pairs sometimes perform a duet), proclaim territory, and effect social integration at communal roosts. Although birds call at any time of day, there is usually 5 to 15 minutes of intense calling when birds first arrive in their territories each morning. Often call from buildings or other elevated perches, but occasionally from the ground. Males call twice as much as females. Much noisy chattering at communal roosts, night and morning.

DISTRIBUTION
Afghanistan, Baluchistan, southern Russian Turkestan, Pakistan, India, Bangladesh, the Andaman Islands, Burma and Malaysia. Successfully introduced to New Zealand, Australia, South Africa and many Pacific islands including Hawaii, New Caledonia, Fiji and the Solomon Islands. Introduced to the South Island of New Zealand in 1870 but extinct there before the turn of the century. Introduced to the North Island in 1875. Now present north of a line from Wanganui to Waipukurau; a few pockets also persist in Wairarapa and odd birds recorded from the Hutt Valley. Especially abundant in central Hawke's Bay, Taupo, Bay of Plenty, Waikato, Auckland and North Auckland. Occasional records from the South Island, possibly escaped cage birds.

RECOGNITION
Little larger than a starling and easily distinguished by its generally brown colour with darker head and, in flight, conspicuous white wing patches. Patch of yellow skin near eye noticeable at close quarters. Purposeful starling-like walk. Frequently feeds on or beside roads. Fearless of cars and adept at avoiding them.

Early releases of the Indian myna in New Zealand were of birds imported from Australia in groups of up to 200.

Saddleback *Philesturnus carunculatus* (Gmelin, 1789)

ENDEMIC
North Island Saddleback
P.c. rufusater (LESSON, 1828).
South Island Saddleback
P.c. carunculatus (GMELIN, 1789).

OTHER NAME: *Tieke.*

SIZE: *250 mm.*

DESCRIPTION
ADULT: *Sexes alike, except female slightly smaller and usually with smaller wattles. Glossy black. Back to upper tail coverts, scapulars and wing coverts form bright chestnut saddle edged at front with narrow gold band. Undertail coverts bright chestnut. Iris dark brown. Bill and feet black. Orange fleshy wattles grow from soft skin in gape. Nostrils have covering flap of black skin. In South Island saddleback no gold band at front of saddle and wattles smaller.*
JUVENILE: *Saddle duller and lacks gold band. Rest of body dull black with brownish tinge. Wattles very small. South Island saddleback uniform chocolate brown.*

MOULT
Not known.

VOICE
Chatter song consists of long initial note followed by 3 to 20 short, rapidly delivered notes. Given by both sexes, very frequently by female. Rather lengthy version often heard at roosting time. Male also has repertoire of 1 to 4 rhythmical songs, each consisting of a phrase repeated 4 to 8 times. Very frequently this is prefaced by 2 high-pitched zeet *notes. On Cuvier Island, each song type was sung by a small group of neighbouring males. Where 2 song groups overlapped the individual birds had a 2-song repertoire and so on up to a maximum of 4 songs. Each song group centred around an original male coloniser of the island. Young males do not inherit song patterns but learn them from territorial neighbours where they settle to breed. Some new territory holders make small errors in learning their neighbour's songs and some of these are subsequently copied accurately by later settlers. In this way the dialect song types often split into 2. Both sexes have between 4 and 6 quiet songs, mostly melodious and flute-like, but sometimes harsh and vibratory. Quiet songs are constantly interchanged between birds of a pair.*

DISTRIBUTION
North Island saddleback: *Hen, Middle Chicken, Cuvier, Red Mercury, Kapiti, Stanley and Lady Alice Islands. Possibly Fanal and Cavalli Islands.*

South Island saddleback: *Confined to a few islands off Stewart Island.*

RECOGNITION

Glossy black bird with bright chestnut saddle and orange wattles.

THE SADDLEBACK CONSTANTLY forages for insects throughout the forest from the ground to the top of the canopy. On the forest floor it turns over litter and digs into rotting logs; on large trunks and branches it prises off bark; in the canopy it pecks open dead wood and searches leaves for caterpillars. Favourite foods at all levels are wetas and boring beetle grubs. It eats the fruits of coprosmas, five-fingers and especially kawakawas, whenever they are available.

The saddleback holds large items of food, such as wetas, against a branch with one foot and pulls them apart with its strong, pointed beak. Like starlings and mynas it has a jaw hinge mechanism which allows its bill to be opened with much greater force than is usual in birds of this size. It uses this adaptation to prise off pieces of bark, split dead sticks, and separate leaves by inserting its bill into small crevices and then forcefully opening the mandibles. The flap of skin partially roofing its nostrils is thought to prevent powdered dead wood from falling into them.

It is such a noisy and vigorous feeder that it attracts fantails which fly very close below it to catch the dislodged insects. In winter, especially, each saddleback is accompanied almost constantly by a fantail.

The saddleback was once widespread in the North and South Islands. Towards the end of the last century it declined rapidly, surviving only on Hen Island and a few islands off Stewart Island. Since 1964, North Island saddlebacks have been transferred successfully to Middle Chicken, Cuvier, Red Mercury, Lady Alice and Kapiti Islands. It is a bird of forest, thick scrub, and regenerating forest. It seldom flies above the canopy and travels around the edges of clearings rather than across them.

Juvenile saddlebacks are usually solitary and mobile after the break-up of families in the autumn, but they pair and establish a territory if there is space in the habitat. Once the pair-bond is formed they usually stay together for life. After breeding

in a territory they remain there permanently.

Border skirmishes and fighting are rare in a stable set of territories. Birds proclaim their territories almost exlusively by song. However, if one bird dies the rest display aggressively as they rearrange pairs and territorial boundaries.

In one display, the bird points its bill at the ground, presents its saddle to its opponent, fans its tail out wide and calls a melodious flute-like warble. In another the two birds fence with their bills, causing their inflated wattles to wobble in front of their opponent's eyes. At rare intervals when two, three, or four pairs meet there is much excited bowing, fanning, and warbling intermixed with rapid running along branches and courtship feeding. At the same time the birds make piping calls.

Courtship feeding occurs between members of a pair throughout the year. The male utters a characteristic note causing the female to approach and receive food. The male invites the female to a nest hole by holding his wings arched high above his back. He prances along the branch towards the hole and back to the female with a chip of bark in his bill.

Each night the pair separate and roost in separate holes. Before roosting the birds utter a chatter song which seems to be infectious. A similar song precedes the formation of the pair in the morning. Juveniles sometimes roost in thick ground cover and occasionally adults roost in kiekie clumps.

The nest is a loosely woven structure of fibrous matter placed in a tree hole. The underbark of the whau tree is a favourite material. Saddlebacks lay two eggs, rarely three, and usually rear only one brood each year. The eggs of the North Island saddleback are very pale brown and blotched all over with brown and pale brown, especially at the larger end. The eggs of the South Island subspecies are ovoid and pale grey with dark and pale brown blotches all over, mostly at the larger end. Both male and female incubate and rear the chicks. Most broods seen being fed in the field contained one or two fledglings. P.F.J.

At their loosely woven tree-hole nest, both male and female North Island saddlebacks share incubation of the eggs.

Kokako
Callaeas cinerea
(Gmelin, 1788)

ENDEMIC
North Island Kokako
C.c. wilsoni (Bonaparte, 1851).
South Island Kokako
C.c. cinerea (Gmelin, 1788).

OTHER NAMES: *Blue wattled crow, blue gill, orange wattled crow, organ-bird.*

SIZE: *380 mm.*

DESCRIPTION
ADULT: *Sexes similar, except male slightly larger. Body steel grey or blue-grey merging into olive-dun grey on wing coverts and rump. Black face mask from base of bill behind eye and across forehead. Wing and tail feathers dark grey with some olive shading. From edges of gape, fleshy wattles fold under base of bill, sometimes overlapping underneath, sky blue in North Island kokako, orange with blue bases in South Island kokako. Iris dark brown. Bill, legs and feet black.*
NESTLING: *Initially uniform dark grey. Black face mask develops about 2 weeks after hatching. Wattles form from 1 week and begin to change colour from fleshy pink to lilac at fledging.*

MOULT
Adults undergo post-nuptial moult in late summer or autumn. Tail and wing feathers replaced at same time as those of head and body.

VOICE
Rich flute-like song. Sings very loudly and for long periods, particularly in early morning. Full song consists of slow series of long melodic syllables, short clucks and buzzes. Pairs sing complex duet, often matched by songs of the same pattern from birds of adjacent areas. Song varies geographically. Pairs usually remain in close visual contact, so individuals may be silent for long periods. Contact calls, when given, include variety of quiet clucks, buzzes and a sound like the meow of a cat. Harsh alarm call by nestlings and adults.

DISTRIBUTION
North Island kokako: *Significant numbers in Puketi Forest; isolated records from Warawara Forest and the Tangihua and Tatumoe Ranges; small numbers in the Hunua Range and Coromandel Range; northern Great Barrier Island; the Kaimai-Mamaku plateau and southern Bay of Plenty, especially in the northern part of Mamaku State Forest; the northern parts of the Urewera forest; larger forest areas of the King Country, especially north Pureora and the western ranges; North Taranaki.*
South Island kokako: *Unconfirmed sightings from the Nelson area, near Havelock; the Tasman Mountains; the Paringa River; Mt Aspiring National Park; the Catlins area, southeast Otago; and Stewart Island.*

RECOGNITION
Could be confused with a tui at a distance, but considerably larger. Wattles characteristic though not always obvious. May eat noisily when picking fruit and leaves. Runs squirrel-like through the canopy or leaps upwards from branch to branch.

Small numbers of North Island kokako are found in isolated pockets, but sightings of the South Island bird are rare.

THE KOKAKO'S WEAK FLIGHT and largely vegetarian diet confine it to the forest. It prefers lowland and mountain forest because of their rich diversity of foods. In the north, kokakos live in kauri forest, but the largest numbers are thought to inhabit mixed stands of kauri, podocarp and hardwood. In the Rotorua and Taranaki areas most birds live in mixed broadleaf and tawa forest, while on the Volcanic Plateau most kokakos are found in podocarp-tawa forest. The South Island kokako probably used a range of habitats and was frequently found close to the ground. It was seen at the edges of the bush and in the open glades along wide rivers. It also inhabited open spaces with low scrub from sea level to over 1000 m above sea level.

A sedentary and mainly vegetarian bird such as the kokako needs foods from many sources and changes its diet as the seasons progress. In autumn, winter and spring its diet is mainly vegetarian, but in summer insects form more than half its diet, especially a scale insect *Ctenochiton viridis*. When they are available it eats mostly succulent fruits. In Pureora Forest it takes the berries of totara, miro, matai, kahikatea and rimu, as well as many of the fruiting hardwoods. In all areas at all times of the year, but particularly in spring between the period of winter fruit abundance and summer insect abundance, the kokako eats many leaves, especially those of epiphytes and lianas. It takes hanging spleenwort, hounds-tongue fern, filmy ferns, orchids and mosses, as well as the leaves of kaikomako, supplejack, putaputaweta, broadleaf and passion flower. It also eats the new growth and cones of podocarps.

The kokako feeds like a parrot, taking foliage or fruit to a perch. Holding the food in one claw it balances with one foot grasping the perch.

Breeding and future survival

The age of first breeding is not known, but may begin at two years. Most nests found contained eggs laid from early November until early December. Incubation takes 20 days and fledging a further 30 to 34 days. Kokako rear one clutch a season and do not always nest again if predators kill eggs or chicks. The clutch size is normally three, but nests containing one or two eggs have also been recorded. The eggs have a cream-coloured background with brown speckles.

The nest is a large structure, normally built in the cover of dense foliage, such as supplejack, lawyer or passion flower, in a medium-sized tree between three and 10 m in height. The base of the nest is of twigs and lengths of supplejack, beneath a cup of smaller twigs lined with a thick bed of moss. Its diameter is about half a metre, and the cup itself is about 15 cm across. As the chicks mature the sides of the cup tend to get flattened until, at fledging, the nest is often little more than a platform.

The female does all the incubation, leaving the nest for short periods to be fed by the male or to feed herself. The male also feeds her at the nest, visiting every half hour to hour. On hatching, the chicks are fed regularly about every 15 minutes by both adults. While young, they are fed leaf, berry and insect pulp and, as they develop, progress to whole fruit and insects. After fledging, juveniles normally stay with their parents for much of the following autumn.

The pair-bond is maintained through mutual preening and feeding and lasts all year round, probably for life. Occasionally the birds display before mating. The male dances around the female, arching his head, fanning his tail and wings and uttering bubbling sounds. While singing, the male often gives a similar display from a prominent perch, during which the sound of his wings flapping can be clearly heard.

Kokakos are territorial, though the establishment and maintenance of an area is through song and mutual avoidance. When boundary disputes occur the birds may chase back and forth across the boundary. Fighting is rare, although sometimes they fight with beaks and claws. Occasionally three or more pairs may interact in a boundary area.

There has been a large reduction in the range and abundance of the kokako since the arrival of Europeans. According to Maori tradition it was common in all suitable forests of the North Island and subfossil records tend to support this. The South Island kokako was found over a large area of the South, Stewart, Resolution and Stephens Islands. Now the South Island kokako is almost extinct. The North Island kokako remains in apparently healthy populations in some areas but is dwindling in others. Opossums threaten the kokako because the diets of the two species overlap greatly, and the reduction in range of kokako appears to mirror the increase in range of opossums. Introduced predators—stoats, weasels and rats—have reduced the breeding potential considerably, a three year study indicating an average production of only one fledgling between ten pairs over a year. Long-term survival depends on maintenance of sufficient habitat free of disturbance and the control of opossums.   J.R.H.

White-browed Wood-swallow *Artamus superciliosus* (GOULD,1837)

Only male white-browed wood-swallows have been sighted in New Zealand.

IN AUSTRALIA THE white-browed wood-swallow prefers open grassland and eucalypt woodlands, although it also ranges through a variety of habitats, including arable farmland. It occasionally appears in coastal areas when inland droughts are severe.

It forages mainly in the air. Loose flocks fly over crops or insect plagues. It also feeds on the ground and in nectar-bearing flowers where it may take nectar as well as insects. Its prey includes spiders, cicadas, hemiptera bugs, lepidoptera adults and larvae, and locusts.

White-browed wood-swallows often perch on the terminal branches of trees and make repeated aerial forays from them. When at rest they sometimes spread their tails and swing them from side to side, though the function of this behaviour is unclear. Roosting birds cluster together in tight groups on tree trunks.

They usually nest in loose mixed colonies. Birds arrive back at the breeding grounds in late September or early October. Nesting begins in late October and continues through to late January. However, this varies and adequate rainfall in particular appears to influence when and where the birds breed. The nest is a flimsy structure of twigs, lined with grasses and rootlets, usually in a stump or the fork of a tree within five metres of the ground. Both sexes incubate and feed the two or three young. Two broods may be reared. M.D.D.

VAGRANT

OTHER NAMES: *Blue martin, summer-bird.*

SIZE: *190 mm.*

DESCRIPTION
ADULT: *Upper parts slaty grey; paler on rump, tail and wings. Forehead, lores and side of face black. Prominent white eyebrow stripe extending along side of crown and broadening to rear. Throat and chin black. Rest of underparts rich chestnut, becoming paler on undertail coverts. Axillaries and underwing coverts white. Rest of underwing light grey. Tail tip white. Iris dark*
brown. Bill light blue with black tip. Legs and feet black.
ADULT FEMALE: *Head and upper parts grey; pale on rump and tail, which is tipped white. Lores black. Faint eyebrow stripe. Chin and throat grey. Rest of underparts dull chestnut, becoming paler on undertail coverts. Axillaries and underwing coverts white. Rest of underwing light grey. Iris brown. Bill light blue with black tip. Legs and feet black.*
JUVENILE: *Upper parts grey, mottled with white, particularly on wing. Underparts brown-grey. Bill brown.*

MOULT
In Australia, young birds speckled until their first moult.

VOICE
Loud, querulous chirp; throaty drawn-out tchew; *and rasping squawk. Pleasant trilling song. Contact calls between a pair or in a flock consist of soft chatter. Mobbing call is harsh chatter.*

DISTRIBUTION
Widespread in Australia, generally inland, wintering north of the Tropic of Capricorn and migrating south for the summer. In New Zealand, no sightings since 1973. Recorded from Naseby State Forest, Central Otago: 1 male in December 1971 which was banded; 4 males in the summer of 1971–72; and the banded male and 1 other in
November 1972. The last sighting of either bird was in late July 1973.

Masked Wood-swallow

Artamus personatus (GOULD,1841)

THE PAIR OF MASKED wood-swallows which appeared at Naseby in March 1973 with two juveniles may have bred in New Zealand or have flown to New Zealand with their young from Australia. Both adults fed the juveniles on insects, including blowflies, till the end of March.

In Australia masked wood-swallows generally inhabit open savannah and lightly forested areas, although they apparently tolerate arid land better than white-browed wood-swallows. The two species feed together in flocks.

They forage in the air, making forays from prominent perches. Their almost entirely insectivorous diet includes grasshoppers, spiders, lepidoptera and diptera. New Zealand observations suggest they occasionally eat nectar. At night the birds roost in large groups and mutual preening is common.

Masked wood-swallows nest in colonies, often with white-browed wood-swallows. The irregular breeding season depends on the local climate, but usually occurs from October to January. Nests are usually within one or two metres of the ground, in shrubs or stumps, and consist of a rough arrangements of twigs, lined with fine grass. Two or three oval eggs are laid. M.D.D.

The nomadic masked wood-swallow, on its nest in native Australian eucalypt.

VAGRANT

OTHER NAMES: *Bush martin, blue martin, skimmer, blue jay.*

SIZE: *190 mm.*

DESCRIPTION
ADULT MALE: *Upper parts dark grey, paler on rump and upper tail coverts. Tail grey, usually with white tip. Forehead, lores, narrow line over eye, face, chin and throat black. Throat fringed by white collar of varying width and sometimes absent. Rest of underparts pale grey, except for white axillaries,*
underwing coverts and undertail coverts. Iris black. Bill light blue with black tip. Legs and feet black.
ADULT FEMALE: *Upper parts dark grey, tinged with brown. Tail grey with white tip. Lores black. Face, chin and throat grey-black. Indistinct grey-white collar. Underparts wine-coloured. Undertail coverts, axillaries and underwing coverts white. Rest of underwing grey. Iris dark brown. Bill bluish grey with black tip. Legs and feet black.*
JUVENILE: *Upper parts similar to female, with white speckling. Underparts brown-grey.*

MOULT
In New Zealand a female masked wood-swallow was evidently moulting in early August. Two juveniles observed in New Zealand had not completed moult by June.

VOICE
Similar to white-browed wood-swallow: soft chattering contact calls; and harsher calls when mobbing.

DISTRIBUTION
Through Australia, particularly common in the interior. Winters north of the Tropic of Capricorn and migrates south to breed.
Nomadic; may live in an area for several years and then disappear for several years. In New Zealand, recorded at Naseby State Forest, Central Otago: one pair January to July 1972; another pair with 2 flying young March to July 1973.

Australian Magpie *Gymnorhina tibicen* (LATHAM, 1801)

The white-backed magpie defends its territory fiercely during breeding.

INTRODUCED
Black-backed Magpie
G.t. tibicen (LATHAM, 1801).
White-backed Magpie
G.t. hypoleuca (GOULD, 1837).

OTHER NAMES: *None.*

SIZE:
Black-backed magpie: *400 mm.*
White-backed magpie: *420 mm.*

DESCRIPTION
ADULT MALE: *Head black. Hind neck, back, rump and tail coverts white, with black band 7 to 10 cm wide across back in black-backed magpie. Tail white with outer third black. Scapulars, primaries and secondaries black. Primary coverts mainly black with outer vanes of each feather white on inner half. Remaining coverts white. Underparts glossy black except white vent, undertail coverts, and axillaries. Outermost underwing coverts black but all others white. Iris yellowish brown. Bill bluish white with black tip. Legs black. Hybrid white-backed and black-backed magpies vary from having black band to few black feathers on back. Albino recorded.*
ADULT FEMALE: *Like adult male except feathers of hind neck, back and rump pale grey with blackish shafts.*
JUVENILE: *Like adult female except undersurface brownish black and feathers usually have broad pale tips which produce indistinct mottling. Pale tips wear off with time so breast becomes darker. Primaries become brown with wear. Beak leaden to dull black at least until mid-winter.*
NESTLING: *Greyish white down overlies pinkish skin of head and back. Gape pinkish. Tips of primaries appear after 2 days. Traces of grey appear in otherwise pink legs at about 11 days.*

MOULT
Young moult contour feathers within 3 months of leaving nest. Subsequent darkening of breast in late winter or early spring results from abrasion of pale tips of otherwise brownish black feathers. Full moult begins August or September when nearly 1 year old and continues until February though most have completed by mid-December. Annual moult of adults usually occurs between October and March, though some adults do not finish until May.

VOICE
Song is medley of flute-like notes rendered quardle oodle ardle wardle doodle. *Heard throughout year, especially early in morning during spring. Often uttered with head vertical and wings partly open, sometimes in duet. Harsh call may be used in territorial disputes. Young have loud insistent begging call.*

DISTRIBUTION
Australia and New Guinea. Introduced to New Zealand in 1864.
Black-backed magpie: *Most abundant in Hawke's Bay especially near Hastings; also, North Auckland, near Lake Taupo, Poverty Bay, Taranaki, Wanganui, Manawatu, and North Canterbury.*

White-backed magpie: *Most of the North Island; Canterbury, Otago, and sparsely distributed in northern Marlborough and Southland.*

RECOGNITION

Contrasting black and white plumage; black below and mainly white above except for black head, black wings (white on coverts) and black outer third of tail. Black-backed magpie has black band across back. Large pale crow-like bill. Melodious song carries well. Rapid wing-beats. Aggressively chases other birds such as harriers.

MAGPIES LIVE MAINLY in open grassland and cultivated paddocks with nearby trees in which to shelter. They are also found in city parks and playing fields, on the edges of native and exotic forest, on tussock grassland, and occasionally on mountains up to 1700 m. They sometimes feed along open beaches.

Females rarely breed successfully until they are three years old; males may be even older. Nest building begins as early as June and laying normally starts in July or August, continuing through to November. Clutches lost early in the season are usually replaced, but second broods are rare.

Nests are usually high in exotic trees such as pines, macrocarpas, eucalypts or willows, but occasionally in native trees such as tawa, beech, kanuka or cabbage trees. Where trees are scarce, nests may be sited only one and a half metres from the ground in gorse or hawthorn hedges. Occasionally, nests are built on man-made structures such as power pylons.

The female builds the nest alone, though the male occasionally carries material. It is a bulky structure made mainly of twigs, sometimes cemented with mud, and contains a central cup lined with finer material such as dry grass, wool, feathers and pine needles. Apart from a wide variety of natural materials, magpies sometimes incorporate man-made items in their nests. These include barbed wire, string, cloth, cardboard, matchboxes, cotton wool, rubber, old spoons, glass and pieces of china.

The eggs vary in colour and markings from clutch to clutch, but they usually have a bluish green background with streaks, spots and blotches which may be green brown or reddish. The number of eggs in a clutch varies from two to five, but is usually three or four. The female incubates, sometimes fed at the nest by the male, for 20 to 21 days. The chicks, fed by both parents, fledge in about four weeks and depend on their parents for up to two months. In New Zealand, magpies rarely rear more than two chicks and often only one.

Black-backed magpies in southeastern Australia live in groups of five differing but intergrading types. Successful breeding occurs only in permanent groups. These consist of two to 10 birds (rarely more than three breeders) which jointly defend a two to eight hectare territory containing adequate food and shelter all year round. At the other extreme are the flock birds which do not breed or defend a territory. The three intermediate groups consist of adults which keep together and hold, or attempt to hold, territories of varying degrees of impermanence. Birds in marginal groups sometimes attempt to breed, but they are rarely successful.

Though magpies feed mainly on insects, they also take other invertebrates, such as spiders, slaters, centipedes, millipedes, small snails and earthworms and occasionally small vertebrates, including lizards, mice, small birds and even carrion. Vegetable food includes seeds, especially those of clovers, grasses and *Solanum nigrum*, as well as grass blades and clover leaves. They have been recorded taking wheat, peas and tawa berries.

Magpies usually feed on open pastures—both dry and marshy—or on ploughed paddocks, but sometimes along the shoreline. They obtain most of their food at the soil surface, though occasionally they probe quite deeply. They turn over small stones, leaves and loose turfs and, in grassland, sometimes make short runs or jumps to capture flying insects. When searching for earthworms magpies often run a short distance, then remain motionless, before making a sudden thrust with their bills. They sometimes regurgitate indigestible material in the form of pellets.

Relations with humans

The playfulness sometimes noted in pet magpies occasionally appears in wild birds. One stopped feeding and rolled over on its back in the middle of a paddock. Magpies, however, are noted more for aggressiveness than playfulness. They have been known to attack other birds, people, sheep, dogs, a horse and hedgehogs. Because of complaints that they were driving away native birds and even attacking children, legal protection was removed from magpies in 1951. They have also been accused of killing new-born lambs and of pecking the eyes from cast sheep. Finally, they are disliked by electricity supply authorities because they settle on power lines where they may cause short circuits if they peck at nearby lines or make contact with pieces of wire carried as nesting material. Electrocuted magpies, falling to the ground with their feathers alight, have occasionally been blamed for starting fires in dry vegetation.

Magpies are sometimes kept as pets or to control insect pests in glass houses and gardens, though they sometimes pull up seedlings. Magpies build nests and even lay eggs in captivity, and one captive magpie was said to be at least 18 years old when it died. Some tame magpies are reported to 'talk' and others imitate a wide range of household noises.

P.C.B.

Rook *Corvus frugilegus frugilegus* LINNAEUS, 1758

SINCE ITS INTRODUCTION in 1862 the rook has spread slowly. Eighty years after the species was released almost the entire breeding population of rooks in New Zealand was still confined to limited areas of Hawke's Bay and Canterbury. New country has been occupied in two ways: by colonising new territory just beyond that already occupied and, more rarely, by the appearance of small rookeries in districts remote from those already occupied. Some of these isolated rookeries were started by the deliberate transfer of birds; others may result from unrecorded liberations or the settling of birds that have wandered far beyond their normal range. Despite recent poisoning, the rook population of Hawke's Bay is probably about 25 000 birds, far more than exist in the rest of New Zealand. There are about 2500 rooks in Canterbury and probably fewer than 1000 in isolated colonies elsewhere, giving a total of less than 30 000 birds.

Rooks prefer cultivated land and grazed pastures, but they also frequent open spaces in cities and, in Napier, the seashore. They visit piggeries, and favour trees with ripening nuts, especially walnuts. Rooks require tall trees for nesting, usually small clumps with good all-round views; they avoid forests and scrub.

The breeding season

Rooks normally breed in colonies, sometimes containing hundreds of pairs. They are usually at least two years old before breeding, though a few nest when only one year old, especially in rookeries recently reduced by poisoning. They begin building nests in August and lay from late August to late October in Hawke's Bay, a week or two later in Canterbury. It is rare for rooks to rear more than one brood each year, though they replace clutches lost early in the season.

The nests are untidy, bulky structures built in the tops of tall trees, usually pines or eucalypts, but occasionally in poplars, elms, oaks, wattles, macrocarpas and, at Napier, Norfolk Island pines. The male provides most of the material and the female arranges it. Nests found in Hawke's Bay have had a base of coarse twigs and mud on which finer twigs and leaves were placed to form a deep central cup lined with pine needles, eucalypt bark, tufts of grass and sometimes wool.

The clutch varies from one to seven, often three or four, eggs which are pale blue to pale green with light to dark brown blotches. In Canterbury, birds under study laid in the morning, usually one egg each day, though occasionally up to five days separated eggs.

The female incubates for about 17 days while the male feeds her on the nest. About half the eggs hatch. Chicks hatch approximately 24 hours after the first pipping of the egg and, depending on clutch size, it takes from 24 to 27 hours for all the eggs of a clutch to hatch. The eggs hatch in the order they were laid. At first, the male feeds newly hatched chicks and the brooding female; then, after 20 days, both parents feed the chick. The adults carry food for chicks in their throat pouches. All the chicks of a brood leave the nest at the same time at about 33 days old. Over half of successful broods lose one or more chicks. Usually only one or two fledge. Many nestlings die in the first four days, usually those that hatched last.

Rooks are highly gregarious throughout the year; they group into rookeries for nesting in spring, and into much larger communal roosts in winter. A winter roost, with its contributing rookeries, is called a 'parish', and a large district, such as Hawke's Bay, may contain several such parishes. Once the young fledge, the birds desert the rookery and congregate wherever food is abundant. They may spend the night in temporary roosts nearby.

Roosts and feeding behaviour

With the onset of winter, the birds abandon the temporary roosts in favour of a traditional winter roost, often a pine plantation, which may be used on a seasonal basis for 20 years or even longer by birds from several different rookeries. By mid-winter, a large roost may contain up to 5000 or more rooks. The birds continue to visit their breeding rookeries early each morning before dispersing to feed in the surrounding countryside. Some visit the rookery again briefly in the late afternoon. Birds from the more distant rookeries may journey 20 km or more, night and morning, between their breeding rookeries and the winter roost. As spring approaches, rooks spend more and more time at the breeding rookeries, and roost there once the first eggs are laid. Some winter roosts are abandoned altogether in spring, but others also serve as breeding rookeries for some of the birds that roost there in the winter.

Rooks have elaborate courtship displays, especially before laying. These involve bowing, drooping of wings and fanning of tails by males, and quivering of wings by females. In Hawke's Bay, males sometimes raped, or attempted to rape, incubating females whose mates were away gathering food. This behaviour was especially prevalent at hatching time and probably contributed to the loss of eggs and young.

Rooks eat a wide range of both animal and vegetable materials. Animal foods consist mainly of insects and earthworms, but include carrion and spiders. They take a wide variety of insects but most of them belong to the orders Diptera, Coleoptera, Lepidoptera and Hymenoptera. Plant materials eaten include walnuts, acorns, cereal grain (especially maize), legume and pumpkin seeds and the leaves of grasses and clovers.

The relative importance of the animal and vegetable components of the rook's diet varies seasonally. In Hawke's Bay, both wild and caged rooks preferred invertebrates and walnuts to other foods, but walnuts were available only in autumn and winter, and invertebrates became scarce in periods of drought or frost. When walnuts and invertebrates became scarce, rooks congregated in large flocks on crops and foods put out for stock.

In the autumn rooks bury walnuts in open paddocks, and return in late autumn and winter to search for and recover their store. They hold the nut on the ground with one foot while they hammer a hole through the hard shell with the tip of the bill to reach the kernel.

Rooks are resourceful and energetic in seeking animal foods. They jump and run to catch flying insects; peck food from the surface of the ground; tear dung open with their bills when searching for fly larvae; turn mown pasture, loose turf or dung to expose insects and earthworms; and dig or probe deep into the ground for soil animals. Birds feeding on newly sown crops follow the rows, methodically extracting each seed from the soil.

Rooks are generally disliked by farmers because they eat newly sown seeds, particularly of cereals (especially maize) but also of pumpkins and peas. They regularly carry off walnuts and may damage ripening peas by ripping open the pods and trampling the vines; occasionally they peck apples, pears and potatoes. They steal food put out for domestic stock, and tear up pasture while searching for grubs.

Rooks were declared Pests of Local Importance in Eastern Hawke's Bay in 1971 (and subsequently in several other districts). This designation, never before applied to a bird in New Zealand, gave legal responsibility for rook control to Pest Destruction Boards which poisoned more than 35 000 during 1971–77. P.C.B.

INTRODUCED

OTHER NAME: *Crow.*

SIZE: *450 mm.*

DESCRIPTION
ADULT: *Black with purplish sheen, especially on head, neck, mantle and breast. Very distinctive greyish, featherless area of roughened skin surrounds base of bill and extends to eye. Iris dark brown. Bill and feet black. Female tends to be smaller with less massive bill. Breeding female has brood pouch. Part albinos recorded.*
JUVENILE: *Like adult except purplish sheen less marked and face and throat fully feathered. Numerous elongated, stiffish, forwardly directed, bristle-like feathers cover inner third of culmen and conceal nostrils. Because of abrasions, birds nearly a year old lack gloss, and wing and tail feathers distinctly brownish.*
NESTLING: *Down dark grey and sparse. Skin very dark. Inside of mouth pink; no spots. Outside of gape pale flesh tinged with yellow.*

MOULT
Most adult and one-year-old rooks collected in Hawke's Bay in November had begun to moult primaries, and the moulting of body feathers probably continues until about March. Juveniles probably moult body feathers and wing coverts in first summer (January), but retain wing and tail feathers until about following November. By this time many juveniles have already lost some nasal bristles and also many of the small feathers that formerly covered the skin between the 2 halves of lower mandible.

VOICE
Characteristic caw or kaah, with variations, especially at rookeries and roosts. High-pitched kiow often heard above frantic cawing that results from disturbing a large rookery. Hungry nestlings have persistent begging call.

DISTRIBUTION
Western Eurasia, including the British Isles, south of 60°N to 63°N in Scandinavia and Russia and 56°N in Siberia, east to Siberia and Mongolia and south to Central France, northern Italy, Austria, the Balkans, the Crimea, the Caucasus, Iran and Sinkiang. Winter range extends to the Mediterranean Basin (including North Africa), Iraq, Arabia, Iran and northwestern India. In New Zealand, found in Hawke's Bay from Tutira in the north to Pahiatua in the south; also reported from near Palmerston North, Miranda, Tolaga Bay, Waitotara, Pirinoa, Banks Peninsula, Christchurch, Ashburton, Blenheim, and Middlemarch; but some of these rookeries may no longer exist. Stragglers recorded from North Auckland, Morrinsville, Taupo, East Cape, Horowhenua, Wellington, Nelson, Motunau, and the Chatham Islands.

> ### RECOGNITION
>
> Plumage uniformly black. Larger and heavier than magpie. Featherless, greyish white skin around face. Except when frightened, flies with even, unhurried wing-beats which, together with short neck and heavy bill, distinguishes it from other large black birds. Calls characteristic *caw*.

The rook, originally introduced to control insects, was the first bird in New Zealand to become the responsibility of a Pest Destruction Board.

Extinct birds

New Zealand has an unenviable record for the extinction of endemic species—especially since the arrival of man, his associated predators, and the development of land for farming. These few species indicate how rapidly isolated species, even plentiful ones, can disappear. Included is one recent, accidentally introduced species which was deliberately exterminated before becoming well established after its habits suggested its danger as a pest. Though considered extinct, these species—and other extinct subspecies noted in the main texts— are recorded to encourage observers to maintain their vigilance and provide an example of what can happen to other species without careful management in the future.

New Zealand Little Bittern *Ixobrychus novaezelandiae* (POTTS, 1871)

OTHER NAMES: *None.*

Until 1979, the New Zealand little bittern was classified as a subspecies of the Australian little bittern *Ixobrychus minutus*, but recent studies of museum specimens have convinced some ornithologists that it is—or was—a distinct species. It is clear that the New Zealand bird is closely related to, and almost certainly derived from, the Australian species.

The New Zealand little bittern has been described as a small (300mm) secretive, swamp inhabitant, appreciably smaller than the Australian species, and lacking the continuously black back or uniform buff wing coverts and undersurface. In the New Zealand species the contrasting pattern of chestnut buff and dark brown on the upper wings was obvious during flight. All sightings were from the South Island in the 1800s, most of them on Westland. A bird seen at Meremere, South Auckland, in 1963 is now considered to have been a small, immature Australasian bittern. No records this century have been made of the New Zealand species.   M.J.W.

Auckland Island Merganser *Mergus australis*
HOMBRON & JACQUINOT, 1841

OTHER NAMES: *None.*

Australasia's only sea duck, the Auckland Island merganser, was one of only two species occurring in the southern hemisphere. The earliest remains were found in the South Island, dated as being later than AD 1500, and the last specimen was taken in 1902. Recent expeditions to the Auckland Islands, however, have failed to locate it.

The origin and distribution of the Auckland Island merganser is a puzzle. It is probably an isolated derivative of the northern hemisphere species which gradually lost its plumage differences, the bright colours of the drake being replaced by the more camouflaging plumage of the female. It most closely resembles the Chinese merganser *Mergus squamatus*, but how that form could travel so many miles and not colonise Australia is a mystery. The other southern hemisphere merganser is the Brazilian merganser; with its shiny green plumage, it resembles the northern form.

The Auckland Island bird had a much wider distribution than the name implies and occurred throughout the mainland. Subfossil remains were found on the South Island, and at Stewart Island; a reference in last century's literature suggests it also inhabited Campbell Island. It was recorded from both the main Auckland Island and from Adams Island. There is considerable doubt as to the primary habitat of the merganser, and evidence from the food of the animal does not provide more clues. A reference states that the bird ate small freshwater fish (*Galaxias brevipennis*); and the gut of a preserved bird was found to contain macerated fish bones, the mandibles of a marine worm, and a small gastropod. What seems likely is that the Auckland Islands were probably at the extreme edge of the merganser's range and, in order to survive in an abominable climate, it had to adapt to a different habitat.

With the arrival of the Polynesians, followed by the Europeans, the merganser seems to have been driven southwards to its last known predator-free refuge on Adams Island. If that island were the species last retreat, then the collecting of 26 specimens over 20 years would have had a huge impact on the small numbers surviving on that island.   M.J.W.

New Zealand Quail *Coturnix novaezelandiae* QUOY & GAIMARD, 1830

OTHER NAME: *Koreke.*

The extinction of the New Zealand quail is as deplorable as it is unexplained. It was the only native New Zealand game bird belonging to the order Galliformes, which includes pheasants and partridge as well as quail. This bird was a very dark, warmly brown and very spotted quail with a short black bill. Its near relative is the stubble quail of Australia, and some studies have suggested that the birds belong to the same species. Though its rapid decline in the 1850s and disappearance during the sixties is well recorded, quail were reported to be present in the South Island till 1875.

In the early days of the colony the New Zealand quail was 'excessively' abundant in open country and its reproductive potential was apparently high. There are numerous records of the presence of quail, its wide distribution in both islands and the large numbers hunted and killed. Whatever combination of environmental and biological factors was responsible (including excessive hunting), all that remain are a few dozen stuffed birds, specimen skins and a few egg shells in some 18 museums.   K.E.W.

Laughing Owl *Sceloglaux albifacies* (GRAY, 1844)

OTHER NAMES: *Whekau, hakoke (North Island), rock owl.*

The 'doleful shrieks' of the laughing owl, which varied seasonally, were heard incessantly on rainy nights. Apparently it was easily kept in captivity, and reports say that it cooeyed in the evening, yelped like a young dog and mewed and chuckled. It was distinguished from the morepork by its larger size, white face, brown iris, shorter tail and yellower plumage—more clearly streaked and mottled on the back. The underparts and head were less streaked and mottled.

The laughing owl has been recorded in the southern half of the North Island and mainly east of the Southern Alps in the South Island. It lived in and around rocky areas, either in open country or at the margins of scrub or forest, and apparently hunted for its food over and on open ground. It ate earthworms, insects, lizards, small birds and mammals, including mice and Polynesian rats. The most recent record was a sighting at Manapouri in 1950 but egg fragments were found at Waianatarua (Canterbury) in 1960. Its decline coincided with European settlement but whether this was due to introduced predators or changes in land usage is unknown. Probably both factors are important.   M.H.

Red-vented Bulbul *Pycnonotus cafer bengalensis* BLYTH, 1846

OTHER NAMES: *None.*

A native of India and Southeast Asia, the red-vented bulbul is a slender bird with black, brown and grey plumage. It has a slightly curved bill, a distinct triangular crest, a conspicuous white rump, a narrow white band at the tail's tip and, not always visible, a red undertail.

This bird was introduced to Auckland about 1952. It was promptly labelled a pest because of its reported tendency to damage crops and fruit, and was successfully exterminated by mid-1955, under the auspices of the Department of Agriculture. It is thought the bird was released from a ship visiting Waitemata Harbour. Fifty-four bulbuls are known to have established themselves in inner city suburbs, north to Takapuna and south to Stanley Bay and Mt Eden. In Asia the red-vented bulbul, with its cheerful song and splash of scarlet feathers, is a popular cage bird.   E.G.T.

Huia *Heteralocha acutirostris* (GOULD, 1837)

OTHER NAMES: *None.*

Presumed extinct since 1907, the huia belongs to the same ancient wattlebird family as the saddleback and the kokako. It was a medium-sized slender bird and its plumage was generally black with a greenish gloss. It had a distinct broad white band across the tip of the tail feathers, and an orange wattle. The differently formed bills in the two sexes enabled them to assist each other in their search for food. The male used his short, stout bill to chisel at decaying logs to expose prey; the female, with her longer, slender, and more strongly curved bill, could probe and extract grubs from areas the male was unable to reach. Though the larvae and pupae of the huhu beetle (*Prionoplus reticularis*) formed the bulk of their diet they are known to have eaten berries and insects.

In pre-European times the huia seems to have undergone a restriction in its range and by 1843 was said to be confined to the deepest parts of the primeval forest around Port Nicholson and along the ranges north to Hawke's Bay. Extensive forest fires in the late 1800s greatly reduced the huia habitat. In addition large numbers of birds were taken for collections and for cash reward. The tail feathers were highly prized by the Maori, who wore them in their hair as a sign of rank; huia skins were worn as ornaments attached to the ears.

The huias were tame and fearless birds, and responded to an imitated call note by coming to within a metre or so of the caller. Consequently they were easily snared, killed with sticks or shot.   D.G.M.

New Zealand Thrush *Turnagra capensis* (SPARRMAN, 1787)

OTHER NAMES: *Piopio, korohea.*

The New Zealand thrush, in the medium-sized range of perching birds, had a plumage of olive-brown, rufous, yellow and yellowish-white. Its bill and feet were dark brown, and its iris yellow. The undersurface and forehead of the South Island thrush *T.c. capensis* had a striped appearance, whereas the colours of the North Island thrush *T.c. tanagra* were of a more solid nature. Both species appeared to be omnivorous.

The first specimen of the South Island thrush collected by Europeans was a bird shot at Cascade Cove, Dusky Sound, on 2 April 1773, during Cook's second voyage. The subspecies was still abundant when European settlers arrived but, by 1872, ornithologists were lamenting the substantial diminution in its numbers. Now, more than half a century has elapsed since the last confirmed sighting. The probable extinction of the subspecies has occurred since the arrival of European man, and is directly attributable to his activities and those of his mammalian predators.

The North Island thrush, described as 'unquestionably the best of our native songsters', was not common in European times and the few records available indicate that it was confined to the more remote and rugged forested areas in the south of the island. By 1888 it was said to be one of New Zealand's rarest species, and by 1905 was noted as almost extinct. Though there have been many reports, including those from the Waikaremoana area in the 1950s, extensive searches over recent years have failed to yield positive results. The final decline of the North Island thrush was perhaps encouraged by forest destruction and introduced predators.   D.G.M.

Classification by order and family

Species that are closely related are grouped into a genus; related genera are grouped into a family, and related families into an order. Altogether there are 27 orders of birds, grouped into the class Aves. In the New Zealand region, there are representatives of 58 families in 18 orders. These groups are described below.

ORDER APTERYGIFORMES

Kiwis

This order consists of a single endemic New Zealand family. The bill is long, with nostrils at the tip. Wings are rudimentary and the birds have no distinct flight or tail feathers.

FAMILY APTERYGIDAE

Kiwis: pages 36–39

The smallest of the flightless ratite birds, the kiwi has a long, slender, slightly curved bill. The base is covered with a hard cere. Kiwis stand apart from all other living birds in that their nostrils are placed at the tip of the bill; the rudimentary wings are hidden in the body feathers; and the tail is apparently absent.

ORDER SPHENISCIFORMES

Penguins

This order consists of a single family. The wings are modified into flippers adapted for swimming, the feathers reduced to small scale-like structures. Penguins are found in the southern oceans as far north as southern Australia, northern New Zealand, the Galapagos Islands, Argentina and South Africa.

FAMILY SPHENISCIDAE

Penguins: pages 40–53

There are 16 species of penguins, and 12 breed in the New Zealand region. Three species are confined to the Antarctic sector. These southern hemisphere birds have webbed feet set far back on their bodies. Their plumage is a compact waterproof coat of small glossy feathers. Penguins are grey, blue or black above and generally white below. Stout of body, they have paddle-like wings for swimming. They do not fly. The six basic penguin groups are described below.
Aptenodytes: The two species are large birds easily distinguishable from all other penguins by the long, downward-curved and pointed bill, the long narrow flippers, and orange patches on the side of the neck. Both species are circumpolar in distribution—one is strictly Antarctic, whereas the other breeds on various islands in the subantarctic.
Pygoscelis: The bill is short to moderately long; the tail long, of 12 to 16 feathers. Allied to Megadyptes, it differs in the narrower latericorn and the greater amount of feathering at the base of the bill. There is no yellow eyebrow band or crests. It comprises three species found in the Antarctic and subantarctic seas.
Megadyptes: The bill is characteristically long and moderately stout; the tail short, of 20 feathers. This genus is readily recognised by the yellow eyebrow bands surrounding the head. There is a single endemic species in the New Zealand region.
Eudyptula: The bill is moderately long, and stout; the tail moderately long, of 13 to 16 feathers. Eudyptes are distinguished from all other penguins by the stout red bill, with deep grooves and swollen latericorn, and the presence of yellow eyebrow crests which do not unite behind the head. The general colour is black above and white below. Five species are found in cold temperate seas, two being circumpolar and three endemic species confined to the New Zealand region.
Eudyptula: The bill is moderate, the upper mandible hooked at the tip; the flippers are short. The tail is very short, consisting of 16 feathers, almost concealed by the upper tail coverts. This group differs conspicuously from all other penguins by its small size and the absence of eyebrow stripes. The general colour is blue above and white below. There are six subspecies: five in New Zealand and one in Australia.
Spheniscus: These are moderately sized penguins, with black feet, black plumage above and white below, except for one or two black chest bands. They are usually confined to South Africa and South America.

ORDER PODICIPEDIFORMES

Grebes and dabchicks

This order consists of one family, the members of which are found throughout the world.

FAMILY PODICIPEDIDAE

Grebes and dabchicks: pages 54–57

Of the 19 species of grebes found throughout the world four live in New Zealand. Two species, the Australian little grebe and the hoary-headed grebe are recent arrivals. The bill is straight, compressed and pointed, and these weak-flighted birds have short rounded wings and no tail. The feet, set far back on the body, have broadly lobed toes and flattened claws. The sexes are alike.

ORDER PROCELLARIIFORMES

Tube-nosed seabirds

The order is made up of four families, and representatives of all breed in the New Zealand region. The bill, strongly hooked at the tip, is covered with separate horny plates; the nostrils are tubular. The front toes are fully webbed, with the hind toe absent or very small. Flying the seas, they seldom come ashore except to breed.

FAMILY DIOMEDEIDAE

Albatrosses: pages 58–66

Of the 13 species of albatrosses, nine inhabit temperate southern seas, with seven breeding in the New Zealand region. Albatrosses are large stout-bodied birds, with long narrow wings and the power of effortless gliding flight. The feet are webbed, with the hind toe absent. The large bill has a hooked tip, and the nostril tubes are short, placed on either side of the culminicorn. Southern albatrosses fall into three basic groups, with adults showing the following characteristics.
Sooty albatrosses: There are two species. The bill is black, the lower mandible with long lateral grooves containing coloured skin. All birds have dark plumage.
Mollymawks: The five species, two endemic to New Zealand, feature a variety of coloured bills; there are no grooves on the lower mandible, and the latericorn widens between nostril and base. There is a strip of coloured skin at the base of the bill and gape. The back and tail are always dark.
Great albatrosses: There are two species, one endemic to New Zealand. The bill is uniformly light horn, with no coloured skin at the base. The lower mandible is without grooves, and the latericorn does not widen behind the nostril. The back is generally white.

FAMILY PROCELLARIIDAE

Fulmars, petrels, prions and shearwaters: pages 67–101

The 66 species of this family are found throughout the oceans of the world, but they are more numerous in the south. Thirty-two species breed in the New Zealand region and a further 12 have been recorded as visitors. The size and shape of the bill varies, but it is always hooked at the tip. Two nasal tubes join on the culminal ridge, with the openings directed forwards. Feet are webbed, with a hind toe present. There are, in the New Zealand region, five broad groups within this family.
Fulmars: Within this group there are five genera. Fulmars range in size from large to small birds, and have relatively long, broad wings. They nest in the open, on cliff ledges or in rock clefts. The bill is robust, with nostril tubes united into a single opening; the septum does not reach the aperture.
Gadfly petrels: There are two genera within this group, which consists of small to medium-sized, highly pelagic birds. The wings are shorter in relation to body length than those of fulmars and shearwaters, and broader at the base and more pointed at the tip. The tail is long and wedge-shaped. The strongly hooked, black bill is short and stout with prominent nostrils in which the nasal openings are directed forward. The tarsi are rounded. These birds seldom alight on the water, do not dive, and tend to avoid ships. They nest in burrows excavated in soft ground. There are four endemic species in the New Zealand region.
Prions: This group comprises six species of small blue-grey petrels with white underparts, black-tipped tail, and a dark open W visible on the upper surface of the spread wings in flight. Both the bill and feet are blue, the bills varying in width. These birds nest in burrows and crevices.
Procellaria *petrels:* Four species of large petrels belong to this group; three species are entirely black, the other grey above and white below. They have heavy, pale or bi-coloured bills, with large hooked tips. The nasal tubes are prominent, with the apertures directed forward. These petrels nest in burrows in soft ground. Two endemic species inhabit the New Zealand region.
Shearwaters: Of the two genera, only one, *Puffinus,* breeds in the New Zealand region. Seven of the 14 species occurring in the southern oceans breed in the New Zealand region and a further four species are visitors. These slender-bodied birds have narrow pointed wings. The bill is long, narrow and slender, generally dark, and hooked at the tip; the nostrils open obliquely upwards; the tarsus is flattened laterally. These birds dive readily for food, and nest in burrows in soft ground. Two endemic shearwater species inhabit the New Zealand region.

FAMILY HYDROBATIDAE

Storm petrels: pages 102–105

There are 21 species worldwide with six occurring, and five breeding, in the New Zealand region. They are small dark birds with slender bills, the nostril tubes united into a single opening similar to fulmars. They are distinguished by fluttering butterfly-like flight and their legs dangle while they feed from the surface. Storm petrels nest in burrows, in soil or dense tussock.

FAMILY PELECANOIDIDAE

Diving petrels: pages 106–107

Four species live in the southern oceans; of these, two breed in the New Zealand region. They are small, chunky, short, black-billed petrels, black above and white below. The paired nostrils open upwards. The feet are blue, and short wings produce a direct, rapid, bumblebee-like flight for short distances. They dive for food, and nest in burrows in soft soil.

ORDER PELECANIFORMES

Pelicans, gannets, boobies and allies

The members of the six families in this order are the only birds with all four toes webbed. All fish for food.

FAMILY PHAETHONTIDAE

Tropic birds: page 108

Of the three species that occur throughout the tropical seas, one breeds and another is a rare vagrant in the New Zealand region. Tropic birds, almost-white seabirds with elongated central tail streamers, have short wings and weak feet. The bill is stout, pointed and droops slightly; in adults, the edges of the bill are serrated. Tropic birds feed by plunge-diving for fish and squid. They nest in loose colonies, laying their eggs on open ground, under ledges and bushes, and in hollow trees. Both sexes incubate the eggs.

FAMILY PELECANIDAE

Pelicans: page 109

Eight species live throughout the world, and one of these breeds in Australia. It rarely visits New Zealand. Large, heavily built birds, the pelicans have a long bill with an extendable throat pouch. Their flight is heavy but buoyant, with much gliding. They nest in colonies and their white eggs are incubated by both sexes.

FAMILY SULIDAE

Gannets and boobies: pages 110–113

Gannets are birds of temperate waters, whereas the six booby species inhabit tropical waters. One gannet and one booby breed in the New Zealand region; another booby is a rare straggler. Gannets are distinguished from boobies mainly by a feathered chin and heavily scaled front toes. All have streamlined bodies and long wings. The bill is straight with a slight droop at the tip. The edges of the bill are smooth in juveniles and serrated in adults. Gannets and boobies feed on fish and squid by plunge-diving and swimming under water. They generally nest in colonies and their eggs are incubated by both sexes.

FAMILY PHALACROCORACIDAE

Shags and cormorants: pages 114–126

Of the 33 world species, 13 species breed in the New Zealand region; and eight of these are endemic. Two groups are generally recognised. The freshwater shags, usually called cormorants, all have black feet, whereas the marine shags have coloured feet. The latter group can be divided into spotted shags, which have grey plumage and yellow feet, and island shags, which have black and white plumage and pink feet. All birds of this family have straight unserrated bills with hooked tips. They feed by diving from the surface and swimming under water. They nest in colonies, either in trees or on the ground. The eggs are incubated by both sexes.

FAMILY ANHINGIDAE

Darters: page 127

There are two world species, with one species breeding in Australia. It occurs as a very rare straggler to the New Zealand region, and has a long, snake-like neck and a small head. The serrated bill is straight and pointed. The plumage of male and female birds differs.

FAMILY FREGATIDAE

Frigate birds: page 128

There are five species throughout the tropical seas, with two straggling to New Zealand. Frigate birds have a small body, huge wings, forked tail and weakly webbed feet. The all-dark male is smaller than the female, and when courting it inflates a bright red throat pouch. Frigate birds rarely enter the sea, and feed parasitically by forcing other seabirds, particularly terns and boobies, to disgorge their food.

ORDER CICONIIFORMES

Herons, ibises and spoonbills

Two of the six families in this order are found in the New Zealand region. They are large birds with long legs and a long bill. Adapted for wading in shallow water, they feed mainly on fish, amphibia and crustaceans. They have three forward toes and one long hind toe.

FAMILY ARDEIDAE

Herons, egrets and bitterns: pages 129–135

There are 64 species worldwide. Four species breed in New Zealand, and one is extinct. A further five species are rare to common visitors from Australia. They are waterbirds, with long legs, a long neck and narrow straight-pointed bill. The mid toe has a serrated claw. Bitterns have shorter legs than herons, and the inner toe is longer than the outer. Their plumage is cryptic, and they tend to skulk in the vegetation. In egrets and herons the outer toe is longer than the inner toe. They have powder-down patches on the breast, rump and thighs. Conspicuous in most habitats, they often breed in colonies.

FAMILY THRESKIORNITHIDAE

Ibises and spoonbills: pages 136–137

Two of the world's 27 ibises are relatively regular visitors to New Zealand. Of the six species of spoonbill, only one breeds and another is a rare straggler. These medium-sized wetland birds have long bills (curved in ibises; straight with a spatulate tip in spoonbills). The neck and legs are extended in flight. The mid toe is not serrated in spoonbills, and they do not have powder-down patches. There are variable amounts of bare skin on the face and head. The birds generally nest in colonies.

ORDER ANSERIFORMES

Duck-like birds

There are two families belonging to this order: the screamers, which are confined to South America, and the cosmopolitan geese, swans and ducks.

FAMILY ANATIDAE

Swans, geese and ducks: pages 138–151

There are 147 species throughout the world. Of the 11 species that breed in the New Zealand region, four are endemic and four introduced. Another six species are occasional visitors, and one endemic species is extinct. They are waterbirds (some more or less terrestrial), with relatively short legs. The front toes are connected by webs. The wings are relatively small, broad, and mostly pointed. Covered with soft skin, the bill is generally flattened and typically broad, high at the base, and rounded with a horny nail at the tip. Generally, swans, geese and ducks are solitary breeders, and the clutch is large. The nests are lined copiously with down.

ORDER FALCONIFORMES

Hawks, falcons and vultures

Of the five families that belong to this order two are found in the New Zealand region. The bill is short, the culmen strongly downcurved to a sharp overhanging tip. At the base of the bill is a waxy cere through which the nostrils open. The feet are bare, with sharp talons. The female is larger than the male.

FAMILY ACCIPITRIDAE

Eagles, hawks and harriers: pages 152–153

Only one of the 217 species worldwide breeds in New Zealand. The upper mandible is not toothed, and the nostrils are oval. These birds have large rounded wings and are typically plumaged in blended greys and browns. Generally, they have long tails. They are usually solitary breeders.

FAMILY FALCONIDAE

Falcons: pages 154–155

Of the 61 species worldwide, one endemic species breeds in the New Zealand region; another is a rare visitor. The upper mandible is toothed, and the nostrils are round. These birds have long pointed wings and long tails. Flight is swift, with a rapid wing-beat. Usually, they are solitary nesters.

ORDER GALLIFORMES

Megapodes, quails, pheasants and allies

Only one of three families is represented in New Zealand. All are ground-living birds, with three forward toes and one short hind toe.

FAMILY PHASIANIDAE

Pheasants and quails: pages 156–163

One endemic species is now extinct. Nine of the world's 213 species have been introduced, but the status of two is now uncertain. They are heavily built ground-living birds, with short, rounded wings and a stout bill. The tarsi are partially or entirely naked and often armed with spurs. Flight is characterised by short bursts of direct fast flight. The sexes are usually different. These birds nest on the ground, and the female usually incubates and rears the young.

ORDER GRUIFORMES

Cranes, rails, coots and allies

There are 12 families in this order. Members of one family breed in New Zealand; one other family is a rare straggler. They are ground-living birds, usually with long legs, no webs on the feet, and rather short or pointed bills. The nostrils are not separated by a bony partition.

FAMILY GRUIDAE

Cranes: page 164

There are 15 species throughout the world, and one straggles to New Zealand. They are large, long-legged, dagger-billed birds similar to herons in appearance. They fly with the neck extended; their voice is loud and resonant. Nests are found in vegetation on the ground, or built on water; both sexes participate in nesting duties.

FAMILY RALLIDAE

Rails: pages 165–173

There are 141 species throughout the world. Eight species now breed in New Zealand, of which two are endemic. In addition, one is extinct, and two species are considered to be rare stragglers. Though sizes vary greatly, the body is generally laterally compressed, which is an adaptation for moving through dense vegetation. They are poor flyers, with short, rounded wings. The bill is strong, compressed, and with a bright frontal shield in some species. The legs are short, with long toes; these are lobed in the coots. The tails, which are weak, are often flicked up and down. They nest among vegetation, on the ground or on water. Both sexes incubate and rear the young.

ORDER CHARADRIIFORMES

Waders and gulls

There are 17 families in this order; seven breed in the New Zealand region, and representatives of two further families are visitors. This is a widely variable order of small to medium-size, gregarious waders and shorebirds. They generally nest on the ground, and feed both on the ground and on the water's surface. Many species undertake long migrations.

FAMILY HAEMATOPODIDAE

Oystercatchers: pages 174–176

With seven species in existence throughout the world, three are found in New Zealand; two of these are endemic. They are bulky shorebirds, their plumage either black, or black and white. The bill is long, straight and orange-red, and laterally compressed. The legs are strong, with short toes, and a low hind toe. The nest is a scrape in ground, and both sexes share nesting duties.

FAMILY CHARADRIIDAE

Lapwings, plovers and dotterels: pages 177–189

Of the 64 species worldwide, there are 14 found in New Zealand. Seven have been recorded breeding and four are endemic; a further seven species are visitors, two of which are very rare stragglers. These squat birds have a large head, narrow rounded bill, and a short neck. Generally the hind toe is poorly developed or absent. They feed along the shore or on open ground. Flight is fast and sustained, without soaring. They nest in a scrape on the ground, and both sexes share nesting duties.

FAMILY SCOLOPACIDAE

Turnstones, curlews, sandpipers and snipe: pages 190–211

One endemic species breeds in the New Zealand region and a further 30 species are visitors. Some of these visitors occur annually in large numbers; others are rare stragglers. Most species of this family live and breed in the high latitudes of the northern hemisphere, and migrate to the southern hemisphere to escape the northern winter. In New Zealand they are generally in dull eclipse plumage. The bill is moderately to very long, generally straight, but curved in some species. The hind toe is short. These species are gregarious and most feed on mud flats. Both sexes share nesting duties.

FAMILY RECURVIROSTRIDAE

Stilts and avocets: pages 212–214

There are seven species throughout the world, three of these occurring in New Zealand. Two species breed in New Zealand, one of which is a rare endemic species. Another is an occasional visitor. These birds have long slender legs, and short toes. In the stilts the hind toe is absent. The long thin bill is upturned in the avocets, and straight in the stilts. The head is small and the neck moderately long. They nest on the ground near water, and both sexes incubate and rear young.

FAMILY PHALAROPODIDAE

Phalaropes: page 215

Three species live in the Arctic and migrate to the southern hemisphere in winter; two of them occur in New Zealand. These small, elegant waders have five lobes on their three toes, an adaptation to their aquatic way of life. Females are larger and more colourful in breeding plumage than males, and courtship and nesting roles are reversed. Phalaropes take food from the surface of the water with their straight, slender bill while swimming. They seldom come ashore to feed.

FAMILY GLAREOLIDAE

Pratincoles and coursers: page 216

There are 16 species, from Eurasia to Australia, with one a rare visitor to New Zealand. These waders have a fairly short bill, pointed at the tip. Their eyes are large. Pratincoles usually have relatively short legs, a short hind toe and long pointed wings; they are aerial feeders and eat insects. The sexes are alike. The eggs are usually incubated on plain ground by the female, but both sexes share the rearing of the young.

FAMILY STERCORARIIDAE

Skuas and jaegers: pages 217–220

There are five species throughout the oceans of the world, and all have been recorded in the New Zealand region. Two breed in the New Zealand region, two are regular visitors and one is a very rare straggler. These strong flyers breed in the high latitudes of the northern and southern hemispheres. They are gull-like in appearance; the bill is black, and strongly hooked. The feet are black and webbed, with sharp, hooked claws. There is a distinctive white patch at the base of the primaries. The nest is a scrape, and birds may nest singly or in loose colonies. Both parents incubate and rear the young.

FAMILY LARIDAE

Gulls: pages 221–223

Of some 44 species worldwide three breed in the New Zealand region, one of which is endemic. The upper mandible is decurved at the tip and overlaps the lower mandible. There is a prominent ridge at the distal junction of the lower mandibles. The tail is square to rounded, and feet are webbed, with a short hind toe. They generally nest in colonies, and the male and female share nesting duties.

FAMILY STERNIDAE

Terns: pages 224–236

There are 47 species worldwide; of these eight (two of which are endemic) breed in the New Zealand region. A further seven species are visitors. Terns have long pointed wings that are narrower than those of gulls. The bill is straight, with both mandibles of equal length, and the tail is forked or notched. These birds have short legs and webbed toes. Generally, they nest on the ground in colonies. Both sexes share nesting duties.

ORDER COLUMBIFORMES

Pigeons and doves

There are three families in this order, one of which is found in New Zealand. These bulky, thickly feathered land birds can swallow water without raising their heads. The bill is short, straight, swollen at the tip and base, and well adapted for eating fruit and seeds. The hind toe is at the same level as the other toes. The tarsus is covered with small plates and is usually feathered on the upper part.

FAMILY COLUMBIDAE

Pigeons and doves: pages 237–240

Of the 303 species throughout the world, only four live in New Zealand; three of these were introduced. These heavy birds have a small head and a short neck. Their wings are rounded and they are strong flyers. The nest is usually a flimsy platform of sticks and the white eggs are incubated by both the male and female. The young are fed on 'pigeon's milk'—a liquid from the lining of the crop.

ORDER PSITTACIFORMES

Cockatoos and parrots

These birds are variously classified into three to 11 families, three of which are represented in the New Zealand region. Their plumage is usually rich and colourful. The bill is hooked, with the curved upper mandible fitting neatly over the lower, and the tongue is thick. The head is large and broad, the neck short, and the nostrils set in a bare fleshy cere. The feet are short and stumpy, and have two toes pointing forward and two backward. All species nest in holes or hollows and lay white eggs. The young are fed by both parents.

FAMILY CACATUIDAE

Cockatoos: pages 241–243

Unlike Australia, which has a wide variety of 11 species, the New Zealand region has only two of the 17 species found throughout the world. One is a rare endemic species and the other is introduced. Cockatoos are large, thickset birds, usually with heavy bills and a conspicuous crest. They have rounded wings, and are generally good flyers. The endemic kakapo, however, has been reduced to flightlessness. The sexes are similar in appearance, and share incubation.

FAMILY NESTORIDAE

New Zealand parrots: pages 244–245

Of the three species, two are endemic to New Zealand; the other, at nearby Norfolk Island, is recently extinct. The bill is much compressed, its length greater than its depth: the lower mandible is only slightly curved. The cere is partly covered with hairy feathers. The shafts project from the tail feathers.

FAMILY PLATYCERCIDAE

Broad-tailed parrots: pages 246–251

These birds are confined to Australasia and New Caledonia. There are six species in New Zealand—one is introduced, and of the three endemic species one is possibly extinct. They are slender, medium-to-small, green, red, and blue parrots. The bill is deeper than it is long, and the lower mandible is curved upwards. Their flight is fast and direct, and the sexes are usually similar.

ORDER CUCULIFORMES

Cuckoos and turacos

Two families of birds belong to this order, one of which is found in New Zealand. The birds' feet have two toes forward and two back, though the fourth toe may go both ways. The bill is pointed and slightly arched and there is no cere over the nostrils.

FAMILY CUCULIDAE

Cuckoos, koels and coucals: pages 252–255

Only two of about 130 species throughout the world breed in the New Zealand region; a further four are fairly rare visitors or stragglers. These slender birds have a long tail, pointed wings and a narrow downcurved bill. They are mostly parasitic, laying their eggs in the nests of other birds. Others, such as the coucals, rear their own young. Cuckoos are rather solitary birds, mostly tree-dwelling,

and many are migratory. They call monotonously in the breeding season.

ORDER STRIGIFORMES

Owls

This order is variously classified as one or two families. These nocturnal birds of prey have large heads, and the eyes are directed forward for binocular vision. The face is surrounded by a disc of feathers; the bill is short and strongly hooked, with a cere at the base. The tarsus is mainly feathered, and the outer toe is reversible. The tail is short, and the flight feathers have softened edges, which makes their flight silent. All have white eggs.

FAMILY STRIGIDAE

Owls: pages 256–258

There are 146 species throughout the world. In the New Zealand region, one species is introduced, one a rare visitor, and one a breeding species; one endemic species is possibly extinct. The nostrils are hidden by stiff bristles. Plumage is variable shades of brown. All owls have large eyes, with light coloured irides, with the exception of barn owls, which have dark eyes. Generally, both parents incubate.

ORDER APODIFORMES

Swifts

Two families belong to this order, one of which visits New Zealand. These fast-flying birds have long, sickle-like, pointed wings; short tails; short legs and small feet.

FAMILY APODIDAE

Swifts: page 259
There are over 70 species throughout the world; one is a sporadic visitor to the New Zealand region and another is a rare straggler.

ORDER CORACIIFORMES

Kingfishers, rollers and allies

Two of the world's nine families occur in New Zealand. They are generally brightly coloured birds; the three front toes are fused to a greater or lesser extent. These birds nest in holes, burrows or hollows, and their eggs are commonly white.

FAMILY ALCEDINIDAE

Kingfishers: pages 260–262

Of the 90 species throughout the world, only two breed in New Zealand; one of these is introduced. The bill is long, with a rounded culmen, and a ventral ridge on the lower mandible, ascending towards the tip. These birds have a large head, short neck, and compact body. The wings are generally short and rounded. Both sexes share nesting duties.

FAMILY CORACIIDAE

Rollers: page 263

One of the 16 species worldwide occurs as an occasional visitor from Australia. Rollers have a large head, short neck and long wings. Their legs are short, the feet weak.

ORDER PASSERIFORMES

Perching birds

This order consists of some 56 families; 19 are found in New Zealand, and three of these are endemic. The birds of this worldwide order, sometimes called passerines or songbirds, comprise three fifths of all known living birds. Their bills are straight or curved, never hooked. The tarsi are generally long and weak; and four unwebbed toes are joined at the same level, three in front and one behind. Their specialised voice box structure and musculature enables them to sing. All have altricial young reared in the nest.

FAMILY XENICIDAE

New Zealand wrens: pages 264–266

In this endemic family of four species, one is extinct and another is extremely rare. They are tiny birds, and the bill is straight and much shorter than the tarsus. The wings are rounded with the secondaries almost as long as the primaries. The tail is very short and the tarsi, generally, are not scaly.

FAMILY ALAUDIDAE

Larks: page 267

One of the 78 species worldwide occurs as an introduced bird to the New Zealand region. These grey-brown, black or buff birds have long, pointed wings and strong legs. The legs are scaled at the back as well as the front, and the hind claw is long, straight and spur-like. They build their nests on the ground and live in open grassland.

FAMILY HIRUNDINIDAE

Swallows and martins: pages 268–269

There are some 80 species throughout the world. Of the two species that occur in New Zealand, one breeds. These birds have long pointed wings with nine primaries only, a slim body, and a short neck. The bill is short, with a wide gape; the birds feed on insects in flight. The nest is constructed of mud under shelter.

FAMILY MOTACILLIDAE

Pipits and wagtails: page 270

Of the 54 species worldwide, one widespread pipit has local races in the New Zealand region. Pipits and wagtails are mainly terrestrial. They have nine, instead of the usual 10, primary flight feathers found on songbirds. The hind claw is curved (and also long in pipits). Flight is generally strong and many species migrate. They usually build cup-shaped nests, often on the ground.

FAMILY CAMPEPHAGIDAE

Cuckoo-shrikes: pages 271–272

There are 70 species of cuckoo-shrike. Two of these have visited the New Zealand region and one is a very rare straggler. The bill is short, decurved at the tip, rather wide at the base, and notched near the tip. The wings are long and pointed, and their flight undulating.

FAMILY PYCNONOTIDAE

Bulbuls: page 308

This family consists of 123 species; one has been introduced to New Zealand. Many have strong head patterns and/or brightly coloured undertail coverts. These restless, agile birds are mainly tree-dwelling fruit-eaters and insect-eaters. They have rounded wings and long tails. The nests are cup-shaped, and the male and female share nesting duties.

FAMILY PRUNELLIDAE

Accentors: page 273

There are 13 species throughout the world; one has been introduced to New Zealand. The bill is straight, pointed, and wide at the base. The tarsus is short and similar in length to the mid toe and claw. Accentors have rounded wings and the tail is shorter than the wing. They move on the ground by walking or short jumps, and are secretive birds with quiet habits. Their eggs are blue.

FAMILY MUSCICAPIDAE

Flycatchers, warblers, thrushes and allies: pages 274–287

There are about 1340 species worldwide in this very large and varied family, which forms the major component of the passerines. In New Zealand 13 species have been recorded: nine are endemic species, two were introduced and one is a rare straggler. Most of the members of this family are insect-eating birds characterised by 10 primary flight feathers. They catch insects on the wing or by gleaning them from leaves and twigs, or by dragging them out from under bark and leaf litter. The bill is slender and slightly arched, the culmen ridged; most have bristles at the base of the bill. The wings have a short first primary. All build a cup-shaped nest and lay spotted eggs.

FAMILY ZOSTEROPIDAE

Silvereyes: page 288

About 80 species belong to this family; one is found in New Zealand. These small birds have a sharp bill equal or shorter in length than the head. Silvereyes have lightly brush-tipped tongues, and obtain nectar from blossoms; they eat insects, soft fruit and berries. They have a narrow ring of white feathers around their eyes, and nine primary flight feathers. These gregarious, wholly tree-dwelling birds often travel in large feeding flocks, and some are migratory. They build flimsy cup-shaped hanging nests and lay plain pale blue eggs.

FAMILY MELIPHAGIDAE

Honeyeaters: pages 289–292

There are 162 species worldwide. Three endemic species and one rare straggler are recorded for New Zealand. The bill is slender, curved and medium to long with a tube-like brush-tipped tongue—an adaptation to feeding on nectar. They also eat insects and fruit. The first primary is half the length of the second primary. They are largely tree-dwelling and their flight is undulating. Nests are cup-shaped.

FAMILY EMBERIZIDAE

Buntings: pages 293–294

There are 548 species which occur naturally worldwide (with the exception of Australasia). Two species have been introduced and breed in New Zealand, one of which is very localised. These finch-like birds have short pointed bills, incurved cutting edges, and sharply angled mandibles. The tail is long.

FAMILY FRINGILLIDAE

True finches: pages 295–298

There are about 120 species throughout the world, with the exception of Australasia. Four species have been introduced to New Zealand. The plumage of these small finches shows great variation—some are cryptically coloured and others brilliant. They have nine instead of the usual 10 primary flight feathers. The shape of the bill varies from short and pointed, to stout, massive and even hooked, according to the diet of the species. Most eat seeds, but some also eat insects and fruit. Members of the family are frequently gregarious. The nest is built in a cup shape.

FAMILY PLOCEIDAE

Sparrows and weavers: page 299

About 147 species belong to this family worldwide; one has been introduced to New Zealand. Sparrows have inconspicuous, drab plumage, and short thick cone-shaped bills. They are mainly seed-eaters. They build untidy dome-shaped nests in the open, but with a preference for roof cavities and other holes and crevices.

FAMILY STURNIDAE

Starlings and mynas: pages 300–301

There are about 110 species worldwide; two have been introduced to New Zealand. This Old World, largely tropical family of active gregarious birds has silky or glossy plumage which is often black. The bill is straight, rather long and slender, and the tail is usually short and square. The birds either live in trees or walk or run on the ground, and are omnivorous. Their flight is swift and direct. Many species mimic other birds and most species are garrulous, making a variety of harsh, grating notes or musical whistles. They nest in hollows or crevices or build massive domed nests of grass and fibre.

FAMILY CALLAEIDAE

New Zealand wattlebirds: pages 302–303

This is an endemic New Zealand family of three species. One species is extinct and the other two are threatened. The bill shape is variable: sharp and pointed and straight in saddlebacks; curved in the huia; short, heavy, and hooked in kokako. All have coloured wattles at their gape. Their wings are short and rounded, and they are poor flyers. The tail is long and drooping. Wattlebirds feed on insects and fruit.

FAMILY ARTAMIDAE

Wood-swallows: page 304

There are 10 world species in this family, two of which have occurred as rare stragglers in New Zealand. They have blue-grey bills with a black tip. Their wings are long and pointed, and they catch their food—insects—in flight. They sometimes feed at blossoms; assisted by their brush tongue, they gather nectar and pollen. Nests are flimsy and cup-shaped. Wood-swallows are gregarious, and often gather to roost at night piling in tight bunches into a crevice or tree hollow, or on a bare branch.

FAMILY CRACTICIDAE

Bell magpies: page 305

Of the 10 species throughout the world, one has been introduced to New Zealand from Australia. These crow-like, mostly black and white, birds have loud, often tuneful voices. The bill is straight, powerful and slightly to strongly hooked. They are usually gregarious and mostly tree-dwelling birds, but often feed on the ground. Their flight is strong. Nests are coarse cups of twigs and the eggs are green-blue marked with reds and browns.

FAMILY TURNAGRIDAE

New Zealand thrushes: page 308

This endemic family of one species is now presumed extinct. The bill is stout, arched and compressed, with bristles at the base. The tail is long and drooping. They are poor flyers, and feed mainly on the ground.

FAMILY CORVIDAE

Crows: pages 306–307

Of some 106 species worldwide, one has been introduced to New Zealand. These large, noisy and usually omnivorous birds are generally plumaged in black. The bill is strong and downcurved, and the nostrils are usually covered by a mat of hairy bristles. They feed mainly on the ground, often in groups. Nests are coarse cups of sticks, and the eggs toned green or blue. Nestlings grow plumage like that of adults.   F.C.K. & C.J.R.R.

Index of scientific names

A

Acanthisitta:
  chloris 264
  chloris chloris 264
  chloris granti 264
Accipitridae 152, 310
Acridotheres tristis 301
Alauda arvensis arvensis 267
Alaudidae 267, 312
Alcedinidae 260, 312
Alectoris:
  chukar 156
  chukar chukar 156
  chukar koroviakovi 156
Anarhynchus frontalis 188
Anas:
  aucklandica 146
  aucklandica aucklandica 146
  aucklandica chlorotis 146
  aucklandica nesiotis 146
  clypeata 147
  gibberifrons gracilis 145
  platyrhynchos platyrhynchos.........143
  rhynchotis variegata 14P
  superciliosa superciliosa 144
Anatidae 138, 310
Anhinga melanogaster 127
Anhingidae 127, 310
Anous:
  minutus 234
  stolidus 235
Anseriformes 138, 310
Anthochaera carunculata
  carunculata 292
Anthornis:
  melanura 290
  melanura melanocephala 290
  melanura melanura 290
  melanura obscura 290
Anthus:
  novaeseelandiae.................270
  novaeseelandiae aucklandicus........270
  novaeseelandiae novaeseelandiae ..270
  novaeseelandiae steindachneri 270
Apodidae 259, 312
Apodiformes 259, 312
Aptenodytes:
  forsteri 40
  patagonicus 41
Apterygidae 36, 309
Apterygiformes 36, 309
Apteryx:
  australis 38
  australis australis 38
  australis lawryi 38
  australis mantelli 38
  haastii 39
  owenii 39
Apus pacificus pacificus 259
Ardea:
  novaehollandiae novaehollandiae..129
  pacifica 130
Ardeidae 129, 310
Arenaria interpres.................201
Artamidae..................... 304, 313
Artamus:
  personatus 304
  superciliosus.....................304
Athene noctua 258
Aythya:
  australis australis 151
  novaeseelandiae.................150

B

Bartramia longicauda.................196
Botaurus stellaris poiciloptilus 135
Bowdleria:
  punctata 274
  punctata caudata 274
  punctata punctata 274
  punctata rufescens 274
  punctata vealeae 274
  punctata stewartiana 274
  punctata wilsoni 274
Branta canadensis moffitti 140
Bubulcus ibis coromandus.................134

C

Cacatua galerita 241
Cacatuidae 241, 312
Calidris:
  acuminata 206
  alba 210
  alpina 207
  alpina sakhalina 207
  bairdii 205
  canutus 203
  ferruginea 208
  fuscicollis 207
  mauri 208
  melanotos 205
  ruficollis 209
  tenuirostris........................204
Callaeas:
  cinerea 303
  cinerea cinerea 303
  cinerea wilsoni 303
Callaeidae 302, 313
Calonectris diomedea borealis.............93
Campephagidae 271, 312
Carduelis:
  carduelis britannica 297
  chloris chloris 296
  flammea cabaret 298
Cereopsis novaehollandiae 141
Charadriidae 177, 311
Charadriiformes..................... 174, 311
Charadrius:
  alexandrinus ruficapillus 181
  bicinctus 180
  bicinctus bicinctus 180
  bicinctus exilis 180
  hiaticula 184
  leschenaultii 185
  melanops 186
  mongolus 185
  obscurus 182
  veredus 186
Chenonetta jubata 151
Chlidonias:
  hybrida 225
  leucopterus........................224
Chrysococcyx lucidus lucidus 254
Ciconiiformes 129, 310
Circus approximans.................152
Coenocorypha:
  aucklandica 202
  aucklandica aucklandica 202
  aucklandica huegeli 202
  aucklandica iredalei 202
  aucklandica meinertzhagenae........202
  aucklandica pusilla 202
Colinus virginianus 158
Columba livia 237
Columbidae 237, 311
Columbiformes 237, 311
Coraciidae 263, 312
Coraciiformes 260, 312
Coracina novaehollandiae 271
Corvidae 306, 313
Corvus frugilegus frugilegus.........306
Coturnix novaezelandiae 308
Cracticidae 305, 313
Cuculidae 252, 312
Cuculiformes 252, 312
Cuculus:
  pallidus 252
  pyrrhophanus prionurus 252
  saturatus 253
Cyanoramphus:
  auriceps 251
  auriceps auriceps 251
  auriceps forbesi 251

malherbi 247
novaezelandiae.................248
novaezelandiae chathamensis.......248
novaezelandiae cyanurus 248
novaezelandiae hochstetteri.........248
novaezelandiae novaezelandiae ...248
unicolor 250
Cygnus:
  atratus 139
  olor 138

D

Dacelo novaeguineae 262
Daption:
  capense...............................70
  capense australe 70
  capense capense.................70
Dendrocygna eytoni 138
Diomedea:
  bulleri 64
  bulleri bulleri 64
  bulleri platei 64
  cauta 65
  cauta eremita 65
  cauta salvini 65
  cauta steadi 65
  chlororhynchos.....................63
  chlororhynchos bassi 63
  chlororhynchos chlororhynchos 63
  chrysostoma 62
  epomophora 60
  epomophora epomophora 60
  epomophora sanfordi 60
  exulans 58
  exulans chionoptera 58
  exulans exulans 58
  melanophrys 61
  melanophrys impavida 61
  melanophrys melanophrys.............61
  nigripes 63
Diomedeidae 58, 309

E

Egretta:
  alba modesta 131
  garzetta immaculata 130
  intermedia 133
  sacra sacra 132
Emberiza:
  cirlus cirlus 294
  citrinella caliginosa.................293
Emberizidae 293, 313
Erythrogonys cinctus.................182
Eudynamys taitensis 255
Eudyptes:
  chrysocome 49
  chrysocome chrysocome 49
  chrysocome moseleyi 49
  chrysolophus 48
  chrysolophus chrysolophus.........48
  chrysolophus schlegeli 48
  pachyrhynchus 50
  robustus 51
  sclateri 52
Eudyptula:
  minor 46
  minor albosignata 46
  minor chathamensis 46
  minor iredalei 46
  minor minor 46
  minor variabilis 46
Eurystomus orientalis pacificus........263

F

Falco:
  cenchroides cenchroides 154
  novaeseelandiae.................154
Falconidae 154, 310

Falconiformes 152, 310
Finschia novaeseelandiae 275
Fregata:
  ariel ariel 128
  minor 128
Fregatidae..................... 128, 310
Fregetta:
  grallaria 105
  tropica 105
Fringilla coelebs gengleri 295
Fringillidae..................... 295, 313
Fulica atra australis 173
Fulmaris glacialoides 67

G

Galliformes 156, 310
Gallinago hardwickii 203
Gallinula:
  tenebrosa 172
  ventralis 172
Gallirallus:
  australis 168
  australis australis 169
  australis greyi 169
  australis hectori 169
  australis scotti 169
Garrodia nereis 103
Gelochelidon nilotica macrotarsa 225
Gerygone:
  albofrontata 279
  igata 278
Glareola maldivarum 216
Glareolidae 216, 311
Gruidae 164, 311
Gruiformes 164, 311
Grus rubicunda 164
Gygis alba 236
Gymnorhina:
  tibicen 305
  tibicen hypoleuca 305
  tibicen tibicen 305

H

Haematopodidae 174, 311
Haematopus:
  chathamensis 176
  ostralegus finschi 174
  unicolor 175
Halobaena caerulea 84
Halcyon sancta vagans 260
Hemiphaga:
  novaeseelandiae.................238
  novaeseelandiae chathamensis........239
  novaeseelandiae novaeseelandiae ..239
Heteralocha acutirostris 308
Himantopus:
  himantopus leucocephalus 212
  novaezealandiae 214
Hirundapus caudacutus
  caudacutis 259
Hirundinidae 268, 312
Hirundo tahitica neoxena 269
Hydrobatidae 102, 310
Hydroprogne caspia 226
Hylochelidon nigricans nigricans 268
Hymenolaimus malacorhynchos 149

I

Ixobrychus novaezelandiae..............308

L

Lalage sueurii tricolor.................272
Laridae 221, 311
Larus:
  bulleri 223
  dominicanus........................221

novaehollandiae scopulinus 222
Leucocarbo:
  atriceps 124
  atriceps purpurascens 124
  campbelli 122
  carunculatus 118
  chalconotus 119
  colensoi 123
  onslowi 121
  ranfurlyi 120
Limicola falcinellus sibirica 211
Limosa:
  haemastica.............................193
  lapponica baueri 194
  limosa melanuroides 192
Lophortyx californica brunnescens ..159
Lugensa brevirostris 84

M

Macronectes:
  giganteus 68
  halli 69
Megadyptes antipodes 42
Meleagris gallopavo 162
Meliphagidae 289, 313
Mergus australis 308
Mohoua:
  albicilla 276
  ochrocephala 277
Motacillidae 270, 312
Muscicapidae 274, 313
Myiagra cyanoleuca 286

N

Nestor:
  meridionalis.............................244
  meridionalis meridionalis 244
  meridionalis septentrionalis...........244
  notabilis.................................245
Nestoridae 244, 312
Ninox novaeseelandiae
  novaeseelandiae.......................257
Notiomystis cincta 289
Notornis mantelli 170
Numenius:
  madagascariensis 190
  minutus 192
  phaeopus 191
  phaeopus hudsonicus 191
  phaeopus variegatus 191
  tahitiensis 190
Numida meleagris 163
Nycticorax caledonicus 133

O

Oceanites oceanicus.........................102
Oceanodroma leucorhoa leucorhoa ..102

P

Pachyptila:
  belcheri 85
  crassirostris 88
  desolata desolata 86
  salvini salvini 86
  turtur.......................................87
  vittata vittata 85
Pagodroma:
  nivea 71
  nivea major 71
  nivea nivea 71
Passer domesticus domesticus...........299
Passeriformes 264, 312
Pavo cristatus 161
Pelagodroma:
  marina....................................104
  marina albinclunis 104

marina dulciae 104
marina maoriana 104
Pelecanidae........................... 109, 310
Pelecaniformes...................... 108, 310
Pelecanoides:
  georgicus 107
  urinatrix 106
  urinatrix exsul 106
  urinatrix urinatrix 106
Pelecanoididae 106, 310
Pelecanus conspicillatus 109
Perdix perdix 157
Petroica:
  australis 282
  australis australis 283
  australis longipes 283
  australis rakiura 283
  macrocephala..........................284
  macrocephala chathamensis 284
  macrocephala dannefaerdi 284
  macrocephala macrocephala 284
  macrocephala marrineri 284
  macrocephala toitoi 284
  traversi 281
Phaethon:
  lepturus dorotheae 108
  rubricauda roseotincta 108
Phaethontidae...................... 108, 310
Phalacrocoracidae 114, 310
Phalacrocorax:
  carbo 114
  carbo steadi 114
  melanoleucos brevirostris...............117
  sulcirostris 115
  varius 116
  varius varius 116
Phalaropodidae 215, 311
Phalaropus:
  fulicarius 215
  lobatus 215
Phasianidae......................... 156, 311
Phasianus:
  colchicus 160
  colchicus colchicus 160
  colchicus mongolicus 160
  colchicus torquatus 160
Philesturnus:
  carunculatus 302
  carunculatus carunculatus 302
  carunculatus rufusater 302
Phoebetria palpebrata 66
Platalea:
  flavipes 137
  leucorodia regia 137
Platycercidae 246, 312
Platycercus:
  elegans...................................247
  eximius 246
Plegadis falcinellus 136
Ploceidae 299, 313
Pluvialis:
  fulva 177
  squatarola 178
Podiceps:
  cristatus australis 57
  poliocephalus 56
  rufopectus 54
Podicipedidae 54, 309
Podicipediformes 54, 309
Porphyrio porphyrio melanotus 171
Porzana:
  pusilla affinis 166
  tabuensis plumbea 167
Procellaria:
  aequinoctialis 92
  cinerea 89
  parkinsoni 90
  westlandica 91
Procellariidae 67, 309
Procellariiformes 58, 309
Procelsterna cerulea 235
Prosthemadera:
  novaeseelandiae.........................291
  novaeseelandiae chathamensis........291

novaeseelandiae novaeseelandiae ..291
Prunella modularis occidentalis 273
Prunellidae 273, 313
Psittaciformes...................... 241, 312
Pterodroma:
  alba 75
  axillaris 81
  cookii 80
  externa cervicalis 75
  externa externa 74
  inexpectata 76
  lessonii 73
  leucoptera caledonica 78
  longirostris 82
  macroptera gouldi 72
  magentae 78
  mollis mollis 77
  neglecta neglecta 79
  nigripennis 83
  pycrofti 82
  solandri 74
Puffinus:
  assimilis 101
  assimilis assimilis 101
  assimilis elegans 101
  assimilis haurakiensis 101
  assimilis kermadecensis 101
  bulleri 93
  carneipes 95
  gavia 100
  griseus 96
  huttoni 99
  nativitatis 95
  pacificus 94
  puffinus puffinus 98
  tenuirostris 98
Pycnonotidae 308, 312
Pycnonotus cafer bengalensis 308
Pygoscelis:
  adeliae 43
  antarctica 45
  papua 44

R

Rallidae................................ 165, 311
Rallus:
  modestus 165
  pectoralis muelleri 166
  philippensis 165
  philippensis assimilis 165
  philippensis dieffenbachii 165
  philippensis macquariensis 165
Recurvirostra novaehollandiae 212
Recurvirostridae 212, 311
Rhipidura:
  fuliginosa.................................280
  fuliginosa fuliginosa 280
  fuliginosa penitus 280
  fuliginosa placabilis 280

S

Sceloglaux albifacies........................308
Scolopacidae......................... 190, 311
Scythrops novaehollandiae 253
Spheniscidae 40, 309
Sphenisciformes 40, 309
Spheniscus magellanicus...................53
Stercorariidae....................... 217, 311
Stercorarius:
  longicaudus 220
  maccormicki 217
  parasiticus 220
  pomarinus 219
  skua lonnbergi 218
Sterna:
  albifrons sinensis 231
  albostriata 227
  bergii cristata 229
  fuscata 233
  nereis 230

paradisaea 231
striata 232
vittata bethunei 228
Sternidae 224, 311
Stictocarbo:
  featherstoni 126
  punctatus 125
  punctatus punctatus 125
  punctatus steadi........................125
Streptopelia:
  chinensis tigrina 240
  risoria 240
Strigidae 256, 312
Strigiformes 256, 312
Strigops habroptilus 242
Sturnidae 300, 313
Sturnus vulgaris vulgaris 300
Sula:
  bassana serrator........................110
  dactylatra personata 113
  leucogaster plotus 112
Sulidae 110, 310
Synoicus ypsilophorus 158

T

Tachybaptus novaehollandiae...........56
Tadorna:
  tadornoides 141
  variegata 142
Thalassoica antarctica 67
Thinornis novaeseelandiae 188
Threskiornis molucca 136
Threskiornithidae 136, 310
Tringa:
  brevipes 199
  flavipes 196
  hypoleucos 197
  incana 198
  nebularia 199
  stagnatilis 197
Turdus:
  merula merula 287
  philomelos clarkei 286
Turnagra:
  capensis 308
  capensis capensis 308
  capensis tanagra 308
Turnagridae 313
Tyto alba delicatula 256

V

Vanellus miles novaehollandiae 178

X

Xenicidae 264, 312
Xenicus:
  gilviventris 266
  longipes 265
  longipes longipes 265
  longipes stokesii 265
  longipes variabilis 265
Xenus cinereus 200

Z

Zosteropidae........................ 288, 313
Zosterops lateralis lateralis 288

Index of common names

A

Akiaki 222
Albatross
  black-footed 63
  light-mantled sooty 66
  northern royal 60
  royal 60
  snowy 58
  southern royal 60
  wandering 58
Amokura 108
Avocet, red-necked 212
  Australian 212

B

Bellbird 290
  Chatham Island 290
  Three Kings 290
Bird-of-providence 74
Bittern
  Australasian 135
  Australian brown 135
  brown 135
  New Zealand little 308
Black burrower 94
Black cap 232
Blackbird 287
Blightbird 288
Blue 304
Blue-billy 85, 235
Bob-white 158
Booby
  blue-faced 113
  Brewster's 112
  brown 112
  common 112
  masked 113
  whistling 113
  white 113
  white-bellied 112
Bos'un bird 108
Brainfever bird 252
Brolga 164
Bulbul, red-vented 308
Bunting
  cirl 294
  yellow 293

C

Callie 159
Canary, bush 277
Cape hen 92
Caterpillar-eater, white-shouldered 272
Chaffinch 295
Chukar 156
  Indian 156
  Persian 156
Chukor 156
Cockatoo
  sulphur-crested 241
  white 241
Coot, Australasian 173
Cormorant
  black 114
  Cook Strait 118
  great 114
  imperial 124
  little 117
  little black 115
  little pied 117
  pied 116
  yellow-faced 116
Crake
  marsh 166
  spotless 167
Crane
  Australian 164
  blue 129, 132
Creeper, brown 275
Crow 306
  blue wattled 303
  orange wattled 303
Cuckoo
  ash-coloured 252
  bronze 254
  channel-billed 253
  fan-tailed 252
  hawk 253
  Himalayan 253
  long-tailed 255
  oriental 253
  pallid 252
  shining 254
  see also Cuckoo-shrike
Cuckoo-shrike
  black-faced 271
  large 271
Curlew
  American 191
  Australian 190
  bristle-thighed 190
  eastern 190
  far-eastern 190
  Hudsonian 191
  little 191, 192
  long-billed 190
  pygmy 192

D

Dabchick
  Australian 56
  hoary-headed 56
  New Zealand 54
Dancing dolly 104
Darter 127
Diving petrel
  Chatham Island 106
  common 106
  Kerguelen 106
  New Zealand 106
  South Georgian 107
  subantarctic 106
  see also Petrel, Storm petrel, Taiko
Dollar bird 263
Dotterel
  Auckland Island banded 180
  banded 180
  black-fronted 186
  large sand 185
  Mongolian 185
  New Zealand 182
  oriental 186
  red-breasted 183
  red-capped 181
  red-kneed 182
Dove
  Barbary 240
  domestic collared 240
  Java 240
  laceneck 240
  Malay spotted 240
  ring 240
  ringed turtle 240
  rock 237
  spotted 240
  spotted turtle 240
Duck
  Australian white-eyed 151
  blue 149
  brown 146
  grass whistle 138
  grey 144
  maned 151
  mountain 141
  paradise 142
  teal 146
  white-eyed 151
  wood 151
  see also Tree duck, Whistling duck
Dunlin 207
Dunnock 273

E

Egg bird 233
Egret
  cattle 134
  eastern great white 131
  intermediate 133
  large 131
  little 130
  plumed 133
  white 131

F

Falcon
  bush 155
  eastern 155
  New Zealand 154
  southern 155
Fantail 280
  black 280
  Chatham Island 280
  North Island 280
  pied 280
  South Island 280
Fernbird 274
  Chatham Island 274
  Codfish Island 274
  North Island 274
  Snares 274
  South Island 274
  Stewart Island 274
Flip-flap 125
Flood-bird 253
Flycatcher, satin 286
Frigate bird 128
  greater 128
  lesser 128
Fulmar
  Antarctic 67
  giant 68, 69
  silver-grey 67
  southern 67

G

Gannet
  Australasian 110
  Australian 110
  brown 112
Gill, blue 303
Godwit
  American black-tailed 193
  Asiatic black-tailed 192
  eastern bar-tailed 194
  eastern black-tailed 192
  Hudsonian 193
  Pacific 195
Gogo 235
Goldfinch 297
Goldie 297
Gooney, black 63
Goose
  Cape Barren 141
  giant Canada 140
  pig 141
  see also Solan goose
Grass bird 274
Grebe
  Australasian little 56
  Australian little 56
  black-throated 56
  crested 57
  hoary-headed 56
  southern crested 57
Greenfinch 296
Greenshank 199
  little 197
Grenadier 232
Groundlark 270
Guineafowl 163
  crowned 163
  helmeted 163
  tufted 163
Gull
  black-billed 223
  Buller's 223
  Dominican 221
  kelp 221
  mackerel 222
  red-billed 222
  silver 222
  southern black-backed 221

H

Hakoakoa 218
Hakoke 308
Hard head 151
Harrier
  Australasian 152
  marsh 152
  swamp 152
Hawk
  bush 155
  man-o'-war 128
  quail 153
Hedgesparrow 273
Heron
  blue 132
  blue reef 132
  buff-backed 134
  eastern reef 132
  great white 131
  nankeen night 133
  reef 132
  rufous night 133
  Pacific 130
  white 131
  white-faced 129
  white-necked 130
Hihi 289
Honeyeater, wattled 292
Honker 140
Hoverer 154
Huahou 203
Huia 308

I

Ibis
  Australian white 136
  glossy 136
  white 136

J

Jackass, laughing 262
Jackie 222
Jaeger
  long-tailed 220
  parasitic 220
  pomarine 219
Jay, blue 271, 304
JC bird 104
Johnny 44

K

Kahawai bird 232
Kahu 152
Kaka 244
  North Island 244
  South Island 244
Kaka-kereru 244
Kaka-korako 244
Kaka-kura 244
Kaka-pipiwarauroa 244
Kakaiki 248
Kakapo 242
Kakariki 251
Kaki 214
Karakahia 151
Karearea 155
Karoro 221
Karuhiruhi 116
Kawau-tua-whenua 114
Kawaupaka 117
Kea 245
Kereru 239
Kestrel
  Australian 154
  nankeen 154
Kingfisher
  great brown 262
  New Zealand 260
  sacred 260
Kiwi 36
  brown 38
  great spotted 39
  large grey 39
  little grey 39
  little spotted 39
  North Island brown 38
  South Island brown 38
  Stewart Island brown 38
Knot 203
  eastern (Asiatic) 204
  great 204
  greater 204
  lesser 203
  red 203
Koekoea 255
Kohoperoa 255
Koitareke 166
Kokako 303
  North Island 303
  South Island 303

Kookaburra 262
laughing 262
Korara 46
Koreke 308
Korimako 290
Korohea 308
Korure 76
Kotare 260
Kotuku 131
Kotuku-ngutupapa 137
Kuaka 106, 195
Kuku 239
Kukupa 239
Kuru whengi 148

L

Lark, native 270
Laughing jackass 262
Linnet, green 296
Longbill 203
Lory, red 247
Lowry, red 247

M

Magpie
Australian 305
black-backed 305
white-backed 305
Makomako 290
Mallard 143
Man-o'-war bird 128
Pacific 128
Man-o'-war hawk 128
Martin
Australian tree 268
blue 304
bush 304
tree 268
Matata 274
Matuhituhi 265
Matuku-moana 132
Matuku-hurepo 135
Maui-potiki 284
Mavis 286
Merganser, Auckland Island 308
Merle 287
Minah 301
Mockie 290
Moho 170
Moho-pereru 165
Mohoua 277
Mohoua houa 277
Mollymawk
black-browed 61
Buller's 64
Chatham Island 65
grey-headed 62
New Zealand black-browed 61
northern Buller's 64
Salvin's 65
shy 65
southern Buller's 64
white-capped 65
yellow-nosed 63
Moorhen, dusky 172
Morepork 257
see also Owl
Muttonbird 72, 99
big-hill 74
New Zealand 97
Tasmanian 98
Myna
common 301
Indian 301
Mynah 301

N

Native companion 164
Native hen, black-tailed 172
Nelly 68, 69
Ngiru-ngiru 284
Ngutu-parore 189
Noddy 232
black 234
blue-grey 235
brown 235
common 235
greater 235
grey 235
lesser 234
white 236
white-capped 234

O

Oi 72
Organ-bird 303
Owl
Australian barn 256
barn 256
boobook 257
brown 258
delicate 256
German 258
laughing 308
lesser masked 256
little 258
New Zealand 257
rock 308
screech 256
white 256
see also Morepork
Oystercatcher
Chatham Island 176
South Island pied 174
variable 175

P

Pakaha 99, 100
Pakura 171
Papango 150
Parakeet
alpine 247
Antipodes green 250
Antipodes Island 250
Antipodes red-crowned 248
Chatham Island red-crowned 248
Chatham Island yellow-crowned 251
Forbes' 251
Kermadec 248
Lord Howe Island 248
New Zealand 248
New Zealand red-crowned 248
orange-fronted 247
red-crowned 248
Reischek's 248
yellow-crowned 251
Parara 85
Parekareka 125
Parera 144
Pari 142
Parrot
brown 244
bush 244
ground 242
night 242
owl 242
Parson bird 291
Partridge
chukar 156
common 157
grey 157
Hungarian 157
Pass bird 170
Pateke 146
Paturiwhata 183
Peacock 161
Peafowl 161
Indian 161
Pediunker 89
Pee-oo 66
Peewee-lark 272
Pelican
Australian 109
spectacled 109
Penguin
Adélie 43
bearded 45
big-crested 52
blue 46
Chatham Island blue 46
chinstrap 45
Cook Strait blue 46
crested 49
emperor 40
erect-crested 52
fairy 46
Fiordland 50
Fiordland crested 50
Gentoo 44
jackass 53
Johnny 44
king 41
little 46
little blue 46
macaroni 48
Magellanic 53
Moseley's rockhopper 49
New Zealand crested 50
northern blue 46
ringed 45
rockhopper 49
royal 48
Snares 51
Snares crested 51
Snares Island 51
southern blue 46
thick-billed 50
tufted 49
white-flippered 46
yellow-eyed 42
Petrel
Antarctic 67
black 90
black-capped 75
black-winged 83
blue 84
brown 89
brown-headed 74
Cape 70
Chatham Island 81
Christmas Island 75
Cook's 80
frigate 104
greater snow 71
grey 89
grey-faced 72
Hall's giant 69
Juan Fernandez 74
Kerguelen 84
Kermadec 79
Leach's 102
Leach's fork-tailed 102
lesser snow 71
little blue 235
magenta 78
mottled 76
New Caledonian 78
northern giant 69
Parkinson's 90
Peale's 76
phoenix 75
pintado 70
providence 74
Pycroft's 82
scaled 76
snow 71
soft-plumaged 77
Solander's 74
southern giant 68
Stejneger's 82
Sunday Island 75
Westland black 91
white-chinned 92
white-headed 73
white-naped 75
white-necked 74
Wilson's 102
see also Diving petrel, Storm petrel, Taiko
Phalarope
grey 215
northern 215
red 215
red-necked 215
Pheasant 160
black-necked 160
melanistic mutant 160
Mongolian 160
ring-necked 160
Pigeon
Cape 70
Chatham Island 239
feral 237
New Zealand 238, 239
rock 237
Snares Cape 70
Pihoihoi 270
Pintado 163
Piopio 308
Pipipi 275
Pipit 270
Antipodes 270
Auckland Islands 270
New Zealand 270
Pipiwharauroa 254
Piropiro 284
Piwakawaka 280
Plover
Asiatic golden 177
black-bellied 178
black-fronted 187
double banded 180
grey 178
least golden 177
lesser golden 177
Mongolian 185
New Zealand shore 188
oriental 186
Pacific golden 177
red-capped 181
ringed 184
spur-winged 178
upland 196
wrybilled 189
see also Sand plover
Poaka 212
Pohowera 180
Popokatea 276
Pratincole
eastern 216
eastern collared 216
oriental 216
Prion
Antarctic 86
broad-billed 85
cliff 88
Crozet Islands 86
dove 86
fairy 87
fulmar 88
lesser broad-billed 86
Marion Island 86
medium-billed 86
narrow-billed 87
Salvin's 86
slender-billed 85
thick-billed 88
thin-billed 85
Pukaki 171
Puke 171
Pukeko 171
Putangitangi 142
Puteketeke 57
Putoto 167
Puweto 167

Q

Quail
Australian 158
bobwhite 158
brown 158
California 159
Californian 159
New Zealand 308
swamp 158
Tasmanian 158
Virginian 158

R

Rail
Auckland Island 166
banded 165
Chatham Island 165
Dieffenbach's 165
Macquarie Island 165
Rainbird 76
Ranguru 81
Redbill 174, 175, 176
Redpoll 298
lesser 298
Rifleman 264
North Island 264
South Island 264
Riroriro 278
Roa 39
Robin 282
black 281
bush 283
Chatham Island 281
North Island 283
Snares Island 284
South Island 283
Stewart Island 283
Roller, broad-billed 263

Rook 306
Rosella 246
crimson 247
eastern 246
Rowi 38
Ruru 257

S

Saddleback 302
North Island 302
South Island 302
Sand plover
eastern 186
eastern long-legged 186
Geoffroy's 185
greater 185
grey-rumped 199
lesser 185
long-billed 185
short-billed 185
see also Plover
Sanderling 210
Sandpiper
American grey-rumped 198
avocet 200
Baird's 205
Bartram's 196
black-bellied 207
Bonaparte's 207
common 197
curlew 208
eastern broad-billed 211
great 204
grey-rumped 199
marsh 197
pectoral 205
red-backed 207
rufous-necked 209
sharp-tailed 206
Siberian pectoral 206
terek 200
upland 196
western 208
white-rumped 207
Scaup 150
New Zealand 150
Scooper 85
Screamer 255
Screecher 255
Sea-swallow 231, 232
Shag
Auckland Island 123
black 114
blue 125
blue-eyed 124
Bounty Island 120
bronze 119
Campbell Island 122
carunculated 118
Chatham Island 121
crested 125
double-crested 126
emperor 124
frilled 117
Gray's 119
king 118
little 117
little black 115
little river 117
Macquarie Island 124
Marlborough Sounds 118
needle-beaked 127
ocean 125
pied 116
Pitt Island 126
rough-faced 118
spotted 125
Stewart Island 119
subantarctic king 124
white-throated 117
Shearwater
allied 101
black 95
Buller's 93
Christmas 95
Christmas Island 95
common 98
Cory's 93
flesh-footed 95
fluttering 100
Forster's 100
great grey 89
grey-backed 93
Hutton's 99
Kermadec little 101
little 101
Manx 98
Mediterranean 93
New Zealand 93
Norfolk Island little 101
North Atlantic 93
North Island little 101
pale-footed 95
short-tailed 98
slender-billed 98
sooty 96
subantarctic little 101
wedge-tailed 94
Shelduck
Australian 141
chestnut-breasted 141
paradise 142
Shoemaker 92
Shoveler
New Zealand 148
northern 147
Shufflewing 271
Silvereye 288
Skimmer 304
Skipjack 104
Skua
Antarctic 217
Arctic 220
brown 218
long-tailed 220
McCormick's 217
pomarine 219
pomatorhine 219
south polar 217
southern 218
southern great 218
subantarctic 218
Skylark 267
Snake-bird 127
Snipe 202
Antipodes Island 202
Auckland Island 202
Australian 203
Chatham Island 202
Japanese 203
Latham's 203
Snares Island 202
Stewart Island 202
Solan goose 110
see also Goose
Spadger 299
Sparrow
English 299
house 299
Sparrowhawk 155
Spoonbill 148
royal 137
yellow-billed 137
Spoonie 148
Starling 300
Stilt
black 214
pied 212
white-headed 212
Stinker 68, 69
Stint
curlew 208
eastern little 209
red-necked 209
Stitchbird 289
Storm bird 252, 253
Storm petrel
Australian white-faced 104
black-bellied 105
fork-tailed 102
grey-backed 103
Kermadec 104
Leach's 102
New Zealand white-faced 104
white-bellied 105
white-faced 104
Wilson's 102
see also Petrel, Diving petrel, Taiko
Summer bird 271, 304
Swallow 269
tree 268
welcome 269
Swallow-plover 216
Swallowtail 232
Swamp hen 171
Swan
black 139
mute 138
white 138
Swift
fork-tailed 259
spine-tailed 259
white-rumped 259
white-throated needle-tailed 259

T

Taiko 90
Chatham Island 78
see also Petrel, Diving petrel, Storm petrel
Takahe 170
Takahi-kare-moana 104
Takapu 110
Takaraka 42
Tara 227, 232
Tara-iti 230
Taranui 226
Tarapo 242
Tarapunga 222
Tarepo 242
Tattler
Alaskan 198
American 198
grey-rumped 199
grey-tailed 199
Siberian 199
wandering 198
Tauhou 288
Tawaki 50, 52
Tchaik of the Moriori 78
Teal
Auckland Island 146
black 150
brown 146
Campbell Island 146
grey 145
Teetotum 278
Tern
Antarctic 228
Arctic 231
Asiatic little 231
black-fronted 227
black-lored 231
Caspian 226
crested 229
eastern little 231
fairy 230, 236
greater crested 229
gull-billed 225
little 231
long-legged 225
love 236
marsh 225
noddy 235
Pacific 236
sooty 233
swift 229
whiskered 225
white 236
white-fronted 232
white-winged black 224
white-winged marsh 224
wideawake 233
Ternlet
grey 235
white-shafted 231
Tete 145
Thrush
New Zealand 308
North Island 308
song 286
South Island 308
swamp 274
Tieke 302
Tikkitak 232
Tit 284
Auckland Island 284
black 284
Chatham Island 284
North Island 284
pied 284
Snares 284
South Island 284
white-breasted 284
yellow-breasted 284
Titerack 234
Titi 76, 80, 97, 99
Titipounamu 264
Titi-wainui 87
Toanui 95
Tokoeka 38
Tom Pudding 56
Tom Thumb bird 265
Tomtit
North Island 284
white-breasted 284
Torea 174
Torea-pango 175
Toroa 58, 60, 61
Toutouwai 282
Tree-duck
Eyton's 138
plumed 138
see also Duck, Whistling duck
Triller, white-winged 272
Tropic bird
red-tailed 108
white-tailed 108
yellow-billed 108
Tui 291
Chatham Island 291
Turkey
wild 162
Turnstone 201
ruddy 201
Tuturiwhatu 180
pukunui 183
Tuturuatu 188

W

Wanderer 58
Warbler
Chatham Island 279
grey 278
Water hen, black-tailed 172
Wattle bird, red 292
Waxeye 288
Weka 168
buff 169
North Island 169
Stewart Island 169
western 169
Weweia 54
Whale bird 233
Whalebird 85
Whekau 308
Whimbrel 191
American 191
Asiatic 191
eastern 191
little 192
Whio 149
Whistler 101, 254
Whistling duck, plumed 138
see also Duck, Tree duck
White-eye 288
Whitehead 276
Windhover, Australian 154
Wood-swallow
masked 304
white-browed 304
Woodhen 169
Woodrail 169
Wren
bush 265
green 265
North Island bush 265
rock 266
South Island bush 265
Stead's bush 265
Wrybill 188

Y

Yellowhammer 293
Yellowhead 277
Yellowlegs, lesser 196
Yellowshank 196

Acknowledgments

PHOTOGRAPHS: The names of photographers and photographic libraries are listed after the number of the page on which their photographs are reproduced. (The letter *t* = top, *c* = centre, *b* = bottom.)

Cover Front cover: Brian Chudleigh; back cover, from top left, clockwise: Photobank/C. R. Veitch, Rod Morris, Rod Morris, J. A. Mills, Rod Morris. **1** Len Robinson/NPI. **8** Brian Chudleigh. **10-11** Gavin Woodward. **12** Brian Chudleigh.**13** D. V. Merton. **15** *t*, Brian Chudleigh; *c and b*, Rod Morris. **18** G. R. Chance. **19** Stuart L. G. Rees. **20** Wynston Cooper ARPS. **21** D. S. Horning. **22** M. F. Soper. **23** *t*, Rod Morris; *b*, C. J. R. Robertson. **26** *t and b*, Brian Enting. **27** *t*, Geoff Moon; *b*, Brian Enting. **28** *t*, M. F. Soper; *b*, Brian Enting. **29** M. F. Soper. **30** *t*, Brian Enting; *b*, Rod Morris. **31** *t and b*, Geoff Moon. **33** National Library of Australia. **34-5** Walter Imber. **36** *t*, Photobank/C. R. Veitch; *c and b*, P. H. McKenzie. **37** Robin Smith Photography Ltd. **38** *t*, C. E. Barwell; *b*, M. F. Soper/Bruce Coleman Ltd. **39** *t*, Geoff Moon; *b*, Rod Morris. **40** John Boyd/Oxford Scientific Films. **41** G. W. Johnstone. **42** M. F. Soper. **43** P. M. & J. L. Sagar. **44** G. W. Johnstone. **45** John Darby. **46** John Warham. **47** Ian McVinnie. **48** John Warham. **49** M. F. Soper. **50** C. E. Barwell. **51** P. M. & J. L. Sagar. **52** P. J. Moors. **53** Cindy Buxton/Oxford Scientific Films. **55** Geoff Moon. **56** *t*, Graeme Chapman; *b*, F. G. Craven/NPI. **57** Graeme Chapman. **58-9** John Warham. **60** R. B. Goffin. **61** John Warham. **62** G. W. Johnstone. **63** *t*, Peter Steyn/Ardea; *b*, Brian Hawkes/Jacana. **64** P. M. & J. L. Sagar. **65** P. J. Moors. **66** John Warham. **67** *t*, Barry M. Allwright/NPI; *b*, G. W. Johnstone. **68** G. W. Johnstone. **69** Nigel Brothers. **70** H. A. Best. **71** G. W. Johnstone. **72** Dave Garrick. **73** M. F. Soper. **74** P. J. Fullagar/NPI. **75** Mark J. Rauzon. **76** P. M. & J. L. Sagar. **77** John Warham. **78** *t*, F. Hannecart; *b*, M. D. Dennison. **79** D. V. Merton. **80** P. C. Harper, **81** Dave Garrick. **82** D. V. Merton. **83** Dave Garrick. **84** Peter Steyn/Ardea. **85** M. F. Soper/NPI. **86** *t*, Dave Garrick; *b*, Trevor Pescott. **87** P. C. Harper. **88** P. M. & J. L. Sagar. **89** M. F. Soper. **90** Photobank/C. R. Veitch. **91** Ian McVinnie. **92** Jouve/Jacana. **93** *t*, John Warham; *b*, P. C. Harper. **94** D. V. Merton. **95** *t*, A. Habraken; *b*, Sigurd Halvorsen/Bruce Coleman Ltd. **96-7** *both* P. M. & J. L. Sagar. **98** *t*, J. R. Napier/NPI; *b*, R. Vaughan/Ardea. **99** Geoffrey Harrow. **100** P. M. & J. L. Sagar. **101** P. C. Harper. **102** *t*, S. Roberts/Ardea; *b*, Peter Johnson/NHPA. **103** M. F. Soper. **104** H. A. Best. **105** *t*, M. F. Soper; *b*, J. Disney & P. J. Fullagar/NPI. **106** M. F. Soper. **107** Dave Garrick. **108** *t*, Tony Beamish/Ardea; *b*, Chris N. Challies. **109** W. D. F. MacKenzie/NPI. **110** Peter A. Morath. **112** Mark J. Rauzon. **113** Photobank/C. R. Veitch. **114** M. J. Ladbrook. **115** Graeme Chapman. **116** M. F. Soper. **117** C. E. Barwell. **118** M. F. Soper. **119** Geoff Moon. **120** C. J. R. Robertson. **121** Rod Morris. **122** R. B. Goffin. **123** D. S. Horning. **124** G. W. Johnstone. **125** Rod Morris. **126** Photobank/C. R. Veitch. **127** H. & J. Beste/NPI. **128** *t and b*, Vincent Serventy/NPI. **129** Geoff Moon. **130** *t and b*, W. J. Labbett/NPI. **131** Brian Chudleigh. **132** Len Robinson/NPI. **133** *t*, W. J. Labbett/NPI; *b*, G. A. Foreman. **134** J. B. & S. Bottomley/Ardea. **135** G. R. Chance. **136** *t*, D. & M. Trounson/NPI; *b*, John Fennell. **137** *t*, Tim Newbery/NPI; *b*, M. F. Soper. **138** *t*, Graeme Chapman; *b*, G. R. Chance. **139** Brian Chudleigh. **140** M. F. Soper. **141** *t*, F. M. Dowling/NPI; *b*, Graeme Chapman. **142** John Fennell. **143** G. R. Chance. **144** Graeme Chapman. **145** M. F. Soper. **146** *b*, M. F. Soper. **146-7** Photobank/C. R. Veitch. **147** *b*, Tom & Pam Gardner/NPI. **148** Kenneth W. Fink/Ardea. **149** Rod Morris. **150** M. F. Soper. **151** *t*, Graeme Chapman; *b*, D. H. Brathwaite. **153** M. F. Soper. **154** R. F. Kenyon/NPI. **155** M. F. Soper/Bruce Coleman Ltd. **156** M. F. Soper. **157** J. A. Bailey/Ardea. **158** *t*, J. S. Dunning/Ardea; *b*, G. Rogerson/NPI. **159** M. J. Ladbrook. **160** S. Roberts/Ardea. **161** D. & M. Trounson/NPI. **162** R. N. Thomas. **163** M. F. Soper. **164** L. J. Millar/NPI. **165** M. R. Quinn. **166** *t*, Rod Morris; *b*, L. G. Chandler/NPI. **167** Graeme Chapman. **168** L. J. Richards. **169** M. D. Dennison. **170** J. A. Mills. **171** L. J. Richards. **172** *t*, Graeme Chapman; *b*, M. F. Soper. **173** Geoff Moon. **174** C. E. Barwell. **175** M. F. Soper. **176** M. F. Soper. **177** Graeme Chapman. **178** Tom & Pam Gardner/NPI. **179** M. J. Ladbrook. **180** R. J. Wasley. **181** Graeme Chapman. **182** *t*, Graeme Chapman/NPI; *b*, M. F. Soper. **183** M. R. Quinn. **184** Ralf Richter/Ardea. **185** *t*, D. & M. Trounson/NPI; *b*, Brian Chudleigh. **186** E. E. Zillman/NPI. **187** Graeme Chapman. **188** M. F. Soper. **189** M. F. Soper. **190** *t*, D. & M. Trounson/NPI; *b*, B. L. Sage/Ardea. **191** M. F. Soper. **192** *t*, Tom & Pam Gardner/NPI; *b*, Brian J. Coates/Bruce Coleman Ltd. **193** B. N. Kleeman. **194-5** Noel Gleeson. **195** M. F. Soper. **196** *t*, Kenneth W. Fink/Ardea; *b*, B. L. Sage/Ardea. **197** *t*, M. D. England/Ardea; *b*, H. & J. Beste/NPI. **198** M. F. Soper. **199** *t and b*, Graeme Chapman. **200** G. K. Brown/Ardea. **201** Graeme Chapman. **202** Rod Morris. **203** *t*, H. & J. Beste/NPI; *b*, Photobank/C. R. Veitch. **204** Tom & Pam Gardner/NPI. **205** *t*, Edgar T. Jones/Ardea; *b*, S. J. Krasemann/Bruce Coleman Ltd. **206** Graeme Chapman. **207** *t*, Richard Vaughan/Ardea; *b*, J. A. Bailey/Ardea. **208** *t*, D. & M. Trounson/NPI; *b*, Kenneth W. Fink/Ardea. **209** Geoff Moon. **210** Alan Rogers/NPI. **211** Graeme Chapman. **212** Graeme Chapman. **213** C. E. Barwell. **214** Ian McVinnie. **215** *t*, J. B. & S. Bottomley/Ardea; *b*, J. A. Bailey/Ardea. **216** T. S. U. de Zylva/Frank W. Lane. **217** P. M. & J. L. Sagar. **218** P. M. & J. L. Sagar. **219** William Burlace. **220** *t*, Trevor Marshall/Ardea; *b*, Brian Hawkes/Jacana. **221** L. J. Richards. **222** Geoff Moon. **223** John Fennell/Bruce Coleman Ltd. **224** M. D. England/Ardea. **225** *t*, Graeme Chapman; *b*, Thomas Lowe/NPI. **226** Rod Morris. **227** M. F. Soper. **228** P. M. & J. L. Sagar. **229** Len Robinson/NPI. **230** Geoff Moon. **231** *t*, B. L. Sage/Ardea; *b*, Ake Lindau/Ardea. **232** Ian McVinnie. **233** Chris N. Challies. **234** Photobank/C. R. Veitch. **235** *t*, E. E. Zillman/NPI; *b*, Photobank/C. R. Veitch. **236** M. F. Soper. **237** M. F. Soper. **238** Brian Enting. **239** Rod Morris. **240** *t and b*, Bruce Coleman. **241** Graeme Chapman. **242** Rod Morris. **244** Brian Enting. **245** Rod Morris. **246** Len Robinson/NPI. **247** M. F. Soper. **248** D. V. Merton. **249** Photobank/C. R. Veitch. **250** John Warham. **251** Photobank/C. R. Veitch. **252** *t*, Graeme Chapman/NPI; *b*, Graeme Chapman. **253** *t*, E. E. Zillman/NPI; *b*, H. & J. Beste/NPI. **254** L. J. Richards. **255** Robin Smith Photography Ltd. **256** Keith Ireland/NPI. **257** Geoff Moon. **258** M. J. Ladbrook. **259** N. W. Vincent/NPI. **260-1** Geoff Moon. **262** Graeme Chapman. **263** John Warham/NPI. **264** M. F. Soper. **265** D. V. Merton. **266** *t and b*, M. F. Soper. **267** John Fennell. **268** J. Purnell/NPI. **269** T. A. Waite/NPI. **270** Geoff Moon. **271** T. A. Waite/NPI. **272** Graeme Chapman. **273** M. F. Soper. **274** Geoff Moon. **275** L. J. Richards. **276** John L. Craig. **277** M. F. Soper/Bruce Coleman Ltd. **278** M. R. Quinn. **279** Photobank/C. R. Veitch. **280** T. C. Dennison. **281** Photobank/C. R. Veitch. **282** Geoff Moon. **283** Rod Morris. **284** *t*, M. F. Soper; *b*, John Warham. **285** Photobank/C. R. Veitch. **286** *t*, Graeme Chapman; *b*, B. N. Kleeman. **287** T. A. Waite/NPI. **288** T. C. Dennison. **289** *t and b*, Brian Enting. **290** Photobank/C. R. Veitch. **291** M. F. Soper/Bruce Coleman Ltd. **292** Graeme Chapman. **293** Geoff Moon. **294** Geoff Moon. **295** Brian Chudleigh/NPI. **296** L. J. Richards. **297** Brian Chudleigh. **298** Stephen Dalton/NHPA. **299** B. N. Kleeman. **300** M. F. Soper. **301** Geoff Moon. **302** Photobank/C. R. Veitch. **303** Photobank/C. R. Veitch. **304** *t*, I. R. McCann/NPI; *b*, Frank Park/NPI. **305** T. C. Dennison. **307** J. B. & S. Bottomley/Ardea.

REFERENCES: The publishers wish to acknowledge their indebtedness to the following books and journals that were used for reference. This is an abbreviated list; a full bibliography of the many sources consulted by the contributors will be published separately, at a later date, in conjunction with the Ornithological Society of New Zealand.

Books: *Annotated Checklist of the Birds of New Zealand* by F. C. Kinsky, Convener (Reed); *Antarctic Ecology* ed. by M. W. Holdgate (Academic Press); *Atlas of the South Pacific* by Department of Lands and Survey (Government Printer, Wellington); *Atlas of the World* (Reader's Digest); *Biography and Ecology in New Zealand* ed. by G. Kuschel (Junk); *The Biology of Penguins* ed. by B. Stonehouse (Macmillan); *Bird Distribution in New Zealand* by P. C. Bull, P. D. Gaze, C. J. R. Robertson (Ornithological Society of N.Z.); *Bird Islands of New Zealand* by R. A. Wilson (Whitcombe and Tombs); *Bird Life on Island and Shore* by H. Guthrie-Smith (Whitcombe and Tombs); *Bird Secrets* by G. A. Buddle (Reed); *Bird-song and New Zealand Songbirds* by J. C. Anderson (Whitcombe and Tombs); *The Birds Around Us* by R. H. D. Stidolph (Hedleys Bookshop); *Birds in the Australian High Country* ed. by H. J. Frith (Reed); *Birds of Australia* by J. D. Macdonald (Reed); *Birds of Canada* by W. E. Godfrey (National Museum of Canada); *Birds of New Zealand* by G. R. Williams (Reed); *Birds of the Antarctic and Subantarctic* by G. E. Watson (American Geophysical Union); *Birds of the British Isles* by D. A. Bannerman (Oliver and Boyd); *Birds of the Ocean* by W. B. Alexander (Putnam); *Birds of the Palaearctic Fauna* by C. Vaurie (Witherby); *Birds of the Soviet Union* by G. P. Dementiev; *Birds of the Water, Wood and Waste* by H. Guthrie-Smith (Whitcombe and Tombs); *The Birds of the Western Palaearctic* by S. Cramp and K. Simmons (Oxford University Press); *Book of British Birds* (Drive Publications Ltd, London); *British Birds of Prey* by L. Brown (Collins); *Buller's Birds of New Zealand* ed. by E. G. Turbott (Whitcombe and Tombs); *The California Quail* by A. S. Leopold (University of California Press); *Checklist of Birds of the World* by J. L. Peters (Harvard University Press); *Eagles, Hawks and Falcons of the World* by L. Brown and D. Amadon (McGraw-Hill); *A Field Guide to Australian Birds* by P. Slater (Rigby); *A Field Guide to the Birds of Australia* by G. Pizzey (Collins); *The Habits of the Flightless Birds of New Zealand* by R. Henry (Government Printer); *The Handbook of Australian Sea-birds* by D. L. Serventy, V. N. Serventy and J. Warham (Reed); *A Handbook of Birds of Western Australia* by D. L. Serventy and H. W. Whittell (Patterson Press); *The Handbook of British Birds* by H. F. Witherby, F. C. R. Jourdain, N. F. Ticehurst, B. W. Tucker (Witherby); *Handbook of North American Birds* ed. by R. S. Palmer (Yale University Press); *The Herons of the World* by J. Hancock and H. Elliot (London Editions Ltd); *History of the Birds of New Zealand* (2 Editions & Supplement) by W. L. Buller (published by the author); *Kapiti Bird Sanctuary* by A. S. and A. Wilkinson (Whitcombe & Tombs); *Life Histories of New Zealand Birds* by E. F. Stead (Search Publishing Co.); *More New Zealand Bird Portraits* by M. F. Soper (Whitcombe and Tombs); *Muttonbirds and Other Birds* by H. Guthrie-Smith (Whitcombe and Tombs); *The Natural History of Canterbury* ed. by G. A. Knox (Reed); *The Naturalisation of Animals and Plants in New Zealand* by G. M. Thomson (Cambridge University Press); *A New Dictionary of Birds* ed. by A. L. Thomson (Thomas Nelson and Sons); *A New Guide to the Birds of New Zealand* by R. A. Falla, R. B. Sibson and E. G. Turbott (Collins); *New Zealand Atlas* ed. by Ian Wards (Government Printer, Wellington); *New Zealand Bird Portraits* by M. F. Soper (Whitcombe and Tombs); *New Zealand Birds* (2 editions) by W. R. B. Oliver (Reed); *New Zealand's Nature Heritage* ed. R. Knox (Hamlyns); *Oceanic Birds of South America* by R. C. Murphy (Macmillan); *Owls of the World* ed. by J. A. Burton (Dutton Ltd); *Parrots of the World* by J. M. Forshaw (Lansdowne); *Pigeons and Doves of the World* by D. Goodwin; *A Population Study of Penguins* by L. E. Richdale (Clarendon Press); *Rails of the World* by S. D. Ripley (M. F. Feheley Ltd); *Reader's Digest Complete Book of Australian Birds* ed. by H. J. Frith (Reader's Digest Pty Ltd); *Refocus on New Zealand Birds* by G. J. Moon (Reed); *Seabirds – an Identification Guide* by P. Harrison (Croom Helm); *Sexual Behaviour of Penguins* by L. E. Richdale (University of Kansas Press); *Southern Albatrosses and Petrels – an Identification Guide* by P. C. Harper and F. C. Kinsky (Price Milburn); *Subantarctic Campbell Island* by A. M. Bailey and J. H. Sorenson (Denver Museum); *The Sulidae* by J. B. Nelson (Oxford University Press); *The Swans* by P. Scott (Michael Joseph); *A Treasury of New Zealand Bird Song*, K. and J. Bigwood (Reed); *Tutira* by H. Guthrie-Smith (Blackwood & Sons); *Waterfowl in Australia* H. J. Frith (Angus and Robertson).

Journals: *Alauda* (Société d'Etudes Ornithologiques); *American Museum Novitates; Antarctic* (New Zealand Antarctic Society); *Antarctic Research Series; Ardea* (Netherlands Ornithologists' Union); *Auk* (American Ornithologists' Union); *Australasian Seabird Group Newsletter; Australian Bird Bander; Australian Journal of Science; Australian National Antarctic Research Expedition (A.N.A.R.E.) Scientific Report Series; Australian Wildlife Research; Biological Conservation* (Applied Science Publishers Ltd, U.K.); *Biometrika* (Biometrika Trust, University College, London); *Bird Banding; Bird Study* (British Trust for Ornithology); *British Antarctic Survey Bulletin; British Australian New Zealand Antarctic Research Expedition (B.A.N.Z.A.R.E.) Reports; British Birds* (British Birds Ltd); *Bulletin of the American Museum of Natural History; Bulletin of the British Ornithological Club; Bulletin of the International Council for Bird Preservation (I.C.B.P.)* Cambridge, U.K.; *Bulletin of the Peabody Museum of Natural History; C.S.I.R.O. Wildlife Research; Cape Expedition Series; Comité National Français de Recherches Antarctiques (C.N.R.F.A.) Report Series; Condor* (Cooper Ornithological Club); *Corella* (Australian Bird Study Association); *Discovery* (Peabody Museum of National History, Yale University); *Durban Museum Novitates; Ecology* (Ecological Society of America); *Emu* (Royal Australasian Ornithologists' Union); *Environmental Pollution* (Applied Science Publishers Ltd U.K.); *Falklands Islands Dependencies Survey Scientific Reports; Forest and Bird* (Royal Forest and Bird Protection Society of N.Z.); *Giervalk-Gerfaut* (Koninklijk Belgisch Instituut voor Natuurwetenschappen); *Heredity* (Genetical Society of Great Britain); *Ibis* (British Ornithologists' Union); *International Zoo Yearbook; Journal für Ornithologie* (Deutsche Ornithologen Gesellschaft); *Journal of Animal Ecology* (British Ecological Society); *Journal of Applied Ecology* (British Ecological Society); *Journal of Wildlife Management* (Wildlife Society, Bethesda, Md.); *Journal of the Zoological Society*, London; *L'Oiseau* (Société Ornithologique de la France); *Lands and Survey Research Series; Limosa* (Netherlands Ornithological Union); *Living Bird; Mauri Ora; Miscellaneous Reports of the Yamashina Institute for Ornithology; Nature* (Macmillan Journals Ltd, U.K.); *New Zealand Bird Notes; New Zealand D.S.I.R. Bulletins; New Zealand Journal of Agricultural Research; New Zealand Journal of Ecology; New Zealand Journal of Marine and Freshwater Research; New Zealand Journal of Science and Technology; New Zealand Journal of Science; New Zealand Journal of Zoology; New Zealand Science Review; Notornis* (Ornithological Society of New Zealand); *Ornis Scandinavica* (Scandinavian Ornithologists' Union); *Ostrich* (South African Ornithological Society); *Pacific Science* (University of Hawaii); *Proceedings of the California Academy of Sciences; Proceedings of the International Ornithological Congress; Proceedings of the New Zealand Ecological Society; Proceedings of the Royal Society of New South Wales; Proceedings of the S.C.A.R. Symposia on Antarctic Biology; Proceedings of the U.S. National Museum; Raptor Research* (Society for the Preservation of Birds of Prey, California); *Records of the Auckland Institute and Museum; Records of the Canterbury Museum; Records of the Dominion Museum; Records of the National Museum of New Zealand; Records of the Queen Victoria Museum; Science* (American Association for the Advancement of Science); *Tane; The Ring* (Polskie Towarzystwo Zoologiczne; (International Ornithological bulletin); *Transactions and Proceedings of the New Zealand Institute; Transactions and Journal of the Royal Society of New Zealand; Wildlife – A Review* (N.Z. Wildlife Service); *Wilson Bulletin* (Wilson Ornithological Society).

Typesetting by Graphicraft Typesetters Ltd,
Lockhart Road, Hong Kong.

Colour separations by Hong Kong Graphic Arts Service Centre,
Westlands Road, Quarry Bay, Hong Kong.

Printed and bound by Toppan Printing Company,
Westlands Road, Quarry Bay, Hong Kong,
for Reader's Digest Services Pty Ltd, 26–32 Waterloo Street,
Surry Hills, NSW 2010.